The Art of Compiler Design
Theory and Practice

Thomas Pittman

James Peters
University of Arkansas

PRENTICE HALL, Englewood Cliffs, NJ 07632

Library of Congress Cataloging-in-Publication Data

Pittman, Thomas.
    The art of compiler design : theory and practice / Thomas Pittman,
James Peters.
        p.   cm.
    Includes bibliographical references and index.
    ISBN 0-13-048190-4
    1. Compilers (Computer programs)   I. Peters, James F. II. Title.
QA76.76.C65P57   1992
005.4'53--dc20   91-21591
                                                               CIP

Acquisitions editor: *Tom McElwee*
Editorial/production supervision
    and interior design: *Richard DeLorenzo*
Copy editor: *Brenda Melissoratos*
Cover design: *Butler Udell Design*
Prepress buyer: *Linda Behrens*
Manufacturing buyer: *David Dickey*

© 1992 by Prentice-Hall, Inc.
A Simon & Schuster Company
Englewood Cliffs, New Jersey 07632

The author and publisher of this book have used their best efforts
in preparing this book. These efforts include the development,
research, and testing of the theories and programs to determine
their effectiveness. The author and publisher make no warranty of
any kind, expressed or implied, with regard to these programs
or the documentation contained in this book. The author and
publisher shall not be liable in any event for incidental or
consequential damages in connection with, or arising out of, the
furnishing, performance, or use of these programs.

Printed in the United States of America

10 9 8 7 6 5 4 3 2 1

ISBN 0-13-048190-4

Prentice-Hall International (UK) Limited, *London*
Prentice-Hall of Australia Pty. Limited, *Sydney*
Prentice-Hall Canada Inc., *Toronto*
Prentice-Hall Hispanoamericana, S.A., *Mexico*
Prentice-Hall of India Private Limited, *New Delhi*
Prentice-Hall of Japan, Inc., *Tokyo*
Simon & Schuster Asia Pte. Ltd., *Singapore*
Editora Prentice-Hall do Brasil, Ltda., *Rio de Janeiro*

7   Automated Bottom-Up Parser Design   198

7.1   Introduction 198
7.2   LR(k) Parsers 202
       7.2.1 Constructing the LR(k) State Machine 203
       7.2.2 An LR(2) Parser 205
       7.2.3 Apply and Shift Operations 205
7.3   Conflicts 206
7.4   Example: Conflict Resolution in G2 207
7.5   Saving States on the Stack 207
7.6   Other LR(k) Parsers: SLR 210
7.7   LALR(k) Parsers 211
7.8   Bottom-Up Parser Implementation 213
7.9   Error Recovery 213
7.10   Attribute Evaluation in an LR Parser 215
       Summary 216

8   Transformational Attribute Grammars   222

8.1   Introduction 222
8.2   Program Representation as Trees 223
8.3   Tree-Transformational Grammars 224
       8.3.1 Nongenerative Grammars 227
       8.3.2 A TAG Example 228
       8.3.3 Evaluation Order 229
       8.3.4 Information Flow and Storage 230
       8.3.5 Tree-Valued Attributes 231
       8.3.6 Nondeterministic Parsing 233
8.4   Combining String and Tree Grammars 234
8.5   Type-Checking in TAGs 235
8.6   Code Optimization by Transformation 236
       8.6.1 Data-Flow Analysis 237
       8.6.2 Using Attribute Grammars for Data-Flow Analysis 240
8.7   Alternatives to Tree Representations of Intermediate Code 241
       8.7.1 Data-Flow in Quads 243
       8.7.2 Data-Flow Analysis Through Loops 244
8.8   A Survey of Useful Optimizing Transformations 247
       8.8.1 The Class of Simulated Execution Optimizations 249
       8.8.2 Analysis for Constant Folding 250
       8.8.3 Common Subexpression Detection Using Value Numbers 253
       8.8.4 Left–Motion Hoisting 256
       8.8.5 Right–Motion Hoisting 258
       8.8.6 Useless Code and Other Right-to-Left DFAs 262
       8.8.7 Mathematical Identities and Code Selection 262
       8.8.8 Loop Structure Analysis 264

5   **Semantic Analysis and Attribute Grammars**   **130**

5.1   Introduction   130
5.2   Attribute Grammars   131
      5.2.1 Inherited and Synthesized Attributes   132
      5.2.2 Attribute Value Flow   136
5.3   Nonterminals as Attribute Evaluation Functions   137
5.4   Symbol Tables as Attributes   138
5.5   A Micro-Modula Attribute Grammar   139
5.6   Using Attributes with the TAG Compiler   142
5.7   Scope and Kind of Identifiers   142
      5.7.1 Identifier Scope Grammar   142
      5.7.2 Identifier Scope Example Analysis   145
      5.7.3 Other Symbol Table Issues   149
5.8   Implementing Attributes in Recursive Descent   150
5.9   Implementing a Symbol Table   150
      Summary   152

6   **Syntax-Directed Code Generation**   **159**

6.1   Introduction   159
6.2   Computer Hardware Architecture   160
6.3   Stack Machine Expression Evaluation   161
6.4   The "Itty Bitty Stack Machine"   163
6.5   Attributed Code Generation   166
      6.5.1 Operator Precedence and Associativity   169
      6.5.2 Semantics of Program Structures   169
      6.5.3 The Forward Branch Problem   171
6.6   Generating Code for Procedures and Functions   176
6.7   Block-Structured Stack Frame Management   177
      6.7.1 Frames and Frame Pointers   177
      6.7.2 Static and Dynamic Links   178
      6.7.3 The Display Vector of Frame Pointers   179
6.8   Other Data Types   182
6.9   Structured Data Types   184
      6.9.1 Pointer Types   184
      6.9.2 Record Structures   185
      6.9.3 Array Semantics   186
6.10   Other Data Structures   188
6.11   Input and Output in the Itty Bitty Stack Machine   189
6.12   Limits to Syntax-Directed Semantics   189
6.13   Generating Code in Hand-Coded Compilers   190
6.14   Applications of Syntax-Directed Semantics   190
      6.14.1 A Tiny Basic Interpreter   191
      6.14.2 A Micro-Modula Pretty-Printer   192
      Summary   193

2.8.1 Limits of Finite-State Automata 33

2.8.2 Counting on Context-Free Grammars 35

2.8.3 Sensitive to the Context 38

Summary 39

3   Scanners and Regular Languages   **48**

3.1   Introduction to Lexical Analysis 48

3.2   Regular Expressions 49

3.2.1 The Algebra of Regular Expressions 50

3.2.2 Formal Properties of Regular Expressions 51

3.3   Transforming Grammars and Regular Expressions 54

3.4   Finite-State Automata 57

3.5   Nondeterministic Finite-State Automata 59

3.6   Transforming Grammars to Automata 60

3.7   Transforming Automata 63

3.8   Transforming Automata to Grammars 71

3.9   Left-Linear Grammars 72

3.10   Implementing a Finite-State Automaton on a Computer 72

3.11   Special Implementation Problems for Scanners 77

3.11.1 Input Alphabet Size 77

3.11.2 Halting States in the Scanner Automaton 78

3.11.3 Stripping Spaces and Comments 78

3.11.4 Token Output 79

3.12   String Table Implementation 82

3.13   Reserved Words 87

Summary 90

3.14   Using Scanner Generators 90

4   Parsers and Context-Free Languages   **99**

4.1   Introduction 99

4.2   Push-Down Automata 100

4.2.1 Halting Condition Equivalence 102

4.2.2 Constructing a PDA from a Context-Free Grammar 103

4.3   The LL(k) Criterion 105

4.3.1 *First* and *Follow* Sets 106

4.3.2 Selection Sets 109

4.4   Left-Recursion 110

4.5   Common Left-Factors 112

4.6   Extending CFGs with Regular Expression Operators 114

4.7   Using a Parser Generator 116

4.7.1 Using YACC 118

4.8   Recursive-Descent Parsers 118

4.9   Recursive-Descent Parsers as Push-Down Automata 119

Summary 121

Contents

Preface   **x**

1   The Compiler Theory Landscape   **1**

1.1   Introduction 1
1.2   Languages and Translators 2
1.3   The Role of Grammars 3
1.4   Some Examples 5
1.5   Structure of a Compiler 7
       1.5.1 Lexical Analysis 9
       1.5.2 The String Table 10
       1.5.3 Parsing 11
       1.5.4 Constraining 11
       1.5.5 The Symbol Table 12
       1.5.6 Code Generation 12
       1.5.7 Optimization 13
              Summary 14

2   Grammars: The Chomsky Hierarchy   **18**

2.1   Introduction 18
2.2   Grammars 19
       2.2.1 Alphabets and Strings 19
       2.2.2 Nonterminals and Productions 20
       2.2.3 Some Example Grammars 20
2.3   The Chomsky Hierarchy 24
2.4   Grammars and Their Machines 24
       2.4.1 Turing Machines 25
       2.4.2 Linear-Bounded Automata 26
       2.4.3 Push-Down Automata 27
       2.4.4 Removing Empty Productions 28
       2.4.5 A Comparison of Context-Free and Context-Sensitive 28
       2.4.6 Finite-State Automata 29
2.5   Empty Strings and Empty Languages 30
2.6   Canonical Derivations 30
2.7   Ambiguity 32
2.8   The Art of Thinking in Grammars 33

8.9   Implementing Abstract-Syntax Trees 267
8.10   Implementing TAG-Driven Tree Transformers 276
        Summary 280

9   Code Generation and Optimization   **287**

9.1   Introduction 287
9.2   Loop Optimizations 288
        9.2.1 Range Analysis Through Loops 288
        9.2.2 Induction Variables 290
        9.2.3 Loop Unrolling 291
9.3   Register and Memory Allocation 292
        9.3.1 Algorithms for Register Allocation 293
        9.3.2 Register Allocation in Expressions 295
        9.3.3 Data-Flow Analysis for Better Register Allocation 308
        9.3.4 Register Allocation in Loops 311
        9.3.5 Addressing Modes 311
        9.3.6 Branch Address Selection 312
        9.3.7 Branch Chains 314
9.4   Complexities of Code Generation 319
        9.4.1 Instruction Selection 320
        9.4.2 Strength Reduction 323
9.5   Specialized Instructions 324
        9.5.1 RISC and Pipeline Processor Scheduling 325
        9.5.2 Vector Processors 328
9.6   Varieties of Code Optimization 333
        9.6.1 Peephole Optimizations 333
        Summary 334

10   Nonprocedural Languages   **339**

10.1   Introduction 339
10.2   Compiling an Applicative Language 340
        10.2.1 Some Lisp Concepts 342
        10.2.2 Tail-Recursion 343
        10.2.3 Implementing an Applicative Language Compiler 345
10.3   A Transformational Attribute Grammar Compiler 352
        10.3.1 TAG Compiler Parts 353
        10.3.2 Iterators in a Grammar 354
        10.3.3 Reporting Syntax Errors to the User 355
        10.3.4 Automatic Scanner Construction 357
        10.3.5 Parsing in the TAG Compiler 360
        10.3.6 Tree Transformation 365
        10.3.7 Syntax Error Halts 367
        Summary 368

Appendices   **372**

A   Itty Bitty Modula Syntax Diagrams 372
B   The TAG Compiler TAG 376
C   Itty Bitty® Stack Machine Instruction Set 400
D   Code Generation Tables 405

Index   **408**

Listings

Listing 1.1. Failed attempt to "comment out" some code in Modula-2.   7

Listing 3.1. Modula-2 implementation of a simple finite automaton.   74
Listing 3.2. Encoding a finite automaton's transitions in program code.   76
Listing 3.3. Encoding a finite automaton's state in the Program Counter.   77
Listing 3.4. Three ways of encoding semantic actions in scanner code.   81
Listing 3.5. A linear-search string table implementation.   83
Listing 3.6. A hashing string table implementation.   85
Listing 3.7. A search-tree string table implementation.   88

Listing 4.1. The grammar G_{28} acceptable to the TAG compiler.   116
Listing 4.2. The TAG compiler grammar grammar.   117
Listing 4.3. Recursive-descent parser for grammar G_{28}.   120

Listing 5.1. "Micro-Modula" syntax grammar.   140
Listing 5.2. "Micro-Modula" attribute grammar, with type-checking.   141
Listing 5.3. "Micro-Modula" attribute grammar header for TAG compiler.   143
Listing 5.4. Changes to "Micro-Modula" syntax to add functions.   143
Listing 5.6. Implementation of an attribute grammar production in Modula-2.   151

Listing 6.1. "Micro-Modula" attribute grammar, generating code for IBSM.   167
Listing 6.2. Generating backpatch code for IF-statements.   172
Listing 6.3. Procedure header attributes for parameterless functions.   180
Listing 6.4. Tiny Basic syntax grammar, with informal semantic actions.   191
Listing 6.5. Pretty-printing Micro-Modula.   192

Listing 7.1. LR parser table interpreter.   214

Listing 8.1. A simple TAG for constant folding.   229
Listing 8.2. Two ways to construct an abstract-syntax tree in the   235
Listing 8.3. A small program for data-flow analysis.   238
Listing 8.4. Forward data-flow analysis using intersection.   238

Listing 8.5. Backward data-flow analysis using set union. 239
Listing 8.6. A small data-flow analysis grammar. 241
Listing 8.7. Quads for the program of Listing 8.3, showing basic blocks. 242
Listing 8.8. Live variable analysis grammar, including 246
Listing 8.9. Constant folding analysis and transformation grammar. 251
Listing 8.10. Common subexpression elimination grammar fragment. 257
Listing 8.11. Right-motion hoisting grammar fragment. 259
Listing 8.12. Two grammar fragments for strength reduction. 263
Listing 8.13. Grammar fragment for loop-constant code motion. 266
Listing 8.14. A tree node implementation module. 269
Listing 8.15. A virtual-memory tree node module. 273
Listing 8.16. A sample tree-transformer, from TAG in Listing 8.13. 278

Listing 9.1. Unrolling a WHILE loop once. 292
Listing 9.2. Linearizing an array. 292
Listing 9.3. Simulating a zero-address stack in registers. 296
Listing 9.4. A module for generating register-based code from IBSM. 299
Listing 9.5. Using RegGenCode in a tree-flattening grammar. 309
Listing 9.6. A branch address selection queue. 315
Listing 9.7. Building branch chains in a code generator grammar. 319

Listing 10.1. A Tiny Scheme source-to-tree grammar. 347
Listing 10.2. A code-generating grammar fragment for Tiny Scheme. 348
Listing 10.3. Error messages in a TAG grammar fragment. 356
Listing 10.4. The scanner compiler grammar from the TAG compiler. 359
Listing 10.5. The code generator grammar from the TAG compiler. 362
Listing 10.6. A library routine to parse one tree template detail. 367

Listing B.1. The TAG Compiler TAG. 376
Listing C.1. Code to Build a Display on the IBSM Stack. 404

Preface

No useful modern complex information system ever evolved from the accumulation of chance events. The complexity of compilers as useful information systems can be understood in simple terms only because of careful design. Not only is the undesigned compiler nonfunctional, but compiler theory itself depends on a subtle relationship between linguistic principles originally developed for natural (human) languages and computers considered as finite-state automata. Understanding and exploiting this relationship requires a thorough grounding in the theoretical principles that underlie grammar theory, and a good grasp of their mechanical implementation. Thus, teaching compiler design involves also a complex information system that must be carefully designed to present the concepts in a coherent and logical sequence, so that the student finds compiler design both relevant and manageable.

This book is not an encyclopedic compendium of all possible ways to build all possible compilers, but a sequential introduction to the fundamental issues of compiler design in sufficient depth that the diligent student will be thoroughly equipped to construct practical and efficient compilers either by hand or using modern compiler generation tools, or some combination of the two. More importantly, the student will understand what is going on in the tools and why grammars must be composed in certain ways to achieve the intended results. This is the principle of design. Therefore, while most modern parser generators use bottom-up parsing techniques, we explore the more restrictive top-down parsing theory in considerable depth before advancing to a relatively brief (but complete) single chapter on bottom-up parsers. The goal in each chapter is always to instill an understanding of the concepts first, then to apply them in practical ways.

We believe *The Art of Compiler Design* stands out among comparable works in four important ways. First, it is rooted solidly and consistently in grammars. Beginning with the theoretical relationship between grammars and language recognizers, we continue throughout the entire book to apply the technology of grammars to all aspects of compiler design. The second distinction is the consistent and practical use of attribute grammars as a vehicle for compiler semantics. This uncompromising stand leads naturally to a compiler-compiler specified entirely in an attribute grammar that compiles itself; indeed, this is the focus of the final chapter. On the other hand, the third unique quality of this book is its very practical nature. Compiler *design* must be specified in attribute grammars, but compiler *construction* requires executable code, and every important theoretical principle is illustrated in generous listings written in a real programming language, always showing the very natural relationship between the grammars and the machine code. Finally, our choice of Modula-2 as the programming language for illustrative code walks a narrow line between conceptual abstraction and concrete efficiency. Applying the optimizations taught in the later chapters can make programs written in Modula-2 more efficient at lower cost than comparable code in lower-level languages such as C.

This book may be used in a one-term beginning compiler course by concentrating on the first six or seven chapters, or the whole book may be spread over a full year for better coverage of the more advanced topics. The one-term course of study is suited for either a semester or quarter schedule; it has been optimized and classroom-tested to allow the steady progress of student projects culminating by the end of the term in a functional "Itty Bitty Modula" compiler that can be used in a final project to compile a *second* parser such at the pretty-printer or Tiny Basic interpreter outlined at the end of Chapter 6.

Some of the sections and problems are designed to be optional. While we firmly believe in a good theoretical basis for compiler design, there are some interesting mathematical side trails along the way which may be passed up if time or aptitude make them inappropriate. These have been marked with a little professor icon in the margin as you see here. Other sections are relevant to the major issues of compiler design, but the material is difficult to comprehend on the first-year level at which this book is aimed. These sections are identified with a little "Ex Calibur" icon in the margin as you see here. Similarly, there are some problems that are particularly challenging. The reader who tackles these problems will come away with agreater appreciation of the intricacies of compiler design, but a good understanding of the subject material does not require the extra time and effort that these problems take. They are also identified by the Ex Calibur icon in the margin.

While we can hardly mention all the people who contributed to this text, the first name that comes to mind is Brad Blaker, without whose encouragement and early assistance *The Art of Compiler Design* would never have happened. We also appreciate Bill Hankley, Austin Melton, and the patient students at Kansas State University for persevering through the early drafts, and Frank DeRemer for planting and nurturing many of the seminal ideas expressed here. The comments and suggestions from Thom Boyer, Dick Karpinski, Brian Kernighan, Marvin Zelkowitz, Wayne Citrin, Norman C. Hutchinson, Johnson M. Hart, Bernhard Weinberg, Will Gillett, and especially Dean Pittman, Chota, and Dave Schmidt were particularly helpful in making this into the book you are now reading.

Thomas Pittman
James Peters

Chapter 1

The Compiler Theory Landscape

Aims

- Survey the purpose of and approach to compiling.
- Introduce grammar concepts in language specification.
- Give an overview of a compiler structure.
- Introduce the basic data structures used by a compiler.
- Distinguish between lexical analysis and parsing.
- Survey the front and back ends of a compiler.

1.1 Introduction

Compiler design is one of the few areas of computer science where the abstract theory radically changed the way we write programs. The earliest compilers were largely written by ad-hoc "seat-of-the-pants" methods, using conventional programming techniques. The advent of grammar-driven parsers changed all that. We no longer see any real compiler that is not written first as a context-free grammar which is then mechanically translated into code.

This book is about modern compiler design, and so it is about grammars. Every part of a good compiler is related in some way or other to the grammars used to specify it. We show that the grammatical specification of the compiler *is* that compiler, written in a very high level language, and we show both how to write compilers in grammars and how to write grammar-compilers to compile the grammars into compilers. Grammar theory drives the design, so the designs are clean and easily implemented. The diligent reader can learn from this book how to write a complete compiler for a small but realistic programming language in a few days.

1

1.2 Languages and Translators

Like natural languages (English, French, Russian), computer languages define a way of structuring words into sentences for communicating information. A natural language communicates feelings of the heart, facts about the world, questions about those facts and feelings, and commands that should be followed by the listener or reader. A computer language is typically restricted to commands that are to be followed by the machine receiving them.

A natural language restricts the form of what can be said, but not what can be said. For example, it is meaningful in English to say, "Peter hit the ball" but not "ball Peter the hit." One is grammatically correct; the other is not. Similarly, we could say "Pièrre frappa la balle" in grammatically correct French. A bilingual reader would immediately recognize that the English and French sentences say the same thing — that is, they have the same meaning — but that would not necessarily be obvious to a person conversant in only one of those languages. The word "frappa" has no meaning to the English speaker, and the word "hit" means nothing to the French. Even if the dictionary meaning of the verbs were recognized, the grammars of the respective languages still define verb tense, which is indicated in the form of the words: both are in the past tense.

When an Englishman wishes to communicate to a Frenchman and neither knows the other's language, it is necessary to bring in a translator. In the natural world, a translator is a person who receives a message in one language and repeats that same message in some other language. A human translator from English to French would read, "Peter hit the ball" and write "Pièrre frappa la balle." If the translator happened upon the expression "ball Peter the hit," he would probably respond that it makes no sense. Because it has no meaning in English, it cannot be translated into a French sentence with any meaning.

A compiler is a computer program that acts like our human translator. It reads statements in one computer language, and if they make sense in that language, it translates them into statements with the same meaning in another computer language. There are rules defining what makes sense in each language, and the compiler applies these rules to determine if its input makes sense and to ensure that the output makes sense. A sequence of statements in a computer language is a program, and the compiler translates the program from one computer language (called the source language) into a program — that is, a sequence of statements — in another computer language (called the target language).

There are actually several kinds of computer languages and computer language translators. The simplest translator reads words in a simple computer language, and translates these words directly to the numbers that computers use for their instruction codes. This is called an *assembler*, and the source language is called *assembly language*. The name derives from the fact that most machine instructions are composed of several parts, and the assembly language uses a separate word or number for each part; the assembler assembles these parts into one numerical code. An assembler consists of little more than a table lookup routine, where each word of the source language is looked up in a table for its numerical equivalent, which is then output as part of the target language program. Assembly language generally gives the programmer precise and direct access to every capability of the computer hardware, but it is much harder to write correct programs in assembly language than in most other computer languages.

The term *compiler* is generally reserved for the more complex languages, where there is no immediate and direct relationship between the source language words and the target language. The target language for most compilers is usually the same machine language that is the target for assemblers — indeed, the purpose of computer language translators is to ease the process of creating programs in machine language — but most of the early compilers and even some modern compilers compile to assembly language and then let an assembler finish the translation to machine language. The source language for a compiler, however, is usually what we call a "high-level language" or HLL. High-level languages are characterized by resembling problem-solving notations rather than machine languages. For example, for business applications, Cobol ("COmmon Business Oriented Language") uses terminology easily understood by accountants and middle managers. Scientific problems are often stated in formulas for which Fortran ("FORmula TRANslator") is considered appropriate. Some programmers now favor a language with the more abstract structures of an HLL, but with all the low-level control offered by an assembler; for this purpose they use the language C (so named because it was the next language after an earlier language called B). Recent advances in programming methodology dictate a modular software design, a characteristic featured in Modula-2.

An *interpreter* is somewhat like a translator in that it reads a program in an HLL, but the translation is immediate, just as a human interpreter makes a verbal translation that is heard and understood immediately. Where a compiler will translate a computer program into machine code that executes at a later time, an interpreter actually executes the program as it is read. In one sense the interpreter never really completes the translation process; it is as if the human translator of our earlier example were to hear the command "Peter, hit the ball!" but instead of responding, "Pièrre, frappez la balle!" he just went and hit the ball himself. Because the interpreter does not have to be concerned with a target language, it can often process a line of source program much faster than a compiler. An interpreter must read its input program over and over to compute the results, but a compiler translates it only once. Compilers take longer to get the output from the first time a computer program is run, but subsequent runs are much faster than with the interpreter because no additional translation is needed.

Most of the focus of this book is on compiler design, but some of the exercises encompass interpreters also.

1.3 The Role of Grammars

One of the characteristics we study in a natural language such as English or French is its *grammar*. The grammar of a language defines the correct form for sentences in that language. For example, the English language might have some rules such as

sentence	→ noun-phrase verb noun-phrase
verb	→ "hit"
noun-phrase	→ article noun
	→ proper-name
article	→ "a" | "the"
noun	→ "ball" | "bat"
proper-name	→ "Peter"

This grammar says that a sentence can consist of a verb between two noun phrases. That is, the abstract concept of a sentence represented by the word "sentence" in the grammar may be rewritten as, or replaced by, the sequence of three abstract concepts, noun phrase, verb, and another noun phrase. A noun phrase can be a proper name like "Peter," or it can be an ordinary noun like "ball" with an article ("the" or "a"). The verb in our example is of course "hit." Similarly, in a computer language the grammar defines the correct form for sentences in that language by specifying how to rewrite the abstract concepts of the language as ever more concrete sequences of symbols. Each rewrite rule of the grammar is represented by an arrow connecting a word with one or more other words. Of course, what we mean by "sentence" is carefully defined in a computer language.

Starting with the word "sentence," this little grammar can generate not only the sentence "Peter hit the ball" but also "a ball hit Peter" and the somewhat nonsensical sentence "Peter hit Peter." When a grammar defines alternatives (either by means of multiple arrows, or else by the "or-bar" separator "|"), any one of the alternatives may be chosen arbitrarily in rewriting an occurrence of the name on the left of the arrow. The language generated by the grammar is the set of all the sentences that can be generated by successively choosing all possible alternatives in all combinations. This language has exactly 25 possible sentences.

A programming language is usually specified by two separate grammars, one to define the words of the language, the other to define how the words go together. A grammar could similarly be written to define the target language, and recent research has focused on building compilers automatically from the source and target grammars, but with mixed results. Therefore, we adhere to the more traditional compiler design methodology, using *attribute grammars* to define explicitly how the translation is to take place. Several grammars may be used to define a compiler, with each grammar specifying the functions of one component of the compiler.

The primary grammar is the *phrase-structure grammar*, and it specifies the central part of a compiler or interpreter, called the *parser*. The phrase-structure grammar specifies how the "words" of the computer language are allowed to fit together to form syntactically valid programs. "Parsing" is the natural-language term that describes the process of analyzing a sentence in that language according to its grammatical form; we use the term in exactly the same way with respect to computer languages. Our tiny English-language grammar is a phrase-structure grammar.

A secondary grammar is often used to specify the correct form or spelling of the "words" of the computer language. This is called the *lexical grammar*, from the Latin word for "word." The part of the compiler that analyzes the individual words of the input program is called the *scanner*. We might define a lexical grammar for English-language words something like this:

$$
\begin{aligned}
\text{word} \quad &\rightarrow \text{letter word} \\
&\rightarrow \text{letter}
\end{aligned}
$$

where we mean "letter" to stand for exactly one letter of the 26 letters of the alphabet at a time. Although this grammar generates a lot of nonsense words, it shows that a grammar need not be complex to generate a very large language. Indeed, the language of this grammar is infinite: as long as we choose the first alternative in adding single letters to the beginning of a word, the word can get as long as we like.

The translation process in a compiler is specified by values (called "attributes") and by attribute evaluation functions and assertions attached to the lexical and phrase-structure grammars. Other attribute grammars may be used to specify how the compiler can improve the speed or size of the compiled program. We could use assertions, for example, to prevent the nonsensical sentence "Peter hit Peter" by constraining the grammar to generate at most one proper name in a sentence.

This entire book focuses on the grammatical approach to compiler construction. It is our opinion that a grammar is a high-level language specification of a compiler — indeed, it *is* the compiler. In other words, all of the compiler design should go into writing the grammars that define the components of the language and its translation. That properly done, the rest of compiler design is mechanical and can be automated. The tools for automatically building compilers from grammars alone are fully described in this book, for these tools are themselves a compiler, and their design is an important part of the Art of Compiler Design.

1.4 Some Examples

One of the rewards of directing our attention to the construction of compilers as a logical extension of language specification is that we will be more likely to appreciate the clean design of grammar-specified and strongly-typed languages. Fortran was designed in a rather haphazard way to represent mathematical formulas and simple control structures. Without the grammatical specification to drive the language design, we find it excruciatingly difficult to write deterministic and fast scanners for Fortran compilers. Consider, for example, the following two lines, both legal in the original Fortran (note that spaces were insignificant in Fortran, and could be omitted entirely):

```
DO10K=1.9
DO10K=1,9
```

The first line is an assignment statement, assigning the real value 1.9 to the floating-point variable DO10K; the second is the beginning of a loop construct that ends on the statement labeled 10, with the control variable K, which steps from one to nine. There is nothing to distinguish the line with statement label 10 as the terminator of a loop, so the compiler has no way to recognize whether or not the first is a miskeyed attempt to program the second (or the other way around). Indeed, it is reported that the first Venus probe was lost in a crash landing due to just such a programming error (a comma or period substituted for the other in such a way that it radically changed the meaning of the Fortran program controlling the space probe). Furthermore, in this example the compiler must examine all but the last character of this statement before it can even begin to consider what to do with the first — that is, whether this statement begins with the keyword DO or an identifier for a real variable.

Fortran is every language designer's favorite whipping boy; we mention only one other classic puzzle in the language, by way of example of the difficulties that could have been eliminated by a sound and unambiguous grammatical specification. In the following

four-line nonsense program, is line 10 an assignment statement or a format specification for the output statement?

```
      DIMENSION FORMAT(72)
 10   FORMAT(X3H)=(I5)
      WRITE(6,10)K
      END
```

Fortran was not, however, the only offender. When Fortran was invented there was no grammatical definition of a computer language. The concept of a context-free language was only beginning to be understood in connection with natural languages at that time. But John Backus, one of the designers of Fortran, went on to adapt the new concepts in what now bears his name: *Backus-Naur Form* (BNF, sometimes also called "Backus-Normal Form") is a way of writing the grammar for a programming language. It was first used in the specification of Algol 60. The grammars we use in this book appear a little different from BNF, but the difference is cosmetic only. In BNF our example of an English-language grammar fragment would look like this:

<sentence>	::=	<noun-phrase> <verb> <noun-phrase>
<verb>	::=	hit
<noun-phrase>	::=	<article> <noun>
	::=	<proper-name>
<article>	::=	a | the
<noun>	::=	ball | bat
<proper-name>	::=	Peter

Niklaus Wirth sought to simplify the compiler design aspects of Algol while preserving some of its formal qualities; the result in 1970 was the language Pascal. Pascal was carefully designed with a formal grammar, but an error crept in, making the grammar ambiguous. The problem revolves around the optional **else**-clause in an **if**-statement, because his grammar could not specify formally how to relate an **else** to nested **if**-statements when not all of them had an **else**-clause. Wirth was aware of the problem and offered an ad-hoc solution ("it goes with the inner **if**") instead of correcting the error in the grammar. There is an important reason for this: the language would have been much more clumsy to use without the ambiguity. A significant number of conditionals in actual programs require the **else**-clause, and a significant number also have no use for it; to require the **else**-clause in all cases would have made programs harder to write and less readable, but to have eliminated it would have crippled the language. The clause therefore is optional and the language is ambiguous. A feature of the language thus serves the convenience of the user rather than formal correctness.

Wirth's next system programming language, Modula-2, resolved this problem in a readable and grammatically correct way. Modula-2 preserves the optional **else**-clause without Pascal's ambiguity, but it appears that Wirth did not really learn his lesson. Modula-2 has a different problem: a compiler for it cannot be built with a pure finite-state scanner. Programmer convenience is again served by the ability to "comment out" sections of code — including comments — even at the cost of implementation

simplicity. Unfortunately, this results in an ill-defined (if not ambiguous) scanner grammar. Most implementers, following Wirth's lead, resolve this difficulty by ignoring it. This has the effect that not all sections of code can be successfully be commented out by adding comment delimiters at the beginning and end. Listing 1.1 shows a pathological example where the attempt to remove code by commenting it out will compile without error but have surprising results.

```
MODULE pathological;                         MODULE pathological;
      (* Original program *)                 (* First 2 statements commented out *)
FROM InOut IMPORT WriteString;               FROM InOut IMPORT WriteString;
VAR anyString: ARRAY[0..99] OF CHAR;         VAR anyString: ARRAY[0..99] OF CHAR;
BEGIN                                        BEGIN
                                             (****** begin new comment region
 IF 1<2 THEN anyString := "Hello!"            IF 1<2 THEN anyString := "Hello!"
 ELSE anyString :=                            ELSE anyString :=
  '*) WriteString("Surprise!"); (*'            '*) WriteString("Surprise!"); (*'
 END (* IF *);                                END (* IF *);
 WriteString(anyString);                      WriteString(anyString);
                                                     end new comment region ******)
 WriteString("  What happened?");             WriteString("  What happened?");
END pathological.                            END pathological.
```

```
Hello!  What happened?                       Surprise!  What happened?
```

Listing 1.1. Failed attempt to "comment out" some code in Modula-2.
Note newly executable statement (underlined) formerly part of a string constant.

1.5 Structure of a Compiler

A compiler comprises four essential components, outlined in bold in Figure 1.1: the scanner, the parser, the constrainer, and the code generator. The *scanner* reads the source text file as a string of characters and recognizes from it a stream of words and symbols, called *tokens*. The tokens output by the scanner are input to the *parser*, which recognizes the phrase structure of the source language and builds an *abstract syntax tree* (AST) to pass on. The *constrainer* enforces type and declaration rules, leaving *decorations* on the AST. The constrainer is often considered to be a part of the parser, because they work so closely together. The *code generator* constructs from the AST the target machine code. The scanner and the constrainer typically each build a private data structure to help in their recognition process. The scanner builds a *string table*, in which it stores the spelling of identifiers, character string constants, and the like. The constrainer builds a *symbol table*, containing semantic information about the identifiers, collected as they are declared or encountered in the source program.

In addition to these four essential components, a compiler may also include one or more *optimization* modules. There are two kinds of optimization, distinguished largely by the degree to which each optimization depends on characteristics of the target machine

code. *Machine-independent* optimization normally operates on the AST to reshape it in ways that result in more efficient code, without regard to the peculiarities of the target machine code. *Peephole* optimization, the most common form of machine-dependent optimizer, operates on the target machine code that comes out of the code generator, making specific local improvements to it. The name derives from the fact that this form of optimization examines only a small number of instructions at a time (as if it were "peeping" through some kind of keyhole with a limited view), and makes the changes right at the point of observation.

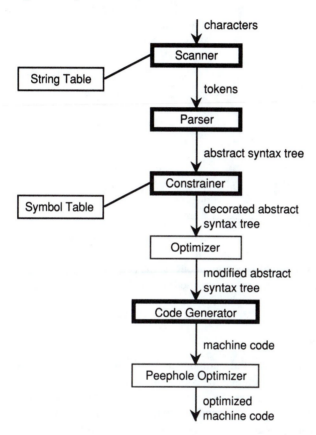

Figure 1.1. The components of a compiler.

Although we show the scanner, parser, constrainer, and code generator in a row like stations in a factory assembly line, the actual structure of a compiler is often somewhat different because of the way most computers operate. As shown in Figure 1.1, it would appear that the scanner, parser, constrainer, optimizers, and code generator are independent programs, each reading an input file, doing some internal processing, and then writing an output file to be read by the next program. Real compilers tend to consist of a main program that is the parser, which calls the scanner, constrainer, and code generator as subroutines, as in Figure 1.2. Each call to the scanner returns with a single token, each call to the constrainer finds a single identifier in the symbol table or validates the operand types for a single expression operator, and each call to the code generator sends a single semantic action to emit one or more single instructions of object code.

The Compiler Theory Landscape   Chap. 1

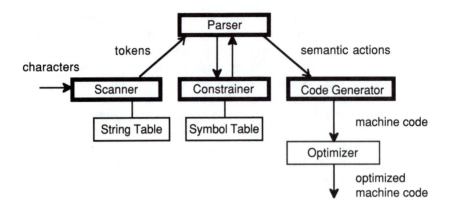

Figure 1.2. The structure of a compiler.

1.5.1 Lexical Analysis

Although language manuals often define a programming language in a single grammar all the way down to the individual characters that make up its component parts, it is usually more efficient to separate the character recognition process from the structure recognition, which requires separately defined lexical and phrase-structure grammars. For theoretical reasons the parser is unable to match identifiers that must be spelled the same in their declarations and references. Therefore it is also convenient to isolate the spelling of the identifiers (and various kinds of constants) from the phrase structure recognition done by the parser. We do this in a module called the scanner.

The scanner is specified by a grammar that defines all of the valid tokens in the source language. A *token* represents any special character, number, word, or string of characters that the parser expects as a single atomic symbol. The word "token" refers to a single symbol in the language defined by any grammar, although we usually restrict the term to the parser grammar. The scanner is a procedure that analyzes the input text file and recognizes the valid tokens in it, that is, strings of characters (each in the language of the lexical grammar) which are reported to the parser as individual tokens. Illegal tokens are also identified, and appropriate error recovery action is taken to resume compilation; a compiler is often more useful if it tries to analyze as much of the source program as possible, rather than stopping at the first error.

The function of the scanner is called *lexical analysis*, because it analyzes the lexemes, or words, of the input language. Each lexeme recognized is converted into a single token in the output stream of the scanner. Usually the scanner is called to get one token, which it returns to the parser as soon as it is recognized. Thus, the stream of tokens is never actually collected into a file or other data structure; we only view it that way as a convenience in distinguishing the parts of the compiler. At any one instant, only one such token exists, and it is the one the parser is working on next.

A typical programming language may be defined with 50 to 100 different tokens, where each token is typically represented in the source file by a string of several characters. In addition, the source may have a lot of white space (space characters, line

ends, and tab characters) for readability, as well as comments which do not contribute to the meaning of the program (from a computer perspective). The scanner removes all these before passing the tokens to the parser. The result is that there is a reduction by an order of magnitude or more between the input text file and the stream of tokens emitted by the scanner. Often most of the compile time is spent in the scanner. Therefore, it is important to maximize its efficiency. One of the reasons for separating the scanner from the parser is that a lexical grammar to recognize the tokens is simpler and can be processed more efficiently than the class of grammar required for the parser.

In a modern programming language, the tokens are readily identifiable as those parts of the input program with the next larger granularity from individual characters. Figure 1.3 shows this hierarchy from characters to tokens to AST.

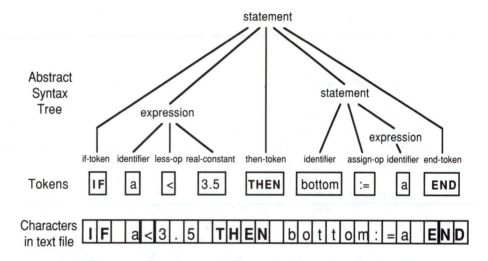

Figure 1.3. An example of characters, tokens, and abstract syntax tree.

1.5.2 The String Table

The tokens that the scanner passes to the parser have been cleansed of any additional distinguishing features such as how the identifiers are spelled and the values of the constants; the parser grammar is not concerned with these details. Nevertheless the information cannot be summarily discarded as comments and extra space characters between tokens are. Indeed, one of the functions of the compiler is to associate a particular memory location with each unique variable identifier, and to treat these consistently throughout the procedure or program. Thus the spelling of the identifiers is relevant and must be checked.

The original Fortran compiler restricted all identifiers to no more than the number of characters that could fit in one computer word, but modern programming languages tend to allow relatively long identifiers. Aside from the inefficiency of allocating memory space in the symbol table for the maximum number of characters even though few

identifiers ever reach that maximum, it is clumsy and slow to compare long strings of characters for equality every time a name must be found in the symbol table. One way to solve both problems is to encode the spelling of each unique identifier into a single integer or pointer; that value can be used to access the spelling when it is needed (generally only in error messages and load maps), and comparison for equality of a pair of single atomic values is much faster than string comparisons. The spelling of the identifiers is stored packed in a *String Table*. A pointer or index into the string table serves as a ready unique reference to the identifiers. One of the tasks of the scanner is to manage the string table, inserting new identifiers and other character strings, and finding strings already there so that their unique index can be passed to the constrainer.

1.5.3 Parsing

The parser is the driving engine for the compiler, and controls the scanner and the code generator. It recognizes the phrase structure or *syntax* of the input program represented as a stream of tokens. We normally think of the output from the parser as an abstract syntax tree, but often no such tree is ever built. Instead, the flow of execution of the parser traces a path through the abstract or imaginary tree, visiting every node in it in some specified way. Thus, if we recorded the execution trace graphically, it would be an AST when the compiler finished, but at any instant, only a fragment of the AST exists — perhaps the path from the root to the current node in the tree — and that is hard to identify specifically.

In principle, the AST corresponds to the syntax diagrams familiar to high school English students: each token is represented by a part of the tree, and the whole structure is defined by the interconnections between the parts.

There are two deterministic parsing algorithms in common use. The oldest is "top-down," which builds the AST by starting at the top (most mathematical trees are drawn with the root node at the top) and building the tree down from that root node. This method is also much simpler to program by hand from the grammar. "Bottom-up" parsing starts with the tokens and constructs the tree branch by branch, joining branches into larger and larger trees as more of the program is recognized, until all of the subtrees finally connect into one AST representing the whole program. Both top-down and bottom-up parsing read the source tokens in left-to-right order, but the grammar rules are applied in a different order; this leads to the equivalent terms for top-down: "LL" (from "Left-to-right scan, Leftmost derivation"), and bottom-up: "LR" (from "Left-to-right scan, Rightmost derivation in reverse").

1.5.4 Constraining

Often considered as part of the parser, but really implemented in a totally different manner from the syntax-checking functions of the parser, is the constrainer, or "static semantics" phase of the compiler. The term "semantic analyzer" is often used to refer to the constrainer combined with some parts of code generation, but we prefer to distinguish those functions. The constrainer is a necessary part of recognizing valid source programs from erroneous ones, but it is not possible to construct it automatically from the same class of grammars that we use to construct the parser. Constraints that must be checked

include such things as verifying that all identifiers have been declared before they are used, that identifiers used in procedure calls were not declared as enumerated type constants, that expressions of type integer are not assigned nor compared to variables of type Boolean, and so on. In the program fragment of Figure 1.3, the constrainer would verify that identifier *a* is either a constant or variable of type real, and that *bottom* has been declared as a real variable. We use attribute grammars for constraint checking. Because attribute grammars are a natural extension of the context-free grammars used in constructing the parser, this is a reasonably painless way to implement the constraints.

1.5.5 The Symbol Table

The *symbol table* is the repository of semantic information attached by the compiler to individual identifiers in the program being compiled. Such information is often called "attributes," although we will avoid that term to prevent confusion with attribute grammars. An entry in the symbol table must contain at least some reference to the identifier's spelling (if not the characters of the word), a value usually representing the memory location or access path of the variable or procedure named by that identifier, and such flags as are necessary to distinguish variables, procedures, and other identifiers.

1.5.6 Code Generation

A compiler is generally divided into two halves. The *front end* of a compiler is concerned with recognizing a valid input source program file (analysis), while the *back end* is concerned with generating code for the target machine (synthesis). The scanner, the parser, and the constrainer comprise the front end; the back end consists of the code generator and any optimization modules. In the case of an interpreter, the back end would be the part that produces the computed results, although that term is not generally applied to interpreters.

It is up to the compiler designer to define the particular sequences of instructions in the target machine that correctly translate each identifiable node in the AST. There have been reported in the literature several attempts to specify the grammar and semantics of the target machine language, so that an appropriate compiler-compiler could deduce the necessary code generation rules, but these have not been particularly successful in practice. We adopt the more traditional position of requiring the compiler designer to specify these transformations.

The code generator is that part of the compiler that implements the actual generation of output code from the internal representation of the source program. In one-pass compilers, such as many of the projects given in this book as exercises, the code is generated "on the fly" from semantic-action specifications in the parser grammar: whenever a source construct is recognized that is to result in target machine code, the code is generated immediately. This imposes some restrictions on the kinds of languages that can be compiled and the efficiency of the generated code.

The target language for most compilers is the native machine language of the target machine. The earliest compilers generated assembly language in a text file, which was then fed to an assembler. There are some advantages to this in simple one-pass compilers, but they are easily overcome by the inefficiencies of the extra assembler step; our

exercises concentrate on direct generation of machine language (also called "native code"), although a few of the exercises deal with source-to-source translation, that is, from one high-level programming language to another.

Computer hardware is designed according to a variety of performance and architectural specifications; some of these have profound effects on the kind of code that must be generated for the same source program. It is beyond the scope of this book to cover all the common architectures in detail. Because it is the simplest machine to generate code for, we treat a zero-address stack machine in depth. Register architectures and memory-to-memory operations are treated in connection with code optimization. We believe that a good grounding in the fundamental concepts of code generation will transfer to almost any architecture, regardless of the particular operational details. The diligent reader will find ample opportunity for generating code for a variety of target architectures.

1.5.7 Optimization

Optimization is the process by which a compiler modifies its internal data structures or the generated code in order to cause some improvement in execution time or code space. Although the earliest compilers had already done substantial optimization, a great deal of research has gone into the study of optimization algorithms since then. Some of the algorithms in common use are based on sound theory, but many optimization strategies in practice turn out to be ad hoc code. There is very little of the kind of automatic generation that has reduced compiler front-end design to a mechanical translation of an attributed context-free grammar. In other words, writing correct optimizers is far from the trivial task that writing correct parsers has become.

Different code generation strategies in the compiler design can give rise to greater or fewer opportunities for optimization. A fairly sophisticated code generator in one compiler may implicitly accomplish what is left to the optimizer of a compiler with a much simpler code generator. Thus, a code generator that tracks register contents could eliminate redundant load instructions that might otherwise be left for peephole optimization. On the other hand, the application of a particular optimization transformation to the AST of a program may give rise to other optimization opportunities that could not otherwise be detected. For example, back-substitution of the procedure body into its calling sites could give rise to constant expression evaluation and dead code elimination in the case of constant parameters that can be evaluated at compile time.

The tiny computer that is the target for the majority of the compiler construction exercises in this book lacks the variety of instruction forms that gives rise to most machine-dependent optimization transformations. Nevertheless, most of the classical machine-independent optimization algorithms are still relevant.

In the construction of a practical compiler, the scanner and parser are usually built automatically from grammars; recent advances in attribute grammars are beginning to bring automation to the constrainer, too. Code optimization and optimization are still largely a manual exercise in programming. Accordingly, the effort to build a complete compiler tends to be concentrated mostly in the code generation and optimization phases and, to the degree it is not automated, also in the constrainer. Compilers with little or no optimization and languages with limited constraint requirements are much easier to implement and thus tend to dominate the marketplace. The implementer of a new compiler may expect to spend as much effort on the constrainer as on the scanner and parser combined. A simple code generator, as for the compiler exercises in this book, will be no more difficult than the constrainer, but a reasonable optimizer will often require more effort than all the rest of the compiler together.

Symbols

$\rightarrow$ Reads "rewrite as" in a grammar rewrite rule, as in
$$vowel \rightarrow \text{"}a\text{"} \mid \text{"}e\text{"} \mid \text{"}i\text{"} \mid \text{"}o\text{"} \mid \text{"}u\text{"}$$
which expresses that the syntactic form called a vowel may be rewritten as either the literal letter "*a*" or "*e*" or "*i*" or "*o*" or else "*u*."

| Reads "or" in a grammar rewrite rule to express an alternative way of rewriting.

::=   BNF equivalent to the arrow ($\rightarrow$).

< >   BNF symbols used to identify a syntactic name and to distinguish it from tokens in the language, as in
$$<vowel> ::= a \mid e \mid i \mid o \mid u$$
In this text we prefer to quote the tokens and leave the syntactic names as undistinguished identifiers because it is more consistent and easier to automate.

Acronyms

AST   Abstract syntax tree, the implied output of a parser.

BNF   Backus-Naur Form (or Backus-Normal Form), a way of writing grammars.

HLL   Higher-level language, such as Fortran or Modula-2.

LL   Left-to-right scan that expands the Leftmost nonterminal, a simple parsing strategy.

LR   Left-to-right scan that expands the Rightmost nonterminal in reverse, a more powerful parsing strategy.

Keywords

code generator   A compiler procedure that constructs code for the target machine based on information (typically isolated semantic action calls or an AST) generated by the front end.

compiler   A program that translates an input source program (usually a text file) into an output target program (usually some machine language "object module").

back end   generates code for the target machine. The parts of the back end are the code generator and optionally one or more optimizers.

front end   recognizes a valid input program file and analyzes its structure. The front end consists of a scanner, a parser, and a constrainer.

constrainer	A compiler procedure that enforces type and declaration rules in the source program.
grammar	A set of rules for writing valid sentences in a language.
lexical	grammar specifies the correct form of tokens or words of a computer language.
phrase structure	grammar specifies how words of a computer language fit together to form syntactically valid programs.
HLL	Higher-level language, whose notation is more closely related to the problems to be solved than the target machine language.
input program	A text file or stream of characters.
interpreter	A program that executes an input source program without translating it into any particular machine language output.
lexeme	A token or word in the source program language, consisting of a character or sequence of characters.
lexical analysis	The scanner actions that recognize and identify lexemes (words) of a language.
parser	The part of a compiler that analyzes a sentence (program) in a computer language according to its phrase structure.
parsing	The parser actions that identify the phrase structure or syntax of an input program.
bottom-up	construction of an AST starts with tokens in the leaves and builds the AST branch by branch until the root is reached; LR is a bottom-up parsing strategy.
LL	means Left-to-right scan of an input string with the decision of which grammar production to apply based on the Leftmost nonterminal (called a leftmost derivation).
LR	means Left-to-right scan of an input stream with a Rightmost derivation in reverse, where the rightmost nonterminal is expanded.
top-down	construction of AST starts at the top with the root node and builds down to to the token leaves; LL is a top-down parsing strategy.
scanner	A compiler procedure that recognizes valid tokens from the string of characters that is an input source text.
string table	A data structure used by the scanner to store the spelling of identifiers and string constants.
symbol table	A data structure used by the constrainer to store semantic information about the identifiers in a source text.
token	Any single, atomic symbol that the scanner recognizes. Tokens can be numbers or string constants or punctuation characters like ";" or reserved (key) words like "IF" or multiple character symbols like ":=" or identifiers (such as for procedure, variable, or constant names).

translator	A program to translate a source text into a target (machine) language.
assembler	translates low-level symbolic code into machine code.
compiler	translates HLL source into a target machine code to be executed later.
interpreter	immediately executes its source text without translating it into any machine code.
tree	A hierarchical data structure (a directed acyclic graph with a single path from the root to any other node).
AST	Abstract syntax tree, is constructed by the parser where the interior nodes represent nonterminals and the leaves represent tokens.

Exercises

1. List all the sentences generated by the little English-language grammar. Show how you derived each sentence from the original word "sentence."

2. Change the English-language grammar so that a proper noun cannot occur on both sides of the verb.

Review Quiz

Indicate whether the following statements are true or false.

1. Scanners perform lexical analysis.

2. An assembly language is an HLL.

3. A parser first constructs a string table, which it then uses to construct an AST.

4. A parser recognizes phrase structure in an input stream.

5. An interpreter is a form of compiler that runs slowly.

6. An attribute grammar defines how the symbol table is used.

Compiler Project

1. Make a list of all possible tokens in Itty Bitty Modula — a subset of Modula-2 limited to IF and WHILE control structures, integer and Boolean operators, but with no sets or constant identifiers or separate modules. Note that you should consider all identifiers to be represented by a single generic "identifier" token. If necessary, refer to Appendix A for a syntax diagram of Itty Bitty Modula.

2. Make a list of the ASCII characters necessary to compose all the tokens in your list.

3. Speculate about the constraints on identifiers and expressions that an Itty Bitty Modula compiler should enforce. Note that word order and phrase structure are syntactic issues for the parser, not semantics for the constrainer.

Further Reading

Allen, J. *Natural Language Understanding*. Reading, MA: Benjamin/Cummings, 1987. See section 17.4, "Grammars and Generators."

Dowty, D.R., Karttunen, L., & Zwicky, A. (eds.). *Natural Language Parsing*. New York: Cambridge University Press, 1985.

Gazdar, G. "Phrase Structure Grammar." In *The Nature of Syntactic Representation*, ed. Jacobson, P. & Pullman, G.K. Dordrecht: D. Reidel, 1982, pp. 131-186.

Wirth, N. "From Modula to Oberon." *Software—Practice and Experience*. Vol. 18, No. 7 (July 1988), pp. 661-670.

Chapter 2

Grammars:
The Chomsky Hierarchy

Aims

- Understand the structure of a grammar.
- Survey the Chomsky hierarchy.
- Distinguish between context-sensitive, context-free, and regular grammars.
- Examine the structure of parse trees.
- Explore the relationships between grammars and their machines.
- Introduce the canonical derivations.
- Explore the limitations of finite-state automata.
- Examine methods of counting in grammars.
- Practice the art of thinking in grammars.

2.1 Introduction

In this chapter we explore the central theme of the book: grammars. Because the front end of a compiler may be largely constructed automatically from the grammars that specify the language, it is important that our understanding of them be grounded in rigorous mathematical theory. One of the characteristics of a grammar relates to the complexity of the language it generates. Following the work of Noam Chomsky in natural languages, we distinguish four levels of language complexity, commonly known as "the Chomsky Hierarchy." With each language level is identified a class of automata that can recognize strings in a language of that level. We are particularly interested in the two higher (most restricted) levels in the Chomsky hierarchy, regular and context-free, because we can automatically construct efficient scanners and parsers from grammars in these two classes.

2.2 Grammars

A *grammar* is defined mathematically as a 4-tuple; that is, it consists of four distinct components: the alphabet, the nonterminals, the productions, and a goal symbol. These are represented here by the symbols Σ, N, P, and S, enclosed in parentheses and separated by commas:

(Σ, N, P, S)

Three of these symbols represent sets, and the fourth identifies a particular element of the second set. A grammar, therefore, consists of three mathematical sets and one distinguished element of one of them.

2.2.1 Alphabets and Strings

The first set, Σ, is the *alphabet*, or set of *terminals*. It is a finite set consisting of all the input characters or symbols that can be arranged to form sentences in the language. In the English language the alphabet is normally thought of as the 26 letters from *A* to *Z*, but in our definition we would also have to include the punctuation symbols and the space between letters, because these are important parts of correct English sentences.

Most programming languages are encoded as strings of text characters, so the alphabet for them is the set of text characters, usually some well-defined computer set such as ASCII (pronounced "*ask-key*," it stands for the *American Standard Code for Information Interchange*).

A compiler is usually defined with two grammars. The alphabet for the scanner grammar is ASCII or some subset of it, but the alphabet for the parser grammar is the set of tokens generated by the scanner, not ASCII at all. We abstract away or remove the individual spelling of the identifier tokens; that is, identifiers are recognized and reported by the scanner as a generic "identifier" token at each occurrence. Thus, the set of tokens is still finite — indeed, it is often smaller than the scanner alphabet.

Many of our examples and exercises focus on particular aspects of grammars, so we often use very restricted alphabets consisting of a few lower-case letters from the beginning of the Roman alphabet, defined explicitly: {*a, b, c, d*}. In grammars for realistic languages we usually represent the alphabet as individual characters quoted as character constants, such as the alphabet for real number constants:

{'+', '−', '.', 'E', '0', ..., '9'}.

The terminals in the alphabet can be assembled into strings of any length according to the rules of the grammar. We use the term *string* to refer to a sequence of zero or more terminals in any particular order. Although we never contemplate infinite strings, a string can be arbitrarily long, so there are an infinite number of possible strings for any given (finite) alphabet. A particular language may define in its grammar only a finite number of strings (possibly even none), but the interesting programming languages are all infinite, or practically so.

For an example of strings, let $\Sigma = \{a, b, c, d\}$. Possible strings of terminals from Σ include *aaa, aabbccdd, d, cba, abab, ccccccccccacccc,* and so on. The empty string is usually denoted by $\in$. The set of all possible strings in Σ, including the empty string $\in$, is denoted by Σ^* (read "sigma star"). Σ^* is called the closure of the alphabet. Σ^* denotes any of the strings of alphabet symbols, including the empty string. The asterisk is called the Kleene star after the logician Stephen Cole Kleene. We use the Kleene star in several different contexts to mean "zero or more of" whatever it is appended to; in this case it means "strings of zero or more terminals from the alphabet Σ." A language is some specified subset of Σ^*.

2.2.2 Nonterminals and Productions

The second set composing the mathematical definition of a grammar is the set of *nonterminals*, shown in the 4-tuple as "*N*." This is a finite set of symbols not in the alphabet. The nonterminals are not sets of strings, but symbols that can be thought of as representing or standing for sets of strings which are subsets of Σ^*. A particular nonterminal, the *goal symbol*, represents exactly all the strings in the language. Nonterminals are also called syntactic categories or grammar variables. We often use capital letters from the front of the Roman alphabet as nonterminals in our examples and exercises, with "A" (or sometimes "S") as the goal symbol. In real programming language grammars, identifiers that suggest meanings to be associated with the nonterminals are preferred as symbols for the nonterminals. The set of terminals and nonterminals, taken together, is called the *vocabulary* of the grammar.

The *productions* of a grammar ("*P*" in our 4-tuple) is a set of rewriting rules, each written as two strings of symbols separated by an arrow. The symbols on each side of the arrow may be drawn from both terminals and nonterminals, subject to certain restrictions in the form of the grammar. Simpler languages can be described by simpler grammars, that is, grammars limited by more restrictions. The more complex languages require fewer restrictions in the form of the productions to define them.

2.2.3 Some Example Grammars

Let's consider a very simple language that can be defined with the simplest of all possible grammars, involving the most restrictions on its form. Here is a complete grammar for all strings containing two of the letters *a, b,* and *c* (possibly both the same letter) in any order:

$$G_1 = (\{a, b, c\}, \{A, B\}, \{A{\rightarrow}aB, A{\rightarrow}bB, A{\rightarrow}cB, B{\rightarrow}a, B{\rightarrow}b, B{\rightarrow}c\}, A)$$

In this grammar, the alphabet Σ is the set of lower-case letters, $\{a, b, c\}$; the nonterminals are the set of capital letters, $\{A, B\}$, of which the letter A is the goal symbol. The set of productions is the following list:

A→*a*B	B→*a*
A→*b*B	B→*b*
A→*c*B	B→*c*

The nonterminal A represents "all the strings in the language," and the nonterminal B represents "all the strings of one character." Beginning with the goal symbol A, we can apply the rules of the productions to rewrite it (or parts of it) until we end up with a string of terminals. We always begin with the goal symbol, which in this grammar is A (the goal symbol is also often called the *start symbol* because we start with it):

A

Any of the first three rules or productions can be applied to this initial string; let us arbitrarily choose the second, and replace the A with "*b*B":

*b*B

We continue to apply rules as long as that is possible. Because there are no longer any A's to rewrite, the first three rules can no longer be applied, but any of the last three can, because any one of them could replace the B in our working string. Let us choose the last rule, again arbitrarily, and rewrite the string:

bc

Now we have no more nonterminals in the string, only terminals, so the process terminates.

This sequence of steps is called a *derivation*. The result is that we have *derived* a string in the language. The derivation may also be written on a single line, thus:

A $\Rightarrow$ *b*B $\Rightarrow$ *bc*

The double arrow "$\Rightarrow$" is pronounced "derives" and represents one step in the derivation. Thus, A derives the string *b*B, which derives the terminal string *bc*. As long as there are nonterminals in the working string, the process does not terminate; when only terminals remain, the application of rewriting rules terminates. This is the reason the symbols are called, respectively, "nonterminals" and "terminals." At any point in the process we can choose any rule that has its left-hand side somewhere in the string; we replace that left-hand side by the right-hand side of the same rule.

Sometimes it is convenient to abbreviate a derivation by using the Kleene star:

A $\Rightarrow^*$ *bc*

The starred double arrow means that the string "*bc*" can be derived from the nonterminal A by zero or more derivation steps.

We can derive a second string in the language by choosing different productions:

A $\Rightarrow$ *a*B $\Rightarrow$ *aa*

By making different choices along the way it is easily seen that the only strings we can generate from this grammar are the nine two-letter strings we defined as our language. G_1 is an example of the kind of grammar used to define a scanner, although in this case the language is finite. Most scanner grammars define infinite languages.

For a second example, take the grammar $G_2 = (\Sigma, N, P, E)$, where the alphabet Σ is the set $\{n,+,*,),(\}$, N is the set of nonterminals $\{E,T,F\}$, and P is the following set of productions (numbered for later reference):

D.1.   E→E+T
D.2.   E→T
D.3.   T→T*F
D.4.   T→F
D.5.   F→(E)
D.6.   F→*n*

The first production has a single nonterminal, E, on the left-hand side, and a string consisting of the two nonterminals E and T separated by the terminal "+" on the right-hand side. This production means that whenever this grammar is used to generate a string in the language it defines, any time the nonterminal E appears in the working string, that nonterminal may be rewritten as the string "E+T" leaving the rest of the string unchanged. Starting with the goal symbol E, we can apply the first production to rewrite it as "E+T" and then apply it again to rewrite just the E at the left end of the working string, giving a new working string, "E+T+T" and so on:

$$E \Rightarrow E+T \Rightarrow E+T+T \Rightarrow ...$$

The grammar G_2 can be used to derive the string $n+n*n$ from the goal symbol E as follows:

E	goal symbol
E+T	apply rule D.1
E+T*F	apply rule D.3
T+T*F	apply rule D.2
F+T*F	apply rule D.4 to leftmost T
F+F*F	apply rule D.4 again
F+F*n	apply rule D.6 to rightmost F
F+n*n	apply rule D.6 to rightmost F again
$n+n*n$	apply rule D.6 one more time

We can also diagram the process as a tree, called the *derivation tree* or *parse tree* or *abstract syntax tree* (see Figure 2.1a). We write

$$E \Rightarrow^* n+n*n$$

to mean that nonterminal E derives the string $n+n*n$ in zero or more steps. Each of the nine lines of this derivation is called a *sentential form*, and the last line is called a *sentence* in the language. A sentence in the language is any string in Σ^* that can be derived from the goal symbol in one or more steps. A sentential form ω is any string in $(\Sigma \cup N)^*$ — that is, containing any number of terminals and nonterminals — that satisfies the relations,

$$S \Rightarrow^* \omega \Rightarrow^* \sigma$$

where S is the goal symbol and σ is a sentence in Σ^*. In other words, a sentential form is any string of terminals and nonterminals that can be derived from the goal symbol on the way to a sentence in the language. Any *cut* across the parse tree of a sentence is a sentential form, provided that it does not go around (that is, below) any terminals. Figure 2.1b shows an example of the cut that marks the sentential form "F+F*F". Note that if the gray line of the illustration failed to curve up and catch the terminal "+" but fell below it, then it would not be a proper cut: "FF*F" is not a sentential form in this language.

The alert reader will notice that in this grammar the order in which the productions are applied when there is a choice of more than one does not make any difference. For example, in the derivation of $n+n*n$, the second step could be the application of rule D.3 to the nonterminal T, or it could be application of rule D.2 to the nonterminal E:

$$E \Rightarrow E+T \Rightarrow E+T*F \Rightarrow ... \qquad \text{apply D.3}$$
$$E \Rightarrow E+T \Rightarrow T+T \Rightarrow ... \qquad \text{apply D.2}$$

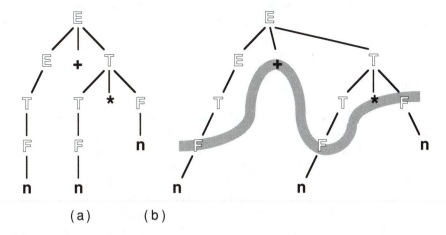

(a)   (b)

Figure 2.1. The parse tree for the Derivation E $\Rightarrow$* $n+n*n$. The gray line (b) represents a cut, showing the sentential form, F+F*F.

The same productions must all be applied eventually (in whatever order) to derive the same terminal string, but there is considerable freedom in the specific order. This is a property of unambiguous context-free grammars that we will exploit later.

The leaf nodes (branch tips) of the parse tree, read in left-to-right order, form the sentence parsed by this tree, also called its *frontier*. If two different parse trees can be constructed for the same sentence, then the grammar is said to be *ambiguous*.

Both of our example grammars have had exactly one nonterminal symbol on the left-hand side of each production. This form is characteristic of the grammars used to construct compilers. However, there is also an important class of grammars without this restriction. Our third example grammar generates all nonempty strings with equal numbers of a's, b's, and c's in alphabetical order:

$$G_3 = (\{a,b,c\}, \{A,B,C\}, P, A)$$

where P is the set of productions,

A→aABC	CB→BC
A→aBC	
bC→bc	aB→ab
cC→cc	bB→bb

To generate the string *aabbcc* the following derivation works:

$$A$$
$$a\text{ABC}$$
$$aa\text{BCBC}$$
$$aa\text{BBCC}$$
$$aab\text{BCC}$$
$$aabb\text{CC}$$
$$aabbc\text{C}$$
$$aabbcc$$

Note that by rewriting a string of symbols (such as in the production, $aB \rightarrow ab$), this grammar forces the generated string to be in alphabetical order, even though at one point in the derivation it is not.

2.3 The Chomsky Hierarchy

In the mid-1950s the linguist Noam Chomsky defined four levels of grammars, by which he hoped to analyze natural human languages. As a natural linguist he failed, but the "Chomsky Hierarchy" has served us well as a formal basis for describing the artificial languages we use to program computers.

Chomsky defined four levels of language complexity, which he numbered (in the fine tradition of computer professionals, who always begin their numbering schemes at zero) from 0 to 3, and four classes of grammar to generate languages in those levels. Subsequent language research has identified four corresponding classes of *automata* (singular: *automaton*) or abstract machine types, which can recognize exactly those strings that are in the languages generated by their respective grammars. Table 2.1 gives the four levels.

Chomsky Language Class	Grammar	Recognizer
3	Regular	Finite-State Automaton
2	Context-Free	Push-Down Automaton
1	Context-Sensitive	Linear-Bounded Automaton
0	Unrestricted	Turing Machine

Table 2.1. The Chomsky Hierarchy of languages and automata.

2.4 Grammars and Their Machines

An automaton consists of a control mechanism with a finite number of *states*, and some form of *tape*, which may be read and advanced as in a magnetic tape player, and possibly also written (recorded) and moved in either direction. A finite alphabet defines the symbols that may be on the tape, the same as the alphabet in a language definition. The initial content of the tape is a string of characters in the alphabet; it is the *input* to the automaton. Beginning with a designated *start state*, the automaton sequences through its states, based on what it finds on the tape and the rules in its control. These steps are called *transitions*. At any time the automaton may *halt*, and by doing so it is said to *accept* the input string. It may also *block*, that is, reach a state for which it has no rules by which to proceed with the current tape input; if this happens, the automaton is said to *reject* the input. The different classes of automata are distinguished primarily by the kind of tape they have.

2.4.1 Turing Machines

The least restrictive of all language types is Level 0 in the Chomsky hierarchy, which is called an *unrestricted* grammar; it is recognized by the most general of all automata, the Turing machine. The *Turing machine* (often abbreviated *TM*), shown in Figure 2.2, is an abstract model of a computational device devised by Alan Turing in the 1940s; it consists of a read-write head that can be positioned anywhere along an infinite tape. The automaton can be in any one of its finite set of states, but only by arriving in that state by a sequence of transition rules from the start state. Each transition rule specifies for a single state and a single character of the alphabet under the read-write head, three actions: the next state to advance to, a new character (possibly the same) to write back onto the tape, and a direction to move the tape by one character position. The tape may also be left in the same position, and any transition rule may also specify that the machine halt at the end of its transition, signifying that it accepts the input as a string in the language it recognizes. If there is no transition for a particular state and tape symbol, the TM blocks and rejects the input. A Level 0 language is also called a recursively enumerable language because it is the set of those strings that can be enumerated (listed) by a TM.

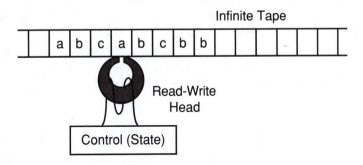

Figure 2.2. The Turing machine.

Turing machines are an important basis for much of the theory in computability and computational complexity, but as a practical tool for compiling programs in a production environment they are hopelessly inefficient. In fact, it is provable that we cannot know, for an arbitrary starting tape, whether a TM will terminate (either halt or block) with a result. Thus, Level 0 is not a useful class of languages for compiler design, so we do not devote much space to its discussion. We mention it here because all other automata that recognize language levels in the Chomsky hierarchy are variations and restrictions of Turing machines.

2.4.2 Linear-Bounded Automata

Level 1 in the Chomsky hierarchy is called *Context-Sensitive*. Context-sensitive languages may be recognized correctly by an automaton with a finite read-write tape, called a *linear-bounded automaton* (LBA), as shown in Figure 2.3.

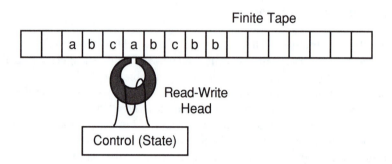

Figure 2.3. The linear-bounded automaton.

A context-sensitive grammar has two restrictions: the left-hand side of each production must have at least one nonterminal in it, and the right-hand side must not have fewer symbols than the left. In particular, there can be no empty productions. An *empty production* is of the form $N \rightarrow \epsilon$, that is, a nonterminal on the left and the empty string on the right. The one exception to the second restriction is if the left-hand side consists of the goal symbol only, and the goal symbol does not occur on the right-hand side of any other production, then the right-hand side may be empty. This exception is necessary to generate the empty string in the language. G_3 is an example of a context-sensitive grammar. In fact, grammars G_1 and G_2 are also context-sensitive in form, but they are more restricted; we normally describe a language by the highest Chomsky level it fits, that is, the most restrictive grammar that can generate the language.

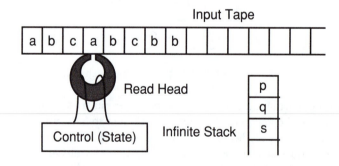

Figure 2.4. The push-down automaton.

2.4.3 Push-Down Automata

Level 2 in the hierarchy is called *context-free*. A context-free language may be correctly recognized by a *push-down automaton* (PDA), which can only read its input tape but has a stack that can grow to arbitrary depth where it can save information (see Figure 2.4). An automaton with a read-only tape and two independent stacks is equivalent to a Turing machine.

A *stack* is a linear data structure that permits access only at one end, something like the stack of papers on a busy executive's desk, or the mechanical plate server in a cafeteria. In principle the stack can grow to any arbitrary depth, but in practice we limit it to some particular large size — usually based on the size of memory in the computer. There are two operations on a stack, *push* and *pop*, both of which operate on the top of the stack, as illustrated in Figure 2.5. Push adds one item to the top of the stack, obscuring the previous top element, and pop takes the top element off the stack, exposing the next element for access by a subsequent pop.

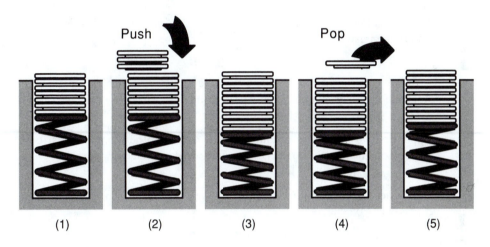

Figure 2.5. How a Stack Works. **Push**ing three plates (2) onto a plate stack, then **Pop**ping one plate off (4)

Every PDA step pops a symbol off the stack. It can then immediately push the same or other symbols back onto the stack, or none at all. The PDA may optionally read and advance its input tape on any move, or halt (and accept). Because the PDA makes its state transitions based on the symbols it finds on the stack top as well as under the read head, it can use the stack for temporary storage of what has been read.

A context-free grammar is more restricted than a context-sensitive one in that it allows at most a single nonterminal (and no terminals) on the left-hand side of each production. We use the phrase "context-free grammar" in this book so often that it is convenient to abbreviate it "CFG." G_2 is an example of a CFG. Unlike context-sensitive grammars, we can relax the requirement about empty productions in context-free grammars because we can prove it does not alter the fundamental strength of the language. Any CFG with empty productions can be transformed into an equivalent CFG having at most a single empty production meeting the empty-production restriction of context-sensitive grammars. Chapter 7 shows how to construct deterministic (linear-time) PDAs automatically from a large class of context-free grammars.

2.4.4 Removing Empty Productions

Empty productions can be removed from a context-free grammar by the following transformation. For every empty production in the grammar

$$A \rightarrow \in$$

find and copy all the productions with A on the right-hand side, deleting A from the copy. Then if A is not the goal symbol, delete the empty production. If A is the goal symbol and A also occurs on the right-hand side of some production, choose a new nonterminal G for a goal symbol, and add the two productions

$$G \rightarrow A$$
$$G \rightarrow \in$$

The original empty production can then be safely removed. Consider for example the simple grammar

$A \rightarrow AaB$	$B \rightarrow Ba$
$A \rightarrow \in$	$B \rightarrow \in$

Applying the first step to the empty production in B, we add two new productions

$A \rightarrow Aa$	$B \rightarrow a$

Applying it to the empty production in A adds two new productions (one from the original grammar, one from the new production added in the first step)

$A \rightarrow aB$	$A \rightarrow a$

Then a new goal symbol G is added, giving a final grammar in correct form, with no excess empty productions:

$G \rightarrow A$	$G \rightarrow \in$
$A \rightarrow AaB$	$B \rightarrow Ba$
$A \rightarrow Aa$	$B \rightarrow a$
$A \rightarrow aB$	$A \rightarrow a$

2.4.5 A Comparison of Context-Free and Context-Sensitive

The major difference between context-free and context-sensitive grammars is implied by their names: all context-free productions are applied without regard to any context or symbols that may be near a nonterminal being rewritten. A context-sensitive production may include any number of context symbols on the left-hand side, so productions can be written to rearrange the symbols in the sentential form, as we did in G_3 to get the b's and c's sorted into alphabetical order. Context-free productions can only expand (or in some cases by extension, contract) nonterminals where they are. Thus no production in a CFG can affect the symbols in any other nonterminal in the working string. This makes context-sensitive languages both more powerful and much harder to recognize than context-free.

All modern programming languages are specified with context-free grammars, but as we shall see, most of them have context sensitivity built into their language definition. An example of such sensitivity is the requirement in Pascal and Modula-2 that identifiers be declared before they are used: the existence of such a declaration is the *context* in which the use of the identifier is allowed. Rather than open up a Pandora's box of context-sensitivity, we adopt very carefully restricted extensions to context-free grammars. These extensions are called *attributes*. Thus, we hope to preserve all of the linear (fast) compile-time benefits afforded by context-free grammars, without discarding the language features that would otherwise seem to require the lower Chomsky levels.

2.4.6 Finite-State Automata

The highest and most restrictive level in the Chomsky hierarchy is Level 3, a *regular* language (sometimes also called a *"regular set"*), may be recognized by a *finite-state automaton* (FSA, but also called a finite-state machine, or FSM), shown in Figure 2.6. The FSA has no infinite storage and is allowed to read its input only once in a single pass. Anything that must be remembered about the context of a symbol on the input tape must be preserved in the state of the machine. Because it is finite, there is a limit to the amount of information that can be stored in the machine state. Regular grammars are the most restrictive of all, and allow only one symbol on the left-hand side of each production (a nonterminal), and only one or two symbols on the right-hand side. The first symbol on the right must always be terminal; the second, if present, is always nonterminal. Like context-sensitive and proper context-free, a regular grammar does not allow empty productions, except for the single production with the goal symbol on the left when the goal symbol does not occur on the right of any production.

As in context-free grammars, we can relax this rule without changing the language strength, but because regular grammars properly formed relate so directly to their equivalent FSAs, we use a different term to refer to the more relaxed grammar: a *right-linear* grammar is a grammar where every production has exactly one nonterminal on the left, and zero or more terminals on the right, followed by at most one nonterminal. In every production with a nonterminal on the right, it is always the rightmost symbol — hence the term *right*-linear. A grammar in the same form but with the nonterminal on the left end of the right-hand side is called *left-linear*. Chapter 3 shows how to transform regular, right-linear, and left-linear grammars into each other, and how to construct equivalent FSAs from them.

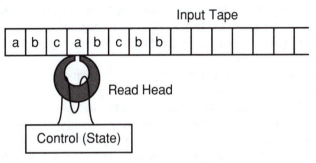

Figure 2.6. The finite-state automaton.

2.5 Empty Strings and Empty Languages

It is important as we consider the languages generated by various grammars, that we do not confuse a grammar that generates the *empty string* ϵ as one of the strings in its language with a grammar for an *empty language*; that is, it generates no strings at all. G_4 is a grammar that generates exactly one string, the empty string:

$$G_4 = (\{a\}, \{A\}, \{A \rightarrow \epsilon\}, A)$$

G_5 generates no strings at all, not even the empty string:

$$G_5 = (\{a\}, \{A,B\}, \{A \rightarrow B, B \rightarrow aA\}, A)$$

On first glance it would appear that G_5 generates strings of a's, but every partial string contains a nonterminal. The process never terminates, so it never results in a terminal string. The language is empty, because the grammar cannot generate any strings consisting only of zero or more terminals. When the grammar is less trivial, it is easier to overlook productions that cannot generate any strings, such as G_6:

$$G_6 = (\{a,b,c\}, \{A,B,C\}, P, A)$$

where P is the set of productions

$$A \rightarrow BC$$
$$A \rightarrow aC$$
$$B \rightarrow bB$$
$$C \rightarrow cC$$
$$C \rightarrow a$$

Although this grammar has a production that seems to generate strings of b's, there is no way to get rid of the nonterminal B in that production, so both the nonterminal and the production are useless. The grammar generates only strings of c's with an a at each end. The first production is also useless, since it can never be applied in a derivation of a sentence.

2.6 Canonical Derivations

Earlier we introduced the concept of a *derivation*, where a nonterminal A is said to *derive* a string ω of terminals and nonterminals, if by successive application of production rules a nonterminal A is transformed into ω, that is, $A \Rightarrow^* \omega$. Consider again the grammar G_2, where E is the goal symbol. We can say that E derives the sentence in the language, $n+n*n$ by applying rules D.1, D.2, and D.3 each once, rule D.4 twice, and rule D.6 three times. We can show this process graphically by building a *parse tree* (also called a *derivation tree*), as in Figure 2.7.

Because of its two-dimensional graphical representation, Figure 2.7 shows all eight rule applications at once. Computers tend to be sequential devices, operating on sequential files, so this graphical representation is somewhat awkward except for illustrative purposes. We can, however, linearize the process by applying one rule at a time. This gives several opportunities to choose which rule to apply first. In an unambiguous CFG as this is, the order in which the same rules are applied makes no difference to the resulting parse tree for the same final string derived. Consider, for example, the two strategies in Figure 2.8. One is called the *leftmost derivation* because it always applies a rule to the leftmost nonterminal in the sentential form. The other is called the *rightmost derivation* because it always applies a rule to the rightmost nonterminal. Both derive the string *n+n*n* and both construct the same parse tree. It is not possible to derive this string in G_2 without applying these same rules in some order and constructing this same parse tree.

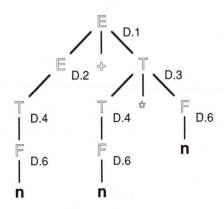

Figure 2.7. The Parse tree for Deriving *n+n*n* in the Language of G_2.

The order in which the rules are applied, however, is significant in the sequence of sentential forms that takes us from the goal symbol E to the sentence *n+n*n*. The two derivations in Figure 2.8 are called *canonical derivations*, because they form the basis or rule (the Latin word for "rule" is *canon*) for the two classes of parser construction. Leftmost derivations are the easiest to implement in handwritten compilers. When a Leftmost derivation is used on an input string read from Left to right, the parse tree is constructed from the top down, that is, beginning with the goal symbol E; such a compiler is called a *top-down* or "LL(*k*)" compiler. Rightmost derivations can handle a

E			E	
E + T	D.1		E + T	D.1
T + T	D.2		E + T * F	D.3
F + T	D.4		E + T * *n*	D.6
n + T	D.6		E + F * *n*	D.4
n + T * F	D.3		E + *n* * *n*	D.6
n + F * F	D.4		T + *n* * *n*	D.2
n + *n* * F	D.6		F + *n* * *n*	D.4
n + *n* * *n*	D.6		*n* + *n* * *n*	D.6

(a) (b)

Figure 2.8. Leftmost (a) and Rightmost (b) Canonical Derivations for the string *n+n*n* in G_2.

larger and less restrictive subset of context-free grammars. When a <u>R</u>ightmost derivation is used in reverse on an input string read from <u>L</u>eft to right, the parse tree is constructed from the bottom up, that is, beginning with the sentence $n+n*n$; such a compiler is called a *bottom-up* or "LR(k)" compiler. In much of this book we focus on top-down parsers, although Chapter 7 discusses some of the implementation differences between top-down and bottom-up parsers. Most automatic parser generators are bottom-up because LL(k) grammars are somewhat more restrictive than any of the bottom-up techniques.

2.7 Ambiguity

An *ambiguous* grammar is one in which there exists a string in its language with two different parse trees. Consider the grammar G_7 which generates the same language as G_2. Figure 2.9 shows two different parse trees for the same string, $n+n*n$ (it is usually easy enough to infer the vocabulary and goal symbol of a grammar from the set of productions, so we often abbreviate the grammar specification to just the list of productions).

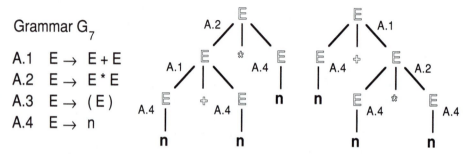

Grammar G_7

A.1 $E \rightarrow E + E$
A.2 $E \rightarrow E * E$
A.3 $E \rightarrow (E)$
A.4 $E \rightarrow n$

Figure 2.9. Ambiguous grammar G_7, with two different parse trees for the same input string $n+n*n$.

Both parses of the string $n+n*n$ with G_7 require the same rules, but the order in which the rules are applied in a top-down parse (leftmost derivation) results in differing parse trees. If rule A.1 is applied first to the goal symbol E, the result is the tree on the right, in which the plus operator adds the first n to the product of the other two n's. If rule A.2 is applied first to the goal symbol E, the result is the tree on the left, in which the star operator multiplies the last n by the sum of the first two n's. It is impossible to define exactly what characteristics make a grammar ambiguous, but we can prove some grammars to be unambiguous. A grammar can be proved to be ambiguous by showing two different parse trees for some string in its language, but finding such an example for a particular grammar may not be particularly easy.

The programming language Pascal has one production that makes it ambiguous. $G_8 = (\Sigma, \{S\}, P, S)$ is a fragment of the language as a stand-alone grammar, where P is the set of productions

$\qquad$ S→"**if**" e "**then**" S "**else**" S
$\qquad$ S→"**if**" e "**then**" S
$\qquad$ S→ p

and Σ={"**if**", "**then**", "**else**", e, p}. The compound statement

if e **then if** e **then** p **else** p

has nested **if** statements, but only one of the **if**s has the optional **else** part; the question is, which one? Pascal arbitrarily defines it to be the innermost **if** statement, but the sentence could as easily parse the other way. It makes a difference in the meaning of the statement, for if the **else** part goes with the inner **if**, then it will not be executed if the outer **if** expression evaluates to false, no matter how the inner expression evaluates; to execute the **else** part, the outer expression must be true and the inner false. On the other hand, if the **else** part goes with the outer **if**, then it depends only on the outer expression in all cases.

2.8 The Art of Thinking in Grammars

In this book we devote a lot of time to the mechanics of constructing computer programs that recognize the languages specified by particular context-free and regular grammars. This can be done automatically; that is, computer programs exist to build the recognizer automata from the grammatical definitions. Less time is spent in showing how to write the grammars. There is a reason for that: we have algorithms for building the automata, but no algorithms exist for writing correct grammars for arbitrary language requirements. It is an art. Like most artistic endeavors, however, we can study some of the known techniques and tools that contribute to good grammar design.

One important tool is a good understanding of the limits and capabilities of the different Chomsky levels for describing language features. We focus on Levels 1-3; Level 0 is unrestricted in what can or cannot be specified in the language and needs no further attention. The major distinction between the three higher Chomsky levels is the flexibility in counting symbols in the generated strings. By "counting" we mean the mathematical sense of puting the elements of a set (for example, a particular class of tokens in a string of the language) into one to one correspondence with the elements of another set (perhaps another class of tokens in the same string). A language like Modula-2 or Pascal that requires parentheses to be matched, left to right, counts the left parentheses by matching them to an equal number of right parentheses. Because parentheses can be nested to any depth, the counting is (in principle) unlimited.

2.8.1 Limits of Finite-State Automata

A finite automaton is not able to count, or match, any symbols in the alphabet, except to a finite number. Although most computers are in fact FSAs (no computer actually has an infinite stack or an infinite-length data tape), the complexity of the system seen as a vast number of states makes this perspective unuseful — much like trying to survey a forest by counting all the leaves on the trees. Therefore, we limit our consideration of FSAs and regular grammars to applications that require counting only small numbers of things.

One example of a regular grammar that counts a small number of items is G_1. The language is specified to consist of all strings in Σ^* with exactly two characters. The grammar must therefore count to two.

Another example is counting the number of digits in an integer constant literal in order to validate the correct form of the literal. In the set of all possible strings of zero or more digits (for simplicity we assume the alphabet contains only digits), integer constants are only those strings with at least one digit. Therefore, it is only necessary to count the first digit in a grammar to generate them. Zero-length strings are not in the language but all other strings of digits are, regardless of their length. Note that we are concerned here only with the *form* of the integer constants. It is conceivable (and a very real possibility) that an integer is of the correct form, but too large to represent in an integer variable of the target machine; we consider that to be a semantic issue, not the scanner's problem, and not something we would attempt to prevent in a regular grammar (but see Exercise 6).

Not quite so obvious is the counting necessary to guarantee that the number of symbols in the string is odd or even. It is necessary to count only to two to determine oddness, so a regular grammar is sufficient. The following productions come from a regular grammar that defines a language consisting of all strings with an even number of *a*'s and an odd number of *b*'s:

A→*a*B	C→*a*D
A→*b*C	C→*b*A
A→*b*	D→*a*
B→*a*A	D→*a*C
B→*b*D	D→*b*B

Of the four nonterminals, A represents all the strings in the language, that is, all the strings with an even number of *a*'s and an odd number of *b*'s. A string in this language may, by the first production, consist of an initial *a* followed by any string represented by the nonterminal B. Therefore, B represents all strings with an odd number of *a*'s (that is, the even number in A, less the initial *a*) and an odd number of *b*'s. Similarly, C represents all strings with an even number of *a*'s and an even number of *b*'s. Zero is an even number, so the nonterminal A could also consist only of one *b* and no *a*'s (the third production in A). By the same reasoning, nonterminal D consists of all strings with an odd number of *a*'s and an even number of *b*'s, possibly only the single token *a*.

A good rule of thumb is that whenever a symbol must be counted in a regular grammar, the number of nonterminals required is the highest the count must reach; if several independent counts must be maintained, then the total number of nonterminals required for counting is the product of all the individual requirements. In this case, we wished to count two symbols (*a*'s and *b*'s) and each must count up to two; 2×2=4, so because there are no other requirements than just counting, the number of nonterminals required is four. If the specification had called for the number of *a*'s to be exactly divisible by three, then that would have required three nonterminals to count the *a*'s, and for each of those three, two to count the *b*'s, for a total of six.

A regular grammar can enforce a certain order of the symbols in the generated string also. If a nonempty string may consist of any number of *a*'s, *b*'s, and *c*'s, but the *a*'s must precede all the *b*'s, and the *b*'s must precede all the *c*'s, then a simple grammar suffices:

A→*a*A	A→*a*
A→*b*B	A→*b*
A→*c*C	A→*c*
B→*b*B	B→*b*
B→*c*C	B→*c*
C→*c*C	C→*c*

Here we use one nonterminal to count the number of *c*'s (up to one), another to count the *b*'s before the first *c*, and yet another to generate *a*'s before the first *b*. Because there are three stages of letters (*a*'s, then *b*'s, then finally *c*'s), but counting only one of each, three nonterminals are required, the sum of the counts for each stage. If the first stage required an odd number of *a*'s, then it would require two nonterminals, for a total of four (2+1+1).

In this last example, it is also possible to see another important aspect of "thinking in grammars." The nonterminal A, because it is the goal symbol, represents all the strings in the language: we can think of it as representing "any number of *a*'s, followed by any number of *b*'s, followed by any number of *c*'s." The nonterminal B represents only substrings of *b*'s and *c*'s, with no *a*'s; as soon as the first *b* is generated there can be no more *a*'s, and the nonterminal B remembers that. Similarly the nonterminal C remembers that a *c* has been generated, so there can be no more *a*'s or *b*'s.

In the previous example, the nonterminal A represents any (as yet ungenerated) string with even *a*'s and odd *b*'s; B represents ungenerated strings with both *a*'s and *b*'s odd, so once A generates a single *a* the remaining ungenerated string has one less *a*, so it has an odd number — just what B represents. Therefore the production rewriting A with a generated *a* includes nonterminal B in its rightpart.

2.8.2 Counting on Context-Free Grammars

Because the push-down automaton has an infinite-depth stack, it can successfully count any number of symbols in an input string, matching them to an equal number of other symbols. We speak of "counting," but we do not mean storing away some numeric representation of the number of symbols; counting in the mathematical sense means matching one-to-one with the cardinal numbers, so we focus on the matching aspect. For example, a grammar to count *a*'s and *b*'s, and thereby force them to have equal numbers, can be done with a simple CFG:

A→*a*A*b*A
A→*b*A*a*A
A→*ab*
A→*ba*

Although this grammar is ambiguous, it illustrates the important distinction of counting: because we cannot force which production to choose when there is a choice (unless we are trying to match a particular terminal string), any matching of symbols must be compelled by both symbols appearing in equal numbers in the same productions. In this example there is no way to compel the selection of any one of the four productions (because all four rewrite the nonterminal A), so the only way to get the same number of *a*'s and *b*'s is to put one *a* and one *b* in the same production, for every production in which any of them appear. This way you can never generate an *a* without generating a *b* at the same time. In practice it is necessary only that the terminals to be matched be derived from (as it were) a "common ancestor," that is, a single production that derives exactly one of each. For example, the context-sensitive grammar G_3 introduced earlier generates equal numbers of *a*'s, *b*'s, and *c*'s, but the three symbols that appear together in the same production consist of the terminal *a*, and the nonterminals B and C. The two nonterminals generate exactly one terminal each (their respective lower-case letter), so they are effectively matched.

The grammar G_2 generates all arithmetic expressions with addition and multiplication where the conventional operator precedence applies, but parentheses can be used to override the precedence. Note again the significance of giving the nonterminals somewhat meaningful names such as "E" (for "expression"), "T" (for "term"), and "F" (for "factor"), thereby reflecting the fact that they represent meaningful components of the generated language.

Let's examine the parenthesis matching first. Observe that G_2 generates only parentheses in matched pairs, because the two appear only one each in the same production (Rule D.5). Furthermore, the left parenthesis always precedes its matching right parenthesis, which is compelled by their order in the production. This does not mean that all left parentheses must precede all right parentheses, for indeed that is not the case: the string $(n)+(n)$ is in the language just as $((n+n))$ is. However, when we trace the generation of the two strings (see Figure 2.10), we see that the parentheses are always properly nested as they are generated.

E	E
E+T	T
T+T	F
F+T	(E)
F+F	(T)
(E)+F	(F)
(E)+(E)	((E))
(T)+(E)	((E+T))
(T)+(T)	((T+T))
(F)+(T)	((F+T))
(F)+(F)	((F+F))
(n)+(F)	$((n$+F))
(n)+(n)	$((n$+$n))$

Figure 2.10. Two derivations generating properly nested parentheses.

This "proper nesting" is characteristic of context-free languages: we can require symbols to match in the properly nested order, but we cannot match them in the same left-to-right order. We can write a CFG to generate palindromes (where the first half of the string matches the second half in reverse), but we cannot write a context-free grammar to match the spelling of the same word twice. To do that requires a context-sensitive grammar.

Suppose, for example, that we wanted to write a CFG to generate strings consisting of any number of a's and b's in any order, followed by a single c, followed finally by the same sequence of a's and b's in the same order as the first sequence. Remembering that to get the second string to match the first we must generate the matching symbols one each in the same production, we might try something like grammar G_{12}.

G_{12} 　　　 A→aAa
　　　　　 A→bAb
　　　　　 A→c

Unfortunately this generates palindromes, with the second sequence backward from the first. If we try changing the first two productions so that the nonterminal A is at one end or the other, the pairs of symbols do not get separated by the required middle c. Adding additional nonterminals does not solve the problem.

One thing is apparent in this analysis: a recursive production (which is the only way to generate strings of arbitrary length) is going to generate multiple copies of all other symbols but the recursive nonterminal by ejecting copies of them on whatever side of that nonterminal they occur in the production. Thus the recursive production

A→$aAbc$

generates a's out the left side and bc pairs out the right side as shown in Figure 2.11. Because every application of this recursive production results in another copy of the nonterminal in the working string (A in this case), there must be at least one other production rewriting the same nonterminal that is *not* recursive, such as A→e, or else the production can never generate any strings. Anything the nonrecursive productions generate will be in the center of the generated string, between the left and right halves. In our palindrome example (G_{12}), the only nonrecursive production generates exactly one c, and that is the center of the palindrome. This is an important concept, and it will be helpful later in the study of regular expressions and also in building LL(k) parsers.

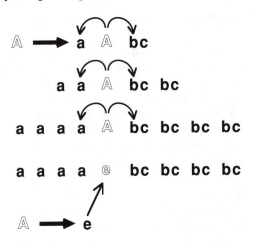

Figure 2.11. Generating matched repetitive patterns, with terminator.

2.8.3 Sensitive to the Context

Although we do not attempt to construct linear-bounded automata (LBAs) from context-sensitive grammars automatically, it is sometimes instructive to see what these kinds of grammars afford that CFGs do not. As noted, one quality requiring context sensitivity is the ability to repeat strings of symbols in the same order. A context-sensitive grammar G_{13} to generate a language consisting of all pairs of identical substrings in a and b, each started and ended by a single letter c, follows:

$$G_{13} = (\{a,b,c\}, \{S,A,B,F,G\}, P, S)$$

where P is the set of productions in Figure 2.12.

$S \rightarrow c$GF	S
$G \rightarrow a$GA	cG F
$G \rightarrow b$GB	caGAF
$G \rightarrow cc$	caGaF
$F \rightarrow c$	cabGBaF
$Aa \rightarrow a$A	cabGaBF
$Ab \rightarrow b$A	cabGabF
$Bb \rightarrow b$B	$cabb$GBabF
$Ba \rightarrow a$B	$cabb$GaBbF
$AF \rightarrow a$F	$cabb$GabBF
$BF \rightarrow b$F	$cabb$GabbF
	$cabbccabb$F
	$cabbccabbc$
(a)	(b)

Figure 2.12. Productions for G_{13} (a) and the derivation of *cabbccabbc*.

The nonterminal G generates pairs of symbols $(a,$A$)$ or $(b,$B$)$. The nonterminal F flags the end of the rightmost substring and serves as context to tell nonterminals A and B when to turn into (derive) terminals. A and B are generated in the middle of the string, then "walk" their way to the right, exchanging places with all terminal a's and b's until they reach the flag F. Finally, when the string is complete, G and F turn into c's. If F turns into a terminal too soon, the remaining A's or B's cannot generate terminals (that is, the derivation would generate no sentence); similarly, the A's and B's cannot become terminals until they finally reach the right end of the string at the flag. Although more A's and B's can be generated from the center before previously generated A's or B's have reached the end and converted, they cannot get out of order with respect to them, because there is no way for nonterminal A's or B's to be exchanged until the earlier ones have reached their final resting place and become terminals.

This is an interesting problem, mostly because it is an over-simplified representation of the language requirement for declaration before use: let the c's represent all the rest of the program; the first substring in a and b is a variable or procedure declaration for some identifier, and the second substring is its use in the body of the program. For a grammar to formally verify that every identifier is declared before use, it must do the same thing as

Grammars: The Chomsky Hierarchy   Chap. 2

spell a substring the same way twice in the sentence. Type-checking the parameters on a procedure call is essentially the same problem. Because a CFG cannot do this, we conclude that a CFG cannot type-check variable and procedure declarations. Until researchers discover a way to efficiently convert context-sensitive grammars into deterministic automata, and experience develops for writing context-sensitive grammars to define these language requirements, we must find another way to deal with variable declaration checking. All modern compilers use a constrainer with a symbol table for this purpose.

This particular example also illustrates some of the characteristic writing styles that yield workable context-sensitive grammars. The key concept is to generate the symbols (or nonterminals representing those symbols) at the point where the generator nonterminal is active (typically by a recursion as used in CFGs), then use context-sensitive productions to sort or re-arrange the symbols that are still in nonterminal form. By including only some of the possible symbol permutation transformations, exactly the desired effect can be achieved. Finally, some flag generated at startup can trigger the conversion to terminals, which (if necessary) can propagate like dominoes falling over. Figure 2.13 shows the propagation paths for grammar G_3, another example of this kind of grammar thinking.

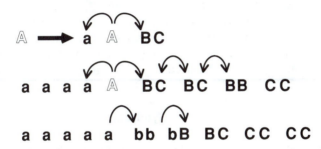

Figure 2.13. Sorting symbols in a context-sensitive grammar.

Summary

A grammar is a mathematical description for a language. This description is in the form of a 4-tuple (Σ, N, P, S), where Σ is an alphabet, N is set of nonterminals, P is a set of productions, and S is a goal symbol. Writing grammars is an art. This means that it depends not only on knowledge of language principles and design skills, but also on a certain elusive creativity that is more easily caught than taught. Grammar-writing design skills stem from a sense of language structure and a perception of language form which enables a designer to mold alphabet and nonterminals into a description of a language.

The Chomsky hierarchy provides a useful organization of the languages we wish to treat. In this chapter, the languages in the Chomsky hierarchy have been correlated with language recognizers and their corresponding grammars. This book concentrates on the mechanization of regular and context-free grammars, but in this chapter context-sensitive grammars are also used to aid in understanding the art. A context-sensitive grammar is restricted only in the length of the rightpart of its productions. That is, for every production $\alpha \rightarrow \beta$, the number of symbols (terminals and nonterminals) in β must be at least that of α, with one exception to allow for the empty string in the language. Context-free languages are a proper subset of the set of context-sensitive languages. The grammar for a context-free language is more restrictive than that for a context-sensitive language. That is, every production of a context-free grammar must have exactly one nonterminal (and no terminals) on the left. Regular languages are further restricted in their grammars to at most one nonterminal on the right side of the arrow, and that nonterminal must be consistently at the right end.

A language recognizer is a procedure for defining a set of strings. Recognizers are modeled with three basic parts: input tape, finite state control unit, and perhaps some form of memory. The control unit is analogous to a computer program, which determines which direction its input head is moved across the tape in terms of the current input symbol it has read. The recognizer for a context-free language is a push-down automaton (PDA). A PDA is named after its memory unit, a stack.

The recognizers for regular languages are finite-state automata (FSAs), which are the simplest recognizers. An FSA has no memory unit. We specify an FSA by defining a finite set of control states, a set of input symbols, an initial state, and a finite set of final states. A final state indicates acceptance of an input string. An FSA gives us another way of specifying the set of strings of a regular language.

In sum, we have seen two ways to specify the strings of a language: with a recognizer and with a grammar. In practice a compiler is a recognizer; it is constructed mechanically from the corresponding grammar. It is much more important, therefore, to hone our grammar-writing skills than to focus directly on automaton design techniques.

Symbols

Σ The finite set of all input characters or symbols that can be used to construct sentences in a particular language.

Σ^* The set of all possible strings consisting of zero or more symbols from Σ.

$\in$ The empty string.

N   The set of nonterminals (not in Σ), metalinguistic symbols, which represent subsets of Σ^*.

P   The set of rewrite rules (productions) for a grammar.

$\Rightarrow$ Derives, a single step in a derivation.

$\Rightarrow^*$ Zero or more derivation steps.

Acronyms

ASCII   American Standard Code for Information Interchange, a common representation of alphanumeric text characters in computers.

CFG   Context-free grammar.

FSA   Finite-state automaton, the recognizer for a regular language.

FSM	Finite-state machine, equivalent to an FSA.
LBA	Linear-bounded automaton, the recognizer for a context-sensitive language.
PDA	Push-down automaton, the recognizer for a context-free language.
TM	Turing machine, the most unrestricted of all automata.

Keywords

alphabet	The set of symbols Σ of which sentences in a language are composed.
ambiguous grammar	A grammar with more than one parse for at least one sentence in the language, or at least two leftmost or rightmost derivations of that sentence.
derivation	A sequence of steps in deriving a string in a language by applying one rewrite rule at each step.
canonical	One of two derivations that apply rules in a specified order.
leftmost	replaces the leftmost nonterminal at each step in a derivation.
rightmost	replaces the rightmost nonterminal at each step in a derivation.
frontier	The leaf nodes of a parse tree, representing a sentence.
grammar	The tuple (Σ, N, P, S), where Σ = alphabet (set of terminals) N = set of nonterminals (metalinguistic symbols) P = set of productions (rewrite rules) S = goal symbol (a nonterminal)

grammar types:

context free	A grammar that permits applications of its productions without regard to any context or symbols other than the nonterminal being rewritten. Each production has the form $A \rightarrow \beta$ where A is in N and β is in $(N \cup \Sigma)^*$
context sensitive	A grammar where each production is of the form $A \rightarrow B$ with $|A| \leq |B|$ where $|A|$ denotes the length of A. Note: this means B cannot be the empty string, unless A is the goal symbol and does not occur on the right of any production.
left linear	A grammar where all productions are of the form $A \rightarrow Bx$ or $A \rightarrow x$ where x is in Σ^* and A,B are in N.
regular	A right linear grammar where all productions are of the form $A \rightarrow xB$ or $A \rightarrow x$

where x is in Σ and A, B are in N. The production $A \rightarrow \in$ is also permitted if A is the goal symbol and does not appear on the right-hand side of any production.

right linear	A grammar where all productions are of the form $$A \rightarrow xB$$ or $$A \rightarrow x$$ where x is in Σ^* and A, B are in N.
unrestricted	A grammar with productions of the form $$\alpha \rightarrow \beta$$ where α and β are arbitrary strings of grammar symbols and $\alpha \neq \in$
language	(1) A set of strings of finite length over an alphabet Σ. (2) A specified subset of Σ^*. (3) A set strings generated by a grammar (see grammar). (4) A set input strings accepted by a language recognizer (see recognizer).
language type:	
0	Phrase-structured language generated by an unrestricted grammar.
1	Context-sensitive language generated by a context-sensitive grammar.
2	Context-free language generated by a context-free grammar.
3	Regular language generated by a regular grammar
nonterminal	An identifier or symbol not in Σ^* but representing a subset of Σ^*.
parse tree	In two-dimensional form, a diagram representing the steps to rewrite the goal symbol as a sentence. Also called an abstract syntax tree (AST).
production	(1) A rewriting rule that describes one step of how the sentences of a language are to be generated. (2) A pair of strings $\alpha \rightarrow \beta$ where α contains at least one nonterminal and β can be a mixture of terminals and nonterminals.
recognizer	A real or abstract machine that accepts (recognizes) exactly all the strings in a language.
recognizer type:	
0	Turing machine (TM), which defines a phrase-structured or recursively enumerable language.
1	Linear-bounded automaton (LBA), which defines a context-sensitive language.
2	Push-down automaton (PDA), which defines a context-free language.
3	Finite-state automaton (FSA), which defines a regular language.
sentence	A string in the language.
sentential form	Any line in a derivation.

stack	A linear data structure such that all insertions ("pushes") and deletions ("pops") are made at the same end of the structure.
terminal	A symbol used to construct sentences in a language. A member of the alphabet Σ.
vocabulary	The set of terminals and nonterminals (Σ and N).

Exercises

1. Indicate which of the following are true or false.

   (a) All context-free grammars are context-sensitive.

   (b) All right-linear grammars are context-free.

   (c) All regular grammars are right-linear.

   (d) All regular grammars are left-linear.

   (e) All left-linear grammars are context-free.

   (f) All left-linear grammars are context-sensitive.

   (g) All regular grammars are context-sensitive.

   (h) All right-linear grammars are context-sensitive.

2. Classify the following grammars as unrestricted, context-sensitive, context-free, right-linear, left-linear, or regular. Some grammars may fit more than one category. Indicate *all* the categories to which each grammar belongs.

(a)	(b)	(c)	(d)
$S \rightarrow aB$	$S \rightarrow Cba$	$S \rightarrow abC$	$S \rightarrow aBC$
$S \rightarrow c$	$S \rightarrow C$	$S \rightarrow A$	$S \rightarrow A$
$C \rightarrow cA$	$C \rightarrow Bc$	$A \rightarrow aB$	$A \rightarrow aBA$
$B \rightarrow bC$	$B \rightarrow Cb$	$A \rightarrow aA$	$A \rightarrow a$
$B \rightarrow b$	$B \rightarrow b$	$B \rightarrow bC$	$B \rightarrow BC$
$A \rightarrow aA$	$A \rightarrow Ba$	$B \rightarrow b$	$B \rightarrow b$
$A \rightarrow a$	$A \rightarrow Aa$	$C \rightarrow c$	$C \rightarrow c$

(e)	(f)	(g)	(h)
$S \rightarrow ab$	$S \rightarrow aA$	$S \rightarrow a$	$S \rightarrow ab$
$S \rightarrow B$	$S \rightarrow \in$	$S \rightarrow b$	$S \rightarrow B$
$B \rightarrow bc$	$A \rightarrow bcS$	$S \rightarrow \in$	$B \rightarrow bc$
$B \rightarrow \in$			

(i)	(j)	(k)	(l)
$S \rightarrow ab$	$S \rightarrow Aab$	$S \rightarrow ABC$	$S \rightarrow aAbc$
$S \rightarrow B$	$S \rightarrow B$	$AB \rightarrow A$	$S \rightarrow \in$
$B \rightarrow bc$	$A \rightarrow Ba$	$A \rightarrow aB$	$A \rightarrow Bc$
$B \rightarrow ab$	$B \rightarrow bc$	$aBC \rightarrow abC$	$B \rightarrow bB$
	$B \rightarrow \in$	$C \rightarrow cd$	$B \rightarrow cS$

3. (a) Indicate which, if any, of the above grammars are ambiguous.

   (b) Prove the grammars you selected in (a) are ambiguous.

4. (a) Construct the parse tree for grammar G_2 deriving the string $(n+n)*n$. Give both the leftmost and rightmost derivations.

   (b) Show that grammar G_2 cannot derive the string $n+*n$.

   (c) Show that grammar G_3 cannot derive the strings *aaccbb* and *abbccc*.

5. (a) Construct a regular grammar that generates all strings of *a*'s and *b*'s having both an odd number of *a*'s and an odd number of *b*'s.

   (b) Derive the string *aababb* using the grammar you constructed.

6. (a) Construct a regular grammar that generates all strings of *a*'s and *b*'s in which all *a*'s occur in groups of three.

   (b) Derive the string *baaabaaabb* using the grammar you constructed.

7. (a) Write a regular grammar to generate all possible combinations of zeros and ones where the string is six or fewer characters long.

   (b) Derive the string 01001 using the grammar you constructed.

8. (a) Write a regular grammar for Modula-2 string constants. A string constant consists of any string not containing single quote enclosed in single quotes, or any string not containing double quote enclosed in double quotes. To simplify things, assume that the only characters in the alphabet are: *a*, *b*, ', and ".

   (b) Derive the string 'aba"aab" ' using the grammar you constructed.

9. (a) Write a context-free grammar that generates all palindromes of *a*'s and *b*'s. A palindrome is a string that reads the same backward and forward (for example, *abaababaabaaba*).

   (b) Derive the string *abbaabba* using the grammar you constructed. Draw the parse tree.

10. (a) Write a context-free grammar for Modula-2 comments. A comment must begin with '(*' and end with '*)'. To simplify things, assume that the only characters are: *a*, *b*, *, (, and). Note that comments can be nested.

   (b) Derive the string $(*ab*a**(b*)$ using the grammar you constructed, giving both the leftmost and rightmost canonical derivations. Draw the parse tree.

11. (a) Write a context-free grammar for all strings of *a*'s and *b*'s in any order, such that there are more *a*'s than *b*'s. It follows that there must be at least one *a*.

   (b) Derive the string *baaba* using the grammar you constructed, giving both the leftmost and rightmost canonical derivations. Draw the parse tree.

12. (a) Write a context-sensitive grammar for all strings of *a*'s, *b*'s, and *c*'s in any order, such that there are more *a*'s than *b*'s and more *b*'s than *c*'s. It follows that there must be at least two *a*'s and at least one *b*.

   (b) Derive the string *caabaaba* using the grammar you constructed.

13. (a) Write a context-sensitive grammar for all strings of *a*'s, *b*'s, and *c*'s having an equal number of *a*'s, *b*'s, and *c*'s in any order.

   (b) Derive the string *cacbab* using the grammar you constructed.

14. (a) Write a context-sensitive grammar for strings of a's and b's such that each string consists of two identical substrings. For example, *aabaab* is one such string.

    (b) Derive the string *babbbabb* using the grammar you constructed.

15. (a) Write a context-sensitve grammar for all strings of a's and b's such that each string consists of three identical substrings. For example, *aabaabaab* is one such string.

    (b) Derive the string *abaaabaaabaa* using the grammar you constructed.

16. (a) Write a right-linear grammar for Pascal's real constants (for example, 5, 4E5, +3.8, –29.6E15, 7E–3). Note that the decimal point is always preceded and followed by digits, and there are at most two digits in the exponent. For simplicity, let d stand for any digit.

    (b) Derive the string –49.72E–12 using the grammar you constructed.

17. Describe the languages generated by the following grammars. Try to capture the nature of the language in English, rather than merely writing down an English transcription of the grammar.

(a)	(b)	(c)	(d)
S → cA	S → 0 S	S → abcA	S → 0
A → cA	S → S 0	S → Aabc	S → 1
A → 0A	S → 1 S	A → ∈	S → 1 S
A → 1A	S → S 1	Aa → Sa	
A → c	S → 0	cA → cS	(e)
A → 0	S → 1		S → a
A → 1			S → * S S
			S → + S S

18. Select the appropriate grammar level and automaton for each of the following languages

    (a) All strings of zeros and ones in equal numbers, in any order.

    (b) All strings of zeros, ones, and twos in equal numbers, in any order.

    (c) All strings consisting of two identical substrings of a's and b's where each substring has a's and b's in any order (for example, *abaaabaa*).

    (d) All strings consisting of one a, one b, and two c's in any order (for example, *cbca*).

    (e) All strings consisting of matching parentheses (for example, "(( )) ( )").

    (f) All strings of paired zeros and ones, that is, each zero immediately preceding or following its matching one.

19. Rewrite the following context-sensitive grammar as an equivalent context-free grammar.

    S → ABS
    S → AB
    AB → BA
    A → 0
    B → 1

Review Quiz

Indicate whether the following statements are true or false.

1. We can define a finite-state machine that recognizes the empty language.

2. A language that consists only of the empty string is a type 3 language in the Chomsky hierarchy.

3. It is not possible to construct a finite-state machine that recognizes strings defined by
$$A \rightarrow 0A \mid 1B \mid 0 \mid \in$$
$$B \rightarrow 1B \mid \in$$

4. The grammar in question 3 is context-free.

5. The language defined by the grammar in question 3 is regular.

6. The grammar in question 3 is left-linear.

7. Every right-linear grammar is regular.

8. The strings in a regular language will be accepted as input by at most one FSM.

9. Every regular grammar is right-linear.

10. Every grammar defines a language that has a corresponding recognizer.

Compiler Project

1. Write a regular grammar to generate each of the following classes of Itty Bitty Modula tokens.
(a) All identifiers.
(b) All reserved words; assume the identifiers 'INTEGER', 'BOOLEAN', 'TRUE', and 'FALSE' are reserved words (they are predeclared identifiers in standard Modula-2).
(c) Unsigned integers, and hexadecimal and octal constants.
(d) All operators and punctuation symbols.
(e) String constants (see Exercise 8).
(f) Itty Bitty Modula comments, but do not allow the substrings '(*' or '*)' within a comment.

2. Write a context-free grammar to generate the phrase structure of Itty Bitty Modula. If necessary, refer to the syntax diagrams in Appendix A. Let your alphabet be the token list you prepared at the end of Chapter 1.

3. Write a tiny program in Itty Bitty Modula, and construct its derivation tree using your grammar. Show both leftmost and rightmost canonical derivations for your program.

Further Reading

Aho, A.V., & Ullman, J.D. *The Theory of Parsing, Translation, and Compiling: Vol. I. Parsing.* Englewood Cliffs, NJ: Prentice Hall, 1972. See ch. 2, "Elements of Language Theory," especially section 2.1 on recognizers and section 2.2 on the generators and recognizers for regular languages.

Chomsky, N. "Three Models for the Description of Language," *IRE Transactions on Information Theory*, Vol. 2, No. 3 (1956), pp. 113-124.

Chomsky, N. & Miller, G.A. "Finite State Languages." *Information and Control*, Vol. 1, No. 1 (1963), pp. 91-112.

Cohen, D.I.A. *Introduction to Computer Theory.* New York: Wiley, 1986. See ch. 5 on finite automata, and Part II, *Pushdown Automata Theory,* especially ch. 19 on context-free languages. Also see ch. 30, "The Chomsky Hierarchy."

Fass, L.F. "Learning Context-Free Languages from Their Structured Sentences." *ACM SIGACT News*, Vol. 15, No. 3 (1983), pp. 24-35. The learning problem is concerned with devising techniques for determining a grammar G that generates a context-free language L based on sample information. This article is especially good, because it offers a formal treatment of concepts given in Chapter 2.

Fass, L.F. "On the Inference of Canonical Context-Free Grammars." *ACM SIGACT News*, Vol. 17, No. 7 (Spring 1986), pp. 55-60. This paper introduces various forms of context-free grammars.

Haines, L. *Generation and Recognition of Formal Languages.* Ph.D. dissertation, MIT, 1965.

Hopcroft, J.E. & Ullman, J.D. *Introduction to Automata Theory, Languages, and Computation.* Reading, MA: Addison-Wesley, 1979. See ch. 9, "The Chomsky Hierarchy," especially sections 9.1, "Regular Grammars" and 9.2, "Unrestricted Grammars."

Parikh, R.J. "On Context-Free Languages," *Journal of the ACM*, Vol. 13, No. 4 (1966), pp. 570-581.

Reis, A. "Regular Languages under F-gsm Mappings," *ACM SIGACT News*, Vol. 18, No. 3 (Spring 1987), pp. 41-45. F-gsm is a generalized sequential machine with final states where the output associated with a transition can be of any length and an output is defined for an input only if the input leads from the start state to a final state.

Stearns, R.E. "A Regularity Test for Pushdown Machines," *Information and Control*, Vol. 11 (1967), pp. 323-340. This paper gives an an account of how to determine if the set of input strings recognized by a PDA is regular. It does this by extracting a finite-state machine, which is equivalent to the PDA, which recognizes the strings in a regular language.

Tennent, R.D. *Principles of Programming Languages.* Englewood Cliffs, NJ: Prentice Hall, 1981. See section 1.3 on phrase structure, and section 2.6.2 on ambiguous syntactic descriptions.

Whitney, G.E. "The Generation and Recognition Properties of Table Languages," *Information Processing 68.* Amsterdam: North-Holland, 1969, pp. 388-394. Section 3 presents recognition as the dual of generation of the strings of a language.

Chapter 3

Scanners and Regular Languages

Aims

- Develop a theoretical foundation for scanner grammars.
- Introduce the formal properties of regular expressions and regular languages.
- Explore the practical implications of the algebra of regular expressions.
- Describe a technique to convert between regular expressions and regular grammars.
- Develop a finite-state automaton from a regular expression or grammar.
- Explore the implementation of a finite-state automaton as a scanner.
- Consider efficient methods of implementing string tables used by scanners.

3.1 Introduction to Lexical Analysis

The front end of a compiler reads and parses source text. Most of its runtime is spent on lexical analysis in the *scanner*, which reads characters from the input file, reducing them to manageable *tokens* (words or special symbols). It is therefore incumbent upon a compiler designer to exert some effort in making the scanner efficient. At the same time, we are concerned with a clean formal definition that leads to a correct implementation. Efficiency must not displace correctness.

We begin the definition of the compiler's scanner with a grammar. The language defined by the scanner grammar is the set of all strings of characters in the external (text) alphabet that form tokens in the language to be compiled. For example, any string that is an identifier is a token, and is therefore a sentence in the scanner language. The scanner recognizes that one token then "halts" and accepts.

This is a simple language, and a regular grammar is sufficient to fully define all the strings in the language. Consequently, a finite-state automaton (FSA) is adequate to implement the scanner.

48

In this chapter we present the methods for constructing finite-state automata automatically from regular grammars, and we show several ways to program a scanner from the formal specification of an FSA. We also show how to attach to the grammar those semantic actions necessary to support the compiler use of recognized tokens, and we show how these actions can be processed in the scanner implementation.

We begin, however, by introducing another notation for expressing a regular language. The notation more intuitively captures our notions about the form of tokens, and we show that notation to be equivalent to regular grammars.

3.2 Regular Expressions

Consider the integer constant literal. The numerals 0 and 384 are examples of integer-constant literals. An integer-constant token might be defined loosely in English as, "At least one decimal digit, followed by zero or more additional digits." We recognize the phrase "zero or more" in connection with the Kleene star notation, so we might represent the definition of an integer constant as "*dd**" where *d* represents a digit. A constant is thus one digit, followed by zero or more digits.

Similarly, an identifier in Pascal and Modula-2 consists of one letter (let's represent it by *a*), followed by zero or more of either letters or digits. If we use the vertical bar "|" to mean "either/or," then we can express the idea "either an *a* or a *d*, but not both" by writing "*a|d*". Now we can represent an identifier succinctly as "*a(a|d)**". This compact notation is called a *regular expression*. Regular expressions are a powerful and intuitive notation for defining a regular language.

Many people are familiar with regular expressions from their association with the popular UNIX® operating system. Therefore, because we use a notation slightly different from some others, and as an aid to encouraging the reader's familiarity with the grammatical notation that is the core of this text, we introduce regular expressions by means of a context-free grammar describing their form:

RE = ({"|", "*", ")", "(", σ}, {RegExpn, Term, Primary, Factor}, P, RegExpn)

where σ (sigma) represents any symbol in the alphabet of the language the regular expression defines, and P is the set of productions in Table 3.1.

3.1	RegExpn	→ RegExpn "|" Term	{*alternation*}
3.2	RegExpn	→ Term	
3.3	Term	→ Term Primary	{*concatenation*}
3.4	Term	→ Primary	
3.5	Primary	→ Factor "*"	{*iteration*}
3.6	Primary	→ Factor	
3.7	Factor	→ "(" RegExpn ")"	{*grouping*}
3.8	Factor	→ σ	{*any terminal*}

Table 3.1. The productions of a grammar for regular expressions.

Regular expressions have four metasymbols, "|", "*", ")", "(", in addition to the characters of the alphabet represented by σ. The grammar gives the syntax of regular expressions, but not the meaning. The meaning (hinted in the comments) is fairly simple: the vertical bar signifies *alternation*, or the selection of alternatives. That is, any Term to the right of a bar can be arbitrarily chosen instead of the RegExpn to its left. Because the production is recursive, the first two productions taken together generate a sequence of one or more Terms, separated by bars; of the whole sequence, exactly one Term is selected. Thus "*a|b*" means "either *a* or *b*, but not both." The regular expression "*a|b|c*" means "either *a* or *b* or *c*, but only one of them."

Similarly, a Term is a sequence of Primarys with no punctuation or metasymbols between them; the sequence denotes *concatenation*. The regular expression "*ab*"means "*a* followed by *b*."

A Factor can be a symbol in the alphabet or a parenthesized expression. If a Factor has a star affixed to its right, we call it *iteration*. The star means that the Factor is repeated zero or more times. Thus, "*a**" means "any number of *a*'s, or none at all." Note that the star operator is most binding, so that in the sequence "*a|bc**" only the *c* is iterated; alternation is least binding, so *bc** taken together is the alternative of *a* in the same regular expression.

It is sometimes convenient to use two or three additional metasymbols to express other kinds of iteration. To accommodate them, we add two productions to the grammar:

3.9 Primary → Factor "+"
3.10 Primary → Factor "?"

The plus "+" iterator means that its Factor is repeated one or more times (not zero or more times as with the star); the question mark means none or once. These are secondary iterators because they can be defined entirely in terms of the original grammar:

a+	means *a a**
a?	means *a* | ∈

It follows immediately from the definition that $(a+)? = (a?)+ = a*$.

3.2.1 The Algebra of Regular Expressions

Alternation and concatenation exhibit some of the characteristics of a mathematical *field*, with algebraic laws governing it such as those that govern addition and multiplication. A binary operation ⊕ is *commutative* if $a⊕b=b⊕a$ for all *a* and *b*. An operation ⊕ is *associative* if $(a⊕b)⊕c=a⊕(b⊕c)$ for all *a*, *b* and *c*. An operation • *distributes over* ⊕ if $a•(b⊕c)=a•b⊕a•c$ for all *a*, *b* and *c*. Concatenation distributes over alternation, but not vice versa; that is, $a(b|c)=ab|ac$ but $a|bc≠(a|b)(a|c)$. Both concatenation and alternation are associative, so that $a(bc)=(ab)c$ and $a|(b|c)=(a|b)|c$; only alternation, however, is commutative: $a|b=b|a$ but $ab≠ba$. Alternation has no identity element, but the identity for concatenation is the empty string ∈; thus $a∈= ∈a = a$. Another law, only vaguely evocative of the arithmetic laws we are familiar with, is *absorption* for alternation: $a|a=a$ for all *a*. Some algebraic identities for regular expressions are summarized in Table 3.2.

We can now illustrate how these identities can be used to manipulate regular expressions. Consider the regular expression

a(ba|ca) | (ac|ab)a

(*r*, *s*, and *t* are any regular expressions)

1. $r \mid s = s \mid r$ (commutativity for alternation)
2. $r \mid (s \mid t) = (r \mid s) \mid t$ (associativity for alternation)
3. $r \mid r = r$ (absorption for alternation)
5. $r(st) = (rs)t$ (associativity for concatenation)
6. $r(s \mid t) = rs \mid rt$ (left distributivity)
7. $(s \mid t)r = sr \mid tr$ (right distributivity)
8. $r\epsilon = \epsilon r = r$ (identity for concatenation)
9. $r^*r^* = r^*$ (closure absorption)
10. $r^* = \epsilon \mid r \mid rr \mid \dots$ (Kleene closure)
11. $(r^*)^* = r^*$
12. $rr^* = r^*r$
13. $(r^* \mid s^*)^* = (r^*s^*)^*$
14. $(r^*s^*)^* = (r \mid s)^*$
15. $(rs)^*r = r(sr)^*$
16. $(r \mid s)^* = (r^*s)^*r^*$

Table 3.2. Algebraic identities for regular expressions.

Applying the identities, we can simplify it in the following way:

$= (aba\mid aca) \mid (aca\mid aba)$ (6,7)
$= aba\mid(aca \mid (aca\mid aba))$ (2)
$= aba \mid ((aca\mid aca) \mid aba)$ (2)
$= aba\mid(aca\mid aba)$ (3)
$= aba\mid(aba\mid aca)$ (1)
$= (aba\mid aba)\mid aca)$ (2)
$= aba\mid aca$ (3)
$= a(b\mid c)a$ (6,7)

This is a more succinct and readable definition of the set of strings defined by the original regular expression.

3.2.2 Formal Properties of Regular Expressions

A regular expression can be defined informally as a compact notation for specifying a set of strings over the same alphabet. For example, if our alphabet is {0, 1}, the notation $(0\mid1)^*$ represents all strings of zeros and ones. Formally, we define a regular expression as follows:

Definition 3.1. A regular expression is a formal expression that is
    a) a single character in the alphabet Σ
    b) the empty string ϵ
    c) the empty set { }

or, given sets of strings R and S taken from Σ^*, we can obtain a regular expression by a finite number of applications of the following operations:

union operation:

$$R \mid S = \{x \mid x \text{ in R or } x \text{ in S}\}$$

concatenation operation:

$$RS = R \cdot S = \{xy \mid x \text{ in R, } y \text{ in S}\}$$

closure operation:

$$R^* = \{\ \} \mid R \mid RR \mid RRR \mid \dots$$

In effect, then, a regular expression can either be a single character from some alphabet or built up by a combination of one or more uses of the union, concatenation, and closure operations. For example, the single character "0" from the alphabet {0, 1} is a regular expression. Notice that the regular expression "0" represents the set {0}, which is a language in its own right. The set {0} is an example of a regular language.

Definition 3.2. A regular language is a set of strings L over an alphabet such that L can be defined by a regular expression.

In other words, a language L is regular if there exists a regular expression that represents the strings in L.

This means that if R and S are regular expressions, then R and S define regular languages L(R) and L(S). Also notice that the sets used to construct regular expressions are sets of strings taken from Σ^*. Each of these sets taken from Σ^* is finite. These sets are interesting because each of them is a regular language. We can prove that this is true by using mathematical induction and the following lemma:

Lemma 3.1. Every set containing a single string has a corresponding regular expression.

Proof. The proof of this lemma requires mathematical induction on the length of the string and is left for Exercise 22.

This lemma is needed in the induction step of the proof of Theorem 3.1:

Theorem 3.1. Every finite set of strings is a regular language.

Proof. (by induction): Basis step: by definition, the empty set { } is a regular expression and by definition a set of strings that is defined by a regular expression is regular. That is, { } is a regular language. Similarly, the empty string $\in$ is a regular expression and therefore the set {$\in$} is also regular. Finally, a character a is a regular expression representing the set {a}, so {a} is a regular language because it is represented by a regular expression.

Induction hypothesis: Assume the set of strings L with k elements is represented by a regular expression r. That is, assume that L is a regular language.

Induction step: Prove that any language L' with $k+1$ strings can be represented by a regular expression. To prove this, we can express L' as the union of L and {a}. That is, we express L' as the union of a language L with k strings and a language L" with one string in it ({a}, for example). We know by the induction hypothesis that L corresponds to the the regular expression r. By Lemma 3.1, we also know that language L" has a corresponding regular expression (call it r"). By definition, we know $r \mid r$" is a regular expression. This means the language L' has a corresponding regular expression, which is what we wanted to prove.

It may be asked if the converse to Theorem 3.1 is also true. We state this idea in Proposition 3.1 (a proposition is an assertion that may be true or false):

Proposition 3.1. Every regular language is finite.

Analysis. See Exercise 23.

Finally, notice that regular languages are closed with respect to union, concatenation, and Kleene star. That is, we can show that if L1 and L2 are regular languages, then we get another regular language by computing L1 | L2 or L1·L2 or L1* or L2*. This fact is summarized as follows:

Theorem 3.2. If L1 and L2 are regular languages, then L1|L2, L1·L2 and L1* are also regular languages.

Proof. This theorem can be proved by appealing to the definition of regular language. The details of the proof are left for Exercise 24.

The Kleene star operation on a set R represents an infinite union of concatenations as in

$$R^* = \{ \ \} \mid R \mid RR \mid RRR \mid ...$$

Less grandiose unions may also be defined, such as

$$R^3 \mid R^5 = RRR \mid RRRRR$$

By definition, we have

Definition 3.3. For a language L, $L^0 = \{\in \}$, the language with the empty string.

This leads to another theorem:

Lemma 3.2. If L is a regular language then L^n is also a regular language.

Proof. See Exercise 25.

Now you can also prove

Theorem 3.3. If L is a regular language, then the following are also regular languages:

    (a) $L^n \mid L^m$ for $n, m \geq 0$
    (b) $L^1 = \{\in \}L$

3.3 Transforming Grammars and Regular Expressions

A regular language can be defined by either a regular expression or a regular grammar. In other words, for every regular grammar, there exists a regular expression that defines the same language, and for every regular expression there exists a regular grammar that generates the same language. However, some regular languages are much more easily defined by a grammar, whereas others are more clearly defined by a regular expression. Therefore, it is important to be able to convert between the two. We now establish their equivalence by construction.

The productions of a regular grammar differ from regular expressions in one critical aspect: a grammar is a set of rules for *rewriting* the goal symbol, whereas the expression merely describes the finished string. The regular expression tends to be more intuitive in its description; that is, it is usually easier to see just what strings are in the language by examining the regular expression than by examining the grammar.

The first step in transforming a regular expression into a grammar is to make it into a rewrite rule. This is done by attaching a goal symbol. Thus, for any regular expression ω, choose some nonterminal S and make it the goal symbol of the new grammar, then write one production:

$$S \rightarrow \omega$$

The regular expression will normally contain some or all of the metasymbols; these are not defined in a regular grammar, so the second step of the transformation removes them.

Let x and y be any regular expressions, possibly empty or including nonterminal symbols. For every production of the form

$$A \rightarrow xy$$

choose some new nonterminal B and write instead

$$A \rightarrow xB$$
$$B \rightarrow y$$

For every production in our partially transformed grammar of the form

$$A \rightarrow x^*y$$

write instead the four productions

$$A \rightarrow xB$$
$$A \rightarrow y$$
$$B \rightarrow xB$$
$$B \rightarrow y$$

The extra nonterminal is necessary only if the iteration is nested inside another structure, but multiple nonterminals are only tedious, not detrimental. For every production of the form

$$A \rightarrow x|y$$

write instead

$$A \rightarrow x$$
$$A \rightarrow y$$

Continue with these transformations, applying the algebraic identities as necessary, until the resulting grammar is right-linear, that is, it contains no regular expression metasymbols and at most one terminal in each production. Note that the construction guarantees that there will never be more than one nonterminal on the right-hand side of any production, and it will be on the right end. Similarly, there will be at most one terminal on the right-hand side of any production (if not, just apply the first transformation rule until that is the case). The rules for transforming regular expressions into right-linear grammars are summarized in Rules R.1-R.3 of Table 3.3.

There may remain some productions with no terminal, making the grammar right-linear, not regular. We now show how to change a right-linear grammar into a regular grammar. A right-linear grammar with more than one terminal in any single production can be transformed by the first rule above. We are concerned here with the productions with no terminal. For every production of the form

$$A \rightarrow B$$

find and copy all the productions with B on the left-hand side, replacing it with A in the copy. Then delete the offending production.

For empty productions we can apply the transformation in Chapter 2, that is, for every empty production

$$A \rightarrow \epsilon$$

find and copy all the productions with A on the right-hand side, deleting A from the copy. Then if A is not the goal symbol, delete the empty production. If A is the goal symbol and A also occurs on the right-hand side of some production, choose a new nonterminal G for a goal symbol, and add the two productions

$$G \rightarrow A$$
$$G \rightarrow \epsilon$$

Continue to apply these two transformations until the resulting grammar is regular. The rules for transforming right-linear grammars into regular grammars are summarized in Rules R.4-R.6 of Table 3.3.

Rule #	Regular Expression Productions:		Grammar Productions:	
R.1	$A \rightarrow xy$		$A \rightarrow xB$	$B \rightarrow y$
R.2	$A \rightarrow x^*y$		$A \rightarrow xB\|y$	$B \rightarrow xB\|y$
R.3	$A \rightarrow x\|y$		$A \rightarrow x$	$A \rightarrow y$
R.4	$A \rightarrow B$	$B \rightarrow x$	$A \rightarrow x$	$B \rightarrow x$
R.5	$A \rightarrow \epsilon$	$B \rightarrow xA$	$B \rightarrow xA$	$B \rightarrow x$
R.6	$S \rightarrow \epsilon$ {S *is goal symbol*}		$G \rightarrow S$	$G \rightarrow \epsilon$

Table 3.3. Transforming regular expressions to regular grammars.

Consider for example a regular expression that we wish to transform into a regular grammar:

$$a\,(a|d)^*$$

We begin with a goal symbol S:

$S \rightarrow a\ (a|d)^*$

The outer regular expression structure is a concatenation, so Rule R.1 applies:

$S \rightarrow a\ A$
$A \rightarrow (a|d)^*$

Rule R.2 can be applied to the second production, where x is the contents of the parentheses and y is empty. This gives us:

$S \rightarrow a\ A$	
$A \rightarrow (a|d)\ B$	$B \rightarrow (a|d)\ B$
$A \rightarrow \in$	$B \rightarrow \in$

The distributive law can be applied to the two alternations, followed by Rule R.3:

$S \rightarrow a\ A$	
$A \rightarrow a\ B$	$B \rightarrow a\ B$
$A \rightarrow d\ B$	$B \rightarrow d\ B$
$A \rightarrow \in$	$B \rightarrow \in$

The grammar is now right-linear. The two empty productions can be eliminated by Rule R.5, leaving the regular grammar:

$S \rightarrow a\ A$	$S \rightarrow a$
$A \rightarrow a\ B$	$A \rightarrow d\ B$
$A \rightarrow a$	$A \rightarrow d$
$B \rightarrow a\ B$	$B \rightarrow d\ B$
$B \rightarrow a$	$B \rightarrow d$

To convert a regular grammar to a regular expression it is necessary only to reverse the process. In other words, if there are more than one production for a single nonterminal A, then replace them all with a single production, collecting the rightparts into a single rightpart separated by bars "|" as in Rule R.3 of Table 3.4. If the resulting production is recursive, then apply the commutativity law to rearrange the terms, so that all the recursive nonterminals are together, and then apply the distributive law to factor them out; group the remaining terms using the associative law, so that the result is in the form of Rule R.2, then replace it with the iteration form. This puts a single star around all of the subexpressions that were formerly recursive productions. Other than the goal symbol, any nonrecursive nonterminal with only one production can be replaced anywhere it occurs in the rightpart of another production by its rightpart, according to Rule R.1. When the goal symbol defines the only production, with no nonterminals in its rightpart, that right-hand side is the desired regular expression.

Rule #	Grammar Productions:		Regular Expression Productions:
R.1	$A \rightarrow x\mathrm{B}$	$B \rightarrow y$	$A \rightarrow xy$
R.2	$A \rightarrow x\mathrm{A}|y$		$A \rightarrow x^*y$
R.3	$A \rightarrow x$	$A \rightarrow y$	$A \rightarrow x|y$

Table 3.4. Transforming regular grammars to regular expressions

Consider a simple regular grammar, which we wish to convert to a regular expression:

$S \rightarrow a\,A$ $S \rightarrow a$

$A \rightarrow a\,A$ $A \rightarrow a$

$A \rightarrow d\,A$ $A \rightarrow d$

We apply Rule R.3 to both nonterminals first, so that we have one "production" each:

$S \rightarrow a\,A \mid a$ $A \rightarrow a\,A \mid a \mid d\,A \mid d$

Depending on the commutative law to rearrange the terms, and the associative law to add parentheses, we collect all the terms recursive in A together on the left:

$S \rightarrow a\,A \mid a$ $A \rightarrow (a\,A \mid d\,A) \mid (a \mid d)$

The distributive law allows us to factor out the recursive A, so that the production is now in the form to apply Rule R.2:

$A \rightarrow (a \mid d)A \mid (a \mid d)$

which, when applied, eliminates the recursion for the iterator:

$A \rightarrow (a \mid d)^{*}\,(a \mid d)$

Note that the transformation removes both the recursive nonterminal A and the or-bar next to it. This regular expression can now be substituted in the production for S, giving

$S \rightarrow a\,(a \mid d)^{*}\,(a \mid d) \mid a$

The resulting regular expression is somewhat verbose, but the application of the algebraic laws can simplify it somewhat. First, we can apply the concatenation identity $a = a\epsilon$ to the a on the right side of the alternation, then apply the distributive law to factor out the leading a on both sides of the alternation, giving

$a\,((a \mid d)^{*}\,(a \mid d) \mid \epsilon)$

From the definition of x^{+} we get

$a\,((a \mid d)^{+} \mid \epsilon)$

and then immediately

$a\,(a \mid d)^{*}$

3.4 Finite-State Automata

For every language defined by a regular grammar or regular expression, there exists a deterministic finite-state automaton to recognize the same language. A finite-state automaton is defined as a 5-tuple; that is, it has five different components:

$M = (\Sigma, Q, \Delta, q_0, F)$

The alphabet Σ for the FSA is the same as that for the regular grammar (it is also the same as the set of all σ in the specification of regular expressions). Q is a finite set of *states*, of which q_0 is one specific state called the *start state*; F is a subset of Q called the set of *final states* or *halting states*. A halting state is any state in which the FSA can halt. A finite set of *transition rules*, Δ, defines how the automaton advances from one state to the next on the basis of the symbols in the input "tape." The transitions are a partial function of the current state and the next input symbol:

$$\Delta: Q \times \Sigma \rightarrow Q$$

For any state A and input symbol *a*, a transition that advances to state B upon reading *a* is written as

$$\delta(A,a)=B$$

A *configuration* is a pair (q,ω), where q∈Q is the current state of the FSA and ω∈Σ* is the rest of its (unread) input. An automaton in the configuration (q, ∈), where q∈F is a final state, halts and *accepts*. In other words, if the FSA is in a halting state when there are no more symbols in the input string, the FSA is said to accept the string. Otherwise, if it is in a state for which there is no defined transition for the next input symbol, the FSA *blocks* and *rejects* the string as not a member of its language. It also rejects the string if there are no more input symbols but the FSA is not in a halting state.

Two automata are said to be *equivalent* if they accept the same language. They are called *isomorphic* if they are equivalent and have the same states and transitions, except for the names of the states. In other words, isomorphic FSAs differ only in the particular names of their states. An FSA is *reduced* if there exists no equivalent FSA with fewer states. The simple finite automaton shown graphically in Figure 3.1 is reduced. The automaton in Figure 3.2a is isomorphic to it, and the automaton in Figure 3.2b is equivalent.

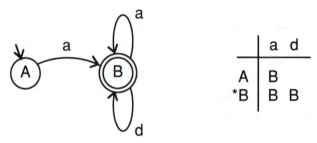

Figure 3.1. A simple finite automaton, showing both the graphical and tabular representation.

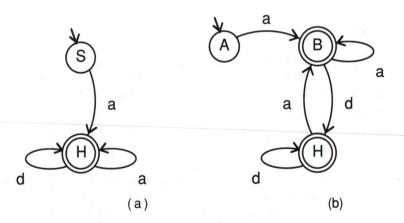

(a)   (b)

Figure 3.2. Two equivalent finite automata.

Consider again the language consisting of all strings that start with a and contain any number of additional a's and d's. A simple two-state FSA to recognize this language is shown graphically in Figure 3.1. The formal definition is

$$M = (\{a, d\}, \{A, B\}, \{\delta(A,a)=B, \delta(B,a)=B, \delta(B,d)=B\}, A, \{B\})$$

The alphabet Σ consists of the two symbols a and d. There are two states, A and B; A is the start state, and B is the only member of the set of final states, shown by the double circle in Figure 3.1. There are three transitions, shown in the diagram by arcs labeled with the input symbol on which the FSA makes that transition. The automaton is reduced because no equivalent automaton with fewer states exists.

The same FSA is also shown in tabular form in Figure 3.1. The rows in the table represent the states, and the columns the input symbols. A blank entry in a particular row and column represents a transition that is not possible, that is, where the FSA would block. Halt states are identified by an asterisk on the state name.

Let us run this automaton on the input string ada. The initial configuration is (A,ada). There is a valid transition from state A on input symbol a, so after one move, the configuration is (B,da). The next transition takes it to (B,a), and then to (B,$\in$). B is a final state, so it accepts the string ada. If we attempt to run the same FSA on the input string dd, we discover there is no transition from state A on input symbol d, so it blocks and rejects dd as not in the language.

3.5 Nondeterministic Finite-State Automata

Although we are interested in implementing only deterministic automata in compilers, it is instructive to study nondeterministic FSAs, primarily because the path from grammar to scanner leads through nondeterminism.

From any given state and for any given input symbol, a deterministic automaton has at most one possible transition. A *nondeterministic finite-state automaton* (NDFA) differs from the deterministic model in two respects: for any given state and input symbol, the NDFA can have more than one possible transition. The NDFA can arbitrarily choose any available transition. Of course some of the choices may lead to blockages, but the NDFA is said to accept the input string if there exists at least one sequence of transitions from the start state to a final state that reads the whole string.

The second difference is that the NDFA is allowed to make a state transition without reading an input token; we call this an *empty transition*. States can have both empty and nonempty transitions from them, and the NDFA arbitrarily chooses any one of the empty transitions, or else any available transition on the current input symbol.

Nondeterministic finite automata are represented in tabular form with a *set* of destination states at each row and column; an extra column is also added for empty transitions. Figure 3.3 shows a simple NDFA that recognizes the language consisting of all strings that start with a and contain any number of additional a's and d's. This NDFA is equivalent to the deterministic FSA in Figure 3.1.

The NDFA in Figure 3.3 is nondeterministic in state B. From the configuration (B,da) this automaton can move to any of the configurations (A,a), (B,a), (A,da), or (C,da). Of these, only the first two lead to accepting the rest of the input string; states A and C have no transitions on d, so they both block.

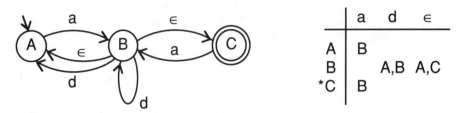

Figure 3.3. A nondeterministic finite automaton.

3.6 Transforming Grammars to Automata

We write scanner specifications using regular grammars and regular expressions; everything else is mechanical. Regular grammars bear a special relationship to finite automata. An NDFA can be constructed directly from the grammar by making the following constructions:

- The alphabet is the same.
- For each nonterminal in the grammar, create a state in the NDFA with the same name. The goal symbol S will also be the start state S.
- Add one new state, and make it the only final state.
- Then for each production in the grammar

    A → xB

construct a transition in the NDFA

    $\delta(A, x) = B$

- For each production in the grammar

    A → x

construct a transition in the NDFA

    $\delta(A, x) = F$

where F is the final state.

The resulting automaton is likely to be nondeterministic because it is possible to have two different productions in a regular grammar with the same nonterminal in its leftpart and the same terminal in its rightpart. Later we will see how to make the NDFA deterministic.

A finite automaton can be constructed from a regular expression by converting it to a regular grammar, or else the regular expression can be converted directly into its recognizing NDFA by the following algorithm: define a "black box" with a state at each end and the regular expression inside; attach a start state to the left end and a halt state to the right end by adding empty transitions from the start state to the black box, and from the black box to the halt state, as shown in Figure 3.4. Then for each black box in the incomplete automaton, apply one of the transformations F.1-F.5 in Figure 3.5 to break it into smaller black boxes until there are no black boxes left. Figure 3.6 shows the process for the regular expression "*a (a|d)**".

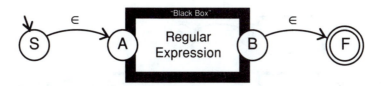

Figure 3.4. Starting to Convert a Regular Expression into an NDFA.

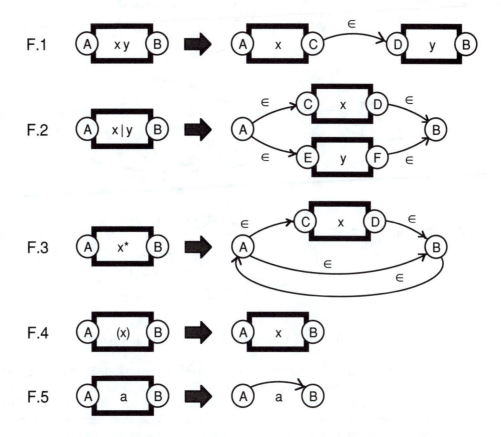

Figure 3.5. Rules for converting regular expressions into state Transitions.

In constructing the NDFA graph from a regular expression, it is often tempting to omit many of the empty transitions and superfluous states by inspection; however, as in converting regular expressions to grammars, if care is not taken in the case of nested or

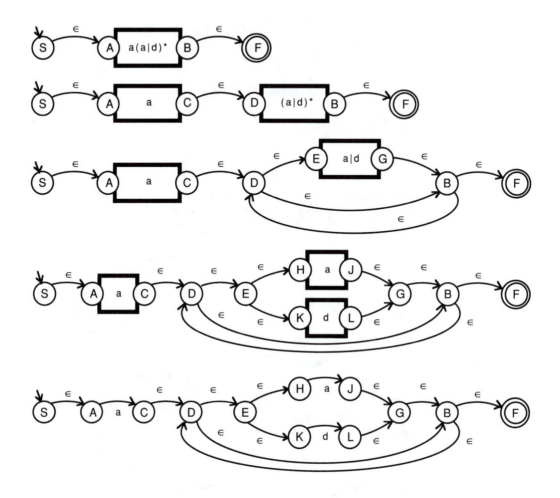

Figure 3.6. Converting a regular expression into an FSA.

concatenated iterators it is possible to change the language. Rule F.3 creates new states C and D with empty transitions from A to C and from D to B; it is easily seen that omitting these new states and their transitions, keeping only the empty transitions from A to B and back, works for many simple iterators such as in the regular expression "*a* (*a*|*d*)*" where the FSA recognizes the same language as the regular expression, as shown in Figure 3.7. Consider, however, the regular expression "(*a**b)*" in which every nonempty string ends with at least one *b*. Using "False R.3" results in an FSA that recognizes strings containing only *a*'s, as in Figure 3.8 — clearly a change in the language.

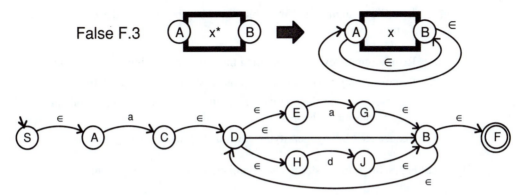

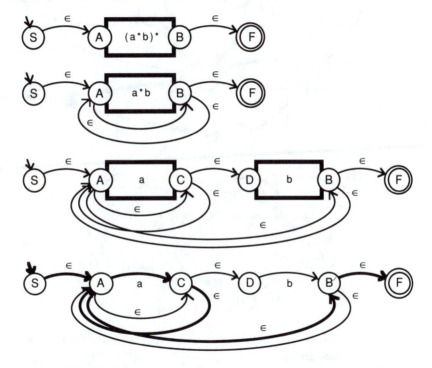

Figure 3.7. Omitting empty moves often seems safe, as with *a* (*a*|*d*)* but...

Figure 3.8. Omitting empty moves changes the language with (*a*b)*. State transitions for the invalid string with a single *a* (heavy arcs) are S-A-C-A-B-F.

3.7 Transforming Automata

As we said before, nondeterministic automata are not very useful in compiler design. There are four steps required to transform a nondeterministic NDFA to a reduced deterministic FSA, summarized in Table 3.5. They begin with the elimination of two classes of empty transitions.

1. Remove empty cycles by merging the states of each into a single state.
2. Remove empty moves by copying target states onto origin states.
3. Remove nondeterminism by constructing a new FSA whose states represent sets of states in the NDFA.
4. Reduce the FSA by identifying equivalence classes among the states.

Table 3.5. Steps to construct a deterministic finite-state automaton.

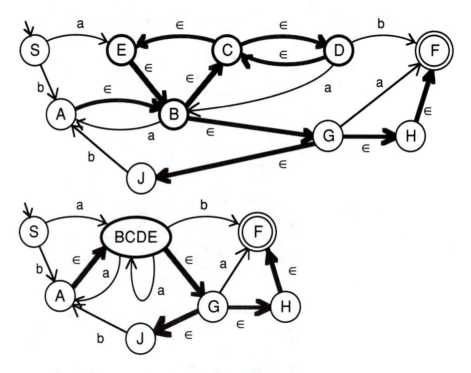

Figure 3.9. Reducing an empty cycle (E-B-C-D-C-E) to a single state (BCDE).

Rule F.3 for constructing an NDFA from a regular expression introduces an *empty cycle*, that is, two or more states with empty transitions between them in such a way that any state can advance to any other state in the cycle on an empty transition. It is clear that an FSA in any such state can advance to any other state in the cycle without reading any input, so all the states in an empty cycle are equivalent. Therefore, without changing the language recognized by the FSA, we can consider all the states in an empty cycle to be a single state; any transitions from any state in the original cycle become transitions from the new single state, and any transitions to any state in the original cycle become transitions to the single state. Any resulting empty moves from any state to itself (including any from the new single state to itself) are redundant and can be safely removed. This is shown graphically in Figure 3.9, where there are empty transitions between states C and D (forming a two-state empty cycle), and between E, B, and C (forming a three-state empty cycle). Because these two cycles have the state C in common, there is a larger empty cycle, E-B-C-D-C-E, which can be safely collapsed into one single state, labeled BCDE. Note that all of the transitions into any of the original states now go to the merged state, and all of the transitions from any of them remain as transitions from the merged state, except for the empty cycle itself. Nonempty transitions between the merged states (such as from D to B on a) are handled just like any other transitions; notice, however, that because both ends of the transition were on states of the empty cycle, the transition remains as a transition from state BCDE (formerly D) to itself (formerly B) on a.

Empty cycles can be found most easily in the tabular representation of an NDFA. All empty transitions are represented by entries in the $\in$ column; for each entry, you construct a tree of empty moves connecting states beginning with that entry (see Figure 3.10b). As soon as one of the transitions in the tree folds back to a state already in the

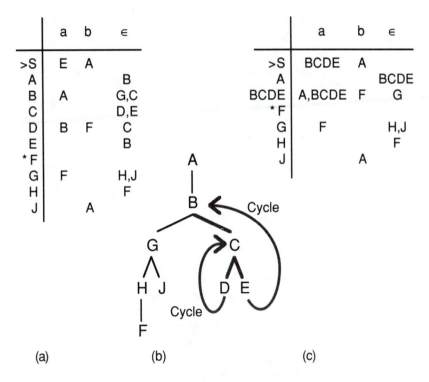

(a)   (b)   (c)

Figure 3.10. Identifying and merging empty cycles in a state table. The table in (a) is the original NDFA; the graph in (b) shows all the empty moves in a single tree, with empty cycles shown in gray. The table in (c) collects the four states of the empty cycles into a single merged state BCDE.

tree, as from state D back to state C in Figure 3.10, you have discovered a cycle: every state in the loop is in the cycle, but states leading into or from the cycle on one-way empty moves are not in the empty cycle. Thus, C-D-C is a cycle, and B-C-E-B is a cycle, but the empty transition from A to B is not part of the cycle, nor is the empty transition from B to G. Furthermore, although there is a transition from J to A, it is not an empty move, so no empty cycle is created by it; we examine only the empty move column of the table.

In this example we could independently merge states C and D into a single state CD, then observe that CD is in the cycle B-CD-E-B and merge it again to the single state BCDE, or else we could merge the cycle B-C-E-B into a single state BCE which is now part of the cycle BCE-D-BCE. Either approach gives the same result as observing that the state C is common to both cycles, and therefore together they form a single empty cycle.

When the states in an empty cycle are merged, every occurrence of any one of their state names is replaced with the merged state name; in this case the transition from the start state S to E on the token *a* becomes a transition from S to BCDE on *a*, and the empty transition from A to B is preserved as an empty transition from A to BCDE. The four transitions out of the cycle — from B to G on empty, from B to A on *a*, from D to B on *a*, and from D to F on *b* — are preserved as transitions out of the newly merged state BCDE. Only the empty transitions starting and ending in the newly merged state — that is, the original empty cycle transitions — are deleted. If any state in the original cycle is a halting state, then that feature is copied into the merged state also, and it becomes a halting state. In this example that is not the case.

Once all the empty cycles have been removed by combining their states into single states, any remaining empty transitions can be removed. An empty move from any state A to another state B means that if the automaton is in state A, it can make any valid transition out of B as well as any out of A, because it can advance to B without reading or otherwise affecting its configuration. Because there are no remaining empty cycles, the reverse is not true; that is, once the FSA has made the empty move from A to B, there is no way to return to A without reading input. The empty move is removed by *copying the destination* state onto the origination state; that is, all the transitions out of B become also transitions out of A. Graphically it is like lifting a copy of B with all the arrow tails also copied and lifted with it, and stretching the copy over to A, as shown in Figure 3.11. Arrow heads into B are not copied in this process, but if state B is a halting state, the copy carries that feature with it. Note that the original transitions out of state A are preserved; we only add some more transitions out of A.

The tabular representation in Figure 3.12 is even more intuitive: everything on line B is copied onto line A. This includes other empty transitions, but the empty transition that caused the copy is deleted. If there are already transitions from state A on some input token *a* and also from state B on the same token, then the new state A will nondeterministically have both transitions on token *a*. If the row being copied is a halting state as in the second step in Figure 3.12, the line it is copied to becomes a halting state also. Note that copying the extra transitions removes only the empty transition that caused it; the state that was the destination of the empty move remains. It may become inaccessible by this step, but we will correct that problem in a later step.

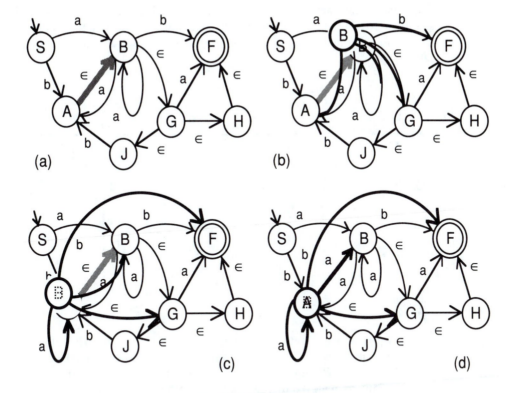

Figure 3.11. Removing an empty transition by copying its destination state. The initial NDFA (a) with an empty move from state A to state B, is transformed by "stretching" a copy of B (b) over on top of A (c). Arcs with their tails rooted in B are also copied, but not arcs with their heads at B. Finally, the empty move is removed (d).

All of the empty moves are removed by successive applications of this step. The alert reader will notice that some manual effort can be saved by starting with empty transitions that lead to states with no empty transitions out of them. Otherwise some of the copying effort is duplicated. The end of such a chain always exists, for otherwise there would be a cycle. We know, however, that the previous step removed all the empty cycles.

Once the empty transitions have all been removed, we proceed to construct a deterministic FSA from the NDFA. We do this by defining a deterministic FSA whose states represent *sets of states* in the original NDFA. Each state in an FSA captures the recognition of that part of the input string that has been read. In the NDFA a given partial input string could lead to any of several states; the new deterministic FSA will have exactly one state defined for each possible partial input string. The construction is simple and straightforward in the table representation of an FSA; the graphical representation does not lead to understandable and error-free constructions. It is not recommended.

A new table is begun, with the start state as its first entry. There is only one start state, so the start state in the constructed FSA is labeled by that state name. In Figure 3.13 the start state is state A. For every state q added to the new table, the transition out of that state on any particular token x is the *union* of all the transitions on x in all of the states of the NDFA in the set represented by deterministic state q. In this example A has a transition to either itself, D, or F on b, so the union of these states names the new state: ADF.

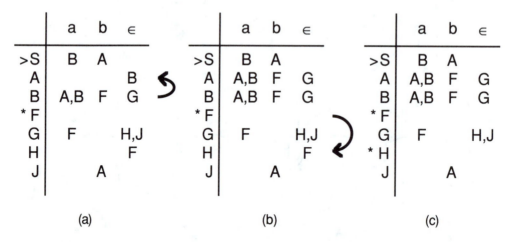

	a	b	∈
>S	B	A	
A			B
B	A,B	F	G
*F			
G	F		H,J
H			F
J		A	

(a)

	a	b	∈
>S	B	A	
A	A,B	F	G
B	A,B	F	G
*F			
G	F		H,J
H			F
J		A	

(b)

	a	b	∈
>S	B	A	
A	A,B	F	G
B	A,B	F	G
*F			
G	F		H,J
*H			
J		A	

(c)

Figure 3.12. Removing empty transitions by copying their destination states. The empty transition from A to B is removed by copying row B onto row A (a). Then the empty transition from H to F is similarly removed by copying row F onto row H (b), leaving H as a halting state.

As each new state is added as the target state of a transition in the table under construction, it is also added to the list of states labeling rows, if not already there. In our example (Figure 3.13), the start state contributes states B and ADF to the list. Similarly, state B has a transition to C and F, so the new state CF is added.

State ADF is the union of states A, D, and F. Because F is a halt state, ADF is also a halt state. In the NDFA state A goes to B on a, but D goes to E; the union of these (F has no transition on a, so it contributes nothing) goes to the state labeled BE. Similarly, on input token b, ADF goes to the union of {A,D,F} (from A), {E,D,H} (from D), and {D,H} (from F), which is the set {A,D,E,F,H}; we write ADEFH.

As we come to state BE, we find that the transition on b from the union of states B and E yields the state CF, which is already in the new set. The transitions out of state ADEFH also contributes no new states. The resulting deterministic FSA therefore has nine states.

The final step in constructing a deterministic FSA from the NDFA is to *reduce* it to the minimum number of states. Although properly a part of making the FSA deterministic, it is often a good idea because it helps keep the scanner down to a manageable size. The FSA is reduced by defining *equivalence classes* of states, where two states are assigned to the same equivalence class if the FSA exhibits the same behavior in the two states; that is, for every given partial string, if the FSA recognizes the string from one of the two states it will recognize it from the other, and conversely. Initially,

Scanners and Regular Languages   Chap. 3

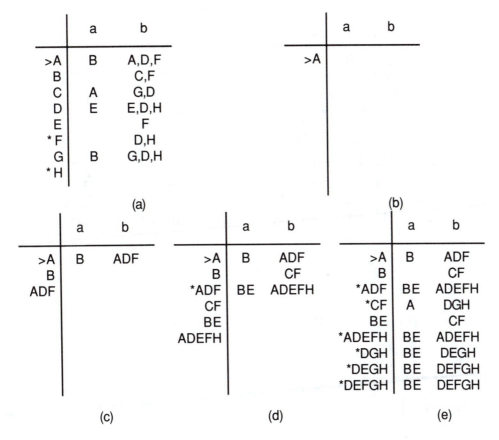

	a	b
>A	B	A,D,F
B		C,F
C	A	G,D
D	E	E,D,H
E		F
*F		D,H
G	B	G,D,H
*H		

(a)

	a	b
>A		

(b)

	a	b
>A	B	ADF
B		
ADF		

(c)

	a	b
>A	B	ADF
B		CF
*ADF	BE	ADEFH
CF		
BE		
ADEFH		

(d)

	a	b
>A	B	ADF
B		CF
*ADF	BE	ADEFH
*CF	A	DGH
BE		CF
*ADEFH	BE	ADEFH
*DGH	BE	DEGH
*DEGH	BE	DEFGH
*DEFGH	BE	DEFGH

(e)

Figure 3.13. Constructing a deterministic FSA from the NDFA (a). Beginning with a start state (b), fill out its transitions. For each new state that is the destination of a transition, add it to the state names (c). Each set of states that is the destination of a transition in the NDFA names a new state (d), or a state already named; the process ends when no new states are added (e).

we divide the states into two classes, where the only distinction is whether a state is final or not, as shown in Figure 3.14. Of the two classes, the halting states recognize the empty string, and the other states do not.

Whenever two states in an equivalence class can be distinguished by a transition on the same token to two different equivalence classes, it means that in a configuration where that token is the next input, the FSA responds differently to the remainder of the input string. There is at least one substring that one state goes on to accept and the other rejects. Therefore, they belong in separate classes. After the first division in our example, all of the halting states go to the other class on a, and to their own class on b, so there is no distinction. However, state A in the nonhalting class goes to state B (in its own class) on a, while states B and BE block; although all three states go to a state in the class of halting states on b, they are distinguished by their transitions on a.

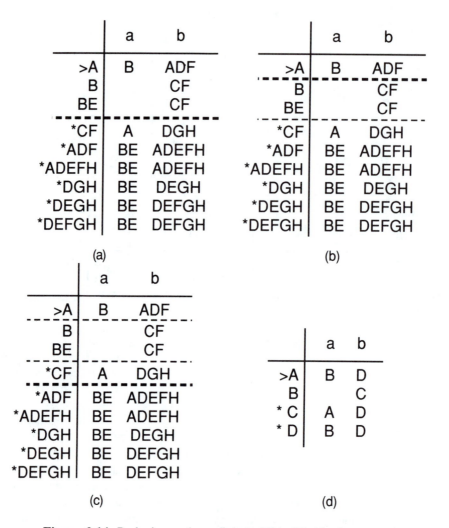

Figure 3.14. Reducing a deterministic FSA. Divide the states into two classes, halting and nonhalting (a). Any class with some states that block on a particular input and some that do not can be further subdivided (b). States in the same class that make transitions on the same input to two different classes can also be separated (c). When no further subdivisions are possible, each class becomes a state in the reduced FSA (d).

After this division, we observe that state CF of the halting states moves on *a* to the class containing state A, while all the other halting states go to state BE, which is now in a different class; this distinguishes state CF into its own equivalence class. All subdivisions of equivalence classes are made on the basis of transitions across class boundaries.

When no further divisions in the equivalence classes can be made, the FSA is said to be *reduced*. In the example in Figure 3.14 the last five states of the unreduced table advance to three different states on input token b, but all three states are in the same equivalence class; no distinction can be made on that basis. We conclude therefore that the reduced FSA has four states, which we have renamed in the last panel of Figure 3.14 for clarity.

It may not be worth the trouble to reduce the FSA for a scanner. Equivalent states are generally the result of alternatives in the regular expressions used to define the scanner. A typical programming language scanner such as for Modula-2 may come out with a dozen equivalent states out of a total 50 to 200 states.

3.8 Transforming Automata to Grammars

Although there is seldom any reason to do so while constructing a compiler, it is interesting to note that a finite-state automaton can be converted into its equivalent grammar fairly readily. The rules for constructing an FSA from a grammar are simply applied in reverse. For every transition

$$\delta(A, x) = B$$

we write a production in the grammar

$$A \to x\ B$$

and for every halting state F, we add a production

$$F \to \in$$

to the grammar. Applying this construction to the reduced FSA of Figure 3.14, we get the following nine productions of a right-linear grammar:

$A \to a\ B$	$C \to a\ A$	$D \to a\ B$
$A \to b\ D$	$C \to b\ D$	$D \to b\ D$
$B \to b\ C$	$C \to \in$	$D \to \in$

Applying Rule R.5 by back-substituting the empty productions for C and D into copies of their references, we get the regular grammar

$$G = (\{a, b\}, \{A, B, C, D\}, P, A)$$

where P is the set of productions

$A \to a\ B$	$C \to a\ A$	$D \to a\ B$
$A \to b\ D$	$C \to b\ D$	$D \to b\ D$
$A \to b$	$C \to b$	$D \to b$
$B \to b\ C$	$B \to b$	

Because we already have a way to construct regular expressions from regular grammars, it is therefore possible to convert any of the three (regular grammar, regular expression, and deterministic finite-state automaton) into any other equivalent member of the set. Normally we begin with a regular grammar or regular expression and construct an FSA from it.

3.9 Left-Linear Grammars

Until now we have been concerned only with right-linear and right-regular grammars. Occasionally it becomes necessary to deal with a left-linear grammar, usually to convert it into an equivalent right-linear grammar. The simplest algorithm to accomplish this consists of converting it to a regular expression by applying a mirror image of Rules R.1-R.3 in Table 3.4, then (if necessary) converting the regular expression back to a right-linear or regular grammar by the usual method.

The mirror-image rules recognize that in a left-linear grammar, the nonterminal on the right-hand side of each production is at the left. The rules are briefly summarized in Table 3.6. Note that Rule L.2 only works for going from left-linear grammars to regular expressions; to go to a grammar from nested iterators requires a second nonterminal as in Table 3.3.

Rule #	Grammar Productions:		Regular Expression Productions:
L.1	$A \rightarrow Bx$	$B \rightarrow y$	$A \rightarrow yx$
L.2	$A \rightarrow Ax$	$A \rightarrow y$	$A \rightarrow yx*$
L.3	$A \rightarrow x$	$A \rightarrow y$	$A \rightarrow x|y$

Table 3.6. Transforming from left-linear to regular expressions.

3.10 Implementing a Finite-State Automaton on a Computer

Most compilers are implemented as programs on a conventional computer. Although we use compiler-generators to construct most of our compilers directly from grammars and regular expressions, it is instructive to know how to build a scanner by hand from the same grammar. Indeed, all that is necessary is to know how to implement a finite-state automaton as a computer program because all the steps from a grammar or regular expression to the FSA are already understood.

A computer is a finite-state automaton with output. Neglecting the output for the moment, we observe that the input "tape" is in fact the terminal keyboard (or rather the set of all input keyboards currently connected either locally or remotely). For simplicity we assume a single local keyboard. The FSA is not able to go back over the input tape, nor is the computer able to "rewind" or back up the keyboard input. Once a character has been read from the keyboard, it is not available again.

The *alphabet* Σ of the computer as an FSA is the set of all characters that can be typed on the keyboard, plus a special symbol ∘, representing the input condition "nothing has been typed." Because computers are so much faster than the humans who type into the keyboard, most of the input tape represented by the keyboard will be filled by the symbol ∘. Where the human operator might be typing, "The quick brown fox ..." the computer will see an input tape that looks more like this:

All of the computer registers, memory, and on-line disk storage are used to encode the *state*. This results in an incredibly large number of possible states: not counting registers and disk storage, a computer with a megabyte of internal memory has $2^{8,388,608}$ or about $10^{2,500,000}$ possible states. That's a one with over 2 million zeros after it, an astronomical number that is inconceivably many times larger than the number of subatomic particles in the known universe. It is therefore not particularly instructive to consider an ordinary computer solely in terms of a finite-state machine.

A computer can be *programmed*, however, to emulate a much smaller FSA. A computer running a nonrecursive computer program with no output is also a finite-state automaton. All the variables of the program, together with the program counter (which is the current instruction address in the hardware), encode the state. The constants and the executable code together represent the *transition rules*. The start state is the condition of the program when it first begins to execute the first instruction. Often computers are said to have "undefined" contents in the program variables when the program starts; that really means that the contents are defined by the previous program in memory, or that the programmer is not told what the contents are. To the extent that this is true, we may have to note that a particular program with uninitialized variables will have slightly different start states depending on what was previously in memory.

We construct a scanner FSA with even less state information: one variable of an enumerated type. The enumerated type lists all the possible states of our FSA, and the variable encodes just exactly those states, and nothing else. To keep things simple, we construct this program from the table representation of an FSA and store the table explicitly in an array in the program. The array is formally a variable, but because it never changes during program execution after it is initialized, it does not represent state. We use one Boolean variable to signal termination of the FSA; it is always true while the program is running, so it also represents no state information. A temporary variable holds the current input symbol, but only long enough to use it to index the state tables; although properly part of the state information, it is not used in that way by this program.

The program listing in Listing 3.1, written in Modula-2, shows the necessary components of the FSA in Figure 3.1. The enumerated type State identifies all the possible states in the FSA, namely AA and BB. The current state variable CurrentState, of type State, represents the entire state of the FSA. The array NextState encodes the state transition rules. The enumerated type Alphabet, imported from module ReadInputTape, identifies all the input symbols. The halting states are listed explicitly in the constant set HaltStates.

Two function procedures are used in this program, but not declared; their purpose is to read the next symbol from the input tape, and to determine if the input has reached the end. We show them imported from module ReadInputTape along with type Alphabet.

In this program there are three possible terminations. If the NextState table shows no valid transition for the current state and input token, the FSA blocks and rejects the string; if the end of the input string is reached (function atEnd returns true) and the FSA is in a halting state it accepts; if it reaches the end of the string and the FSA is not in a halting state it rejects. The main loop of the program tests for these three termination

```
MODULE ReadInputTape;
  EXPORT Alphabet, atEnd, nextInput;
  TYPE Alphabet = (a, d);
  PROCEDURE atEnd: BOOLEAN;
  PROCEDURE nextInput: Alphabet;
END ReadInputTape;

MODULE FSA;
  FROM ReadInputTape IMPORT Alphabet, atEnd, nextInput;
  FROM InOut IMPORT WriteString;
  TYPE State = (AA, BB);
  CONST HaltStates = State{BB};
  VAR CurrentState: State;
    notDone: BOOLEAN;
    theInputToken: Alphabet;
    NextState: ARRAY State, Alphabet OF RECORD
        isValid: BOOLEAN;
        theState: State; END;

  PROCEDURE InitializeTable;
  BEGIN
    NextState [AA, a].isValid := TRUE;
    NextState [AA, d].isValid := FALSE;
    NextState [BB, a].isValid := TRUE;
    NextState [BB, d].isValid := TRUE;
    NextState [AA, a].theState := BB;
    NextState [BB, a].theState := BB;
    NextState [BB, d].theState := BB;
  END InitializeTable;
BEGIN (* FSA program *)
  InitializeTable;
  CurrentState := AA;
  notDone := TRUE;
  WHILE notDone DO
    IF atEnd() THEN
      notDone := FALSE;
      IF CurrentState IN HaltStates
        THEN WriteString ('Accept')
        ELSE WriteString ('Reject') END
    ELSE
      theInputToken := nextInput();
      notDone := NextState [CurrentState, theInputToken].isValid;
      IF notDone
        THEN CurrentState :=
          NextState [CurrentState, theInputToken].theState
        ELSE WriteString ('Reject') END
    END (* IF atEnd *)
  END (* WHILE notDone *)
END FSA.
```

Listing 3.1. Modula-2 implementation of a simple finite automaton.

conditions, and otherwise advances to the next state on the input symbol. Each time through the main loop except the last reads exactly one input symbol and advances exactly one state transition.

Listing 3.1 is not the most efficient implementation of an FSA in a computer programming language. Because we are often — in the case of a scanner, almost always — concerned with execution efficiency, we look for ways to improve its performance without degrading the rigor of its design. The first and most obvious way is to include the information about invalid transitions in the CurrentState variable, so that only one table lookup is necessary. We do this by defining one more state representing an *error state* and eliminating the record definition in the table (because the Boolean field is no longer needed). If the FSA ever enters the error state, it represents the fact that the formal FSA blocked. The main loop is therefore improved somewhat as follows:

```
WHILE (CurrentState <> ErrorState) AND NOT atEnd() DO
  CurrentState := NextState [CurrentState, nextInput()]
  END (* WHILE notDone *);
IF CurrentState = ErrorState THEN WriteString ('Reject')
  ELSIF CurrentState IN HaltStates THEN WriteString ('Accept')
  ELSE WriteString ('Reject')
  END
```

Testing for the termination conditions on each iteration of the loop is unavoidable (although it still can be improved a little bit more as we shall see later); table lookup — especially in a two-dimensional table — is quite expensive in computational terms.

We can make a significant improvement in some computers by encoding the table in the program code. This makes the program much larger and more difficult to construct, but it saves execution time. The result of this improvement is shown in Listing 3.2. The CASE statements are still the machine-language equivalent of table lookup, but there are two advantages: first the CASE table is single-dimensioned, which is usually more efficient. Also, many of the cases degenerate into code that could be more efficiently written as IF–THEN–ELSE statements. For example, the code for state BB makes no decisions at all (it remains in state BB for all input), so it could be replaced with an empty statement; similarly state AA need only test the input to see if it is the token *a*:

```
CASE CurrentState OF
  AA: IF theInputToken = a THEN CurrentState := BB
        ELSE CurrentState := ErrorState
        END (* "CASE" in State AA *) |
  BB: (* do nothing in State BB *)
  END (* CASE CurrentState *)
```

The FSA state itself can be encoded in the program counter for maximum speed. The result is that the program code represents not only the state transition table, but also the FSA state. The CASE statements that test the state variable are thus eliminated and replaced with duplicate code. Again the program gets larger and faster; it is often the case in computer programming that we can trade off space for speed (or vice versa). Listing 3.3 shows this improvement. Notice that we have in no way compromised the formal correctness of the FSA definition: the input alphabet is still the same, the state names are still completely identified — each now only by the comment labeling the region of code representing that state — and the transition table is still encoded in the program code as it is in Listing 3.2.

```
MODULE FSA;
  FROM ReadInputTape IMPORT Alphabet, atEnd, nextInput;
  FROM InOut IMPORT WriteString;
  TYPE State = (AA, BB, ErrorState);
  CONST HaltStates = State{BB};
  VAR CurrentState: State;
    notDone: BOOLEAN;
    theInputToken: Alphabet;
BEGIN (* FSA program *)
  CurrentState := AA;
  WHILE (CurrentState <> ErrorState) AND NOT atEnd() DO
    theInputToken := nextInput();      (* read input tape *)
    CASE CurrentState OF
      AA: CASE theInputToken OF
            a: CurrentState := BB |
            d: CurrentState := ErrorState
            END (* CASE in State AA *) |
      BB: CASE theInputToken OF
            a,d: CurrentState := BB
            END (* CASE in State BB *)
      END (* CASE CurrentState *)
    END (* WHILE notDone *);
  IF CurrentState = ErrorState THEN WriteString ('Reject')
    ELSIF CurrentState IN HaltStates THEN WriteString ('Accept')
    ELSE WriteString ('Reject')
    END (* IF Accept/Reject *)
END FSA.
```

Listing 3.2. Encoding a finite automaton's transitions in program code.

One difficulty with encoding the state in the program counter is that an arbitrary FSA requires GOTOs to advance from state to state. This is not a problem in the machine language of most computers, but modern programming languages discourage the use of GOTOs in source code. We were lucky in our trivial example to be able to do it with nothing more than an IF-THEN-ELSE construct; in the general case that is not possible. On the other hand, manually writing the code to implement such an FSA correctly is quite difficult; we should normally only expect scanner-compilers to do this. The input source language for a compiler-compiler is a grammar or regular expression (not code in a programming language like Modula-2), so GOTOs are not a problem.

At first glance it would appear that Listing 3.3 is nothing but a direct transcription of the regular expression defining the language, and in this case that is true. In general, however, the deterministic FSA recognizing the language of a simple regular expression may not be simple, and the construction may well be far from straightforward. It is insufficient, for example, to begin the recognizer for the language defined by the regular expression $(a|b)*aaba$ with a simple WHILE loop. The construction of a correct recognizer for this regular expression is left as an exercise.

```
MODULE FSA;
  FROM ReadInputTape IMPORT Alphabet, atEnd, nextInput;
  FROM InOut IMPORT WriteString;
  TYPE State = (AA, BB, ErrorState);
  CONST HaltStates = State{BB};
  VAR CurrentState: State;
    notDone: BOOLEAN;
    theInputToken: Alphabet;
BEGIN (* FSA program *)
  IF atEnd()                              (* start in state AA *)
    THEN                   (* state AA is not a halting state *)
      WriteString ('Reject')
  ELSIF nextInput() <> a        (* read input tape in state AA *)
    THEN                          (* block on error input *)
      WriteString ('Reject')
  ELSE                            (* advance to state BB *)
    WHILE NOT atEnd() DO
      IF nextInput() IN Alphabet{a, d}
        THEN END                  (* only read input in state BB *)
      END (* WHILE *);
    WriteString ('Accept')
  END                           (* end of state BB *)
END FSA.
```

Listing 3.3. Encoding a finite automaton's state in the Program Counter.

3.11 Special Implementation Problems for Scanners

When it comes to real-world scanner implementations, we encounter three special problems not formally addressed.

3.11.1 Input Alphabet Size

The first problem relates to the size of the input alphabet. In a typical scanner FSA the number of states is about 60 or so; if the whole ASCII alphabet is used as its input, there are 128 characters. The result is a scanner table with 8,000 entries; a direct code implementation would be much larger. This may be acceptable in a mainframe but not in many of today's smaller computers.

The usual way to solve this problem is to define equivalence classes of characters, so that all digits are treated as if they were but a single symbol in the input alphabet, all letters except "E" (which is used in real constants) as another, all special symbols not specifically defined in the language (for example the accent grave "`" is seldom specified as a language character) as yet another single alphabet symbol. This will usually reduce the alphabet to less than half its original size at the cost of a single small table lookup.

The alphabet for the FSA in Figure 3.1 has only two symbols, *a* and *d*. If we understand them to be the equivalence-class collections for *letter* and *digit*, respectively, then it is easy to see that this machine recognizes all Modula-2 (or Pascal) identifiers: the identifier must begin with a letter and thereafter may have any number of letters and digits. The table to convert the ASCII character set into an alphabet suitable for this FSA will have 128 one-byte entries, each containing either the enumeration constant *a* or *d*, or else some other symbol to be recognized as an error.

3.11.2 Halting States in the Scanner Automaton

The second implementation problem has to do with recognizing the end of a token string. Each of the implementations of a finite-state automaton so far has called on an unspecified function `atEnd()` to determine the end of the input string. In the real world such functions do not exist, and it falls upon the scanner itself to determine the end of a token.

Consider what happens if the scanner built from the regular expression d^+d^+ is reading the input string "12435". If the scanner expects to find two integer constants, where does the first end and the second begin? It could as easily be 124 followed by 35, or 12 followed by 435, or even just a single integer 12435. Pascal and Modula-2 do not allow this situation to occur by requiring one or more spaces between adjacent numbers and identifiers. But the problem still remains, where does the FSA stop reading input characters and halt?

The problem is limited to recognizing the end of the input string in halting states that have transitions out of them. There are two solutions.

One solution is to get the next input character into a buffer variable on each read, then in every halting state with transitions out of it, look at the buffer variable to see if the next character will precipitate one of those transitions. If so, read the character and take the transition; if not, halt.

The other solution is more general. Ignoring halting states altogether, run the FSA until it blocks on an input character. If the FSA is at that time in a final state, halt and accept; if not, reject. In either case, save the character that caused the block and use it to start up the FSA for the next token. Neither method will detect the erroneous string "123*abc*" but report it as a number followed by an identifier.

3.11.3 Stripping Spaces and Comments

Comments and spaces are not tokens in most languages. The scanner removes them from the source text as it scans, and never reports them to the parser. In Pascal and Modula-2, comments may occur "anywhere a space character is permitted" (except within string constants), and they have the same semantic value as a space character.

A regular expression or grammar can be written for a comment, but the semantic action for the recognized comment is empty. Similarly, a trivial regular expression or grammar can be written for the space character. By attaching the regular expression for a space character to the front of the composite regular expression for a token, spaces are explicitly allowed and deleted by the scanner. Consider the subset of Modula-2 tokens defined in the following regular expression:

T.1 $a(a|d)* \mid dd* \mid \text{"("} \mid \text{")"} \mid \text{"+"} \mid \text{"–"} \mid \text{"*"}$

This defines the set of identifiers and positive integer constants, parentheses, and the operators for integer addition, subtraction, and multiplication. It would look like this with comments and spaces specified:

T.2 $(\text{" "}|c)* \; (a(a|d)* \mid dd* \mid \text{"("} \mid \text{")"} \mid \text{"+"} \mid \text{"–"} \mid \text{"*"})$

where c is the regular expression for a comment. Thus, any number of space characters and comments in any order can precede any other single token.

In languages like Pascal and Modula-2 it is important to do this design in the token grammar or regular expression because the comment delimiter uses the same characters as other valid tokens. It can profoundly affect the FSA implementation. When a deterministic FSA is constructed from the regular expression with comments, a new halting state to recognize the left parenthesis will be distinguished from the halting state that recognizes the other single-character tokens, as shown in Figure 3.15. The new state has a transition out of it on an asterisk, which if taken goes on to become a comment prefixed to another (possibly different) token.

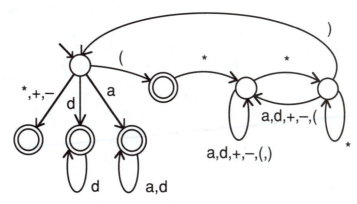

Figure 3.15. The Separation of Comments from Other Tokens in the FSA.

3.11.4 Token Output

The final problem in the implementation of a scanner is much more serious and has been touched on only in passing: output. A scanner not only reads and recognizes its input string, it generates an output token for every valid input string it recognizes. A formal finite-state automaton has no output. We solve this by extending our definition of an FSA to attach *semantic actions* to the state transitions. As a part of each transition is defined a list of zero or more semantic actions associated with that transition. Although there is no theoretic restriction on the functions of a semantic action, in practice we limit them to collecting the characters of an identifier or string token, and emitting a token symbol for each recognized string in the scanner's language.

Consider again the subset of Modula-2 tokens defined in T.2, defining the set of identifiers and positive integer constants, parentheses, and the operators for integer addition, subtraction, and multiplication. Each of these seven tokens should be identified by the scanner to the parser as a unique token in the parser's input alphabet, perhaps as values of an enumerated type

```
TYPE Token = (id, num, left, right, plus, minus, star);
```

Semantic actions to pass these token values to the parser can be attached to the regular expression in appropriate places. We write them into the regular expression enclosed in bracket metasymbols to distinguish them from alphabet symbols. The result looks somewhat like this:

a [id](a|d)* | d [num]d* | "(" [left] | ")" [right] | "+"[plus] | "–"[minus] | "*"[star]

The same semantic actions can be written into the (right-linear) grammar for the same language in a similar way:

S →a A	[Tok=id]	A →d A
S →d N	[Tok=num]	A →a A
S → "("	[Tok=left]	A → ∈
S → ")"	[Tok=right]	N → d N
S → "+"	[Tok=plus]	N → ∈
S → "*"	[Tok=star]	S → "–" [Tok=minus]

The scanner FSA constructed from either the grammar or the regular expression preserves the semantic actions in its transition rules, as shown in Figure 3.16. In a programming language such as Modula-2 these semantic actions consist of nothing more than an extra line of code at the transition that distinguishes each such token. In the table implementation, a third field encodes the semantic actions to be performed on each transition. If the table entry is a procedure pointer, the procedure could be called when it is not NIL; if it is an enumerated type value, a CASE statement can be used to select the appropriate action code; if it is a value of type Token, it could be assigned to the output token variable directly, as shown in Listing 3.4.

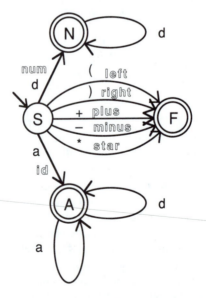

Figure 3.16. Semantic actions (Outline) in an FSA.

```
WHILE notDone DO             (* direct assignment to output token *)
  ...
  theInputToken := nextInput ();
  NextToken :=
    NextState [CurrentState, theInputToken].SemanticAction;
  CurrentState := NextState [CurrentState, theInputToken].theState
  ...

WHILE notDone DO             (* in-line code appropriate to semantics *)
  ...
  theInputToken := nextInput ();
  CASE NextState [CurrentState, theInputToken].SemanticAction OF
    id:
      Stuff (theInputToken);       (* see section on string tables *)
      NextToken := id   |
    num:
      Value := value * 10 + ORD (theInputToken) - ORD ('0');
      NextToken := num   |
    plus: NextToken := plus   |
      ...
    END (* semantic action CASE *);
  CurrentState := NextState [CurrentState, theInputToken].theState
  ...

WHILE notDone DO             (* using procedure pointer in table *)
  ...
  theInputToken := nextInput ();
  SemProcPtr :=
    NextState [CurrentState, theInputToken].SemanticAction;
  IF SemProcPtr <> NIL
    THEN SemProcPtr (theInputToken) END;              (* call it *)
  CurrentState := NextState [CurrentState, theInputToken].theState
  ...
```

Listing 3.4. Three ways of encoding semantic actions in scanner code.

Thus, we have a deterministic way to attach semantic actions to our scanner definitions. By convention in this book we distinguish semantic actions from pure grammars by means of the enclosing square brackets. The compiler-generator introduced in Chapter 4 recognizes this syntax for semantic actions, and builds the appropriate target code to handle the semantics. The particular syntax for semantic actions that we use differs somewhat from this example, but the concept is essentially the same. Other implementations of compiler-generators use other notations to achieve the same end, but the differences are primarily notational.

Note that in every case the scanner automaton reads (and recognizes) exactly one token from its input stream, then "halts." Halting in the scanner means that it stops reading input and returns the token value to the parser, not that the computer stops running. The language of the scanner is the set of all possible tokens, taken one at a time, so the scanner does not advance past the single input token it recognizes in a given call. When the parser is ready for another token, it will restart the scanner in its start state and receive another token when it halts.

3.12 String Table Implementation

As the scanner abstracts out the token id from the particular spelling of any given identifier, that spelling must be preserved for later use in error messages, memory map listings, and intermodule linkages. It is inefficient to require the parser to attend to such details because most references to an identifier are not so much concerned with its spelling as with its uniqueness in its context. The fewer times the compiler must touch the individual characters of its input text, the faster it will run. Therefore, it is up to the scanner to save the spelling of the identifiers and string constants, and to make them available only upon request. This is accomplished by a data structure called the *string table*.

In its essence, a string table is a large packed array of characters, where each identifier and constant string is tagged and stored end-to-end. Tags may include length or terminator codes and possibly links to the next item in the search queue. Variable-length identifiers are handled without waste, so there is no longer any reason to limit source language identifier length. The string's position in the table is passed on to the parser and constrainer as a unique reference to the identifier. Thus, all subsequent comparisons for identifier equality are made on a simple integer index, rather than by a costly variable-length character string comparison.

The semantic action code for identifiers within the scanner stores each new character into the table in the next available entry as the character is read by the FSA. If later the identifier is found to already exist in the table, the space can be quickly reclaimed by ignoring the new entry. If it is truly new, the end of table pointer is advanced to the end of the new string and the string is linked into the table.

In the simplest implementation (see Listing 3.5), the entire table is searched for a match to each new string. Because the new string is inserted at the end, the search will always terminate with a match, possibly at the new string.

A linear search is not particularly fast, and because a substantial number of the tokens in a program are identifiers, there is ample incentive to find a faster algorithm.

The generally accepted algorithm for fast symbol table searches is called "hash coding." The strings in the string table are divided into some large number n of independent lists, as shown in Figure 3.17. The number is usually chosen so that the median compiled program size puts a small number of identifiers (with an average number that is typically close to one) in each list (called a *hash bucket*). Each list element points to a string in the string table.

A *hash function* is an algorithm designed to compute from some data (typically the characters making up a string) a small number (called a *hash code*) such that when the hash function is applied to an average mix of strings, the individual hash codes will be evenly distributed over the range $0..n-1$. It is called a *collision* when two or more strings hash to the same index (and therefore fall into the same bucket). Multiple collisions in a hash table reduce its efficiency. This is unavoidable when the table has more strings than

```
(* Global declarations used by UniqueIdent *)
CONST EOS = 0C;                                (* end of string code *)
VAR                              (* each string terminated by EOS *)
  StringTable: ARRAY[1..MaxStrings] OF CHAR;
  TableEnd: INTEGER;    (* start of new symbol, end of old table *)
  NextStringTableEntry: INTEGER;    (* end of working new symbol *)
PROCEDURE UniqueIdent():INTEGER;
VAR SearchAt, NewSymbol, StringStart: INTEGER;
BEGIN
  SearchAt := 1;
  NewSymbol := TableEnd;      (* the new string is already at end *)
  StringTable[NextStringTableEntry] := EOS;      (* terminate it *)
  WHILE SearchAt < NewSymbol DO  (* dont compare string to self *)
    StringStart := SearchAt;
    WHILE (StringTable[SearchAt] = StringTable[NewSymbol]) AND
       (StringTable[SearchAt] <> EOS) DO (* string compare loop *)
    INC(SearchAt);
    INC(NewSymbol)
    END (* string compare loop *);
    IF (StringTable[SearchAt] = StringTable[NewSymbol]) THEN
      NewSymbol := StringStart;                (* found string *)
    ELSE                        (* not this one, advance to next *)
      NewSymbol := TableEnd;
      WHILE StringTable[SearchAt] <> EOS DO INC(SearchAt) END;
      INC(SearchAt)
      END (* found string IF *)
    END (* string search loop *);
  IF NewSymbol = TableEnd THEN          (* add new string to table *)
    INC(NextStringTableEntry);
    TableEnd := NextStringTableEntry;
  ELSE                                  (* throw new string away *)
    NextStringTableEntry := TableEnd
    END (* add new string IF *);
  RETURN NewSymbol
END UniqueIdent;
```

Listing 3.5. A linear-search string table implementation.

buckets, but an even distribution of strings in the buckets keeps the search time relatively low. Typical hash functions consist of summing the ordinal values of all characters modulo n, or bit-rotating the intermediate sum between characters to minimize collisions between similar symbols. Compiler designers must keep in mind a common programming style that uses the same string of characters in front of every related identifier; this makes a mess of string table hashing functions that attempt to skimp on computation time by (for example) examining only the first three characters of an identifier. Modulo sums have the advantage that only one division at the end is adequate. Bit rotation of the sum can be effected by adding the working sum to the new character value twice; only when the sum exceeds a fairly high threshold is a (usually slower) divide necessary to bring it back into range.

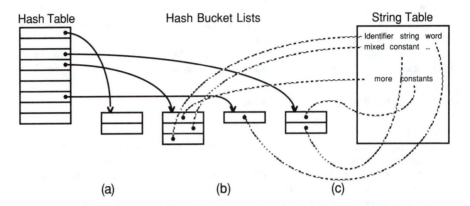

Hash Table	Hash Bucket Lists	String Table

Identifier string word
mixed constant ...

more constants

(a)   (b)   (c)

Figure 3.17. Hash table structure. The hash table (a) is an array of pointers indexed by the hash function of individual strings in the string table (c). Each hash table entry points to a hash bucket (b), which is a list of string table index values. A hash bucket contains references to all the strings that hash to the same hash table index.

Instead of a linear search through the whole string table to see if each newly scanned identifier is already there, only the strings in a single hash bucket must be searched. For a hash table loading factor under 50% (that is, there are half as many total strings as hash buckets) the search time is effectively reduced to a constant. Additional calculation is required to compute the hash function for every identifier, hence the concern for its efficiency. Code for the state that scans the next character of an identifier and adds it to the hash code might look something like this:

```
theInputChar := nextInput();
CASE SemanticAction[CurrentState, theInputChar] OF
...
  DoIdentChar:
    HashCode := HashCode + HashCode + ORD(theInputChar);
    IF HashCode > 16000 THEN
      HashCode := HashCode MOD HashTableSize END;
    StringTable[NextStringTableEntry] := theInputChar;
    INC(NextStringTableEntry);
...
```

With only a small number of strings in each hash bucket to search, conventional character string comparison algorithms are generally adequate. Linked lists for the buckets are rather prodigal of memory space (possibly doubling the space used by each identifier). Considerable improvement can be achieved by constructing the buckets out of short arrays of integers. An array size of one or two elements more than the average bucket size is adequate, if the arrays are then linked into lists to handle overflow. This extension is not shown in Listing 3.6.

```
(* Global declarations used by UniqueIdent *)
CONST EOS = 0C;                            (* end of string code *)
  HashTableSize = 256;    (* depends on mem avail & avg prog size *)
TYPE
  HashBucket = POINTER TO BucketElement; (* linked list of elts *)
  BucketElement = RECORD
    theString: INTEGER;                  (* index into StringTable *)
    nextElement: HashBucket;   (* link to next element in bucket *)
    END;
VAR                                (* each string terminated by EOS *)
  StringTable: ARRAY[1..MaxStrings] OF CHAR;
  TableEnd: INTEGER;     (* start of new symbol, end of old table *)
  NextStringTableEntry: INTEGER;            (* end of new symbol *)
  HashCode: INTEGER;                      (* hashed new symbol *)
  HashTable: ARRAY [0..HashTableSize] OF HashBucket;
                                       (* unused entries = NIL *)
PROCEDURE UniqueIdent():INTEGER;
VAR
  SearchAt, NewSymbol: INTEGER;
  thisBucket: HashBucket;
BEGIN
  NewSymbol := TableEnd;      (* new string already stored at end *)
  StringTable[NextStringTableEntry] := EOS;      (* terminate it *)
  HashCode := HashCode MOD HashTableSize;
  thisBucket := HashTable[HashCode];
  IF thisBucket = NIL THEN      (* create new bucket if not there *)
    NEW (thisBucket);
    HashTable[HashCode] := thisBucket;
    WITH thisBucket^ DO
      theString := NewSymbol;
      nextElement := NIL END
  ELSE WHILE thisBucket <> NIL DO WITH thisBucket^ DO
    SearchAt := theString;
    WHILE (StringTable[SearchAt] = StringTable[NewSymbol]) AND
        (StringTable[SearchAt] <> EOS) DO  (* strg compare loop *)
      INC(SearchAt);
      INC(NewSymbol)
      END (* string compare loop *);
                                       (* listing continues *)
```

Listing 3.6a. A hashing string table implementation (Part 1).

Slightly better performance can be achieved at a significant increase in complexity and table space by building and saving a search tree with one node for every character in every string. The structure is called a *trie* (pronounced "tree" as in "re*trie*val"—the pun probably intended). Each node contains 37 (or 63 for case-sensitive languages like Modula-2) links to the next comparison node, one for each possible letter or digit in the identifier, plus one for the terminator. String comparison then can proceed concurrently with character reading.

```
     IF StringTable[SearchAt] = StringTable[NewSymbol] THEN
       NewSymbol := theString;                       (* found string *)
       thisBucket := NIL
     ELSIF nextElement = NIL THEN     (* not in table, so add it *)
       NewSymbol := TableEnd;
       NEW(nextElement);
       WITH nextElement^ DO
         theString := NewSymbol;
         nextElement := NIL;
         thisBucket := NIL
         END (* nextElement WITH *)
     ELSE                             (* not this one, advance to next *)
       NewSymbol := TableEnd;
       thisBucket := nextElement
       END (* found string IF *)
     END (* thisBucket WITH *) END (* string search loop *) END;
   IF NewSymbol = TableEnd THEN       (* add new string to table *)
     INC (NextStringTableEntry);
     TableEnd := NextStringTableEntry;
   ELSE                               (* throw new string away *)
     NextStringTableEntry := TableEnd
     END (* add new string IF *);
   RETURN NewSymbol
END UniqueIdent;
```

Listing 3.6b. A hashing string table implementation (Part 2).

As each character of an identifier is scanned, it is used to index into the current tree node. If the indexed element points to another tree node, that node becomes current for the next character. When the indexed node element points to a string in the string table, it is unique so far; subsequent characters of the new identifier are compared to the selected identifier in the string table. If they fail to match, the tree is extended to the point of diversion and the new identifier continues to be added to the end of the string table. When the last character of an identifier has been read, the comparison is also complete, and if it is new, the identifier has already been entered into the table. Figure 3.18 shows the structure of such a tree. Because of the previously mentioned popular identifier-naming convention, it is not normally practical to limit the tree to the first few characters (although this is common practice in noncompiler applications of the search algorithm), for large numbers of identifiers would collide in such cases. Listing 3.7 assumes that input characters have been translated into a character code where letters and digits are contiguous. With standard ASCII an extra translation (table lookup) step is required to reduce the range on the node index. Table 3.7 gives relative size and speed comparisons for the three string table search algorithms.

Further performance improvements can be obtained by keeping the entire source file in memory; then instead of building a separate string table, index directly into the source code array. Thus, no character moving and no system calls for reading input character by character are needed. On many computers a file can be read very quickly as a block directly into the memory data structure where it will be used, without involvement of the CPU.

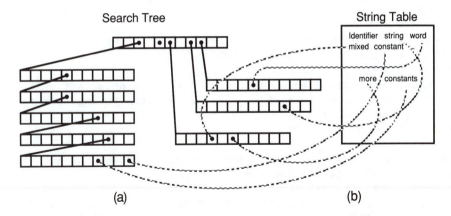

Search Tree   String Table

Identifier string word
mixed constant

more constants

(a)   (b)

Figure 3.18. Tree-search string table structure. Each path through the search tree (a) defines the spelling of one identifier in the string table (b), up to uniqueness. Each character index in each node in the tree either points to another node, or to a string.

Algorithm	Table Size (bytes)*		Time to Scan Existing 12-byte Identifier**	
	50 Ids	500 Ids	50 Ids	500 Ids
Linear Search	600	6,000	2,960	29,060
Hash Table***	1,400	10,400	250	540
Tree Search	5,720	36,000	250	250

*Assuming an average string size of 12 bytes, including terminator.
**Instruction time for hypothetical register machine. Assumes file is in memory.
***Assuming 100-word Hash table, 4-byte words.

Table 3.7. Relative performance of different string table algorithms.

3.13 Reserved Words

Most programming languages are defined with a set of reserved words, sometimes also called word-symbols. Examples in Modula-2 are "PROCEDURE", "IF", "THEN", and "END", but not "INTEGER" or "TRUE" (which are just identifiers that can be redeclared within a program). A *reserved word* is a word-symbol that is recognized by the scanner and reported to the parser as a distinct token. Because they have the same form as identifiers, reserved words pose a special problem in the design and implementation of a deterministic FSA scanner.

```
(* declarations used by tree search *)
CONST EOS = ';';                                   (* end of string code *)
TYPE
  TreePointer = POINTER TO TreeNode;
  TreeNode = ARRAY['0'..'z'] OF RECORD
    CASE UniqueHere: BOOLEAN OF
      FALSE: NextNode: TreePointer |    (* link next node in tree *)
      TRUE:  theString: INTEGER;        (* index into StringTable *)
      END (* variants *)
    END (* TreeNode *);
VAR
  theInputChar: CHAR;               (* each string terminated by EOS *)
  StringTable: ARRAY[1..MaxStrings] OF CHAR;
  TableEnd: INTEGER;     (* start of new symbol, end of old table *)
  NextStringTableEntry: INTEGER;     (* current end of new symbol *)
  UniqueIdent: INTEGER;                 (* the returned string ID *)
  SearchTree, CurrentNode: TreePointer;

  matchedString, treeDepth: INTEGER;
  newNode: TreePointer;
  charindex: CHAR;

BEGIN                 (* see EndIdentifier below for startup code *)
  theInputChar := nextInput();
  CASE SemanticAction[CurrentState, theInputChar] OF
    ...
    DoIdentChar:
      StringTable[NextStringTableEntry] := theInputChar;
      IF matchedString = 0 THEN WITH CurrentNode^[theInputChar] DO
        IF UniqueHere THEN                        (* matched so far *)
          matchedString := theString
        ELSIF NextNode = NIL THEN                (* new from here on *)
          matchedString := TableEnd;
          UniqueHere := TRUE;
          theString := matchedString;
          CurrentNode := NIL
        ELSE                             (* still matching in tree *)
          CurrentNode := NextNode;
          INC(treeDepth);
          END (* UniqueHere or NextNode = NIL *)
        END (* WITH CurrentNode^[...] *)
      ELSIF CurrentNode <> NIL THEN (* match old string so far, *)
        IF StringTable[NextStringTableEntry-TableEnd+matchedString]
            <> theInputChar THEN   (* but no longer; branch off *)
        WHILE treeDepth < NextStringTableEntry-TableEnd DO WITH
          CurrentNode^[StringTable[matchedString+treeDepth]] DO
                                          (* listing continues *)
```

Listing 3.7a. A search-tree string table implementation (Part 1).

```
          INC(treeDepth);
          UniqueHere := FALSE;
          NEW(NextNode);
          FOR charindex := '0' TO 'z' DO
            WITH NextNode^[charindex] DO
              UniqueHere := FALSE;
              NextNode := NIL
              END (* WITH NextNode^[charindex] *)
            END (* FOR *);
          CurrentNode := NextNode
          END (* WITH CurrentNode^[...] *)
        END (* WHILE treeDepth < *);
    WITH CurrentNode^[StringTable[matchedString+treeDepth]] DO
      UniqueHere := TRUE;
      theString := matchedString;
      END (* WITH CurrentNode^[...] *);
    WITH CurrentNode^[theInputChar] DO
      matchedString := TableEnd;
      UniqueHere := TRUE;
      theString := matchedString;
      CurrentNode := NIL
      END (* WITH CurrentNode^[theInputChar] *);
    END (* no longer matching IF *)
  END (* matching so far IF *);
INC(NextStringTableEntry);

EndIdentifier:
  IF matchedString = 0 THEN WITH CurrentNode^[EOS] DO
    IF UniqueHere THEN matchedString := theString
                                      (* matched existing *)
    ELSE                      (* string is new, so add it *)
      matchedString := TableEnd;
      UniqueHere := TRUE;
      theString := matchedString;
      END (* UniqueHere *)
    END (* WITH *) END (* matchedString = 0 *);
  IF matchedString = TableEnd THEN (* extend table over new *)
    StringTable[NextStringTableEntry] := EOS;
    INC(NextStringTableEntry);
    TableEnd := NextStringTableEntry
  ELSE
    NextStringTableEntry := TableEnd;
    END (* matchedString = TableEnd *)
  UniqueIdent := matchedString;   (* set up for next search *)
  treeDepth := 1;
  CurrentNode := SearchTree;
  ...
```

Listing 3.7b. A search-tree string table implementation (Part 2).

The straightforward implementation of an FSA that recognizes both identifier tokens and particular reserved word tokens works with a little care. When a reserved word is recognized, the semantic actions will report both the reserved-word token and the generic identifier token; the implementation must assure that the reserved word token value takes precedence. The presence of a large number of reserved words in the token language, however, tends to proliferate scanner states.

The scanner may also be implemented without explicit recognition of the reserved words. At the back end of the scanner, if the token is recognized as an identifier, a second test is applied to see if it is a reserved word. No lengthy table search is necessary for this test if the string table is preloaded with the reserved words at the front and the token values can be recovered from the string table index. Token values can be encoded as characters in the string table itself, provided that they are not mistaken for identifier matches — this is not a problem if the token values map onto nonalphanumeric characters. The code to add to the end of the scanner is then just the following two lines:

```
IF NextToken = IDtoken
  THEN NextToken := Token(StringTable[UniqueIdent-2]) END
```

where `IDtoken` is a constant of type `Token`, and the variables `NextToken`, `StringTable`, and `UniqueIdent` are declared as in Listing 3.7.

3.14 Using Scanner Generators

Few modern compilers are handwritten. Parser generators are used to construct the parser from a context-free grammar, and every parser generator comes with a companion scanner generator.

In this book we concentrate our attention on the TAG compiler, which builds not only the scanner and parser of a compiler, but also the constrainer and code generator (TAG stands for Transformational Attribute grammars, which are discussed later in this book. See Appendix B for a fuller description of the TAG compiler). The TAG compiler constructs the scanner from two parts. The first part is a scanner grammar that takes regular expressions for individually named tokens. Semantic actions can be encoded right in the grammar. The rest of the scanner is implicitly derived from the parser grammar. Most tokens can be spelled out in the parser grammar as quoted literals, and the TAG compiler extracts these and adds them to its scanner construction.

Summary

Everything we did in this chapter leads to the development of scanners. A scanner is an implementation of some regular grammar or regular expression through a corresponding finite-state automaton (FSA). By construction we showed that for every regular expression and every regular grammar there is a corresponding FSA. We also showed by construction that every set of strings accepted (or recognized) by an FSA can be represented by a regular grammar or regular expression. In effect, there is an intimate relationship between FSAs and regular expressions.

A regular expression is a concise notation for representing a certain class of strings drawn from an alphabet, which typically encompass most of the token requirements of a programming language. The union, concatenation, and Kleene star operations give rise to a rich variety of regular expressions.

We developed in this chapter two techniques for mechanically translating an FSA specification into the programming language code to implement a scanner in a compiler.

Finally, a scanner depends on the use of a string table to store the spelling of identifiers and string constants. A string table can be implemented as a large packed array of characters. We examined several methods for maintaining the string table efficiently.

Symbols

| | The union operator (alternation) for regular expressions, read "or." For example, the union of the regular expressions R and S is written as R|S.

* The closure operator for regular expressions (called the Kleene star), read "any number of" or "0 or more of."

L^* reads "concatenate language L any number of times with itself."

L^i reads "concatenate language L with itself i times."

\+ "1 or more of."

? "0 or 1 of."

Δ A finite set of transition rules.

Q A finite set of states.

Σ The alphabet for a grammar or automaton.

Acronyms

FSA Finite-state automaton, the recognizer for regular languages.

FSM Finite-state machine, equivalent to an FSA.

NDFA Nondeterministic finite automaton.

Keywords

absorption The algebraic law that R|R = R for every regular expression R (also called the idempotent property of regular expressions).

accept (1) A language L is said to be accepted by a a finite automaton M if and only if every string x in L is accepted by M.

(2) A string x is accepted by a finite automaton if there is a sequence of transitions from the start state and ending in a final state, such that each character read by a transition matches the corresponding character in x.

alphabet	The set of symbols Σ of which sentences in a language are composed.
alternation	$R\vert S = \{x : x$ in R or x in S$\}$ for regular expressions R and S.
distributivity	The algebraic law that $R(S\vert T)=RS\vert RT$ for regular expressions R, S, and T (that is, concatenation distributes on the left over alternation). The concatenation operator is also right-distributive over alternation.
empty transition	A transition from one state in an NDFA to another without reading an input symbol.
equivalence class	A set of states Q_e in an FSA M such that M exhibits the same behavior for any two states of Q_e, that is, relative to any partial string x, if M recognizes x from q in Q_e, it will also recognize x from q' in Q_e.
finite automaton	(1) A finite set of states and a set of transitions from one state to the next state based on input symbols taken from an alphabet.
	(2) A 5-tuple (Q,Σ,δ,q_0,F) with Q being a a finite set of states; Σ, a finite input alphabet; δ, a mapping $Q\times\Sigma\rightarrow Q$; q_0, a start state; and F, a finite set of final states.
halting state	(1) A state reached in a finite automaton whenever the last character of an accepted input string has been processed by the automaton.
	(2) Any q in Q that is also in F for a finite automaton (Q,Σ,δ,q_0,F).
hash bucket	A list identified by a hash code.
hash code	Output from a hash function.
hash collision	The computation by a hash function of identical hash codes for two distinct input strings.
hash function	A (usually pseudo-randomized) mapping from an input string to an integer (typically a small positive integer).
iteration	A symbol repeated in a regular expression.
regular expression	A notation for expressing strings in a regular language, using the operations iteration, alternation, and concatenation, and parentheses for grouping.
regular language	(1) A language that can be described by a regular expression.
	(2) A language that can be generated by a regular grammar.
	(3) The set of strings accepted by a finite state automaton.
regular set	A regular language.
scanner grammar	A regular grammar defining the set of all strings in the external (text) alphabet that form tokens in a language to be compiled.

semantic action	A rule that specifies some side effect incidental to the recognition of a string, such as entering the string into a string table, or defining an output token.
string table	A data structure used by a scanner to save the spelling of identifiers and string constants.

Exercises

1. Write regular expressions for the following languages.

    (a) All strings of letters that contain the five vowels in order. Each vowel is to occur only once in the entire string.

    (b) All strings of letters that consist of substrings that contain the five vowels in order. Each vowel may occur many times throughout the string. Also, allow each vowel to occur more than once at its position. For example,

    bghaaatrasdfeewqprilkohmoooozu

    is an acceptable substring (as well as an acceptable string).

    (c) All strings of zeros and ones with an even number of zeros and an odd number of ones.

    (d) All strings of zeros and ones that do not contain the substring 011.

    (e) All strings of ones, twos and threes such that neither 1, 2, nor 3 occur more than once in the string.

    (f) All strings of ones and twos such that ones are never repeated (that is, no 11's). There must be at least one 1 or 2; empty strings are not allowed.

    (g) All strings of ones and twos such that no digit is ever repeated (that is, no 11's or 22's). There must be at least one 1 or 2; empty strings are not allowed.

    (h) All strings of a's and b's where the string is five or fewer characters long. Empty strings are allowed.

2. Describe the languages denoted by the following regular expressions. Try to capture the essence of the language in a natural description, instead of merely transcribing the regular expression symbols into English.

    (a) 0(0|1)*0 (c) (0|1)*0(0|1)(0|1)

    (b) ((∈|0)1*)* (d) 0*10*10*10*

    (e) (00|11)*((01|10)(00|11)*(01|10)(00|11)*)*

    (f) (00|11)*(01|10)((01|10)(00|11)*(01|10)(00|11)*)*
    ((01|10)(00|11)*1|0)|(00|11)*1

3. Rewrite the following regular expressions to eliminate the + and ? operators.

    (a) 0|(01?|10)+

    (b) (((1|(010)+)?)|(1|0|(10)?))+

4. Simplify the following regular expressions by successive applications of the algebraic laws.

(a) 012|32|(10|01)|013

(b) (12|13)(0|1)|((2|3)|((3|1)(1|0)))

5. Identify which of the following FSAs are equivalent and which are isomorphic.

(a)	0	1
S	A	B
A	S	C
*B	C	S
C	B	A

(b)	0	1
S	B	A
*A	C	D
B	D	C
C	A	B
D	B	A

(c)	a	b
E	F	G
F	E	H
*G	H	E
H	G	F

(d)	0	1
J	M	K
*K	L	N
L	K	M
M	N	L
N	M	K

6. Convert the following regular grammars to regular expressions.

(a)	(b)	(c)	(d)
A → aB	A → 0B	A → 1B	S → 0A
A → bA	A → 1C	A → 0C	S → 1B
B → aC	B → 0C	B → 0C	S → 1
B → cD	B → 1C	B → 1B	A → 0S
C → c	C → 0D	C → 1B	A → 1C
D → d	C → 1D	C → 1	B → 0C
	D → 0A		B → 1S
	D → 1A		C → 1A
	D → 0		C → 0B
			C → 0

7. (a) Convert the regular grammars of Exercise 6 to nondeterministic finite-state automata.

(b) Convert the NDFAs of Exercise 7a to reduced deterministic FSAs.

8. Convert the following regular expressions to regular grammars.

(a) (12|2)*(12|1|2)

(b) 1*(0|01)*

(c) a*|(bca*(ab|ba))

(d) ((0|1)*(10|01))*1|(11|00)

9. (a) Convert the regular expressions of Exercise 8 to nondeterministic finite-state automata.

(b) Convert the NDFAs of Exercise 9a to reduced deterministic FSAs.

10. Convert the following nondeterministic finite-state automata to deterministic finite-state automata.

(a)

	a	b	c	ε
S	A,B	C,D	D	A,B,D
A	A		C	B
B	A	D		C
*C	B	A		A
*D	C	B		S

(b)

	a	b	c	ε
S	A	B	C	
*A	S	B,C		C,D
B	A	B	A,D	A
*C	A,B	B		A,D
D		A,C	B	S

(c)

	a	b	c	ε
S	C,D	A	D	
A	A	B	C	D
*B		C	D	C
C	A,B		C	
D	C	B		A

11. (a) Construct a deterministic finite-state automaton from the regular expression, (a|b)*aaba.

(b) Write a scanner to implement your FSA.

12. From each of the following FSAs construct an equivalent regular grammar.

(a)

	a	b	c
S	A	B	
A	A		C
*B		C	D
C	B		C
D	C	B	

(b)

	a	b	c
S		A	D
A	A	B	C
B		C	D
C	B		C
*D	C	B	

13. Give a formal definition of a language L accepted by a finite-state automaton M.

14. Give an example of a language L that is not accepted by the FSA in Figure 3.16. Also specify a string x in L such that $\delta(q_0, x) \neq p$ in F, the set of final (halting) states shown in Figure 3.16. Give the grammar for L.

15. Give an example of a language L' that is not accepted by the FSA in Figure 3.16 but does have at least one string x that is accepted by the same FSA. Give the grammar for L'.

17. Give the regular grammars for each of the regular expressions in Exercise 1.

18. Give the FSAs for each of the regular languages in Exercise 1.

20. Prove that the language recognized by an FSA can be represented by a regular expression.

21. Prove that for every regular expression R, there exists a finite automaton M that accepts the set of strings represented by the regular expression R.

22. (Lemma 3.1) Prove that every set containing a single string has a corresponding regular expression. Hint: use a proof-by-construction technique.

23. (Proposition 3.1) Prove or disprove that every regular language is finite.

24. (Theorem 3.2) Prove that if L1 and L2 are regular languages, then L1|L2, L1·L2 and L1* are also regular languages.

25. (Lemma 3.2) Prove that if L is a regular language, then L^n for $n \geq 0$ is also a regular language.

26. (Theorem 3.3) If L is a regular language, then the following are also regular languages.

    (a) $L^n \mid L^m$ for $n, m \geq 0$

    (b) $L^1 = \{\in\}L$

27. Show that for a regular expression R, R* is equal to (R*)*.

28. Prove each of the identities in Table 3.2.

29. Show for regular expressions R and S that RS does not always equal SR by giving an example where RS does equal SR.

30. A semigroup is a pair (T, ⊕) where T is a nonempty set of elements and ⊕ is an associative, binary operation defined on T. Give two examples of semigroups defined in this chapter.

31. Prove that if R is a regular set then there exists a right-linear grammar G such that the language L(G) defined by G is R.

Review Quiz

Indicate whether the following statements are true or false. Assume that R, S, and T represent regular sets of sentences drawn from Σ^* and that $\{\in\}$ is the set containing the empty string $\in$.

1. An empty language is a regular expression.
2. If R = S*T then R = SR | T.
3. (R*S)* = (R|S)*S | {∈}.
4. Every finite string can be represented by more than one regular expression.
5. Every regular language contains {∈} as a subset.
6. Every regular expression defines a regular language.
7. All regular expressions with the Kleene star implicitly use the concatenation operation.
8. (R {∈} S {∈} T)* = (RST)*(RST)*
9. { } {∈} = { }

Compiler Project

1. Write a regular expression to generate the language of all of the Itty Bitty Modula tokens specified in the grammar you wrote for Chapter 2, or else all of the tokens shown in ovals in the syntax diagrams in Appendix A. The regular expression should generate sentences consisting of exactly one token each. Be sure to take spaces and comments into account. Show appropriate semantics.

2. Mechanically construct (that is, do not rethink the problem) a finite-state automaton to recognize Itty Bitty Modula tokens, working from either
   (a) Your regular expression (see number 1 above), or
   (b) Your regular grammar for the same language.

3. Write a scanner procedure that implements exactly the FSA of number 2 above. Test your scanner using the following main program (or its equivalent, if you are writing in Pascal or some other language).

```
MODULE MainProgram;
   ...              (* You fill in other TYPEs and VARs *)
VAR NexToken: Token;
   ...              (* You fill in Getoken and other procedures *)
BEGIN
  InitializeScanner;
  REPEAT
    Getoken;
    WriteInt(ORD(NexToken));
    WriteLn;
    UNTIL NextToken = Dot;
END MainProgram.
```

Further Reading

Chomsky, N. "On Certain Formal Properties of Grammars." *Information and Control*, Vol. 2 (1959), pp. 137-167. See section 5, which discusses regular grammars.

Clifford, A.H. & Preston, G.B. *The Algebraic Theory of Semigroups.* Providence, RI: American Mathematical Society, 1961. See section 1.1 for basic definitions related to semigroups.

Cohen, D.I.A. *Introduction to Computer Theory.* New York: Wiley, 1986. See ch. 7 on Kleene's theorem and ch. 10 on regular languages.

DeRemer, F.L. "Lexical Analysis." In *Compiler Construction* ed. F.L. Bauer & J. Eikel. New York: Springer-Verlag, 1974. See section 3.1.3 on converting regular grammars to regular expressions.

Ginzburg, A. *Algebraic Theory of Automata.* New York: Academic Press, 1968. See ch. 4 on regular expressions, especially sections 4.1 through 4.6, which develop a proof of Kleene's theorem.

Gries, D. *Compiler Construction for Digital Computers.* New York: Wiley, 1971. See ch. 9 for a thorough discussion of ways to organize string tables (called symbol tables by Gries).

Hopcroft, J.E. & Ullman, J.D. *Introduction to Automata Theory, Languages, and Computation.* Reading, MA: Addison-Wesley, 1979. See section 2.5 on regular expressions.

Kleene, S.C. "Representation of Events in Nerve Nets and Finite Automata." In *Automata Studies.* Princeton, NJ: Princeton University Press, 1956, pp. 3-42.

Knuth, D.E. "On the Translation of Languages from Left to Right." *Information and Control*, Vol. 8, No. 6 (1965), pp. 607-639. See p. 611 for discussion about regular (finite automaton) languages. This article gives a variety of interesting grammars.

McKeeman, W.M. Symbol Table Access. In *Compiler Construction* ed. F.L. Bauer & J. Eikel. New York: Springer-Verlag, 1974. See section 7 on hash table access and section 8 on hash functions.

Mossenbock, H. "Alex — A Simple and Efficient Scanner Generator." ACM *SIGPLAN Notices*, Vol. 21, No. 12 (December 1986), pp. 139-148. See pp. 146-147 for an example of a scanner grammar. Alex has been implemented in Modula-2.

Sebesta, R.W. & Taylor, M.A. "Minimal Perfect Hash Functions for Reserved Word Lists." ACM *SIGPLAN Notices*, Vol. 20, No. 12 (December 1985), pp. 47-53. See p. 49 for the new perfect hash function, which you might want to try in terms of the reserved words in Modula-2.

Shyu, Y.-H. "From Semi-Syntactic Analyzer to a New Compiler Model." ACM *SIGPLAN Notices*, Vol. 21, No. 12 (December 1986), pp. 149-157. See p. 152 for complete finite-state automaton for a scanner.

Chapter

Parsers and Context-Free Languages

Aims

- Introduce LL(k) grammars.
- Formulate transformation rules for removing left-recursion and left-factoring to obtain context-free grammars that are LL(k).
- Determine the relationship between context-free grammars and corresponding push-down automata.
- Introduce *First*, *Follow*, and *Selection* sets used to determine if a nonterminal in a grammar is LL(k) and if a grammar itself is LL(k).
- Extend context-free grammars with regular expression operators.
- Learn how to transform an extended LL(1), context-free grammar into a recursive descent parser.

4.1 Introduction

A scanner of a compiler recognizes terminal symbols of a language from the sequence of characters in an input string. These terminal symbols are the words of the language recognized by a compiler. The language defined by a scanner is the set of words that the scanner recognizes. This is the lexical level of a programming language. A parser is a push-down automaton (a stack machine, usually abbreviated as PDA) that recognizes the phrase structure of a language — how the words of a language go together correctly to form syntactically correct programs.

Most programming languages permit sentence constructions with nested and matched parentheses. As shown in Chapter 2, such languages are context-free and are defined by context-free grammars (CFGs). Every language recognized by a PDA is context free. This can be proved rather easily by constructing the rules of a CFG from the transitions of a PDA. The rules of a CFG for a language accepted by a PDA are designed so that each production of the CFG corresponds to a PDA transition. We also show in this chapter that every context-free language is accepted by a nondeterministic PDA.

The focus in this chapter is on context-free languages that are accepted by a class of deterministic PDAs. These languages are defined in terms of what are called LL(k) context-free grammars. An LL(k) grammar permits deterministic, top-down parsing by looking ahead k symbols in an input string. The "LL" notation describes the parsing strategy being used. That is, the LL parsing strategy scans an input string from left to right, and the LL parser constructs a leftmost derivation. This chapter introduces a technique for transforming an LL(1) grammar into what is known as recursive descent parser written in a conventional programming language.

4.2 Push-Down Automata

A push-down automaton is formally defined as a 7-tuple:

$$P = (\Sigma, Q, \Delta, H, h_0, q_0, F)$$

where all the components are the same as in an FSA, with the addition of two new components, a finite *stack alphabet* H, and an initial symbol h_0 in H, which is the initial contents of the stack. Like an FSA, the PDA halts and accepts when it reaches the end of the input string in a final state (a state in the set F). It can also halt and accept *on empty stack*. If it reaches the end of the input string under any other circumstance, or if it blocks, it rejects the input.

The stack alphabet may or may not have symbols in common with the input alphabet — we will work with both kinds — but the stack itself can grow to arbitrary depth. We do not call it an infinite stack (for then it would take infinitely long to fill it), but there is no fixed finite limit to its depth.

The set of transition rules Δ is a partial function from states, input alphabet, and stack alphabet to state and stack alphabet strings. That is, a transition rule δ in the set Δ has the following functionality:

$$\delta: Q\times(\Sigma\cup\epsilon)\times H \rightarrow Q\times H*$$

This means that every transition is defined for a particular state; it either reads one input token or not, but it always pops one symbol off the stack, then advances to a new state and pushes a string of zero or more symbols back onto the stack. A transition rule is similar to a transition rule for an FSA

$$\delta(q_i, \alpha, \eta) = (q_j, x)$$

where q_i and q_j are states, α is some token in the input alphabet or ϵ, η is a token in the stack alphabet, and x is a (possibly empty) string in the stack alphabet. The string x could easily be the symbol η again, if this transition does nothing to the stack. A *configuration* (q, ω, x) represents the state q of a PDA with a string ω of unread symbols waiting to be input and a particular string x on the stack.

Parsers and Context-Free Languages   Chap. 4

As with FSAs, a PDA may be nondeterministic. A nondeterministic PDA differs from a deterministic PDA by having more than one possible transition for any given configuration. That is, two or more transition rules from the same state with the same stack symbol either read the same input token, or one of them reads nothing.

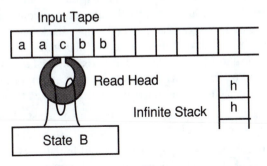

Figure 4.1. An example of a push-down automaton.

For an example, let $P_0 = (\{a,b,c\}, \{A,B,C\}, \Delta, \{h,i\}, i, A, \{\})$ be a deterministic PDA (see Figure 4.1), where Δ is the following set of transitions:

$$\delta(A,a,i) = (B,h) \qquad\qquad \delta(A,c,i) = (A,\in)$$
$$\delta(B,a,h) = (B,hh) \qquad\qquad \delta(B,c,h) = (C,h)$$
$$\delta(C,b,h) = (C,\in)$$

This PDA recognizes all the strings generated by the grammar $\{S \rightarrow aSb, S \rightarrow c\}$, that is, an equal number of a's and b's, separated by a single c. It starts in state A with an i on the stack and halts on an empty stack. Let's give it the input string $aacbb$. In five transitions it halts and accepts (note the top of the stack is to the left, as illustrated also in Figure 4.2):

Configuration	PDA Actions
(A, *aacbb*,*i*)	initial configuration; read a, pop i, push h, go B
(B, *acbb*,*h*)	read a, pop h, push hh, go B
(B, *cbb*,*hh*)	read c, pop h, push h, go C
(C, *bb*,*hh*)	read b, pop h, go C
(C, *b*,*h*)	read b, pop h, go C
(C,$\in$,$\in$)	halt

Figure 4.2. The stack growth of a push-down automaton.

4.2.1 Halting Condition Equivalence

It is easy to see that halting on a final state is equivalent to halting on empty stack; that is, for every PDA that halts on a final state, we can construct an equivalent PDA (that accepts the same language) that halts on empty stack, and vice versa. Let P_1 be a PDA that halts on empty stack; that is, its set of final states F is empty. We construct a new PDA P_2 identical to P_1 except that it has two additional states q_f (which we designate its final state) and q_g (which we designate its start state), one additional stack symbol h_f (which we designate the initial stack element), and the additional transition rules

$$\delta(q_g, \in, h_f) = (q_0, h_0 h_f) \qquad \text{(the top of the stack is on the left)}$$
$$\delta(q_i, \in, h_f) = (q_f, h_f) \qquad \text{for every } q_i \text{ in } Q_1, \text{ the states of } P_1$$

The first of these new rules pushes the old initial stack symbol h_0 on top of the new initial stack symbol h_f and advances to the old start state q_0 reading no input. From there P_2 operates as P_1 did, until it reaches the condition that in P_1 was an empty stack. In P_2 the stack still has h_f on it; every state of P_1 has a transition from this configuration to the halt state q_f (represented in the second line above), so P_2 halts in exactly the same configurations, but one transition later. Because the new transitions we added all read no input and require the new stack symbol h_f in order to advance, they cannot affect the previous functions of P_1. If we were to apply this transformation to the example PDA P_0, the result would be

$$P_0' = \{a,b,c\}, \{A,B,C,E,F\}, \Delta', \{h,i,f\}, f, E, \{F\})$$

where Δ' is the augmented set of transitions

$\delta(A,a,i) = (B,h)$	$\delta(A,c,i) = (A,\in)$
$\delta(B,a,h) = (B,hh)$	$\delta(B,c,h) = (C,h)$
$\delta(C,b,h) = (C,\in)$	
$\delta(E,\in,f) = (A,if)$	$\delta(A,\in,f) = (F,f)$
$\delta(B,\in,f) = (F,f)$	$\delta(C,\in,f) = (F,f)$

Now, given any PDA P_2 that halts on a final state, we similarly construct a new PDA P_3 to halt on empty stack, as follows. To P_2 we add one new state q_g and for every symbol h_i in H, we add the transitions

$$\delta(q_g, \in, h_i) = (q_g, \in)$$
$$\delta(q_f, \in, h_i) = (q_g, \in) \qquad \text{for every final state } q_f \text{ in } P_2$$

Thus whenever the PDA P_2 would halt by reaching a halting state q_f, P_3 drops into the special state q_g that clears out the stack (and therefore halts).

Applying this transformation to P_0', we get

$$P_0'' = \{a,b,c\}, \{A,B,C,E,F,G\}, \Delta'', \{h,i,f\}, f, E, \{\})$$

where Δ'' is the set of transitions (augmented again)

$\delta(A,a,i) = (B,h)$	$\delta(A,c,i) = (A,\in)$
$\delta(B,a,h) = (B,hh)$	$\delta(B,c,h) = (C,h)$
$\delta(C,b,h) = (C,\in)$	
$\delta(E,\in,f) = (A,if)$	$\delta(A,\in,f) = (F,f)$

$$\delta(B, \in, f) = (F, f) \qquad \delta(C, \in, f) = (F, f)$$
$$\delta(G, \in, h) = (G, \in) \qquad \delta(F, \in, h) = (G, \in)$$
$$\delta(G, \in, i) = (G, \in) \qquad \delta(F, \in, i) = (G, \in)$$
$$\delta(G, \in, f) = (G, \in) \qquad \delta(F, \in, f) = (G, \in)$$

4.2.2 Constructing a PDA from a Context-Free Grammar

The input alphabet of the PDA is the same as the grammar's alphabet. The stack alphabet of this PDA consists of $(\Sigma \cup N)$, that is, all the tokens of the input alphabet plus all the nonterminals of the grammar. The initial stack symbol is the goal symbol of the grammar. This PDA has only one state q and it halts on empty stack. The transitions of the PDA are constructed as follows: for every terminal x in Σ, add one transition rule:

N.1 $\quad \delta(q, x, x) = (q, \in)$

which reads the token and pops the same token off the stack. For every production $A \rightarrow \omega$ in G, add one transition rule:

N.2 $\quad \delta(q, \in, A) = (q, \omega)$

which replaces the nonterminal on the top of the stack with the string ω (of terminals and nonterminals) from the right part of the production, without reading any input.

It is easily seen that this PDA implements a top-down parse. Starting with the goal symbol on the stack, it nondeterministically continues to rewrite the leftmost nonterminal until the leftmost symbol in the sentential form (that is, the top of the stack) is a terminal matching the first token of the input string. The transition that reads that token is taken, and the process repeats until the entire input string has been read or the PDA blocks. The PDA blocks if and only if there is no sequence of transitions leading to a match of the next input token to the top of stack, which means that no string in the language matches the input string. Note that the current sentential form is fully represented on the PDA stack only until the first symbol is read from the input. Thereafter the sentential form is divided between that part of the input that has been already read and the current stack. We have just shown Theorem 4.1 by construction:

Theorem 4.1. If L is a context-free language, there exists a nondeterministic PDA that accepts it.

Lemma 4.1. If L is a language accepted by a PDA, then L is context-free.

Proof. The proof is by construction. Briefly, if we let M be a PDA. The rules of a grammar are constructed from the transitions of M. The actual construction of these rules is left for Exercise 17.

Theorem 4.2. If L_1 and L_2 are context-free languages, then their union $L_1 + L_2$ is also context-free.

Proof. This is can be shown by construction by applying the result from Theorem 4.1 twice, constructing a new PDA from the PDA_1 which recognizes L_1 and the PDA_2 which recognizes L_2 and using the result from Lemma 4.1 (see Exercise 18).

Note: Theorem 4.2 can also be proved by constructing a new context-free grammar that is an amalgam of CFG_1 for L_1 and CFG_2 for L_2.

Theorem 4.3 If L_1 and L_2 are context-free languages, then the concatenation of of all strings from L_1 and L_2 (written $L_1 \cdot L_2$) is also a context-free language.

Proof. This can be proved by construction. Without loss of generality, assume that L_1 and L_2 are defined by CFG_1 and CFG_2, respectively, as follows:

$$CFG_1 = (\Sigma_1, P_1, N_1, A) \quad \text{defines } L_1$$
$$CFG_2 = (\Sigma_2, P_2, N_2, A) \quad \text{defines } L_2$$

where (Σ_1, P_1, N_1, A) and (Σ_2, P_2, N_2, A) are, respectively, the alphabet, set of productions, set of nonterminals and goal symbol for CFG_1 and CFG_2. We have deliberately given the same name to the goal symbols for these two grammars, namely, A. We need to distinguish the nonterminals of these two grammars, so we will subscript all nonterminals in CFG_1 with a 1 and nonterminals in CFG_2 with a 2. Now these grammars have the following form:

$$CFG_1 = (S, P, N, A_1) \quad \text{defines } L_1$$
$$CFG_2 = (S, P, N, A_2) \quad \text{defines } L_2$$

Then introduce a new nonterminal A in the following rewrite rule:

$$A \rightarrow A_1 A_2$$

where A_1 is the goal symbol for CFG_1 and A_2 is the goal symbol for CFG_2. Then any string in $L_1 \cdot L_2$ can be derived with the new grammar (call it CFG_A). If w is a string derived by CFG_A, w will have the form

$$w = \{ \, string\_in\_L_1 \, \}\{ \, string\_in\_L_2 \, \}$$

Because the nonterminals in the original grammars are distinguishable in terms of their subscripts, there is no ambiguity in knowing which rewrite to choose next during a derivation.

Consider the grammar G_{19} that generates all strings of a's followed by an equal number of b's:

P.1 $S \rightarrow a \, S \, b$
P.1 $S \rightarrow \in$

The transitions for the constructed PDA are

4.1	$\delta(q, \in, S) = (q, aSb)$	(from N.2, P.1)
4.2	$\delta(q, \in, S) = (q, \in)$	(from N.2, P.2)
4.3	$\delta(q, a, a) = (q, \in)$	(from N.1)
4.4	$\delta(q, b, b) = (q, \in)$	(from N.1)

Parsing the input string *aabb* starts the PDA with the initial configuration $(q, aabb, S)$, shown in Table 4.1, line 1. It is easily seen that the only transitions that are applicable are Rules 4.1 and 4.2; we choose Rule 4.1, yielding the new configuration on line 2. Now the only possible transition is Rule 4.3, yielding (q, abb, Sb). Again faced with the same choice, suppose we choose Rule 4.2. That leaves us with the configuration on line 4a, from which no transition is applicable: the choice was ill-made. If instead we choose a second application of Rule 4.1, it can be followed by Rule 4.3, yielding the configuration (q, bb, Sbb) on line 5. A third application of Rule 4.1 now runs aground on the configuration (q,*bb*,*aSbb*), but Rule 4.2 successfully leaves a configuration (line 6b), from which two applications of Rule 4.4 quickly read the remaining input and empty the stack.

As we noted in Chapter 3, nondeterministic automata do not make very efficient computer programs, and this PDA is no exception. The alert reader probably has already noticed that some of the nondeterministic choices of transition rules could be determined by looking at the next token in the input string and comparing it to the available choices. Indeed, this is exactly what we do in LL(k) predictive parsing.

	Input String (dot is at next read)	Stack	Transition Rule
1	.*aabb*	S	
2	.*aabb*	*aSb*	4.1
3	*a.abb*	*Sb*	4.3
4a	*a.abb*	*b*	4.2?
4b	*a.abb*	*aSbb*	4.1
5	*aa.bb*	*Sbb*	4.3
6a	*aa.bb*	*aSbbb*	4.1?
6b	*aa.bb*	*bb*	4.2
7	*aab.b*	*b*	4.4
8	*aabb.*		4.4

Table 4.1. Nondeterministic parse of *aabb*.

4.3 The LL(*k*) Criterion

The PDA that we constructed from the grammar has two transitions that make it nondeterministic. Both read no input and pop the nonterminal S off the stack, replacing it with something else.

One of the transitions pushes a string starting with the terminal *a* onto the stack. With an *a* on the top of the stack, the next input symbol must also be an *a* if the parser is not to block. The other transition pops off the S and leaves nothing in its place. Except for the starting configuration, every S pushed onto the stack is part of a string that follows the S with the terminal *b*. When that S is popped and replaced with an empty string, the *b* will be on the top of the stack, so the next input symbol must also be *b* to prevent the parser PDA from blocking.

In this example, therefore, the two nondeterministic choices force different input symbol requirements on the next transition. Turning that around, if we look at the next input token (without reading it), we can intelligently select the transition that does not block on that input in the next move. That is, if the next input token is *a*, then choose the transition of Rule 4.1 because it makes the following transition of Rule 4.3 possible; but if the next input token is b, then choose Rule 4.2 because it makes the following application of Rule 4.4 possible. Looking at the next token without reading it is called *lookahead*. Any grammar from which a deterministic top-down PDA can be constructed if it looks ahead k symbols in the input tape is called an LL(k) grammar.

A grammar G is LL(k) if for any two leftmost derivations

$$S \Rightarrow^* uAz \Rightarrow uxz \Rightarrow^* uvw$$
$$S \Rightarrow^* uAz \Rightarrow uyz \Rightarrow^* uvw$$

where u, v, and w are (possibly empty) strings of terminals, x, y, and z are strings of terminals and nonterminals, and $|v|$ (the length of the string v) is k symbols, then $x = y$. That means there are not two different productions A→x and A→y that result in the same k symbols in the generated string from the point of application. Note that we do not require that x or y themselves generate the k symbols of v, but only that whatever they generate, followed by as many terminals generated by the string z as is necessary to make up k tokens, result in identical strings. Put another way, the top-down parser constructed from grammar G, after reading the tokens in the prefix u and faced with the choice between productions A→x and A→y, will be able deterministically to select one or the other based on the next k symbols in the (as yet) unread input string exactly when the grammar is LL(k).

Returning to our example, we can see that the grammar is LL(1) because all nondeterminism can be removed by looking one symbol ahead. In Production P.1 of grammar G_{19}, the *first* token in the rightpart of the production (that is, a) was the lookahead symbol that enabled us to choose the transition (that is, Rule 4.1) based on that production. In Production P.2 there are no tokens in the rightpart — indeed, the rightpart is empty — but we were able to observe the tokens that *follow* its nonterminal in the rightparts of other productions. Thus, the derivation in grammar G_{19}

$$S \Rightarrow^* \underline{aSb} \Rightarrow aaSbb \Rightarrow^* aabb$$

requires the application of production S→aSb in the underlined step because, for the corresponding PDA, the next symbol (k=1) in the (remaining unread input) string abb at that point in the parse is an a, which is the *first* token in the selected production. On the other hand, the derivation

$$S \Rightarrow^* \underline{aSb} \Rightarrow ab \Rightarrow^* ab$$

requires the application of production S→ε because in the PDA the next (and only remaining) symbol in the input string at that point in the parse is a b, which is the token that *follows* S in Production P.1.

4.3.1 *First* and *Follow* Sets

In order to prove a grammar to be LL(k), we construct some sets of strings k symbols in length, based on the productions in the grammar. We construct $First_k(w)$ for all rightparts w in the grammar's productions, and $Follow_k(N)$ for all nonterminals N in the grammar. From these we can construct *selection sets* for all productions, and then go on to prove the LL(k) criterion for that grammar.

The $First_k$ of any string w is the set of all terminal strings of k tokens or fewer that can be derived from w. The $Follow_k$ of a nonterminal N is the set of all terminal strings of k tokens that can follow whatever N derives. The selection set $Select_k$ of a production is the set of lookahead strings of k tokens that govern the selection of that production in a deterministic top-down parser.

For any strings of terminals and nonterminals u, v, and w, the set $First_k(w)$ is constructed by Rules F.1-F.4 in Table 4.2. Note that in these rules, $First_k$ applies variously to individual strings or to sets of strings, depending on the context.

Rule F.1 says that we can construct the $First_k$ of a string consisting of two substrings by constructing the $First_k$ of each substring, forming all strings consisting of one element of the $First_k$ from the first substring concatenated with one element of the $First_k$ from the second substring, then taking the first k tokens from each string. When there are fewer than k tokens in a concatenated string, the whole string is in the set. Thus, if the $First_2(u)$ is the set $\{ab,cd,d,dd,\in\}$ and the $First_2(v)$ is the set $\{cc,d,\in\}$, then the $First_2(uv)$ is formed by concatenating each of the five strings in $First_2(u)$ with each of the three strings in $First_2(v)$, and taking the first two characters of each of the 15 resulting strings

$$abcc \quad abd \quad ab, \quad cdcc \quad cdd \quad cd, \quad dcc \quad dd \quad d, \quad ddcc \quad ddd \quad dd, \quad cc \quad d \quad \in$$

which is the set, $\{ab,cd,dc,dd,d,cc,\in\}$ after removing the duplications.

Rule F.2 says that the $First_k$ of a nonterminal is the union of the $First_k$ of the rightparts of all productions having that nonterminal on the left. Rule F.3 says the $First_k$ of a token by itself is that token in a set by itself. By extension, the $First_k$ of a string of tokens k or fewer symbols long is the singleton set that is that string. Rule F.4 formally allows us to have strings less than k symbols long in the $First_k$ sets.

For an example, consider the simple grammar G_{20}

$$A \to Ba \qquad\qquad B \to b \qquad\qquad B \to c$$

The $First_1$ of the string Ba is by Rule F.1, equal to $First_1(First_1(B)First_1(a))$. $First_1(B)$ is by Rule F.2, the union of $First_1(b)$ and $First_1(c)$, which in turn by Rule F.3, are $\{b\}$ and $\{c\}$, respectively. Thus, $First_1(B)$ is the set $\{b,c\}$, so $First_1(Ba)$ is $First_1(\{ba,ca\}) = \{b,c\}$.

The $Follow_k(A)$ for a nonterminal A is constructed by Rule F.5, also in Table 4.2. Rule F.5 means that to construct the $Follow_k(A)$, you search the grammar for all productions in which A occurs in the rightpart, adding to the $Follow$ set the $First_k$ of everything to the right of that A, including the $Follow_k(B)$, where B is the nonterminal on the left.

Recursively defined sets such as $First$ and $Follow$ can give rise to logical problems with having more than one solution; we avoid these problems by specifying that $First$ and $Follow$ are the minimal solution sets.

F.1 $First_k(uv) = First_k(\ First_k(u)\ First_k(v)\ )$
F.2 $First_k(N) = \cup\ (First_k(w)\ )$ for all w such that N→w is a production
F.3 $First_k(x) = \{x\}$ for any terminal x in the alphabet of the grammar
F.4 $First_k(\in) = \{\in\}$

F.5 $Follow_k(A) = \cup\ (First_k(\ First_k(v)\ Follow_k(B)\ )\ )$ for all productions B→uAv

Table 4.2. Definition of $First$ and $Follow$ sets.

By definition, the goal symbol S also always has the special string "$\perp$" representing the end of the string (which is the end of input to the PDA) in its *Follow* set; this represents the obvious but easily overlooked fact that the end of the string follows the whole generated string. For a compiler, the end-of-string symbol represents the end of the source file; the parser of the command line interpreter in an operating system might recognize the end of the input line as the end of string. The end-of-string symbol "$\perp$" is assumed to be the equivalent of k tokens long, and thus entirely fills its $Follow_k$ strings. Because every string in the language is implicitly followed by "$\perp$" and the $Follow_k$ sets are recursively defined to reach back (if necessary) to the goal symbol to pick up the end of string, it follows that the $Follow_k$ sets consist only of strings k symbols long. No *Follow* set will be empty, nor will any contain the empty string.

As an example of *Follow*, consider the simple grammar G_{21}

$$S \rightarrow Bx \qquad\qquad A \rightarrow aA$$
$$B \rightarrow yAzA \qquad\quad A \rightarrow b$$

To compute the $Follow_1$ of A we find all occurrences of nonterminal A on the right-hand side of any production: there are three. One of these is followed by z, so z is in the $Follow_1$ set. The other two are at the end of their respective productions, so each looks to the $Follow_1$ of their respective leftparts, namely, A and B, thereby including them in the $Follow_1$(A) set. The $Follow_1$ of B is easily seen to be x because there is only one instance of B in a rightpart of a production, and it is followed by x. Thus, x is also in the $Follow_1$ set for A. The other A at the end of its production finds an A also on the left. Right-recursive nonterminals contribute nothing to the *Follow* sets and can be ignored. The $Follow_1$(A) in this example is therefore the set $\{x,z\}$. If there had also been in the grammar a production

$$B \rightarrow AA$$

then $Follow_1$(A) also would have included $First_1$(A), which in this case is the set $\{a,b\}$ by Rule F.2.

Returning again to the grammar G_{19} for all strings of a's followed by an equal number of b's, let's construct for it the $First_1$ and $Follow_1$ sets:

$$S \rightarrow aSb \qquad\qquad First_1(aSb) = First_1(First_1(a)\ First_1(Sb)) = \{a\}$$
$$S \rightarrow \in \qquad\qquad\quad First_1(\in) = \{\in\}$$

The $First_1$(Sb) recursively requires $First_1$(aSb), which is what we are calculating, but because whatever that set eventually comes out to be, it will be concatenated to the right of an a and $First_1$ of that set of composite strings will be the a alone (ignoring the recursive set). In general, $First_1(xy)$ where x is a token is $\{x\}$, regardless of what y is.

The only nonterminal in this grammar is S, and $Follow_1$(S) contains two elements $\{\perp,b\}$. The end-of-string symbol is included because S is the goal symbol; the token b comes from the first production and the application of Rule F.5:

$$First_1(First_1(b)\ Follow_1(S)\ )$$

As in the construction of $First_1$(aSb), because the $First_1$(b) set contains no strings shorter than $k=1$, it is not necessary to calculate the rest of the expression, for it cannot contribute to the set.

4.3.2 Selection Sets

For each production in a grammar A→w, we construct the selection set

$$Select_k(A \rightarrow w) = First_k(First_k(w)\ Follow_k(A)\ )$$

A nonterminal A in a grammar is LL(k) if no two selection sets for productions in A (that is, with A on the left) have any elements in common. A grammar is LL(k) if every nonterminal in its grammar is LL(k).

Any grammar that is LL(k) is also LL($k+1$). This is obviously the case: if k lookahead symbols are enough to determine any choice of productions, then looking at yet one more symbol cannot be less deterministic. The converse, however, is not true.

All LL(0) grammars generate finite languages. This should be evident when you consider that there can be no meaningful choices in an LL(0) grammar. A choice between two productions that generate different strings would have to be made on the basis of looking ahead at the input string (to see which string is to be generated). The only way for a language to be infinite is with recursion, and recursion cannot terminate if there is no alternate (nonrecursive) production in the same nonterminal. Thus, an LL(0) grammar necessarily generates exactly one string of finite length (or else none at all).

In grammar G_{19} there are two productions in S; we calculate their selection sets:

$$
\begin{aligned}
S \rightarrow aSb \quad Select_1(S \rightarrow aSb) &= First_1(First_1(aSb)\ Follow_1(S)) \\
&= First_1(\{a\}\{\perp,b\}) = First_1(\{a \perp,ab\}) = \{a\} \\
S \rightarrow \in \quad Select_1(S \rightarrow \in) &= First_1(First_1(\in)\ Follow_1(S)) \\
&= First_1(\{\in\}\{\perp,b\}) = \{\perp,b\}
\end{aligned}
$$

The two selection sets for S have no elements in common, so S is LL(1), and therefore the grammar is LL(1).

For another example, consider G_2, the context-free grammar for simple expressions from Chapter 2. For simplicity we have added one new nonterminal G, which will be the goal symbol, and a new production to show the end of string explicitly. We construct the $First_1$, $Follow_1$, and $Select_1$ sets in Table 4.3.

The $First$ sets are most easily constructed bottom-up, that is, by beginning with productions that have terminals for the first symbol of their rightparts — in this case, the two productions in F. That makes it easier to calculate the $First$ sets for other productions that contain references to those nonterminals.

		$First_1$	$Follow_1$	$Select_1$
D.0.	G→E⊥	{ n, (}		{ n, (}
D.1.	E→E+T	{ n, (}	{ ⊥, +,) }	{ n, (}
D.2.	E→T	{ n, (}		{ n, (}
D.3.	T→T*F	{ n, (}	{ ⊥, +, *,) }	{ n, (}
D.4.	T→F	{ n, (}		{ n, (}
D.5.	F→(E)	{ (}	{ ⊥, +, *,) }	{ (}
D.6.	F→n	{ n }		{ n }

Table 4.3. *First*, *Follow*, and *Selection* sets for G_2.

Calculating *First* for Production D.4 is the simple union of all the *First* sets for nonterminal F, but D.3 poses a different problem: we cannot know the *First*(T*F) until we know the *First*(T), and that is what we need the *First*(T*F) for! An intuitive analysis resolves the problem in short order. Nonterminal T is recursive on the left; that is, as long as we choose Production D.3, the partial string will have T on the left, although it will generate "*F" on the right for each time through. The only way to exit the recursion is by choosing D.4, leaving a string of F's separated by asterisks. In particular, the first symbol is F, so the recursive T contributes no elements to the *First*(T*F) set. Similarly, Production D.1 contributes no elements to the *First*(E+T) set; they all come from Production D.2.

The *Follow* sets are more easily constructed top-down, starting with the goal symbol G. In this case, the end-of-string mark is explicitly written into the grammar as a terminal, so there is nothing to write for the *Follow*(G). But because there are no choices for this production and it never generates the empty string, no *Follow* set is necessary.

The *Follow* of E is readily identified by scanning the rightparts of the grammar for occurrences of E: there are three, each one followed by a terminal. That makes it easy. *Follow*(E) is just the set of all three terminals.

The nonterminal T also occurs three times in the rightparts of productions, but only one of them is followed by a terminal. Certainly the terminal "*" is in *Follow*(T), but what about the other two references? In both of them there is nothing at all after the nonterminal T. However, the LL(k) criterion requires not that we *generate* k symbols, but only that we look at the next k symbols, however they are generated. That means that the *Follow* of T must include whatever follows the rightpart of which it is the rightmost symbol. This is expressed in Rule F.5 by the recursive reference to the *Follow* of the nonterminal on the left, in both cases here, E. That is, *Follow*(T) includes all the elements of *Follow*(E) as well as the "*" already encountered.

Similarly, the *Follow* of F includes all the elements of *Follow*(T), and none others because it only occurs at the end of productions in T.

The selection sets are now readily constructed from the *First* and *Follow* sets. Because none of the *First* sets contain any string shorter than k, we do not even need to consider *Follow* sets; the selection sets are exactly the *First* sets. Unfortunately, both productions in E have the same elements, so nonterminal E is not LL(1). Similarly, nonterminal T is not LL(1). For either of these reasons, the grammar G_2 is not LL(1). Nor is it LL(2) or LL(3). Often a programming language grammar, if it is not LL(1), is also not LL(k) for any k.

4.4 Left-Recursion

The critical problem with grammar G_2 is that the productions in E and T are both left-recursive; that is, the nonterminal E on the left side of D.1 also occurs on the left end of the rightpart, and similarly for T in D.3. There is no way for the parser to know by a finite lookahead how many times to apply the recursion before taking the production that terminates the recursion (see Figure 4.3). Thus, no left-recursive production is LL(k).

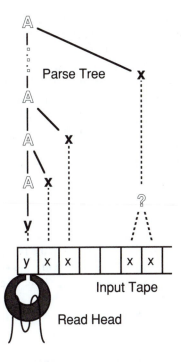

Figure 4.3. The problem with left-recursion. While it is evident that the symbol y under the read head must come from the nonrecursive production, and that each x following it must come from the application of the recursive production, it cannot be known from the top how many times to apply the recursion, without knowing how many x's there are.

Consider the following simple left-linear grammar:

A→Ax
A→y

This grammar generates all strings that begin with y, followed by any number of x's. Because it is left-linear, we can write a regular expression for the same language, following the transformation L.2 in Chapter 3:

y x*

From this regular expression, we can construct a right-linear grammar,

A→yB
B→xB
B→ε

This grammar is no longer left-recursive, but it generates the same language. If we let x and y represent any fixed string of terminals and nonterminals, then it is easy to see that the same transformation can convert any left-recursive context-free grammar into a right-recursive form by adding a new nonterminal B as shown. But is the new grammar LL(k)?

Assuming for the moment that x and y are terminals, we calculate the selection sets:

	$First_1$	$Follow_1$	$Select_1$
A→yB	{ y }	{ ⊥ }	{ y }
B→xB	{ x }	{ ⊥ }	{ x }
B→ε	{ ε }		{ ⊥ }

The *Follow* of B clearly contains the *Follow* of A (from the first production); as noted before, the second production cannot add any elements to the set. The *Select* sets can now be constructed from *First* in two of the productions. In the third, where the *First* set contains only the empty string, the *Select* set is the same as the *Follow* set.

Thus, we see that in this simple case, we have succeeded in making the grammar LL(1). If we let x and y represent any fixed string of terminals and nonterminals, and embed the nonterminal A in a larger grammar, it is necessary to demonstrate that $First_k(x)$ has no common elements with $Follow_k(A)$. In general, this is the case with common programming languages, usually by design.

When we converted our simple left-linear grammar to right-linear, we stopped short of making it a regular grammar, which would also have put it into proper CFG form. The reason is that it would not have been LL(1):

$$A \rightarrow yB \qquad\qquad B \rightarrow xB$$
$$A \rightarrow y \qquad\qquad\quad B \rightarrow x$$

Clearly, the two productions in A start with the same terminal y, and the two productions in B start with the same terminal x. One of the reasons for allowing the extension to context-free grammars that permits empty productions is that it is necessary for converting most kinds of left-recursion to LL(k).

The absence of left-recursive nonterminals is a requirement for LL(k) grammars, which we express in Theorem 4.4:

Theorem 4.4. If G is an LL(k) grammar, then G has no nonterminals that are left-recursive.

The remarks at the beginning of this section provide an informal proof of this theorem. A formal proof is left as an exercise (see Exercise 25).

4.5 Common Left-Factors

We now examine the special situation of the same strings at the left end of two productions in more detail. Consider the simple right-linear grammar

$$A \rightarrow xy$$
$$A \rightarrow xz$$

Because both productions begin with the token x, it is the only element of the selection sets for both productions; the grammar is clearly not LL(1). If we were to write a regular expression for this language, it would start out as

$$xy \mid xz$$

but the distributive law of regular expressions can be applied to convert this to

$$x (y \mid z)$$

which we can then rewrite as the regular grammar

$$A \rightarrow xB$$
$$B \rightarrow y$$
$$B \rightarrow z$$

Now each production in B begins with a different token, which defines the selection sets for B; the new grammar is LL(1). Also, as we did with recursion, we observe that the LL(k) property is not lost if x, y, and z represent arbitrary strings of terminals and nonterminals, provided that $First_k(y)$ and $First_k(z)$ have no elements in common.

We summarize the two transformations for converting a context-free grammar that is not LL(k) to one that is:

1. Convert any left-recursion of the form on the left into right-recursion of the form on the right, where B is a new nonterminal and x and y are any strings of terminals and nonterminals. Note that if there is more than one nonrecursive production in A, the new nonterminal B must be added to the end of each of them. Similarly, a new right-recursive production in B must be created for each left-recursive production in A that it replaces:

$$A \rightarrow Ax \qquad A \rightarrow yB$$
$$A \rightarrow y \qquad B \rightarrow xB$$
$$B \rightarrow \epsilon$$

2. Convert any common left-factors of the form on the left into the form on the right, where B is a new nonterminal and x, y, and z are any strings of terminals and nonterminals:

$$A \rightarrow xy \qquad A \rightarrow xB$$
$$A \rightarrow xz \qquad B \rightarrow y$$
$$B \rightarrow z$$

Returning to G_2, let us convert it to LL(1) by applying these rules. We observe that E and T are both left-recursive. We introduce two new nonterminals, S and P, and calculate the new selection sets on the transformed grammar G_{27}, shown in Table 4.4. The x of the transformation rule, which represents the repeated part, stands for the string "+T" in Production D.1. The y of the rule is the terminator, which is "T" in D.2. Transforming D.3 and D.4 is identical. No transformation of D.5 and D.6 is necessary.

The new grammar can be read intuitively just as before, by thinking of the new nonterminals as "Sum" and "Product": an expression is a term followed by a sum part. A sum part is either a plus followed by a term and another sum part, or else it is empty. Similarly a term is a factor followed by a product part, which in turn is either an asterisk followed by a factor and another product part, or else empty.

	$First_1$	$Follow_1$	$Select_1$
G→E⊥	{ n, (}		{ n, (}
E→TS	{ n, (}	{ ⊥,) }	{ n, (}
S→+TS	{ + }	{ ⊥,) }	{ + }
S→∈	{ ∈ }		{ ⊥,) }
T→FP	{ n, (}	{ ⊥, +,) }	{ n, (}
P→*FP	{ * }	{ ⊥, +,) }	{ * }
P→∈	{ ∈ }		{ ⊥, +,) }
F→(E)	{ (}	{ ⊥, +, *,) }	{ (}
F→n	{ n }		{ n }

Table 4.4. *First*, *Follow*, and *Selection* sets for G_{27}, transformed from G_2.

Ambiguous grammars pose a different kind of problem. No ambiguous grammar can be LL(k), because the two different choices for the ambiguous productions lead to the same sentence in the language. It is possible that the ambiguity is not endemic in the language, but merely a mistake in writing the grammar. In such a case the ambiguity can be resolved by removing the superfluous parse trees from the possible parses of the ambiguous strings. Generally this can be done by applying the rules for removing common left-factors.

If on the other hand, the grammar reflects a language ambiguity as is the case with Pascal's optional **else**-clause, then there is no way to make the grammar unambiguous and therefore LL(k), short of redefining the language.

4.6 Extending CFGs with Regular Expression Operators

As we manipulated left-recursive and common left-factor grammars to make them LL(k), we used regular expressions to represent the intermediate forms. It is perfectly feasible — and indeed quite useful — to leave the regular expression operators in the grammar. That is, we extend context-free grammars with the regular expression metasymbols to express repetition and alternation. This has the advantage of a clear notation that expresses more intuitively the sequence of terminals and nonterminals than does endlessly verbose productions of recursive nonterminals.

Using the transformations from Table 3.5 for converting regular grammars to regular expressions, and treating every symbol in the rightpart of a production as a token with respect to the transformation process, we obtain for G_2 the extended grammar, G_{28}

$$E \rightarrow T \ (\text{``+''} \ T)*$$
$$T \rightarrow F \ (\text{``*''} \ F)*$$
$$F \rightarrow \text{``(''} \ E \ \text{``)''} \ | \ \text{``}n\text{''}$$

It is much easier to read from this grammar that an expression (E) starts with a term (T), followed by any number of additional terms connected by pluses; a term is one or more factors connected by asterisks, and a factor is either an expression enclosed in parentheses, or else the token n.

Note that we begin with this grammar to put the terminals inside quotation marks to prevent confusion between the terminals and the metasymbols. Note further that it is not possible in general to convert a context-free grammar into a single regular expression. If we were to succeed, that would be evidence that a CFG was unnecessary and the language should have been described with a regular grammar.

Extended grammars are much simpler to write, and as we shall see later, they transform naturally into handwritten parser code. Do they preserve the LL(k) criterion? The answer is yes, but calculating the selection sets is somewhat more complex.

It is important to realize that selection sets are relevant only for productions that have a choice. Any nonterminal that has no choices is automatically LL(k) for all k, and the selection sets need not be considered. Looking at the extended version of G_2 it initially appears that no selection sets are needed. This is not the case, for there are three points in the grammar where a decision must be made. The most obvious is the alternation: a factor is either an expression enclosed in parentheses or a terminal n; choose one. Less obvious, but no less a decision point, is each of the two iterators: each time around the iteration, the decision must be made whether to go around again or to terminate.

Each alternation and each iterator in an extended CFG defines a *decision point*. For each decision point, selection sets must be constructed for each alternative. In the case of alternation, a selection set must be constructed for each alternative. In the case of iteration, a selection set must be constructed for the body of the iteration, and another for its *Follow*. At each decision point, all the selection sets must have no common elements.

Let w be a fragment of the rightpart of an extended CFG, and x and y any strings of terminals and nonterminals, possibly including properly nested regular expression metasymbols:

S.1　If $w = x|y$　　$Select_k(x) = First_k(\, First_k(x)\, Follow_k(w))$
　　　　　　　　　　$Select_k(y) = First_k(\, First_k(y)\, Follow_k(w))$
S.2　If $w = x*$　　$Select_k(repeat) = Select_k(x) = First_k(\, First_k(x)\, Follow_k(w))$
　　　　　　　　　　$Select_k(quit) = Follow_k(w)$

We make some observations about the kinds of strings that can make up x and y. In an alternation, at most one of the alternatives can have ϵ in its *First* set, for the empty string allows the selection set to pull in the elements of the *Follow* set, and if more than one alternative does this, they will have common elements. Similarly, the body of an iteration cannot have ϵ in its *First* set, because that would pull in the entire *Follow* set, with which it can have no common elements.

One can usually tell fairly quickly whether a string is *nullable* — that is, if it can generate the empty string — and thus save some effort in discovering that an extended grammar is not LL(1). Any string enclosed by an asterisk or question mark operator is nullable, and any alternation with a nullable alternative is nullable. Concatenation of two nullable strings is nullable, but if either is not nullable, the concatenation is not nullable. A token is not nullable. A nonterminal is nullable if the rightpart of its production (taken as a single extended grammar production) is nullable and not otherwise.

Returning to grammar G_{28} we construct the selection sets to see if it is still LL(1):

　　$E \rightarrow T$ ("+" T)*　　　　　　Decision point: iteration.
　　　　$Select(body) = \{$"+"$\}$,
　　　　$Select(exit) = Follow(($"+"T$)*) = Follow(E) = \{$")"$, \bot\}$
　　$T \rightarrow F$ ("*" F)*　　　　　　Decision point: iteration.
　　　　$Select(body) = \{$"*"$\}$,
　　　　$Select(exit) = Follow(($"*"F$)*) = Follow(T) = \{$"+"$\} \cup \{$")"$, \bot\}$
　　$F \rightarrow$ "(" E ")" | "n"　　　　　　Decision point: alternation.
　　　　$Select(left) = \{$"("$\}$,
　　　　$Select(right) = \{$"n"$\}$

Thus we see that the selection sets at each decision point have no common elements. The extended grammar is indeed LL(1). Note that the constructed selection sets are the same pairs that we constructed for the unextended grammar. That gives the satisfying feeling that adding regular expression operators to our context-free grammar has fundamentally changed neither the language nor the decision points where a deterministic PDA implementing the grammar must invoke lookahead to recognize the language.

4.7 Using a Parser Generator

All of the steps we take to prove a grammar is LL(1) can be mechanized, so can the steps to convert the grammar to a deterministic PDA. A program that mechanizes this process is called a *parser generator*. Several parser generators exist for instructional and production compiler construction. In Chapter 10 we discuss the structure of a particular parser generator, the "TAG compiler." This is a compiler of compilers; that is, it accepts as its source language an extended grammar (extended further with tree transformations and attributes, both of which are discussed in later chapters), and produces as output a parser implemented as a Modula-2 or Pascal program. Using the attribute semantic actions, it is possible to specify a complete compiler as a grammar, then to compile the grammar under the TAG compiler.

The TAG compiler expects its input grammar in a slightly different form than we have been using. When we write several productions in the same nonterminal, we have been repeating the nonterminal on the left of each production, depending on the line end to signal the end of the production. The TAG compiler's source language (like many modern programming languages) places no significance on line ends; therefore, we must delimit productions in another way. All the productions in a single nonterminal must occur together, but only the first of them has that nonterminal specified. The last production in each nonterminal is terminated by a semicolon.

Nonterminals may be any identifier beginning with a letter and containing letters and digits, except for a few reserved words. All terminals are quoted, except for a few explicitly defined by regular expressions in the scanner section. Comments in the grammar are enclosed in braces, as in Pascal. Grammars must begin with the reserved word "tag", followed by the grammar name and a colon; the name is repeated at the end of the grammar with the reserved word "end" and a period. The full specification for grammars to be accepted by the TAG compiler is given in Appendix B.

Listing 4.1 is the grammar G_{28} rewritten in a form acceptable for the TAG compiler, using the token NUM (representing whole numbers) for n. Listing 4.2 gives an abbreviated grammar for grammars; it is itself in the form acceptable to the TAG compiler.

```
tag G2:
scanner
  ignore -> " ";              {ignore spaces only}
  NUM -> ("0".."9")+ ;        {define number token}
parser
  G -> E ".";                 {use dot as explicit end of string}
  E -> T ('+' T)*;            {regular expression extensions OK}
  T -> F P;                   {right-recursive form OK also}
  P -> "*" F P
    -> ;                      {for empty production, leave blank}
  F -> "(" E ")" | NUM;
end G2.
```

Listing 4.1. The grammar G_{28} acceptable to the TAG compiler.

```
tag TagGrammar:            {abbreviated for syntax only}
scanner    {this is the scanner defn section for this grammar}
ignore                     {reserved word -- defines chars to ignore}
  -> " " | ""              {ignore spaces and ends of lines}
  -> "{" ""..."~" "}";      {ignore brace-delimited comments}
CHR                         {--define character token used in scanner}
  -> ('"' '"'|"'" "'")       {endline is two single- or double-quotes}
  -> "'" (" "..."&"|"("..."~") "'"
          {anything except single-quote}
  -> '"' (" "..."!"|"#"..."~") '"';
          {anything except double-quote}
STR                         {--define string token used in parser}
  -> "'" (" "..."&"|"("..."~")+ "'"
          {any string without '}
  -> '"' (" "..."!"|"#"..."~")+ '"';
          {any string without "}
ID                          {--define identifier token used in parser}
  -> ("a"..."z"|"A"..."Z")
          {start with letter, }
      ("a"..."z"|"A"..."Z"|"0"..."9")*;
          { then letters & digits}
parser     {this is the parser definition section for this grammar}
TagGrammar                  {the first nonterminal is the goal symbol}
  -> "tag" ID ":"           {give a name (ID) to the grammar}
      ("scanner"            {optional scanner def'n has two parts...}
        ("ignore" ("->" scanre)+ ";")?   {chars to ignore, and...}
        (ID ("->" scanre)+ ";")+)? {...named tokens, ended by semi}
      "parser" (parsrule)+     {parser definition follows scanner}
      "end" ID ".";          {the ID must match grammar name at front}
scanre                      {a scanner regular expression is...}
  -> scanalt ("|" scanalt)*;      {...alternatives sep'd by "|"}
scanalt -> (scanterm)*;    {an alternative is a sequence of terms}
scanterm -> "(" scanre ")"    {a term is a reg exp'n in parens...}
  -> CHR (".." CHR)?;       {...or else a char or character range}
parsrule -> ID "->" parsre     {a parser rule is a production...}
      ("->" parsre)* ";";   { followed by rightparts with arrows}
parsre -> parsalt ("|" parsalt)*; {each rightpart is a reg expn}
parsalt -> (parsterm)*;    {note: a parser alternative can be empty}
parsterm -> ID             {note: IDs cannot be directly iterated...}
  -> parsfact ("*"|"+"|"?"|); {they must be paren'd in parsfact}
parsfact -> "(" parsre ")"    {either a regular exp'n in parens,}
      | STR;                  {...or else a quoted token string}
end TagGrammar.
```

Listing 4.2. The TAG compiler grammar grammar.

4.7.1 Using YACC

The most popular parser generator in wide use has the somewhat whimsical name, "Yet Another Compiler Compiler" (usually abbreviated in lower case as "yacc"). Although YACC uses a simplified bottom-up parsing algorithm rather than the more restrictive top-down algorithms discussed in this chapter, its widespread availability justifies mention here. LL(1) grammars are a proper subset of the class of LR grammars that YACC accepts, so any valid LL(1) grammar constructed according to the rules in this chapter will be accepted by YACC. YACC will also accept some grammars with left-recursion and common left-factors, which an LL algorithm would reject. If it rejects a grammar, the reasons it offers may not be meaningful from a top-down perspective, but you can be sure the grammar is not LL(1). YACC cannot handle the extensions to context-free grammars that we use for constraint checking and code generation in the next two chapters. For those purposes YACC forces the compiler designer to include fragments of C source code. That is not, however, a problem at this time.

Syntactically, the form of a YACC grammar is very similar to the TAG notation we use here. The scanner definition is defined separately (using the program LEX), and named scanner tokens are explicitly declared in YACC using the "%token" directive. Instead of a right-pointing arrow "→", YACC expects a simple colon ":" to separate the leftpart (nonterminal name) of a production rule from its rightpart. Multiple rules are collected into a single rightpart, separated by alternation bars, a form accepted also by the TAG compiler, or else the nonterminal name may be repeated. Terminal symbols are quoted (using apostrophes) and nonterminal references are simple identifiers, again just like the TAG compiler. Each production is similarly terminated by a semicolon.

Our purpose here is not to give a tutorial in YACC — any system supporting YACC will also have documentation adequate for running it — but to expose the reader to those few differences that make the material in this book transferable.

4.8 Recursive-Descent Parsers

Although the focus of this book is on using appropriate tools to construct parsers mechanically from context-free grammars, LL(1) grammars have an important advantage for the implementation of handwritten compilers. There exists a one-to-one mapping that transforms an extended LL(1) CFG into recursive code in a conventional programming language such as Modula-2. The transformation is simple:

Each *nonterminal* in the grammar is represented exactly by a parameterless procedure in the program. Conventionally we use the same identifier to name the procedure as the nonterminal itself. The *goal symbol* procedure is called by the main program. The main program also initializes the scanner and reads the lookahead token into a global variable, which by convention we call NextToken. All the productions for a nonterminal are collected into a single production with alternatives, in the extended form, and the rightpart of that production forms the basis for the body of code in the procedure that implements the nonterminal. There is no need at this time for local variables in the procedure.

For each element or structure of an extended rightpart of a production, there is exactly one Modula-2 (or Pascal: the differences are trivial) program element or structure. Every *nonterminal* in the grammar is represented by a procedure call to the procedure of the same name. Every *terminal* is represented by a call to the scanner. But because the next token to be read is already in the lookahead symbol, the parser must first match it to the terminal in the grammar, then replace it with a new lookahead symbol. The form for any terminal x is

```
IF NextToken=x THEN Getoken ELSE Error END
```

For each alternation $x|y$, where x and y are any strings, the selection sets for x and y must be tested:

```
IF NextToken IN Select(x) THEN x
ELSIF NextToken IN Select(y) THEN y
ELSE Error END
```

Of course, the selection sets are constant sets precalculated by the programmer and are not written as function calls.

For each iteration $x*$ the selection sets must be calculated to prove the grammar is LL(1), but only the selection set for x is used in the program code:

```
WHILE NextToken IN Select(x) DO x END
```

In both of these structures, x represents whatever Modula-2 code the string transforms into by the same rules.

An empty string translates into no code at all, although appropriate error testing may require checking the follow set in such a case.

Consider, for example, the LL(1) grammar G_{28} in Listing 4.1. The Modula-2 recursive-descent parser implementing the same grammar is given in Listing 4.3 (the scanner procedure `Getoken` is not shown).

In many places in the Modula-2 code the lookahead token is tested several times for the same value. This is an artifact of the very mechanical translation from grammar to Modula-2. Usually an optimizing compiler (or an industrious but careful programmer) can eliminate the redundant tests.

4.9 Recursive-Descent Parsers as Push-Down Automata

We began this chapter with a formal introduction to push-down automata. Although we showed how to construct a recursive-descent parser from an LL(1) context-free grammar, it remains to be seen whether such a program properly constitutes a PDA.

A PDA, as you recall, is a 7-tuple, consisting of an input alphabet Σ, a set of states Q, a set of transitions Δ, a stack alphabet H, an initial stack symbol h_0 and state q_0, and a (possibly empty) set of final states F. In the parser, the input alphabet is clearly the set of tokens returned by the scanner.

A computer executing a program written in Modula-2 can be thought of as having a finite number of states, which are the line numbers of — or more precisely, the machine instruction locations corresponding to — the source program statements. At any time, exactly one simple statement is active, and the program advances from statement to statement in a well-defined way. The advancement from statement to statement corresponds to the transitions from state to state.

```
MODULE G2;
TYPE Token = (Plus, Star, Left, Right, NUM, Dot);
VAR NextToken: Token;
FROM Somewhere IMPORT Getoken, InitScanner, Error;
PROCEDURE E; (* with F, P, and T nested to avoid forward refs *)
  PROCEDURE F;
  BEGIN
    IF NextToken IN Token{Left} THEN              (* first alternative *)
      IF NextToken = Left THEN Getoken            (* read the token "(" *)
        ELSE Error END;
      E;   (* recursively call nonterminal E *)
      IF NextToken = Right THEN Getoken           (* read the token ")" *)
        ELSE Error END
    ELSIF NextToken IN Token{NUM} THEN            (* second alternative *)
      IF NextToken = NUM THEN Getoken             (* read the token "NUM" *)
        ELSE Error END
    ELSE Error END                                (* neither of the above *)
  END F;
  PROCEDURE P;
  BEGIN
    IF NextToken IN Token{Star} THEN (* first alternative *)
      IF NextToken = Star THEN Getoken
        ELSE Error END;
      F; P;
    ELSIF NextToken IN Token{Plus, Right, Dot} (* Follow1 of P *)
      THEN                       (* second alternative is empty *)
    ELSE Error END
  END P;
  PROCEDURE T;
  BEGIN
    F; P
  END T;
BEGIN (* E *)
  T;
  WHILE NextToken IN Token{Plus} DO
    IF NextToken = Plus THEN Getoken
      ELSE Error END;
    T
    END (* WHILE *)
END E;
BEGIN (* G2 *)
  InitScanner;
  Getoken;
  E;
  IF NextToken = Dot THEN (* Accept *) ELSE Error END;
END G2.
```

Listing 4.3. Recursive-descent parser for grammar G_{28}.

Any programming language that allows recursion must save the return addresses on some form of stack in memory. This is the stack of our PDA. The stack alphabet, therefore, is a subset of the state numbers, representing the procedure call statement locations. Most of the transition rules leave the stack unchanged. Although formally required to pop off the top stack symbol, all such rules immediately push it back on. The exceptions are the procedure call statements, which also push on their own statement number, and the END statement of each procedure. The END statement, instead of advancing to the next statement sequentially in the source, goes back to the statement following the procedure call (whose address it popped).

The initial stack symbol is the command line interpreter in the operating system — or whatever a terminated program normally returns to on completion of its execution. This PDA halts on empty stack. The start state is the BEGIN of the main program.

Thus, by showing how each formal component of a PDA is modeled in a recursive-descent parser, we have established that our correctly coded handwritten parsers are indeed push-down automata. Once again we maintain formal correctness at no loss of expedience.

Summary

The focus of this chapter has been the techniques and tools for constructing parsers mechanically from context-free grammars. This chapter examined the relationship between push-down automata and context-free languages. By definition, the strings in a context-free language are derived from a corresponding context-free grammar. We showed that for every context-free grammar, there exists a nondeterministic push-down automaton that accepts the language defined by the context-free grammar.

This chapter introduced LL(k) grammars, a limited subset of CFGs. For every LL(k) grammar, there exists a deterministic, push-down automaton that accepts any string in the language defined by the grammar, by constructing a leftmost derivation and looking ahead at no more than k input symbols at every step in the derivation. Grammars without the LL(k) property also exist. Many of them can be converted to LL(1) by removing left-recursion and common left-factors.

This chapter also gave practical steps for the construction of parser programs from LL(1) grammars. This can be done automatically by using a parser generator, or a recursive-descent parser may easily be written by hand with little thought by substituting specified programming language constructs for grammar components.

Acronyms

LL(k)   <u>L</u>eft-to-right scan of input, parsing by the <u>L</u>eftmost canonical derivation, looking ahead at no more than k input symbols.

NDPDA   Nondeterministic push-down automaton.

PDA   Push-down automaton.

TAG   Transformational attribute grammar, the input language for a compiler-compiler featured in this book.

Keywords

ambiguous	A grammar that cannot be deterministically parsed (that is, at one or more steps in a derivation, there will be more than one rule that can be applied in the derivation).
configuration	(q, w, c), representing the state q of a PDA with string w of unread symbols waiting to be input and a particular string c on the PDA stack.
compiler compiler	A parser generator with additional provisions for semantics.
decision point	An alternator or iterator in the rightpart of a rewrite rule in an extended CFG.
extended grammar	A grammar written with regular expression operators in one or more productions.
left-factors	Two or more productions with the same strings at the left end of the rightpart and the same nonterminal on the left-hand side as in (see Section 4.5) $A \rightarrow 0B11$ $A \rightarrow 01$
left-recursive	A production of the form $A \rightarrow Ax$ (see Section 4.4).
LL(k) grammar	A grammar from which we can construct a deterministic, top-down PDA that looks ahead at most k symbols in the input tape.
LL(1) grammar	The most common form of LL(k) grammar, and the easiest to convert manually into a PDA using a programming language.
lookahead	Looking at the next token in the input without reading it.
lookahead set	See selection set.
nullable string	A string of terminals and nonterminals that can generate the empty string as part of a sentence of the language.
parser	(1) A recognizer (acceptor of all strings of a language), which outputs a parse or derivation of each accepted input (see recognizer). (2) A syntax analyzer.
parser generator	A software tool used to produce a syntax analyzer from an input grammar which is usually a context-free grammar.
PDA	Push-down automaton
deterministic	has only one possible transition for any given configuration.
nondeterministic	means a given configuration can have more than one transition.
PDA transition	A partial function of the form $\delta: Q \times (\Sigma \cup \in) \times H \rightarrow Q \times H^*$ where δ is in the set Δ of PDA transition rules, Q is a set of states, Σ is a language alphabet, and H is the PDA stack alphabet. It is a partial function because not all combinations of states and alphabet symbols have transitions defined for them.
phrase structure	How words go together to form syntactically correct programs.

production	Rewrite rule.
recognizer	(1) A procedure that accepts all strings belonging to a language and rejects all others.
	(2) An automaton.
recursive-descent	A parser for an LL(1) grammar where every nonterminal is represented exactly by a parameterless procedure and every terminal in the grammar is represented by a call to the scanner.
selection set	Contains the prefixes of length k of strings that can be derived from a nonterminal A in $Select_k(A \rightarrow w)$. Also called a lookahead set.
semantic analysis	Determining what a program means computationally.
set	Primitive mathematical concept meaning a collection of objects.
$First_k(w)$	Set of all terminal strings of k or fewer tokens that can be derived from string w (see Section 4.3.1 for rules for constructing this set).
$Follow_k(N)$	Set of all terminal strings of k or fewer tokens that can come after any substring derivable from nonterminal N.
$Select_k(A \rightarrow w)$	$= First_k(First_k(w)Follow_k(A))$. Also called the selection set, it contains the prefixes of length k of strings that can be derived from A.
TAG compiler	A compiler-compiler that accepts as its source language an extended grammar and produces as output a parser.
top-down parse	Starting with the goal symbol on the stack, continue to rewrite the leftmost nonterminal in the sentential form at each step, choosing always the production that ultimately results in matching the input string.

Exercises

1. (a) Show that P_0 accepts the string c and rejects the strings $aacb$ and abc.

   (b) Show that P_0' accepts the strings $aacbb$ and c and rejects abc.

   (c) Show that P_0'' accepts the strings $aacbb$ and c and rejects abc.

2. Convert the following PDA, which halts on an empty stack, to an equivalent PDA that halts on a final state.

   $P = (\{a, b\}, \{q\}, \Delta, \{S, A, B, a, b\}, S, q, \{ \})$, where:

   $\Delta = \{ \ \delta(q, \epsilon, S) = (q, aA),$
   $\delta(q, \epsilon, S) = (q, bB),$
   $\delta(q, \epsilon, A) = (q, aA),$
   $\delta(q, \epsilon, A) = (q, bB),$
   $\delta(q, \epsilon, B) = (q, b),$
   $\delta(q, a, a) = (q, \epsilon),$
   $\delta(q, b, b) = (q, \epsilon) \ \}$

3. Convert the following PDA, which halts in a final state, to an equivalent PDA that halts on an empty stack.

P = ({*a*, *b*, *c*}, {p, q, r}, Δ, {S, A, B, *a*, *b*, *c*, *h*}, h, p, {r}), where:

Δ = { δ(q, ∈, S) = (q, *a*Ac),
       δ(q, ∈, S) = (q, *b*B),
       δ(q, ∈, A) = (q, *a*A),
       δ(q, ∈, A) = (q, *b*B),
       δ(q, ∈, B) = (q, *b*),
       δ(q, *a*, *a*) = (q, ∈),
       δ(q, *b*, *b*) = (q, ∈),
       δ(q, *c*, *c*) = (q, ∈),
       δ(p, ∈, h) = (q, Sh),
       δ(q, ∈, h) = (r, h) }

4. Construct nondeterministic PDAs from the following CFGs.

(a)

S → 01A0
S → 0B1
A → 01A
A → 01
B → 0B1
B → 0S1

(b)

S → A*ac*B
S → *ab*
A → C*ba*
B → *bc*
C → *c*A*b*B
C → *c*

5. Trace the steps of the PDA given below in recognizing the following strings.

P = ({0, 1}, {S, A, B, C}, Δ, {S, A, B, C, 0, 1}, h, S, {C}), where:

Δ = { δ(S, 0, h) = (A, h),   (a) 0011001
       δ(S, 1, h) = (B, h),
       δ(A, 0, h) = (S, h),   (b) 1100110
       δ(A, 1, h) = (C, h),
       δ(B, 0, h) = (C, h),
       δ(B, 1, h) = (S, h) }

6. Trace the steps of the NDPDA given below in recognizing the following strings.

P = ({*a*, *b*, *c*}, {q}, Δ, {S, A, B, C, *a*, *b*, *c*}, S, q, { }), where:

Δ = { δ(q, ∈, S) = (q, *a*Abc),   (a) *aabcabbbc*
       δ(q, ∈, S) = (q, S*b*B),
       δ(q, ∈, A) = (q, *a*Ab),   (b) *abcbcabbcbb*
       δ(q, ∈, A) = (q, B*ab*),
       δ(q, ∈, B) = (q, B*b*C),
       δ(q, ∈, B) = (q, *b*C),
       δ(q, ∈, C) = (q, *c*),
       δ(q, ∈, C) = (q, ∈),
       δ(q, *a*, *a*) = (q, ∈),
       δ(q, *b*, *b*) = (q, ∈),
       δ(q, *c*, *c*) = (q, ∈) }

7. Construct $First_1$, $Follow_1$, and $Select_1$ sets for the following grammars and indicate whether the grammars are LL(1) or not.

(a)	(b)	(c)	
S → 0AS	A → aB	S → +B	G → dG
S → 10	A → bC	S → –B	G → eC
A → 1	B → b	S → dA	G → ϵ
A → 0SA	B → aA	B → dA	C → +H
	B → bD	A → dA	C → –H
	C → aD	A → .F	C → dD
	C → bA	A → eC	H → dD
	C → a	A → ϵ	D → dE
	D → aC	F → dG	D → ϵ
	D → bB		E → ϵ

8. Construct $First_2$, $Follow_2$, and $Select_2$ sets for the following grammars and indicate whether the grammars are LL(2) or not.

(a)	(b)
A → aB	A → aAa
A → bC	A → bAb
A → b	A → aa
B → aD	A → bb
C → aB	A → a
C → bC	A → b
C → b	
D → aE	
D → a	
E → aB	
E → bC	
E → b	

9. Construct $First_3$, $Follow_3$, and $Select_3$ sets for the following grammars and indicate whether the grammars are LL(3) or not.

(a)	(b)
S → aSc	P → P "&" P
S → aAb	P → P "V" P
S → cB	P → P ">" P
A → abA	P → P "=" P
A → a	P → "–" P
B → bB	P → "P"
B → bcB	P → "Q"
	P → "R"

10. Determine how much lookahead (that is, LL(1), LL(2), etc.) the following grammars require by constructing the appropriate *First*, *Follow*, and *Select* sets.

(a)

$A \rightarrow \in$
$A \rightarrow 10B$
$B \rightarrow A11$
$B \rightarrow 0$

(b)

$A \rightarrow 01B$
$A \rightarrow 0C$
$B \rightarrow 0C10$
$C \rightarrow 10D$
$D \rightarrow 01$
$D \rightarrow 0$

11. Eliminate any left-recursion or common left-factors in the following grammars.

(a)

$S \rightarrow SaA$
$S \rightarrow bB$
$A \rightarrow aB$
$A \rightarrow c$
$B \rightarrow Bb$
$B \rightarrow d$

(b)

$S \rightarrow aA$
$S \rightarrow bB$
$A \rightarrow bA$
$A \rightarrow bB$
$B \rightarrow cB$
$B \rightarrow c$

(c)

$S \rightarrow Aa$
$S \rightarrow b$
$A \rightarrow SB$
$B \rightarrow ab$

(d)

$S \rightarrow Ab$
$S \rightarrow Ba$
$A \rightarrow aA$
$A \rightarrow a$
$B \rightarrow a$

(e)

$S \rightarrow A0$
$S \rightarrow B10$
$A \rightarrow B0B$
$A \rightarrow B1B$
$B \rightarrow 0$
$B \rightarrow 1$

(f)

$S \rightarrow 0A$
$S \rightarrow 1B$
$A \rightarrow AB$
$A \rightarrow A1$
$A \rightarrow 01$
$B \rightarrow 01$
$B \rightarrow 00$

(g)

$E \rightarrow E+E$
$E \rightarrow E*E$
$E \rightarrow (E)$
$E \rightarrow n$

12. Convert the following simple grammar to an extended grammar.

$S \rightarrow 0A$
$S \rightarrow 1B$
$A \rightarrow A10$
$A \rightarrow 0$
$B \rightarrow 01S$
$B \rightarrow 1$

13. Construct $Select_1$ sets for the following extended grammars and indicate whether the grammars are LL(1) or not.

(a)

$S \rightarrow (aA \mid bB)*$
$A \rightarrow (aa)* b$
$B \rightarrow (ba) \mid a*$

(b)

$S \rightarrow 0(0\mid1)* \mid (A\mid0B)$
$A \rightarrow (01\mid\in) \mid (1B)*$
$B \rightarrow (01 \mid 00)*$

(c)

$R \rightarrow (``+"\mid``-")? \; d^+ \; (``."d^+)? \; (``E" \; (``+"\mid``-")? \; d \; d?)?$

Parsers and Context-Free Languages   Chap. 4

14. The following grammar represents the ambiguous **if**-statement in Pascal. Write an unambiguous CFG with the same syntax of the Pascal **if**-statement; that is, i generates the same language. Note that Pascal is defined so that the **else-** clause always goes with the innermost **if**-statement to which it can apply. Prove your grammar is LL(1) and therefore unambiguous, or else show why it cannot be LL(1).

$$G \rightarrow S.$$
$$S \rightarrow i\,x\,t\,S\,e\,S$$
$$S \rightarrow i\,x\,t\,S$$
$$S \rightarrow p$$

15. Give an example of a grammar that is

    (a) LL(2) but not LL(1)   (b) LL(3) but not LL(2)
    (c) without left recursion but not LL(k) for any k.

16. Determine if the following grammar is LL(k) and if so, give the value of k.

    $$A \rightarrow yB \mid zB \mid y \mid z \qquad\qquad B \rightarrow xB \mid yB \mid y \mid \epsilon$$

17. Complete the proof of Lemma 4.1.

18. Give a proof by construction for Theorem 4.2 in terms of PDAs.

19. Give a proof by construction for Theorem 4.2 in terms of context-free grammars.

20. Using the construction method in Exercise 19, write out the context-free grammar for the union of the languages defined by the CFGs in Exercise 4. Give two sample derivations of strings in $L_1 + L_2$.

21. Using the construction method shown in the proof for Theorem 4.3, write out the context-free grammar for the product $L_1 \cdot L_2$ of the two languages defined in Exercise 4.

22. Show that if L is a context-free language, then L* is a context-free language. Hint: use the proof-by-construction technique.

23. Write two sample derivations of strings in L* using

    (a) the CFG in exercise 4a to write out the context-free grammar for L* and

    (b) L* from part (a)

24. Does the assertion in Exercise 22 mean that if L is LL(1), then L* is also LL(1)? Justify your answer.

25. (Theorem 4.4) Prove that if G is an LL(k) grammar, then G has no left-recursive nonterminals. Hint: prove the contrapositive of this theorem: if G has left-recursive nonterminals, then G is not LL(k) for any k.

26. Show that the converse of Theorem 4.4 is not true. Hint: assume the converse is true and find a counterexample.

27. Prove that if for each nonterminal A in a context-free grammar G, the lookahead sets $Select_k(\,A \rightarrow w\,)$ are disjoint, then the grammar G is LL(k).

28. (Ambiguity Rule) Prove that if G is an LL(k) grammar, then G is unambiguous. Hint: use proof-by-contradiction technique.

29. Show that the converse of the ambiguity rule is not true. Hint: the proof technique used in Exercise 26 will also work in this exercise.

used in Exercise 26 will also work in this exercise.

Review Quiz

Indicate whether the following statements are true or false.

1. If L is a context-free language, then L* is also a context-free language.
2. If a context-free grammar is LL(1), its selection sets do not have to be disjoint.
3. The parser for an LL(k) grammar works deterministically if it looks ahead at $k-1$ input symbols to the right of its current input position.

The next three questions concern the following grammar named G:

$$A \rightarrow Ax \mid Ay \mid xB \mid y$$
$$B \rightarrow xyB \mid xxB \mid \in$$

4. The grammar G is left-recursive without common left prefixes.
5. The grammar G is not left-recursive but does have common left prefixes.
6. We can remove the left-recursion in G by using the method known as left-factoring.
7. The language recognized by a PDA is context-free.
8. If L is context-free language, then we can always find a PDA that accepts L.
9. A grammar that is left-recursive is not an LL(k) grammar for any k.
10. The grammar

$$A \rightarrow 0A \mid 0B \mid \in$$
$$B \rightarrow 0B \mid 1B \mid 0 \mid 1$$

is not LL(1).

Compiler Project

1. Prove the CFG you wrote in Chapter 2 is LL(1) by constructing the selection sets for each production. If the grammar is not LL(1), transform it so that it is.
2. Enter your grammar into a computer file and feed it to a parser generator such as the TAG compiler or YACC. You may have to modify the form of your productions to be acceptable to the parser generator. If you have done step 1 correctly, the parser generator should accept your grammar without further modification.
3. Compile your parser.
4. Write some small programs and parse them with your compiled parser. Show that correct programs are accepted, but syntax errors are rejected by your parser.

Further Reading

Aho, A.V. & Ullman, J.D. *Theory of Parsing, Translation, and Compiling*, Vol. 1, Parsing. Englewood Cliffs, NJ: Prentice Hall, 1972. See section 5.1 on LL(k) grammars, *First* and *Follow* sets.

Cohen, D.I.A. *Introduction to Computer Theory*. NY: Wiley. See ch. 18 on the relation between PDAs and CFGs, especially ch. 19 on context-free languages.

Dwyer, B. "Improving Gough's LL(1) Lookahead Generator." ACM *SIGPLAN Notices*, Vol. 20, No. 11 (November 1985), pp. 27-29. Uses the closure of a relation *begun_by* to form a *First* set of each vocabulary symbol and forms a *Follow* set for each nonterminal using the closure of the ends relation. In his algorithm (see p. 28), Dwyer represents each production as a linked list.

Gough, K.J. "A New Method of Generating LL(1) Lookahead Sets." ACM *SIGPLAN Notices*, Vol. 20, No. 6 (June 1985), pp. 16-19. Explains what Dwyer says. What Gough calls a lookahead set, we call a selection set.

Graham, S.L., et al. "An Improved Context-Free Recognizer." ACM *Transactions on Programming Languages and Systems*, Vol. 2, No. 3 (July 1980), pp. 415-462. See especially section 2, pp. 417-427, where a new algorithm is given in 14 lines of Pascal-like code, using what is called a recognition matrix.

Schreiner, A.T. & Freidman, H.G. *Introduction to Compiler Construction with Unix*. Englewood Cliffs, NJ: Prentice Hall, 1985. See ch. 3 on language recognition and discussion of yacc.

Sudkamp, T.A. *Languages and Machines: An Introduction to the Theory of Computer Science*. Reading, MA: Addison-Wesley, 1988. See ch. 4 on parsing, ch. 8 on PDAs and CFGs, especially ch. 15 on *First*, *Follow* and lookahead sets $LA_k(A)$.

Chapter 5

Semantic Analysis and Attribute Grammars

Aims

- Extend context-free grammars with attributes and semantic rules.
- Extend to two forms of attributes, LL(1) recursive-descent parsers.
- Introduce assertions to constrain the values of attributes.
- Develop a model attribute grammar and corresponding recursive-descent parser to illustrate the techniques.
- Use attributes to enforce predeclaration of identifiers and strong type-checking.

5.1 Introduction

Correctly parsing the syntax of the input source program in a compiler, given the grammatical specification of that syntax, is easy. But a programming language consists of more than syntax and phrase structure. Modern languages require declarations for the identifiers used in a program, and the usage of a variable or procedure name must be consistent with its declaration. As we observed in Chapter 2, matching identifiers to their declarations requires a context-sensitive language.

Rather than fully open the can of worms labeled "Linear Bounded Automata" and have all that nondeterminism and incomplete formalism squirm out all over everything, we will take the much more conservative approach of laying on top of context-free grammars and deterministic push-down automata just barely enough functionality to solve the immediate problem. And thus are born attribute grammars.

5.2 Attribute Grammars

In noncomputer usage, an attribute of an object or person is some feature, quality, or characteristic that describes that object or person, such as a person's sense of humor or an object's color. Treating the nodes of a parse tree as objects, we might describe the sentence fragment denoted by the nonterminal at some node by certain attributes such as its numerical value (if it is an expression), or the location in memory of the procedure or variable named by it (if it is an identifier), or the set of identifiers visible to it (in a scoped language like Pascal or Modula-2). These attributes are in no way defined by the context-free grammar (CFG) that defines the syntax of the string, but they surely are part of the language we hope to compile. Therefore, we find it useful to extend the CFG with the attributes and the constraints they impose on the language.

An *attribute grammar* is a triple: A = (G, V, F) consisting of a context-free grammar G, a finite set of distinct attributes V, and a finite set of *attribute assertions*, or predicates F about the attributes. Each attribute is associated with a single nonterminal or terminal of the grammar, and each assertion is associated with a single production and therefore makes reference only to the attributes associated with the terminals and nonterminals on the left and right sides of that production. A string in the language of G is also in the language of A if and only if all the assertions hold true for all of the attributes attached to the terminal and nonterminal nodes of the parse tree for that string. The *constrainer* is that part of the compiler that verifies that all the assertions are true with respect to the program being compiled.

Consider, for example, the tiny expression grammar

$$E \rightarrow T + T \mid T \text{ "OR" } T$$
$$T \rightarrow num \mid \text{"TRUE"} \mid \text{"FALSE"}$$

applied to the string "3+4" as in Figure 5.1. Each term T might have a type attribute t, either *int* if it is an integer constant, or *bool* if it is Boolean. The expression nonterminal could have an assertion relating these two attributes: they must be the same.

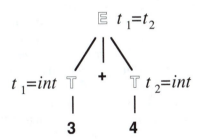

Figure 5.1. Simple parse tree with attributes.

The attributes are (at least conceptually) static values — not variables — descriptive of the terminal or of the string generated by their respective nonterminals, but their values might be different for different strings in the language, and for different instances of their terminals or nonterminals. An attribute value is thus constrained by the assertions that refer to it. Assertions may compel a specific attribute value, as in the example, or they may merely limit an attribute to some range of values.

The possibility of attribute values ranging over several different numbers may be interesting in theory, but it has little practical use. The assertions are therefore commonly divided into two categories: those that constrain an attribute to a single value for each instance, called *attribute evaluation functions*, and *predicates* that are not so restricted. Attribute evaluation functions, like the assertion $t_1=int$ in the example of Figure 5.1, resemble assignment statements in that they constrain the attributes to a single value. Predicates, like the assertion $t_1=t_2$ in the example (if the parse tree is read bottom-up), do not compel any single specific value, but only that the two values be equal. A predicate imposes additional constraints on one or more attributes already constrained by evaluation functions. It may constrain an attribute to a single value (as in our example), or it may relate it to an expression (perhaps involving other attributes), such as $a_1>a_2+3$. Attribute predicates are essentially the same as predicates in the predicate calculus, where the predicate $P(x) =$ "x loves Sally" asserts that for some specified object x defined elsewhere, it has a certain relationship (being in love) with a specific object named Sally.

Often the two categories of assertions are formalized in the definition of an attribute grammar; we consider it an unnecessary distinction except as an implementation detail. If the parse tree in the example is read from right to left (instead of bottom-up), then the assertion $t_1=t_2$ is an evaluation function and the assertion $t_1=int$ is a predicate. We do, however, separate evaluation functions from predicates in our terminology when that clarifies the semantic issues in a particular context.

We write an attribute grammar as a context-free grammar, in which we attach zero or more *attributes* to each of the nonterminals. Classical attribute grammar notation uses a record-field format, where each reference to an attribute specifies both the nonterminal and attribute names, as in "*nonterminal.attribute*". We observe that the attribute assertions are most conveniently written locally to the production in which they apply. The combination of distinctive names and positional notation is familiar to most programmers, thus making for a more compact and readable grammar.

One of the functions of an attribute grammar is to specify formally the flow of context information through the grammar, without *appearing* to make a context-sensitive grammar of it. This is important because we have efficient algorithms for constructing push-down automata mechanically from CFGs, but we lack these tools for linear-bounded automata. It can be shown formally, however, that although an attribute grammar is not a context-sensitive grammar in the formal sense, it defines a context-sensitive language (although perhaps restricted somewhat). Attribute evaluation functions and attribute predicates, however, transfer directly onto the implementation of the parser automaton, without destroying the algorithmic construction.

5.2.1 Inherited and Synthesized Attributes

Attributes come in two flavors: an *inherited* attribute is defined by assertions in the productions whose rightparts contain references to the nonterminal to which it is attached; a *synthesized* (also called *derived*) attribute is defined within the productions of the nonterminal to which it is attached, or is intrinsic to the terminal to which it is attached.

As shown in Figure 5.2, inherited attributes *inherit* their values from the parent in the parse tree; we write them into the grammar with an arrow pointing down ($\downarrow$*attname*). Synthesized attributes may be further distinguished into those that are used only locally to the productions in which they are defined, and those that are passed up the parse tree to the parent node. The latter we write in the grammar with an arrow pointing up ($\uparrow$*attname*). In the example of Figure 5.1, t_1 and t_2 would both be synthesized attributes if the parse tree is evaluated bottom-up.

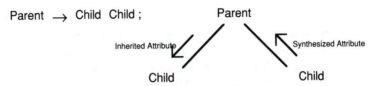

Parent $\longrightarrow$ Child Child ;

Parent

Inherited Attribute

Synthesized Attribute

Child

Child

Figure 5.2. Inherited and synthesized attributes in a parse tree, showing the flow of attribute information.

Attribute grammars sprang fully formed from the pen of Donald Knuth in 1968, but we are only now beginning to make effective use of them in compiler design. Nevertheless, Knuth's example of attribute evaluation remains the best tutorial in the concept. Consider this context-free grammar defining fixed-point binary numbers:

$$N \rightarrow S\ \text{"."}\ S$$
$$S \rightarrow SB$$
$$\rightarrow B$$
$$B \rightarrow \text{"0"}$$
$$\rightarrow \text{"1"}$$

Obviously we could write a simple regular grammar for the same language, but our purpose here is to show how inherited and synthethized attributes can be attached to the nonterminals.

The goal symbol N represents the entire binary number. We attach to it the synthesized attribute v, representing the numerical value of the number:

$$N \uparrow v$$

The symbol v represents the *value* of any number generated by the nonterminal N. For any particular parse tree in this language, the terminal string derived from the goal symbol will have a particular value v, and the root node N is attributed with that value.

The nonterminal B represents a binary digit; it has its own value v (not to be confused with the attribute with the same name attached to N). The value a digit contributes to the overall value of a binary number N, however, depends on the digit's position in the number. The digit's value is scaled by a power of two that depends on how far from the binary point it is. This scale factor f cannot be synthesized from information available to the digit itself, but must be inherited from its parent, the nonterminal S:

$$B \downarrow f \uparrow v$$

We can define an assertion relating the value v to the scale factor f. Specifically, if the digit is a one, its value must be equal to the scale factor f. When the digit is zero the scale factor is irrelevant; the value of the digit can be asserted to be zero.

The nonterminal S represents a string of binary digits; it too has a value v that depends on its position in the string, which is a function of the inherited scale factor f. But where is this scale factor to come from? It must be based on the length of the string and its position, relative to the binary point. The position can be determined within the productions for N and S, but the length l of a string can only be synthesized as the string is constructed digit by digit within the productions for S. Therefore, we attach to S not only the scale factor inherited (perhaps indirectly) from the root, but also the synthesized length of the string and its value:

$$S \downarrow f \uparrow v \uparrow l$$

Now we can write the attribute assertions associated with the productions in each nonterminal. These assertions are only used to construct the value of the number (that is, by constraining it to a single value), so we could with equal correctness refer to the assertions as attribute evaluation functions:

$$N \uparrow v \quad \rightarrow S \downarrow f_1 \uparrow v_1 \uparrow l_1 \text{ "."} S \downarrow f_2 \uparrow v_2 \uparrow l_2 \quad [v = v_1 + v_2;\ f_1 = 1;\ f_2 = 2^{-l_2}]$$

$$S \downarrow f \uparrow v \uparrow l \quad \rightarrow S \downarrow f_1 \uparrow v_1 \uparrow l_1\ B \downarrow f_2 \uparrow v_2 \quad [f_1 = 2f;\ f_2 = f;\ v = v_1 + v_2;$$
$$l = l_1 + 1]$$

$$\rightarrow B \downarrow f \uparrow v \quad [l = 1]$$

$$B \downarrow f \uparrow v \quad \rightarrow \text{ "0"} \quad [v = 0]$$

$$\rightarrow \text{ "1"} \quad [v = f]$$

As we did with the semantic actions in regular grammars, the assertions are enclosed in square brackets. We usually give distinctive names (here subscripted) to the attributes attached to the nonterminals in the rightparts of the grammar, so that there is no confusion as to which "v" is being referred to in the assertions.

Reading the first production of this grammar, we observe the value v of a number to be the sum of the values v_1 (integral part) and v_2 (fractional part). The integral and fractional parts have already been properly scaled by the scale factors sent down the parse tree. The scale factor inherited by the binary digit string in the integer part of the number is one, but the scale factor inherited by the fractional binary digit string is based on the number of digits between its right end and the binary point, which is the string's length.

For any string S composed of a substring followed by a binary digit (the first production in S), the scale factor f_2 of the binary digit B is the same as that of the string, but the substring is scaled at twice that value because it is one binary digit to the left of it. The length of the string is one greater than the length of the substring, and the value v of the string is the sum of the values of the substring and the digit. When a binary string consists of just a single digit B, the scale factor is the same and the derived value is the same: we can abbreviate these assertions in the grammar by using the same attribute names on both nonterminals.

Finally, as we observed previously, the value of a binary digit is that digit times its scale factor; this value is zero if the digit is zero.

Figure 5.3 shows the flow of attribute values through the parse tree for this grammar. Note that although it is shown as three passes, with the values of different attributes evaluated sequentially at different times, the fully attributed parse tree has all of the attributes attached to their respective nodes in a single tree, such that all of the assertions are simultaneously true. We consider it an artifact of the implementation in this example that the attribute evaluation cannot be completed in one pass. Indeed, for this attribute grammar, it is barely capable of evaluation at all. The evaluation order requires a minimum of three passes through the tree: one bottom-up pass to evaluate string length, one top-down pass to evaluate scale factors, and finally another bottom-up pass to evaluate the values.

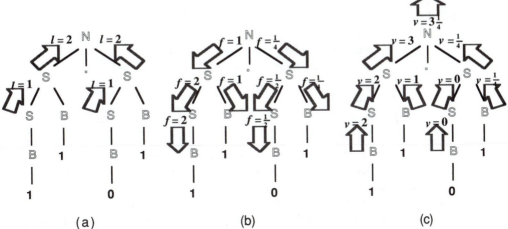

Figure 5.3. The flow of attributes in the parse tree for the string "11.01". Length flows up (a), then scale factor flows down (b), then value flows up (c).

It is conceivable that attribute evaluation functions could be defined in such a way that they are mutually dependent, such as u and v, x and y in this tiny grammar:

$$A \qquad \rightarrow B \downarrow x \uparrow y \qquad\qquad [x=y]$$
$$B \downarrow u \uparrow v \quad \rightarrow a \qquad\qquad [v=u]$$

We call such a dependency *circular* because inherited attribute x depends on synthesized attribute y, which is the same as v, which in turn depends on u, and u matches x again. Much research has gone into determining how to avoid circular attribute dependencies, as well as finding efficient strategies for attribute evaluation order.

As we noted at the beginning of this discussion on evaluating binary numbers, this is a contrived example, mostly to show the differences between synthesized and inherited attributes. It also alerts us to the potential problem of attribute evaluation order. In practice, we do not attempt to write compilers that require such complex attribute evaluation strategies. For example, if we chose a different set of attributes in the binary number example, a single bottom-up pass would be sufficient to evaluate the value attributes completely. Suppose we omit the attributes f and v from the nonterminals S and B, replacing them with the single derived attribute i, representing the integral value of the binary digit or string (considered as a whole number); the grammar now simplifies to

$$N \uparrow v \qquad \rightarrow S \uparrow i_1 \uparrow l_1 \text{ "."} S \uparrow i_2 \uparrow l_2 \quad [v = i_1 + 2^{-l_2} \cdot i_2]$$
$$S \uparrow i \uparrow l \quad \rightarrow S \uparrow i_1 \uparrow l_1 \text{ B} \uparrow i_2 \qquad [i = 2i_1 + i_2; \ l = l_1 + 1]$$
$$\qquad\qquad \rightarrow B \uparrow i \qquad\qquad\qquad [l = 1]$$
$$B \uparrow i \qquad \rightarrow \text{"0"} \qquad\qquad\qquad [i = 0]$$
$$\qquad\qquad \rightarrow \text{"1"} \qquad\qquad\qquad [i = 1]$$

Furthermore, because it now requires only a single bottom-up pass, the attribute evaluation can proceed concurrently with the parsing. This is not always the case, but the more carefully we choose our attribute evaluation functions, the more efficient we can make the compiler operation.

5.2.2 Attribute Value Flow

In a typical optimizing compiler, we normally encounter four kinds of attribute evaluation requirements or information flow:

1. Bottom-up
2. Top-down
3. Left-to-right
4. Right-to-left

Those attributes that derive their values from some intrinsic property of the subtree under consideration (like the length attributes l in the binary number grammars) will normally use a bottom-up evaluation order. Attributes that depend on some part of the context or environment in which the subtree is situated will often require some form of top-down evaluation. Few attributes are strictly top-down throughout the whole grammar; they tend to be limited to compiler switches and other global information available before the compilation begins. Most inherited attributes depend on synthesized attributes evaluated elsewhere in the grammar. This category is generally divided into left-to-right and right-to-left information flow. Information flowing from left to right is derived from the left subtree of a particular node in the parse tree, and then inherited into the right subtree. Usually an attribute value is inherited by the nonterminal, possibly modified within that production (or below it in the tree), and a new attribute is derived from the modified value.

Figure 5.4 shows an ambiguous CFG for binary integers, to which a left-to-right attribute evaluation flow has been attached. Each substring of binary digits appends its own value to the right end of the inherited value attribute. Empty substrings just pass the value through unchanged. A parse tree for the string "10011" shows the flow of values.

In this chapter we look closely at languages like Pascal and Modula-2 which require prior declaration of identifiers before use. Predeclaration of identifiers is an example of left-to-right information flow because the declarations are to the "left" of the usage references. In Chapter 8 we deal with optimization topics that include concern for how a variable is next going to be used, clearly a right-to-left flow of information.

Both top-down and bottom-up parsers can evaluate purely synthesized (bottom-up) attributes at parse time. Because the source program is parsed from left to right, most left-to-right attribute evaluation is also possible in both top-down and bottom-up parsers, though some care is necessary in bottom-up parsers to make the information flow consistent. In general, attributes that require information logically "to the right" of the parser's lookahead symbol cannot be evaluated at parse time. Chapter 8 discusses the evaluation of attributes in an abstract syntax tree constructed by the parser in memory; this is much more flexible than attribute evaluation at parse time, though also more prodigal of memory and CPU time.

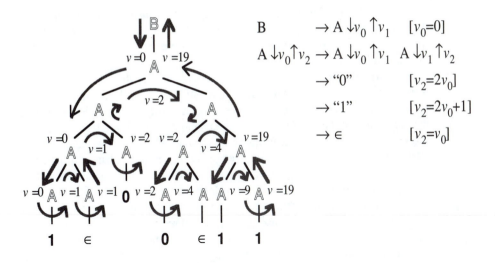

$$B \rightarrow A \downarrow v_0 \uparrow v_1 \quad [v_0=0]$$
$$A \downarrow v_0 \uparrow v_2 \rightarrow A \downarrow v_0 \uparrow v_1 \; A \downarrow v_1 \uparrow v_2$$
$$\rightarrow \text{``0''} \quad [v_2=2v_0]$$
$$\rightarrow \text{``1''} \quad [v_2=2v_0+1]$$
$$\rightarrow \in \quad [v_2=v_0]$$

Figure 5.4. The flow of attributes from left to right for the string "10011".

Most programming languages can be compiled in one pass (albeit to inefficient code) with strictly left-to-right and bottom-up attribute flow. Exercises 1d and 1e illustrate the effects of bad and good attribute grammar design on information flow.

5.3 Nonterminals as Attribute Evaluation Functions

Once we establish a direction for attribute information flow by designating some attributes to be inherited and others to be synthesized, attribute evaluation functions can be readily collected or isolated into empty productions in the grammar, whose only purpose is thus to encapsulate the semantics. Consider again the tiny attribute grammar

$$
\begin{array}{lll}
E & \rightarrow T\uparrow t_1 \; \text{``+''} \; T\uparrow t_2 & [t_2=t_1] \\
T\uparrow t & \rightarrow num & [t=int]
\end{array}
$$

The attribute predicate $[t_2=t_1]$ could be encapsulated in another production with a new nonterminal X:

$$
\begin{array}{lll}
E & \rightarrow T\uparrow t_1 \; \text{``+''} \; T\uparrow t_2 \; X\downarrow t_1 \downarrow t_2 & \\
X\downarrow t_1 \downarrow t_2 & \rightarrow \in & [t_2=t_1] \\
T\uparrow t & \rightarrow num & [t=int]
\end{array}
$$

This has the effect of specifying explicitly that it is a predicate asserting equality rather than an evaluation function. To force it to be an evaluation function, we simply designate a different flow of information:

$$
\begin{array}{lll}
E & \rightarrow T\uparrow t_1 \; \text{``+''} \; T\uparrow t_2 \; X\downarrow t_1 \uparrow t_2 & \\
X\downarrow t_1 \uparrow t_2 & \rightarrow \in & [t_2=t_1] \\
T\uparrow t & \rightarrow num & [t=int]
\end{array}
$$

Now the first nonterminal T asserts t_1 to be *int* (by construction), and that value is passed down to X, which asserts t_2 to be the same. This in turn is passed up the tree to E, which implicitly asserts it to be the same as the t_2 that the second instance of nonterminal T has asserted to be *int*.

Although the example is trivial, it is easily seen that the reference to the nonterminal X with its inherited and synthesized attributes effectively stands in for the assertion $t_2=t_1$. We use this equivalence in two ways. First, it gives an obvious way to encapsulate the constraints of the language as a separate and distinct part of the grammar, thus making the grammar more readable. Rather than cluttering up the syntax grammar with random attribute assertions, they can be collected and named in a logical manner. It also has the side effect of aiding the implementation choice between predicate and evaluation functions for particular attributes because the information flow is explicit in the notation.

The second benefit of this equivalence is more important, for it offers us a consistent notation for arbitrarily complex attribute evaluation functions and predicates. We have been using ordinary arithmetic and comparison operators in attribute assertions with the normal mathematical meaning of these operators. Conventional operators, however, are inadequate for all the functions needed in a compiler. One kind of attribute assertion that cannot be expressed using ordinary operators involves the concept of a symbol table.

5.4 Symbol Tables as Attributes

A major function of an attribute grammar is to restrict the language of syntactically correct strings to those that meet certain semantic constraints. One constraint in a strongly typed language is that the declared or inferred type of any variable or subexpression be consistent with its use. Another common constraint is that any identifier be declared before use. The syntax grammar you developed in Chapter 4 for your project compiler has no way to enforce predeclaration of identifiers in the program to be compiled; we simply ignored that problem. Strong typing could be enforced in your first grammar by disallowing, in the language syntax, any expressions with a type violation. The result is a trivial language, not true Pascal or Modula-2. We now consider what attributes to add to the grammar, so that these two constraints can be properly enforced in a larger subset of the language.

A classical *symbol table* is a data structure associating a set of identifiers with values. Each identifier has been encoded by the scanner as a unique integer, which in the constrainer is considered to be a synthesized attribute of the terminal ID. On the other hand, the values associated with the identifiers in the symbol table are typically complex records of information. Some of the data that must be associated with an identifier include what kind it is (such as, type name, variable name, procedure, or constant), where it resides in the target machine memory (in the case of variables and procedures), what type it is, and so on. Each symbol in the symbol table must be in some sense unique, so the symbol table may be thought of as a dynamic function from integers to value records.

The symbol table has two fundamental modes of access: one to add a new identifier with its value, verifying that the identifier is not already there; and the other to find a particular identifier and retrieve its value. We define these two access functions as attribute evaluation functions in the form of nonterminals, where the symbol table, the identifier, and the value record are the attributes. The same notation for inherited and derived attributes in nonterminal reference is used, but enclosed in brackets to signify that this is a predefined attribute evaluation function, not a nonterminal. The symbol table access functions are written thus:

[into ↓*oldsymtab* ↓*ident* ↓*value* ↑*newsymtab*]
{add *ident:value* to *oldsymtab* and return *newsymtab* with *ident* in it}
[from ↓*symtab* ↓*ident* ↑*value*]
{look up *ident* in *symtab* and return its *value*}

The evaluation function into asserts (by construction) that *newsymtab* is a symbol table identical to *oldsymtab*, except that it also contains the entry relating *ident* to *value*. It further asserts that there is no conflicting symbol *ident* in *oldsymtab*. Similarly, from asserts that *ident* is in the symbol table *symtab*, and that it is associated there with *value*. Note that we continue to avoid viewing the attributes as *variables* that can be modified in time, but rather as *values* which may be related to new values according to the evaluation functions — which are in reality just assertions. So although we might easily come to view the symbol table as a partially filled array of records in some conventional programming language — and indeed, the implementation may well be such a data structure in the compiler's data space — to allow our understanding to become clouded by such a representation would eliminate all of the formal and conceptual advantages conferred by attribute grammars, and we may as well go back to hacking compilers in some low-level programming language such as C. In practice, we do not really copy the entire symbol table for every use of into, but only add the new symbol to the top and return a pointer to the new top of the table. If the table is implemented as a linked list of records, this results in no inefficiency at all.

Identifiers are terminals in the language of the parser (the scanner recognizes their form and passes the single token ID for any identifier), but declaration and type-checking require that we recognize the different identifiers as different. In Chapter 3 we showed how to add semantic actions to the scanner grammar, and from there how to add them to the FSA that implements the scanner. One such semantic action generates a unique integer identifier number for each unique identifier in the string table. The identifier number is returned by the scanner as a synthesized attribute. Note that the string table maintained in the scanner is not related to (and should not be confused with) the symbol table. The string table contains the spelling of identifiers, whereas the symbol table is concerned with abstract attributes and symbol properties. In the past, the symbol table typically contained identifier spelling also (as another symbol property), but this is impractical in modern languages, where identifiers often exceed the six- or eight-character length limitation of the early compilers.

5.5 A Micro-Modula Attribute Grammar

We now extend G_2 from Chapter 2 (page 21) to include variable declarations and assignment statements, and add some Boolean operations to make type-checking interesting, thereby turning it into a "Micro-Modula" grammar as shown in Listing 5.1.

```
M  -> "MODULE" ID ";" "VAR" V "BEGIN" B "END" ID "." ;
V  -> ID ":" T ";" V                    {zero or more variable declarations}
   -> ;
T  -> "INTEGER"                         {two predeclared types}
   -> "BOOLEAN" ;
B  -> ID ":=" E ";" B                   {assignments only in body}
   -> ;
E  -> S C ;                             {simple expression, or else...}
C  -> "=" S                             {...a comparison of equality}
   -> ;
S  -> F P ;                             {note, this grammar is LL(1)}
P  -> "*" F P
   -> "AND" F P
   -> ;
F  -> "(" E ")"
   -> ID
   -> NUM                               {integer and Boolean constants}
   -> "TRUE"
   -> "FALSE" .
```

Listing 5.1. "Micro-Modula" syntax grammar.

To this grammar we now attach the attributes necessary for type-checking. First we note that the token ID has one synthesized attribute *idn*, which uniquely identifies the spelling of the identifier. There are two identifiers in the goal symbol production; Modula-2 requires that they be the same identifier, that is, that they have the same *idn*. It is easy to write an attribute assertion to enforce this, either by giving them the same name in the production as we have done (see Listing 5.2), or else by explicitly writing a predicate of equality. Elsewhere in the grammar the attribute on identifiers is used to distinguish them in the symbol table. Note that in Listing 5.2, up arrows ↑ are typed as the ASCII circumflex character ""^"" and down arrows ↓ are typed as exclamation points "!".

We also need an inherited (left-to-right) symbol table attribute to be carried throughout the grammar. Let us assume that the goal symbol inherits an empty symbol attribute *vacantTbl*, and that each nonterminal inherits a *tblIn*; the declaration nonterminal also derives from it a (usually modified) *tblOut*, which is inherited as *tblIn* by the next nonterminal to its right. Similarly, type-checking imposes a left-to-right attribute evaluation order within expressions.

Consider the attribute grammar in Listing 5.2. An expression E consists of a simple expression S, followed by a comparison C, which may be another simple expression separated by "=" or else empty. In the case of empty, the type of the expression E is the same as the type of its component simple expression S, but that cannot be known in one pass in the production for E; therefore, that type is passed down to C, which returns it unchanged in the production $C \rightarrow \in$. On the other hand, if C is the rest of a comparison, the type of the two subexpressions must be the same, either integer or Boolean (expressed in the grammar by the equality predicate), and the type of the comparison is Boolean.

```
M !vacantTbl              -> "MODULE" ID^idn ";"
                             "VAR" V!vacantTbl^tblOut
                             "BEGIN" B!tblOut
                             "END" ID^idn "." ;
V !tblIn ^tblOut          -> ID^idn ":" T^type ";"
                             [ into !tblIn!idn!type^nutbl ]
                             V!nutbl^tblOut
                          -> [ tblOut=tblIn ];
T ^type                   -> "INTEGER" [ type=1 ]
                          -> "BOOLEAN" [ type=2 ];
B !tblIn                  -> ID^idn ":=" E!tblIn^type ";"
                             [ from !tblIn!idn^type ]
                             B!tblIn
                          -> ;
E !tblIn ^type            -> S!tblIn^stype C!tblIn!stype^type ;
C !tblIn !typeIn ^typeOut
                          -> "=" S!tblIn^ctype
                             [ typeIn=ctype; typeOut=2 ]
                          -> [ typeOut=typeIn ];
S !tblIn ^type            -> F!tblIn^type P!tblIn!type ;
P !tblIn !type            -> "*" F!tblIn^type P!tblIn!type
                             [ type=1 ]
                          -> "AND" F!tblIn^type P!tblIn!type
                             [ type=2 ]
                          -> ;
F !tblIn ^type            -> "(" E!tblIn^type ")"
                          -> ID^idn
                             [ from !tblIn!idn^type ]
                          -> NUM^value [ type=1 ]
                          -> "TRUE"  [ type=2 ]
                          -> "FALSE" [ type=2 ];
```

Listing 5.2. "Micro-Modula" attribute grammar, with type-checking.

The type of a simple expression S is the same as its component factor F, so that synthesized attribute is passed on up unchanged. At the same time it must be the same as the type of any product component P to the right of that factor. Within the production for product P, if the product is empty there is nothing to say about its type. But if the product is multiplication, then the factor must derive the same type inherited by the product, and the recursive product inherits the same type, and that type must be integer (encoded here as the number 1). If the operator is AND then all the types concerned must be Boolean (encoded as 2).

The type of a constant factor is synthesized as a constant (1 or 2, depending on whether the constant is a number, or one of the keywords TRUE or FALSE), but the type of a variable must be sought from the symbol table.

Variables are declared in the production V, where each identifier is associated with either the word INTEGER (which derives the type attribute 1) or the word BOOLEAN (which derives the type attribute 2). The identifier is entered into the inherited symbol table with its type, and the new symbol table is passed on recursively to any declarations to the right of this one, and thence up and out to the body of the program, where it is inherited by assignment statements and their component expressions.

In the body of an assignment, the identifier on the left of the assignment operator is looked up in the symbol table, and the type it returns is asserted to be equal to the type derived by the expression on the right-hand side, implicitly by reference to the same attribute name.

5.6 Using Attributes with the TAG Compiler

The TAG Compiler is designed to generate appropriate constraint-checking code from an attribute grammar source. Unlike the little grammars we have been writing here, however, it is strongly typed. Inherited and synthesized attributes must be declared in the production header with a type name, much as Modula-2 and Pascal require the declaration of variables.

The two predefined types that concern us at this time are int (integer numbers) and symtab (symbol tables). The built-in attribute evaluation functions must also be declared with their attribute types. Built-in semantic evaluation functions used in the scanner part of the TAG are predeclared in the same way. As in strongly-typed programming languages, the predeclared type requirement permits the compiler to make reasonable consistency checks, and thereby to detect and report some of the more common coding errors.

The header information for the grammar in Listing 5.2 would look like Listing 5.3. A special syntax uses the @ symbol to evaluate attributes within iterated regular expressions; this is explained at length in Chapter 10. Right now its only use is to evaluate integer values. Note also that VacantTable has been replaced in the grammar by an empty table constructor "<>".

5.7 Scope and Kind of Identifiers

So far the only identifiers we entered into the symbol table have been local variable names. In serious programming languages there are also procedure and function names, types, and constants, each of which must be handled slightly differently. Furthermore, in block-structured languages like Pascal and Modula-2, an identifier need not be unique in the symbol table if the same identifiers are not declared at the same scope level. We consider these two enhancements together by adding just one more kind of identifier to our micro-Modula, namely parameterless functions.

5.7.1 Identifier Scope Grammar

We add two new nonterminals (A and H) and change three other productions (M, B, and F) to add the new feature to the syntax (see Listing 5.4). The new nonterminal H defines the syntax of a function procedure, having a name and type, its own local variables and possibly nested function declarations, and a body of statements. We add the RETURN

```
tag MicroModula:
predeclared
  into !symtab !int !int ^symtab;
  from !symtab !int ^int;
  charval ^int;             {scanner func to return ordinal of a char}
  initbl;                   {scanner func to start an identifier}
  addtbl !int;              {scanner func to add a char to string table}
  strindex ^int;            {scanner func to look up ident in table}
scanner
  ignore                    -> " "|"";        {delete spaces & line ends}
  ID ^name:int              -> [initbl]
    ("a".."z"|"A".."Z")[charval^this; addtlb!this]
    (("a".."z"|"A".."Z"|"0".."9")
                            [charval^this; addtbl!this])*
    [strindex^name];
  NUM ^value:int            -> [value=0]
    (("0".."9")[charval^this; value@=value*10+this-48])+;
parser
M                           -> "MODULE" ID^idn
                               "VAR" V!<> ^tblOut
                               "BEGIN" B!tblOut
                               "END" ID^idn "." ;
V !tblIn:symtab ^tblOut:symtab
                            -> ID^idn ":" T^type ";"
... {etc.}
end MicroModula.
```

Listing 5.3. "Micro-Modula" attribute grammar header for TAG compiler.

```
A   →   " (" ")"                              {function call}
    →   ∈ ;                                   {variable reference}
H   →   "PROCEDURE" ID ":" T ";" "VAR" V
           H "BEGIN" B "END" ID ";" H
    →   ∈ ;
M   →   "MODULE" ID "VAR" V H "BEGIN" B "END" ID "." ;
B   →   ID ":=" E ";" B
    →   "RETURN" E
    →   ∈ ;
F   → "(" E ")"
    → ID A
    → NUM
    → "TRUE"
    → "FALSE"  .
```

Listing 5.4. Changes to "Micro-Modula" syntax to add functions.

statement to the definition of a statement; it is necessarily at the end of the block. Finally the productions for factor F are modified to allow function calls to be syntactically distinguished from variable references, in keeping with the Modula-2 syntactic form. This is essential so that we can determine from the syntax whether to compile the identifier as a variable reference or a function call. In Chapter 8 we show how to deal with compiling homonyms — that is, different semantic forms that are syntactically identical, such as between variable references and parameterless function calls in Pascal.

The symbol table to support the new feature also grows somewhat more complex. We must introduce a concept of *lexical level* (or *lex level*) as a property of identifiers in the table; the same identifier may occur several times in the symbol table if each occurrence has a different lex level. The current lex level is maintained as a property of the symbol table itself, so that it need not be specified in the attribute evaluator `into`, but we need another attribute evaluation function `open` to open a new scope by raising the current lex level of the symbol table. Because this always returns a new symbol table, the lex level may be lowered (and all symbols in the higher level discarded automatically) by simply making no further reference to any table derived from the higher level.

Now it is also necessary to distinguish two kinds of identifiers in the symbol table, namely, variables and functions. Both have the same type values, but a variable name must not be used in a function call, and a function name must not appear on the left side of an assignment statement, nor in an expression without the empty parameter list parentheses. Where we were previously able to encode the two types INTEGER and BOOLEAN as the simple numeric values 1 and 2, respectively, we must now include also the kind. This is done by making each value in the symbol table into a record containing both type and kind fields. The TAG compiler has a mechanism for encoding records, but its complexity would detract from our purpose here. Instead, we manually encode the two fields as the tens and units digits of a decimal integer, respectively, as shown in Table 5.1. An identifier entered into the symbol table now carries two pieces of information in its value: the *kind* and the *type*. When the value is retrieved, the information must be extracted again into its separate components. Ordinary integer multiplication and division perform the packing and unpacking functions acceptably well for our purposes.

Kind	3	Variable
	4	Function
Type	1	Integer
	2	Boolean

$$packedvalue = kind * 10 + type$$
$$kind = packedvalue / 10$$
$$type = packedvalue - kind * 10$$

Table 5.1. Packing *kind* and *type* into a single integer.
Example: integer variable = 31, Boolean function = 42.

In addition to the constraint checking to validate the use of identifiers and the obvious semantics of the new syntax, two new attribute evaluations are required to implement functions in Micro-Modula. One of these pertains to the management of the symbol table. A new scope is opened on entry to each function declaration after the function name is declared, so that the function name is still available after the scope has been closed. Opening a new scope has the additional advantage that symbols declared in the new scope are automatically discarded when that scope is closed, a requirement for block-structured languages.

The other new attribute assertion is somewhat more obscure, but something like it is required to verify that the type of the expression in the RETURN statement matches the type of the function, and that the RETURN has not been omitted. Because this grammar requires the RETURN statement be the last statement, we could have compelled that syntactically by putting it in the function header production for H. Our approach is more general and can be adapted for use in larger languages where the placement of the RETURN statement is not so constrained. We do it by adding an inherited type attribute to the body nonterminal B; it carries the function type down into the body, where it can be compared to the type of the RETURN expression, or asserted to be zero if there is none.

5.7.2 Identifier Scope Example Analysis

Without the variable scope problems introduced by nested function declarations, it is evident that the symbol table attribute evaluation functions correctly implement type checking in Micro-Modula. The grammar in Listing 5.5 is not so obvious. Consider the small program in Figure 5.5 as we trace the attribute flow, with specific attention to the symbol table. The numbered circles identify interesting points to snapshot the symbol table and other attributes.

At snapshot point 1 (see Table 5.2), the symbol table is in the attribute named vartable of the production for nonterminal M; it contains just the three global variables, a, b, and c, derived from the recursive nonterminal V, and to be inherited by the function header nonterminal H. The nonempty first production for nonterminal H puts the function name into the symbol table (deriving nextable), then opens a new scope on that and sends the result down to V again. Nonterminal V declares one variable a and returns with the symbol table (also called vartable), which is the basis of snapshot 2.

Back in H again, it enters H recursively, puts the name and type of the second function into the symbol table (at lex level 1 because it is nested within function First), then opens another new scope at lex level 2 and declares the local variables a and b. Both of these are already in the symbol table (see snapshot 3 in Table 5.3), but at lower lex levels (1 and 0, respectively), so there is no problem adding the new identifiers.

Snapshot 3 also represents the state of the symbol table passed through all the body of function Second. Thus, when in the first assignment statement the parser encounters the reference to variable b, the symbol table is searched (most recent symbols first), and the local variable b of type integer is found before reaching to the global (Boolean) variable b. On the other hand, in the expression part of the assignment, factor F finds global variable c (since there are neither local nor intermediate identifiers by that name).

```
G   ->  "MODULE" ID^idn ";"  "VAR" V !<> ^vartable
        H!vartable ^bodyTable
        "BEGIN" B !bodyTable !0  "END" ID^idn "." ;
H !tblIn:symtab ^tblOut:symtab
    ->  "PROCEDURE" ID^idn ":"  T ^type ";"
        [ into !tblIn !idn !type+40 ^nextable ]
        [ open !nextable ^nutbl ]
        "VAR" V !nutbl ^vartable
        H !vartable ^bodyTable
        "BEGIN" B !bodyTable !type  "END" ID^idn ";"
        H !nextable ^tblOut
    -> [ tblOut=tblIn ];
V !tblIn:symtab ^tblOut:symtab
    ->  ID^idn ":" T ^type ";"
        [ into !tblIn !idn !type+30^nutbl ]
        V !nutbl ^tblOut
    -> [ tblOut=tblIn ];
T ^type:int
    -> "INTEGER" [ type=1 ]
    -> "BOOLEAN" [ type=2 ];
B !tblIn:symtab !typeR:int
    -> ID^idn ":=" E !tblIn ^type ";"
       [ from !tblIn !idn ^typeID; ]
       [ typeID/10=3; type=typeID-30 ]
       B !tblIn !typeR
    -> "RETURN" E !tblIn ^typeR ";"
    -> [ typeR=0 ];
E !tblIn:symtab ^type:int
    -> S !tblIn ^stype  C !tblIn !stype ^type ;
C !tblIn:symtab !typeIn:int ^typeOut:int
    -> "=" S !tblIn ^ctype [ typeIn=ctype; typeOut=2 ]
    -> [ typeOut=typeIn ];
S !tblIn:symtab ^type:int
    -> F !tblIn ^type  P !tblIn !type ;
P !tblIn:symtab !type:int
    -> "*" F !tblIn ^type  P !tblIn !type [ type=1 ]
    -> "AND" F !tblIn ^type  P !tblIn !type [ type=2 ]
    -> ;
A !typeID:int ^type:int
    -> "(" ")" [ typeID/10=4; type=typeID-40 ]
    -> [ typeID/10=3; type=typeID-30 ];
F !tblIn:symtab ^type:int
    -> "(" E !tblIn ^type ")"
    -> ID^idn [ from !tblIn !idn ^typeID ]
       A !typeID ^type
    -> NUM^value [ type=1 ]
    -> "TRUE"  [ type=2 ]
    -> "FALSE" [ type=2 ];
```

Listing 5.5. Micro-Modula attribute grammar, with functions.

```
MODULE NestedFunctions;
VAR a: INTEGER; b: BOOLEAN; c: INTEGER;


  PROCEDURE First: INTEGER;
  VAR a: BOOLEAN;


    PROCEDURE Second: INTEGER;
    VAR a: INTEGER; b: INTEGER;
    BEGIN
      b := c;
      a := First()*Second();
      RETURN a*b;
    END Second;


BEGIN
  a := First()=Second();
  RETURN 5;
END First;

PROCEDURE Third: INTEGER;
VAR c: BOOLEAN;
BEGIN
  c := (First()=a)=b;
  RETURN c;
END Third;
```

```
BEGIN (* NestedFunctions *)
  a := 1;
  c := 2;
  b := (First()=3)=Third();
END NestedFunctions.
```

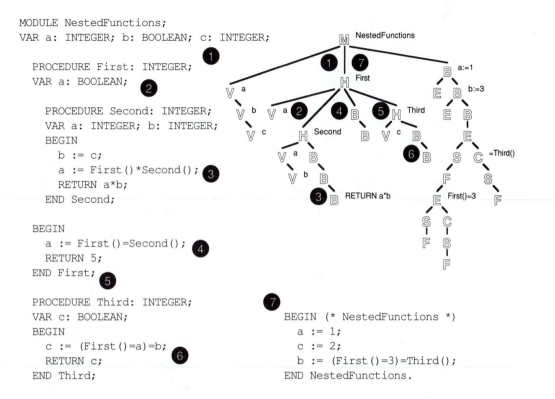

Figure 5.5. A Micro-Modula program and parse tree, showing attribute flow.

Symbol	Lex Level	Value		Current Lex Level = 0
a	0	31		
b	0	32		
c	0	31		

Symbol	Lex Level	Value		Current Lex Level = 1
a	0	31		
b	0	32		
c	0	31		
First	0	41		
a	1	32		

Table 5.2. Attribute flow in Micro-Modula program (snapshots 1-2).

3

Symbol	Lex Level	Value
a	0	31
b	0	32
c	0	31
First	0	41
a	1	32
Second	1	41
a	2	31
b	2	31

Current Lex Level = 2

4

Symbol	Lex Level	Value
a	0	31
b	0	32
c	0	31
First	0	41
a	1	32
Second	1	41

Current Lex Level = 1

5

Symbol	Lex Level	Value
a	0	31
b	0	32
c	0	31
First	0	41

Current Lex Level = 0

6

Symbol	Lex Level	Value
a	0	31
b	0	32
c	0	31
First	0	41
Third	0	41
c	1	32

Current Lex Level = 1

7

Symbol	Lex Level	Value
a	0	31
b	0	32
c	0	31
First	0	41
Third	0	41

Current Lex Level = 0

Table 5.3. Attribute flow in Micro-Modula program (snapshots 3-7).

When nonterminal H (parsing function Second) has finished its work, it passes the symbol table containing only the added name of the function (attribute nextable in H) down to the function declaration to its right, which (because it is empty) returns it unchanged as tblOut. Thus, it is passed back still unchanged to the previous invocation of nonterminal H (still parsing function First). Continuing still unchanged, this symbol table is passed down to the body of the function, as shown in snapshot 4 in Table 5.3. Note that when we say "unchanged" we mean that all the "copies" of the symbol table attribute represented at each point of the parse tree have the same value.

Snapshot 5 once again shows the contents of the symbol table attribute passed out of nonterminal H parsing the body of function First, and down to the recursive invocation of nonterminal H parsing the function Third. The identifier Second with all its local variables, and all the local variables of First are gone — indeed, they were never in this copy of the symbol table. Thus, consistently with the scope visibility rules of Modula-2 and Pascal, function Second is not visible within function Third (see snapshot 6), nor, as snapshot 7 shows, is it visible in the body of the main program.

5.7.3 Other Symbol Table Issues

This example shows only parameterless procedures. Introducing parameters into the type picture complicates it considerably. Value parameters are treated locally exactly as local variables, where the only difference is that they are assigned an initial value in the course of the procedure call. The number and type of the parameters are also reflected in the functionality of the procedure, which Modula-2 considers as part of the procedure type. Strong type-checking prohibits calling a procedure with the wrong number or types of parameters. Because our symbol table encoding mechanism lacks the space to represent an arbitrary number of parameter types in the single procedure type record, we leave that problem as an exercise in the next chapter.

Reference parameters (identified in Modula-2 by the keyword VAR in the parameter list) introduce several new kinds of problems. Many modern languages (C, for example) do not even allow reference parameters. One of the problems with reference parameters is that the syntax of the procedure call must be parsed differently for the two kinds of parameters: value parameters can accept any expression of the correct type, whereas reference parameters must be passed a variable reference only. Because we concentrate in this chapter on syntax-directed semantics, reference parameters are deferred to Chapter 8.

Every programming language includes a standard library of predefined functions and procedures, many of which often have magical properties requiring special compiler attention. Other library routines are no different (from the compiler's perspective) than user-coded procedures; their declarations need only be inserted into the default (empty) symbol table in such a way that they occur at a lexical level just outside the main program. The magical procedures typically require special productions in the attribute grammar to cope with their particular properties. Modula-2, for example, has several polymorphic library procedures, that is, procedures that accept parameters with any of a class of data types. One of these is the INCL procedure, which accepts as its first parameter any variable of a set type; the second parameter must be an ordinal expression value compatible with the base type of the set. Thus, if the set is a SET OF CHAR, then the value must type CHAR, and so on. User-coded procedures are not allowed to be polymorphic in Modula-2, so the compiler must include special constraints to check the parameters to polymorphic library routines. Ada programmers may write polymorphic procedures, but other library routines in Ada require special constrainer attention. As much effort can be spent defining those library productions in a reasonably typical compiler as in all the rest of the language constraints.

Modula-2 introduced to strongly typed languages a separate compilation feature, using syntax similar to its data encapsulation mechanism, the MODULE. The implementation of internal modules affords few surprises, requiring only that a new (empty) symbol table be opened at the module boundary. The enclosing environment must be linked to the new symbol table in some way that is opaque to symbol searches, but accessible to the semantic processing of IMPORT and EXPORT clauses. Separately compiled definition and implementation modules imply a virtual environment just outside the compilation unit, usually implemented as files of symbol definitions and code objects. We do not consider the special problems associated with processing module declarations to be particularly instructive here, but the industrious student may find it an interesting and challenging exercise.

5.8 Implementing Attributes in Recursive Descent

In Chapter 4 we showed a one-to-one mapping of LL(1) context-free grammars onto recursive-descent parsers written in a programming language like Modula-2. Synthesized attributes and left-to-right inherited attributes with their evaluation functions can be added directly to recursive-descent parsers as easily as they were added to the grammars from which the parsers were constructed.

Each *inherited attribute* is passed as a value parameter in the procedure call that implements the nonterminal reference. Each *derived attribute* is passed as a reference (VAR) parameter in the procedure call. Each *attribute evaluation function* is an assignment in the parser code, assigning the computed value to the specified attribute. Each *attribute predicate* is implemented as a conditional test whose alternative is *Error*. All synthesized attributes not in the parameter list are implemented as local variables in the parser code.

Consider, for example, the nonterminal C in our Micro-Modula attribute grammar:

```
C ↓tableIn:symtab  ↓typeIn:int  ↑typeOut:int
    → "=" S↓tableIn↑ctype [ typeIn=ctype; typeOut=2 ]
    → [ typeOut=typeIn ];
```

The Modula-2 code to implement this production is straightforward, as seen in Listing 5.6. The remainder of the implementation of Micro-Modula is left as an exercise to the reader.

5.9 Implementing a Symbol Table

As similar as their functions appear, the symbol table is not (and should not be) the same as the the string table. The string table manages character strings, abstracting from them a simple ordinal handle to be used for further reference. Each new identifier or string constant must be compared, character by character, with those already in the table to prevent wasteful duplications. This also performs at one time the identity matching that is so important in the symbol table. Nothing is stored in the string table but the spelling of the strings themselves and the structures required for efficient management.

The symbol table is a data structure for storing several data associated with particular identifiers. In a block-structured language the identifiers can be replicated in the symbol table with different data.

There are some points of contact, however. Historically, the string table was embedded in the symbol table. That is, instead of abstracting the strings out into a separate table, the full identifier character strings were stored in the symbol table, and symbol table searches actually did string comparisons on the identifier spelling. This was prevented from wasting excessive time by limiting the identifiers to a short (six or eight) number of characters.

```
PROCEDURE C (tblIn: symtab; typeIn: INTEGER; VAR typeOut: INTEGER);
VAR ctype: INTEGER;
BEGIN
  IF Nextoken = '=' THEN
    Getoken;
    S (tblIn, ctype);
    IF typeIn <> ctype THEN Error END;
    typeOut := 2
  ELSE
    typeOut := typeIn
  END
END C;
```

Listing 5.6. Implementation of an attribute grammar production in Modula-2.

Another point of contact is that a function of both tables is to search for an identifier. In fact, the string table exists to simplify that search in the symbol table. The string table experiences growth only as new identifiers are encountered, but the symbol table may grow and contract with the block structure of the program. The string table asks only of its data structure with respect to a particular item, "Is it there?" The symbol table asks not only if it is there, but also what the value record stored with the identifier is.

Because the symbol table may duplicate identifiers in block-structured languages, it is not always practical to use the same kinds of search optimizations as we did in Chapter 3 for the string table. The major difficulty is that as each procedure scope is closed, all of the symbols at the current level must be deleted from the table. There are several ways to accomplish this short of maintaining a simple linear stack-structured table.

As with the string table, the most direct search optimization is and remains the hash table. However, to retain the scope nesting, each lex level in the symbol table must have its own hash table. Two strategies compete for efficiency, depending on the relative size of the tables and the number of up-level searches. Fairly simply, whenever a new lex level is opened, the entire hash table from the previous level can be copied into it. New identifiers added build upon the old table, and redeclared identifiers simply replace the previous declaration in the table. This way only one table is searched, yielding maximum search efficiency regardless of how far up the scope chain the found identifier lies. The disadvantage is that the entire hash table with all its buckets must be recopied each time a new scope is opened. This is not a conceptual problem, for we see attribute evaluation as copies anyway, but it does take a little bit of time. Fortunately it only happens at module, procedure, and record boundaries.

Alternatively, a new hash table can be opened at each lex level and linked to the next level down in a list. When a symbol is not found in the current scope hash table, the links are chased, searching in each hash table in turn until the symbol is found. When few identifiers are declared in each of many lex levels, this degenerates into the linear stack in efficiency. Program statistics, however, show that most symbol references are concentrated at the local and global ends of the list. Considerable improvement in performance can be achieved if the global hash table is searched immediately upon failure to find a symbol in the local table, and then only if not found is the symbol sought in the intermediate linked list. Whenever a global symbol is redeclared in some local scope, a flag is set in the global table to eliminate the shortcut. Redeclaration of global identifiers is typically quite rare, so the flags can be set permanently without serious loss of efficiency.

Another symbol table structure depends on assistance from the string table manager. If identifiers are sequentially numbered (a simple step in the scanner), the symbol table can be maintained as a linear vector (array) of record pointers indexed directly by the identifier number. There is never any search, for any identifier's information record is one access away. Each time a new scope is opened, the pointer array is copied to a new vector. In terms of performance, this method is equivalent to a perfect hash table, with no collisions within buckets — that is, every bucket has at most one item. The table must, however, be as long as the highest identifier number.

Summary

Attribute grammars provide a convenient tool for specifying the semantics of programming languages. Attribute grammars also provide a formalism for implementing compilers and compiler writing systems. A variety of compiler-generators have been created via attribute grammars: MUG1 and MUG2 (Modularer Übersetzer Generator, both complete compiler generators), GAG-A (attribute grammar based generator), HLP 84 (Helsinki Language Processor 84 is a language processor toolbox), and TAG (introduced in this book) as well as 33 other existing compiler-generator systems listed by Deransart in 1988. Attribute grammars are not only useful for automating compiler generation but also have proven useful in generating text editing environments (see Horowitz & Teitelbaum, 1986) and in program optimization, a topic we will develop more fully in Chapter 8.

An attribute grammar consists of a context-free grammar and a set of semantic rules attached to each production of the grammar. Associated with each nonterminal are zero or more attributes whose values are defined or constrained by the semantic rules. The meaning of an input string (belonging to a language) is identified with the value of the attributes of the goal symbol of an attribute grammar. There are two classes of attributes: synthesized and inherited. Synthesized attributes pass information up the parse tree, and inherited attributes pass information down the parse tree. A combination of synthesized and inherited attributes pass information between siblings in the tree.

Using a "Micro-Modula" grammar to illustrate the techniques, this chapter showed how specific programming language constraints can be checked in a attribute grammar. It introduced a type-checking method by storing information about identifiers in a symbol table. Finally, this chapter extended the way Chapter 4 mapped LL(1) context-free grammars onto recursive-descent parsers, showing how synthesized and inherited attributes are added to recursive-descent parsers. Inherited attributes are passed as value parameters in procedure calls, and synthesized attributes are passed as reference (VAR) parameters. Attribute predicates are implemented as conditional tests.

Symbols

$\downarrow$ Inherited attribute, written $\downarrow$*attname*.

$\uparrow$ Synthesized (derived) attribute, written $\uparrow$*attname*.

Keywords

assertion

A statement or expression constrained to evaluate true in the context of a production. A string being parsed is not in the language of the grammar if any assertion evaluates false. We distinguish two kinds of assertions, attribute evaluation functions and predicates:

attribute evaluation
function

constrains its attributes to single values known independently, such as $a_1=10$.

predicate

imposes additional constraints on one or more attributes already constrained by evaluation functions. A predicate may constrain an attribute to a single value, or it may relate it to an expression (perhaps involving other attributes), such as $a_1 > a_2$.

attribute

A quality or characteristic that describes an object. In an attribute grammar, the object is a nonterminal or the substring it stands for. Each nonterminal in a context-free grammar can have associated with it a set of attributes describing some features or qualities of the object represented by that nonterminal.

evaluation order

(1) Bottom-up when attributes derive their values from some intrinsic property of the subtree being considered.
(2) Top-down when attributes depend on some part of the context in which a subtree is situated.
(3) Left-to-right when information is derived from the left subtree of a node in the parse tree and then inherited into the right subtree.
(4) Right-to-left when information is derived from the right subtree of a node in the parse tree and then inherited into the left subtree.

inherited	(1) An attribute defined by assertions (attribute evaluation functions) in the productions whose rightparts contain references to the nonterminal to which it is attached.
	(2) Symbolized by $\downarrow$*attname*.
synthesized	(1) An attribute that is defined within the productions of the nonterminal to which it is attached or is intrinsic to the terminal to which it is attached.
	(2) Also called a derived attribute.
	(3) Symbolized by $\uparrow$*attname*.
attribute grammar	A triple (G, V, F) where
	G = context-free grammar
	V = finite set of distinct attributes
	F = finite set of attribute assertions
constrainer	That part of a compiler that verifies that all the assertions are true with respect to the program being compiled.
Micro-Modula	A tiny (micro) subset of Modula-2, used to illustrate the use of attribute grammars.
symbol table	A data structure associating a set of identifiers with values. A symbol table may be accessed by
	1. adding a new identifier with its value if the identifier is not already in the symbol table.
	2. finding an identifier and retrieving its value.

Exercises

1. For each of the following attribute grammars, indicate whether overall, general attribute value flow is bottom-up, top-down, left-to-right, right-to-left, circular, or none of these.

(a)

G	$\rightarrow$ A$\downarrow$1
A$\downarrow n$	$\rightarrow$ B$\downarrow$3n A$\downarrow$7n
	$\rightarrow$ "c" C$\downarrow n{-}1$
B$\downarrow n$	$\rightarrow$ "a" B$\downarrow n{+}4$ "b" C$\downarrow$2n
	$\rightarrow$ "b"
C$\downarrow n$	$\rightarrow$ "c"

(b)

G	$\rightarrow$ A$\uparrow x$	
A$\uparrow x$	$\rightarrow$ B$\uparrow u\uparrow v$ A$\uparrow y$	$[x{=}uy{+}v]$
	$\rightarrow$ "c" C$\uparrow z$	$[x{=}2z]$
B$\uparrow u\uparrow v$	$\rightarrow$ "a" B$\uparrow r\uparrow s$ "b" C$\uparrow x$	$[u{=}2r{+}x{-}s;\ v{=}s{+}1]$
	$\rightarrow$ "b"	$[u{=}1;\ v{=}2]$
C$\uparrow x$	$\rightarrow$ "c"	$[x{=}3]$

(c)

G   → A↓0↑r

A↓x↑z   → B↓y↑z A↓x↑y

          → "c" C↓x↑y   [z=10y+3]

B↓x↑w   → "a" B↓10y+2↑z "b" C↓x↑y   [w=10z+1]

          → "b"   [w=10x+2]

C↓x↑y   → "c"   [y=10x+3]

(d) (inefficient memory allocator)

D   → V↓0↑m

V↓a↑m   → N↓a T↓a+k↑n↑k V↓n↑m

          → ∈   [m=a]

T↓a↑x↑k → N↓a T↓a+k↑x↑k

          → "b"   [x=a; k=1]

          → "i"   [x=a; k=2]

          → "r"   [x=a; k=4]

N↓a   → "s"

(e) (better memory allocator)

D   → V↓0↑m

V↓a↑m   → "s" T↓a↑n↑k N↓n V↓n+k↑m

          → ∈   [m=a]

T↓a↑x↑k → "s" T↓a↑y↑k N↓y   [x=y+k]

          → "b"   [x=a; k=1]

          → "i"   [x=a; k=2]

          → "r"   [x=a; k=4]

N↓a   → ∈

(f)

G   → E↑r

E↑x   → E↑v "+" T↓v↑f   [x=v+f]

          → T↓0↑x

T↓n↑m   → T↓x↑m "*" F↓n+m↑x

          → F↓n↑m

F↓x↑y   → F↓v↑y D↑v

          → D↑v   [y=x+v]

D↑v   → "0"   [v=0]

          → "1"   [v=1]

(g)

G   → E↓0↑r

E↓s↑r   → E↓a+s↑r "+" T↓1↑a

          → T↓1↑a   [r=a+s]

T↓m↑v   → T↓m↑p "*" F↓p↓1↑v

          → F↓m↓1↑v

F↓p↓s↑v → F↓p↓2*s↑n D↓s↑b   [v=n+b*p]

          → D↓s*p↑v

D↓s↑v   → "0"   [v=0]

          → "1"   [v=s]

2. For each of the attribute grammars in Exercise 1, construct the parse tree for the specified string and (if possible) annotate each nonterminal node with its attribute values.

(a) *abbcabbccc*

(b) *abbccc*

(c) *aabbcbcabbccc*

(d) *ssisssbsrsi*

(e) *srsissbsssrsr*

(f) 011*1+1

(g) 1101+11*10

3. Transform the attribute grammars (c) and (g) of Exercise 1 to give the same derived attribute *r* for all strings in the language, but using only synthesized attributes.

Review Quiz

Indicate whether the following statements are true or false.

1. For a given attribute grammar, the set of attributes associated with a particular nonterminal is the union of the sets of inherited and synthesized attributes.

2. An attribute grammar is really a context-sensitive grammar.

3. In an attribute grammar, every nonterminal has one or more attributes associated with it.

4. The constrainer of a compiler verifies that every nonterminal in the corresponding grammar has at least one synthesized attribute.

5. An assertion like $x < y$ associated with attributes x and y in a production is an example of what is known as predicate.

6. Predicates never constrain an attribute to some specific value.

7. Attribute evaluation functions cannot be collected together into empty productions in an attribute grammar.

8. Homonyms are different semantic forms that are syntactically identical.

Compiler Project

1. (a) Modify your Itty Bitty Modula grammar to omit procedures and functions for this first part, but leave in INTEGER and BOOLEAN intrinsic types. Add the necessary attributes and attribute evaluation functions to your grammar so that it correctly enforces all the type rules of standard Modula-2.

(b) Test your grammar by compiling it on the TAG compiler, or by writing a recursive-descent parser to implement it. Your compiler should accept correct program fragments such as

```
TYPE a=BOOLEAN; VAR b:a; ...
IF b THEN ...
b := (3>2) AND (TRUE>FALSE); ...
```

but reject as not in the language erroneous source text such as

```
TYPE a=BOOLEAN; VAR a:INTEGER;          (* redeclaring a *)
IF a=TRUE THEN ...     (* where a is declared as a TYPE *)
b := 3>TRUE;           (* b is undeclared *)
                       (* incompatible types in expression *)
IF 3 THEN ...          (* inappropriate condition type *)
```

2.   (a) Add parameterless functions to your grammar, with the semantics to support up-level variable references.

   (b) Test your new grammar. Be sure that references to variables out of scope report as errors, and that redeclared identifiers correctly mask nonlocal declarations.

3.   Design a library file format, and then add a separate compilation feature to your compiler, including DEFINITION MODULE, IMPLEMENTATION MODULE, and IMPORT clauses. Assume that all symbols declared in the DEFINITION MODULE are automatically exported to the library; do not attempt an EXPORT clause at this time.

Further Reading

Deransart, P., Jourdan, M., & Lorho, B. *Attribute Grammars: Definitions, Systems and Bibliography*. Lecture Notes in Computer Science 323. New York: Springer-Verlag, 1988. See sections 1 and 2 of Part I, which give the fundamental definitions and properties of attribute grammars; also see, especially, Part II which reviews existing compiler generators based on attribute grammars (there are 40 of them).

Horowitz, S. & Teitelbaum, T. "Generating Editing Environments Based on Relations and Attributes." *ACM Transactions on Programming Languages and Systems*, Vol. 8, No. 4 (October 1986), pp. 577-608. See sections 2.1 for overview of attribute grammars and 4.2, 4.3 on relationally attributed grammars.

Jazayeri, M. & Pozefsky, D. "Space-Efficient Storage Management in an Attribute Grammar Evaluator." *ACM Transactions on Programming Languages and Systems*, Vol. 3, No. 4 (October 1981), pp. 388-404. See section 1 for a good overview of attribute grammars and pseudocode for calculating stack offsets for attributes on pp. 396-397.

Katayama, T. "Translation of Attribute Grammars into Procedures." *ACM Transactions on Programming Languages and Systems*, Vol. 6, No. 3 (July 1984), pp. 345-369. See section 3, which shows the translation method where parameters in procedure calls are associated with attributes.

Kennedy, K. & Ramanathan, J. "A Deterministic Attribute Grammar Evaluator Based on Dynamic Sequencing." *ACM Transactions on Programming Languages and Systems*, Vol. 1, No. 1 (July 1979), pp. 142-160. Gives a deterministic method for evaluating all attributes in a "semantic" parse tree; see especially section 4.

Kleene, S.C. *Mathematical Logic*. New York: Wiley, 1967. See ch. 2 for a discussion of predicates (also known as predicate functions).

Knuth, D.E. "Semantics of context-free languages." *Mathematical Systems Theory Journal*, Vol. 2 (1968), pp. 127-145.

Knuth, D.E. "Semantics of context-free languages: Correction." *Mathematical Systems Theory Journal*, Vol. 5 (1971), p. 95.

Robinson, J.A. *Logic: Form and Function*. New York: Elsevier North Holland, 1979. See ch. 6 for a discussion of assertions and the idea of logical consequence.

Chapter 6

Syntax-Directed Code Generation

Aims

- Translate a source text into target code using code generation sequences defined in the grammar that specifies the syntax for the source text.
- Use the instruction set of a small virtual computer to gain insight into the workings of a target computer machine language.
- Extend the Micro-Modula grammar from Chapter 5 to generate executable object code in compiling Micro-Modula programs.
- Solve the forward branch problem using backpatching, which makes a one-pass compiler possible.
- Explore code generation for various control structures.
- Investigate code to access record, array, and pointer data structures.

6.1 Introduction

The whole purpose of a compiler is to translate the source program into the target machine language, also called the *object code*. The object code must have the same semantics as the source program — that is, it must compute the same results — even though the syntax is very different. So far (in the first five chapters) we have been concerned only with the syntactic correctness of the source program, including the forms that would be called syntax if we had used a context-sensitive grammar to describe them (that is, declaration before use, correct types, and the like). These are the concerns of the *front end* of a compiler, the part that recognizes a syntactically correct source program. Now we turn our attention to the *back end*, which in the case of a compiler is concerned with generating the object code. Other programs that use compiler front-end methods with different back ends are interpreters and "pretty-printers" (which analyze the syntax of a source program and print it with appropriate indentation).

159

There has been some recent research in formal methods for describing the target machine by an attribute grammar, then letting a theorem-proving engine (using artificial intelligence techniques) figure out the correct translator to convert the source program into object code. These efforts tend to ignore entropic considerations, and thus have not yet produced workable production compilers in any significant quantity.

We focus instead on the more traditional method of (manually) selecting appropriate target code sequences for each syntactic source form, which is called *syntax-directed code generation*. We call it "syntax-directed" because the code generation sequences are defined in the grammar that specifies the syntax of the source. In other words, the parser is able to choose appropriate sequences of machine language operations strictly on the basis of syntax of the source code being parsed, and not dependent in any way on grammar semantics, except for constant values and machine addresses of variables or procedures.

6.2 Computer Hardware Architecture

There are a variety of computer hardware architectures that are imposed upon compiler designers. Although formal language design methods have long dominated source language definition, it is market pressure (driven by machine-language code hackers) that motivates hardware design the most — and the hardware shows this influence. The baroque instruction sets that characterize the computer environment have two effects.

First, just exactly the right instruction required to implement a particular source code construct may not exist in the target machine for which the compiler is being designed, so the compiler must generate a sequence of other instructions to have the same effect.

Second, there may be more than one way to achieve the same effect for any given source code construct, so the compiler must choose one of them. A good compiler makes the choice dynamically, based on various criteria of "goodness" such as memory space or speed, but a simple compiler is more likely to make some arbitrary choice as preselected by the compiler designer. Chapter 9 covers some of the complexities in code selection.

Apart from scheduling requirements relevant only to high performance computers, the most significant difference in computer architecture with respect to code generation is the number and kind of addressing modes available. The earliest computers had only one place from which to fetch data for their instructions: main memory. To add two numbers you had to specify two (or three) locations in memory; for each machine instruction, data values were fetched from memory and the results put back into memory. Significant performance improvements were achieved when one of those memory addresses was eliminated in favor of an *accumulator*. A single value was fetched ("loaded") from memory into the accumulator or stored from the accumulator back into memory, and the arithmetic operations specified only a single address; the second operand was always the accumulator (see Figure 6.1). Further improvements came about by letting both operands come from *general-purpose registers*. With more than one register to specify, instructions once again required two addresses, but a register address took up few precious bits in the instruction word, and register access is faster than memory access in most computers. Among well-known computers, the Digital Equipment PDP-11 probably has the cleanest architecture with very nearly full *orthogonality*, which means that any instruction can find either or both of its operands in a register or in memory.

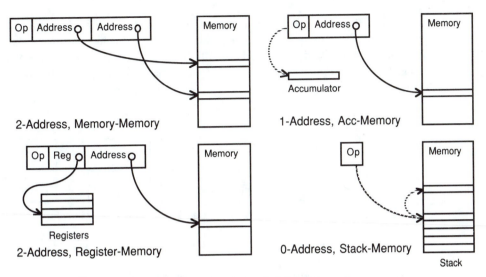

Figure 6.1. A variety of addressing modes.

With the coming of smaller computers, an ever-smaller instruction word size became more valuable, so computer architects also sought ways to limit the number of bits to specify an operand. Using a register was one method; designating a small region in memory (typically 64 or 256 words long) to be addressed by fewer bits is another; using a register or memory location as an indirect reference to the operand is also popular. Many small computers give the option of several addressing modes. Choosing an appropriate and efficient addressing mode (when there is a choice) is often quite difficult in a compiler.

6.3 Stack Machine Expression Evaluation

If one address is better than two, then perhaps zero addresses are best of all. A *zero-address* computer maintains all of its data on top of an *operand stack*. We saw in Chapter 4 how a push-down automaton (PDA) with a stack was an efficient formal machine for parsing context-free languages. We now show that a stack architecture also simplifies expression evaluation. Consider the simple expression 3*4+5*2 to be evaluated sequentially. The first operation the computer can complete in a left-to-right evaluation is the subexpression 3*4 giving the intermediate result 12. This value cannot immediately be added to the other term of the sum, for that term is itself a product of two factors, yet to be evaluated. If you start from the right you have the same problem. There is no way to escape the fact that an intermediate value must be computed and saved.

With enough registers available, intermediate results can be stored in registers — up to a limit — but ultimately all compilers must force subexpressions into temporary data space in memory. Many compilers merely dump this duty on the programmer with an error message something like, "Simplify this expression." When the programmer is involved, the temporary data space is allocated to variables. When the compiler does it automatically, the temporary data space is still allocated, but anonymously. A much simpler method is afforded by an expression stack.

Consider the sequence of operations on the expression stack in Figure 6.2. Values are pushed onto the stack in left-to-right order, as they are encountered in the expression. Whenever both operands for an add or multiply operation are the top two elements of the stack, that operation removes (pops) the two operands and pushes the result of the operation.

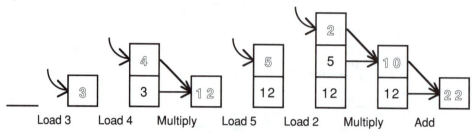

Figure 6.2. Stack evaluation of the expression 3*4+5*2.

The Polish mathematician Lukasiewicz proved that any expression with parentheses and operator precedence (such as used in our familiar arithmetic) could be represented equivalently without parentheses or precedence by placing the operator in front of its operands. Thus, the expressions 3*4+5*2 and (3*4)+(5*2) can both be represented parenthesis-free as +,*,3,4,*,5,2. With characteristic chauvinism, his work was reported in the American press by a person who could remember only the originator's nationality and not his name; he therefore called it "Polish notation" and the name stuck. Moving the operator to the right of its operands preserves the equivalence, and the resulting notation is often called "reverse Polish" or "postorder Polish" but usually just "Polish." The same expression represented in reverse Polish is 3,4,*,5,2,*,+.

Figure 6.3 shows the parse tree for the same expression 3*4+5*2 constructed using grammar G_2. Notice that a left-to-right, postorder tree walk visits each node in the tree in exactly the same order as the semantic operations decorating those nodes must be executed (which also happens to be the same order the parser constructed them). That means that as we enter each node from the top, we walk on down the left subtree before the right, finally making our formal visit to each node as the last thing before exiting out the top. In this case, entering the first production for E at the top of the parse tree, we immediately descend to the E node below and to its left, continuing on to T, T, and F. There at the leaf node (the token 3) we "visit" F and generate "Load 3" on the way out. Reaching the upper T in the left subtree, we again continue down its right subtree to F and generate "Load 4" on the way out. Finally reaching this T for the last time, we generate its "Multiply" before heading back up to E. Continuing down the right branch of the top E, we generate two more loads and another multiply before leaving the top E with its "Add."

Thus, it is easily seen that we can attach the obvious semantic action attributes to the grammar in the productions where the syntax calls for them, and get exactly the intended computation for a stack architecture. This is what we mean by the term, "syntax-directed translation."

Because of its inherent simplicity and direct correspondence to postorder tree walking and a context-free parse, we concentrate in this chapter on zero-address stack evaluation of expressions. Chapter 9 addresses some of the ways to deal with nonstack architectures.

$E \rightarrow E + T$ ["Add"]

$E \rightarrow T$

$T \rightarrow T * F$ ["Multiply"]

$T \rightarrow F$

$F \rightarrow (E)$

$F \rightarrow num$ ["Load *num*"]

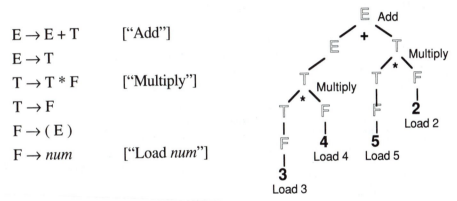

Figure 6.3. Grammar G_2 with semantic actions and parse tree for 3*4+5*2.

6.4 The "Itty Bitty Stack Machine"

It is essential that the compiler designer have a thorough understanding of the target computer machine language. Most real computers have substantial and complex instruction sets, and a tutorial on any particular machine language is outside the scope of this book. In order to introduce the basic concepts of code generation with as little extraneous noise as possible, we define a small pure stack machine, which we call the IBSM (for "Itty Bitty Stack Machine"). This computer has fewer than 30 operations; we are concerned with about half of them, listed in Table 6.1. The full instruction set is defined in Appendix C.

Note that only one of these instructions, LoadCon, has any explicit operand at all, and it is only to load a constant from the following word of memory onto the stack. All the other instructions are truly zero-address, and take all their operands off the stack.

As we saw earlier, Multiply and Add pop two operands off the stack, perform their respective operations, then push the result; the Boolean operators Or and And work similarly. The comparison operators, Equal, Less, and Greater also pop two operands, compare them as implied by the name, and then push a one (true) or zero (false) back on. Negate takes but a single operand off the top of the stack and pushes its arithmetic negative. Load pops an address (which is of course just a number) off the top of the stack, uses the value of that number to address some location in memory, then pushes a copy of the contents of that memory cell. Similarly, Store pops off a value and an address, and stores the value into the memory cell indicated by the address. Zero is a synonym for LoadCon 0; that is, it has the same meaning (effect on the machine) but is spelled differently (that is, it has a different operation code). The control structures are less intuitive and will be discussed more fully later.

It is traditional to write comments in a separate column to the right of the mnemonic and any operand it may have. Because no assembler program exists to convert IBSM mnemonics into machine code, and because (except for the exercises in this chapter aimed

Code	Mnemonic	Function
30	Zero	*push the constant* 0
28	LoadCon *<value>*	*push <value>*
27	Load	*pop address, push memory(address)*
26	Store	*pop value, pop address, store value in memory(address)*
11	Multiply	*pop* a, *pop* b, *push* b*a
12	Add	*pop* a, *pop* b, *push* b+a
14	Or	*pop* a, *pop* b, *push* b or a
15	And	*pop* a, *pop* b, *push* b and a
16	Equal	*pop* a, *pop* b, *push* 1 *if* b=a *else push* 0
17	Less	*pop* a, *pop* b, *push* 1 *if* b<a *else push* 0
18	Greater	*pop* a, *pop* b, *push* 1 *if* b>a *else push* 0
20	Negate	*pop* a, *push* −a
1	BranchFalse	*pop offset, pop value, if value=0 then add offset to PC*
3	Call	*pop address, push return address, go to subroutine*
4	Enter	*pop number, allocate space for that many variables*
5	Exit	*pop number, deallocate that many params & return to caller*
8	Dupe	*push a copy of the stack top*
9	Swap	*pop two values, push them back on in reverse* order
24	Stop	*stop run*
25	Global	*subtract frame pointer from top of stack*

Table 6.1. Some Itty Bitty Stack Machine operations.

at making you familiar with the instruction set) nobody ever writes IBSM machine instructions by hand anyway, we can tolerate considerable freedom in the representation of these instructions. You are encouraged in the exercises here to annotate your code liberally.

To execute the evaluation of the simple expression 3*4+5*2 we must generate exactly the seven instructions for a stack machine, in the same order. Note that the stack contents, shown in the comments field of each line, follow Figure 6.2 exactly:

Instruction Mnemonic	Resulting Stack Contents (top to the left)
LoadCon 3	3
LoadCon 4	4,3
Multiply	12
LoadCon 5	5,12
LoadCon 2	2,5,12
Multiply	10,12
Add	22

If an operand is a variable instead of a constant, the address of the variable is loaded as a constant, then the Load instruction fetches its value. An assignment statement a:=b therefore compiles to the sequence

Instruction Mnemonic	Resulting Stack Contents (top to the left)
LoadCon <address of a>	address of a
LoadCon <address of b>	address of b, address of a
Load	value of b, address of a
Store	(*empty*)

The Store instruction requires two values on the stack: the top value is the value to be stored, which was pushed by the previous Load (which in turn fetched it from the variable b); the second item popped is the address in memory of the variable a, pushed by the first LoadCon instruction. The order of values on the stack for Store requires the address below (pushed before) the value to be stored. Thus, the address must be pushed, then the expression value computed, before the value can be stored. As we shall see shortly, that is just the order we can generate these values. Now, consider the assignment a:=a−1. Because IBSM has no subtract instruction, we compose one from the two operations, Negate and Add, representing the algebraic identity defining subtraction: $a-b = a+(-b)$.

Instruction Mnemonic	Resulting Stack Contents (top to the left)
LoadCon <address of a>	address of a
LoadCon <address of a>	address of a, address of a
Load	value of a, address of a
LoadCon 1	1,a, address of a
Negate	−1,a, address of a
Add	a−1, address of a
Store	(*empty*)

In real computers the instructions to be executed are only numbers in memory, each number signifying the operation to be performed at the time it is fetched. Thus, to generate code for the IBSM we must generate the sequence of numbers that encode the operations desired. Let us assume that the variable a is located in the memory cell addressed by the number 3. The assignment a:=a−1 therefore compiles to the sequence of numbers

28	LoadCon <address of a>
3	
28	LoadCon <address of a>
3	
27	Load
28	LoadCon 1
1	
20	Negate
12	Add
26	Store

We can show the semantics of code generation in the grammar in much the same way we handled all other semantics: by enclosing them in brackets. The production (rewrite rule) for multiplication in Micro-Modula (see Listing 5.1 for the full grammar), with code generation added, looks like this:

```
P → "*" F [" 11 "] P
```

This rule can be read to mean that after parsing the factor that follows the asterisk in a multiplication, the compiler should emit the number 11 into the output code file. The code to be generated is enclosed in quotes just like the tokens; the enclosing brackets prevent confusion of tokens and code. The TAG compiler accepts any quoted string of characters inside the brackets as output code and writes exactly that string of characters out to the output code file. Thus, to separate the number 11 that means Multiply from the other numbers preceding and following it, we include the extra spaces.

Some parser generators permit semantic actions only at the end of the right-hand part of a production. This is not a problem, because nonterminals can go anywhere, and empty productions can be used to generate code. Indeed, it is often easier to collect code generation productions into one place in the grammar for ease of reading and editing. Without loss of correctness, therefore, we could write two productions that have the same effect as the single one above, but have the further property that all of the semantics follow the rightpart of the production in which it occurs:

```
P → "*" F M P
M → [" 11 "]
```

Note that without the semantics, M is an empty production: it recognizes no input tokens. Applying the algorithm for removing empty productions from context-free grammars (see Chapter 2) leaves the original grammar.

Often the code generator must generate not a sequence of numbers in a text file, but some specially formatted binary object module file. It is not our purpose here to go into the complexities of such file formats, but they are easily handled by appropriate semantic action routines in the form of empty productions.

6.5 Attributed Code Generation

Direct output of text strings for code generation works adequately for simple syntax-directed code such as arithmetic operators. But much of the output code depends on semantic information, particularly including data normally stored in the symbol table. Indeed, even the operators in most modern languages are overloaded in such a way that different types of operands result in different machine instructions. For example, the multiplication operator "*" in Pascal and Modula-2 can be applied variously to integers, reals, and sets — each with fundamentally different machine operations to implement it. Syntax-directed code generation no longer works in this kind of situation, and we postpone its proper consideration until Chapter 8.

We consider here a more immediate problem, namely, the location of variables in memory. The code generator must be able to emit the appropriate numbers to direct the hardware to load and store the specific memory cells allocated to particular variables. And as the variable declarations are parsed, they must be allocated space in memory and their locations recorded in the symbol table for future reference.

Returning to our Micro-Modula grammar from Chapter 5, we find we must augment the attributes of the variable declaration nonterminal V to include the address of the next available variable location, and we must augment the information stored in the symbol table to include the address of this variable. Listing 6.1 extends the attribute grammar of Listing 5.2 to handle the new semantics of code generation.

```
predeclared
        into !SymTab !{name}int !{value}int ^SymTab;
        from !SymTab !{name}int ^{value}int;
        number !int {value to output};
        newline;
parser                    {no check for valid identifier class}
G !vacantTable:SymTab
        -> "MODULE" ID^identno ";"
           [ "3 100 0 100 -1 100"; newline ]
           "VAR" V!vacantTable!3^tableOut^varsOut
           O!28 O!varsOut O!4
           "BEGIN" B!tableOut
           O!24 [ "-1 -32"; newline ]
           "END" ID^identno "." ;
V !tableIn:SymTab !locIn:int ^tableOut:SymTab ^locOut:int
        -> ID^identno ":" T^type ";"
           [ value=type+locIn*1000 ]
           [ into !tableIn!identno!value^newtable ]
           V!newtable !locIn+1 ^tableOut ^locOut
        -> [ locOut=locIn; tableOut=tableIn ];
T ^type:int
        -> "INTEGER" [ type=1 ]
        -> "BOOLEAN" [ type=2 ];
B !tableIn:SymTab
        -> ID^identno
           [ from !tableIn!identno^value ]
           [ loc=value/1000 ]
           O!28 O!loc ":=" E!tableIn^type O!26 ";"
           [ type=value-value/10*10 ]
           B!tableIn
        -> ;
E !tableIn:SymTab ^type:int
        -> S!tableIn^stype C!tableIn!stype^type ;
C !tableIn:SymTab !typeIn:int ^typeOut:int
        -> "=" S!tableIn^ctype O!16
           [ typeIn=ctype; typeOut=2 ]
        -> [ typeOut=typeIn ];
S !tableIn:SymTab ^type:int
        -> F!tableIn^type P!tableIn!type ;
```

Listing 6.1. "Micro-Modula" attribute grammar, generating code for IBSM, part 1.

```
P !tableIn:SymTab !type:int
        -> "*" F!tableIn^type O!11 P!tableIn!type
           [ type=1 ]
        -> "AND" F!tableIn^type O!15 P!tableIn!type
           [ type=2 ]
        -> ;
F !tableIn:SymTab ^type:int
        -> "(" E!tableIn^type ")"
        -> ID^identno
           [ from !tableIn!identno^value ]
           [ loc=value/1000; type=value-loc*1000 ]
           O!28 O!loc O!27
        -> NUM^value O!28 O!value [ type=1 ]
        -> "TRUE" O!28 O!1  [ type=2 ]
        -> "FALSE" O!28 O!0 [ type=2 ];
O !value:int
        -> [ number!value; newline ].
```

Listing 6.1. "Micro-Modula" attribute grammar, generating code for IBSM, part 2.

We have added to this grammar one new nonterminal O to generate output object code; its single inherited attribute is the value to generate. The only production for this nonterminal is empty, so its inclusion in the rest of the grammar does not change the language in any way. The semantics for the nonterminal O, however, introduces two new semantic action routines: number generates one decimal integer in the output file, and newline, which generates an end of line. The output file is initialized for IBSM by the second line of the goal symbol production, G. It allocates 100 words of data space for the stack, before the beginning of the code. The intrepid reader may refer to Appendix C for details on the operation of the Itty Bitty Stack Machine interpreter.

As when we extended Micro-Modula to add type and function declarations (although they have not been included in our extension here), we are packing two items into the value assigned to each symbol in the symbol table. One is the type of the variable, the other its allocated location in memory. Nonterminal V allocates the space by adding one to the (left-to-right) pass-through attribute that counts the total number of variables. In a more complex language we would be obliged to count not variables but actually allocated memory words (or bytes, depending on the machine architecture); here they are equal. The location of the new variable is packed into the symbol table value by multiplying it by 1,000 and adding the integer value that encodes the type. When an identifier occurs on the left side of an assignment (B) or in an expression (F), it is found in the symbol table, and the value is unpacked. The type is checked as before, but the location part is used to generate the LoadCon instruction with that address. On the left side of an assignment the address is all that is required; a Store instruction follows the computation of the expression on the right side. Note the sequence in the code generation: the address of the variable to which a value is to be assigned is calculated first, as it must be pushed on the runtime stack first by the generated code. Then the expression generates any code that it may, followed by the Store instruction that stores the value into the variable.

Within the production for Factor (F), a variable reference generates the LoadCon for the address, followed by a Load to fetch its value onto the runtime stack. The constants TRUE and FALSE simply push onto the runtime stack the appropriate Boolean constant values (one or zero); an integer constant must generate the code to push whatever number is returned from the scanner.

Note that except for the packing and unpacking of the value associated with each identifier in the symbol table, the type-checking semantics of the attribute grammar is unchanged. Type-checking and code generation are essentially independent.

6.5.1 Operator Precedence and Associativity

Normal rules of arithmetic give multiplication and division greater operator precedence than addition and subtraction. That is, in an expression combining addition and multiplication without parentheses, the multiplication is done first, before the addition. We express this precedence in the grammar of the syntax by showing expressions to be constructed of the sum of terms, and terms in turn the product of factors, and not the other way around. Thus, when we add the semantics to the grammar as we have done above, the multiplication is performed within terms, and the addition is performed within expressions, after the multiplication. In essence, the further down the parse tree an operator appears, the higher its precedence.

The associativity of operators is easily seen to relate similarly to the structure of the parse tree. We normally associate arithmetic operators to the left, so that $a-b+c$ is interpreted the same as $(a-b)+c$ and not as $a-(b+c)$. This makes a difference with operators that lack the algebraic property of associativity, such as subtraction and division. Grammar G_2 is left-associative in both addition and multiplication. The parse tree for $a+a+a$ puts the left addition below the right, so that the code generated for it does the left addition before the right addition (see Figure 6.4a). When we converted the grammar to LL(1) we avoided just flipping the grammar over (Figure 6.4d), which would have made it right-associative. The construction we used preserves the left-associative property, provided that the semantics applies the addition to just the nonterminal T (Figure 6.4b). With the same grammar, improper placement of the semantics renders the addition right-associative (Figure 6.4c).

6.5.2 Semantics of Program Structures

As we saw earlier, Polish notation affords a clean and correct way to convert infix expressions to executable code in a stack machine. It is easily extended to handle simple statements like assignments and procedure calls. Program structure — notably IF-THEN-ELSE and WHILE loops — require a little more care.

Since the time of Dijkstra's famous paper, "GOTOs Considered Harmful," modern program language design has tended to avoid the use of unstructured jumps. Unfortunately the hardware designers have not been willing and able to follow the lead of language designers, and the fundamental control operation in computer hardware continues to be the machine equivalent of a GOTO, usually called a "branch" instruction.

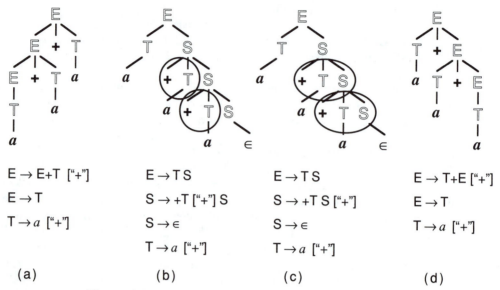

$$E \rightarrow E+T \ [\text{``+''}]$$
$$E \rightarrow T$$
$$T \rightarrow a \ [\text{``+''}]$$

$$E \rightarrow T \ S$$
$$S \rightarrow +T \ [\text{``+''}] \ S$$
$$S \rightarrow \in$$
$$T \rightarrow a \ [\text{``+''}]$$

$$E \rightarrow T \ S$$
$$S \rightarrow +T \ S \ [\text{``+''}]$$
$$S \rightarrow \in$$
$$T \rightarrow a \ [\text{``+''}]$$

$$E \rightarrow T+E \ [\text{``+''}]$$
$$E \rightarrow T$$
$$T \rightarrow a \ [\text{``+''}]$$

(a)　　　　　(b)　　　　　(c)　　　　　(d)

Figure 6.4. Parse tree associativity for addition. The two grammars (a) and (b) on the left are left-associative; (c) and (d) are right-associative.

The classical branch instruction tests some condition in the current machine state, and then if the condition renders a "true" result, execution transfers to some specified other location in memory; otherwise it continues with the next instruction in sequence. Different machines have different kinds of conditions to test, often including also a complement for each tested condition. For example, one branch might jump if the accumulator is zero, another if it is not zero. Often a computer has a set of *condition codes*, which encode the results of different instructions, most notably a single compare. A variety of branch instructions then test for various useful combinations of bits in the condition codes. Virtually every machine design includes also an unconditional branch; that is, the implied condition tested always returns true. There are also different ways to specify the address where execution continues when the branch is taken. The earliest hardware specified a full memory address. With the trend toward shorter instructions and larger memory address spaces, several abbreviations became popular, depending as they did on the locality of most branches: few branches in any program go very far from point of branch. The most popular form jumps a fixed offset from the branch instruction, so that relocating the instruction in memory as part of its program segment does not invalidate the branch address. It is called *relative addressing*, and programs with only relative branches are called *self-relocating* (or sometimes, *position-independent*) because they can be relocated anywhere in memory without modification.

The branch instruction in the Itty Bitty Stack Machine (described fully in Appendix C) is relative, in that the offset popped off the stack is added to the program counter (that is, the address of the next instruction) in case of a branch. There is only one condition to test, and only one version of that test. The condition is whether or not the second word on the stack is zero. Zero is the representation of the Boolean value **false**, and the branch instruction branches exactly when that value is **false**; that is, when the number popped off the stack is zero. Following one of the three comparison operators, this is sufficient to handle conditionals and all common forms of loop code. An unconditional branch in IBSM is composed of an instruction to push a zero onto the stack, followed by the branch-if-zero.

Consider a simple conditional

IF b THEN x ELSE y END

where b is any Boolean expression, and x and y are any sequences of statements. The code to implement this in IBSM, not unlike that for any conventional computer, is the following sequence of instructions and pseudocode:

1		<code to evaluate b>	*test condition*
2		LoadCon <offset e–t>	*skip **then**-part if false*
3		BranchFalse	
4	t:	<code to do x>	***then**-part starts here*
5		LoadCon 0	*skip over **else**-part*
6		LoadCon <offset j–e>	
7		BranchAlways	
8	e:	<code to do y>	***else**-part starts here*
9	j:	<whatever follows>	*both parts come here when done*

The computer must evaluate the Boolean expression b (line 1) to determine whether to execute the THEN-part or the ELSE-part. The THEN-part follows immediately in the source and object code, so if the condition evaluates to **true**, no branch is taken; that is, when the branch instruction executes it does nothing but advance to the next instruction on line 4. If the expression evaluates to **false**, the branch to the ELSE-part must be taken. This means that the branch instruction adds to the program counter an offset that must be the difference in addresses from the next instruction after the branch (line 4, which is also the beginning of the THEN-part, labeled "t:") to the first instruction of the ELSE-part (line 8, labeled "e:"). The difference is shown in the pseudocode as "e–t." On completion of the THEN-part (done only if the condition was true), execution must skip over the ELSE-part before continuing. This is unconditional, so to branch over the ELSE-part, a zero condition is pushed onto the stack as a constant. The offset is constructed the same way as previously, by loading a constant representing the difference between the address of the join (line 9, labeled "j:") and the beginning of the ELSE-part.

In both cases the offsets are program constants; that is, the number of instructions to jump over is fixed at compile time, so the compiler can know what constant to push. However, that number cannot be known until the compiler has compiled all the statements to be jumped over, which is after the LoadCon instruction where it is used has been generated. This is the *forward branch* problem that must be solved in any compiler.

6.5.3 The Forward Branch Problem

There are two approaches to the forward branch problem, both in common use. One is to compile the program twice, only generating code the second time through. The first time through all the branch destinations are noted and recorded for use during the second time through. A compiler that takes this approach is called a "two-pass" compiler because it makes two passes through the program. A variant of this method converts all incomplete forward references into special linker commands, and relies on a subsequent link-relocator step to resolve the forward references. Although reading the source text twice takes more time, two-pass compilers are necessary to compile languages that do not require declaration before use because it cannot always be known on the first pass what code to generate for an arbitrary identifier reference.

The second method keeps a record of each incomplete forward branch as it compiles, then when the target address becomes known, goes back in the output code and patches the offset or branch address with the correct value. This method is called *backpatching*, and it makes a one-pass compiler possible. We favor this method with block-structured languages like Pascal and Modula-2, although it does require some nonsequentiality in the output file.

Any computation of address offsets must be based on the addresses of instructions generated, which in turn requires that the address values be carried about through the code generation productions as attributes. It is feasible to synthesize a size attribute, which is accumulated as it flows up the parse tree, and which would thus provide adequate information for generating offsets to relative branches. We prefer, however, a left-to-right absolute address attribute, so that it can also be used later when we need an absolute address of procedures for the symbol table. A fragment of the attribute grammar to generate code for IF– and other statements (without type-checking) might look something like Listing 6.2. In this grammar the `Emit` nonterminal tracks the location counter while emitting object code.

```
Stmt !locIn:int ^locOut:int
      -> "IF" BoolExpn !locIn^locEx
         Emit !28!locEx^locOff1
         Emit !0!locOff1^locBrf
         Emit !1!locBrf^locThen
         "THEN" Stmts !locThen^locLdz
         Emit !30!locLdz^locLdc
         Emit !28!locLdc^locOff2
         Emit !0!locOff2^locBra
         Emit !1!locBra^locElse
         "ELSE" Stmts !locElse^locOut "END"
         BackPatch !locOut!locOff1!locElse-locThen
         BackPatch !locOut!locOff2!locOut-locElse
      -> OtherStmt !locIn^locOut;
BackPatch !locn:int !locOff:int !value:int
      -> [ "-1 "; number!locOff; newline; ]
         [ number!value; newline; ]
         [ "-1 "; number!locn; newline; ];
Emit !value:int !locIn:int ^locOut:int
      -> [ number!value; newline; locOut=locIn+1 ].
```

Listing 6.2. Generating backpatch code for IF-statements.

We assume that this compiler will be generating code for the standard IBSM loader, which recognizes a "−1" followed by a number as redirecting the load address to that number. Thus, we do not have to backspace or rewind the output file, nor buffer it wholly in memory. The `BackPatch` nonterminal generates one word at the specified address (using this address redirection), then restores the address location counter to the current address (passed to it in the first inherited attribute, `locn`).

Let's look at how a short program fragment might compile with this grammar. Given the statement sequence

```
a:=3;
IF a<b THEN  b:=1  ELSE  b:=5  END;
c:=0;
```

we assume the current location counter is 147, and that the local addresses of a, b, and c are respectively 11, 12, and 13. We arrive on the scene just as the parser is ready to accept the IF token, so the output file looks like this (with the location counter values and instruction mnemonics shown for clarity, although they do not appear in the output file):

```
    . . .
(147)  28              LDC 11 (address of a)
(148)  11
(149)  28              LDC 3
(150)  3
(151)  26              ST     (into a)
(152)
```

The parser now arrives in nonterminal `Stmt` with `locIn=152`. The next token is IF so the scanner accepts that token and nonterminal `BoolExpn` is invoked with inherited attribute `locIn=152` to parse the Boolean expression a<b, generating the following code:

```
(152)  28              LDC 11 (address of a)
(153)  11
(154)  27              LD     (value of a)
(155)  28              LDC 12 (address of b)
(156)  12
(157)  27              LD     (value of b)
(158)  17              LESS
(159)
```

We now return to the nonterminal `Stmt` from `BoolExpn` with derived attribute `locEx=159`, and emit three more words of instruction:

```
(159)  28              LDC 0  (placeholder for offset)
(160)  0
(161)  1               BRF    (Branch if False)
(162)
```

The synthesized attribute `locOff1` has the value 160, the address of the zero that will eventually be replaced by the forward branch offset. Synthesized attribute `locThen` has the value 162, the address of the beginning of the Then-part of the If-statement, and at the same time, the base from which the branch offset must be calculated. If we ran the IBSM on this code and watched the contents of the stack, it would take on the values in Figure 6.5 (assuming b=4).

```
         3                      12    4                     stack data
    11   11   --   11   3    3    3    1    --
147  149  151  152  154  155  157  158  159  161  location
    Time →
```

Figure 6.5. Execution Trace for "a:=3; IF a<b THEN ..."

The nonterminal `Stmts` is invoked recursively, with the current address 161 in the inherited attribute `locThen`. Code is generated for the assignment statement, and the synthesized attribute `locLdz` is evaluated with the value 167. Four more words of generated code, and the output file looks like this:

```
(162)  28            LDC 12  (address of b)
(163)  12
(164)  28            LDC 1
(165)  1
(166)  26            ST      (1 into b)
(167)  30            ZERO    (push FALSE onto stack)
(168)  28            LDC 0   (placeholder)
(169)  0
(170)  1             BRF     (BranchAlways)
(171)
```

Note that the IBSM does not have a proper "Branch Always" instruction; the effect is composed from the Zero and BranchFalse instructions. At this point the parser accepts the ELSE token and returns to the `Stmts` nonterminal with a new inherited attribute `locElse`=171. Although not shown here, the `Stmts` nonterminal will see that attribute as its own inherited attribute (perhaps named "`locIn`"), in the same way it saw the previous value 162, and after generating the code for "b:=5", return the synthesized attribute value 176 that is named `locOut` in `Stmt`:

```
(171)  28            LDC 12  (address of b)
(172)  12
(173)  28            LDC 5
(174)  5
(175)  26            ST      (5 into b)
(176)
```

This is now where the backpatching gets interesting. Nonterminal `BackPatch` is given three inherited attributes: the first is the current location, so that it can restore the load address for the next sequential word after the backpatch. The second attribute is the memory address to be patched, and the third attribute is the value to patch into that location. Local attributes `locOff1` and `locOff2` preserve the addresses of the placeholder zeros; one invocation of `BackPatch` for each one is required. According to the pseudocode, the first patch requires the difference between the address of the else-part and the then-part, 171–162=9. `BackPatch` emits for this three lines in the output file after the last code generated:

```
(175)   26                      ST      (5 into b)
        -1 160                  (address of offset)
(160)   9                       (value of offset)
        -1 176                  (restore current address)
(176)
```

The second invocation of nonterminal BackPatch takes inherited attributes locOff=169 (the address saved in locOff2) and value=14 (=176–162), and three more lines are added to the output file:

```
        -1 169                  (address of offset)
(169)   14                      (value of offset)
        -1 176                  (restore current address)
```

Finally nonterminal Stmt exits with derived attribute locOut=176, the address of the next machine instruction to be generated. The assignment following the IF generates five more words, leaving the output file fragment for these three statements looking like this (in three columns, with comments no longer showing):

```
28              1              26
11              28             -1 160
28              12             9
3               28             -1 176
26              1              -1 169
28              26             14
11              30             -1 176
27              28             28
28              0              13
12              1              28
27              28             0
17              12             26
28              28
0               5
```

If you were to take a conventional memory dump, however, after the file had been loaded into memory, you would see the offset values placed correctly, somewhat like this (memory addresses and data shown in decimal):

```
0147   .. .. .. .. .. .. .. 28 11 28
0150   03 26 28 11 27 28 12 27 17 28
0160   09 01 28 12 28 01 26 30 28 14
0170   01 28 12 28 05 26 28 13 28 00
0180   26 .. .. ..
```

The basic WHILE-loop introduces only the new concept of the backward branch. An attribute evaluation function must calculate the (negative) offset for the branch, but because both locations are already fixed at the time of generation, no backpatching is necessary. Of course, the forward branch for when the loop condition evaluates to False still requires a backpatch to set its offset correctly. For the loop

WHILE b DO x END

the generated code must be somewhat like this:

```
t:    <code to evaluate b>        test condition at loop front
      LoadCon  <offset e–b>       quit if false
      BranchFalse
b:    <code to do  x>             execute loop body
      LoadCon  0                  branch back to loop front
      LoadCon <offset t–e>
      BranchAlways
e:    <whatever follows>          come here when done
```

The productions of an attribute grammar to effect this code are left as an exercise for the student.

6.6 Generating Code for Procedures and Functions

In most conventional programming languages, procedures and functions differ only in whether a value is returned. Otherwise, the parameters (if any) are evaluated the same, the calling sequence is the same, and the code on entry and exit from the procedure or function is the same. That is probably why Wirth abandoned the separate keyword FUNCTION in going from Pascal to Modula-2.

One of the earliest innovations in computer architecture (back in vacuum-tube days) was the concept of a subroutine (procedure) call, where the hardware saves the address of the instruction to return to after the subroutine is finished. Virtually every modern computer instruction set now contains two instructions to implement efficient subroutine calls and returns. The Call instruction (sometimes also called "Jump to Subroutine") saves the address of the next instruction in some specified location (usually on a hardware stack, but often in a register instead), then does an unconditional jump or branch to the subroutine address. The Return instruction restores program control to the saved address. Modern high-level languages often require additional housekeeping instructions to pass parameters, allocate local variable storage within the subroutine, and to permit recursion. There are three code sequences to be concerned with: the subroutine entry, the exit, and the call. Usually there is more than one call to a given subroutine, so it is considered advantageous to concentrate as much of the entry and exit code within the subroutine rather than replicating these instructions in every calling sequence.

Entry to a procedure is in principle the same as entry to a program, but without the code file setup semantics that initialize the output code module. This is replaced instead by some code to set up an array of pointers called a "display." Each pointer contains the address of the local variable space for a procedure within which the current procedure is nested. In nonnested languages like C and Fortran, the display needs only two entries, local and global, so most of the cost of setup is avoided. In the IBSM, constructing the display involves some 33 instructions packed into 16 words. The semantics of code generation, however, is not concerned with the display construction details (a "cookbook recipe" will suffice our purposes). Exit code is just two instructions, one to push a constant representing the number of formal parameters, and the second to effect the exit. The specifics of the hardware entry and exit code are not particularly relevant here, and each computer is different. The interested reader is referred to Appendix C for the full details of procedure entry and exit in the Itty Bitty Stack Machine.

The calling sequence for a procedure consists in pushing the expression values for each value parameter (if any) onto the stack, followed by the address of the called procedure with its parent frame pointer, then the Call instruction. The parent frame pointer is used for constructing the display, which affords access to nonlocal variables.

Function calls push space for the return value first, before pushing the arguments. Functions also have a RETURN statement, which must store the value to be returned into the function result space saved on the stack by the caller, then exit. Figure 6.6 shows the general structure of the call, entry, and exit code for function procedures in the IBSM.

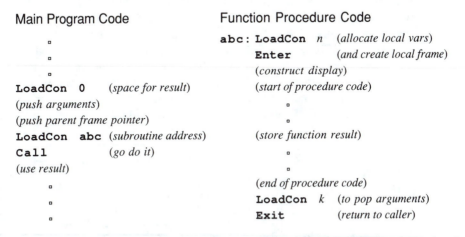

Figure 6.6. Function call, entry, and exit code in IBSM.

6.7 Block-Structured Stack Frame Management

In a block-structured language like Modula-2 or Pascal, a statement can refer to variables not only locally in the procedure most nearly containing the statement, but also to any variables in any procedure containing the immediate procedure. In Chapter 5 we observed how this affects the symbol table management. Now we must be concerned with how the executing program can gain access to (thereby to load or store values in) those variables. Unstructured languages like C and Fortran do not have this problem because only two levels are visible at all times: global (called "COMMON" in Fortran) and local; no procedure can access the variables of any other procedure except by reference passed as a parameter.

6.7.1 Frames and Frame Pointers

Each procedure or function is allocated on entry (that is, when it is called) some memory where its local variables are stored. This memory block is called a *frame*, and is typically of fixed size because it can be determined at compile time how many variables using how many words of memory there are. A procedure that is called recursively allocates a new frame on each incarnation, so there is no interference between the variables of each incarnation. Some languages allow "static" variables that are not allocated space in the local frame; these are effectively global variables that are visible only to the procedure in which they are declared. Because they act as globals except for visibility, we can with impunity give them no special consideration here. Most implementations of Fortran make all variables static.

The local variable frame is usually accessed by a hardware *frame pointer* which is either a special register dedicated to that purpose (as in the Itty Bitty Stack Machine) or else a general address register used for that purpose by convention. Local variables are then addressed by fixed offsets from the current frame pointer. It is these offsets that we have been storing in the symbol table, along with type and kind. The local frame typically also contains saved registers (also called "state") from the procedure's caller. The frames are usually allocated dynamically and linked together into a linked list, or else allocated sequentially on a stack. Figure 6.7 shows a linked list of local variable frames for nested procedures A and B in the main program. When a procedure or function terminates and returns to its caller, it deallocates its local variable frame, restoring the hardware pointer to the frame of its caller as well as recovering any other saved state such as registers. This process is automated somewhat in IBSM by a single instruction, Exit.

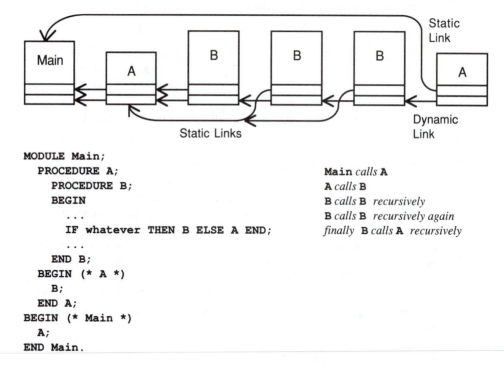

```
MODULE Main;                              Main calls A
  PROCEDURE A;                            A calls B
    PROCEDURE B;                          B calls B recursively
    BEGIN                                 B calls B recursively again
      ...                                 finally B calls A recursively
      IF whatever THEN B ELSE A END;
      ...
    END B;
  BEGIN (* A *)
    B;
  END A;
BEGIN (* Main *)
  A;
END Main.
```

Figure 6.7. A linked list of variable frames, showing program listing and execution trace at the time of the frame snapshot.

6.7.2 Static and Dynamic Links

In a recursive but nonstructured language like C the global variables — usually in a fixed location in memory, or else accessed by another dedicated register — and the local frame are all there is. In a block-structured language like Modula-2 it is often necessary to reach not only local and global variables, but also variables local to intermediate procedures. To touch those, the program must gain access to that procedure's frame pointer. Often the next frame in the linked list representing the sequence of callers does not give access to the next level of enclosing procedure scope. For example, if a procedure calls itself recursively, there may be several linked frames for that same procedure, such as the frames for procedure B in Figure 6.7, but an up-level (nonlocal) variable reference must bypass all those frames in search of the frame containing the referenced variable, perhaps in procedure A. Thus, the frames are usually connected together with a second chain of links, representing the scope visibility chain. This second chain is called the *static links*, and the chain of callers represents the *dynamic links*. Dynamically scoped languages like Lisp access only the dynamic links for nonlocal variables, but programming such a language is so fraught with potential errors that few languages deviate from the static scoping found in Pascal and Modula-2 — indeed, even some dialects of Lisp are returning to static scoping.

6.7.3 The Display Vector of Frame Pointers

The easiest way to access a nonlocal variable is to build, on entry to each procedure, a vector of frame pointers called a *display*. In a statically scoped language the *lex level* is the number of containing procedures in the source text, which can be determined at compile time. Thus, the display is a fixed-length array with as many elements as the current lex level, each element pointing to the frame pointer of one containing procedure, in lex-level order. In the IBSM the display consists not of pointers but of (negative) offsets from the current frame pointer. The sequence of IBSM instructions to construct the display is not particularly instructive, so the code is shown here only in decimal absolute. The interested reader can refer to the full listing in Appendix C. Listing 6.3 is a fragment of an attribute grammar for Micro-Modula showing how to set up parameterless function headers (type-checking has again been omitted for clarity). Procedure headers differ only slightly, in obvious ways. Within a procedure or function, local variables could be accessed as before, by a **LoadCon** of the address offset followed by the **Load** or **Store**. All memory references in the IBSM are made relative to the current procedure's frame pointer, which is set up on entry. Nonlocal variables can be reached only indirectly through the display. Because there is no syntactic way to distinguish local variables from nonlocal, we generate display access code for local variables also. The sequence of IBSM instructions to construct the address of a local or nonlocal variable is

LoadCon <offset>	{*position of var in its frame*}
LoadCon <display + lexlevel>	{*index into display*}
Load	{*get offset to var's frame*}
Add	

The current **offset** and **lexlevel** are whatever is indicated in the symbol table for this variable. The **lexlevel** is zero for global variables, one for the variables within its first level of contained procedures, etc. The **lexlevel** is typically passed around the parse as an inherited attribute, and stored into the symbol table when a variable is declared. The constant **display** represents the relative address of the display in the local frame. It is the equal to the number of local variables +3 because the local variables are allocated space in the local frame before the display. When this sequence is followed by **Load**, the variable value is fetched for use in an expression. If it is followed instead by some later **Store**, the value immediately above the offset on the stack is stored into the addressed variable.

```
H !tblIn:SymTab !locIn:int !lex:int ^tblOut:SymTab ^locOut:int
  -> "PROCEDURE" ID ^identno ":"  T ^type ";"
     [ value=type+locIn*1000+lex*100+type+40 ]
     [ into !tblIn !identno !value ^nextable ]
     [ open !nextable ^newtable ]
     "VAR"  V !newtable !0 !lex+1 ^vtable ^nvars
     Emit !30 !locIn ^loc1   {jump over nested fns}
     Emit !28 !loc1 ^loc2
     Emit !0 !loc2 ^loc3
     Emit !1 !loc3 ^locn
     H !vtable !locn !lex+1 ^btable ^locd
     BackPatch !locd !loc2 !locd-locn
     Display !locd !nvars !lex+1 ^locb
     "BEGIN" B !locb !type !lex+1 !nvars ^locx
     Emit !28 !locx ^loc6    {LoadCon nargs+1}
     Emit !1 !loc6 ^loc7
     Emit !5 !loc7 ^locz
     "END" ID ^identno ";"
     H !nextable !locz !lex ^tblOut ^locOut
  -> [ locOut=locIn; tableOut=tableIn ];

{set up procedure/function entry and allocate local vars}
Display !locIn:int !nvars:int !lex:int ^locOut:int
  -> Emit !28828 !locIn ^loc1
     Emit !nvars !loc1 ^loc2
     Emit !lex !loc2 ^loc3
     Emit !44968 !loc3 ...
```
[continue to output the following numbers, for a total of 15 *words:*
      13288,30,21481,268,1149,26473,7102,52,32044,31124]
```
     Emit !53661 !loc14 ^locOut ;
```

Listing 6.3. Procedure header attributes for parameterless functions.

It is the function of the caller to properly set up a pointer to the called procedure's next link up the static chain, which we call the "parent pointer." The parent pointer is a reference to the frame pointer of the next static level out from the procedure being called. If the call is recursive to itself, the next level out is the same as the next level out of the caller. The parent pointer is the same as the caller's parent pointer if the call is to a sibling at the same lex level as itself. When the procedure being called is contained (nested) within the caller, the parent pointer is the caller's own frame pointer. Otherwise, a call is being made recursively or to an "uncle" up the scope chain one or more steps. Figure 6.8 shows the stack after several procedure calls (including one recursive call).

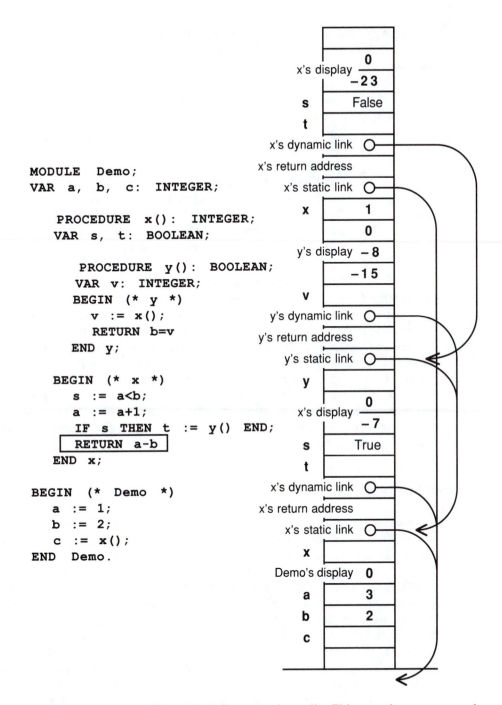

```
MODULE  Demo;
VAR a,  b,  c:  INTEGER;

    PROCEDURE  x():  INTEGER;
    VAR s,  t:  BOOLEAN;

        PROCEDURE  y():  BOOLEAN;
        VAR v:  INTEGER;
        BEGIN  (*  y  *)
            v  :=  x();
            RETURN b=v
        END  y;

    BEGIN  (*  x  *)
        s  :=  a<b;
        a  :=  a+1;
        IF  s  THEN  t  :=  y()  END;
        RETURN  a-b
    END  x;

BEGIN  (*  Demo  *)
    a  :=  1;
    b  :=  2;
    c  :=  x();
END  Demo.
```

Figure 6.8. The IBSM stack during recursive calls. This snapshot represents the stack during the execution of the marked RETURN statement in the inner call to procedure X.

In each case the parent pointer is calculated from the current display, and pushed onto the stack before calling the procedure or function. The sequence of instructions to call a procedure is:

```
              Zero                        {create space for the return value}
<push whatever arguments, if any>
              Zero                        {calculate the value of my frame pointer...}
              Global                      {...which is  –(0–FP)}
              Negate
              LoadCon  <display + lexlevel>          {index into display}
              Load                        {get offset to parent pointer}
              Add                         {leave parent pointer on the stack}
              LoadCon  <address of proc>
              Call                        {go to the procedure}
```

The lex level of the procedure name in the symbol table indexes the display to get the correct offset for its parent pointer. The preceding three instructions convert the current frame pointer into a word on the stack. This code is for functions that return a value. When calling procedures that return no value, you should not push the initial zero.

Shown only graphically in Figure 6.8, the static link of procedure x actually has the somewhat unintuitive value -1, which is the frame pointer for its parent, the main program. Global variables are offset from this frame, which is set by the initial ENTER instruction in the main program at one less than the current (initial) stack pointer value, zero. Note also that variables are allocated on the stack in reverse order when separated by commas in a single declaration. This is a natural artifact of the recursive allocation scheme (see also Exercises 1d and 1e in Chapter 5).

6.8 Other Data Types

So far we have considered only variable types INTEGER and BOOLEAN, which occupy one word of memory each. There are a variety of data types in common use, including complex data structures. Most of them are represented in standard Modula-2, so we address them in that context.

In addition to INTEGER and BOOLEAN, Modula-2 (and Pascal) offer three other kinds of simple data types: CHAR, enumerated types, and REAL. BOOLEAN is a special case of enumerated type because the compiler generates values of type BOOLEAN from relational expressions without explicit reference to the type name, and conditionals (IF, REPEAT, and WHILE) require values of type BOOLEAN. Otherwise, it follows all the general rules for any enumerated type. In particular, any enumerated type is defined by an ordered list of constant names. These are properly constant identifiers, but in our restricted language we have forced them to be reserved words in the type BOOLEAN. The constant names would ordinarily go into the symbol table as constants, linked to the entry in the symbol table for the type. The constant identifiers for any enumerated type are assigned sequential values beginning with zero (as we noted, FALSE is 0 and TRUE is 1), and the semantics for code generation treats them just like numeric constants. Unfortunately, because there is a syntactic ambiguity that fails to distinguish constant and variable identifiers (that is, the same syntax — *identifier* — generates different code), there is a limit to what syntax-directed code generation can do for us with constant identifiers. We have avoided general enumerated types in Itty Bitty Modula for this reason.

The scalar type CHAR does not have the syntactic ambiguity problem, and its implementation is straightforward. Constants of type CHAR are syntactically distinguished by being enclosed in quotes. The code generated to implement a character constant is the same as that to implement a numeric constant, except that the constant value is the numeric equivalent of the ASCII character code (or whatever is appropriate to the hardware and operating system). Variables of type CHAR are indistinguishable from other scalar variables, except in the type code stored in the symbol table. Strong type-checking requires that the type codes be consistent, but the code generated need not distinguish them. Of course, when type-checking an arithmetic or Boolean operator, if an operand of type CHAR is parsed, it is an error.

Subranges of scalar types are slightly more complex. Variables of a subrange type are often allocated the full memory space as the base type, but they must be entered into the symbol table as the subrange type so that range-checking code can be generated for them. However, type-checking must be by reference to the base type only. When the compiler is restricted (as we have it so far) to strictly syntax-directed semantics, it is necessary to enter every scalar type into the symbol table as a subrange. The base types are merely subranges of themselves with maximum range. Range-checking code is generated for every assignment, whether or not it is needed. In Chapter 9 we look at optimizations to eliminate unnecessary range-checking code.

Scalar variables are usually allocated one "word" of memory. In a byte-addressed machine it may be convenient to allocate a single byte for enumerated and character variables, as well as for small subranges of INTEGER. Where there is a hardware restriction on odd addresses for larger units, the compiler must take care to do the necessary alignment when allocating memory space, by inserting unused bytes as fillers. Because each variable has a specified type, the type entry in the symbol table should contain (among other things) an indication of how many words or bytes are required in memory for a variable of this type, and perhaps a flag to indicate if word alignment is necessary. Often word alignment is deemed necessary for any type that fills a word or more, so a flag may be omitted in such cases, depending instead on the size to give a clue to word-alignment requirements.

Floating-point variables (type REAL in most languages) are often larger than the single word used to store integers, and when that is the case they are consistently so. Except for the overloading of the arithmetic operators, REAL variables can be considered as special-case opaque records. That is, they occupy several words of memory and are moved as a unit. They have their own semantics (the generated code for floating-point operations is seldom the same as integer), so we have again the ambiguous semantic problem. No more need be said here because code generation for expression evaluation is analogous to integers.

6.9 Structured Data Types

Three major data structures enable the programmer to build an unlimited variety of data organizations in memory by appropriate type definitions. Access to the elements of each structure is controlled explicitly in modern languages, so that all of the semantics in compiling structure access can be syntax-directed. The three structures are *arrays*, *records*, and *pointers*. These may be mixed and nested arbitrarily deep, but the enhanced PDA of an attribute grammar has no trouble wending its way through the labyrinth of access operators by matching the declarations in the symbol table.

To parse what is known as an *L-expression* it is usually most practical to define a single nonterminal in the grammar. An L-expression represents the semantics for accessing a variable on the Left-hand side of an assignment, and can be thought of as an in-line function that returns the address of a variable. In the Itty Bitty Stack Machine an L-expression represents all the code necessary to access a variable, except for the final Load or Store. Considering only the three major structures and our primitive (one word) variable types, the syntax for an L-Expression is

```
Lexpn  →  ID ( "^" | "." ID | "[" Expn "]" )*
```

Thus, we see that an L-expression consists of an identifier, followed by any number of structure-access operators in any order. The three structure-access operators are pointer dereference, record field reference, and array subscript. Because they are independent and each generates syntax-directed code, we can deal with the three operators individually.

6.9.1 Pointer Types

The simplest of the structured data types is the pointer type. Intuitively, the pointer is an index into a giant array, which is all of memory — or at least all of the heap where dynamic variables are allocated. Although a pointer in memory is equivalent to a large integer (one word in IBSM), a pointer type is different from the type it points to. There must, however, be a link from the pointer type to the base type in the symbol table. Figure 6.9 shows how this might be accomplished.

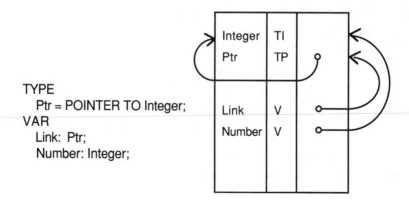

Figure 6.9. Pointer Types in the Symbol Table.

The semantics for a pointer in an L-expression is relatively easy. Each time a pointer is dereferenced (that is, for each occurrence of the dereference operator "^") the current type must also be dereferenced. In Figure 6.9, a reference to the identifier Link is of type Ptr, but a reference to Link^ is of type Integer. Nested pointers to pointers could be dereferenced as many times as the chain is long, or other structure operators inserted according to the declarations. Each dereference must check that the type being dereferenced is a pointer, then set the new working L-expression type to the dereferenced type.

The code to dereference a pointer is also simple. Each dereference operator adds one more fetch from global memory. In the IBSM a memory reference is local to the frame pointer, but the Global instruction converts it. The dereference operator therefore generates exactly two instructions within the L-expression:

	(LoadCon a)	*{get address of pointer a}*
	. . .	
1	Load	*{dereference the pointer}*
2	Global	*{convert local address to global}*
	. . .	
	(Load)	*{get the variable)*

6.9.2 Record Structures

Record structures are like miniature frames. When a record is declared, you must open a new scope in the symbol table and enter the fields as identifiers in this private scope. Each field is marked as a field, but all other semantics are the same as with local variable declarations. In particular, the offset which in the case of a local variable refers to the position of the variable in the local variable frame, in the case of a field refers to the position of the field relative to the record. Thus, the first field in the record has an offset of zero, the second field has an offset equal to the size of the first field, and so on. The size of an object of a record type is the sum of the sizes of the fields; that aggregate size should be stored in the symbol table with the record definition.

At the end of the record declaration, the scope is closed and the entire declaration is saved somewhere, either in some otherwise inaccessible part of the symbol table, or else some place not in the symbol table. When an L-expression calls up a record field by means of the dot operator, the saved scope is opened and the symbol table search for field names is directed to the reopened scope instead of the full visible symbol table. Of course, the type of the L-expression parsed thus far must be a record, and the record type in the symbol table must be linked to the saved field list. In all other ways the semantic processing of type-checking of record fields is the same as for variable identifiers. As a field name is parsed, its type (from the field declaration in the symbol table) becomes the current L-expression working type.

The code to be generated in the IBSM for a record field reference is again exactly two instructions. The first loads a constant, which is the offset within the record, and the second adds it to the working L-expression address:

```
            (LoadCon  a)          {get record address a}
            . . .
      1     LoadCon  <offset>  {get field offset}
      2     Add                    {add it to record address}
            . . .
            (Load)                  {get the variable}
```

In conventional computers with register-based addressing, the record field can be accessed by merely adding the offset to that used to access the variable. This converts a runtime addition to a compile-time addition, and is in the nature of an optimization. The same kind of optimization can be applied to IBSM code, as we shall see when we deal with optimization in Chapter 8.

6.9.3 Array Semantics

Arrays are somewhat more complex than pointers and records. An array is a linear sequence of components in memory, numbered by the subscript type. Thus, an array definition must specify two subtypes: the index type and the component type. The index type must be a scalar type (integer, Boolean, character, any enumerated type, or else a subrange of one of these), but the component type can be any type. The symbol table entry for an array definition must link to both types. The index type must specify its lower bound and the number of its elements (or equivalently, its lower and upper bounds), but these must be included in all scalar types for range-checking anyway. The component type must specify the size of an object of this type, but again, this is required for a variable declaration in all types anyway. The size of an object of the defined array type is the product of the number of elements in the index type and the size of the component type.

Type-checking in an array reference is simply a matter of asserting that the working L-expression is an array type, and checking that the subscript expression is of the same type as the index type declared for the array. The component type of the array becomes the new type of the working L-expression.

The code to generate for an array element reference depends on all of the semantic information stored in the array definition in the symbol table. The working L-expression computation has calculated the address of the array, which is the same as the address of the first element of the array. A simple subscript operation a[k] requires over a dozen separate machine operations to calculate. These will be understood more easily if we first convert the subscript expression to equivalent pseudocode. Given an array defined as

```
VAR  a: ARRAY [lo..hi] OF whatever;
. . . a[k] . . .
```

we must first evaluate the index expression k to find element *k* of the array. Because the array index is based on the constant lo, which may not be zero, we must subtract that base from the calculated value of *k* to normalize the offset to element *k*. Then also a type-safe compiler will validate the range of the index: it must be neither less than lo nor greater than hi. It is more efficient to do this test after subtracting the base, if the index range is stored in the symbol table as a base and number of elements. Finally, the size of the component type in addressable words (or bytes, as dictated by the hardware) is multiplied by the normalized index to determine the physical offset. In Modula-2-like pseudocode, this calculation might look like this:

```
PROCEDURE  SubscriptCalc(A:  ADDRESS;
    k, lo, nelts, eltsize: INTEGER): ADDRESS;
VAR temp: INTEGER;
BEGIN
    temp := k-lo;
    IF temp<0 THEN Error
    ELSIF temp>=nelts THEN Error
    ELSE RETURN A+(temp*eltsize) END
END SubscriptCalc;
```

Abstract IBSM code for the same operations looks like this:

	(LoadCon a)	*{get array address* a}
	. . .	
1	<Expn>	*{evaluate subscript expression}*
2	LoadCon <lobound>	*{subtract off lower bound}*
3	Negate	
4	Add	
5	Dupe	*{make 2 copies for range-checking}*
6	Dupe	
7	Zero	*{be sure it's not < 0}*
8	Less	
9	Swap	
10	LoadCon <numelements>	*{...nor > number of elements}*
11	Greater	
12	Or	*{if either is true,...}*
13	LoadCon 1	
14	BranchFalse	
15	Stop	*{...halt in error}*
16	LoadCon <componentsize>	*{compute offset}*
17	Multiply	
18	Add	*{add it to array address}*
	. . .	
	(Load)	*{get the component)*

We must add to the subscript syntax the code to address the specified element. The first step (line 1) is to evaluate the subscript expression. Because in Modula-2 and Pascal array elements may start at any subscript value, the next step (lines 2-4) is to subtract off the lower bound of the first subscript of the array. A calculated subscript value of 6 for an array declared [3..9] must access the fourth element of the array, not the sixth. The language C forces the lower bound of all subscript ranges to zero, so this step is not needed. Simple constant expression evaluation optimization can move the step to compile time, so it need not become a runtime burden. The offset subscript expression should be range-checked against the number of elements in the array (lines 5-15), or else the original subscript expression can be checked against the upper (and lower) bounds of the index scalar type. It must then be multiplied by the component size to get the offset to the indexed component (lines 16-17). Finally the offset is added to the working L-expression value (line 18) to derive the new working L-expression.

Multiple-dimensioned arrays are equivalent to single-dimensioned arrays of arrays. Indeed, in Modula-2 they are explicitly so. If the language definition distinguishes a two-dimensional array from an array of arrays, the definition in the symbol table can flag which it is. Otherwise, the semantics can treat the comma in the subscript expression as if it were "`] [`" and the comma in the type denoter as if it were the words `OF ARRAY`.

6.10 Other Data Structures

Most other data structures are variations on these three basic themes. Pascal (but not Modula-2) has a file type, but the syntax and semantics are identical to pointer types. A file variable may be slightly larger than an ordinary pointer, so that hidden fields can refer to the appropriate operating system "hooks" for reading and writing, and perhaps also provide for buffering the data.

Modula-2 allows variables of type PROCEDURE to be declared. A procedure variable can be assigned to, passed as a parameter to another procedure, or simply invoked by applying it to a parameter list. A procedure variable must be large enough to hold both the address of the procedure entry point and its current parent frame pointer. Because Modula-2 allows only outer-level procedures to be assigned to variables or passed as parameters, the frame pointer is unnecessary: it will always be the global frame pointer. Other languages may require carrying the frame pointer with the procedure variable. Of course, when this is the case, the frame must not be deallocated while there are open references to it. The management of such a situation is usually considered too complex for its benefits.

Modula-2 and Pascal both have **set** types, which are implemented as a packed array of Boolean. Most computer hardware have instructions that implement set intersection and union (And and Or) on single words. When set types are allowed to grow larger than Modula-2's one-word `BitSet`, an appropriate method of programming multiple-word logical operations must be devised by the compiler designer. Because they offer no particular insight into compiler design not otherwise afforded by structures we are dealing with, and because set operators are represented in the Modula-2 or Pascal source program by overloading the arithmetic operators "*" and "+" (making syntax-directed code generation impossible), we spend no further effort on them.

6.11 Input and Output in the Itty Bitty Stack Machine

As an instructional device, the Itty Bitty Stack Machine has little need for input and output because the correct operation of small test programs can be readily verified by examining the execution trace. For larger programs, however, this could become somewhat inconvenient. Input and output in real computers are generally handled in one of two ways. Some computers have a distinctive I/O (Input/Output) address space and specialized instructions to transfer data to it. Other computers have no distinguished I/O operations, but designate a part of main memory to be considered I/O hardware transfer registers. This is called *memory-mapped* I/O. Of course any computer (including those with I/O instructions) can use memory-mapped I/O if the designer so chooses.

The IBSM is designed to simulate memory-mapped I/O. Physical memory address -1, which is outside the simulated memory address space, is a one-character I/O port. A number stored into this location is converted to a single character that is transferred to console terminal or the standard output. Fetching this address onto the stack reads a single character from the terminal keyboard or standard input file and pushes its ordinal onto the IBSM runtime stack.

As with most computers, the conversion of integers to strings of characters requires a library procedure. As this is outside the focus of this chapter, the implementation of such a procedure is left as an exercise.

6.12 Limits to Syntax-Directed Semantics

Several times in this chapter we have bumped into the edges of what can be done with syntax-directed semantics. In Chapter 5 we studied how to do type-checking by storing information about identifiers in the symbol table. We were able to handle two kinds of semantic information in this way. First, any information that must be validated with respect to the syntactic form must be organized in such a way that it is independent of the semantic kind of the identifier. Thus, we stored the *type* information in the units digit for all identifiers, regardless of whether the identifiers were for variables, types, or functions. Similarly, the *kind* of the identifiers went into the tens digit for all identifiers.

The second piece of information we can handle by syntax-directed semantics in a symbol table is that which is specific to the kind of identifier, but only to the extent that it can be uniquely determined syntactically. Type names are syntactically determined by occurring in TYPE statements and to the right of the colon in VAR and function declarations. Any identifier in one of these positions must be a type name. Similarly, we have recognized variable names syntactically by their occurrence on the left of assignments and within expressions when not followed by parentheses.

Unfortunately, in the real world of programming languages, identifiers can occur in expressions without parentheses and not be variables. They can be declared constants. In Pascal (but not Modula-2) they can be function calls. In Modula-2 a function name in an expression without parentheses is a constant (of type PROCEDURE) and is therefore not formally distinct from other constants.

It is not difficult to do adequate type-checking on constants and (in Pascal) function calls at the same time as variables, using the syntax-directed semantics of an attribute grammar. As we saw, it requires only that the type information be consistently placed in the value record in the symbol table for all kinds of identifiers. But when it comes to code generation the consistency evaporates. In our IBSM model architecture, local variables require three words of generated code — a LoadCon of the variable address, followed by the Load to fetch its value — whereas constants require just the Load of the constant value. Without a syntactic distinction to drive the semantic difference, we cannot generate the two different kinds of code appropriately.

A similar problem crops up even within variables when we allow nonlocal variables. Local variables are accessed by the simple three-word sequence, but nonlocal variables require more or less code depending on how far the variable's frame is. We evaded this problem by forcing all variable references to go through the display, at some cost in code efficiency. This is particularly the more noticeable because most procedures access only local variables, but we have forced all procedures to build the costly display and to pass all variable references through it. Chapter 8 discusses methods for designing semantics-directed code generation within an attribute grammar.

6.13 Generating Code in Hand-Coded Compilers

A one-pass recursive-descent parser differs little from the structure of the attribute grammar, as discussed already in Chapter 5. Emitting output code as character strings in an output file (represented by quoted strings within brackets) is nothing more than an appropriate WriteString procedure call in the Modula-2 code (write in Pascal). The intrinsic attribute evaluation functions number and newline correspond readily with the standard procedures WriteInt and WriteLn (write and writeln in Pascal). If code is buffered into an array data structure, the address corresponds to the subscript of the array, and the code is merely assigned to the appropriate element.

For target machines with more complex instruction sets than IBSM, the component fields of the instruction word can be composed with bit-shifting library routines available in most languages, or else by multiplying and adding as we have done here in packing symbol table values.

6.14 Applications of Syntax-Directed Semantics

Compiler design principles can be applied directly to a wide variety of programming tasks involving formally specified languages. Many programs require user input to be checked for syntactic and semantic consistency before acting on it. The consistency checking is equivalent to the front end of a compiler or interpreter, and the action taken corresponds to the back end. We examine here two different applications to see how syntax-directed semantics can facilitate their implementation. In the one case, a programming language interpreter resembles a compiler in most respects, except that the semantic actions of the back end is to run the program immediately instead of generating code for later execution. In the other case, a pretty-printer depends on syntax-driven cues to determine where line breaks and indentation belong.

6.14.1 A Tiny Basic Interpreter

To illustrate the fundamental properties of a programming language interpreter, we look at a language with no static semantics: integer-only "Tiny" Basic. The Tiny Basic that was popular in the early days of microcomputers had seven statement types and 26 predeclared variables (one letter each); the grammar in Listing 6.4 is somewhat abbreviated.

The most difficult part of implementing this interpreter is maintaining the program code in memory. A simple implementation consists of an array of fixed-length strings, indexed by line number. At startup and after executing the CLEAR command, all the strings are empty (or, less elegantly, filled with spaces). Typing a line number fills the indexed line with whatever else is in the input line. The original microcomputer Tiny Basic implementations had very limited memory: some ran in as little as 2,048 bytes of memory, including the interpreter, the Basic program, and all data space. The Basic program was stored in a character array, with the line numbers separately encoded in binary as two bytes. A reasonable compromise in a Modula-2 implementation might include a line-start array maintained in sorted line number order. Each entry in the line-start array would contain both a line number and an index into the character array. Lengths are not needed because the length of any line is just the difference between its line start index and that of the next line.

```
Comd  → Stmt                              [just do it]
      → NUM textLine                      [insert into memory in linenumber order]
      → NUM                               [remove numbered line from memory]
      → "CLEAR"                           [erase program from memory]
      → "RUN"                             [find first line in memory, and begin executing]
Stmt  → "LET" VAR "=" Expn                [pop expression stack and store into variable]
      → "IF" Expn ("=" | "<" | ">") Expn "THEN" Stmt
                         [pop two values and compare; do statement only if true]
      → "GOTO" Expn                       [pop expression stack; continue from that line]
      → "INPUT" VAR                       [accept number from terminal, store into variable]
      → "PRINT" Expn                      [pop expression and display on the terminal]
      →                                   [empty statement: do nothing]
Expn  → Term (("+"|"-") Term              [pop two; add or subtract; push result] ) *
Term  → Fact (("*"|"/") Fact              [pop two; multiply or divide; push result] ) *
Fact  → VAR                               [push value of variable]
      → NUM                               [push value of number]
      → "(" Expn ")"
```

Listing 6.4. Tiny Basic syntax grammar, with informal semantic actions.

Expression evaluation is simple using a runtime expression stack. Every reference to a variable or constant pushes its value onto the stack. Every operator pops its operands off the stack, performs the operation on the two values, then pushes the result. The IF statement evaluates the comparison, then skips the rest of the statement if the result is false. GOTO evaluates an expression, then finds the line with a line number equal to the result (it's an error if there is no such line), and continues execution with that line. The implementation is left as an exercise.

6.14.2 A Micro-Modula Pretty-Printer

Although this example shows an indented listing output as a text file, another common use for pretty-printing is in a syntax-directed text editor, where the syntax of the language controls the display on the screen. Allowing for the dynamic restructuring of the display on data entry introduces a level of complexity beyond the scope of our analysis here. For the same reason, we investigate only a few control structures, each showing some distinctive aspect of the formatting process. Listing 6.5 is the essential part of an attribute grammar for the pretty-printer.

```
declns ↓indent    →  "PROCEDURE" ID↑name ";"
                     newline ↓indent ["PROCEDURE "; spell ↓name; ";"]
                     (declns ↓indent+1)*
                     "BEGIN" newline ↓indent ["BEGIN"]
                     (stmts ↓indent+1)*
                     "END" ID↑name ";"
                     newline ↓indent ["END "; spell ↓name; ";"]
                  →  "VAR" ID↑name ":"
                     newline ↓indent ["VAR "; spell ↓name; ":"]
                     typeden ↓indent ";"   [";"];

stmts ↓indent     →  "IF" newline ↓indent ["IF "] expn ↓indent+1
                     "THEN" ["THEN"] (stmts ↓indent+1)*
                     ("ELSE" newline ↓indent ["ELSE"] (stmts ↓indent+1)* )?
                     "END"  newline ↓indent ["END"]
                     (";"  [";"]  stmts ↓indent)?
                  →  ID↑name ":="  newline ↓indent [spell ↓name; ":="]
                     expn ↓indent+1 (";"  [";"]  stmts ↓indent)?;

expn ↓indent      →  factor ↓indent+1  (operator factor ↓indent+1)*;

factor ↓indent    →  ID↑name [spell ↓name]
                  →  NUM↑value [number ↓value]
                  →  "(" ["("] expn ↓indent+1 ")"  [")"];

operator          →  "+" ["+"] | "*" ["*"] | "=" ["="] | "<" ["<"];

newline ↓indent   →  [startline] space ↓indent;    {start new line, then space over}

space ↓indent     →  [indent>0; " "] space ↓indent−1 {no space if indent=0}
                  →  [indent=0];
```

Listing 6.5. Pretty-printing Micro-Modula.

The grammar in Listing 6.5 shows no operator precedence in the expressions, because the semantic actions are not concerned with which operator it is, but only that an operator is there. It is also unconcerned with line length. A more sophisticated pretty-printer would carry a left-to-right attribute to capture the remaining space on the current line, and start a new line with an appropriate indentation — one or two steps further in if the inherited indentation attribute is less than some threshold, otherwise back out near the left margin — when there is insufficient space on the current line for the next token.

The final production of this grammar introduces a constraint that may or may not be true in its first production, namely, that the specified indentation may either be zero (at the base of the recursion) or greater than zero (while spacing over from the left margin). The code to support this decision is equivalent to the test for a lookahead symbol in an ordinary LL(1) grammar, but in this case the nonterminal containing the alternation generates the empty string. Chapter 8 develops at length the concept of semantics-driven decisions such as this one.

Summary

Compiling a source text means translating it into the machine language for a target machine. This target machine language program is called object code. One way to do the translation is to define code generation sequences in the rewrite rules of the source language grammar. This technique is known as syntax-directed code generation. When a rewrite rule is applied, the compiler invokes the appropriate code generation routine to create object code. An attribute grammar makes it possible to generate object code that depends partially on semantic information.

This chapter introduced the IBSM (Itty Bitty Stack Machine), a hypothetical computer to illustrate code generation. The grammar for the Micro-Modula language introduced in Chapter 5 (see Listing 5.2) was extended with the new code generation semantics to illustrate the techniques.

Keywords

accumulator	A register that stores data used for arithmetic or logic operations.
backpatching	In a compiler, keeping a record of each incomplete forward branch as it compiles and, when a target address becomes known, going back into the generated output code and inserting the correct value into the branch address.
compiler	A parser that also translates source text into object code.
back end	generates object code.
front end	recognizes a syntactically correct source text.
two-pass	compiler makes two passes (scans) through a source program to resolve forward references.
display	A vector (array) of frame pointers.

goto instruction	(1) A branch instruction,
	(2) An unstructured (unconditional) jump.
I/O	The common abbreviation for computer Input and Output.
lex level	In a statically scoped language, the number of containing procedures at a particular point in the source text, which can be determined at compile time.
memory-mapped	Of computer I/O, the allocation of a part of the memory address space for input and output registers.
object code	Target machine language.
orthogonality	Of computer architecture, the degree to which the addressing modes of an instruction is independent of the operation. A machine is fully orthogonal if every instruction has identical addressing modes.
register	(1) A circuit for the storage of data for a short period of time.
	(2) A kind of memory in a computer that is separately addressable and is more easily and quickly accessed than main memory.
syntax-directed code generation	Code generation sequences defined in a grammar in terms of the syntax of the language, and not selected on the basis of its static semantics.

Exercises

1. Write "assembly language" Itty Bitty Stack Machine code (mnemonics with appropriate comments) for each of the following, and hand-assemble to machine code.

(a) Given two numbers on the top of the stack, pop off (and discard) the smaller, leaving only the larger of the two.

(b) Sum the successive odd integers from 1 to n, where n is given in a variable in memory.

(c) Given an arbitrary number in a variable in memory, calculate its square root by counting the number of successive odd integers that can be subtracted from it before it goes negative. Note: $1+3=4=2^2$, $1+3+5=9=3^2$, and so on.

(d) The IBSM has no single instruction for inverting a Boolean value on the stack, that is, changing **false** (0) to **true** (1) and vice versa. Suggest two different sequences of IBSM instructions to accomplish this.

(e) Given two (local) variable addresses and a number $n>0$ on the stack, move n sequential words from one address to the other. Remove the three values from the stack when you finish. Use only the stack for temporary storage; do not use any auxiliary variables in memory. You could use this code in a compiler to do assignments of data structures.

(f) The IBSM has no instruction for dividing one number by another. Write a procedure that takes two parameters *a* and *b* and returns the quotient *a* DIV *b*. Stop if the divisor *b*=0, but give the correct result for negative *a* or *b*. The simple (but time-consuming) way is to count the number of times you can subtract the divisor from the dividend. A faster routine can calculate *a* DIV *b* by the following algorithm:

```
n := 1;
WHILE b<=a DO
  b := b+b;
  n := n+1;
  END;
q := 0;
WHILE n>0 DO
  IF a<b THEN q := q+q
  ELSE
    a := a-b;
    q := q+q+1;
    END;
  a := a+a;
  n := n-1;
  END;
RETURN q;
```

(g) Modify the code from Exercise 1f to accept a negative dividend and/or divisor also, and give correctly signed results.

2. Write a pair of procedures in some high-level language like Modula-2 to do integer I/O to a character I/O port.

(a) Input should read a particular global (integer) variable repeatedly and assemble the ASCII digits into a number returned as the function result.

(b) Output should decompose its parameter into characters one at a time, and store them into the same global variable. Do not use arrays for intermediate storage.

(c) Translate your procedures into IBSM code. Use the following sequence of IBSM operations to access the character port:

```
LoadCon    1
Negate
Global
<load or store>
```

3. Write an attribute grammar to generate correct IBSM code for a WHILE-loop.

4. (a) Write a formal attribute grammar for the semantics of Tiny Basic.

(b) Write a recursive-descent interpreter for Tiny Basic in Modula-2 or Pascal.

Review Quiz

Indicate whether the following statements are true or false.

1. Syntax-directed code generation means that code generation sequences are defined by the syntax of an acceptable source text rather than semantic analysis embedded in the grammar.

2. The back end of a compiler can be devoted exclusively to code generation.

3. In the IBSM instruction set, the operation Zero means clear memory.

4. You could use syntax-directed code generation to extend Micro-Modula so that it correctly compiles constant identifiers.

5. It is not possible to generate IBSM code that tests a condition and branches if the condition is TRUE.

Compiler Project

1. For your Itty Bitty Modula compiler grammar,

   (a) Add the necessary semantics to generate code for the IBSM. Leave out procedures for your first attempt.

   (b) Compile your compiler in the TAG compiler, or else hand-code the changes into your recursive-descent parser.

   (c) Test your compiler by compiling some small IBM programs and running them on the IBSM. Be sure nested loops and conditionals work correctly.

2. Add to your grammar the syntax and correct semantics for:

   (a) Subranges (with range-checking) and type CHAR.

   (b) Records (but do not attempt to implement the WITH statement).

   (c) Pointers.

   (d) Arrays (this requires subranges).

   (e) FOR-loops.

   (f) Parameterless functions (but do not attempt procedure variables).

   (g) Procedures with up to two parameters (do not attempt VAR parameters).

   (h) ReadChar and WriteChar intrinsic library procedures (using reserved words for the procedure names and inline code).

Further Reading

Cattell, R.G.G. "Automatic Derivation of Code Generation from Machine Descriptions." *ACM Transactions on Programming Languages and Systems*, Vol. 2, No. 2 (April 1980), pp. 173-190. The method given is based on a form of templates called tree productions, which are collected together into machine tables; during code generation, a pattern matching technique is used where nodes in a parse tree are matched against corresponding productions in the machine tables (see section 3 for description of the method).

Ganapathi, M. *Retargetable Code Generation and Optimization Using Attribute Grammars*. Ph.D. dissertation, University of Wisconsin at Madison, 1980. Extends the Graham-Glanville method into a full attribute grammar methodology (see Spector's article for overview).

Ganapathi, M. & Fischer, C.N. "Affix Grammar Driven Code Generation." *ACM Transactions on Programming Languages and Systems*, Vol. 7, No. 4 (October 1985), pp. 560-599. See section 1, especially pp. 562-563, which summarizes the affix grammar strategy.

Hopgood, F.R.A. *Compiling Techniques*. New York: American Elsevier, 1969. See ch. 8 ("Code Generation for Arithmetic Expressions"), which discusses code generation in terms of a hypothetical computer with a single accumulator.

Jacobi, C. *Code Generation and the Lilith Architecture*. Ph.D. dissertation, Swiss Federal Institute of Technology, 1951. The Lilith computer is a stack machine designed with Modula-2 oriented instruction set; see ch. 4 which discusses compiling issues.

Lukasiewicz, J. "Formalization of Mathematical Theories," Paris, 1953. In *Jan Lukasiewicz: Selected Works* ed. L. Borkowski. Amsterdam, Netherlands: North-Holland, 1970. See section 1 where Lukasiewicz introduces his parenthesis-free symbolism in the theory of numbers.

Lukasiewicz, J. *Elements of Mathematical Logic*. Oxford, Eng.: Pergamon Press, 1963. See part I.2 where Lukasiewicz explains the notation he uses in developing a parenthesis-free symbolism for the logic of propositions.

Spector, D. & Turner, P.K. "Limitations of Graham-Glanville Style Code Generation." ACM *SIGPLAN Notices*, Vol. 22, No. 2 (February 1987), pp. 100-108. See section 3.3, which introduces what is called up-down parsing (with a parsing algorithm which is completely table driven) as opposed to left-to-right parsing used by Graham-Glanville.

Chapter 7

Automated Bottom-Up Parser Design

Aims

- Consider bottom-up (shift-reduce) parsing techniques.
- Distinguish various classes of bottom-up grammars and corresponding parsers: LR(k), SLR(k), and LALR(k).
- Learn how to construct an LR(k) state machine.
- Explore LR(1) and SLR(1) state tables.
- Identify error-recovery techniques.
- Develop an LR parse table interpreter.
- Consider attribute evaluation in an LR parser.

7.1 Introduction

We have concentrated our attention thus far on top-down parser techniques because only LL(1) grammars can manually be turned into parsers with any efficiency. The technology has advanced beyond manual compiler construction, so we now turn our attention to deterministic push-down automata (PDAs) that implement a bottom-up (rightmost canonical) parse.

The stack in a top-down parser PDA can be read left to right (where the left end is the top of the stack) as in Figure 7.1a. The stack may be visualized as a cup or bottle, lying on its side so that the bottom is to the right. By considering that part of the input string already read to be attached to the left end of the stack (as if some of the contents of the cup had spilled out onto the table), the combined input and stack is a sentential form in the leftmost canonical parse. This is shown graphically in Table 7.1. Similarly, the stack of a bottom-up parser PDA, when read left to right (where the left end is the bottom of the stack, as in Figure 7.1b), with the remaining unread input considered to be attached to the right end of the stack as if it were spilled from the overturned bottle, tracks the sentential forms of a rightmost canonical parse (see Table 7.2). Note also that a top-down parse starts with the goal symbol in the stack, whereas a bottom-up parse ends with the goal symbol on the stack.

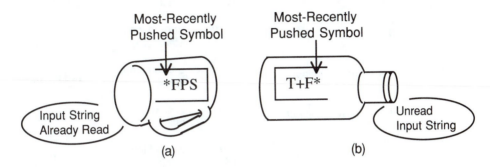

Figure 7.1. Top-down (a) and bottom-up (b) stack orientations. The strings "*FPS" and "T+F*" represent the current contents of the stack at a particular configuration in the parse (T.11 in Table 7.1 and B.8 in Table 7.2, respectively).

Consider again G_{27}, the LL(1) form of grammar G_2:

$E \rightarrow T S$	$P \rightarrow * F P$
$S \rightarrow + T S$	$P \rightarrow \epsilon$
$S \rightarrow \epsilon$	$F \rightarrow (E)$
$T \rightarrow F P$	$F \rightarrow n$

Parsing the input string $n+n*n$ in a top-down parser, the trace is shown in Table 7.1. Notice that if you read the previous input as if it were in a line with the stack (shown in step T.11), the result is a sentential form. The same string is parsed using the same grammar in a bottom-up parser PDA in Table 7.2. Here, however, the stack is on the left, and is read as if in a single line with the yet unread input string to be a sentential form (as illustrated in step B.7).

The top-down parser is sometimes also called a *predictive* parser because (except for the lookahead) it predicts what will be in the input string before it has been read. The bottom-up parser reads the input string into the stack, and applies the productions as soon as their rightparts are recognized among the top symbols of the stack.

As is the case here with this G_{27}, there are often several simultaneous opportunities during a parse to apply a production to the symbols on the top of the stack. For example, at line B.14 in Table 7.2, we chose to apply the production $S \rightarrow +TS$, although we might have as easily chosen $E \rightarrow TS$ or even $S \rightarrow \epsilon$. Like top-down parsing, we depend on occasional lookahead to help choose between available productions, or to read another

Step		Already-Read Input. Unread Input/Stack		Production
T.0	no previous input	$.n +n*n$ $.E$	unread input stack	
T.1		$.n +n*n$ $.TS$	unread input stack	$E \rightarrow T\ S$
T.2		$.n +n*n$ $.FPS$	unread input stack	$T \rightarrow F\ P$
T.3		$.n +n*n$ $.n\ PS$	unread input stack	$F \rightarrow n$
T.4	previous input	$n.+ n*n$ $.PS$	unread input stack	(read input)
T.5	previous input	$n.+ n*n$ $.S$	unread input stack	$P \rightarrow \epsilon$
T.6	previous input	$n.+ n*n$ $.+TS$	unread input stack	$S \rightarrow + T\ S$
T.7	previous input	$n+.n*n$ $.TS$	unread input stack	(read input)
T.8	previous input	$n+.n*n$ $.FPS$	unread input stack	$T \rightarrow F\ P$
T.9	previous input	$n+.n*n$ $.n\ PS$	unread input stack	$F \rightarrow n$
T.10	previous input	$n +n.* n$ $.PS$	unread input stack	(read input)
T.11	previous input	$n +n.* n$ $.*FPS$	unread input stack	$P \rightarrow * F\ P$
T.12	previous input	$n+n*.n$ $.FPS$	unread input stack	(read input)
T.13	previous input	$n+n*.n$ $.n\ PS$	unread input stack	$F \rightarrow n$
T.14	previous input	$n +n*n.$ $.PS$	stack	(read input)
T.15	previous input	$n +n*n.$ $.S$	stack	$P \rightarrow \epsilon$
T.16	previous input	$n +n*n.$ $.$	empty stack	$S \rightarrow \epsilon$

Table 7.1. Stack trace of top-down PDA showing leftmost derivation. The outline string in step T.11 is the sentential form at that step in the derivation.

Automated Bottom-Up Parser Design   Chap. 7

Step	Already-Read Input /Stack.Unread Input			Production
B.0	no previous input empty stack	$\cdot n+n*n$	unread input	
B.1	previous input stack	$n \cdot +n*n$ $n \cdot$	unread input	(read input)
B.2	previous input stack	$n \cdot +n*n$ F.	unread input	$F \to n$
B.3	previous input stack	$n \cdot +n*n$ FP.	unread input	$P \to \in$
B.4	previous input stack	$n \cdot +n*n$ T.	unread input	$T \to F\,P$
B.5	previous input stack	$n+\cdot n*n$ T+.	unread input	(read input)
B.6	previous input stack	$n+n\cdot *n$ T+n.	unread input	(read input)
B.7	previous input stack	$n+n\cdot * n$ T+F.	unread input	$F \to n$
B.8	previous input stack	$n+n*\cdot n$ T+F*.	unread input	(read input)
B.9	previous input stack	$n+n*n.$ T+F* n.		(read input)
B.10	previous input stack	$n+n*n.$ T+F*F.		$F \to n$
B.11	previous input stack	$n+n*n.$ T+F*FP.		$P \to \in$
B.12	previous input stack	$n+n*n.$ T+FP.		$P \to *\,F\,P$
B.13	previous input stack	$n+n*n.$ T+T.		$T \to F\,P$
B.14	previous input stack	$n+n*n.$ T+TS.		$S \to \in$
B.15	previous input stack	$n+n*n.$ TS.		$S \to +\,T\,S$
B.16	previous input stack	$n+n*n.$ E.		$E \to T\,S$

Table 7.2. Stack trace of bottom-up PDA showing rightmost derivation, (reading the trace from the bottom up). The outline string in step B.7 is the sentential form at that step in the derivation.

symbol from the input onto the stack instead of applying a production. Often, however, most of the information we need to decide which production to apply is contained in the parser stack. By delaying the decision of which production to apply until all of the tokens of its rightpart have been read and are represented on the stack guarantees that if a deterministic parse is possible on the basis of k lookahead symbols, then an LR(k) parser can be built. Donald Knuth showed that a finite-state automaton (FSA) can examine the stack so that a bottom-up parser PDA with no more than k lookahead symbols can deterministically choose the correct production to apply if any is possible. This FSA is the basis of all LR(k) parsers. The stack can be arbitrarily deep, and to examine all of it on every parser state transition can be somewhat tedious. Fortunately that is not necessary.

7.2 LR(k) Parsers

Consider the simple grammar, G_{41}:

$$S \rightarrow aAd \qquad A \rightarrow c$$
$$S \rightarrow bBd \qquad B \rightarrow c$$

The grammar is LL(1), so a deterministic parser is clearly possible. In parsing the string bcd with a bottom-up parse, after reading two tokens onto the stack the lookahead symbol is d, which gives no help at all in selecting a production to apply. If the parser mistakenly chooses the production $A \rightarrow c$, then it will block after reading the d, for there is no production to accommodate the string bAd, as shown in Table 7.3. Examination of the stack, however, shows that the only correct choice must be the production $B \rightarrow c$.

previous input empty stack	$\overset{.}{b}cd$	unread input	
previous input stack	$\overset{b.}{b.}cd$	unread input	(read input)
previous input stack	$\overset{bc.}{bc.}d$	unread input	(read input)
previous input stack	$\overset{bc.}{bA.}d$	unread input	$A \rightarrow c$??
previous input stack	$bcd.$ $bAd.$		(read input)
previous input stack	$bcd.$ $bAd.$		(blocks)

Table 7.3. Trace of bottom-up parse attempt for G_{41} ignoring stack contents.

Automated Bottom-Up Parser Design   Chap. 7

There are only a finite number of possible choices at any decision point, so if a deterministic parse is possible at all, a finite-state automaton can traverse and analyze the stack, yielding the decision at the end. Such an FSA for grammar G_{41} is shown in Figure 7.2. Note that G_{41} is LR(0); that is, no lookahead is required to deterministically parse all the strings in the language. Of course, the language is also finite and not very interesting.

The FSA operates as follows. Starting in state 0 at the bottom of the stack, each symbol in the stack advances one state until the top is reached. If it is a halting state, the indicated production is applied by popping off the stack all the tokens of the rightpart of the production, and replacing the nonterminal from the left. If the top of stack is reached in any other state, the next input token is read and pushed onto the stack. In either case the FSA restarted at the bottom in state 0. If the FSA blocks without reaching the top it is an error: the input string is not in the language.

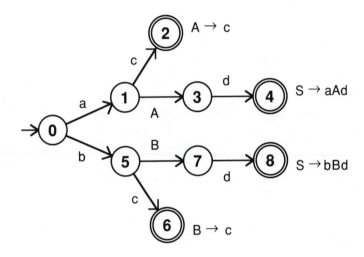

Figure 7.2. An LR(0) stack finite-state automaton for grammar G_{41}.

7.2.1 Constructing the LR(k) State Machine

The finite-state automaton that controls an LR(k) parser is constructed algorithmically from the grammar of the language. The construction is complex and tedious; no serious compiler is constructed by hand.

Each state q in the parser FSA for the language of a grammar G consists of an equivalence class of PDA configurations or *items*. An *item* is written in the form,

$$A \rightarrow u{\bullet}v;\ \sigma$$

where $A{\rightarrow}uv$ is a production in G and σ is a string of k terminals. The dot can be thought of as in some sense representing the read head of the FSA as it walks through the stack. Although intuitively helpful, this is not strictly accurate because the stack actually contains the entire left end of a sentential form, while the item only encodes a single production. An item contains one dot in its rightpart; u and v represent the (possibly empty) strings of terminals and nonterminals on the left and right, respectively, of the dot in this particular item. The string σ is derived from the $Follow_k$ set with respect to the nonterminal in this context, and is used to determine lookahead. Different classes of LR grammars are determined largely by the way σ is computed, as we shall see. The start state q_0 of the FSA is initially the set of all items

$$S \rightarrow \bullet w; \perp$$

where S is the goal symbol of G, $S \rightarrow w$ is a production, and "$\perp$" is the end-of-input token (assumed as previously to be up to k symbols long). For the grammar G_{41} the initial item set in q_0 is the set

$$S \rightarrow \bullet aAd; \perp$$
$$S \rightarrow \bullet bBd; \perp$$

Each time a new state is defined, beginning with the start state q_0, we invoke *closure* on it by adding to the item set the item

$$B \rightarrow \bullet x; y$$

for every item

$$A \rightarrow u \bullet Bv; w$$

and for every y in $First_k(vw)$, where $B \rightarrow x$ is a production in G. Closure adds no items to the initial state q_0 for G_{41}. An item set represents a state in the parser automaton, and closure captures all the possible productions from the grammar that could be applied in a derivation whose parse passes through this state in the PDA. Intuitively, it is similar in concept to constructing a nondeterministic FSA as part of the process for building an FSA from a regular grammar, although not exactly parallel. Closure essentially expands the nonterminals immediately to the right of the dot in any item in the set, reflecting the possible application of that production during the parse of a string in the language.

A transition to another state is defined by advancing the dot to the right past one symbol (terminal or nonterminal) in an item. Thus, for a given nonterminal or terminal x, each item in state q_i

$$A \rightarrow u \bullet xv; y$$

creates a new item

$$A \rightarrow ux \bullet v; y$$

in the new state q_j, and adds to the transition set of the FSA the new transition

$$\delta(q_i, x) = q_j$$

The new state is built with transitions on only one terminal or nonterminal x, and all of the transitions on x from a particular state q_i go to the same state q_j. In the example grammar G_{41} we can construct a transition on a from q_0 to q_1 based on the first item in the item set for q_0. The second item in q_0 gives rise to a transition to a different state, say q_5.

If upon closure the new state has an item list identical to an existing state q_h, then the new state is discarded and q_h is substituted for q_j in each of the new transitions. Note that duplicate states can be determined before invoking closure, if all the items added to a state by closure are so marked and the new state is identical to the unmarked items of another state. The set of unmarked items is sometimes called the *kernel*. Care must be taken to check for exact identity because it is possible that a new state may be created with more or fewer items than an otherwise identical state; these would not be considered to be the same state.

Because there are only a finite number of productions and a finite number of positions for the dot in each production, and a finite number of possible strings of length k, there is necessarily a finite number of states created by this process. The algorithm must therefore terminate.

7.2.2 An LR(2) Parser

Let us construct the FSA for an LR(2) parser that recognizes the language of grammar G_{41} above. The initial state q_0 has two items in it:

$$S \rightarrow \bullet aAd; \perp$$
$$S \rightarrow \bullet bBd; \perp$$

As we noted earlier, closure adds no items because there are no items with a nonterminal immediately following the dot. Now we create a new state q_1 by adding the transition $\delta(q_0,a)=q_1$:

$$S \rightarrow a\bullet Ad; \perp$$

This state initially has only one item because only one item in q_0 had a to the right of the dot. Because there is a nonterminal A to the right of the dot in this item, closure adds one more item from the production $A \rightarrow c$:

$$A \rightarrow \bullet c; d\perp$$

The new *Follow* string is constructed from the previous *Follow* string ($\perp$) appended to the right end of the string following the nonterminal A, which is the token d. Because we are constructing an LR(2) recognizer, we want the $First_2$ of the result, which is the whole string "$d\perp$".

We construct state q_2 by adding the transition $\delta(q_1,c)=q_2$ (closure adds no items):

$$A \rightarrow c\bullet ; d\perp$$

States q_3 and q_4 are similarly constructed from the other possible transition in q_1, and states q_5 through q_8 are constructed analogously from the second item in q_0. Note that the names of the states are quite arbitrary; we simply numbered them in the order of creation. Table 7.4 shows the result of the completed construction, which is the same FSA as Figure 7.2.

7.2.3 Apply and Shift Operations

The FSA halting states are those with an item having the dot at the right end, and that item is the production that the LR parser must apply. The top of the stack exactly matches the rightpart of the production to be applied, and it is replaced by the nonterminal of that production. This is called an *apply* or *reduce* step because the rightpart (also called the *handle*) is reduced to the nonterminal. The FSA then restarts in state q_0 at the bottom of the stack again.

We can use the table just constructed to parse the string bcd in the language of G_{41}. Beginning in state 0 (q_0) with an empty stack, the FSA is at the top of the (empty) stack but not in a "halting" state, so the b is read and pushed onto the stack. Beginning again

State	Items	Transitions
q_0	$S \rightarrow \bullet aAd; \perp$	$\delta(q_0,a)=q_1$
	$S \rightarrow \bullet bBd; \perp$	$\delta(q_0,b)=q_5$
q_1	$S \rightarrow a\bullet Ad; \perp$	$\delta(q_1,A)=q_3$
	$A \rightarrow \bullet c; d\perp$	$\delta(q_1,c)=q_2$
q_2	$A \rightarrow c\bullet ; d\perp$	apply $A \rightarrow c$
q_3	$S \rightarrow aA\bullet d; \perp$	$\delta(q_3,d)=q_4$
q_4	$S \rightarrow aAd\bullet ; \perp$	apply $S \rightarrow aAd$
q_5	$S \rightarrow b\bullet Bd; \perp$	$\delta(q_5,B)=q_7$
	$B \rightarrow \bullet c; d\perp$	$\delta(q_5,c)=q_6$
q_6	$B \rightarrow c\bullet ; d\perp$	apply $B \rightarrow c$
q_7	$S \rightarrow bB\bullet d; \perp$	$\delta(q_7,d)=q_8$
q_8	$S \rightarrow bBd\bullet ; \perp$	apply $S \rightarrow bBd$

Table 7.4. LR(2) parser states for grammar G_{41}.

in state 0, the FSA takes the transition on b to state 5, then reaches the top of the stack, requiring another read, this time pushing c onto the stack. Now we have two tokens on the stack: bc. Restarting the FSA in state 0 at the bottom again, it quickly advances to state 5 on the b, then to state 6 on the c. State 6 is a halting state, associated with the production $B \rightarrow c$, so the c is popped off the stack and replaced with the nonterminal B, leaving a new configuration with bB on the stack. This time the sequence of states from the bottom is 0-5-7. State 7 is a *read* state. That is, it does not apply a production, but rather reads the next token and pushes it onto the stack if the FSA reaches the top of the stack in that state. The FSA is started again with bBd on the stack, yielding the sequence of states 0-5-7-8. State 8 is a halting state, associated with the production $S \rightarrow bBd$, so the top three tokens are popped off the stack and replaced with the nonterminal S. S is the goal symbol, so the parser *accepts* the string.

When the FSA reaches the top of the stack without being in a halting state, it *reads* the next input symbol and pushes it onto the stack. This process is also called *shift* because the input token is shifted to the left from the input to the stack.

7.3 Conflicts

If the FSA reaches the top of the stack in a state that has apply items from two different productions, or an apply item and at least one read item (where the dot is not at the right end of the item string), then an "apply-apply" or "read-apply" conflict (often called a "shift-reduce" conflict to match the alternative terminology) has occurred. In the G_{41} example in Table 7.4 there are no such conflicts. Any apply-apply conflict in an LR(k) parser can be resolved on the basis of *Follow* sets carried along in the construction. These were constructed to be the next k symbols after each production, and because the grammar is LR(k), the conflict must be resolved. A read-apply conflict can be similarly resolved by including the $First_k$ of the string to the right of the dot in the read items. Thus, for an item

$$A \to u \bullet v; \ x$$

the lookahead set to choose to read will include $First_k(vx)$. A parser construction that fails to produce disjoint lookahead sets of k symbols for apply-apply and read-apply conflicts is not LR(k). If there are no such conflicts, then the grammar is LR(0).

7.4 Example: Conflict Resolution in G_2

For another example, illustrating some conflict resolution, let us construct an LR(1) parser for grammar G_2. We use a distinctive goal symbol G to avoid problems with recognizing the accepting state of a grammar in which the goal symbol appears on the rightpart of a production. The kernel of the initial state q_0 therefore contains one item:

$$G \to \bullet E; \ \bot$$

Closure adds all of the productions in E, T, and F, as well as some additional items due to the *Follow* of left-recursive nonterminals E and T. In the interest of a compact representation, items differing only in their *Follow* sets are collected into one line:

$$E \to \bullet E+T; \ \bot,+$$
$$E \to \bullet T; \ \bot,+$$
$$T \to \bullet T*F; \ \bot,+,*$$
$$T \to \bullet F; \ \bot,+,*$$
$$F \to \bullet(E); \ \bot,+,*$$
$$F \to \bullet n; \ \bot,+,*$$

The first transition is on the nonterminal E to state q_1. This takes the first two items (with the dot advanced) as the kernel:

$$G \to E\bullet; \ \bot$$
$$E \to E\bullet+T; \ \bot,+$$

The first item is an apply item, whereas the second is a read item. The read-apply conflict is readily resolved, however because the lookahead set for the apply item is the end of file, whereas the lookahead set for the read item is the "+" token that follows the dot. Note that the dot represents the abstract "read head" of the FSA working its way through the input, so the conflict resolution is based on the strings that follow the dot. We carry the lookahead sets after the semicolon only for those cases where the dot is less than k symbols from the end of the string. In this instance, the apply item has a dot at the right end, so it depends on the lookahead set, whereas the read item has another "+" to go (ignoring the end of file in the distant lookahead set). The two sets are therefore disjoint. The reader can verify that Table 7.5 is the complete construction, and that the other four read-apply conflicts are similarly resolved on the basis of disjoint lookahead sets.

7.5 Saving States on the Stack

It is quite inefficient to run a state machine through every symbol on the stack on each PDA step — indeed, our definition of a push-down automaton in Chapter 2 denies us that luxury. It is easily seen, however, that each move of the LR(k) PDA never pushes more

	Items	Transitions	LA
q_0	$G \rightarrow \bullet E;\ \bot$	$\delta(q_0,E)=q_1$	
	$E \rightarrow \bullet E+T;\ \bot,+$		
	$E \rightarrow \bullet T;\ \bot,+$	$\delta(q_0,T)=q_2$	
	$T \rightarrow \bullet T*F;\ \bot,+,*$		
	$T \rightarrow \bullet F;\ \bot,+,*$	$\delta(q_0,F)=q_3$	
	$F \rightarrow \bullet(E);\ \bot,+,*$	$\delta(q_0,()=q_4$	
	$F \rightarrow \bullet n;\ \bot,+,*$	$\delta(q_0,n)=q_5$	
q_1	$G \rightarrow E\bullet;\ \bot$	apply $G \rightarrow E$	$\{\bot\}$
	$E \rightarrow E\bullet+T;\ \bot,+$	$\delta(q_1,+)=q_6$	$\{+\}$
q_2	$E \rightarrow T\bullet;\ \bot,+$	apply $E \rightarrow T$	$\{\bot,+\}$
	$T \rightarrow T\bullet*F;\ \bot,+,*$	$\delta(q_2,*)=q_7$	$\{*\}$
q_3	$T \rightarrow F\bullet;\ \bot,+,*$	apply $T \rightarrow F$	
q_4	$F \rightarrow (\bullet E);\ \bot,+,*$	$\delta(q_4,E)=q_8$	
	$E \rightarrow \bullet E+T;\ ),+$		
	$E \rightarrow \bullet T;\ ),+$	$\delta(q_4,T)=q_9$	
	$T \rightarrow \bullet T*F;\ ),+,*$		
	$T \rightarrow \bullet F;\ ),+,*$	$\delta(q_4,F)=q_{10}$	
	$F \rightarrow \bullet(E);\ ),+,*$	$\delta(q_4,()=q_{11}$	
	$F \rightarrow \bullet n;\ ),+,*$	$\delta(q_4,n)=q_{12}$	
q_5	$F \rightarrow n\bullet;\ \bot,+,*$	apply $F \rightarrow n$	
q_6	$E \rightarrow E+\bullet T;\ \bot,+$	$\delta(q_6,T)=q_{13}$	
	$T \rightarrow \bullet T*F;\ \bot,+,*$		
	$T \rightarrow \bullet F;\ \bot,+,*$	$\delta(q_6,F)=q_3$	
	$F \rightarrow \bullet(E);\ \bot,+,*$	$\delta(q_6,()=q_4$	
	$F \rightarrow \bullet n;\ \bot,+,*$	$\delta(q_6,n)=q_5$	
q_7	$T \rightarrow T*\bullet F;\ \bot,+,*$	$\delta(q_7,F)=q_{14}$	
	$F \rightarrow \bullet(E);\ \bot,+,*$	$\delta(q_7,()=q_4$	
	$F \rightarrow \bullet n;\ \bot,+,*$	$\delta(q_7,n)=q_5$	
q_8	$F \rightarrow (E\bullet);\ \bot,+,*$	$\delta(q_8,))=q_{15}$	
	$E \rightarrow E\bullet+T;\ ),+$	$\delta(q_8,+)=q_{20}$	
q_{10}	$T \rightarrow F\bullet;\ ),+,*$	apply $T \rightarrow F$	
q_9	$E \rightarrow T\bullet;\ ),+$	apply $E \rightarrow T$	$\{\ ),+\}$
	$T \rightarrow T\bullet*F;\ ),+,*$	$\delta(q_9,*)=q_{16}$	$\{*\}$
q_{11}	$F \rightarrow (\bullet E);\ ),+,*$	$\delta(q_{11},E)=q_{17}$	
	$E \rightarrow \bullet E+T;\ ),+$		
	$E \rightarrow \bullet T;\ ),+$	$\delta(q_{11},T)=q_9$	
	$T \rightarrow \bullet T*F;\ ),+,*$		
	$T \rightarrow \bullet F;\ ),+,*$	$\delta(q_{11},F)=q_{10}$	
	$F \rightarrow \bullet(E);\ ),+,*$	$\delta(q_{11},()=q_{11}$	
	$F \rightarrow \bullet n;\ ),+,*$	$\delta(q_{11},n)=q_{12}$	
q_{12}	$F \rightarrow n\bullet;\ ),+,*$	apply $F \rightarrow n$	
q_{13}	$E \rightarrow E+T\bullet;\ \bot,+$	apply $E \rightarrow E+T$	$\{\bot,+\}$
	$T \rightarrow T\bullet*F;\ \bot,+,*$	$\delta(q_{13},*)=q_7$	$\{*\}$
q_{14}	$T \rightarrow T*F\bullet;\ \bot,+,*$	apply $T \rightarrow T*F$	
q_{15}	$F \rightarrow (E)\bullet;\ \bot,+,*$	apply $F \rightarrow (E)$	
q_{16}	$T \rightarrow T*\bullet F;\ ),+,*$	$\delta(q_{16},F)=q_{18}$	
	$F \rightarrow \bullet(E);\ ),+,*$	$\delta(q_{16},()=q_{11}$	
	$F \rightarrow \bullet n;\ ),+,*$	$\delta(q_{16},n)=q_{12}$	
q_{17}	$F \rightarrow (E\bullet);\ ),+,*$	$\delta(q_{17},))=q_{19}$	
	$E \rightarrow E\bullet+T;\ ),+$	$\delta(q_{17},+)=q_{20}$	
q_{18}	$T \rightarrow T*F\bullet;\ ),+,*$	apply $T \rightarrow T*F$	
q_{19}	$F \rightarrow (E)\bullet;\ ),+,*$	apply $F \rightarrow (E)$	
q_{20}	$E \rightarrow E+\bullet T;\ ),+$	$\delta(q_{20},T)=q_{21}$	
	$T \rightarrow \bullet T*F;\ ),+,*$		
	$T \rightarrow \bullet F;\ ),+,*$	$\delta(q_{20},F)=q_{10}$	
	$F \rightarrow \bullet(E);\ ),+,*$	$\delta(q_{20},()=q_{11}$	
	$F \rightarrow \bullet n;\ ),+,*$	$\delta(q_{20},n)=q_{12}$	
q_{21}	$E \rightarrow E+T\bullet;\ ),+$	apply $E \rightarrow E+T$	$\{\ ),+\}$
	$T \rightarrow T\bullet*F;\ ),+,*$	$\delta(q_{21},*)=q_{16}$	$\{*\}$

Table 7.5. LR(1) parser states for grammar G_2.

than one symbol onto the stack (although it may pop several). Thus, except for that last symbol pushed, the FSA will be retracing its steps throughout the entire stack for every PDA move. If we augment the PDA stack alphabet to include all the states of the FSA, we can insert into the stack after every symbol the FSA state upon reading that symbol, as shown in Figure 7.3. After each PDA read or apply step pushes a new symbol onto the stack, the FSA can be restarted at the state just below (to the left of) the new symbol, from whence it runs just one step, and then pushes the new state on top of the new stack symbol. The PDA is immediately ready to read or apply as indicated by the state pushed by the FSA, and the process repeats. If we now admit the states of the FSA as the states of the PDA, the new PDA matches our definition except that it is allowed to pop several symbols off the stack at once.

Tracing through the G_2 parse of the string $n+n*n$ in Figure 7.3, we observe that the top of the stack (the right-hand end) always contains the current PDA state. On line 0 the state is q_0, which is a read state. This shifts one symbol (the token n) from the input to the stack. The item list for state 0 in Table 7.5 shows an advance to state q_5 upon reading n, bringing the PDA to line 1. State q_5 is an apply state, so all of the symbols in the rightpart of the production (that is, the single n) are popped off the stack and replaced with the corresponding nonterminal F. The last correct state in the stack is the 0, so a transition on F is found in the item list of state q_0, taking the PDA to state 3 on line 2. This is repeated once, but in state q_2 (line 3) the state table calls for a lookahead. The next input symbol is "+", which selects the apply move of the PDA. On line 8 the parser is again called upon to look ahead, and the choice is to read.

	Parser Stack	Unread Next Input	Parser Move
0		0	$n+n*n$	read
1	0 n,5	+$n*n$	apply
2	0 F,3	+$n*n$	apply
3	0 T,2	+$n*n$	lookahead (+), apply
4	0 E,1	+$n*n$	read
5	0 E,1 +,6	$n*n$	read
6	0 E,1 +,6 n,5	*n	apply
7	0 E,1 +,6 F,3	*n	apply
8	0 E,1 +,6 T,13	*n	lookahead (*), read
9	0 E,1 +,6 T,13 *,7	n	read
10	0 E,1 +,6 T,13 *,7 n,5		apply
11	0 E,1 +,6 T,13 *,7 F,14		apply
12	0 E,1 +,6 T,13		lookahead ($\perp$), apply
13	0 E,1		lookahead ($\perp$), apply
14	0 G,1		accept

Figure 7.3. Parsing $n+n*n$ using G_2, leaving the FSA states in the PDA stack.

Whenever the parser is to apply a production, it is not necessary to verify or match the symbols in the stack against those in the production rightpart, for the FSA has already done that. It is sufficient only to count off the appropriate number of symbols on the stack and remove them without further ado. The top state number on the stack after an apply removes the symbols becomes the new parser state just long enough to do a "read" on the newly pushed nonterminal; that is, to find the next state from the item list of the last-revealed state code on the stack.

7.6 Other LR(k) Parsers: SLR

Although the construction for an LR(k) parser is guaranteed to build a deterministic parser if one is possible, it often results in very large state tables. A number of limitations have been devised for LR(k) languages for the purpose of pruning the table size. These are really limitations in that a grammar for which an LR(k) algorithm can construct a deterministic parser may fail under one of the these limitations. Usually, however, a grammar can be designed around the limitations, much as we did for LL(k) grammars in Chapter 4, and the limitations are generally less restrictive than those for LL(k). All variations of LR table construction use the same PDA state sequencer; they differ only in how the tables are constructed, which in turn affects the size of the tables.

In 1965 DeRemer devised a Simple LR, or SLR, parser. The SLR tables can be constructed in fundamentally the same way as LR tables, except that the *Follow* sets are not carried through the construction. Instead, whenever there is an apply-apply or read-apply conflict, the *Follow* of the relevant nonterminals (computed by the LL(k) algorithm of Chapter 4) are used directly. This has two effects. First, item lists can no longer be distinguished by their *Follow* sets. Thus, in our construction for G_2, states q_2 and q_9 would be indistinguishable and therefore not separate states. Similarly, states q_4 and q_{11} are indistinguishable. This indistinguishability propagates to the state pairs, q_8–q_{17}, q_{15}–q_{19}, q_6–q_{20}, q_{13}–q_{21}, q_3–q_{10}, q_5–q_{12}, q_7–q_{16}, and q_{14}–q_{18}. The SLR table (see Table 7.6) thus has only 12 states instead of 22. With more complex languages the reductions are even more dramatic. Now there are only three conflict states: q_1, q_2, and q_{13}. All three are read-apply conflicts, where the symbol to read is a terminal. A grammar is SLR(k) if for every read-apply conflict state with items

$$A \rightarrow x\bullet$$
$$B \rightarrow y\bullet z$$

(where A need not be a different nonterminal from B), $Follow_k(A)$ has no strings in common with $First_k(First_k(z)Follow_k(B))$, and for every apply-apply conflict state with items

$$A \rightarrow x\bullet$$
$$B \rightarrow y$$

$Follow_k(A)$ has no strings in common with $Follow_k(B)$. G_2 is therefore SLR(1) because the $Follow_1(G)$ does not contain "+" and the $Follow_1(E)$ does not contain "*".

A number of actual programming languages have unambiguous grammars that are LR(1) but not SLR(1). Although Modula-2 does not fall into this category, C is such a language. Rather than illustrate the problem within the complexity of an actual language grammar, we show it with an artificial but trivial example, G_{42}:

	Items	Transitions	LA		Items	Transitions	LA
q_0	$G\rightarrow\cdot E$	$\delta(q_0,E)=q_1$		q_2	$E\rightarrow T\cdot$	apply $E\rightarrow T$	$\{\ ),+,\perp\}$
	$E\rightarrow\cdot E+T$				$T\rightarrow T\cdot *F$	$\delta(q_2,*)=q_7$	$\{*\}$
	$E\rightarrow\cdot T$	$\delta(q_0,T)=q_2$					
	$T\rightarrow\cdot T*F$			q_6	$E\rightarrow E+\cdot T$	$\delta(q_6,T)=q_{13}$	
	$T\rightarrow\cdot F$	$\delta(q_0,F)=q_3$			$T\rightarrow\cdot T*F$		
	$F\rightarrow\cdot(E)$	$\delta(q_0,( )=q_4$			$T\rightarrow\cdot F$	$\delta(q_6,F)=q_3$	
	$F\rightarrow\cdot n$	$\delta(q_0,n)=q_5$			$F\rightarrow\cdot(E)$	$\delta(q_6,( )=q_4$	
					$F\rightarrow\cdot n$	$\delta(q_6,n)=q_5$	
q_1	$G\rightarrow E\cdot$	apply $G\rightarrow E$	$\{\perp\}$				
	$E\rightarrow E\cdot +T$	$\delta(q_1,+)=q_6$	$\{+\}$	q_7	$T\rightarrow T*\cdot F$	$\delta(q_7,F)=q_{14}$	
					$F\rightarrow\cdot(E)$	$\delta(q_7,( )=q_4$	
q_3	$T\rightarrow F\cdot$	apply $T\rightarrow F$			$F\rightarrow\cdot n$	$\delta(q_7,n)=q_5$	
q_4	$F\rightarrow(\cdot E)$	$\delta(q_4,E)=q_8$		q_8	$F\rightarrow(E\cdot)$	$\delta(q_8,))=q_{15}$	
	$E\rightarrow\cdot E+T$				$E\rightarrow E\cdot +T$	$\delta(q_8,+)=q_6$	
	$E\rightarrow\cdot T$	$\delta(q_4,T)=q_2$					
	$T\rightarrow\cdot T*F$			q_{13}	$E\rightarrow E+T\cdot$	apply $E\rightarrow E+T$	$\{\ ),+,\perp\}$
	$T\rightarrow\cdot F$	$\delta(q_4,F)=q_3$			$T\rightarrow T\cdot *F$	$\delta(q_{13},*)=q_7$	$\{*\}$
	$F\rightarrow\cdot(E)$	$\delta(q_4,( )=q_4$					
	$F\rightarrow\cdot n$	$\delta(q_4,n)=q_5$		q_{14}	$T\rightarrow T*F\cdot$	apply $T\rightarrow T*F$	
q_5	$F\rightarrow n\cdot$	apply $F\rightarrow n$		q_{15}	$F\rightarrow(E)\cdot$	apply $F\rightarrow(E)$	

Table 7.6. SLR(1) parser states for grammar G_2.

$$S \rightarrow aAa \qquad A \rightarrow c$$
$$S \rightarrow bAb \qquad B \rightarrow cb$$
$$S \rightarrow aBb$$

When you construct the tables by the SLR algorithm, you get a read-apply conflict state with the two items

$$A \rightarrow c\bullet$$
$$B \rightarrow c\bullet b$$

Over the whole grammar, $Follow_1(A)=\{a,b\}$, so the conflict cannot be resolved by appeal to the *Follow* set of nonterminal A. But if the LR algorithm is used, the local *Follow* set carried along for A at this point in the construction contains only a, so the read-apply conflict can be resolved by a single token lookahead.

7.7 LALR(*k*) Parsers

The LR tables are so much larger than SLR tables that some table-building algorithm of intermediate power is desirable. In 1969 Korenjak showed that starting with the LR(*k*) tables, we can merge each set of states with the same kernel into a single state. Because the first part of each item (that is, the part derived from the production string with the inserted dot) is the same in each case, all that is merged is the state number and the lookahead sets. The lookahead set for the merged state is the union of the lookahead sets for all the states that were merged. If the resulting state in each case has no unresolvable conflicts, the grammar is said to be LALR(k). Usually pronounced "laller" (rhymes with "valor"), the acronym paradoxically stands for "Look-Ahead LR," although logically it should be named "Look-Ahead SLR" or "Merged LR" instead. The LALR state table is the same size as SLR, but by preserving the lookahead sets through the construction, it is able to resolve some conflicts that SLR cannot.

As an example, consider again the LR(1) state table for grammar G_2 in Table 7.5. When state q_2 is merged with state q_9, the resulting state q_{29} has the same items, but the lookahead sets have been expanded to include both the end-of-string marker and the right parenthesis:

$$q_{29} \quad \begin{array}{ll} E \rightarrow T\bullet \; ; \perp,),+ & \text{apply } E \rightarrow T \quad \{\perp,),+\} \\ T \rightarrow T\bullet *F; \perp,),+,* & \delta(q_{29},*)=q_{716} \quad \{*\} \end{array}$$

Note that because states q_7 and q_{16} have been merged also, the read transition on "*" goes to the merged state q_{716}.

The LALR(1) construction applied to SLR(1) grammars gives a parser that is isomorphic to that produced by the SLR construction. It is stronger than SLR, however, because some LR(k) grammars that are not SLR(k) are LALR(k). For example, the grammar G_{42} is not SLR(1), but it is LALR(1). The following grammar, G_{43}, however, is LR(1) but neither SLR(1) nor LALR(1):

$$\begin{array}{ll} S \rightarrow aAa & S \rightarrow aBb \\ S \rightarrow bAb & S \rightarrow bBa \\ A \rightarrow c & B \rightarrow c \end{array}$$

When you construct the tables by the SLR algorithm, you get an apply-apply conflict state with the two items

$$\begin{array}{l} A \rightarrow c\bullet \\ B \rightarrow c\bullet \end{array}$$

Over the whole grammar, $Follow_1(A)=Follow_1(B)=\{a,b\}$, so the conflict cannot be resolved by appeal to the $Follow$ sets. But if the LR algorithm is used, the productions in A and B construct different local $Follow$ sets, so the apply-apply conflict can be resolved by a single token lookahead. Merging the states on the basis of their kernel items, however, returns us to the unresolvable apply-apply conflict again.

Most modern parser generators use LALR(1) table-building algorithms. There are more efficient ways to do this than by merging after building the entire LR(1) state table. In particular, each time a new state is to be created by the LR algorithm, the LALR algorithm can check to see if a merge would happen, and if so do it immediately. This means that some of the lookahead sets require extra work to propagate the lookaheads added to the merged state by the merging step. In the example of merging states q_2 and q_9 from G_2, the merger would occur as q_9 was about to be created. But q_7 would already exist as the target of the "*" from q_2, and the LALR construction would have no subsequent reason to create q_{16} as the basis of a new merger. Therefore, the right parenthesis added to the lookahead sets in the merged q_2 must also be propagated to q_7, then to states q_5 and q_4, and thence to states q_8, q_6 and q_3.

7.8 Bottom-Up Parser Implementation

There is no known equivalent to recursive descent for manual bottom-up parser implementation. In general, the parser is a table-driven state machine much like the FSAs we constructed in Chapter 3 to implement a scanner. The major implementation decisions have to do with an efficient encoding of the state table, although there are also some other ways performance can be improved.

The usual LR parser table is two-dimensional, with state number on one axis and stack alphabet symbol (that is, $\Sigma \cup N$, the set of all terminals and nonterminals) on the other. Each entry in the table is one of the following four actions:

> Read; go to state s
> Apply; pop n symbols, push nonterminal P
> Accept
> Error code e

The Read step reads one token from the input (that is, it takes the lookahead symbol, then calls the scanner to replace it), and pushes that token onto the stack with the state s. The Apply step is really a double step because after the n symbols are popped off the stack, the top state on the stack is given the nonterminal P to "read." Thus, P is pushed with a new state as if it had been read, although the input is not affected. The Accept step terminates the parse.

All other entries in the table are filled with Error actions, which report that the input string is not in the language. It is considered good form for the implementer of a compiler to go to considerable effort to make intelligible error messages, so that the user is not faced with a single universal and uninformative SYNTAX ERROR for every possible coding mistake.

Bottom-up parsers are usually constructed automatically by parser generators, so the state machine that interprets the tables is generally a part of the parser skeleton that is copied to each generated parser without significant change. Listing 7.1 gives Modula-2 code for a typical parser machine.

7.9 Error Recovery

Hitherto when our parsers have encountered a syntax error in the input source code, the response has been to "crash and burn," that is, to abandon compilation, report the error, and quit. In the past this was considered somewhat abusive of the typical user, who only got one or two compilation attempts each day on a batch mainframe computer. A compiler that attempted to recover gracefully and to continue parsing as much of the input source as possible had a better chance of enabling the programmer to correct several errors before resubmitting the program for recompilation. Accordingly, considerable research has gone into the analysis of the most frequent coding errors. This analysis not only aids the compiler designer in increasing the probability of recovery from syntax errors, but also aids in the creation of informative error messages, so that the user can more easily make appropriate corrections.

```
FROM Somewhere
   IMPORT MaxStateNo, MaxStack, NTToken,              (* CONSTs, TYPE, VAR *)
      Nextoken, Getoken, Error, GetTheTable;                  (* PROCEDUREs *)
TYPE
   ActionCode = (ReadStep, ApplyStep, Accept, ErrorOff);
VAR
   StackTop: INTEGER;
   Done: BOOLEAN;
   theTable: ARRAY [0..MaxStateNo],NTToken OF RECORD
       theAction: ActionCode;
       Semantics: INTEGER;
       NewNT: NTToken; END;
   theStack: ARRAY [0..MaxStack] OF RECORD
       Symbol: NTToken;
       State: INTEGER; END;
PROCEDURE Parser;
BEGIN
   StackTop := 0;                                    (* Initialize stack *)
   theStack[StackTop].State := 0;
   Done := FALSE;
   GetTheTable(theTable);        (* probably by block read from disk *)
   REPEAT
     WITH theTable[theStack[StackTop].State][Nextoken] DO
       CASE theAction OF
         ReadStep:
           INC(StackTop);                            (* push stack... *)
           WITH theStack[StackTop] DO
             Symbol := Nextoken;                     (* push new token *)
             State := Semantics;                     (* with new state *)
             Getoken                 (* read next lookahead symbol *)
             END (* with *)
       | ApplyStep:
           StackTop := StackTop - Semantics + 1;    (* pop rtpart *)
           WITH theStack[StackTop] DO
             Symbol := NewNT;             (* push nonterminal + state *)
             State := theTable[theStack[StackTop-1]
                .State][NewNT].Semantics;
             END (* with *)
       | Accept:                                 (* = finding goal on top *)
           Done := TRUE
       | ErrorOff:                            (* = finding no read or apply *)
           Error(Semantics);
           Done := TRUE
         END (* Case *)
     END (* With *)
   UNTIL Done
END Parser;
```

Listing 7.1. LR parser table interpreter.

Syntax errors most often consist of single token (or single character) faults in three varieties: missing token, superfluous token, and substituted token. An error recovery heuristic might attempt to supply a missing token, skip over an extra one, or substitute a more appropriate token for one that parses incorrectly. The most care must be exercised in supplying missing tokens. If tokens continue to be inserted, the parser may merely loop in the error states and never read any more input — clearly an inappropriate response. Usually if a single insertion fails to correct the problem so that input can be successfully parsed, the missing token hypothesis must be abandoned.

A variation on the error recovery heuristic that discards superfluous tokens is called "Panic Mode" as it discards tokens willy-nilly until a recognizable production boundary is encountered — usually a semicolon. The stack must also be flushed, so that the parser can resume in the apply state for the StatementList production. This recovery method typically passes over some (usually small) part of the source file before resuming its parse of the input at the next statement after the actual error.

The most sophisticated error recovery technique is called "forward move" by Pennello [Pennello&DeRemer, 1978]. Error productions are added to the grammar, and the parser generator creates error recovery states that attempt to read and discard tokens and apply productions until something works.

With the advent of personal interactive workstations and instant response time, the trend is away from sophisticated error recovery in favor of a crash-and-burn termination that drops the user into a program editor positioned at the token where the error was discovered. Very fast compilation times make this quite practical because the user can request a compilation and have the next error reported in a time comparable to the normal search for an embedded error message in the program listing.

It should be noted that the canonical $LR(k)$ table construction gives the quickest detection of a syntax error. LALR — and to a greater extent SLR — tables cause the parser to advance several states, possibly through several apply steps, before the error is detected. Normally, however, the syntax error will be discovered before reading any more input; this is always true in the case of LALR. In all three constructions the parser will correctly detect erroneous strings; the only difference lies in how quickly they are detected.

7.10 Attribute Evaluation in an LR Parser

It is much more difficult to see intuitively the flow of attribute values in a bottom-up parse than in a top-down parse. As mentioned in Chapter 5, only synthesized and left-to-right inherited attributes can be evaluated during a parse. Attribute values can be added to the stack alphabet of the PDA, or a secondary stack can be defined to hold attribute values. These would be allocated space in a stack frame much like compiled code to manage local variables in a block-structured language.

Attribute evaluation must generally take place during the apply step of the LR-parser machine. At that time the synthesized attributes can be calculated directly from the synthesized attributes of the terminals and nonterminals in the rightpart of the production being applied. Those synthesized attributes being passed on up the parse tree can be stored in the newly created stack frame for the nonterminal being pushed onto the parser stack at that time.

Inherited attributes are much more difficult to implement because it cannot in general be known which nonterminal they were inherited from. In a top-down parse the inherited attributes were assembled in the parent node of the parse tree, but in a bottom-up parse that node does not yet exist. It is likely that the only practical way to pass left-to-right inherited attributes from nonterminal to nonterminal is to construct a packet containing slots for all possible inherited attributes in all possible nonterminals, then to propagate that packet through the parser stack as the stack is built. Each apply step that synthesizes a new attribute value that has a place in the packet puts the new value into the packet before passing the new copy up the stack to the next terminal or nonterminal. Tokens and nonterminals that do not affect any attributes in the packet merely pass a copy unmodified. Ordinarily the packet should not be very large because only a few attributes — typically just the symbol table — require propagation in this way. Figure 7.4 illustrates this process for a single left-to-right attribute in the packet.

$$A\downarrow x_{in}\uparrow x_{out}\rightarrow a\ B\downarrow x_{in}\uparrow x_{temp}\ a \qquad [\ x_{out}=1+x_{temp}\ ]$$

$$B\downarrow x_{in}\uparrow x_{out}\rightarrow b \qquad\qquad\qquad [\ x_{out}=2+x_{in}\ ]$$

Stack:	$\ldots^3a^3b^3$	←Packet values
Stack:	$\ldots^3a^3B^5$	apply $B\rightarrow b$
Stack:	$\ldots^3a^3B^5a^5$	read a
Stack:	$\ldots^3A^6$	apply $A\rightarrow aBa$

Figure 7.4. Attribute evaluation in a bottom-up parse.

Most table-driven parsers collect all the semantic actions into a large CASE statement, indexed by a number stored in the parser table. Where modularity dictates individual procedures for the semantic actions, the CASE statement items will be appropriately parameterized procedure calls. The relative novelty of attribute grammars for specifying compiler semantics and the difficulty of correctly handling arbitrary attribute information flow in a bottom-up parser tend to limit the availability of attribute grammar compiler generators. The most widely used parser generator, YACC, relegates all semantic actions to C code embedded in the grammar.

Summary

The largest class of languages that can be parsed deterministically requires a bottom-up parsing technique. Contrasted with top-down parsing (which derives a sentence in the language by starting at the goal symbol and constructing the parse tree top-down until the frontier of the tree is reached), bottom-up parsing builds the parse tree from the bottom (the frontier, or sentence), working its way upward to the root of the tree.

Bottom-up parsing uses a push-down list (stack). It pushes (shifts) input symbols onto the stack until a handle appears on the top of the stack. A handle is a substring that matches the right-hand side of a rewrite rule in the grammar being used to derive a string. As soon a handle appears on the top of the stack being used by the bottom-up parser, it is reduced by replacing it with the nonterminal from the left-hand side of that rewrite rule. So long as no errors occur, bottom-up parsing continues until all of an input string has been scanned and only the goal symbol remains on the stack.

The LR parsing method introduced by Knuth in 1965 is most general. An LR(k) parser scans its input from left to right and generates an inverse rightmost derivation that needs at most k lookahead symbols to make a parsing decision. Unfortunately, the tables produced during an LR parse proved to be too large for grammars defining actual programming languages. This problem was solved by DeRemer in 1969 with the introduction of SLR (Simple LR) parsers. DeRemer noticed that it was sometimes possible to merge rows of an LR parse table. The large LR parse table problem was solved in another way by Korenjak in 1969 with the introduction of Lookahead LR parsing (LALR). This chapter explored both SLR and LALR parsing techniques. It concluded with an examination of attribute evaluation in an LR parser.

Keywords

apply step	A step in the operation of a bottom-up parser that reduces the handle on the top of the stack to a nonterminal by applying one rewrite rule from the grammar.
bottom-up parsing	In a parser of a context-free grammar, following the rightmost canonical derivation in reverse to construct the parse tree, starting with a string in the language and reducing it to the goal symbol.
handle	A string of terminals and nonterminals on the top of the bottom-up parser stack that matches the the right-hand side of rewrite rule (production) in the grammar.
item	A copy of one rewrite rule in a grammar, modified to contain a dot representing the read head of an FSA in the construction of a bottom-up parser.
closure	adds to an item list all the productions of the grammar for nonterminals where items already in the item list have a dot just to the left of that nonterminal. If A$\rightarrow u{\cdot}Bv$ is an item in the list, then closure would add items of the form B$\rightarrow{\cdot}w$ where B$\rightarrow w$ is a production in the grammar.
complete item	has the dot as its rightmost symbol.
kernel	is those items in the construction of an LR(k) parser state that are derived from advancing the dot across a symbol, before applying the closure operation. Two item sets can be compared for identity by comparing only their kernels.

LALR(k)	Lookahead LR(k) grammar, in which the lookahead set for a merged state is the union of the lookahead sets for all states that were merged.
LR(k) grammar	A grammar for which a parser that does a left-to-right scan of the input string, traversing the rightmost canonical derivation in reverse, can be made deterministic by looking ahead at most k symbols in the input stream.
LR(k) parser	A parser constructed from an LR(k) grammar.
LR parsing	See bottom-up parsing.
merged state	A state in the construction of a LALR(k) parser resulting from combining the items in two LR(k) states that differ only in their lookahead sets.
panic mode	An error recovery heuristic that discards tokens from the input stream until a recognizable rewrite rule boundary is found.
predictive parser	A top-down parser.
read step	A step in the operation of a bottom-up parser that reads the next input symbol and shifts (pushes) it onto the top of the stack.
reduce step	An apply step.
shift step	A read step.
SLR(k)	A grammar for a language that can be recognized by an SLR(k) parser, which is constructed by ignoring the lookahead sets in an LR(k) construction, and using the $Follow_k$ sets for read-reduce conflict resoution.
top-down parser	The parser of a context-free grammar follows the leftmost canonical derivation to construct the parse tree, starting with the goal symbol and expanding it to the string of the language that is its input. Also called a predictive parser.

Exercises

1. Using grammar G_{42} (given in Section 7.6), which defines a language L, give

   (a) a rightmost derivation of a string belonging to L;

   (b) an example of an item;

   (c) the parser states constructed using the SLR algorithm along with an indication of any states where a read-apply conflict occurs;

   (d) the parser states constructed using the LR algorithm.

   (e) a comparison of the state tables for parts (c) and (d).

2. Identify

   (a) the kernels in the state table for part (c) of Exercise 1;

   (b) the kernels in Table 7.5.

3.   Consider the grammar $(\{a,b\}, \{S,A\}, P, S)$ where P is the set of productions

      $S \rightarrow aS \mid bAS \mid a$
      $A \rightarrow abA \mid a \mid b$

Determine if this grammar is

(a) LR(k) for some k (indicate the value of k, if so) or

(b) SLR(k) for some k or

(c) LALR(k) for some k or

(d) LL(k) for some k.

4.   Show that the grammar with the following productions is LALR(k) for some k and indicate the value of k:

      $S \rightarrow Aa \mid dAb \mid cb \mid dca$
      $A \rightarrow c$

5.   Determine if the grammar of Exercise 4 is also SLR(k) for the same value of k, or else show at least one read-apply conflict state in it, that cannot be resolved by $Follow_k$.

6.   Show that not all LALR(k) grammars are LL(k) by finding an example of a grammar that is LALR(k) but not LL(k).

7.   Show that not all LL(k) grammars are LALR(k).

8.   Show that not all LR(0) grammars are SLR(0).

9.   Show that every LL(k) grammar is also an LR(k) grammar.

Review Quiz

Indicate whether the following statements are true or false.

1.   An apply step is the same as a reduce step in an LR parse.

2.   During an LR parse, if the next input symbol is read and shifted, then the input symbol which has been read is popped from the top of the stack.

3.   Not every LALR(k) grammar is an SLR(k) grammar.

4.   Not all SLR(k) grammars are LALR(k) grammars.

5.   An LR(k) grammar is a context-free grammar.

6.   Every LL(k) grammar is an LR(k) grammar.

7.   The grammar with the following productions is LR(0):

      $A \rightarrow Ax$ $A \rightarrow x$

8.   The grammar with the following productions is LR(1):

      $A \rightarrow AaAb$ $A \rightarrow \in$

9.   A grammar is LR(k) if we can determine the handle of each right sentential form a during a rightmost derivation and identify which nonterminal is to replace the handle by scanning a from right to left and going at most k symbols beyond the right end of the handle.

Compiler Project

1. Construct the SLR(1) parser table for your Itty Bitty Modula grammar, leaving semantic actions out. Using a state machine similar to Listing 7.1, test your parser on some tiny Itty Bitty Modula source programs. Verify that syntactically incorrect programs are rejected.

2. Add semantics to your bottom-up parser, following the attribute grammars you developed in Chapters 5 and 6.

3. Design a LALR(1) parser generator. Write an LL(1) attribute grammar for its input and compile it on the TAG compiler, then compile the grammar on your parser generator.

Further Reading

Aho, A.V. & Ullman, J.D. *The Theory of Parsing, Translation, and Compiling; Vol. 2: Compiling.* Englewood Cliffs, NJ: Prentice-Hall, 1973. See section 7.4.1, pp. 622-627, which presents SLR(k) grammars and theory; see section 7.4.2, pp. 627-645, on LALR(k) grammars.

Bermudez, M.E. & Schimpf, K.M. "On the (Non-) Relationship Between SLR(1) and NQLALR(1) Grammars." ACM *Transactions on Programming Languages and Systems*, Vol. 10, No. 2 (April 1988), pp. 338-342. The NQ in NQLALR stands for "not quite." NQLALR grammars were introduced by DeRemer and Pennello in 1982 and are based on similar relations that relate states rather than nonterminal transitions. Bermudez and Schimpf show that SLR(1) grammars are not a subset of NQLALR(1) grammars.

DeRemer, F.L. "Simple LR(k) Parsing." *Communications of the ACM*, Vol. 14, No. 7 (1969), pp. 453-460. Introduces SLR parsing method.

DeRemer, F.L. & Pennello, T. "Efficient Computation of LALR(1) Look-Ahead Sets." ACM *Transactions on Programming Languages and Systems*, Vol. 4, No. 4 (October 1982), pp. 615-649. Introduces NQLALR(1) grammars (see Bermudez and Schimpf), which were thought to contain all SLR(1) grammars.

Hopcroft, J.E. & Ullman, J.D. *Introduction to Automata Theory, Languages, and Computation.* Reading, MA: Addison-Wesley, 1979. See section 10.6 on LR(0) grammars, especially pp. 248-252.

Ives, F. "Unifying View of Recent LALR(1) Lookahead Set Algorithms." ACM *SIGPLAN Notices*, Vol. 21, No. 7 (July 1986), pp. 131-135.

Knuth, D.E. "On the Translation of Languages from Left to Right." *Information and Control*, Vol. 8, No. 6 (1965), pp. 607-639.

Korenjak, A.J. "A Practical Method for Constructing LR(k) Processors." *Communications of the ACM*, Vol. 12, No. 11 (1969), pp. 612-623. Introduces LALR parsing method.

Pennello, T.J. "Very Fast LR Parsing." ACM *SIGPLAN Notices*, Vol. 21, No. 7 (July 1986), pp. 145-151, containing *Proceedings of the SIGPLAN 1986 Symposium on Compiler Construction*. Reports a parsing speed of one-half million lines per minute (up from 40,000 lines per minute) on a computer similar to a VAX 11/780. The improvement was obtained by translating the parser's finite state control into assembly language.

Pennello, T.J. & DeRemer, F.L. "A Forward Move Algorithm for LR Error Recovery." *Fifth Annual ACM Symposium on Principles of Programming Languages* (1978), pp. 241-254.

Chapter

Transformational
Attribute Grammars

Aims

- Introduce tree-transformational grammars.
- Investigate the use of tree grammars in transforming abstract syntax trees into trees with different shapes.
- Distinguish between translation grammars and transformational grammars.
- Introduce transformation attribute grammars (TAGs), which are tree grammars as well as attribute grammars.
- Introduce a simplified approach to attribute evaluation order.
- Indicate how to link the string grammar of a compiler front-end to the tree grammar that specifies optimization and code generation.
- Investigate code optimization by transformation.
- Show how to use attribute grammars for data-flow analysis.
- Give a survey of useful transformational optimizations.

8.1 Introduction

Although we introduced abstract syntax trees (ASTs) in Chapter 1 as a conceptual representation of the syntactic structure of the input source program being compiled, we also noted that compilers often do not actually *build* an AST. In this chapter we study some circumstances where it is desirable to construct a data structure in memory representing the AST.

8.2 Program Representation as Trees

As the name implies, an abstract syntax tree abstracts from the source program just the syntactic structure, without preserving the spelling of the identifiers or keywords, nor the placement of spaces, line breaks, and comments. Thus, in Figure 8.1, the Modula-2 IF-THEN-ELSE-END statement is represented abstractly exactly the same as the Pascal **if-then-else** (except that the subtrees may differ slightly in form). This node connects three program fragments represented as subtrees. The first subtree represents a Boolean expression to be evaluated; the second a statement or sequence of statements to be executed if the evaluated expression is true; and the third is another statement sequence to be executed if the expression is false. Of course the two statement subtrees may themselves be conditional nodes, as well as assignments or other imperatives.

The AST differs from the parse tree in two important respects. First, as we already mentioned, the reserved words and the spelling of the identifiers and constants are gone, leaving only enough to label the structure nodes. In Figure 8.1 this is illustrated by eliminating the reserved words THEN, ELSE, and END, as well as the punctuation and the spelling of identifiers a, b, and anysubroutine.

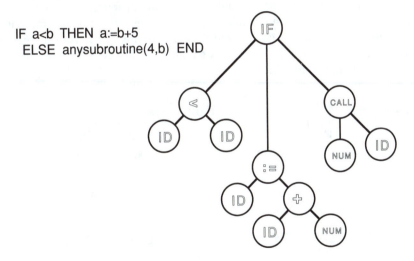

```
IF a<b THEN a:=b+5
   ELSE anysubroutine(4,b) END
```

Figure 8.1. Tree representation of a program fragment.

Second, and more important, is the fact that grammar nonterminals without any semantic actions have been eliminated. In our example in Figure 8.1, there is no reference to the nonterminals Expression or Factor, although they surely were involved in parsing all the expressions. The nonterminal Term is only represented in the node labeled "+", and then only because it results in the semantic action of addition. The AST abstracts only that part of the syntactic structure that preserves the program semantics. A tree-walking automaton could walk the AST, generating code as it visits each node (typically in postorder, but there are significant exceptions), and the generated code would be identical to that produced by a recursive-descent attribute grammar as in Chapter 6.

If our sole purpose were to separate the parsing and code generation, an AST would be a reasonable representation for intermediate code. Once we bring significant code optimization into the picture, an AST is indispensable. This is because many optimizations are most easily performed by transforming (reshaping) the AST.

8.3 Tree-Transformational Grammars

As this text has continuously emphasized the importance of grammars in compiler design, it should come as no surprise that tree transformation is also most easily specified by a grammar; we call such a grammar a *tree-transformational grammar* or TTG. TTGs are a subset of the larger class of tree grammars.

A tree grammar is distinguished from the grammars we have seen so far in that its input alphabet consists of tree nodes and their connections rather than ASCII characters or scanned tokens in a linear string. Because a tree is a two-dimensional structure, the tree grammar must recognize the node structure and not just a linear string of tokens, although we typically represent trees in a prefix Polish notation for writing the productions of the grammar. Figure 8.2 shows a fragment of a tree grammar for recognizing expression trees. Note that this grammar unambiguously shows operator hierarchy without using parentheses or intermediate nonterminals because that is inherent in the tree structure. By this grammar, an expression consists either of an identifier or number leaf node, or else a simple operator node with two expression subtrees. Figure 8.3 shows an expression generated by this grammar.

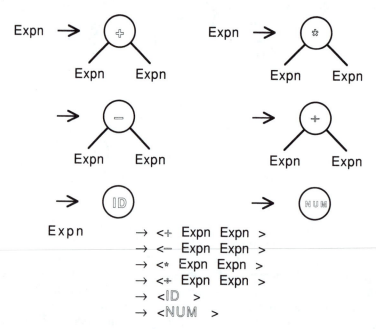

Figure 8.2. A tree grammar fragment for expressions, shown both graphically and in text.

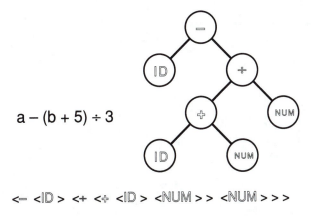

$$a - (b + 5) \div 3$$

<= <ID > <+ <÷ <ID > <NUM > > <NUM > > >

Figure 8.3. An expression tree generated by the grammar of Figure 8.2.

It is not particularly useful in compiler construction merely to recognize (that is, parse) abstract syntax trees generated by a tree grammar. We want to be able to *transform* them into trees with different shapes. Consider the expression tree in Figure 8.3, and suppose that the compiler discovered that the identifier b is declared as a constant 4. The tree could be optimized by transforming the ID node into a NUM node, then replacing any operator node over two NUM nodes with a single NUM leaf node, after computing an appropriate new constant value for it. Figure 8.4 illustrates the steps of this transformation. Figure 8.5 shows a simple TTG for constant folding, which is the evaluation of constant expressions during compilation.

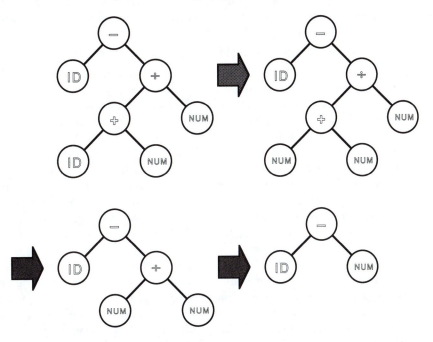

Figure 8.4. Optimizing the expression tree by transforming it.

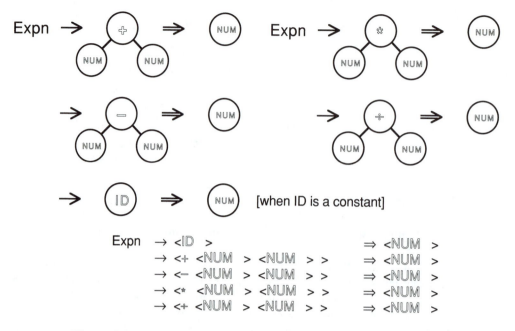

Expn → <ID >   ⇒ <NUM >
     → <+ <NUM > <NUM > >   ⇒ <NUM >
     → <− <NUM > <NUM > >   ⇒ <NUM >
     → <* <NUM > <NUM > >   ⇒ <NUM >
     → <÷ <NUM > <NUM > >   ⇒ <NUM >

Figure 8.5. A simple tree-transformation grammar for constant folding.

A *transformational grammar* T is a context-free grammar G in which every production has two rightparts containing the same nonterminal references, although possibly not in the same order. The second rightpart of each production is indicated by the double arrow ⇒ to its left, separating it from the first rightpart. A production in a transformational grammar might abstractly look something like this:

nonterminal → "first" rightpart ⇒ "second" rightpart

If all the second rightparts are removed, what remains is an ordinary CFG defining what we call the *input language*; if all the first rightparts are removed and the double arrows converted to single arrows, what remains is still an ordinary CFG, defining an *output language*. When a parser constructed to recognize the input language applies a particular production in the grammar, the subtree matched by the rightpart of that production can be replaced by the corresponding rightpart of the same production in the output language, thereby transforming the input language to the output language. The first rightpart is sometimes called the *match template*, and the second rightpart is called the *generator template*. We require a one-to-one correspondence of nonterminals in the two rightparts or templates so that as the parser recursively walks the AST, every nonterminal has a place in the output language. Terminals in the input and output languages have no need for correspondence.

It is not hard to see that the semantic actions of our code generator attribute grammars could easily be written as transformational grammars, where the second rightpart encodes the terminals quoted within the brackets of our notation. Indeed, if we had no need for nonlocal optimization, this would be a natural and effective notation. We shall not attempt to do so, however, but rather go directly to the full power of tree-transformational attribute grammars.

The original work in using attribute grammars for specifying compiler optimizations by transformations of programs represented as trees was done by Eickel, Ganzinger, Giegerich, Ripken, and Wilhelm in development of the MUG2 compiler generator at the Munich Technical University in 1975 [Madsen, 1975]. By 1983, MUG2 had been developed into a complete compiler generator based on attribute grammars. MUG2 uses abstract syntax trees and attributed tree transformations to handle attribute evaluation. In MUG2, an attribute is identified with information attached to the code tree by grammar-specified transformations. This information amounts to special leaf-nodes in the program tree, not attributes in Knuth's sense [Knuth, 1968]. In the United States, the Syntax and Semantics Analysis and Generation System developed by T.F. Payton at Burroughs in 1982 uses tree-transformational grammars in mapping input grammar trees to output grammar trees. Payton's system translates a TTG into an attribute grammar performing the translation and generates the corresponding evaluator [Payton, 1982].

8.3.1 Nongenerative Grammars

Although a fully specified transformational grammar generates both an input language and a possibly very different output language, efficient compilers should not be spending a lot of time walking and transforming trees when no transformation is necessary, that is, when the second rightpart is the same as the first. We distinguish therefore between *translation* grammars that fully generate both the input and output languages, and *transformational* grammars where the input and output languages are essentially the same language. Both translation and transformation grammars have two sets of rightparts, but in transformational grammars (TTGs) we omit productions that transform a tree into itself. Figure 8.5 shows a TTG and not a translation grammar, because it specifies how to transform an operator node over two constants, but not how to transform an operator node over one or more identifiers, nor does it give the circumstances for leaving an identifier unchanged. The transformation in Figure 8.4 appears to apply the transformations opportunistically, wherever there is a template match, and early research compilers constructed from TTGs did just that. We will use a deterministic algorithm for seeking tree transformation opportunities, based on the transformational attribute grammar from which the compiler is constructed.

A *transformational attribute grammar* (TAG) is a tree-transformational grammar that is also an attribute grammar. That is, with each nonterminal in the grammar, zero or more attributes are defined. Both synthesized and inherited attributes are possible, so the attribute evaluation order imposes some restrictions on the grammar: isolated nonterminals cannot pass any attributes up or down the tree. Therefore, we require that although TAGs need not be fully generative, they must generate a tree with the same root as the full program tree and missing only entire subtrees. A TAG cannot generate a disconnected tree, nor any tree part not reachable from the root. A tree-transformational attribute grammar, therefore, is a 6-tuple (Σ, N, P, S, A, E), where

Σ	is an alphabet of tree node names (terminals),
N	is a set of nonterminals,
P	is a set of productions,
S	is a goal symbol associated with the root node of the tree,

A	is a set of attributes, such that each attribute is associated with exactly one nonterminal, and is specified to be either synthesized or inherited, and
E	is a set of assertions restricting and defining the values for the attributes in each production.

Each production in a TAG has five parts:

$$n \text{ "}\rightarrow\text{" } t1 \; s1 \text{ "}\Rightarrow\text{" } t2 \; s2$$

where

n	is a nonterminal, a member of N,
$t1,t2$	are tree templates, witten in text as i ":" "<" σ t_k* ">" "%" e where

        i is an (optional) identifier naming this subtree,

        σ is a member of the node name set Σ, and

        t_k is another subtree template in the same notation, and

        e is an optional tree "decoration" to be defined later.

        The literal symbols ":" and "%" serve to indicate the presence of the optional components associated with them, and the literal symbols "<" and ">" work like parentheses to delimit the tree node and its subtrees.

$s1,s2$	are sequences of semantic actions enclosed in brackets and nonterminal references prefixed by the names of the subtrees to which they apply.

The full grammar specifying a TAG as used in this book is given in Appendix B. At this time we are concerned mainly with its general form.

8.3.2 A TAG Example

As an example, let us examine a small TAG to transform an expression tree by pruning constant subexpressions. It will be organized roughly as in Figure 8.5, but now we add attribute assertions and complete the productions to make the grammar fully generative, as shown in Listing 8.1. We assume that all identifiers are defined in an inherited symbol table.

The grammar walks the expression tree first to discover the constant subtrees. Rather than waste a lot of time pruning subtrees that are parts of larger constant subtrees, a synthesized attribute is carried up to indicate that a subtree is constant (or not), and at the point that an operator joins a constant with a nonconstant, the constant is folded into a NUM node by sending that subtree to the nonterminal Xform. This nonterminal does not walk the whole subtree, but transforms it immediately, replacing it with a constant node, unless it is already one. In this grammar there is no need to define both the shape and name of any tree. The tree templates in the productions are anonymous, and their subtrees are named but show no structure.

Two different kinds of nodes are shown in Listing 8.1 with decorations. Identifier nodes are decorated with their name as found in the symbol table; this permits their properties to be extracted when they are needed. Constant nodes are decorated with their numerical value. The values of constant subexpressions are constructed from the values decorating constant nodes and the values of constant identifiers as found in the symbol table. When a subtree is transformed, the new constant node is decorated with the appropriate composite value.

8.3.3 Evaluation Order

In the constant folding example of Listing 8.1, one nonterminal (Expn) gathers information that enables the decision to transform or not, but another nonterminal (Xform) does the transformation. This is a common and reasonable division of labor.

Expn ↓symbol ↑iscon ↑value
    →   <Plus left rite >
            rite: Expn ↓symbol ↑iscon2 ↑value2
            left: Expn ↓symbol ↑iscon1 ↑value1
            ([iscon1=true; iscon2=false; iscon=false] left: Xform ↓value1
            | [iscon2=true; iscon1=false; iscon=false] rite: Xform ↓value2
            | [iscon1=iscon2; iscon=iscon1; value=value1+value2])

    →   <Minus left rite >
            rite: Expn ↓symbol ↑iscon2 ↑value2
            left: Expn ↓symbol ↑iscon1 ↑value1
            ([iscon1=true; iscon2=false; iscon=false] left: Xform ↓value1
            | [iscon2=true; iscon1=false; iscon=false] rite: Xform ↓value2
            | [iscon1=iscon2; iscon=iscon1; value=value1−value2])

    →   <Star left rite >
            rite: Expn ↓symbol ↑iscon2 ↑value2
            left: Expn ↓symbol ↑iscon1 ↑value1
            ([iscon1=true; iscon2=false; iscon=false] left: Xform ↓value1
            | [iscon2=true; iscon1=false; iscon=false] rite: Xform ↓value2
            | [iscon1=iscon2; iscon=iscon1; value=value1*value2])

    →   <Divd left rite >
            rite: Expn ↓symbol ↑iscon2 ↑value2
            left: Expn ↓symbol ↑iscon1 ↑value1
            ([iscon1=true; iscon2=false; iscon=false] left: Xform ↓value1
            | [iscon2=true; iscon1=false; iscon=false] rite: Xform ↓value2
            | [iscon1=iscon2; iscon=iscon1; value=value1/value2])

    →   <ID >%name
            [from ↓symbol ↓name ↑iscon ↑value]

    →   <NUM >%value
            [iscon=true] ;

Xform ↓value
    → <Plus left rite > | <Minus left rite > | <Star left rite > | <Divd left rite >
    ⇒ <NUM >%value

    → <ID >%name
    ⇒ <NUM >%value

    → <NUM >%value ;   *{no change here}*

Listing 8.1. A simple TAG for constant folding.

Note that Xform does its transformation unconditionally when presented with a node that is not already a constant. The nonterminal Expn will invoke Xform only if it has a constant expression to transform.

In this example the order of information flow during the gathering phase is largely bottom-up, without regard to left-right order. More often there is an inherent flow of information from left to right, or from right to left. Later in this chapter we will examine specific examples of both kinds. When we introduced attribute grammars, we looked at several grammars that required right-to-left or mixed information flow. In the context of a recursive-descent or bottom-up parser, these are simply not practical, but a tree grammar is not constrained by any intrinsic order of tokens in an input file. Indeed, some attribute evaluation tools reported in the literature perform extensive analysis on the attribute grammar to determine an optimal attribute evaluation order. As the time complexity of this analysis is exponential in the size of the grammar, we prefer to observe that the typical compiler designer already has in mind an appropriate attribute evaluation order, and can therefore so inform the compiler-generator without undue imposition.

The grammar in Listing 8.1 specifies its attribute evaluation order in the binary nodes as right-to-left, by the order in which the nonterminals are referenced in the semantic section following the tree template. The fact that the subtrees are listed in the template in left-to-right order has no bearing on the evaluation order.

8.3.4 Information Flow and Storage

The example of Listing 8.1 uses three different kinds of information management, all of them unfortunately called "attributes" somewhere in the literature. Historically first, there is the use of symbol properties stored in the symbol table. Although in classical compiler design the symbol table is a static data structure that grows (and shrinks) according to the current context, whereas we carry a dynamic reference to any of possibly several symbol tables around the parse tree, the organization and construction of the symbol table are not significantly different between the two interpretations. With each symbol in the table is associated one or more values, access to which is made by reference to the symbol. These values have been referred to in the past as symbol "attributes," but to avoid confusion we consistently prefer the term "properties" or sometimes "values." The grammar in Listing 8.1 extracts two properties from the symbol table: a Boolean that identifies the symbol as a constant identifier, and if it is, the value of that constant.

Then we have the inherited and synthesized attributes of the grammar productions, for which we preserve the term. In this grammar, the symbol table is an attribute inherited by the nonterminal Expn, and the symbol properties are synthesized into derived attributes; the composite value of a constant expression subtree is later inherited by the nonterminal Xform.

Finally, and newly introduced with TAGs, is the information attached to nodes of the tree data structure in memory. Some of the literature refers to this attached data as "attributes" and the structure itself as an "attributed graph." We prefer the more colorful and less confusing term "tree decorations" (or just "decorations") for the data, and we call the structure a "decorated tree," although as we increase the connectivity of the nodes to accommodate the information required for global optimization, the term "tree" will become somewhat inaccurate. In the example grammar, the name of an identifier and the value of a constant are decorations on their respective nodes.

A *decoration* is any single piece of data that is properly associated with a particular node in the AST. It can be numeric as in our example, where we decorated two different nodes, one with the numeric value of a constant, the other with a unique symbol reference (typically an index into the string table, as discussed in Chapter 3). A decoration can also be a more complex data object such as a bitset or even a whole subtree. Often we attach to a node a reference to another part of the tree, so that by means of this link we can make ready access to that other part, as in Figure 8.6, where a call node is decorated with a reference to the definition tree for the procedure being called. There is no reason but practicality for a node to be limited to one decoration at a time; even so restricted, the decoration could be a record containing several fields.

8.3.5 Tree-Valued Attributes

As we allow tree-valued decorations on the nodes of the tree, it is also possible to have tree-valued attributes in the grammar. This becomes a powerful tool for collecting into one or two nonterminal productions all the loci involved in a nonlocal optimization transformation.

For example, one desirable optimization involves moving out of a loop all the computations that do not change from iteration to iteration. In the AST, one node typically designates the head of a loop (with the exit test and loop body as one or more specific subtrees), whereas within the body subtree there may be expression trees involving only loop constants (actual constants and variables not modified within the loop), as in Figure 8.7. These loop-constant expression subtrees can often be profitably snipped out of the tree where they are, and grafted back onto the tree outside the loop node. There are two ways to do this with tree-valued attributes.

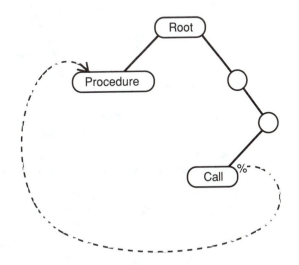

Figure 8.6. Decorating a tree node with a reference to another subtree.

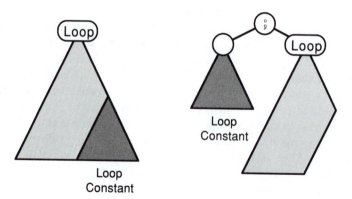

Figure 8.7. Moving loop-constant code out of the body of a loop.

The simplest way to do this is to walk the loop body, snipping out loop-constant expression trees and passing them up the tree as synthesized attributes, as shown in Figure 8.8. These detached snippets are then grafted into place on completion of the tree walk. The other method carries the locus of the node over the loop header node down into

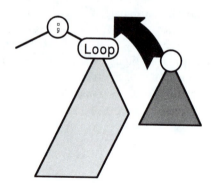

Stmt ↓inloop ↑movecode
    →   <Loop body >
           body: Stmt ↓true ↑bodycon ↑bodycode
    ⇒   <Semicolon bodycode <Loop body > >

    →   <Semicolon notconst loopconst >
           [inloop = false; movecode = <Empty >]   *{no change if not in loop}*

    →   <Semicolon notconst loopconst >
           [inloop = true; movecode = loopconst]
    ⇒   <Semicolon notconst <Empty > >
               →   ...

Figure 8.8. Moving loop-constant code out of a loop by synthesis.

the body of the loop as an inherited attribute, something like a porthole looking back up at the parent node, as shown in Figure 8.9. As loop-constant expressions are recognized, they are grafted onto the parent node immediately as they are removed from the body. Because the inherited attribute is actually a reference to the parent node, transforming it deeply within the tree transforms the remote node. In this simple illustration, only one loop-constant subtree can be extracted; in practice multiple twigs would be fused into a single subtree to be moved.

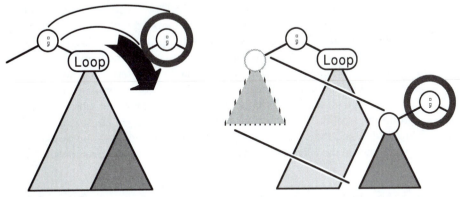

Stmt ↓parent
    →   \<Loop body >
    ⇒   newnode: \<Semicolon moved: \<Empty > \<Loop body > >
           body: Stmt ↓newnode

    →   \<Semicolon notconst loopconst >
           [parent = \<Empty >] *{no change if not in loop}*

    →   \<Semicolon notconst loopconst >
           [inloop ≠ \<Empty >] parent: Graft ↓loopconst
    ⇒   \<Semicolon notconst \<Empty > >
    →   . . .

Graft ↓insertcode
    →   \<Semicolon \<Empty > loopbody >
    ⇒   \<Semicolon insertcode loopbody >

Figure 8.9. Moving loop-constant code out of a loop body by inheriting a reference to a parent node.

8.3.6 Nondeterministic Parsing

One of the problems with using Context-Sensitive grammars for compiler design is that we have no algorithm for constructing deterministic linear-bounded automata. As we import more of the context-sensitivity into context-free grammars by way of attributes, we find the nondeterminism of CSGs also creeping in with it. In the code motion example of Figures 8.8 and 8.9, both grammars required context information to determine whether or not to transform the tree (and move the code out). The context information came as a pair of attributes required by both grammars. An inherited attribute determined whether the outer context was indeed a loop, and although less obvious, a synthesized attribute was required to determine if a particular subtree was indeed loop-constant.

Compared to the string grammars we have been used to, tree grammars themselves are slightly nondeterministic in the sense that several parts of the tree under consideration may require examination before it can be determined whether it matches the source template. If any part of the comparison fails, no matter how far down the tree the parser has already walked, it must back out, abandon this production, and try the next.

A transformational grammar has an implied "otherwise" case that matches any node for which there is no specified production, transforming it into itself. Often tree grammars are explicitly designed to allow less specific templates to match a node that more specific templates failed to match. For example, a constant-folding transformational grammar may have a production that tests an expression node for two constant subtrees, and failing that, tries for one constant subtree. The second case would surely match if it were tried first, but the intent is to match the most specific template possible. This heuristic is sometimes called "the maximal munch" — perhaps an allusion to a child's inclination toward taking the biggest possible bite out of a cookie — because the heuristic gives preference to the biggest (and thus most specific) production template.

8.4 Combining String and Tree Grammars

In a compiler that applies tree transformation for constraints-checking or code optimization, the parser must construct the AST as its semantic action. Although there have been some recent efforts to merge the parsing and back-end functions into a single compiler construction tool, most research has concentrated on smaller parts of the problem without attempting the integration. In this respect we break new ground here in discussing a unified grammatical structure for designing entire compilers.

There are two ways to link the string grammar of the compiler front end to the tree grammar that specifies optimization and code generation. The most direct, and in some ways simplest, approach is to use a translation grammar whose recognition part is a string grammar and whose translation part is a tree grammar [MetaWare, Inc., 1981]. The alternative, which we adopt in this text, is to construct the intermediate code trees as synthesized attributes in the string grammar. This method offers considerably more flexibility in the compiler design, and because we already use attribute grammars for other reasons, at no extra cost. The semantic actions in the parser can now include tree-building components, using substantially the same grammatical structure that was introduced in Chapter 5 and is already familiar. In favor of the translation grammar approach is the fact that it is easier for the compiler construction tool to verify that every nonterminal in every language construct generates some form of intermediate code tree, and that these are properly linked into a full AST. Listing 8.2 compares the two approaches for a fragment of an expression grammar.

Code generation from an AST is very much like code generation from the parser, if you use semantic actions for the generation as we did in Chapter 6. However, just as a transformational grammar can be used to construct an AST, a transformational grammar can specify how to flatten the tree into linear code. The irregularities of real computer hardware make this option less attractive, so we will restrict our code generation efforts to attribute grammars with semantic actions.

Expn	Expn ↑outtree: tree
→ Expn "+" Term	→ Expn ↑etree "+" Term ↑ttree
⇒ <Plus Expn Term >	[outtree= <Plus etree ttree >]
→ Term	→ Term ↑outtree
⇒ Term	
(a) Transformation	(b) Synthesized Attributes

Listing 8.2. Two ways to construct an abstract-syntax tree in the parser. In (a) the source text is "transformed" into a corresponding AST node; in (b) the AST node is constructed as a synthesized attribute.

8.5 Type-Checking in TAGs

Constraint-checking, as we observed in Chapter 5, is dependent on context information inherited in a symbol table, and also on expression type attributes synthesized at the leaves of the expression tree. Where previously we determined the required types of the operands of an expression operator syntactically (**AND** and **OR** are always Boolean, + and * are always integer), this is not always desirable. The Ada programming language explicitly allows the programmer to overload operators, but most programming languages overload the arithmetic operators so that they perform analogous functions on the different numeric types, **integer** and **real**. The constraints on overloaded operators cannot be properly checked syntactically, but they still can be checked in a one-pass parser, provided that the language disallows most kinds of forward symbol references (which is true in Ada as well as Pascal and Modula-2). When there is no requirement in the language that a symbol be declared before it is used — C and Fortran come readily to mind — then strong type-checking is not possible in a one-pass parser. In fact, these two languages are not strongly typed.

If the constrainer is postponed until a second pass over the program, then declaration before use is no longer a requirement for strong type-checking. Because of the cost of scanning and parsing the source text file, a multipass compiler often does the second and subsequent passes over the AST instead of re-reading and parsing the source file. In the case of a constrainer, the nondeterminism of tree parsing is limited by the simplicity of the tree grammar; multiple complex templates in a single grammar rule are generally not necessary for constraint-checking. This does not justify a second pass through the program if the constraints could be checked in the parser, but it reduces the expense of parsing the AST when that is compelled by language declaration order rules (or lack thereof) and other considerations.

There is not much to be said in detail about constraint-checking in a tree grammar that does not follow directly from the general form of a constrainer already laid out in Chapter 5. Typically the parser will have constructed the AST with the identifier leaf nodes decorated with the unique symbol index returned by the scanner; this index is used to construct and search the symbol table exactly as before. The constrainer will transform the

AST slightly to add type decorations to the operator nodes, and to replace identifier nodes with constant, variable, or function reference nodes as appropriate, properly decorated to refer directly to the corresponding variable or procedure declarations in those cases, as shown in Figure 8.10. Although Modula-2 syntactically distinguishes function calls from variable references, Pascal and some other languages do not, so the constrainer must transform the tree appropriately. After the constrainer has completed its transformation of the program tree, the type component of the symbol table can be discarded.

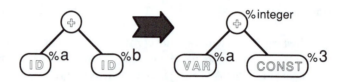

Figure 8.10. Tree transformation by Constrainer of the Expression a+b.

Once syntax-directed constraints-checking has been left behind, we are also free to apply attribute grammars to properly enforcing reference parameter usage, which we could not do under the limitations imposed in Chapters 5 and 6. There are two general approaches to this kind of problem. The purist would define the parser grammar to accept expressions in all parameters, then in the constrainer synthesize a Boolean attribute that asserts a parameter to be a single variable reference; the attribute is evaluated in all cases, but ignored for value parameters and checked only when the symbol table returns a reference parameter type to be matched. The second approach allows the semantics to drive the parser, so that different productions are applied depending on whether a reference or value parameter is required. It is more difficult to get this combined approach correct, but it has the advantage of facilitating one-pass compiling with code generation.

8.6 Code Optimization by Transformation

The earliest high-level language compilers in the mid-1950s already identified a about a dozen useful optimizing code transformations [Backus, 1981]. That list has not grown much in the following 35 years, except where changes in computer architecture have given rise to new opportunities for code improvement. We examine here the classical optimizations, therefore, and show how each one can be naturally specified in a TAG.

Most code optimizations require two steps to effect them. The first step is analytic, collecting the information that identifies the opportunities to apply this particular transformation. The second step actually transforms the AST. Often the two steps can be done in the same pass over the AST; equally often the information must be collected in advance, before any transformation can be applied. In the latter case it may be useful to merge the information-gathering steps of several optimizing transformations into one pass over the AST. Similarly, several tree transformations can frequently be merged into one grammar, representing one pass over the AST. Each unnecessary analysis or transformation pass over the AST represents extra compile time, and it is desirable to minimize these as much as possible within the design objectives of the compiler.

Transformational Attribute Grammars   Chap. 8

8.6.1 Data-Flow Analysis

Many of the transformations require a particular class of analysis called *flow analysis*, or often, *data-flow analysis* (DFA). Flow analysis traces the flow of data, variable usage, or other factors throughout the compilation unit (typically the procedure). Some flow analysis is concerned with information that flows forward through the program. An example of this is constant propagation, where a reference to a variable known to contain a constant value at a particular point in the program execution path can be replaced with that constant. Other flow analysis is concerned with information that flows backward from the end of the program. An example of this is used in the elimination of assignments to variables that will never be used again. TAGs permit the compiler designer to specify explicitly the direction of analysis.

Flow analyses may be further distinguished by whether they apply set union ($\cup$) or set intersection ($\cap$). Because union and intersection are mathematically dual, this distinction tends to be more interesting to the theoretician than to the compiler designer. Most data-flow algorithms can be specified equally with union or intersection operators, depending on the meaning attached to the set attributes involved. It can be shown that the set attributes for a particular class of flow analysis defines a *lattice*, which is a partial ordering of the values such that the union operator returns the least value that is "greater" than or equal to its operands, and the intersection operator returns the greatest value less than or equal to its operands. The lattice *Bottom* is the intersection of all possible values, and in DFA represents "no information" or "everything undefined," whereas the lattice *Top* is the union of all possible values, and may represent a hypothetical program that never completes. The particular meaning assigned to the lattice points depends on the purpose of the attributes and the operation (union or intersection) used to merge set values.

The significant data structure for flow analysis is the bit vector, referred to in Pascal and Modula-2 as a *set*. A set type represents the "powerset" of some ordinal type (typically a subrange of cardinal numbers, say $0..n-1$), and the value of such a set may be any of the 2^n possible collections containing zero or more elements, where an element is either in the collection or not. For example, with the subrange $0..2$ there are three set elements, 0, 1, and 2, and eight different sets possible: $\{\}$, $\{0\}$, $\{1\}$, $\{2\}$, $\{0,1\}$, $\{1,2\}$, $\{0,2\}$, and $\{0,1,2\}$. The natural machine representation for a set is the bit string with (in this case) three bits numbered to match the elements of the subrange base type. An integer i is in the set s exactly when bit i of the bit string is a 1. The empty set is represented by all bits zero. Set intersection is a primitive operation for small sets in most computer hardware: it is the "logical AND" operator. An element is in the intersection of two sets if and only if it is a member of both sets. Similarly, set union is a primitive operation, using the "logical OR" operator. An element is a member of the union of two sets whenever it is in either or both of the two sets.

Many data-flow analyses involve sets of variables. Each variable is given a unique ordinal number, usually by the constrainer when the identifier is added to the symbol table. The numbers need not be contiguous, but the sets can be more compact if they are. However, different variables with the same identifier (perhaps in different scopes) must have different numbers. We are concerned with the actual variables, not their names. Aggregate variables such as arrays and records present a special problem that we will address later.

Consider for an example, the simple program in Listing 8.3. It has three variables, which we arbitrarily number ($a=0$, $b=1$, $c=2$) so they can be represented as contiguous elements of a set. We can do two different kinds of data-flow analysis on this program, one forward and the other backward.

```
      MODULE  DataFlow;
      FROM  IO  IMPORT  ReadInt,  WriteInt;
      VAR  a,b,c:  INTEGER;
 1    BEGIN
 2      a:=5;
 3      ReadInt(b);
 4      IF  b=3  THEN
 5        c:=a-b
 6      ELSE
 7        a:=b;
 8        b:=3  END;
 9      WriteInt(c+b)
10    END  DataFlow;
```

Listing 8.3. A small program for data-flow analysis.

For the first analysis, we propagate through the program sets representing at each point all variables with a known constant value. A variable is in the set if its value is known to be constant at that point in the program. Initially (line 1 in Listing 8.4), all three variables are undefined, so the set is empty (that is, the bit vector is all zeros). After line 2 the variable a has a constant value 5, so the set is $\{0\}$, containing only variable a.

```
      MODULE DataFlow;
      FROM IO IMPORT ReadInt, WriteInt;
      VAR a,b,c: INTEGER;
 1 BEGIN              _____  {}
 2    a:=5;           _____   {0}
 3    ReadInt(b);    ___  {0}
 4    IF b=3 THEN    ___  {0,1}
 5      c:=a-b        _____  {0,1,2}
 6    ELSE            _____  {0}
 7      a:=b;         _____  {}
 8      b:=3 END;    ___  {0,1,2} ∩ {1} = {1}
 9    WriteInt(c+b)
10 END DataFlow;
```

Listing 8.4. Forward data-flow analysis using intersection.

After line 3 variable b is defined, but the value came from input data not known at compile time; it is not known to be constant, so it is not added to the set. At the beginning of line 5, however, variable b is now known to be the constant 3: if it were not 3, the ELSE path would have been taken. The set associated with the beginning of the THEN-part is {0,1}. Because a and b are both known to be constants, their difference is also constant, so variable c is added to the set; it is {0,1,2} at the end of line 5. The ELSE-part (line 7) begins with the set {0} again. The variable b is not a member because all that is known of it is that it is not equal to 3. During the course of the assignment statement on that line, variable a also ceases to have a known constant value, leaving us with the empty set at the end of the line. On line 8, however, b is assigned the constant value 3, so the set at the end of the ELSE-part is {1}.

Now, going into line 9 we have two candidates for the set of constant variables. Any variable not constant coming out of the THEN-part is surely not constant in the following statement; similarly any variable not constant in the ELSE-part must be considered not constant in the following statement. The correct set is, therefore, the intersection $\{0,1,2\} \cap \{1\} = \{1\}$. Although b is constant coming out of both branches of the conditional, it just happens to have the same value in both cases; generally this would not be true, and it would have to be disqualified from the set of known constants. In the expression to be written as output, b is constant, but c is not — indeed, it is not even defined if the execution path came through the ELSE-part. If we had defined our sets differently, we might be able to report a compile-time error here, namely that c is possibly undefined (see Exercise 4).

By way of backward data-flow, let us define a new set attribute to contain a variable exactly when the value in that variable may be used again. Variables that may be used again are called "live" variables. Initially, the only known set value is at the end of the program (line 10 of Listing 8.5), when no more variables are going to be used: the set is empty and all variables are dead. Going into line 9 we now know that variables b and c are used in the output expression; they are added to the live variable set, forming {1,2}.

```
MODULE DataFlow;
FROM IO IMPORT ReadInt, WriteInt;
VAR a,b,c: INTEGER;
 1 BEGIN              _____  {2}
 2   a:=5;            _____  {0,2}
 3   ReadInt(b);      ____  {0,1}∪{1,2} = {0,1,2}
 4   IF b=3 THEN      ____  {0,1}
 5     c:=a-b         _____  {1,2}
 6   ELSE             _____  {1,2}
 7     a:=b;          _____  {2}
 8     b:=3 END;      ____  {1,2}
 9   WriteInt(c+b)    _  {}
10 END DataFlow;
```

Listing 8.5. Backward data-flow analysis using set union.

This set value is propagated equally to both legs of the conditional. The assignment on line 8 disqualifies ("kills") variable b (no previous value of b will be used after this line), but it is added back in on line 7 after killing variable a. Note that we are concerned with the flow of information in *execution* (run time) order, not text order, so assignment to a variable kills that variable in the backward-flowing working set before any use of the same variable in the expression assigned to it would resurrect it again. The working set at the beginning of the ELSE-part is {1,2}. Similarly the assignment in the THEN-part kills variable c but adds a and b to the live variable set.

As the two legs of the conditional meet again at the conditional expression test (that is, just after its evaluation in execution order), we take the union of the two sets. Any variable that is live at the beginning of either leg is surely live coming out of the Boolean expression. This gives us a live set of {0,1}∪{1,2} = {0,1,2}. The Boolean expression tested in the IF statement adds variable b to the set, but because it is already there, no change is made to the set. The input statement on line 3 kills b, and the assignment on line 2 kills a. The live set propagated to line 1 should be empty, reflecting the fact that no variable has a defined value that can be used. Finding variable c in the live variable set is evidence of a program bug, the same one we noted earlier. The reader may wish to add the missing assignment to variable c at the front of the program, then rework the two flow analyses to verify that this correction removes the error (see Exercise 5).

8.6.2 Using Attribute Grammars for Data-Flow Analysis

With a defined set attribute type and appropriate union and intersection attribute evaluation functions, TAGs are a natural notation for specifying DFA. Listing 8.6 shows a grammar fragment for the backward live variable analysis.

The single nonterminal LiveVars in this grammar recursively walks a program tree looking for variable references and assignments. It has one right-to-left attribute that is a flow-through set. Variable references add their respective variable identifier numbers (signified by the name decoration on ID nodes) to the set, and assignments delete the corresponding elements from the set.

Whenever the tree walker parses an assignment node, the variable is excluded from the incoming working set, removing it from the resulting difference set. If the result set is identical to the incoming set, then the identifier was not live coming into this node, so the assignment is useless; a Boolean flag decoration is attached to the node to let a subsequent code generator know that the assignment can be eliminated in such a case. The working set is also sent through the expression subtree, and its result is passed up the tree to the left.

When the tree walker encounters an identifier node, its variable number is simply added to the set passed out. Constants, on the other hand, have no effect on the set. Read statements are similar to assignments with no expression, and write statements flow the attribute sets right on through their expression subtree(s) without further processing. Two-operand expression operator trees and semicolon trees are walked from right to left, so the incoming working set is passed first to the right-hand subtree, and its result is passed to the left subtree.

LiveVars ↓inlive: set ↑outlive: set

→ <Assign <ID >%name expn >
   [exclude ↓name ↓inlive ↑asnset]   *{delete name from incoming set}*
   [useless = (inlive=asnset)]   *{note if it was not there}*
   expn: LiveVars ↓asnset ↑outlive   *{pass result to expression}*
⇒ <Assign <ID >%name expn >%useless
{decorate node to cue codegen}

→ <ID >%name
   [addset ↓inlive ↓name ↑outlive]   *{add name to working set}*

→ <NUM >%value
   [outlive = inlive]   *{ignore constants}*

→ <Read <ID >%name >
   [exclude ↓name ↓inlive ↑outlive]   *{delete name from incoming set}*

→ <Write expn >
   expn: LiveVars ↓inlive ↑outlive   *{pass set thru expression}*

→ <Semi left rite > | <Less left rite > | <Equal left rite > | <Grtr left rite > |
   <Plus left rite > | <Minus left rite > | <Star left rite > | <Divd left rite >
   rite: LiveVars ↓inlive ↑midlive   *{flow sets thru expressions}*
   left: LiveVars ↓midlive ↑outlive   *{...and stmt sequences, R-L}*

→ <IF expn then else >
   then: LiveVars ↓inlive ↑thnlive   *{flow set thru both then & else}*
   else: LiveVars ↓inlive ↑elslive
   [union ↓thnlive ↓elslive ↑expnlive] *{pass their union to expn}*
   expn: LiveVars ↓expnlive ↑outlive

Listing 8.6. A small data-flow analysis grammar.

The interesting node in this grammar is the conditional, because the *then–* and *else*-parts are parallel, not in sequence. That means that the same incoming bitset is passed to both subtrees, and the results must be combined by a set union operation before passing it on to the Boolean expression subtree.

8.7 Alternatives to Tree Representations of Intermediate Code

One of the crucial advantages of an internal representation of the program as a tree is that a generative grammar can be written to visit every node in the program exactly once (in preorder or postorder), and proved correct by conventional program verification techniques. Optimization transformations are therefore more easily proved to be complete and correct, an important consideration in compiler design. Data-flow analysis on a program tree, however, requires that the source program follow the "structured" or GOTO-less programming style. This is a relatively recent language development, and not all languages conform to this restriction. It is remarkable that even some recent languages are not completely structured. For example, the break statement within switch constructs in the programming language C is the functional equivalent of a GOTO because it violates the structured paradigm of "single entry, single exit" in each construct.

Given that there will always be some unstructured languages (most notably including C and Fortran) for compiler designers to cope with, it is worthwhile to review the more traditional intermediate program representation, and to address data-flow considerations in such a structure. The format is known generally as "quads" (or sometimes "triples") with reference to the fact that each element consists of four components: an operator, a destination operand, and up to two source operands.

The quad notation is inspired by the low-level unstructured architecture of most computers. There the control flow is determined by a sequence of operations or instructions, much like the Itty Bitty Stack Machine introduced in Chapter 6. High-level language structures such as while or if-then-else are reduced to conditional and unconditional branches. Similarly, complex expressions are reduced to a sequence of single-operation assignments, using explicit temporary variables to hold intermediate values. Listing 8.7 shows the quads for the sample program of Listing 8.3.

Optimization of a program in the quad notation usually requires the reconstruction of some of the structural information that was discarded in generating the quads. Often programmers use structured programming habits, even if they are not supported or enforced by the language. Although the translation of the program into quads removes any remaining structure, considerable research has gone into program flow analysis with the objective of recovering that structure — or identifying those situations where it is truly absent.

The first step in recovering program structure is to break the linear string of quads into *basic blocks*, which are sequences of quads containing at most one label (on the first line), and at most one branch or call (on the last line). A basic block therefore can only be entered at its first line and only exited after executing the last line. In Listing 8.7 the basic blocks are separated by dashed lines.

B1		a	←	5		
		t1	←	(CALL)	ReadInt	
B2		b	←	t1		
		t2	←	b	=	3
		L1	←	(BRF)	t2	
B3		t3	←	a	−	b
		c	←	t3		
		L2	←	(BRA)		
B4	L1:	a	←	b		
		b	←	3		
		L2	←	(BRA)		
B5	L2:	t4	←	c	+	b
			←	(CALL)	WriteInt	t4

Listing 8.7. Quads for the program of Listing 8.3, showing basic blocks.

Transformational Attribute Grammars   Chap. 8

The next step is to construct a directed graph (not a tree!) in which the basic blocks are nodes, linked by branch instructions and fall-throughs. Figure 8.11 shows the control flow graph for the basic blocks in our small example.

8.7.1 Data-Flow in Quads

Classical DFA was concerned only with the flow analysis within a single basic block. Kildall extended that to the entire graph for the compilation unit, using the lattice model [Kildall, 1972]. A set is attached to each arc in the graph, initially empty. Then the information sets are flowed backward (or forward, as the case may be) until every arc has been updated with new set values. Nodes with two or more inbound arcs (such as B5 in the example) flow their sets equally onto both arcs. Nodes with two or more outbound arcs (B2 in the example) propagate through them the union (or intersection, as the case may be) of the sets from those arcs. Because we cannot in general write a TAG to systematically visit every node in the control graph in the optimum order (even if there were such an ordering), it is necessary to iterate the algorithm until all the sets are stable.

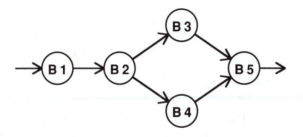

Figure 8.11. Control flow graph for the program of Listing 8.3.

An iterated data-flow algorithm is called *monotonic* if for each iteration the sets consistently increase (elements are never deleted from the set attached to any particular node) or decrease (elements are never added), and cannot change direction. This is often the case with the DFA algorithms used in code optimization. For example, the live variable analysis of Listing 8.6 is monotonic, but the constant variable analysis is not monotonic because a variable visible at a particular point in the program may be found to be constant on the first pass, but an arc from a node in the control graph visited later in the analysis (perhaps the termination of a loop) may leave a different value in a component of its evaluation expression, which a subsequent iteration would take into consideration. A given algorithm is easily proved to be monotonic when only set union (for nondecreasing bit vectors) or intersection (for non-increasing vectors) is used at forks and joins in the graph, and set membership does not depend on the membership of other elements in the set. Other kinds of algorithms may also be monotonic, but it is much more difficult to establish. A monotonic DFA algorithm can always be proved to terminate because finite sets are used (typically limited by the number of variables, expressions, or statements in the source program) and the algorithm will stabilize no later than when all the sets have reached either the empty set (on intersection) or the universal set (on union).

The alert reader will notice that DFA in the directed program graph is equivalent to that in the program tree in all the program constructs we have examined so far, and yet we insist that iteration is required for the control graph, but not generally so for the tree. The fundamental difference lies in what unstructured GOTOs do to the control graph. Figure 8.12 shows two graphs that are not possible with structured program constructs. No algorithm exists for constructing from the source code a tree representation for these graphs that ensures a single visitation of every node in the correct order to guarantee correct DFA, and indeed in one case a single visit graph traversal is inadequate.

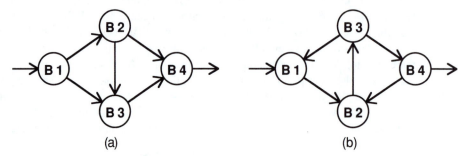

(a)   (b)

Figure 8.12. Two unstructured control flow graphs. Graph (a) is a simplified form of a fragment in C, whereas graph (b) requires undisciplined use of GOTO to achieve interlocking loops.

8.7.2 Data-Flow Analysis Through Loops

Unlike conditional forks (if-then-else and case), DFA through loop structures often cannot be completed in a single pass. The reason is that information flowing forward through the loop to its exit must also be made available at the front of the loop, and information flow backward through the loop to the front must also be made available at the exit. In a directed graph of basic blocks, this problem is explicitly solved by iterating the DFA over the whole graph until it stabilizes. DFA in the tree representation can also be iterated until it stabilizes, but with monotonic algorithms it is generally necessary to process each loop body at most twice. One time through the loop body is sufficient to determine the contribution of statements within the loop body to the set at the other end. The second pass through merges that set with the information flowing in through the entry (in forward DFA).

Consider the use-definition flow analysis example of Listing 8.6. Data flows backwards, so at a loop exit the live variables consist of the union of those live at the entrance to the loop and those live in any code that follows. Figure 8.13 shows the sets in the completed DFA for a small loop. This program fragment has three basic blocks, with block 2 constituting the body of the loop. The live variable set at the entrance to block 3 contains the elements $\{a,b\}$. Considering only the body of the loop and ignoring both blocks that follow it, block 2 has the elements $\{b,c,d\}$ live at its entrance. That is, variables b, c, and d are used within the block before they are killed. The union of these two sets is $\{a,b,c,d\}$, which is the correct set for flow into the loop exit. The same set emerges from the loop entrance on the second pass. Note that variable e is killed (assigned to) within the loop before its first use, so it is not live at the loop entrance.

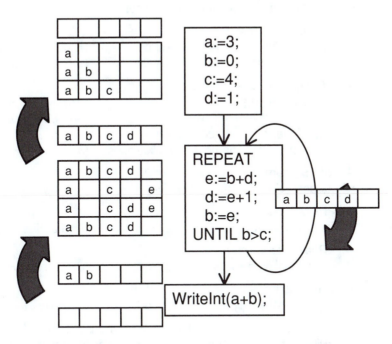

Figure 8.13. Use-definition flow analysis through a loop.

If the first pass of the DFA through the loop body carries as much information as is available, then the sets at the other end will be correct after the first pass; only the sets used within the loop body require the second pass. We state this formally as Lemma 8.1:

Lemma 8.1. A monotonic data-flow algorithm applied to a structured program graph containing a simple loop cannot on subsequent iterations augment any set outside the body of the loop (see Exercise 12 for proof).

Theorem 8.1. Two passes through a structured program tree is sufficient for a monotonic data-flow algorithm.

The proof of Theorem 8.1 follows immediately from Lemma 8.1. We apply this theorem in the extension of the TAG to do live variable analysis (from Listing 8.6), now shown in Listing 8.8. Notice that we have added productions for the **WHILE** and **MODULE** (compilation unit root) nodes. From the root node the program tree is walked twice using the same grammar. The only difference is in processing the loops.

The new production for **REPEAT** nodes saves the bit vector that comes through the body of the loop as a decoration to the tree node, from where it can be used on the next iteration. On the first pass a previous copy of this decoration is not available, so the working live variable set coming into the loop exit is used instead. This is merged with the working set into the loop exit by set union, and the result flows into the Boolean

LiveVars ↓pass: int ↓inlive: set ↑outlive: set

→ <MODULE body >
   body: LiveVars ↓1 ↓empty ↑midlive   *{first pass through program}*
   body: LiveVars ↓2 ↓empty ↑outlive   *{second pass is final}*

→ <Assign <ID >%name expn >
   [exclude ↓name ↓inlive ↑asnset]   *{delete name from incoming set}*
   [useless = (inlive=asnset)]   *{note if it was not there}*
   expn: LiveVars ↓asnset ↑outlive   *{pass result to expression}*
⇒ <Assign <ID >%name expn >%useless   *{decorate node to cue codegen}*

→ <ID >%name
   [addset ↓inlive ↓name ↑outlive]   *{add name to working set}*

→ <NUM >%value
   [outlive = inlive]   *{ignore constants}*

→ <Read <ID >%name >
   [exclude ↓name ↓inlive ↑outlive]   *{delete name from incoming set}*

→ <Write expn >
   expn: LiveVars ↓pass ↓inlive ↑outlive   *{pass set thru expression}*

→ <Semi left rite > | <Less left rite > | <Equal left rite > | <Grtr left rite > |
   <Plus left rite > | <Minus left rite > | <Star left rite > | <Divd left rite >
   rite: LiveVars ↓pass ↓inlive ↑midlive   *{flow sets thru expressions}*
   left: LiveVars ↓pass ↓midlive ↑outlive   *{...and stmt sequences, R-L}*

→ <IF expn then else >
   then: LiveVars ↓pass ↓inlive ↑thnlive   *{flow set thru both then & else}*
   else: LiveVars ↓pass ↓inlive ↑elslive
   [union ↓thnlive ↓elslive ↑expnlive]   *{pass their union to boolexpn}*
   expn: LiveVars ↓pass ↓expnlive ↑outlive

→ <REPEAT body expn >%looplive
   ([pass=1; exitlive=inlive]   *{if pass 1, use working set}*
   |[pass=2; exitlive=looplive])   *{else use from previous pass}*
   [union ↓exitlive ↓inlive ↑expnlive]   *{merge with incoming set }*
   expn: LiveVars ↓pass ↓expnlive ↑bodlive
   body: LiveVars ↓pass ↓bodlive ↑outlive   *{flow set thru body}*
⇒ <REPEAT expn body >%outlive   *{decorate node for next pass}*

Listing 8.8. Live variable analysis grammar, including REPEAT loops.

control expression and thence into the main loop body. The set of live variables flowing out of the body passes up the tree to the left. A copy is also saved as the decoration to this node for the next iteration.

Live variable analysis is not strictly monotonic, because elements are removed from the working set as variables are killed. This means that in two passes over the program tree, if the control expression of the outer of a pair of nested WHILE loops kills a variable (perhaps by passing it as a reference parameter to some function that is known to have the side effect of altering it), the body of the inner loop will see the variable still live. This errs on the side of safety, and then only in those cases using poor programming style. Few useful flow analysis algorithms are truly monotonic, but such a lack of monotonicity, once recognized, can safely be ignored. In very rare cases it will result in slightly more code than is optimal. It is noteworthy that this problem does not occur with REPEAT loops, because there is no control path break between the body of the loop and the evaluation of the control expression. The minimum number of basic blocks in a WHILE loop is two, as shown in Figure 8.14. We will find several kinds of optimization that perform slightly better with REPEAT than WHILE loops. It is curious that DO loops in the original Fortran compiler, which had remarkably sophisticated optimization for its day, worked like REPEAT rather than WHILE. A DO loop always executed at least once, even if the range of its control variable was empty.

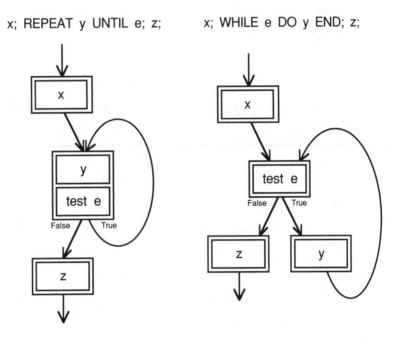

Figure 8.14. The structural difference between REPEAT and WHILE loops.

8.8 A Survey of Useful Optimizing Transformations

With an adequate grasp of the mechanics of analysis and transformation, we are now ready to examine the common optimizations used in compilers. In this section we focus on those that readily adapt to a TAG implementation. Chapter 9 addresses some optimizations that require special considerations.

Table 8.1 gives a summary of 20 different optimizations that have been identified in the literature. For each optimization the requisite analysis and the kind of transformation is indicated. There are essentially four kinds of analyses and three general kinds of transformation. We discuss these in turn.

Ch.	Optimization Name	Required Analysis	Transformation
8	Constant Folding	Simulated Execution	Elimination
8	Dead Code Elimination	Simulated Execution	Elimination
8	Range-Check Elision	Simulated Execution	Elimination
8	Loop-Constant Code Motion	Loop Structure, DFA	Motion
9	Induction Variables	Loop Structure, Sim.Ex.	Selection, Elim.
9	Loop Unrolling	Loop Structure, Statistics	Motion (replic.)
8	Loop Unswitching	Loop Structure	Motion
9	Loop Fusion	Loop Structure	Motion
9	Linearizing Arrays	Loop Structure	Elimination
8	Common Subexpressions	Simulated Execution	Elimination
8	Left– and Right-Hoisting	Sim. Execution, DFA	Motion
8	Copy Propagation	Simulated Execution	Elimination
9	Address Mode Selection	Statistics	Selection
9	Branch Chaining	Statistics	Selection
8	Useless Code Elimination	DFA	Elimination
9	Strength Reduction	*none*	Selection
9	Resource Allocation	DFA, Statistics	Selection
9	Load/Store Optimization	DFA	Motion
8	Mathematical Identities	*none*	Selection, Elim.
9	Back-Substitution	Statistics	Motion

Table 8.1. Twenty optimizing transformations, showing the class of analysis and transformation. The numbers refer to the chapter in which the optimization is discussed.

Data-flow analysis has already been discussed at some length. It is the most commonly required analysis for optimizations. DFA can involve left-to-right or right-to-left traversal of the program tree, and its accumulation of set data may be by union or intersection at the forks. Although this appears to make an elegant division of the genre, it should also be noted that some forms of DFA must be augmented by data that can only fit in a mathematical lattice. Furthermore, because union and intersection are mathematical duals, any analysis involving union can be recast in complementary terms using intersection. Elegant mathematical categories do not always usefully partition the world.

Simulated execution, or as it is sometimes called, *partial evaluation*, is the process of attempting to execute as much of the program as possible at compile time, saving the partial results for completion at run time. It is actually a form of forward flow analysis, carrying not just sets, but also variable and register contents, machine state, and a variety of other information along.

Program statistics is concerned with information that can be gathered in a Data-Flow-like pass through the program, but because it is context-free there is no required order of processing. Generally this counts the number of identifier references in certain contexts, or estimates the number of generated instructions in a subtree, and the like.

Loop structure analysis is concerned with the parameters controlling the loops in a program. Most program execution time is expended in the inner loops of a program, so considerable effort has gone into analyzing loop structure with the goal of improving their performance.

Code elimination is a transformation that generally prunes off and discards superfluous branches from the program tree. Often small transformations in other parts of the program are required to accompany this elimination, to preserve correctness.

Code motion transforms the program tree by moving code out of frequently executed parts of the program (such as loops) into less frequently executed parts. It can also move code closer to where it is used in an effort to minimize the cost of access. Related to this is the replication of some parts of the code in an effort to minimize costly decisions within loops and procedures. Code motion in a TAG consists, as we have seen, of pruning a subtree from one part of the program and grafting it onto another.

Code selection is intimately involved in the selection of output code. It is not so much a transformation of the program tree as the decoration of it in preparation for the final tree-flattening code generation pass.

8.8.1 The Class of Simulated Execution Optimizations

Six of the optimizations listed in Table 8.1 identify simulated execution as their supporting analysis. Analysis by simulated execution can generally take place concurrently with the optimization transformations. The program tree is walked in approximate execution order, with special considerations for loops and forks. Each expression is "evaluated" and each statement "executed" as much as possible to determine at compile time such things as the contents of registers and variables in terms of the source of the information, if not actual values. Where actual values can be known, these are constants, and the tree is transformed to use these constants instead of the variables written into the program. When only the source of the values can be determined, the simulated execution looks for similarities which point to opportunities for saving and reusing intermediate values. The constant value analysis results in constant folding and dead code elimination, and with a little more effort, range-check elision. The common subexpression analysis results in common subexpression elimination, copy propagation, and left-motion hoisting.

8.8.2 Analysis for Constant Folding

The data structure for constant value analysis consists of a value field for each variable to be tracked, and a flag (possibly a distinguished value in the value field, if that is available) to signify that the value is unknown. Generally the analysis is limited to scalar variables, that is, integers, Booleans, characters, enumerated types, and their subranges, but not sets, arrays, or records. Including reals is possible, but not encouraged because numerical analysts prefer to maintain absolute control of real expression evaluation. Doubling the information so that upper and lower bounds are kept for each scalar variable enables range analysis, but for correct handling of loops it is recommended that the loop structure analysis be done first.

As the program tree is walked from left to right, a left-to-right attribute consisting of the range information for all variables is propagated as an inherited then synthesized attribute through each production of the analysis grammar, much as we propagated the symbol table during constraint-checking. Indeed, a symbol table is nearly the best mechanism for implementing this data structure, except that the pair of values for each variable must be updated as new assignments are made, and variables are accessed not by name but by their unique variable number.

In addition to propagating the value set around the tree, expression subtrees synthesize also a range (or value) for the current expression. Whenever the upper and lower bounds of a range coincide (that is, the value is known to be constant), the expression subtree that synthesized this value can be pruned and replaced with a constant node having that value. This pruning is usually deferred until the expression is used in a larger expression that is not constant, or is assigned to a variable or used in some other way such as the control expression of an IF statement. When the control expression of an IF or CASE statement is constant, it is possible to prune not only the subexpression tree, but also all subtrees for cases that cannot be reached because of this constant value. This optimization is called *dead code elimination* because the unreachable code trees are considered "dead" in the sense that they cannot be executed. Dead code elimination gives the programmer the effect of conditional compilation essentially for free because entire chunks of program text will generate no code if contained within the THEN or ELSE part of an IF statement depending on a (possibly global) constant of appropriate value.

When an assignment is made to a scalar variable during the range analysis, the range value for the variable is set to the range derived from the evaluated expression (or if not doing full range analysis, the value and flag are copied). Normally an assignment to a scalar variable will result in the generation of range-check code, but this test can be done at compile time during the range analysis, and if the evaluated range falls safely within one or both bounds, the assignment node can be decorated with a flag signaling to the code generator the elimination of the corresponding tests and error traps. The same compile-time tests can be applied to array subscripts and CASE expression indices.

The grammar fragment in Listing 8.9 shows the basic form of the analysis and transformation for constant folding and the related optimizations, range-check elision and dead code elimination. It is assumed that the parser or constrainer has constructed assignment nodes with a third subtree containing the bounds for range-checking; an empty node in this subtree represents a check that the code generator need not make. The

ConStmt ↓invars: table ↑outvars: table

    →   <Assign <ID >%name expn bounds >
          expn: ConExpn ↓invars ↑evars ↑exlo ↑exhi   *{look for consts in expn}*
          [replace ↓name ↓exlo ↓exhi ↓evars ↑outvars]   *{update value range set}*
          bounds: RngCheck ↓exlo ↓exhi   *{modify range-check subtree}*

    →   <Read <ID >%name >
          [replace ↓name ↓−∞ ↓+∞ ↓invars ↑outvars]   *{update value range set}*

    →   <Semi left rite >
          left: ConStmt ↓invars ↑midvars   *{flow sets thru statements}*
          rite: ConStmt ↓midvars ↑outvars

    →   this:<IF expn then else >
          expn: ConExpn ↓invars ↑evars ↑exlo ↑exhi   *{look for consts in expn}*
          then: ConStmt ↓evars ↑thnvars   *{flow set thru then & else}*
          else: ConStmt ↓evars ↑elsvars
          ([exlo=1; outvars= thnvars; nutree=then]   *{T: replace with then-part}*
          | [exhi=0; outvars= elsvars; nutree=else]   *{F: replace with else-part}*
          | [otherwise; merge ↓thnvars ↓elsvars ↑outvars] *{else pass out union}*
          [nutree=this])
    ⇒   nutree ;

ConExpn ↓invars: table ↑outvars: table ↑loval: int ↑hival: int

    →   <ID >%name
          [lookup ↓name ↓invars ↑loval ↑hival]   *{get name from working set}*
          [outvars=invars]

    →   <NUM >%value
          [outvars=invars; loval=value; hival=value]   *{range is constant}*

    →   this:<Less left rite >
          left: ConExpn ↓invars ↑midvars ↑leftlo ↑lefthi *{flow sets thru subexpns}*
          rite: ConExpn ↓midvars ↑outvars ↑ritelo ↑ritehi
          ([lefthi<ritelo; loval=1; hival=1; nutree =<NUM >%1] *{replace true, synth T,T}*
          | [leftlo≥ritehi; loval=0; hival=0; nutree =<NUM >%0] *{replace F, synth F,F}*
          | [otherwise; loval=0; hival=1; nutree = this])   *{neither, synthesize F,T}*
    ⇒   nutree

    →   this:<Equal left rite >
          left: ConExpn ↓invars ↑midvars ↑leftlo ↑lefthi *{flow sets thru subexpns}*
          rite: ConExpn ↓midvars ↑outvars ↑ritelo ↑ritehi
          ([lefthi<ritelo; loval=0; hival=0; nutree =<NUM >%0] *{replace F, synth F,F}*
          | [leftlo>ritehi; loval=0; hival=0; nutree =<NUM >%0]
          | [lefthi=ritelo& leftlo=ritehi; loval=1; hival=1; nutree =<NUM >%1] *{true, T,T}*
          | [otherwise; loval=0; hival=1; nutree = this])   *{neither, synthesize F,T}*
    ⇒   nutree

Listing 8.9a. Constant folding analysis and transformation grammar.

$\rightarrow$ this:<Plus left rite >
    left: ConExpn ↓invars ↑midvars ↑leftlo ↑lefthi *{flow sets thru subexpns}*
    rite: ConExpn ↓midvars ↑outvars ↑ritelo ↑ritehi
    [loval=leftlo+ritelo; hival=lefthi+ritehi] *{synthesize range of sum}*
    ([loval=hival; nutree =<NUM >%loval] *{replace constant node if so}*
    | [otherwise; nutree = this])
$\Rightarrow$ nutree

$\rightarrow$ this:<Minus left rite >
    left: ConExpn ↓invars ↑midvars ↑leftlo ↑lefthi *{flow sets thru subexpns}*
    rite: ConExpn ↓midvars ↑outvars ↑ritelo ↑ritehi
    [loval=leftlo−ritehi; hival=lefthi−ritelo] *{synthesize range of diff}*
    ([loval=hival; nutree =<NUM >%loval] *{replace constant node if so}*
    | [otherwise; nutree = this])
$\Rightarrow$ nutree

$\rightarrow$ this:<Star left rite >
    left: ConExpn ↓invars ↑midvars ↑leftlo ↑lefthi
    rite: ConExpn ↓midvars ↑outvars ↑ritelo ↑ritehi
    [loval=*min*(leftlo*ritelo, leftlo*ritehi, lefthi*ritelo, lefthi*ritehi)]
    [hival=*max*(leftlo*ritelo, leftlo*ritehi, lefthi*ritelo, lefthi*ritehi)]
    ([loval=hival; nutree =<NUM >%loval] *{replace constant node if so}*
    | [otherwise; nutree = this])
$\Rightarrow$ nutree ;

RngCheck ↓exlo: int ↓exhi: int

$\rightarrow$ <RngChk <NUM >%loval <NUM >%hival >
    [loval≤exlo&hival≥exhi] *{in range...}*
$\Rightarrow$ <RngChk <> <> > *{so delete both checks}*

$\rightarrow$ <RngChk <NUM >%loval <NUM >%hival >
    [loval≤exlo&hival<exhi]
$\Rightarrow$ <RngChk <> <NUM >%hival > *{delete low check}*

$\rightarrow$ <RngChk <NUM >%loval <NUM >%hival >
    [loval>exlo&hival≥exhi]
$\Rightarrow$ <RngChk <NUM >%loval <> > *{delete high check}*

$\rightarrow$ <RngChk <NUM >%loval <NUM >%hival >
    [loval>exlo&hival<exhi] *{not known to be in range}*

$\rightarrow$ <> ; *{no range check to eliminate}*

Listing 8.9b. Constant folding analysis and transformation grammar.

intrinsic attribute evaluation function **replace** creates a new value table in which the range for a particular variable has been replaced with the given two values. Note that some care must be taken in implementing this function because the old table may also be passed down the other branch of a fork and independently updated. Thus, it is important here to retain the reality of attributes as values rather than data structures, which may be altered. The attribute evaluation function merge takes two range tables (generally derived from a single parent) and creates a new table in which the range of each variable is the union of the corresponding ranges in the two input tables. Thus, for each variable, LoOut=min(LoIn1,LoIn2) and HiOut=max(HiIn1,HiIn2). The implementation of these evaluation functions is left to the reader. We note that the lattice Bottom range contains no values (it can be represented by [+∞,−∞] or [1,0] or any other empty range), and is used to initialize the table for all variables when the analysis starts. Alternately, if the analysis starts with an empty table, the Bottom range can be the implied value of any variable not yet entered into the table.

One useful transformation not shown in Listing 8.9 looks for two-operator tree fragments with nonadjacent constant subtrees, such as the example in Figure 8.15. Although moving added constants up toward the root of the expression tree results in no immediate simplification or reduction in code, it turns out that this form of expression tree is common in compiler-generated subscript expressions for which the final operation is a memory reference. Most computers support an indexed offset addressing mode that amounts to a nearly free constant addition as the final operation of the address expression calculation, so propagating constant sum terms out toward the root of the expression tree can result in faster, tighter code in these cases.

The grammar fragment in Listing 8.9 also does not show constant folding in loops. As with DFA, two passes are sufficient to detect constant expressions and variables, but full range checking requires some information about the loop structure. We will address this issue in more detail when we look at that optimization. The reader may wish to modify this grammar to eliminate the range-checking, and to correctly handle constant expressions around loops.

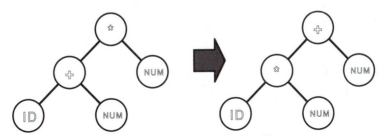

Figure 8.15. Moving added constants toward expression tree root.

8.8.3 Common Subexpression Detection Using Value Numbers

As in constant folding, the working data structure propagated around the program tree for common subexpression elimination (CSE) is a symbol table. In this case, however, the "name" used to access the entries in the table is a subexpression node, not merely a variable number. The "value" of such a name in the table is a reference to the subtree that computes the subexpression. As we walk the tree examining subexpressions, each node is looked up in the table, and if found, the tree is transformed to use a temporary variable in which that value is saved. Our algorithm is a simplification of the "value number" system first published by Cocke and Schwartz in 1970. They numbered the values and constructed a directed acyclic graph (DAG) of the expressions, where we simply use a reference (pointer) to the original subexpression tree. Others have suggested using a data-flow analysis of "available expressions" [Aho&Ullman, 1973], but this is fundamentally the same computation in a less perspicuous notation.

The subexpression node information that is entered as an identifier into the table consists of an operator (node name) and the value numbers of its operands. A binary operator node will thus have three components, and even using numerical value numbers, the resulting record is likely to be too large for convenient and fast table searching. To achieve a reasonable symbol-table lookup performance we recommend that the subexpression characteristics be hashed (see Chapter 3 for a discussion of hash table techniques). With a reasonably large hash table, the lookup time can be reduced to one or two comparisons per access. The number of live entries in the table will typically consist of the visible variables, plus less than a couple dozen available expressions, so a table size of 100-500 is more than adequate, especially in a language like Modula-2, which limits the visibility of nonlocal identifiers.

Global CSE is not often attempted in commercial compilers, because it is thought that it requires iterating data-flow analysis over the whole program. We use a monotonic algorithm, so restricting our program graph to a tree achieves optimal code in two passes. It can be shown, however, that the first pass need only identify the variables modified within the loop. The simulated execution pass can be done only once.

To see how the CSE algorithm works, consider the program tree of Figure 8.16. The nodes of the tree are numbered with Roman numerals to correspond to the sequence of value tables in Table 8.2; value numbers passed as attributes up the tree are shown in outline Arabic numerals. As we begin to walk the tree from the top, the expression table is empty (*i*). Alternatively, it could be initialized to contain the live variables, with value numbers that are merely references to themselves. The first nontrivial node encountered is an assignment.

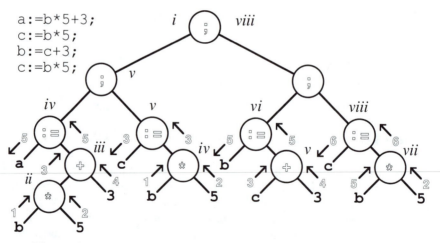

Figure 8.16. Common subexpression elimination illustrated. Small Roman numerals refer to snapshots in Table 8.2. Outline digits are value numbers (see text for detailed explanation).

Travelling down its expression subtree in depth-first simulated execution order, we reach the identifier node b and return a value number 1, referring to this particular value in the variable b (not just any value in b, but the value it contains at this instant in the execution). The constant 5 in the right subexpression of the multiply node returns a value number 2. The multiply node now has a composite value (*,1,2), which is not in the table. It is entered as value number 3 (*ii*), and that value number is passed up the tree to the addition node. There a similar process adds value numbers 3 (just formed) and 4 (the constant 3), to produce a new value number 5 for the composite expression (+,3,4). The assignment operator enters a new value for the variable a into the table, which is the same value number 5 (*iv*).

i	(*empty*)		*vi*		
				b	5
ii				5	2
	b	1		*,1,2	3
	5	2		3	4
	*,1,2	3		+,3,4	5
iii				a	5
	b	1		c	3
	5	2	*vii*		
	*,1,2	3		b	5
	3	4		5	2
	+,3,4	5		*,1,2	3
iv				3	4
	b	1		+,3,4	5
	5	2		a	5
	*,1,2	3		c	3
	3	4		*,5,2	6
	+,3,4	5	*viii*		
	a	5		b	5
v				5	2
	b	1		*,1,2	3
	5	2		3	4
	*,1,2	3		+,3,4	5
	3	4		a	5
	+,3,4	5		c	6
	a	5		*,5,2	6
	c	3			

Table 8.2. The sequence of value number tables for Figure 8.16.

In the second assignment of our example, b is already in the table, with value number 1. That value is used with no alterations to the table. Similarly, the constant 5 returns the value number 2. The multiplication node composes an expression (*,1,2) and finds it also in the table, value number 3. Again, that value is sent up the tree to the assignment operator. This corresponds to the fact that we have (at this point in the program at execution time) already computed the product b*5. The variable c is entered into the table with value number 3 (*v*). The actual code generated for this second multiply would typically be just a store of the register containing that saved intermediate value. In the third assignment, variable c returns the value number 3, and upon lookup, the expression (+,3,4) returns immediately the value number 5. This value number replaces the previous value for variable b (*vi*).

In the final assignment of the example we have again the subexpression b*5, but the value in b has changed. Thus, when the composite expression (*,5,2) is sought in the table, it is not there and must be added (*vii*). The new value number 6 so derived then becomes the value of variable c, replacing its previous contents (*viii*).

At this point in the analysis, value number 3 is inaccessible because it is named by the product of value numbers 1 and 2, and value number 1 is no longer in the table at all. When CSE is applied to basic blocks only, such debris has little opportunity to accumulate and take up excess compile-time storage. But with global subexpression analysis, it is desirable to eliminate value numbers that have been killed in this way. Whenever a variable is given a new value number, any other value numbers containing the old value in their names can also be purged. Although not the case in our example, that can be applied recursively, as these now-dead value numbers also result in killing off others partially named by them.

The grammar fragment in Listing 8.10 shows the basic form of the analysis and transformation for CSE. The new intrinsic attribute evaluation function **compose** takes a node name (shown as a node constructor with no subtrees) and two value numbers and returns a new value number name that can be used to look up that expression in the symbol table. This function works substantially like the string table mechanism discussed in Chapter 3; its implementation is left to the reader. The grammar fragment in Listing 8.10 shows only two expression nodes. Except for the node name, all expressions are treated identically.

Copy propagation is the name given to the optimization that recognizes multiple assignments of the same value to several variables, and eliminates unnecessary register loads. It rarely saves much code or execution time, but it comes essentially free with CSE.

8.8.4 Left–Motion Hoisting

Hoisting is the name given to the optimization that finds identical code in both legs of a fork (IF-THEN-ELSE or all legs of a CASE), and moves it to the common code before or after the fork. Identical code at the beginning of each leg of a fork can be moved forward (left) to just before the conditional branch; code at the ends of the legs can be moved backward (right) to the point where the legs rejoin. Hoisting generally does not make code any faster, but it can save on code space, where that is at a premium.

Left-motion hoisting takes an analysis very much like common subexpression elimination. During a CSE pass through the program, the expression table for the THEN-part of a fork is saved, and during the ELSE-part, each new expression is looked up in that table (but not added if absent). Any expression found in the table for the other leg of the fork is a candidate for hoisting; it should be pruned out of each leg and grafted onto the end of the common code before the fork decision code.

Transformational Attribute Grammars   Chap. 8

CSEStmt ↓invals: table ↑outvals: table

→ <Assign <ID >%name expn >
   expn: CSEExpn ↓invals ↑evals ↑valtree   *{get expn value number}*
   [replace ↓name ↓valtree ↓evals ↑outvals] *{update value number table}*
⇒ <Assign <ID >%name valtree >   *{replace expn tree with new}*

→ unique: <Read <ID >%name >
   [replace ↓name ↓unique ↓invals ↑outvals] *{give it a new value number}*

→ <Semi left rite >
   left: CSEStmt ↓invals ↑midvals   *{flow sets thru statements}*
   rite: CSEStmt ↓midvals ↑outvals

→ <IF expn then else >
   expn: CSEExpn ↓invals ↑evals ↑valtree   *{get expn value number}*
   then: CSEStmt ↓evals ↑thnvals   *{flow set thru then & else}*
   else: CSEStmt ↓evals ↑elsvals
   [mergevals ↓thnvals ↓elsvals ↑outvals] ; *{pass out union}*
⇒ <IF valtree then else >   *{replace expn tree with new}*

CSEExpn ↓invals: table ↑outvals: table ↑valtree: tree

→ vartree: <ID >%name
   [compose ↓<ID > ↓name ↓0 ↑valno]   *{compute a value number}*
   [lookup ↓valno ↓invals ↑tableval]   *{look it up in the table}*
   ([tableval=<>; valtree=vartree]
    [replace ↓name ↓vartree ↓invals ↑outvals]   *{if not there, put it in}*
   | [otherwise; outvals=invals; valtree=tableval])

→ contree: <NUM >%value
   [compose ↓<NUM > ↓value ↓0 ↑valno]   *{compute a value number}*
   [lookup ↓valno ↓invals ↑tableval]   *{look it up in the table}*
   ([tableval=<>; valtree=contree]
    [replace ↓name ↓contree ↓invals ↑outvals]   *{if not there, put it in}*
   | [otherwise; outvals=invals; valtree=tableval])

→ exptree: <Less left rite >
   left: CSEExpn ↓invals ↑midvals ↑leftval   *{flow sets thru subexpns}*
   rite: CSEExpn ↓midvals ↑expvals ↑riteval
   [compose ↓<Less > ↓leftval ↓riteval ↑valno] *{compute a value number}*
   [lookup ↓valno ↓invals ↑tableval]   *{look it up in the table}*
   ([tableval=<>; valtree=exptree]
    [replace ↓name ↓exptree ↓expvals ↑outvals] *{if not there, put it in}*
   | [otherwise; outvals=expvals; valtree=tableval])
⇒ <Less leftval riteval >   *{replace subexpn trees}*

Listing 8.10a. Common subexpression elimination grammar fragment.

```
  →  exptree: <Plus left rite >
     left: CSEExpn ↓invals ↑midvals ↑leftval       {flow sets thru subexpns}
     rite: CSEExpn ↓midvals ↑expvals ↑riteval
     [compose ↓<Less > ↓leftval ↓riteval ↑valno]   {compute a value number}
     [lookup ↓valno ↓invals ↑tableval]             {look it up in the table}
     ( [tableval=<>; valtree=exptree]
      [ replace ↓name ↓exptree ↓expvals ↑outvals]  {if not there, put it in}
      | [otherwise; outvals=expvals; valtree=tableval] )
  ⇒  <Plus leftval riteval >                        {replace subexpn trees}
```

Listing 8.10b. Common subexpression elimination grammar fragment.

A simple but not particularly speedy technique for left-hoisting is to run the CSE algorithm twice, grafting copies of the hoisting candidates into the common code the first time, and letting the normal CSE algorithm prune the originals on the second pass. This method will fail to correctly hoist identical calls on procedures with side effects, but otherwise it is as effective as the more direct method of pruning and grafting in one pass. Because it differs little from the conventional CSE algorithm, we leave the details of implementation to the reader.

8.8.5 Right–Motion Hoisting

Right-motion hoisting in a tree representation of intermediate code is somewhat more complex than left-motion. Consider the program fragment,

```
IF x THEN z:=a+b ELSE z:=a*b END
```

The hoistable common code in this example is the assignment to the variable z. Table 8.3 shows code for a one-address variant of the Itty Bitty Stack Machine (see Appendix C to convert to zero-address), where the hoisting is a simple transformation. In the tree representation, however, the transformation of the tree is far from simple, as shown in Figure 8.17.

Unoptimized Original Code		After Right-Hoisting	
	`LD x`		`LD x`
	`BRF else`		`BRF else`
	`LD a`		`LD a`
	`ADD b`		`ADD b`
	`ST z`		{moved}
	`BR join`		`BR join`
`else`	`LD a`	`else`	`LD a`
	`MPY b`		`MPY b`
	`ST z`		{moved}
`join`	`...`	`join`	`ST z` {hoisted code}
			`...`

Table 8.3. Right-motion hoisting in machine code.

The problem stems from the fact that program execution walks the tree bottom-up, so that left-hoisting can gather leaves and small twigs from the tips of the tree where they are easily pruned, and graft them into the tips of other trees. Because right-hoisting is concerned with the *last* operations to be performed in a subtree, the candidates for hoisting are likely to be interior nodes, while the leaves and small twigs must somehow be left behind! This can be accomplished only by radically transforming the tree, as we have done in Figure 8.17: a conditional statement with two assignment subtrees must become a single assignment with a conditional expression as the value to be assigned. In practice, temporary variables are created to hold the intermediate values.

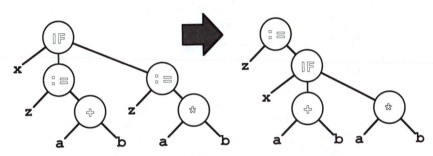

Figure 8.17. The problem of right-motion hoisting in a tree

Listing 8.11 is a fragment of a right-motion hoisting grammar. The fundamental algorithm consists in flowing up the program tree two bundles of code tree fragments. One of these is the collection of code that is to be hoisted; the other is the collection of code that is to be left behind. One of these bundles becomes the transformed node in each production, and the other is passed up as a synthesized attribute. Which bundle is the attribute and which is the transformation depend on whether the current node is to be hoisted or preserved: when the current node is preserved, the bundle of code to be preserved is kept as a subtree to the current node. When the current node is to be hoisted, the bundle to be hoisted is added to it as a subtree, and the preserved code is passed up as an attribute.

RHoist ↓invals: table ↓invref: set ↓invasn: set ↓lastleg: bool ↓hoistme: bool
   ↓parentval: tree ↑outvals: table ↑outvref: set ↑outvasn: set ↑detached: tree

   → myself: <IF expn then else >   {*the root of a hoist tree*}
        else: RHoist ↓empty ↓empty ↓empty ↓false ↓false
              ↓<> ↑elsvals ↑elsvref ↑elsvasn ↑elsdet   {*flow sets thru both legs*}
        then: RHoist ↓elsvals ↓empty ↓empty ↓true ↓true
              ↓<> ↑thnvals ↑thnvref ↑thnvasn ↑thndet
        [union ↓thnvref ↓elsvref ↑midvref]   {*merge the sets for expn*}
        [union ↓thnvasn ↓elsvasn ↑midvasn]   {*not fully recursive here*}
        expn: RHoist ↓invals ↓midvref ↓midvasn ↓lastleg ↓false
              ↓myself ↑outvals ↑outvref ↑outvasn ↑detached
   ⇒ <Semi <IF expn thndet else > then >   {*transform the tree*}

Listing 8.11a. Right-motion hoisting grammar fragment.

→ <Semi left rite >
    rite: RHoist ↓invals ↓invref ↓invasn ↓lastleg ↓lastleg
        ↓<> ↑midvals ↑midvref ↑midvasn ↑ritedet   *{flow sets right-to-left}*
    left: RHoist ↓midvals ↓midvref ↓midvasn ↓lastleg ↓lastleg
        ↓<> ↑outvals ↑outvref ↑outvasn ↑leftdet
    [detached=<Semi leftdet ritedet >]   *{collect detached parts}*

→ myself: <Assign <ID >%name expn >
    ([lastleg=false; valtree=myself; hoistmyself=false]   *{first leg...}*
    ([inset ↓name ↓invasn; midvals=invals]   *{cannot hoist over ass't}*
    | [inset ↓name ↓invref; midvals=invals]   *{cannot hoist over var ref}*
    | [otherwise; into ↓myself ↓invals ↑midvals]   *{ok, put myself into table}*
    | [otherwise]   *{second leg...}*
    [compose ↓<Assign > ↓<ID >%name ↑valno]
    [lookup ↓valno ↓invals ↑tableval; midvals=invals]   *{look me up in table}*
    ([tableval=<>; valtree=myself; hoistmyself=false]
    | [inset ↓name ↓invasn; valtree=myself; hoistmyself=false]
    | [inset ↓name ↓invref; valtree=myself; hoistmyself=false]
    | [otherwise; valtree=tableval; hoistmyself=true]   *{got it; hoist me}*
    tableval: Prune ↓0))   *{also prune other leg}*
    expn: RHoist ↓midvals ↓invref ↓invasn ↓lastleg ↓hoistmyself
        ↓valtree ↑outvals ↑outvref ↑midvasn ↑expdet
    [addset ↓name ↓midvasn ↑outvasn]   *{note this assignment}*
    ([lastleg=hoistself; detached=expdet; xfrm=myself] *{child follows parent}*
    | [otherwise; detached=myself; xfrm=expdet])   *{go our separate ways}*
⇒ xfrm   *{send up new child}*

→ exptree: <Plus left rite >
    ([lastleg=false; valtree=exptree; hoistself=false] *{first leg...}*
    [into ↓exptree ↓invals ↑expvals]   *{put myself into table}*
    | [otherwise]   *{second leg...}*
    [compose ↓<Plus > ↓parentval ↑valno]
    [lookup ↓valno ↓invals ↑tableval; expvals=invals]   *{look me up in table}*
    ([tableval=<>; valtree=exptree; hoistself=false]
    | [hoistme=false; valtree=exptree; hoistself=false]
    | [otherwise; valtree=tableval; hoistself=true]   *{got it; hoist me}*
    tableval: Prune ↓0))   *{also prune other leg}*
    rite: RHoist ↓expvals ↓invref ↓invasn ↓lastleg ↓hoistself
        ↓valtree ↑midvals ↑midvref ↑midvasn ↑ritedet
    left: RHoist ↓midvals ↓midvref ↓midvasn ↓lastleg ↓hoistself
        ↓valtree ↑outvals ↑outvref ↑outvasn ↑leftdet   *{flow sets thru subexpns}*
    exptree: PTangle ↓leftdet ↓ritedet ↓hoistme ↓hoistself ↓tableval ↑detached

Listing 8.11b. Right-motion hoisting grammar fragment.

→ vartree: <ID >%name
    [inset ↓name ↓invasn; hoistme=true]   {cannot hoist over ass't}
    [tempvar ↑varno]   {create new temp var}
    [detached= <ID >%varno]
⇒ <Assign <ID >%varno vartree >   {save var in temp}

→ vartree: <ID >%name
    [otherwise; detached=<>]   {else just follow parent}
    [outvals=invals; outvref=invref; outvasn=invasn];

PTangle ↓leftdet:tree ↓ritedet:tree ↓hoistme:bool ↓hoistself:bool
        ↓oldtree:tree ↑detached:tree

→ exptree: <Plus left rite >
    [hoistme=hoistself]   {child follows parent}
    [detached=<Semi leftdet ritedet >]   {collect detached parts}

→ exptree: <Plus left rite >
    [otherwise; tempvar ↑varno]   {go our separate ways}
    [detached= <Semi <Assign <ID >%varno exptree > <Semi leftdet ritedet >>]
    oldtree: Prune ↓varno   {same var in other leg}
⇒ <ID >%varno ;   {temp var carries value}

Prune ↓varno:int

→ <Plus left rite > | <Assign left rite >
    [varno=0]   {no value to save in var}
⇒ <Semi left rite >

→ exptree: <Plus left rite >
    [varno>0]   {save partial value in var}
⇒ <Assign <ID >%varno <Plus left rite > >;

Listing 8.11c. Right-motion hoisting grammar fragment.

For every node, whether it is to be hoisted or preserved in place is a decision that depends only on its own structure and inherited information. Among that inherited information is a Boolean revealing whether or not the parent node is to be hoisted. Armed with that knowledge, a node can determine how to position the two bundles of subtrees passed up to the parent. There are four possible contingencies, two in which the node and its parent are hoisted or preserved together, and two in which they go their separate ways. Because the decision to hoist depends on whether the parent also hoists, one of these cases is vacuous. However, a parent node can be hoisted, leaving a child behind unhoisted. In this case the two bundles are exchanged in transit, so that the code that goes together stays together. This decision process is illustrated graphically in Figure 8.18. Note that hoisting a subtree node to the right while leaving behind a parent node that depends on the subtree's value corrupts the meaning of the program.

In CSE and left-motion hoisting, an entry in the symbol table is killed by an assignment to the component variable. In right-hoisting, references to variables must also be considered. No variable reference may be hoisted over an unhoisted assignment to it;

variable assignments may be hoisted over neither references nor other assignments to the same variable. This constraint is implemented by two sets flowed from right to left: one contains the set of variables with unhoisted references, and the other is the set of variables with unhoisted assignments. Assignments can only be hoisted when the destination variable is a member of neither set; references to a variable can be hoisted if it is not a member of the assignment set.

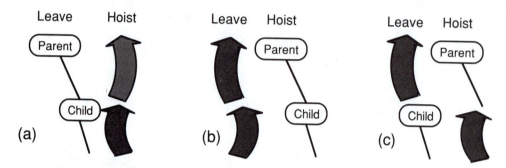

Figure 8.18. The interaction of parent and child nodes in hoisting. In (a) the parent and child are unhoisted; hoisted nodes (if any) are passed up on the right. In (b) the parent and child are both hoisted; unhoisted nodes are passed up. In (c) the parent is hoisted but the child is not; they are separated and sent up with other nodes of similar disposition. It is not possible to hoist a child out from under its parent (see text).

8.8.6 Useless Code and Other Right-to-Left DFAs

Right-motion hoisting is intrinsically a right-to-left mirror image of simulated execution. Useless code elimination also requires a right-to-left analysis that identifies the live variables. Assignments to dead variables are useless and can be removed. We have already looked at live variable analysis.

One of the register allocation strategies is related to live variable analysis in that it seeks to identify which register a value should be in, then works backward to assign the registers for subexpressions so that the value ends up in that register. This will be discussed in more detail in Chapter 9 under the general topic of register allocation. Resource scheduling in high-performance computers makes similar demands.

8.8.7 Mathematical Identities and Code Selection

In most computers there is a variety of different instruction execution times. In particular, multiplication is typically slower than addition or shifting. The clever compiler can exploit mathematical identities such as $n+n=2n$ by replacing multiplication by a constant 2 with adding the multiplicand to itself, or shifting it left one bit position. Multiplication by any constant power of two can be converted into a shift of the appropriate number of places. Such optimizations are called *strength reduction* because they reduce the strength (time, space) of the code to implement a computation.

Transformational Attribute Grammars   Chap. 8

The fragment of a code generation grammar in Listing 8.12 shows two different ways that strength reduction might be applied in the Itty Bitty Stack Machine to convert multiplication by a constant 2 to addition (assuming that it gains a performance advantage). The first rule transforms a multiplication node into an addition node by replicating its subtree; this assumes that a subsequent application of CSE would eliminate the duplication (and that there are no side effects in the subexpression). The other rule is a fragment of the code generation (tree-flattening) grammar, where different code is generated based on the different tree forms. Of course, a compiler would use only one of these methods. Note that the first rule is semantics-driven in form, whereas the second is syntax-driven. With conditional attribute assertions and "maximal munch" tree parsing, either parse could be used in either case.

```
StrenRed        {do this before CSE}

  →  myself: <Star  left  rite >
       left: StrenRed                                    {check subtrees}
       rite: StrenRed                                    {...for strength reduction}
       ( [rite:<CON >%2; xform=<Plus left left >]        {right subtree is constant 2}
       | [left:<CON >%2; xform=<Plus rite rite >]        {left subtree is constant 2}
       | [otherwise; xform=myself]                       {neither subtree qualifies}
  ⇒  xform    {transform the tree}


CodeGen  ↓inlocn:int  ↑outlocn:int                       {in final code generation}

  →  <Star  left  <CON >%2 >
       left: CodeGen ↓inlocn ↑midlocn                    {do left subtree}
       Emit ↓8 ↓midlocn ↑nxtlocn                         {emit DUPE opcode}
       Emit ↓12 ↓nxtlocn ↑outlocn                        {emit ADD opcode}

  →  <Star  <CON >%2  rite >
       rite: CodeGen ↓inlocn ↑midlocn                    {do right subtree}
       Emit ↓8 ↓midlocn ↑nxtlocn                         {emit DUPE opcode}
       Emit ↓12 ↓nxtlocn ↑outlocn                        {emit ADD opcode}

  →  <Star  left  rite >
       [otherwise]                                       {none of the above}
       left: CodeGen ↓inlocn ↑midlocn                    {do left subtree}
       rite: CodeGen ↓midlocn ↑nxtlocn                   {do right subtree}
       Emit ↓11 ↓nxtlocn ↑outlocn                        {emit MPY opcode}
```

Listing 8.12. Two grammar fragments for strength reduction.

Other mathematical identities can be exploited during constant folding. The distributive law for addition and multiplication permits the sum of two products involving the same constant factor to be transformed into the product of a sum. The commutative and associative laws, although not always true in computer arithmetic, can often be applied to collect constant terms for partial evaluation. We have already applied the axiom of negative numbers in the Itty Bitty Stack Machine to perform subtraction; distributing the negative sign through an expression can sometimes save an intermediate store or load in register machines.

Strength reduction optimizations are part of a general class of *code selection* optimizations. In this class the various operation codes of the target hardware are analyzed to select the best sequence of instructions out of several possibilities for each intermediate language construct. For example, in the Itty Bitty Stack Machine the logical NOT operation inverts all the bits of its operand, whereas the NOT operator in Modula-2 inverts only the single bit distinguishing FALSE (0) from TRUE (1). Inverting all the bits of FALSE produces –1, which is different from TRUE. There are several choices for a sequence of IBSM instructions to give a correct NOT operation listed in Table 8.4. One of these would be selected by the compiler designer, depending on hardware execution time and code space for each sequence.

NOT	ZERO	NEG	ONE
ONE	EQUAL	ONE	XOR
AND		ADD	

Table 8.4. Four IBSM code sequences for the Boolean NOT operator.

Unlike the Itty Bitty Stack Machine, many computers lack specific hardware for converting the result of a comparison to a single bit that can be stored into a variable or used as an operand in Boolean operations AND and OR. When this conversion is required, the industrious compiler designer will analyze several different sequences of instructions, seeking an efficient algorithm, just as we did for the Boolean NOT operator in the IBSM.

8.8.8 Loop Structure Analysis

Most of the literature on loop structure analysis deals with reconstructing the structure graph from a linear (basic block or quad) representation of the intermediate code, and for unstructured languages like Fortran there is no alternative. Recognizing the widespread usage of structured programming languages like Modula-2 (and to a certain extent Pascal and C, where the unstructured language features are either limited or usually deprecated), we prefer to preserve as much of the source language structure as possible in the intermediate code for loop analysis. The abstract tree representation of an arbitrary loop in most modern languages requires two distinctive node types, illustrated in Figure 8.19. The entire loop is identified by a LOOP node over its body. Everything under the LOOP node is potentially iterated, which continues until execution reaches the code represented by an EXIT node. If execution completes execution of the code represented by the body subtree without encountering an EXIT, the loop is repeated from the beginning. Some languages may make the representation of an explicit CYCLE node appropriate also; as this contributes no additional difficulty nor understanding, we leave its details to the reader.

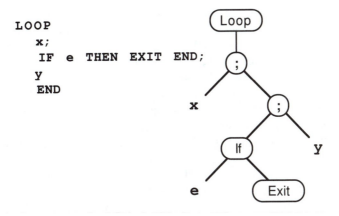

```
LOOP
    x;
    IF e THEN EXIT END;
    y
END
```

Figure 8.19. Loop structure node, showing explicit exit.

The most important result of loop analysis is the identification of what we call *persistent loop variables*, or PLVs. A persistent loop variable is a variable that is live on entry to the loop body, and assigned to within the body. In other words, it is used first, and then modified. Much of the literature is concerned with *induction variables*, which increase (or decrease) by a loop-constant amount for each loop iteration. Induction variables are generally derived from the control variable of a FOR loop, but they may be programmed explicitly in other source forms. The control variable itself is also a PLV; some induction variable optimizations convert derived induction variables into independent PLVs.

Persistent loop variables are readily identified in a single DFA pass through the loop body, either right-to-left or left-to-right. Two sets must be propagated through the DFA to correctly identify PLVs. One of them is the set of variables assigned to, and the other the live references to variables (as seen from the front of the loop). In a left-to-right DFA, a variable is added to the live references set on use if it is not in the assigned set; it is added to the assigned set unconditionally upon assignment. In the right-to-left DFA direction, a variable is added to the live references set only if it is already in the assigned set; assignment removes the variable from the live references set as well as updating the assignment set. Upon completion of the DFA pass, the live variable set is the intersection of the two working sets propagated out of the loop body. As we have already discussed DFA at some length, we leave the specific grammar details as an exercise.

Persistent loop variables are used in identifying loop constants for code motion in a single (subsequent) simulated execution analysis pass through the loop body. This functions somewhat like a cross between constant folding and hoisting and is sometimes actually called hoisting. A variable that is neither loop-constant nor a PLV must be assigned before used within the body of the loop. Therefore, a single set can be propagated forward through the simulated execution, which is the set of variables known not to be loop-constant. It is initialized at the front of the loop body with the set of PLVs and includes any variables assigned along the way. Any expression containing only constants and variable references not in this set can be presumed loop-constant and moved forward out of the loop. Functions with no side effects can also be considered loop-constant if their actual parameters are loop-constant.

Listing 8.13 shows a fragment of a grammar for loop-constant code motion, using the synthetic approach of Figure 8.8. It does not propagate loop-constant code all the way out of nested loops, although it could be modified to do it with a little effort. Of particular interest in this grammar is the IF node whose control expression happens to be loop-constant. The grammar shows moving the expression out of the loop, where it is assigned to a new temporary variable. That variable is tested inside the loop to select one branch or the other. *Unswitching* is an optimization that performs a more radical surgery in this case, forming two loops out of the one, as shown in Figure 8.20. All the code of the loop is duplicated except for the fork. The test is moved outside the loop and selects between one or the other copy, and the THEN-part is preserved in one copy of the loop, whereas the ELSE-part is preserved in the other copy. Thus, although the code size may get substantially larger, all the testing and branching logic is removed from the loops, thereby improving execution time and possibly giving rise to further loop-constant and CSE optimizations that might have been missed due to conflicts between the THEN– and ELSE-parts.

LoopCon ↓notcon:set ↑outnot:set ↑concode:tree

    →   <Loop body >%plv
        body: LoopCon ↓plv ↑newnot ↑moved   *{process loop body}*
        [concode=<>]   *{nothing is propagated out}*
        [union ↓notcon ↓newnot ↑outnot]   *{...except modified var set}*
    ⇒   <Semi moved <Loop body >%plv >   *{attach moved code to front}*

    →   <Exit >
        [outnot=notcon; concode=<>]   *{nothing comes out at all}*

    →   myself: <If expn then else >
        expn: ExpnCon ↓notcon ↑iscon ↑moved   *{do the expression}*
        then: LoopCon ↓notcon ↑notl ↑movet   *{do left subtree}*
        else: LoopCon ↓notcon ↑notr ↑movee   *{do right subtree}*
        [union ↓notl ↓notr ↑outnot]   *{merge modified var set}*
        ([iscon=false; xform=myself]   *{not const: merge all moved}*
        [concode= <Semi moved <Semi movet movee > >]
        | [otherwise; newvar ↑varno]   *{else create a temp var}*
        [xform=<If <VAR >%varno then else >]   *{...to hold constant expn}*
        [concode=<Semi <Assn <VAR >%varno expn > <Semi movet movee > >]
    ⇒   xform   *{replace node as required}*

    →   <Semi left rite >
        left: LoopCon ↓notcon ↑midnot ↑movel   *{do left subtree}*
        rite: LoopCon ↓midnot ↑outnot ↑mover   *{do right subtree}*
        [concode=<Semi movel mover >]   *{merge the moved code}*

Listing 8.13a. Grammar fragment for loop-constant code motion.

→ myself: <Assn <VAR >%varno expn >
       expn: ExpnCon ↓notcon ↑iscon ↑moved   {*do the expression*}
       ([notinset ↓varno ↓notcon; iscon=true]   {*expn&var are constant, so*}
         [concode=myself; outnot=notcon; xform=<>]   {*...move whole assignment*}
       | [otherwise; addset ↓varno ↓notcon ↑outnot]   {*else add var to set*}
         [concode=moved; xform=myself])   {*and pass the moved code*}
⇒ xform   {*replace node as required*}

ExpnCon ↓notcon:set ↑iscon:bool ↑concode:tree

→ <CON >%val
       [concode =<>; iscon=true]   {*yup, it's loop-constant*}

→ <VAR >%varno
       ([notinset ↓varno ↓notcon]   {*var is constant*}
         [concode=<>; iscon=true]
       | [otherwise; concode =<>; iscon=false])   {*not loop-constant*}

→ myself: <Plus left rite >   {*any operator node...*}
       [otherwise]   {*none of the above*}
       left: ExpnCon ↓notcon ↑isconl ↑movel   {*do left subtree*}
       rite: ExpnCon ↓notcon ↑isconr ↑mover   {*do right subtree*}
       ([isconl=isconr; xform=myself; iscon=isconl]   {*both subexpns same, so*}
         [concode=<Semi movel mover >]   {*...keep node together*}
       | [isconl=true; iscon=false; newvar ↑varno]   {*left const: create temp var*}
         [xform=<Plus <VAR >%varno rite >]   {*...to hold constant value*}
         [concode=<Semi <Assn <VAR >%varno left > mover >]
       | [isconr=true; iscon=false; newvar ↑varno]   {*right constant, left not...*}
         [xform=<Plus <VAR >%varno rite >]   {*so do the same...*}
         [concode=<Semi <Assn <VAR >%varno left > mover >])
⇒ xform   {*replace node as required*}

Listing 8.13b. Grammar fragment for loop-constant code motion.

8.9 Implementing Abstract-Syntax Trees

There is little published literature on implementing tree transformers. Most of the material in the remainder of this chapter represents original work with considerable room for improvement. We present it primarily to show one possible implementation, and we encourage our readers to develop more efficient algorithms for their own compilers.

The implementation of an actual abstract-syntax tree in memory requires the use of pointer and record data types for generic tree nodes. In a hand-written compiler, record variants can be used effectively to define the different node structures, but it is often simpler to define a single node record type that is general enough to cover all the different kinds of nodes used in the compiler. For example, if tree nodes can have up to three subtrees, the node record should have three fields for subtree pointers. Another advantage

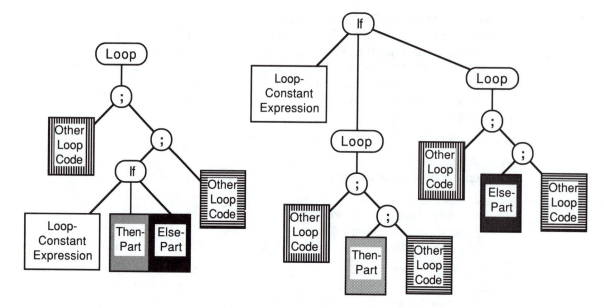

Figure 8.20. Loop unswitching.

of a consistent node structure is that it facilitates the reclamation of dynamic storage as tree fragments are discarded during transformation. Leaving that function to the operating system's DISPOSE procedure is somewhat less efficient than maintaining a list of already-allocated empty nodes. Similarly, when memory constraints force the implementation of virtual memory techniques, the task is simplified with uniform-size nodes.

The minimum requirement for a generic node record structure is a node name defining what kind of node it is, one pointer for each possible subtree, and a pointer of some kind to accommodate a decoration. A variant record either in the decoration field or for the whole node record allows polymorphic decorations: often different parts of the AST (that is, different kinds of nodes) will dictate different types of decoration. Listing 8.8 shows one kind of node (WHILE) decorated with sets, and other kinds (Assign, ID, NUM) decorated with integers. An implementation may also include tag fields in these variants and the code to check for consistent usage if a strongly-typed compiler construction tool is not available; after the compiler is thoroughly tested, the consistency checks and tag fields can be removed if necessary to improve compile time in the production compiler.

The tree node type should be exported from a module that also exports procedures for building and parsing the tree nodes. If sets (that is, the bit vector representation of sets) are implemented as variants of the tree node type, the same module will also export procedures for manipulating them. Listing 8.14 shows a simple implementation of such a module, but with no provisions for storage recovery. Although shown here as an interior module, in practice this would be divided into separately compiled definition and implementation modules in the obvious way.

The tree node constructor BuildTree is fairly straightforward; it returns a tree pointer that can be used directly as the parameter of another BuildTree call, permitting the simple translation of complex tree templates into executable code. Parsing tree nodes is somewhat more complex. Each individual `ParseTree` function call recognizes one node, and returns in reference parameters the subtrees. Complex templates can be parsed by nested IF structures. Both of these procedures are illustrated in the sample transformer of Listing 8.16. The `TransformTree` procedure is used to replace a node structure with some other structure. It cannot transform an empty tree into a nonempty tree node, and vice versa, but these limitations can be enforced mechanically.

```
MODULE Trees;
EXPORT Tree, Sett, NodeKind, Nill,         (* basic types *)
       BuildTree, ParseTree, DisposeTree,   (* procedures *)
       TransformTree,
       IntTree, TreeInt, IntSett,           (* integer coercion *)
       Union, Intersect, SubSett, InSett;   (* set operators *)

CONST
  Nill = NIL;
  SegSize = 64;            (* set segment size, chosen for hardware *)

TYPE
  Tree = POINTER TO Node;
  Sett = Tree;
  NodeKind = (None, Int, Setn, IDn, NUMn, Assign, Readn, Writen,
              IFn, WHILEn, Semi);          (* add others as needed *)

  BitVector = SET OF [0..SegSize-1];
  Node = RECORD
    CASE NodeName: NodeKind OF
      Int: IntValue: INTEGER; |
      Setn:
        BaseValue: INTEGER;
        Link: Sett;
        Segment: BitVector; |
      ELSE
        Left, Middle, Right, Decor: Tree;
    END END;

PROCEDURE Union(a, b: Sett): Sett;
VAR theTree, theRest: Sett;
BEGIN
  IF (a=b) OR (b=NIL) THEN RETURN a
  ELSIF a=NIL THEN RETURN b
  ELSE
    theRest := Union(a^.Link, b^.Link);
    IF (theRest=a^.Link) AND (b^.Segment <= a^.Segment)
      THEN RETURN a
    ELSIF (theRest=b^.Link) AND (a^.Segment <= b^.Segment)
      THEN RETURN b
```

Listing 8.14a. A tree node implementation module.

```
      ELSE
        NEW(theTree);
        WITH theTree^ DO
          NodeName := Setn;
          BaseValue := a^.BaseValue;
          Segment := a^.Segment + b^.Segment;
          Link := theRest;
          END;
        RETURN theTree
    END END;
END Union;

PROCEDURE Intersect(a, b: Sett): Sett;
VAR theTree, theRest: Sett;
BEGIN
  IF a=b THEN RETURN a
  ELSIF (a=NIL) OR (b=NIL) THEN RETURN NIL
  ELSIF a^.BaseValue > b^.BaseValue
    THEN RETURN Intersect(a, b^.Link)
  ELSIF a^.BaseValue < b^.BaseValue
    THEN RETURN Intersect(a^.Link, b)
  ELSIF a^.Segment * b^.Segment = BitVector{}
    THEN RETURN Intersect(a^.Link, b^.Link)
  ELSE
    theRest := Intersect(a^.Link, b^.Link);
    IF (theRest=a^.Link) AND (a^.Segment <= b^.Segment)
      THEN RETURN a
    ELSIF (theRest=b^.Link) AND (b^.Segment <= a^.Segment)
      THEN RETURN b
    ELSE
      NEW(theTree);
      WITH theTree^ DO
        NodeName := Setn;
        BaseValue := a^.BaseValue;
        Segment := a^.Segment * b^.Segment;
        Link := theRest; END;
      RETURN theTree
  END END;
END Intersect;

PROCEDURE InSett(theTree: Sett; Value: INTEGER): BOOLEAN;
BEGIN
  IF theTree=NIL THEN RETURN FALSE
  ELSE WITH theTree^ DO
    IF BaseValue > Value THEN RETURN FALSE
    ELSIF BaseValue+SegSize <= Value THEN RETURN InSett(Link, Value)
    ELSE RETURN (Value MOD SegSize) IN Segment
  END END END;
END InSett;
```

Listing 8.14b. A tree node implementation module.

```
PROCEDURE DisposeTree(theTree: Tree);
BEGIN  (* should recursively dispose theTree and all subtrees *)
END DisposeTree;

PROCEDURE SubSett(a, b: Sett): BOOLEAN;  (* TRUE iff a <= b *)
BEGIN
  IF a=NIL THEN RETURN TRUE
  ELSIF b=NIL THEN RETURN FALSE
  ELSIF a^.BaseValue > b^.BaseValue
    THEN RETURN SubSett(a, b^.Link)
  ELSIF a^.BaseValue < b^.BaseValue
    THEN RETURN (a^.Segment=BitVector{}) AND SubSett(a^.Link, b)
  ELSE
    RETURN (a^.Segment<=b^.Segment) AND SubSett(a^.Link, b^.Link)
  END;
END SubSett;

PROCEDURE BuildTree(name: NodeKind;
                    first, second, third, decn: Tree): Tree;
VAR theTree: Tree;
BEGIN
  NEW(theTree);
  WITH theTree^ DO
    NodeName := name;
    Left := first;
    Middle := second;
    Right := third;
    Decor := decn;
    END;
  RETURN theTree
END BuildTree;

PROCEDURE ParseTree(theTree: Tree; name: NodeKind;
                VAR first, second, third, decn: Tree): BOOLEAN;
BEGIN
  IF theTree=NIL THEN RETURN name=None
  ELSE WITH theTree^ DO
    IF NodeName <> name THEN RETURN FALSE
    ELSE
      first := Left;
      second := Middle;
      third := Right;
      decn := Decor;
      RETURN TRUE
      END
    END
  END
END ParseTree;
```

Listing 8.14c. A tree node implementation module.

```
PROCEDURE TransformTree(theTree, newTree: Tree);
BEGIN
  IF theTree<>NIL THEN
    IF newTree=NIL THEN WITH theTree^ DO
      NodeName := None;
      Left := NIL;
      Middle := NIL;
      Right := NIL;
      Decor := NIL;
      END
    ELSE theTree^ := newTree^ END END
END TransformTree;

PROCEDURE TreeInt(theTree: Tree): INTEGER;
BEGIN
  IF theTree=NIL THEN RETURN 0
    ELSE RETURN theTree^.IntValue END
END TreeInt;

PROCEDURE IntTree(Value: INTEGER): Tree;
VAR theTree: Tree;
BEGIN
  NEW(theTree);
  theTree^.NodeName := Int;
  theTree^.IntValue := Value;
  RETURN theTree
END IntTree;

PROCEDURE IntSett(Value: INTEGER): Sett;
VAR theTree: Sett;
BEGIN
  NEW(theTree);
  theTree^.NodeName := Setn;
  theTree^.BaseValue := Value - Value MOD SegSize;
  theTree^.Segment := BitVector{Value MOD SegSize};
  theTree^.Link := NIL;
  RETURN theTree
END IntSett;
END Trees;
```

Listing 8.14d. A tree node implementation module.

Unlike most set types in Modula-2 and Pascal, the bit vectors we use in flow analysis have an essentially unbounded number of elements. Compiling programs with large numbers of declared variables will require correspondingly large bit vectors for analysis. The same compiler running in a small memory partition and compiling small programs should not be penalized (in time nor space) by the large program requirement for large sets. Therefore, the most practical implementation of such bit vectors is a dynamic linked list of set segments. The implementation of Listing 8.14 illustrates how this is accomplished. Although the set manipulation procedures are shown as recursive, the

Transformational Attribute Grammars   Chap. 8

procedure calling overhead imposed by many hardware and software environments may make an iterated implementation more efficient. Some compilers simply set an arbitrary limit — such as 256 — on the number of variables, assuming that reasonable procedures will not access more than that. This requires that local variables always be numbered from zero, and that nonlocal variables (if they are supported in DFA algorithms at all) be remapped to reference numbers within the upper bound to the extent that there remain unused bit-vector assignments.

The implementation of Listing 8.14 is designed to minimize the number of set segments linked together in a sparse set, by disallowing empty set segments. A singleton set element will use only one segment node, and the intersection operator will omit resulting segments that are empty. Both union and intersection operators attempt to reuse segments as much as possible. The number of elements in a segment should be adjusted for the hardware, to make access to one segment as much as possible an atomic machine operation. This objective must also be balanced against the node size determined by the number of subtree pointers, to minimize wasted memory. Compiling significant programs involves substantial memory usage for in-memory trees, so this is an important consideration.

When a tree transformer is required to operate on more nodes than there is resident memory to contain, the tree node implementation can be readily converted to a virtual memory approach without requiring operating system support other than for a single random-access file. Instead of using NEW and DISPOSE for pointer management, we explicitly allocate node space in a file of node blocks. The Tree type is no longer a pointer but a cardinal index into the file. One advantage of the information-hiding capability of modern programming languages like Modula-2 is that the client routines in the tree transformer need not be altered to accommodate such a radical change in the tree node implementation. Listing 8.15 shows how the file management aspects of a virtual memory version of the tree node module might be implemented.

The function Touch does all the important work in this implementation. Given a virtual tree pointer (that is, an index into the file), it determines if that block is in memory, and if not, finds the least recently used block to swap out for it. It returns an index into the memory array identifying the block that contains this node. A separate information array similarly indexed holds a record showing the time of last touch (from a counter that is incremented on each call), and a flag indicating whether the block requires writing out to disk when it is replaced. There are better swapping algorithms for specific reference distributions, but this works reasonably well for most cases.

```
MODULE Trees;
FROM FileSystem                        (* or its equivalent *)
  IMPORT BinaryFile,    (* = opaque file type *)
    RandomOpen (* filevar: BinaryFile; maxBytes: CARDINAL *),
    RandomRead (* filevar: BinaryFile; position: CARDINAL;
                block: ADDRESS; nBytes: CARDINAL *),
    RandomWrite (* filevar: BinaryFile; position: CARDINAL;
                block: ADDRESS; nBytes: CARDINAL *);
```

Listing 8.15a. A virtual-memory tree node module.

```
EXPORT Tree, NodeKind, Nill,              (* basic types *)
       BuildTree, ParseTree, DisposeTree, (* procedures *)
       IntTree, TreeInt, IntSett,         (* integer coercion *)
       Union, Intersect, SubSett, InSett; (* set operators *)

CONST Nill = 0;
CONST
  BlockSize = 1024;        (* the number of nodes in a block *)
  MemBlocks = 50;          (* the number of blocks in memory *)
  MaxBlocks = 1000;        (* maximum number of blocks in file *)
TYPE
  Tree = CARDINAL;
  ...
  NodeBlock = ARRAY [0..BlockSize-1] OF Node;

CONST BlockBytes = SIZE(NodeBlock);     (* bytes in a block *)

VAR
  NodeFile: BinaryFile;  (* the disk file for swapped-out trees *)
  LastTree: Tree;              (* = the number of allocated trees *)
  NextTime: CARDINAL;                      (* current age *)
  LastBlock: CARDINAL;                     (* file extent *)

  InMemoryTrees: ARRAY [1..MemBlocks] OF NodeBlock;
  InMemoryInfo: ARRAY [1..MemBlocks] OF RECORD
    Blockno: [0..MaxBlocks-1];
    Dirty: BOOLEAN;                  (* write this block if TRUE *)
    Age: CARDINAL;         (* for LRU, smaller numbers are older *)
    END;
  BlockIndex: ARRAY [0..MaxBlocks-1] OF [0..MemBlocks];
                      (* = index to InMemoryTrees, or 0 *)

PROCEDURE Touch(theTree: Tree; MakeDirty: BOOLEAN): CARDINAL;
VAR lru, i, k: CARDINAL;     (* returns index into InMemoryTrees *)
BEGIN
  i := BlockIndex[theTree];
  IF i=0 THEN              (* not in memory; find oldest to swap *)
    lru := NextTime;
    FOR k:= 1 TO MemBlocks DO WITH InMemoryInfo[k] DO
      IF Age<lru THEN
        i := k;
        lru := Age;
        END
      END END;
    WITH InMemoryInfo[i] DO
      IF Dirty THEN RandomWrite(NodeFile, Blockno*BlockBytes,
        InMemoryTrees[i], BlockBytes) END;
      Blockno := theTree DIV BlockSize;
```

Listing 8.15b. A virtual-memory tree node module.

```
      IF Blockno>LastBlock THEN
        RandomWrite(NodeFile, Blockno*BlockBytes,
          InMemoryTrees[i], BlockBytes);
        LastBlock := Blockno;
      ELSE
        RandomRead(NodeFile, Blockno*BlockBytes,
          InMemoryTrees[i], BlockBytes)
        END;
      Age := NextTime;
      Dirty := MakeDirty;
      END
  ELSE WITH InMemoryInfo[i] DO
    Age := NextTime;
    IF MakeDirty THEN Dirty := TRUE END;
    END;
  END;
  NextTime := NextTime+1;
  RETURN i
END Touch;

PROCEDURE NewTree(): Tree;
BEGIN
  LastTree := LastTree+1;
  RETURN LastTree
END NewTree;

PROCEDURE BuildTree(name: NodeKind;
                     first, second, third, decn: Tree): Tree;
VAR theTree: Tree;
BEGIN
  theTree := NewTree();
  WITH InMemoryTrees[Touch(theTree, TRUE)]
      [theTree MOD BlockSize] DO
    NodeName := name;
    Left := first;
    Middle := second;
    Right := third;
    Decor := decn;
    END;
  RETURN theTree
END BuildTree;

PROCEDURE ParseTree(theTree: Tree; name: NodeKind;
                VAR first, second, third, decn: Tree): BOOLEAN;
BEGIN
  IF theTree=Nill THEN RETURN name=None
  ELSE WITH InMemoryTrees[Touch(theTree, FALSE)]
      [theTree MOD BlockSize] DO
```

Listing 8.15c. A virtual-memory tree node module.

```
      IF NodeName <> name THEN RETURN FALSE
      ELSE
        first := Left;
        . . .
END ParseTree;
. . .

PROCEDURE InitTrees;                    (* module initialization code *)
VAR n: CARDINAL;
BEGIN
  RandomOpen(NodeFile, MaxBlocks*BlockBytes);      (* or whatever *)
  LastTree := Nill;
  NextTime := 1;
  FOR n:=1 TO MaxBlocks DO
    IF n<MemBlocks THEN BlockIndex[n-1] := n
      ELSE BlockIndex[n-1] := 0 END END;
  FOR n:=1 TO MemBlocks DO WITH InMemoryInfo[n] DO
    Age := 0;
    Blockno := n-1;
    Dirty := FALSE;
    RandomWrite(NodeFile, Blockno*BlockBytes,
      InMemoryTrees[n], BlockBytes);
    END END;
  LastBlock := MemBlocks-1;
END InitTrees;

BEGIN
  InitTrees;
END Trees;
```

Listing 8.15d. A virtual-memory tree node module.

8.10 Implementing TAG-Driven Tree Transformers

Given a tree node implementation such as that in Listing 8.14, constructing a tree transformer from a TAG becomes again mostly an exercise in mechanical transcription. We start with the recursive-descent construction introduced in Chapter 4, augmented for attribute evaluation as in Chapter 5. Parsing tree templates is accomplished by appropriate calls on the imported function ParseTree; each template is tried in turn, backing out of each failed production until all assertions evaluate to true. The nonterminals, therefore, are most easily implemented as Boolean functions, each of which returns false if no production parses to completion. In some cases flow analysis can show the parse to be deterministic, and the conditional testing can be eliminated. Table 8.5 gives the mechanical translation to Modula-2 for each grammatical form. Listing 8.16 illustrates the translation concretely with the code for the first three productions in the loop constant TAG of Listing 8.13.

Grammar Form	Modula-2 Code

Nonterminal . . .
     → . . . . ;
	```PROCEDURE NonTerminal```
	``` (theTree:Tree; ...):BOOLEAN;```
	```VAR ok: BOOLEAN; any: Tree;```
	```BEGIN```
	``` ok := TRUE;```
	``` . . . .```
	``` RETURN ok```
	```END NonTerminal;```

↓inherited: typename ↑derived: typename	```inherited: typename;``` ```VAR derived: typename;```

→ <Kind left rite >%deco
  . . .
	```IF NOT ok THEN```
	``` ok:=ParseTree(theTree, Kind,```
	``` left, rite, any, deco);```
	``` IF ok THEN ... END END;```

→ atree: <Top <Inner > >
  . . .
	```IF NOT ok THEN```
	``` atree:=theTree;```
	``` ok:=ParseTree(atree, Top,```
	``` temp, any, any);```
	``` IF ok THEN```
	``` ok:=ParseTree(temp, Inner,```
	``` any, any, any, any);```
	``` ... END END;```

atree: NonTerm ↓inhatt ↑synatt	```IF ok THEN ok:=NonTerm(atree,``` ``` inhatt, synatt) END;```
([attr=value] . . . | [otherwise] . . .)	```IF ok THEN IF attr=value THEN ...``` ``` ELSE ... END END;```
[attr= <Kind left rite >%deco]	```IF ok THEN attr:=BuildTree(Kind,``` ``` left, rite, nill, deco) END;```
⇒ atree	```IF ok THEN TransformTree(theTree,``` ``` atree) END;```

Table 8.5. Translating TAG forms to Modula-2.

The TAG implementation of Listing 8.14 and Table 8.5 has one hazard that must be guarded against by other means than shown. The problem comes about when a particular node of the AST is transformed. Because other parts of the tree and other open nonterminals (active procedures) may have references to the node being transformed, the TransformTree procedure must necessarily replace the contents of the node record

```
PROCEDURE LoopCon(theTree:Tree; notcon:Sett;
    VAR outnot: Sett; VAR concode:Tree): BOOLEAN;
VAR ok: BOOLEAN;
    body, moved, expn, thenn, ellse, movet, movee,
      xform, temp: Tree;
    plv, newnot, notl, notr: Sett;
    iscon: BOOLEAN;
    varno: INTEGER;
BEGIN
  ok:=ParseTree(theTree, Loop, body, temp, temp, plv);
  IF ok THEN ok:=LoopCon(body, plv, newnot, moved) END;
  IF ok THEN
    concode := Nill;
    outnot := Union(notcon, newnot);
    TransformTree(theTree, BuildTree(Semi, moved,
      BuildTree(Loop, body, Nill, Nill, plv), Nill, Nill));
    END;
  IF NOT ok THEN
    ok:=ParseTree(theTree, Exit, temp, temp, temp, temp) END;
  IF ok THEN
    outnot := notcon;
    concode := Nill;
    END;
  IF NOT ok THEN
    ok:=ParseTree(theTree, Iff, expn, thenn, ellse, temp) END;
  IF ok THEN ok:=ExpnCon(expn, notcon, iscon, moved) END;
  IF ok THEN ok:=LoopCon(thenn, notcon, notl, movet) END;
  IF ok THEN ok:=LoopCon(ellse, notcon, notr, movee) END;
  IF ok THEN outnot := Union(notl, notr) END;
  IF ok THEN
    IF iscon=FALSE THEN
      xform := theTree;
      concode := BuildTree(Semi, moved,
        BuildTree(Semi, movet, movee, Nill, Nill), Nill, Nill)
    ELSE
      newvar(varno);
      xform := BuildTree(Iff,
        BuildTree(Varr, Nill, Nill, Nill, IntTree(varno)),
        thenn, ellse, Nill);
      concode := BuildTree(Semi,
        BuildTree(Assign,
          BuildTree(Varr, Nill, Nill, Nill, IntTree(varno)),
          expn, Nill, Nill),
        BuildTree(Semi, movet, movee, Nill, Nill), Nill, Nill);
      END END;
  IF ok THEN TransformTree(theTree, xform) END;
  RETURN ok
END LoopCon;
```

Listing 8.16. A sample tree-transformer, from TAG in Listing 8.13.

with a copy of the contents of replacement node. If the replacement tree contains the original node as a subtree, the result of the transformation would be a circular structure as shown in Figure 8.21 instead of the desired tree. This is a likely event in the loop-constant code motion and hoisting optimizations, where a semicolon node is built

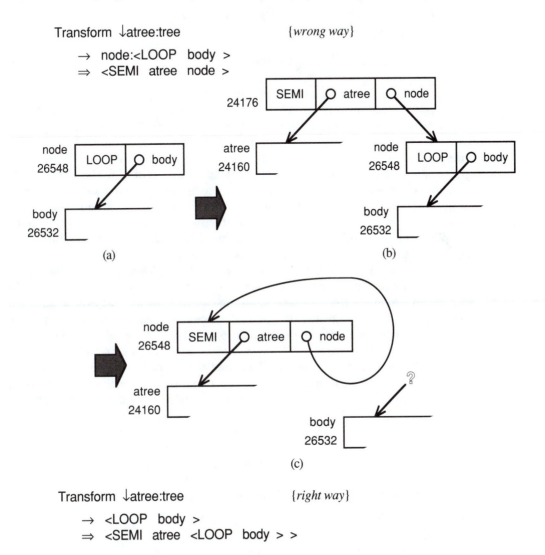

Transform ↓atree:tree   {wrong way}

  → node:<LOOP body >
  ⇒ <SEMI atree node >

Transform ↓atree:tree   {right way}

  → <LOOP body >
  ⇒ <SEMI atree <LOOP body > >

Figure 8.21. Tree transformation the wrong way. The first step (b) builds a new SEMI node over the existing LOOP node (a). The final step (c) copies the new SEMI node over the old tree, resulting in a circular link. The numbers refer to physical memory locations. The second grammar would cause a new LOOP node to be built also, so that when the old tree is replaced by the new one, the connection to the loop body is preserved as in (b).

over the reference node. When manually implementing transformational grammars, the compiler designer must be on guard against this hazard. A mechanical compiler-compiler like the TAG compiler can detect the fault through appropriate data-flow analysis and correct for it by making an extra copy of the reference node. The sample code in Listing 8.16 avoids the problem correctly by reconstructing the reference node (note the difference between the two grammars shown in Figure 8.21).

Summary

This chapter introduced transformational attribute grammars (TAGs) which provide a language for specifying optimizing transformations and code generation. A TAG is a tree-transformational grammar that is also an attribute grammar. A tree-transformational grammar (TTG) specifies a mapping of trees of an input grammar to trees of an output grammar. Recall from Chapter 5 that an attribute grammar (AG) is a context-free grammar extended by attributes associated with each nonterminal. The attributes are evaluated in connection with the application of productions. Attribute values are passed up or down the parse tree. The domain of TAGs is a set of intermediate low-level trees (ILTs), which are tree-structured intermediate transformations of programs produced by compiler front-ends. ILTs differ from parse trees inasmuch as they include low–level, machine-like details, and may omit nonterminals with no semantic actions.

This chapter introduced the notion of a tree grammar which is not constrained by the intrinsic order of the input tokens. Instead, it is the responsibility of the compiler designer to inform the compiler-generator of the appropriate attribute evaluation order. This makes it possible to avoid extensive analysis on the attribute grammar to determine an efficient or optimal attribute evaluation order. This chapter also introduced the construction of intermediate code trees as synthesized attributes in the string grammar as a means of linking the string grammar of a compiler front-end to the tree grammar that specifies optimization and code generation. The use of data-flow analysis for optimizing code transformations was presented. A survey of useful transformational optimizations was also given.

Symbols

$\Rightarrow$	separates rights parts of a TAG production
$\cap$	set intersection
$\cup$	set union

Acronyms

AST	Abstract syntax tree.
CSE	Common subexpression elimination.
DFA	Data-flow analysis.

DFA   Data-flow analysis.

ILT   Intermediate low-level tree.

PLV   Persistent loop variable.

TAG   Transformational attribute grammar.

TTG   Tree-transformational grammar.

Keywords

abstract syntax tree   (1) A parse tree stripped of unnecessary information to obtain a more efficient representation of a source program.

(2) A parse tree that abstracts the syntactic structure from the source program (neither spaces or line breaks nor the spelling of the identifiers and keywords is preserved).

data-flow algorithm

  iterated, monotonic For each iteration, the sets consistently increase or decrease and cannot change direction.

DFA   Data-flow analysis traces flow of data throughout computational unit.

decoration   Any piece of data properly associated with a particular node of an AST.

generator template   Defines the output language.

graph   A graph $G(V,E)$ is a structure consisting of a set of vertices $V=\{v_1,...\}$, edges $E=\{e_1,...\}$ and an incidence function $f: E \rightarrow V \times V$ as in $f(e_i) = (v_j,v_k)$, e_i in E, v_j,v_k in V. The pair (v_j,v_k) marks the endpoints of an edge e_i that connects v_j to v_k.

directed graph   A graph where the endpoints of each edge are ordered. In the graph shown below, edge (u_1,u_2) is in the graph but (u_2,u_1) is not in the graph because there is no edge connecting u_2 to u_1.

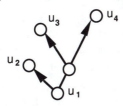

lattice   A set L with intersection $\cap$ and union $\cup$ is called a lattice if and only if L is a partially ordered set and for x, y, z in L the following axioms hold

(1) $x \cap y = y \cap x$ and $x \cup y = y \cup x$ (commutativity)

(2) $(x \cap y) \cap z = x \cap (y \cap z)$ and
$(x \cup y) \cup z = x \cup (y \cup z)$ (associativity)

(3) $x \cup (x \cap y) = x$ and
$x \cap (x \cup y) = x$ (absorption)

match template	Defines the input language in a transformational grammar.
partial order	A binary relation $\leq$ on a set X is a partial order of X when it is reflexive, transitive and antisymmetric. That is, for x,y,z in X, we have

R: $x \leq x$ (reflexive)

T: $x \leq y$ and $y \leq z$ implies $x \leq z$ (transitive)

A: $\ni x,y$ such that $x \leq y$ but not $y \leq x$ (antisymmetric)

Examples: Natural numbers under $\leq$
                 Power set of a set under $\supset$

transformational grammar	A context-free grammar with productions of the form

$$P \to \text{<match template>} \Rightarrow \text{<generator template>}$$

transformations	
code elimination	Prunes, discards superfluous branches from program tree.
code motion	Moves code out of frequently executed parts of program into less frequently used parts.
code selection	Decorates tree in preparation for final tree-flattening code generation pass.
translation grammar	Generates both input and output language.
tree	A connected, nonempty graph is called a tree if it contains no closed path (it is circuit free). Here are two examples of trees:

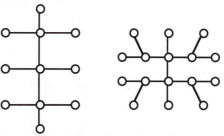

Note: a directed graph is a directed tree if it has a root from which there is a directed path to every other node, and its underlying undirected graph is a tree.

tree grammar	A grammar with an input alphabet consisting of tree nodes and their connections rather than characters or scanned tokens in a linear string.

Exercises

1. Rewrite the following program fragments as trees, using the Polish prefix notation introduced in this chapter. Spell out operator node names, so that "*a+2*" is written as <Plus <ID >%a <NUM >%2 >.

   (a) `(x+y)/(x-y)`

   (b) `next := temp-base*3+1`

   (c) `a := 1; b := -a`

   (d) `IF tx<ty+ent THEN ab:=-1 ELSE ab:=0 END`

   (e) `REPEAT`
   ```
        sum := sum+v*v;
        IF (v>eps) AND (v<ovf) THEN v:=v+delta END
      UNTIL sum>=goal
   ```

   (f) `struct.lnk^^.fld`

2. Apply the grammar from Listing 8.1 to the following expression trees to fold the constants as much as possible. Show the productions applied, including attribute flow. Assume the symbol table contains these identifiers:

dan	TRUE, 6
paul	FALSE, 88
sam	TRUE, 10

   (a) <Minus <ID >%paul <Star <ID >%dan <NUM >%4 >>

   (b) <Plus <Star <ID >%dan <NUM >%3 > <Divd <ID >%sam <NUM >%2 >>

   (c) <Plus <Plus <ID >%paul <NUM >%5 > <ID >%sam >

3. Rewrite the program fragments in Exercise 1 as quads, showing basic blocks.

4. Rework the forward data-flow problem of Listing 8.4, but choose sets that enable your algorithm to catch the use of undefined variables such as c.

5. Modify the program of Listing 8.3 to include an assignment to variable c, then rework the forward and backward data-flow analyses of Listing 8.4 and Listing 8.5 to show the correctness of the modification. Use the corrected forward data-flow algorithm from Exercise 4.

6. Modify the DFA attribute grammar of Listing 8.6 to identify PLVs in a single loop.

Review Quiz

Indicate whether the following statements are true or false.

1. An abstract syntax tree is another form of a parse tree.

2. The input alphabet for a tree grammar consists of scanned tokens in a linear string.

3. A TAG generates a tree with the same root as the program tree.

4. The input and output languages are essentially different languages in a transformational grammar.

5. A TAG is a TTG that is also an AG.

6. A tree grammar is not constrained by any intrinsic order of tokens in an input file.

7. The string grammar of a compiler front end can be linked to the tree grammar that specifies optimization and code generation by using a translation grammar that recognizes a string grammar and whose translation part is a tree grammar.

8. A decoration is any collection of data associated with an AST node.

9. Tree grammars are purely deterministic when compared to string grammars.

10. The maximal munch heuristic is used in a transformational grammar to give preference to the smallest, most specific production template in matching nodes with templates.

Compiler Project

1. Convert your compiler grammar to separate front and back ends, so that the front end builds a tree, and the back end generates IBSM code from the tree.

2. Choose one or more of the optimizations discussed in this chapter, and write a complete TAG for each optimization.

3. Merge your grammars into one TAG and compile it on the TAG compiler, or else write an optimizing compiler in a programming language like Modula-2 from your grammars.

Further Reading

Aho, A.V. & Ullman, J.D. *Theory of Parsing, Translation, and Compiling:Vol. 2, Compiling.* Englewood Cliffs, NJ: Prentice Hall, 1973. Introduces the notion of available expressions in data-flow analysis. An expression A+B is an available expression on entering a block if A+B is always computed before reaching the block but not before a definition of A or B.

Backus, J. "The History of FORTRAN I, II, and III." ACM *SIGPLAN Proceedings of History of Programming Languages* (1981), pp. 25-74.

Cocke, J. & Schwartz, J.T. *Programming Languages and their Compilers. Preliminary Notes,* (2nd rev. version). New York: Courant Institute of Mathematical Science, 1970. Uses graph abstraction technique in code optimizations (see discussion of graph abstraction in the annotation of Kuhn et al., below).

Deransart, P., Jourdan, M., & Lorho, B. *A Survey on Attribute Grammars in Three Parts.* TR 485, Institut National de Recherche en Informatique, 1986. Part I, *Main Results on Attribute Grammars.* See section 4 on "Evaluation by Tree Walk." Part II, *Review of Existing Systems.* See pp. 79ff on MUG2, an overview of a complete compiler generator based on attribute grammars using attributed tree transformations as a tool to specify and perform source level optimizations. Part III, *Classified Bibliography.* See pp. 41ff on data-flow analysis and code generation.

Engelfriet, J. & File, G. "Passes, Sweeps and Visits in Attribute Grammars." *Journal of the ACM*, Vol. 36, No. 4, (1989), pp. 841-869. Pure attribute grammars are defined by nondeterministic evaluators and simple attribute grammars by deterministic evaluators. Eight classes of grammars are given. The time complexity of deciding membership in these classes of attribute grammars is examined.

Engelfriet, J., Rozenberg, G., & Slutzki, G. "Tree Transducers, L Systems and Two-way Machines." *Journal of Computer Systems and Software*, Vol. 20 (1980), pp. 150-202. See for formal discussion of the relationship between attribute grammars and tree-processing transducers.

Even, S. *Graph Algorithms*. London: Pitman, 1979. See ch. 1 on paths in graphs and ch. 2 on trees, especially section 2.1 on tree definitions.

Ganapathi, M. & Fischer, C.N. "Description-Driven Code Generation Using Attribute Grammars." *Proceedings of the 9th Annual ACM Symposium on Principles of Programming Languages*. New York: ACM, 1982, pp. 108-119.

Gokhale, M. *Parallel Evaluation of Attribute Grammars*. Technical Report No. 89-17, Universtiy of Delaware, 1989. A weight is attached to each synthesized attribute and forks a process whenever a weight exceeds a certain threshold.

Kamimura, T. "Tree Automata and Attribute Grammars." In *Automata, Languages and Programming*. Lecture Notes in Computer Science, Vol. 154. New York: Springer-Verlag, 1983, pp. 374-384. Attribute values are treated as strings over a fixed alphabet, and attribute grammars are defined as tree-to-string transducers. Presents tree-walking push-down tree-to-string transducers as a model for attribute transducers.

Kildall, G.A. *Global Expression Optimization During Compilation*. Ph.D. dissertation, University of Washington, Computer Science Group, 1972. Gives algorithms and correctness proof for basic DFA over arbitrary program graph.

Knuth, D.E. "Semantics of Context-free Languages." *Mathematical Systems Theory*, 2:2, New York: Springer-Verlag, 1968, pp. 127-130.

Knuth, D.E. *The Art of Computer Programming: Vol. 1, Fundamental Algorithms*. Reading, MA: Addison-Wesley, 1973. See swapping buffer algorithms, pp. 143-144, 213-215.

Kuhn, R.H. et al. "Dependence Graphs and Compiler Optimization." *Proceedings of the 8th Annual ACM Symposium on Principles of Programming Languages*, 1981, pp. 207-218. Uses graph abstraction (a set of nodes and their arcs are merged into a single node) to organize optimizations (this technique is also used in data-flow analysis (see Cocke&Schwartz, 1970,above) as well as to control the scope of optimization in the SIMPL optimizer described in Zelkowitz&Bail, 1974]). The authors use graph abstraction to isolate sets of statements that can be translated into machine code only when taken as an ensemble.

Madsen, O.L. "On the Use of Attribute Grammars in a Practical Translator Writing System." Report DAIMI, Computer Science Department, Aarhus University, 1975.

Madsen, O.L. "Towards a Practical and General Translator Writing System." Report DAIMI, Computer Science Department, Aarhus University, 1980.

MetaWare, Inc. *Metaware Translator Writing System User Manual*. Santa Cruz, CA, 1981.

Payton, T. et al. "Design Level Debugging of Attribute Grammars." Report, SDC, Burroughs, Paoli, PA, 1982.

Pittman, T. *Practical Code Optimization by Transformational Attribute Grammars Applied to Low-Level Intermediate Code Trees*. Ph.D. dissertation, University of California at Santa Cruz, 1985.

Pittman, T. *Using Transformational Attribute Grammars for Code Optimization*. TR-CS-86-4, Department of Computing and Information Sciences, Kansas State University, 1986. Discusses TAGs, gives sample intermediate code tree ILT showing three out of nine declaration links. Notes two beneficial consequences of using TAG and ILT notations: (1) in the analysis of what was hoistable and (2) in using an ILT to build operator nodes over subexpression subtrees.

Zelkowitz, M.V. & Bail, W.G. "Optimization of Structured Programs." *Software— Practice and Experience*, Vol. 4, No. 1 (1974), pp. 51-57. Optimizes structured blocks from the inside out.

Chapter 9

Code Generation and Optimization

Aims

- Introduce advanced code generation and optimization issues.
- Investigate optimization of loops and resource allocation.
- Consider register allocation in terms of graph-coloring and in expression.
- Illustrate the conversion of zero-address code to register machine code.
- Simulate the execution of code in a compile-time stack.
- Give an example of generating register-based code from IBSM.
- Illustrate processor scheduling implemented in a tree-grammar that constructs a directed acyclic graph.
- Consider compilers designed for RISC, pipeline, and vector processors.

9.1 Introduction

Most of our code generation exercises thus far have been aimed at the Itty Bitty Stack Machine, which has a very simple instruction set. Real computers are not built that way, for a very good reason: strange and wonderful instructions make computers go fast, and fast computers sell better than slow ones. There is no good research relating architectural considerations to each other and to performance; most of the better computer designs spring fully formed from the head of some genius computer designer with an intuitive grasp of what the current technology can do to support the features people seem to be asking for. Compiler writers continue to ask for orthogonal instruction sets to simplify their lives, but speed-critical code is usually written in assembly language, and it is speed hackers, not compiler people, who drive the marketplace.

One important class of optimizations is largely independent of the computer architecture, but also does not often submit very well to a grammatical approach; this is the class of loop optimizations. In Chapter 8 we addressed some of the issues surrounding persistent loop variables (PLVs), loop invariant code motion, and general data flow through loops, and showed how these analyses and optimizations could be expressed in transformational attribute grammars (TAGs). In this chapter we delve more deeply into issues that focus on the special problems involved in making loops execute fast. This includes the conversion of induction variables, loop unrolling and fusion, and linearizing arrays, which can be considered a special case of loop unrolling. There is less published literature covering the implementation of these concepts, and we also treat the topics in less detail than has been our practice, leaving more to the inventive artistry of the reader.

In this chapter we also address the special problems that irregular computer architectures lay on the compiler designer. The most significant of these problems lie in the general areas of memory and register allocation, baroque instructions, and resource scheduling. Each of these problems is particularly difficult to handle in a grammar-based compiler design, but there are some effective compromises that can achieve reasonably good performance for some of these in a grammar-based compiler, and we do touch lightly on other methods for dealing with these issues. It is notable that there is considerable overlap between general loop optimization and the kinds of handling required by vector computers.

9.2 Loop Optimizations

Most computer programs spend nearly all of their runtime within the inner loops which constitute 10% of the total code or less. Effort spent optimizing loops thus has a disproportionate reward.

9.2.1 Range Analysis Through Loops

Of all the optimization analyses with any performance reward that we might consider, the least simple is probably the extension of range analysis through loops. Its rewards are not confined to the code within the respective loops, but extend throughout the program, enabling both full range-check elision and (depending on the target hardware) the substitution of shorter variables and arithmetic operators than those selected by the programmer.

As we have already observed, apart from their use in loops, the range analysis of scalar variables is a simple matter of simulated execution. The range of a persistent loop variable, however, depends also on the number of iterations through the loop, which cannot always be inferred at compile time. We examine here the cases where either it can be inferred, or else bounds on the number of iterations can be established.

The simplest case is clearly the FOR-loop construct, where the number of iterations is set by the programmer-specified range of the control variable. Where the starting and ending values are constants, the number of iterations is also constant. Less often the starting and ending values of the control variable are displaced by constants from the same (nonconstant) expression value, which also yields a constant number of iterations but at considerably more compile-time cost, as in

```
FOR i:=(n-1)*3 TO n*3+8 DO
```

Constant folding transformations that move the added constant parts up toward the root of the expression tree and common subexpression elimination analysis can work together to facilitate the recognition of such loop ranges.

We already know that constant expression analysis is merely a special case of range analysis, so it is a small step to recognize and establish bounds for the control variables in FOR-loops where the starting and ending values differ by nonconstant values. The range analysis will have determined the bounds on the starting and ending values; the lower bound of the starting value and the upper bound on the ending value form the bounds of the control variable without further ado.

In other loop structures the analysis is somewhat more complex. Although it may not be possible to infer reasonable bounds on the number of loop iterations, our concern is not with the number of iterations, but with the ranges of the variables, which are often more limited. Special attention is required only for persistent loop variables; given reasonable bounds on them, the ranges of other variables can be determined by conventional methods.

Most often, although not always, it can be determined that one bound of the PLV within the loop is the initial value established outside the loop. This is the case when the PLV is monotonic; that is, all assignments to it within the loop augment it by a nonnegative (or else nonpositive) value, or multiply it by a positive value, as determined by the range analysis of the modification expression. Unless the PLV is directly referenced in the modification expression, it may be difficult to establish monotonicity. The simple addition of a bounded subexpression (frequently a constant) to the PLV occurs often enough to make its analysis worthwhile. If the control decision of the loop tests a PLV against a bounded expression, that sets another bound on its range, usually at the opposite end from the initial value. Sometimes a programmer will use a constant increment and fixed limit on the PLV that controls a loop instead of a FOR-loop construct, if (as in Modula-2) there is no convenient way to short-circuit the loop execution on alternate criteria; a compiler for such a language might profitably look for such situations to establish also an upper bound on the number of iterations.

When the number of iterations is bounded, the upper (or lower) bound of a monotonic PLV that is neither directly nor indirectly the control variable can still be determined from the product of the upper bound on the number of iterations times the upper bound on the augments in all the PLV assignments. This applies equally to nonmonotonic PLVs because the lower bound can be determined from the product of the lower bound on the most negative augment times the upper bound on the number of iterations.

Error tests included by the programmer can also be used to establish bounds on PLVs, provided that they are in the same execution path with any assignments to the PLVs; the only tests that the compiler can use to this effect are of the form

      IF v>k THEN *ErrorProc*

where the global flow analysis has established that *ErrorProc* is a procedure call that never returns, or else it is a GOTO-like control structure such as EXIT (in Modula-2) or break (in C).

All of the analyses we have discussed so far are nearly linear in compile time; that is, a small fixed number of passes over the program tree, augmented by another small fixed number of extra passes over each loop body at each level of nesting, can gather all of the relevant information. Many of the calculated ranges are admittedly rather pessimistic, but they can be proved correct and safe, and often will yield useful optimizations. Better limits on the the ranges, and particularly bounds on the variables that do not fit any of the criteria identified here, probably require sophisticated theorem-proving techniques and exponential analysis time; it is our opinion that the improvement in performance to be derived from such methods does not justify the extra compile-time costs.

9.2.2 Induction Variables

An *induction variable* is any ordinal variable or compiler-generated temporary variable whose value follows the control variable of a loop in a linear relationship. A programmer-defined induction variable is assigned exactly once in the body of the loop in such a way that any execution path that uses the variable always goes through the assignment first, or else the assignment is unconditional; a temporary induction variable is generally a compiler-generated intermediate value derived from the control variable or another induction variable by the addition or multiplication of loop constants. Although many induction variables are derived in this way from the control variable, the important concept is that they need not be. Consider the following example loop:

```
n:=100;
FOR  i:=1  TO  10  DO
    j:=i*8+k;
    a[j,3]:=n;
    n:=n-10;
END
```

The control variable i is clearly an induction variable, and so is j, which is derived from it by the multiplication and addition of loop constants. Less obvious is the machine-level index to the array a, which is derived from the induction variable j by multiplication times the array slice size and adding the second subscript. In this example, n is also an induction variable, for although it is independently derived, it generally has the value i*(-10)+90. The value of induction variable analysis is that the multiplications required to calculate the iteration values for j and the array subscript can be optimized into additions or subtractions of loop constants, so that they more closely resemble the loop calculation of n (assuming of course that a single addition is less costly than a multiplication possibly followed by an addition, which is usually the case). In this case the compiler would insert an initializing step for j before the loop: j:=k, and then replace the loop body assignment with the (hopefully faster) addition: j:=j+8. The array subscript temporary created by the compiler would undergo a similar transformation. Now the variables take on the same sequence of values as before, but we have eliminated two multiplications from the body of the loop. Furthermore, we can now readily see that the variable j is dead, so its assignment in the loop body can be eliminated altogether, as shown below. It's possible that the remaining addition for the array access may be merged into an indexed addressing mode, giving further performance improvement in a way that was not possible when the multiplication was involved.

Code Generation and Optimization   Chap. 9

```
n:=100;
tv:=k*asize8+abase+3;
FOR i:=1 TO 10 DO
  tv:=tv+asize8;
  a[tv]:=n;
   n:=n-10;
  END
```

The recognition of induction variables requires a slight enhancement of the simulated execution flow analysis used for constant folding and range analysis. Induction variables derived from other induction variables are readily identified, once it can be shown that they lie in the main loop execution path, are not persistent loop variables, and their value is composed from a known induction variable by multiplication and addition of loop constants. PLVs assigned only once are easily seen to be induction variables when their modification is limited to the addition or subtraction of a loop constant. It is our goal to convert all derived induction variables into PLVs. This analysis requires at most one more pass through the body of the loop after the loop constants and PLVs have been identified. The details are left as an exercise.

9.2.3 Loop Unrolling

After moving loop constants out, the simplest and most effective optimization for improving loop execution time is unrolling. A short loop with a fixed number of iterations can be fully unrolled, completely eliminating the loop overhead and making it possible to apply both constant folding and common subexpression elimination to array subscript calculations and other expressions involving the control variable. Even when fully unrolling the loop is not practical, it can be unrolled once, so that two iterations are processed each time through the loop. This small optimization can cut the effective cost of the loop overhead in half and still give ample opportunity for Common subexpression elimination (CSE) to apply across the two iterations.

The easiest kind of loop to unroll is fortunately the one where it is most often effective, and is quite common: a FOR-loop with fixed bounds. The compiler can easily replicate the body of the loop the requisite number of times, with constants substituted for control variable references. When the index range exceeds some implementer-defined limit, it is still possible to establish whether the programmed number of loop iterations is even (or has some other small divisor); with only a little more analysis, the compiler can also make the evaluation for nonconstant index bounds if its range can still be proved constant or a multiple of a small constant. Sophisticated analysis of the index range is probably not justified in most cases, however, except when seeking opportunity to vectorize an inner loop for an array processor.

With loops other than FOR-loops, the analysis is considerably more difficult. The number of iterations may still be inferred from induction variable analysis, but it is not unreasonable to expect a programmer to use a FOR-loop or its equivalent for best performance, when the language supports such a construct. Depending on the target hardware, however, it may still make sense to partially unroll WHILE and REPEAT loops. In these cases there must be a termination test between the iteration segments, but the unrolled loop nonetheless offers the compiler some opportunities for CSE between

the two segments, as shown in Listing 9.1 using Modula-2's LOOP-EXIT construct for
the unrolled loop.

```
WHILE a<b DO                    LOOP
                                    IF a>=b THEN EXIT END;
    b:=b-a*k;                       b:=b-a*k;
    a:=a+1;                         a:=a+1;
    END;                            IF a>=b THEN EXIT END;
                                    b:=b-a*k;  (* a_1*k = a_0*k+k *)
                                    a:=a+1;
                                    END;
```

Listing 9.1. Unrolling a WHILE loop once.

Unrolling the outer loops of a nested set of loops that exactly span a
multidimensioned array is equivalent to interpreting the array references as if the array
were declared with a single dimension. Then, instead of the complex multidimensional
subscript calculation every iteration, a single index steps through the entire array,
avoiding the extra multiplication and addition steps. This is called *linearizing* the array
because it makes code generation equivalent to that of a linear (one-dimensional) array.
The linearized array loop could then be partially unrolled for additional improvements.
Listing 9.2 shows the effects of linearizing an array, again in source language form (note
that array A1 is located at the same memory address as array A).

```
VAR A:ARRAY[1..9,3..17]         VAR A1[ADR(A)]:ARRAY[1..135]
    OF REAL;                        OF REAL;
FOR i:=1 TO 9 DO
    FOR j:=3 TO 17 DO           FOR i:=1 TO 135 DO
        A[i,j]:=0.0 END             A1[i]:=0.0 END
    END
```

Listing 9.2. Linearizing an array.

9.3 Register and Memory Allocation

Most computers have several different kinds of memory explicitly available to the
programmer, often with substantially different performance effects. Usually there is a
small amount of very fast and easily reached memory called *registers*, and a larger amount
of slower memory to hold whole programs and their data. We are not concerned here with
cache memory that is essentially transparent to the program operation. It mimics main
memory, but with a much faster access, deferring only to the slower main memory for
data and instructions that have not been recently touched. We are also not concerned here
with *virtual memory*, which uses disk files to mimic and extend main memory, but at a

slower rate. This is also transparent to the running program because references outside the available physical memory cause an interruption that is handled by the operating system software.

Many computer architectures further subdivide the register and main memory spaces to make some subsets of these more easily reached than others, or to give special significance to some of them. Registers might be divided into *address registers*, which hold main memory addresses, and *data registers*, which hold intermediate calculation values. Main memory can be partitioned into *segments* or *pages*, so that a smaller part of the full memory can be reached more easily than an arbitrary reference.

The main reason for these subdivisions is explained by the concept of *address space*. With n bits you can distinguish 2^n different objects or operations. A memory address space of 65,536 locations requires 16 bits to address it, whereas 4,096 locations require 12 bits and 256 locations requires only 8 bits. In order to pack the most functionality into a limited instruction word size, it is desirable to limit the number of bits in each instruction word allocated to any one function. If, as was the case with early computers, every instruction explicitly addressed two arbitrary locations in memory for the two operands to an addition, then the full address space of a 1,024-word main memory must occupy 20 bits in the instruction. Make one of the operands a single register, and you cut the address component of the instruction word in half. With several registers, there is an address space for the registers also: 3 bits will address 8 registers. Partition a 1-megabyte memory into 65,536-byte segments of which only one or two are accessible at a time and you have removed 3 or 4 bits from the size of the memory access instructions. Sixteen general-purpose registers require 4 bits each to address them, and in instructions that may involve 2 or 3 registers it adds up quickly. Divide the register space into separate address and data registers, and you eliminate 2 or 3 bits from each multiple-register instruction.

To make effective use of register and memory address spaces, the compiler must make decisions about which values to put into registers and when to do it. Human programmers can perceive in a glance clusters of variable usage which could profit from register allocation, but algorithms to reach the same conclusion mechanically are far from trivial. The C programming language leaves the decision to the programmer, which may actually complicate the task of a compiler attempting to do register allocation correctly. The same problem is compounded in computer architectures with various addressing modes. Compilers often get a well-deserved reputation for generating inefficient code because it is so much easier for the compiler designer to simply choose one addressing mode that works correctly, ignoring the opportunities for smaller or faster code that the human programmer might readily see with no effort at all.

9.3.1 Algorithms for Register Allocation

The literature is replete with research in optimal register allocation [Chaitin, 1982; Chaitin et al., 1981; Chow&Hennessy, 1984; Kennedy, 1972]. Considered as a problem in allocating registers to the temporary storage of frequently used variables, it is equivalent to graph-coloring problems. Live variables are represented as regions on the graph, and there is one color for each register to be allocated. The graph is to be colored in such a way that horizontal cuts pass through no two regions of the same color, as shown in Figure 9.1 [Chaitin, 1982].

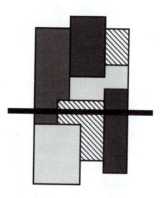

Figure 9.1. Register allocation by graph coloring. The horizontal line represents a particular point in time when three variables are allocated to registers.

Graph-coloring algorithms accomplish their goal by making assumptions about the nature of the register allocation problem, most notably that there are a fixed number of registers available to allocate and that the selection of variables to map into registers is decided elsewhere. Generally there are more candidate variables for register mapping than there are available registers, and the complexity of that decision could dwarf the coloring problem. Furthermore, whereas it is easy to choose some fixed number of registers to be allocated to long-term variable storage, in practice the actual number of available registers varies with the complexity of expressions to be evaluated. We have found an informed demand allocation scheme to give good results without the complexities of graph coloring, and it is also more amenable to a grammatical implementation.

Graph coloring also does not address the question of allocating registers to expression evaluation. With a few exceptions, most modern computers require at least one operand of an arithmetic or logical operation to be in a data register. After applying common subexpression elimination, it is usually desirable to allocate these partial results to registers to make them more accessible for subsequent use without invoking extra memory accesses. The normal way to accomplish this is to create a temporary variable to hold the common subexpression; then submit that variable to the graph-coloring or other register allocation algorithm.

Any register allocation method must be prepared to deal with the problem of running out of registers, especially within an expression evaluation. When that happens, currently active registers are *spilled* to (stored into) memory to make way for new register usage. Registers must also be spilled whenever executing a statement or calling a procedure with side effects that may access the variables held in the registers.

It is here that strongly typed languages like Modula-2 and Pascal make compiler design much easier than low-level languages like C. When the language allows pointer variables free access to any program variable as in C (and also in Modula-2, but only by importing the red-flag SYSTEM.ADDRESS), it is virtually impossible for the compiler to infer that the current register variables are safe; they must all be spilled to their assigned memory locations and reloaded after the pointer has been dereferenced. With strong typing, the compiler can safely assume not only that pointer dereferences threaten no register variables of a different type, but also that a pointer dereference can threaten only dynamic variables, and no local variables at all. A simple data-flow analysis pass through a called procedure can easily determine if that procedure threatens or uses its reference parameters or any nonlocal variables; depending on that procedure's register requirements, only register variables actually used by the called procedure need be spilled to memory, and only those threatened must be reloaded upon return.

Knuth did some studies on expression complexity in typical (Fortran) programs and found that most assignments involved one operator or less, and half were only copying a value to a variable [Knuth, 1971]. Other studies have shown that expression evaluation almost never grows so complex to require five registers for intermediate results. Taking this to heart, many compiler designers have allowed four registers for expression evaluation, which then forces a register spill for the rare complex expression — or else the compiler just gives up and requires the programmer to simplify the expression. Our demand allocation algorithm places no fixed limit (other than the number of hardware registers) on the evaluation, and spills intermediate values or register variables to memory as required by the context.

Given the usual practice of a fixed number of data registers allocated to expression evaluation, there are two different ways to treat the remaining registers. The expression evaluation registers are often considered *volatile*; that is, their values are not preserved across procedure calls. A given compiler may adopt the convention that the other registers are also volatile, or it may choose the somewhat more common convention that some fixed subset of the registers are nonvolatile. A procedure is required by this convention to save and restore any nonvolatile registers it may use. The reasoning in support of such conventions suggests that few procedure calls occur in the middle of active expressions, whereas register variables may be active over many statements, including across procedure calls. In some cases operating system calls are considered to be procedure calls in this respect and do not preserve volatile registers; in other cases the system calls preserve most of the volatile registers also (excepting those that explicitly return values). Usually these conventions are set by the first compiler written for the system, and generally adopted by later compilers as they come along.

9.3.2 Register Allocation in Expressions

A simple one-pass compiler with no flow analysis can do reasonable code generation for a multiple-register machine by simulating the expression stack in the registers. A single flow-through attribute carries an index representing the number of values in the register-based stack, and the registers are ordered so that the first value pushed always goes into (for example) register 0, the second value into register 1, and so on. If the computer supports register-to-register arithmetic, somewhat inefficient zero-address code can be generated with no further ado, as shown in Listing 9.3. Although this example shows a direct conversion from zero-address code to a hypothetical register machine, the code generator could instead generate one-address code, which would eliminate the register-indirect load and store instructions, replacing them and their corresponding address loads with direct loads and stores. We leave the details for an exercise.

Statement to be Compiled: a := (a+b)*(c-3)

IBSM (Zero-Address) Code:		Register Machine Code:		
LDC	A	LDA	0,A	*Load address of* A
LDC	A	LDA	1,A	*Load address of* A
LD		LD	1,@1	*Load* A
LDC	B	LDA	2,B	*Load address of* B
LD		LD	2,@2	*Load* B
ADD		ADD	1,2	*r1+r2→r1*
LDC	C	LDA	2,C	*Load address of* C
LD		LD	2,@2	*Load* C
LDC	3	LD	3,#3	*Load value* 3
SUB		SUB	2,3	*r2−r3→r2*
MPY		MUL	1,2	*r1*r2→r1*
ST		ST	1,@0	*Store into* A

Listing 9.3. Simulating a zero-address stack in registers.

A more structured stack attribute is shown in Figure 9.2, where each cell of this virtual stack at compile time represents the physical location of that value at execution time. The code generator becomes somewhat more complex, because instead of simply generating code to load a register as we did previously, we simulate the execution of the code in the compile-time stack. Actual code is generated only when the information becomes too complex for the virtual stack, or when the result is to be stored back into the destination variable. It is instructive to follow the sequence of steps in Figure 9.2 to see how this works for compiling the assignment statement, a:=(a+b) * (c−3).

In step 1, beginning with an empty virtual stack, the Itty Bitty Stack Machine code that earlier versions of the compiler would have produced results now only in pushing the token "*address of* a" onto the virtual (compile-time) stack. No register code is generated. This is repeated in step 2. Step 3 replaces the top of the virtual stack with the token "*value of* a" in recognition of the IBSM instruction LD. Still no code is generated. The next two steps repeat this process with variable b.

Step 6 requires the simulated computer to add the top two stack cells, but this cannot be shown in the virtual stack. Furthermore, it is not even possible in this computer to add two memory values without putting one of them into a register, so register code is now generated to load register 0 from memory, and the IBSM ADD instruction is reconsidered in step 7, where it results in the memory-to-register ADD instruction. The virtual stack is updated to show that the top cell is the value in register 0. Steps 8 through 12 repeat the process for the second subexpression (b−3). Note that constant values are represented explicitly in the virtual stack. If there is no constant-folding transformation earlier in the compiler, some constant-folding is possible here because the code generator can detect attempts to generate code for arithmetic on two constants in the virtual stack, and simply replace the top of the stack with the appropriate constant token without generating any code.

The final two steps continue the simulation, generating the appropriate register code in each case. It is readily seen that the target machine code is generally very good, and in many cases optimal (as it is here).

	IBSM Code	Virtual Stack	Generated Code
		(empty stack)	
(1)	LDC a	*address of* a	*(no code)*
(2)	LDC a	*address of* a *address of* a	*(no code)*
(3)	LD	*value of* a *address of* a	*(no code)*
(4)	LDC b	*address of* b *value of* a *address of* a	*(no code)*
(5)	LD	*value of* b *value of* a *address of* a	*(no code)*
(6)	ADD	*value of* b *register* 0 *address of* a	LD 0,a
(7)	*ADD*	*register* 0 *address of* a	ADD 0,b
(8)	LDC c	*address of* c *register* 0 *address of* a	*(no code)*
(9)	LD	*value of* c *register* 0 *address of* a	*(no code)*

Figure 9.2a. The virtual stack at compile time.

	IBSM Code	Virtual Stack	Generated Code
(10)	LDC 3	constant 3 / value of c / register 0 / address of a	*(no code)*
(11)	SUB	constant 3 / register 1 / register 0 / address of a	LD 1,c
(12)	*SUB*	register 1 / register 0 / address of a	SUB 1,#3
(13)	MPY	register 0 / address of a	MUL 0,1
(14)	ST	*(empty stack)*	ST 0,a

Figure 9.2b. The virtual stack at compile time.
Italic IBSM operators are held over from previous step.

The critical data structure for generating register code by simulated execution is the virtual stack. It can be implemented as a linked list or as an array of cells. Each cell is a record with a tag field identifying the kind of data contained (variable address, value, constant, or register), and a variant for the variable reference number or address, the constant value, or the register number. Because not all stack cell values will ever be represented in a register (note that the stack in Figure 9.2 grew to four cells, but only two registers were required), it is worthwhile to carry a set of available registers from which to select one when it is needed.

If another register is required and the set of available registers is empty, one of the registers in use must be spilled to memory. Without a backward data-flow analysis (DFA) to inform the selection, the most obvious choice is the register deepest in the virtual stack because it will be the longest before the value in that register is required again. When the register is spilled to memory, its cell in the virtual stack is replaced by a value reference to the temporary memory variable it is stored in at the same time the store instruction is generated. Reload (or direct memory reference in an arithmetic instruction) will occur automatically by the algorithm when that stack cell reaches the top again.

Listing 9.4 shows a module to implement register code generation from IBSM operators passed as parameters. This code will not work perfectly for all register-based architectures, but it does generate adequate (although not always optimum) code for four popular computers, using the constants listed in Table 9.1. The numerical codes for the data tables may be found in Appendix D.

```
MODULE CodeConstants;
(* used in IBSM to general register CPU translator *)

EXPORT
    GenericOpcode,                     (* enumerated list of opcodes *)
    AddressMode;              (* enumerated list of addressing modes *)

TYPE
    AddressMode =
        (non,   (* none or irrelevant *)  con,  (* immediate constant *)
        mem,   (* memory reference    *)  ind,  (* register indirect   *)
        reg,   (* value in register   *)  ccc); (* result of compare    *)

    GenericOpcode = (Nop, Load, Store,      (* memory <--> register *)
        Cmpr, Add, Subt, Mlpy, Neg,         (* arithmetic & compare *)
        Andd, Orr, Jump, Bcc, BackP);       (* cond. branch & logic *)

END CodeConstants;


MODULE TargetMachine;
(* tables defining a particular CPU *)

FROM CodeConstants IMPORT
    GenericOpcode,                     (* enumerated list of opcodes *)
    AddressMode;              (* enumerated list of addressing modes *)

EXPORT
    CPU,       (* a generic number representing the target processor *)
    BigEndian,  (* byte significance in memory: true if msb is 1st *)
    RelBranch, HalfAdd, (* Branch option: true if relative/shifted *)
    HasImmMode,        (* true if has inline constant address mode *)
    WeirdMulti,              (* selects one of n multiply hacks *)
    Register,    (* an integer subrange encompassing all registers *)
    LoReg, HiReg,        (* a range of usable register numbers *)
    AdReg,   (* register for memory addressing, =LoReg if any is OK *)
    ConditionCodes, (* six codes for testing the result of compare *)
    OpCodeIndex, OpCodeTable;   (* the tables for a particular CPU *)

CONST        (* See Table 9.1 and Appendix D for table values *)
TYPE
    Register  = [0..TopReg];
    TableRange = [0..EndTable];
```

Listing 9.4a. A module for generating register-based code from IBSM.

```
VAR            (* these are actually constant tables, not variables *)
  ConditionCodes: ARRAY [0..5] OF CARDINAL;
    (* each entry tests the result of a compare:  <=,<,=,<>,>=,> *)
  OpCodeIndex: ARRAY GenericOpcode, AddressMode OF TableRange;
    (* each entry indexes the start of a sequence in OpCodeTable *)
  OpCodeTable: ARRAY TableRange OF [0..255];
    (* each opcode consists of a sequence of 6+ bytes as follows:
        TotalBytes   - the number of bytes in this instruction
        RegByte      - the byte position of a register number, or cc
        RegPosn      - a multiplier to position it
        AddByte      - the first byte of address, or 2nd reg, or cc
        NumAddBytes  - the number of address bytes, or reg/cc posn
        NumOpBytes   - the number of opcode bytes following
        opbytes...   - the bytes of opcode *)

BEGIN
  (* load up the tables somehow *)
END TargetMachine;


(* Output procedures *)

MODULE TargetGenerator;
(* table-interpreting in-memory code generator *)

FROM TargetMachine IMPORT
  BigEndian,   (* byte significance in memory: true if msb is 1st *)
  Register,      (* an integer subrange encompassing all registers *)
  OpCodeIndex, OpCodeTable;   (* the tables for a particular CPU *)

FROM CodeConstants IMPORT
  GenericOpcode,                     (* enumerated list of opcodes *)
  AddressMode;                (* enumerated list of addressing modes *)

FROM SomeWhere IMPORT
  maxCode;           (* max space to allow for generated object code *)

EXPORT
  EmitTarget;              (* output one target machine instruction *)

VAR ObjectCode: ARRAY [0..maxCode] OF [0..255];

PROCEDURE EmitTarget (theOp: GenericOpcode;
      aMode: AddressMode; regNum, opAddress: INTEGER;
    Location: CARDINAL; VAR NextLoc: CARDINAL);
VAR
  index, opdata, temp, opAdd: CARDINAL;  regNo: Register;
BEGIN
  IF theOp=BackP THEN                    (* backpatching a branch *)
```

Listing 9.4b. A module for generating register-based code from IBSM.

```
      NextLoc := Location;
      opdata := OpCodeIndex[Bcc,mem] + 6;
      Location := NextLoc - OpCodeTable[opdata];
    ELSE                                (* ordinary instruction code *)
      opdata := OpCodeIndex[theOp,aMode];
      NextLoc := Location + OpCodeTable[opdata];
      temp := OpCodeTable[opdata+5];
      FOR index := Location + temp TO NextLoc - 1 DO
        ObjectCode[index] := 0 END;     (* clear unspecified bytes *)
      opdata := opdata + 6;
      FOR index := 0 TO temp - 1 DO            (* insert opcode bytes *)
        ObjectCode[Location+index] := OpCodeTable[opdata+index] END;
      IF aMode > non THEN               (* insert register reference *)
        regNo := regNum;
        index := OpCodeTable[opdata-5];
        temp := regNo*OpCodeTable[opdata-4];
        ObjectCode[Location+index] :=
          ObjectCode[Location+index] + temp MOD 256;
        IF temp>255 THEN
          IF BigEndian THEN
            ObjectCode[Location+index-1] :=
              ObjectCode[Location+index-1] + temp DIV 256
          ELSE
            ObjectCode[Location+index+1] :=
              ObjectCode[Location+index+1] + temp DIV 256
      END END END END;
    IF (aMode = mem) OR (aMode = con) THEN       (* insert address *)
      temp := Location + OpCodeTable[opdata-3] - 1;
      IF BigEndian THEN
        FOR index := OpCodeTable[opdata-2] TO 1 BY -1 DO
          opAdd := opAddress MOD 256;
          ObjectCode[temp+index] := ObjectCode[temp+index] + opAdd;
          opAddress := opAddress DIV 256;
          END
      ELSE FOR index := 1 TO OpCodeTable[opdata-2] DO
        opAdd := opAddress MOD 256;
        ObjectCode[temp+index] := ObjectCode[temp+index] + opAdd;
        opAddress := opAddress DIV 256;
        END END
    ELSIF (aMode = reg) OR (aMode = ind) THEN    (* insert 2nd reg *)
      regNo := opAddress;
      index := OpCodeTable[opdata-3];
      ObjectCode[Location+index] :=
        ObjectCode[Location+index] + regNo*OpCodeTable[opdata-2];
      END;
END EmitTarget;
END TargetGenerator;
```

Listing 9.4c. A module for generating register-based code from IBSM.

```
(* Output procedures *)

MODULE CodeGenerator;
(* IBSM to general register CPU translator *)

FROM TargetMachine IMPORT
  RelBranch, HalfAdd, (* Branch option: true if relative/shifted *)
  HasImmMode,         (* true if has inline constant address mode *)
  WeirdMulti,              (* selects one of n multiply hacks *)
  Register,     (* an integer subrange encompassing all registers *)
  LoReg, HiReg,            (* a range of usable register numbers *)
  AdReg,   (* register for memory addressing, =LoReg if any is OK *)
  ConditionCodes; (* six codes for testing the result of compare *)

FROM TargetGenerator IMPORT
  EmitTarget;              (* output one target machine instruction *)

FROM CodeConstants IMPORT
  GenericOpcode,                   (* enumerated list of opcodes *)
  AddressMode;              (* enumerated list of addressing modes *)

FROM SomeWhere IMPORT
  AllocTempVar, ReleaseTempVars,  (* temp'ry variable allocation *)
  Deepest;                        (* max virtual stack depth *)

EXPORT EmitIBSM, BackPatch;

(* Local definitions *)

TYPE
  regset = SET OF Register;
  stackrange = [0..Deepest];
  stackCell = RECORD
    itsType: AddressMode;
    isNegative: BOOLEAN;
    itsValue: INTEGER;
    END;

VAR
  queuedOpcode: CARDINAL;   (* pending LDC opcode from prev call *)
  busyRegisters: regset;           (* registers currently in use *)
  virtualStack: ARRAY stackrange OF stackCell;
  topStack: stackrange;
  CurrentLoc, hotcc: CARDINAL;

(* Utility procedures *)
```

Listing 9.4d. A module for generating register-based code from IBSM.

```
PROCEDURE PushVirtual (kind: AddressMode; datum: INTEGER);
BEGIN
  INC(topStack);
  WITH virtualStack[topStack] DO
    itsType := kind;
    itsValue := datum;
    isNegative := FALSE;
    END;
END PushVirtual;


PROCEDURE PopVirtual (): INTEGER;
BEGIN
  DEC(topStack);
  RETURN virtualStack[topStack+1].itsValue
END PopVirtual;


PROCEDURE StoreRegister (theReg: Register; theAddress: INTEGER);
  VAR temp: INTEGER;
BEGIN
  EmitTarget (Store, mem, theReg, theAddress,
    CurrentLoc, CurrentLoc);
END StoreRegister;


PROCEDURE SpillRegister (theReg: INTEGER);
  VAR temp: INTEGER;
      here: stackrange;
      gotit: BOOLEAN;
BEGIN
  gotit := FALSE;
  FOR here := 1 TO topStack DO WITH virtualStack[here] DO
    IF (itsType=reg) AND (itsValue=theReg) THEN
      IF NOT gotit THEN
        temp := AllocTempVar();          (* spill this to memory *)
        EmitTarget (Store, mem, theReg, temp,
          CurrentLoc, CurrentLoc);
        gotit := TRUE;
        END;
      itsType := mem;
      itsValue := temp;
    END END END (* of IF,WITH,FOR *);
END SpillRegister;


PROCEDURE CantUseIt (Taken, Weird: BOOLEAN; theReg: Register):
  BOOLEAN;
BEGIN
  RETURN Taken OR Weird AND (WeirdMulti=2) AND NOT ODD(theReg)
    OR Weird AND (WeirdMulti=3) AND (theReg>LoReg)
END CantUseIt;
```

Listing 9.4e. A module for generating register-based code from IBSM.

```
PROCEDURE GetRegister (Weird: BOOLEAN): Register;
  VAR areg: Register;
      hear, there: stackrange;
      usage: ARRAY[LoReg..HiReg] OF CARDINAL;

BEGIN (* GetRegister *)
  areg := LoReg;                              (* try for unused reg *)
  WHILE (areg<HiReg)
      AND CantUseIt(areg IN busyRegisters, Weird, areg)
    DO INC(areg) END;
  IF NOT (areg IN busyRegisters) THEN
    INCL(busyRegisters,areg);
    RETURN areg
    END;
  FOR hear := 1 TO topStack DO WITH virtualStack[hear] DO
    IF itsType=reg THEN                       (* take any reg in stack *)
      areg := itsValue;
      IF NOT CantUseIt(FALSE, Weird, areg) THEN
        SpillRegister(areg);                  (* spill this to memory *)
        RETURN areg
    END END END END (* of IF,IF,WITH,FOR *);
END GetRegister;

PROCEDURE LoadThis (which: stackrange; preferreg: BOOLEAN);
  VAR areg: Register;
BEGIN
  WITH virtualStack[which] DO
    IF (itsType<>reg) OR CantUseIt(FALSE,preferreg,itsValue) THEN
      areg := GetRegister(preferreg);
      EmitTarget (Load, itsType, areg, itsValue,
        CurrentLoc, CurrentLoc);
      itsType := reg;
      itsValue := areg;
    END END;
END LoadThis;

PROCEDURE Flushcc;    (* save compare result not used immediately *)
BEGIN
  IF hotcc>0 THEN LoadThis(hotcc, FALSE) END;
  hotcc := 0;
END Flushcc;

PROCEDURE SwapMaybe (always: BOOLEAN): BOOLEAN; (* TRUE if swap *)
VAR tempCell: stackCell;
BEGIN
  IF NOT always THEN  (* don't swap if top is reg, next not *)
    IF (virtualStack[topStack-1].itsType <> reg)
      AND (virtualStack[topStack].itsType = reg) THEN RETURN FALSE
```

Listing 9.4f. A module for generating register-based code from IBSM.

```
      ELSIF (virtualStack[topStack-1].itsType <> reg)
          OR (virtualStack[topStack].itsType = reg) THEN
        IF virtualStack[topStack-1].isNegative
          OR NOT virtualStack[topStack].isNegative THEN RETURN FALSE
      END END END;
    tempCell := virtualStack[topStack];
    virtualStack[topStack] := virtualStack[topStack-1];
    virtualStack[topStack-1] := tempCell;
    RETURN TRUE
END SwapMaybe;


PROCEDURE DoOpcode (theOp: GenericOpcode);
VAR areg: Register;
  wasNeg: BOOLEAN;
BEGIN
  Flushcc;
  IF SwapMaybe(FALSE) THEN END;
  LoadThis(topStack, (theOp=Mlpy) AND (WeirdMulti>1));
  wasNeg := virtualStack[topStack].isNegative;
  areg := PopVirtual();
  WITH virtualStack[topStack] DO
    IF theOp=Add THEN
      IF wasNeg <> isNegative THEN theOp := Subt END
    ELSIF theOp=Mlpy THEN
      wasNeg := wasNeg <> isNegative;
      IF (WeirdMulti=3) AND ((itsType<>reg) OR (itsValue<>HiReg))
        THEN SpillRegister(HiReg) END; (* special-case 86 regs *)
      END;
    EmitTarget (theOp, itsType, areg, itsValue,
      CurrentLoc, CurrentLoc);
    isNegative := wasNeg;
    itsType := reg;
    itsValue := areg;
    END;
END DoOpcode;


PROCEDURE Compare (ccResult: CARDINAL);
VAR areg: Register;
  wasNeg: BOOLEAN;
BEGIN
  Flushcc;
  IF NOT SwapMaybe(virtualStack[topStack-1].isNegative
      AND NOT virtualStack[topStack].isNegative)
    THEN ccResult := 5-ccResult END;
  LoadThis(topStack, FALSE);
  wasNeg := virtualStack[topStack].isNegative;
  areg := PopVirtual();
```

Listing 9.4g. A module for generating register-based code from IBSM.

```
    WITH virtualStack[topStack] DO
      IF wasNeg <> isNegative THEN (* signs must be same *)
        EmitTarget (Neg, reg, areg, 0,
          CurrentLoc, CurrentLoc) END;
      EmitTarget (Cmpr, itsType, areg, itsValue,
        CurrentLoc, CurrentLoc);
      isNegative := FALSE;
      itsType := ccc;
      IF wasNeg AND (ccResult DIV 2 <> 1) THEN
        itsValue := (ccResult+4) MOD 8 (* invert compare if neg *)
      ELSE itsValue := ccResult END;
      END;
END Compare;


PROCEDURE DoLoad ();
VAR offset, cond: INTEGER;
  areg: Register;
  theOp: GenericOpcode;
BEGIN
  WITH virtualStack[topStack] DO
    IF itsType=con THEN itsType := mem
    ELSE
      LoadThis(topStack, FALSE);
      areg := PopVirtual();
      IF virtualStack[topStack+1].isNegative THEN
        EmitTarget (Neg, reg, areg, 0,
          CurrentLoc, CurrentLoc) END;
      EmitTarget (Load, ind, areg, areg,
        CurrentLoc, CurrentLoc);
    END END;
END DoLoad;


PROCEDURE DoBranch ();   (* always generate long address *)
VAR offset, aLoc, cond: INTEGER;
  theOp: GenericOpcode;
BEGIN
  offset := PopVirtual();
  IF virtualStack[topStack].itsType = con THEN
    IF PopVirtual() = 0 THEN theOp := Jump  (* unconditional *)
      ELSE RETURN END                       (* no branch *)
  ELSE
    theOp := Bcc;
    IF virtualStack[topStack].itsType <> ccc THEN
      LoadThis(topStack, FALSE);
      PushVirtual(con,0);
      Compare(3);                           (* compare top <> 0 *)
      END;
    cond := PopVirtual() END;
```

Listing 9.4h. A module for generating register-based code from IBSM.

```
  IF NOT RelBranch THEN
    aLoc := CurrentLoc;
    offset := offset + aLoc;
    END;
  IF HalfAdd THEN offset := offset DIV 2 END;
  EmitTarget(theOp, mem, cond, offset, CurrentLoc, CurrentLoc);
END DoBranch;

PROCEDURE EmitIBSM (datum: INTEGER; inAddress: CARDINAL;
                    VAR outAddress: CARDINAL);
VAR areg: Register;
BEGIN
  CurrentLoc := inAddress;
  IF queuedOpcode=0 THEN
    queuedOpcode := datum
  ELSE
    PushVirtual(con, datum);
    queuedOpcode := queuedOpcode DIV 32
    END;
  WHILE (queuedOpcode>0) AND (queuedOpcode MOD 32 <> 28) DO
    CASE queuedOpcode MOD 32 OF
      1: DoBranch();
    | 8: WITH virtualStack[topStack] DO          (* DUPE *)
           PushVirtual(itsType, itsValue);
           END;
    | 9: IF SwapMaybe(TRUE) THEN END;            (* SWAP *)
    |11: DoOpcode(Mlpy);                         (* MPY *)
    |12: DoOpcode(Add);                          (* ADD *)
    |14: DoOpcode(Orr);                          (* OR *)
    |15: DoOpcode(Andd);                         (* AND *)
    |16: Compare(2);                             (* EQUAL *)
    |17: Compare(1);                             (* LESS *)
    |18: Compare(5);                             (* GRTR *)
    |20: WITH virtualStack[topStack] DO          (* NEG *)
           isNegative := NOT isNegative;
           END;
    |26: Flushcc;                                (* ST *)
         LoadThis(topStack, FALSE);
         areg := PopVirtual();
         WITH virtualStack[topStack] DO
           EmitTarget (Store, mem, areg, itsValue,
             CurrentLoc, CurrentLoc) END;
    |27: DoLoad();                               (* LD *)
    |29: queuedOpcode := queuedOpcode DIV 32; (* NIBL *)
         PushVirtual(con, queuedOpcode MOD 32);
    |30, 31: PushVirtual(con, queuedOpcode MOD 2) END;
    queuedOpcode := queuedOpcode DIV 32;
    END;
```

Listing 9.4i. A module for generating register-based code from IBSM.

```
    outAddress := CurrentLoc;
END EmitIBSM;

PROCEDURE BackPatch (offset: INTEGER; inAddress: CARDINAL);
VAR aLoc, cond: INTEGER;
BEGIN
  IF NOT RelBranch THEN
    aLoc := inAddress + offset;
  ELSE aLoc := offset END;
  IF HalfAdd THEN aLoc := aLoc DIV 2 END;
  EmitTarget(BackP, mem, 0, aLoc, inAddress, inAddress);
END BackPatch;

BEGIN (* CodeGenerator initialization *)
  topStack := 0;
  busyRegisters := regset{};
  queuedOpcode := 0;
  hotcc := 0;
END CodeGenerator;
```

Listing 9.4j. A module for generating register-based code from IBSM.

Following the definition for the IBSM rather than the logic of Figure 9.2, the Modula-2 code makes no distinction between local variable addresses and constants until the variable is fetched or stored. This code could be called up as semantic action routines in a TAG-based code generator, or else incorporated into a handwritten compiler as subroutines called at code generation time. Listing 9.5 shows a fragment of a TAG showing how the semantic action routines might be used. Note that we adhere reasonably closely to the formal definition of the Itty Bitty Stack Machine in the grammar, and let the code generator convert it to proper register code. A production compiler would normally define a better intermediate pseudo code than IBSM.

9.3.3 Data-Flow Analysis for Better Register Allocation

Simulated execution, as we have seen, is a form of forward DFA that can inform register allocation, enabling it to do substantially better than a naïve register-based stack. Backwards DFA can further minimize register reloading by identifying candidate intermediate values to be held in registers. Simple live-variable analysis, already discussed in Chapter 8, can leave sets of live variables attached to the intermediate code along the way, so that when target machine code is generated it is possible to determine if any calculated values are likely to be reused.

The information for each variable becomes considerably more useful if it is "aged" by distance and fortified by frequency. Instead of propagating a single bit (live or dead) for each variable, a small number, perhaps a small integer in the range [0..255], is carried as a "register preference value." During the backward flow analysis, each use of a variable increments the preference value by a constant, say 8 or 16 (but not past the maximum), and each time the variable is not used, the preference value is decremented by 1 (but not below 1). This decrementation can occur arbitrarily for all nonzero values at each

Code Generation and Optimization   Chap. 9

statement or variable reference because a referenced variable will cause it to be incremented more than it is decremented. The choice of increment value and frequency of decrement can be adjusted for best results.

```
Flatten ↓inAddr:int ↑outAddr:int
  →  <IF expn left rite >
        expn: Flatten ↓inAddr ↑exAddr                {generate code to eval bool}
        [EmitIBSM ↓28 ↓exAddr ↑conAddr]             {generate LDC instruction}
        [EmitIBSM ↓0 ↓conAddr ↑brfAddr]             {for backpatched address}
        [EmitIBSM ↓1 ↓brfAddr ↑preAddr]             {generate BRF instruction}
        left: Flatten ↓preAddr ↑midAddr             {generate left subtree code }
        [EmitIBSM ↓30 ↓midAddr ↑zerAddr]            {generate ZERO instruction}
        [EmitIBSM ↓28 ↓zerAddr ↑konAddr]            {generate LDC instruction}
        [EmitIBSM ↓0 ↓konAddr ↑brAddr]              {for backpatched address}
        [EmitIBSM ↓1 ↓brAddr ↑finAddr]              {generate BRF instruction}
        [BackPatch ↓finAddr-preAddr ↓brfAddr]       {backpatch first BRF}
        rite: Flatten ↓finAddr ↑outAddr             {generate right subtree code }
        [BackPatch ↓outAddr-finAddr ↓brAddr]        {backpatch second BRF}
  →  <Assn theVar expn >
        expn: Flatten ↓inAddr ↑midAddr              {generate code to eval expn}
        theVar: Flatten ↓midAddr ↑postAddr          {variable access code on stack}
        [EmitIBSM ↓9 ↓postAddr ↑finAddr]            {SWAP instruction (no code)}
        [EmitIBSM ↓26 ↓finAddr ↑outAddr]            {generate ST instruction}
  →  <Less left rite >
        left: Flatten ↓inAddr ↑midAddr              {generate left subexpn code }
        rite: Flatten ↓midAddr ↑postAddr            {generate right subexpn code }
        [EmitIBSM ↓17 ↓postAddr ↑outAddr]           {generate LESS instruction}
  →  <Plus left rite >
        left: Flatten ↓inAddr ↑midAddr              {generate left subexpn code }
        rite: Flatten ↓midAddr ↑postAddr            {generate right subexpn code }
        [EmitIBSM ↓12 ↓postAddr ↑outAddr]           {generate ADD instruction}
  →  <Star left rite >
        left: Flatten ↓inAddr ↑midAddr              {generate left subexpn code }
        rite: Flatten ↓midAddr ↑postAddr            {generate right subexpn code }
        [EmitIBSM ↓11 ↓postAddr ↑outAddr]           {generate MPY instruction}
  →  <VAR >%offset
        [EmitIBSM ↓28 ↓inAddr ↑midAddr]             {generate LDC instruction}
        [EmitIBSM ↓offset ↓midAddr ↑outAddr]        {with its address constant }
  →  <Fetch expn>
        expn: Flatten ↓inAddr ↑midAddr              {generate address expn code }
        [EmitIBSM ↓27 ↓midAddr ↑outAddr]            {generate LD instruction}
  →  <CON >%value
        [EmitIBSM ↓28 ↓inAddr ↑midAddr]             {generate LDC instruction}
        [EmitIBSM ↓value ↓midAddr ↑outAddr]         {with its constant }
```

Listing 9.5. Using RegGenCode in a tree-flattening grammar.

CONST CPU	=	11;	86;	370;	68000;
BigEndian	=	FALSE;	FALSE;	TRUE;	TRUE;
HasImmMode	=	TRUE;	TRUE;	FALSE;	TRUE;
RelBranch	=	TRUE;	TRUE;	FALSE;	TRUE;
HalfAdd	=	TRUE;	FALSE;	FALSE;	FALSE;
WeirdMulti	=	2;	3;	0;	1;
LoReg	=	0;	0;	0;	0;
HiReg	=	4;	3;	12;	7;
TopReg	=	7;	7;	15;	15;
AdReg	=	0;	3;	0;	0;
FramePtrReg	=	5;	6;	13;	14;
EndTable	=	208;	203;	156;	236;
ConditionCodes:		7,5,3, 2,4,6;	14,12,4, 5,13,15;	13,4,8, 7,11,2;	15,13,7, 6,12,14;

Table 9.1. TargetMachine constants for some popular computers.

This information is attached to the intermediate code tree within a basic block so that as code is generated during a forward pass, any time a calculated value is to be stored into a given variable or loaded from it, if the variable is live, the result is also kept in the register. When there are more values to save than there are available registers, the variables are ranked by the proximity and frequency of the subsequent references to determine which results will be spilled into memory.

At basic block boundaries, particularly at the join of two blocks, this simplistic flow analysis pass must clear the set of register preference values because the alternate execution path may allocate a different register for the same variable.

When applying live variable analysis to reduce register loads and stores, there is associated with each register a list of the variables of which that register is a valid copy, and a flag signifying whether it is a duplicate of memory or the only copy. The simulated execution of a store to memory during code generation merely adds the destination variable to the list for that register (flagging it as an only copy), removes it from any other register's list, and emits no machine code. The simulated execution of a load operation searches the set of registers for one that lists the variable; only on failing to find one is a new register allocated and a load instruction actually generated. An arithmetic or logical operation involving an only-copy value that is still live must allocate a second register for the operation, or else first update any such variables by storing the contents of the register. Procedure calls that make use of the variables in registers also force their values to be spilled.

Postponing the store operations until the register or its shadow variable is needed can often eliminate the store entirely, as when the only live uses of a variable come in expressions before the register had to be spilled. Although this heuristic cannot in general be proved optimal (whereas the graph-coloring algorithms can be so proved), it can be proved no worse than an algorithm with no lookahead (such as Listing 9.4), and usually will do as well as the graph-coloring algorithm, but in linear time. Note that even without backward DFA to prioritize the register spilling, postponing register storage until required gives significantly better code.

9.3.4 Register Allocation in Loops

Program loops, particularly the small inner loops, are prime candidates for register optimization, for it is here that the small speed improvements gained from eliminating memory loads and stores are most easily felt. All live variables are candidates for holding in registers, and the register preference values calculated through the loop are particularly helpful when there are more live variables than registers.

Persistent loop variables (PLVs) require special handling because it is essential that the final assignment within the loop to each PLV leave it in the same register that it was in on entry to the loop. Similarly, if a register value live throughout the loop (that is, not a PLV) must be spilled to make a register available for a higher-priority usage, it must be reloaded into the same register that it was in on entry. It is simpler (and it may be preferable) to avoid preloading any registers with variables that must be spilled and reloaded during the course of the loop, reserving the registers for those variables that can remain there throughout the whole loop execution.

One of the things a backward DFA can do for PLVs is to choose a target register, then mark the final calculation of the PLV with the designated register, propagating that selection back to intermediate calculations as long as a common accumulator is appropriate. Then instead of an opportunistic register allocation, the allocator can recognize the preselected register, and choose it over the alternatives. The backwards DFA should continue to select intermediate register values for preceding calculations in such a way that the designated register will not be otherwise occupied when it is required. Table 9.2 shows an example of how this could work. The same heuristic can be applied to the allocation of register variables through the join of a fork, or for the calculation of parameters passed to a procedure in registers.

9.3.5 Addressing Modes

Computers with a variety of addressing modes generally do not cause compilers the same kinds of problems as we observed in register allocation. This is because the number of registers is generally far more limited than the number of memory locations accessible through an abbreviated addressing mode. The usual method for dealing with a variety of modes is to arbitrarily choose preferred address spaces for global and local variables, then fall back to the less compact addressing modes when a program's data space exceeds the capacity of the addressing modes. With a little bit of analysis, the compiler can count the references to each variable (giving preference to inner loops or the results of program instrumentation statistics), then distribute the variables in memory to minimize the total number of slow accesses.

Some computers offer register-to-memory and perhaps also memory-to-memory addressing modes for arithmetic operations as well as the memory-to-register mode that we have considered so far. To generate good code for these computers it is necessary to extend the virtual stack data structure to accommodate expressions with a single operator and two operands. The simulated execution of a single arithmetic instruction when the top two elements of the virtual stack contain no operators merely combines the two elements

Source Code	Steps	Allocation Decisions	DataFlow
`agedsum := 0;`	④	agedsum *is a PLV,*	*still allocated to* R4
`FOR i:=1 TO 10 DO`	③	i *is a PLV, still allocated to* R5	⇑
`  temp:=agedsum*0.9;`	**5**	agedsum *is no longer live after this line,*	R4
		so use its register in calculating `temp`.	R4 ⇑
		If `temp` *is not subsequently used in*	⇓ ⇑
		calculating the next value of `agedsum`	⇓ ⇑
		or `temp` *is still live after that, the*	⇓ ⇑
		register can be spilled at that time with	⇓ ⇑
		no extra cost	⇓ ⇑
`agedsum:=temp+val[i];`	②	*this kills* `agedsum`, *but save its register;*	⇓ ⇑
		do not allocate any register to the	⇓ ⇑
		variable `temp` *used in its calculation*	⇓ ⇑
	6	*At code generation ,* `temp` *is still in*	R4 ⇑
		and can be used immediately in the	⇓ ⇑
		calculation of `agedsum`. `temp` *is no*	R4 ⇑
		longer live, so spilling is unnecessary.	⇑
`END;`	①	*Start here for DFA.*	agedsum *allocated* R4
		i *is also a PLV, allocated* R5	

Table 9.2. Preallocation of registers for Persistent Loop Variables. Open numerals ① to ④ chronicle the backward DFA decisions; solid numerals **5** and **6** designate the subsequent allocation decisions made during (forward) simulated execution code generation. Arrows show the flow of register allocation information during the two passes.

into a simple expression, as shown in Figure 9.3 for the assignment `a:=b+a`. When a store operation finds the intended destination matches one of the operands in an expression element, it can generate a memory-based arithmetic operation instead of loading a register for the calculation. Any time the expression exceeds one operator, a register is allocated as before and the code necessary to reduce it to one operator is generated. The guiding principle in setting the complexity limit in such a design is the complexity of the target machine architecture. For a computer supporting only addition and subtraction in the register-to-memory addressing mode, the compiler need not preserve multiplication operators in the virtual stack. If a computer were to have some baroque instruction that did a multiply-add combination into memory, then it would be worthwhile to capture both operators and all three operands in a single virtual stack cell, so that the information would be available if the parameters made it possible to use that instruction.

9.3.6 Branch Address Selection

Branch addresses are usually given more attention in compiler design because the programmer has less control over these addressing modes, and in typical programs on modern computer architectures the range of branches is much more likely to distribute over several modes. Furthermore, a branch instruction often spans other branches, and it is not unusual for later address mode selection decisions to affect the span of previous decisions.

IBSM Code	Virtual Stack			Generated Code
	(empty stack)			
(1) LDC a	address of a			*(no code)*
(2) LDC b	address of b			*(no code)*
	address of a			
(3) LD	value of b			*(no code)*
	address of a			
(4) LDC a	address of a			*(no code)*
	value of b			
	address of a			
(5) LD	value of a			*(no code)*
	value of b			
	address of a			
(6) ADD	value of b	+	value of a	*(no code)*
	address of a			
(6) ST	value of a	+	value of b	*(normalize)*
	address of a			
(7) *ST*	*(empty stack)*			ADD a,b

Figure 9.3. Memory-to-memory code in the virtual stack.

In some computers the conditional branches used to test the result of a compare only come in a short addressing mode, whereas unconditional branches can be either short or long. In such cases the compiler must define an "extra-long" conditional branch macro consisting of the sequence of a conditional branch (with the condition reversed) around an unconditional long branch. This macro is then considered as if it were a single very long instruction for purposes of code generation.

Branch address decisions where the target address is known to be much closer or much more remote than the long/short address space boundary can be made correctly on the first attempt. This is particularly easy in the case of backward branches because the physical address of the target is already known. Forward branches could be informed by a prior program statistics data flow pass that counts the probable number of instruction words, allowing a generous margin for late optimizations. The remaining branches are generally given a default mode, then corrected on a later analysis.

The optimal algorithm has a complexity proportional to the square of the number of branches. It generates minimum branches in all doubtful cases, then reviews the code for each one, substituting long branches where the preliminary decision proved invalid. This may invalidate other branches, so the process must be iterated until it stabilizes. Note that *all* branches must be adjusted every time any mode is changed because the code following the modified branch instruction is moved to accommodate the change, and any branches into the moved code would be incorrect; absolute branches within and relative branches out of the moved code are also invalidated. We do not recommend this algorithm in general, because a linear-time algorithm can give safe decisions without moving and removing generated code. Branches are suboptimal only in a very small percentage of the cases, typically 5% or less, depending on the density of branches in the code and the span of the short addressing mode.

The linear algorithm requires a queue data structure with as many words in it as the span of the short address branch, where each word of the queue can hold one minimum instruction word. Instead of generating code directly to the output file or finished code block, the code generator emits all generated code into one end of the queue. Code is sent to the output file from the other end only when the queue is full. Each unknown branch is generated as a long branch going into the queue, and all branches are reviewed as they emerge from the other end. A backward branch is known to be short if its target is still in the queue when the branch is inserted into the queue; otherwise it is generated long. A forward branch is assumed long going into the queue (no prior analysis is necessary for this), and changed to short before exit when the target address enters the queue. Preliminary branch offsets can be inferred as code is inserted into the queue on the assumption that all words of the queue are finished code; actual address values are calculated as the branches emerge from the queue. We assume target address markers take no space in the queue, and that branches and target address markers are matched one to one (multiple branches to a single address come with corresponding matching multiple address markers). In practice, additional queue words may be allocated for address markers. Similarly, the queue is logically shrunk by the difference in address size every time a target address is inserted into the queue when its matching branch is still in the queue. The code in the queue need not be physically moved if the data structure is large enough to accommodate extra words of code for each logical shrinkage. A separate variable can be used to count the actual code words, so that the logical queue size remains constant. Note that as each branch emerges from the queue, the word count is adjusted by its logical size to note its passage. Listing 9.6 gives the code for a branch address queue.

9.3.7 Branch Chains

One of the more interesting ways to optimize space at the expense of speed in computers with both long and short branch address modes seeks to replace long branches with short branches to other branches with the same ultimate destination. A source program with a succession of ELSIF clauses will generally create an unconditional jump from the end of each clause to the end of the IF construct. The last one or two of these is likely to fall

```
MODULE BranchQueue;
(* For generating fairly good jump addresses. Usage: *)
(* Forward Jumps:                    Backward Jumps:
   -------------------               -------------------
     lab := UniqueLabel();             lab := UniqueLabel();
     EmitJump(TRUE,lab);               EmitLabel(FALSE,lab);
     EmitCode(theOp,opnd,nWords);      EmitCode(theOp,opnd,nWords);
       ...                               ...
     EmitLabel(TRUE,lab);              EmitJump(FALSE,lab);


   then call FlushQueue() at end of compile *)

FROM TargetGenerator IMPORT
   CurrentAddress,     (* logical address of next output code word *)
   EmitToTarget,          (* output one target machine instruction *)
   BackPatch;        (* fixup a previously output ShortBr or LongBr *)

FROM CodeConstants IMPORT
   ShortJumpRange,              (* max short jump from next locn *)
   ShortJumpSize, LongJumpSize,    (* number of generated words *)
   GenericOpcode,    (* list of opcodes, including ShortBr, LongBr *)
   AddressMode;     (* list of address modes, includes: shrt, long *)

EXPORT
   EmitJump, EmitLabel, EmitCode,   (* Inject them into the queue *)
   UniqueLabel,                          (* to get a new label *)
   FlushQueue;                   (* call this at end of compile *)

CONST
   maxtable = 500;

TYPE
   queueRange = [0..maxtable];
   queuedata = (other, justcode, jumped, fordjmp, backjmp,
       alabel, backlab, longlab, shortlab, deleted);

VAR
   QueueTake, QueueInto, QueueSize: queueRange;
   nextLabel: INTEGER;
   CodeQueue: ARRAY queueRange OF RECORD
                         kind: queuedata;
                    theOpcode: GenericOpcode;
              aNumber, theData: INTEGER;
                              END;
```

Listing 9.6a. A branch address selection queue (declarations).

```
PROCEDURE FindLabel (theLabel: INTEGER): queueRange;
VAR index: queueRange;
BEGIN
  index := QueueInto;
  WHILE index<>QueueTake DO
    IF index=0 THEN index := maxtable
      ELSE DEC(index) END;
    WITH CodeQueue[index] DO
      IF (kind>other) AND (aNumber=theLabel) THEN RETURN index END
    END END (* WITH & WHILE *)
END FindLabel;


PROCEDURE UpdateQueue (addwords: INTEGER; additem: BOOLEAN);
VAR recycle: BOOLEAN;  locn: INTEGER;
BEGIN
  IF additem THEN
    IF QueueInto=maxtable THEN QueueInto := 0
      ELSE INC(QueueInto) END;
    QueueSize := QueueSize+addwords;
    END;
  WHILE (QueueInto#QueueTake) AND (NOT additem
      OR (QueueSize>ShortJumpRange) OR
      ((QueueInto+maxtable-QueueTake) MOD maxtable < 5)) DO
    recycle := FALSE;
    WITH CodeQueue[QueueTake] DO CASE kind OF
        other: EmitToTarget(theOpcode, theData, aNumber);
               QueueSize := QueueSize-aNumber |
      jumped,backlab: recycle := TRUE |
      fordjmp: IF theOpcode=ShortBr THEN
                 EmitToTarget(ShortBr, 0, ShortJumpSize);
                 QueueSize := QueueSize-ShortJumpSize;
               ELSE
                 EmitToTarget(LongBr, 0, LongJumpSize);
                 QueueSize := QueueSize-LongJumpSize;
                 END;
               kind := jumped;
               theData := CurrentAddress;
               recycle := TRUE |
      backjmp: WITH CodeQueue[FindLabel(aNumber)] DO
                 locn := theData;
                 kind := deleted;
                 END (* inner WITH *);
               IF CurrentAddress-locn<ShortJumpRange THEN
                 EmitToTarget(ShortBr, locn, ShortJumpSize)
               ELSE EmitToTarget(LongBr, locn, LongJumpSize) END |
        alabel: kind := backlab;
               theData := CurrentAddress;
               recycle := TRUE |
```

Listing 9.6b. A branch address selection queue.

```
      longlab,shortlab: WITH CodeQueue[FindLabel(aNumber)] DO
                  locn := theData;
                  kind := deleted;
                  END (* inner WITH *);
              IF kind=shortlab THEN
                  BackPatch(ShortBr, locn, CurrentAddress)
              ELSE BackPatch(LongBr, locn, CurrentAddress) END |
        deleted: (* this has already been used; ignore it *)
        END END (* CASE & WITH *);
      IF recycle THEN
        CodeQueue[QueueInto] := CodeQueue[QueueTake];
        IF QueueInto=maxtable THEN QueueInto := 0
          ELSE INC(QueueInto) END END;
      IF QueueTake=maxtable THEN QueueTake := 0
        ELSE INC(QueueTake) END;
      END (* WHILE *)
END UpdateQueue;


PROCEDURE EmitCode (theOp: GenericOpcode;
      operand, nWords: INTEGER);
BEGIN
  WITH CodeQueue[QueueInto] DO
    kind := justcode;
    aNumber := nWords;
    theOpcode := theOp;
    theData := operand;
    END;
  UpdateQueue(nWords, TRUE);
END EmitCode;


PROCEDURE EmitLabel (forward: BOOLEAN; theLabel: INTEGER);
VAR mykind: queuedata;  addwords: INTEGER;
BEGIN
  addwords := 0;
  IF forward THEN WITH CodeQueue[FindLabel(theLabel)] DO
    IF kind=fordjmp THEN
      mykind := shortlab;
      theOpcode := ShortBr;
      addwords := ShortJumpSize-LongJumpSize;
    ELSE mykind := longlab END;
    END (* WITH *)
  ELSE mykind := alabel END;
```

Listing 9.6c. A branch address selection queue.

```
    WITH CodeQueue[QueueInto] DO
      kind := mykind;
      theOpcode := BackP;
      aNumber := theLabel;
      theData := 0;
      END;
    UpdateQueue(addwords, TRUE);
END EmitLabel;

PROCEDURE EmitJump (forward: BOOLEAN; toLabel: INTEGER);
VAR mykind: queuedata;  addwords: INTEGER;
BEGIN
    addwords := LongJumpSize;
    mykind := backjmp;
    IF forward THEN mykind := fordjmp
    ELSE WITH CodeQueue[FindLabel(toLabel)] DO
      IF kind=alabel THEN addwords := ShortJumpSize END;
      END END (* WITH & IF *);
    WITH CodeQueue[QueueInto] DO
      kind := mykind;
      IF addwords=ShortJumpSize THEN theOpcode := ShortBr
        ELSE theOpcode := LongBr END;
      aNumber := toLabel;
      theData := 0;
      END;
    UpdateQueue(addwords, TRUE);
END EmitJump;

PROCEDURE FlushQueue ();
BEGIN
    UpdateQueue(0, FALSE);
END FlushQueue;

PROCEDURE UniqueLabel (): INTEGER;
BEGIN
    INC(nextLabel);
    RETURN nextLabel
END UniqueLabel;

BEGIN (* BranchQueue initialization *)
    QueueTake := 0;
    QueueInto := 0;
    QueueSize := 0;
    nextLabel := 0;
END BranchQueue.
```

Listing 9.6d. A branch address selection queue.

within the short branch range, but the first of them may not. If the individual clauses are not excessively long, however, each exit jump may well reach the exit jump of the next clause within the short branch address range. Substituting the nearer target address thus results in the execution of several short jumps instead of one long one. This is normally implemented as a peephole optimization on the generated code, but the tree-flattening code generator can be readily modified, perhaps with some advice from the parser or a statistics DFA pass, to chain the branches as code is generated.

Without concern for branch chaining, the code generator would normally generate a jump when the ELSE (or ELSIF) is reached, and emit the matching label upon return from the recursive StatementList call that generates code for that clause. Branches may be chained if the label is sent to the nonterminal that generates code for the ELSIF clause so that it can emit the label just before generating its own exit jump. It would have to emit the label even if it had no jump of its own, which adds somewhat to the complexity. The general form of the optimization is illustrated in Listing 9.7. Similar logic would apply in joining the execution paths through all the legs of a CASE structure; with a little more effort, nested IF statements that afford the same optimization can also be handled.

At the other end of the speed/space trade-off continuum, branches that are naturally chained can be unchained in the code generator. A natural branch chain can result from nested IF statements, where the THEN-clause of the inner IF jumps over its ELSE-clause, only to jump again over the ELSE-clause of the outer IF statement. To eliminate the second jump requires synthesizing a list of exit labels passed up the parse tree, to be emitted when the next code to be generated is *not* a jump.

Statement
    → "IF" IfStatement ↓0   {*no branch to chain yet*}
    → ... {*other statements...*}

IfStatement ↓chained:int
    → BoolExpn [UniqueLabel ↑myelse; EmitJump ↓myelse]
        "THEN" StatementList
        ([chained#0; EmitLabel ↓chained])?   {*chain incoming branch here*}
        ("ELSIF" [UniqueLabel ↑myexit; EmitJump ↓myexit; EmitLabel ↓myelse]
        IfStatement ↓myexit   {*send down my exit label*}
        |"ELSE" [UniqueLabel ↑myexit; EmitJump ↓myexit; EmitLabel ↓myelse]
        StatementList
        "END" [EmitLabel ↓myexit]
        |"END" [EmitLabel ↓myelse]);

Listing 9.7. Building branch chains in a code generator grammar.

9.4 Complexities of Code Generation

There are essentially two fundamentally opposite approaches to code generation, one easier and the other more optimal. The easy method models the abstract virtual machine in the target machine as much as possible. The alternative looks at the best way to encode a variety of abstract algorithms in the target machine code, then seeks to recognize the components of that abstract algorithm in the intermediate code tree, so that the optimum code sequence for that algorithm can be generated. Practical code generators generally adopt some compromise between these two extremes. We have seen some of the range of choices in this spectrum of options in the case of register allocation. The abstract virtual machine is closely modeled in the register stack implementation, whereas carrying the operator and two operands in a virtual stack structure enables us to come much closer to the best code an expert assembly programmer might write.

It is important to realize that every computer for which a compiler is even a remote consideration has Turing Machine capability; that is, it is capable of computing any problem that is computable (within the limits of its memory size, including on-line file storage). The issue we consider here is not "What can be compiled" (for the answer to that is "Everything"), but "What is the best way to compile it?" A commercial compiler that fails to find the best code for a common program sequence may be displaced in the market by one that succeeds at it.

It is difficult in a general treatise on compiler design like this to give specific details for optimal code generation because every computer instruction set is different, often in subtle but radical ways. Almost always it is necessary to tackle the problem in two phases. The first phase requires becoming familiar with the instruction set of the machine by writing code for it in machine or assembly language, and by reviewing machine language code written by other expert programmers, if that is possible. From this position of insight it is possible to implement a code generator that will emit reasonably good code. The second phase requires examining the generated code from a variety of sample programs, rewriting it by hand to improve performance if possible, and then modifying the code generator — usually by adding special cases — to automatically generate the improved code. This second phase can be iterated arbitrarily often, but it should not be omitted, because even the most carefully designed compiler will yield some surprises when actually put to work on real programs.

The optimal sequence of code for a particular algorithm may not be readily obvious. Although most machine instructions were designed with a particular purpose in mind, many of them have subtle side effects that can be exploited by a clever compiler to achieve performance improvements. Exhaustive search compilers that generate every possible instruction sequence to find the minimum code for a particular effect reportedly turned up some surprising combinations that human programmers never considered.

In the following sections we address first the general issue of code generation for reasonably regular instruction sets, then proceed to some examples of dealing with baroque or unusual instructions.

9.4.1 Instruction Selection

Any serious computer language, including high-level languages such as Modula-2 and Cobol as well as low-level machine languages that are the subject of this chapter, has facilities for the four arithmetic operations, for assigning values to variables and recovering the current value from a variable, for comparing values and making control decisions on the results of the comparisons, and for jumping to closed subroutines and returning from them. Most languages also support a variety of data types or sizes, with rules for conversion between them. Some languages automatically coerce different types into a compatible form, whereas others, like Modula-2 and most machine languages, require explicit conversion.

Not all computer languages support all interesting data types. As designed by Wirth, Modula-2 lacked a data type for complex arithmetic; many smaller computers have no hardware instructions for floating-point, and some even lack an instruction for integer division. The Turing capability of every language guarantees that the missing features can be constructed (simulated) from the available set, and this is an important part of code generation. A compiler with a source language that allows integer division and a target machine without such a feature must generate an appropriate sequence of instructions to do division in software, usually by a call to a compiler-supplied library routine. The target machine instruction set is thus augmented by the library routines supplied by (and thus or otherwise available to) the compiler, and the true target machine of the compiler is the virtual machine so created.

It is the responsibility of the parser and constrainer to identify the precise operation and data type for each source language operator that is compiled. This information may be passed directly to the code generator, or it may be attached to the intermediate code tree as node names and decorations. The virtual target machine language must have at least one operator corresponding to every abstract operation and data type in the intermediate code, and the only difficult job is selecting between alternatives when there are more than one.

Some of the selection work can be done in a tree-walking grammar that seeks particular tree patterns and replaces them with nodes marked to use particular instructions or sequences. If, as is often the case, the multiply operation in the target machine is slower than a shift, a subtree template representing the multiplication by a constant power of 2 can be transformed into a shift left. With a sufficient disparity between multiplication and shifts or addition, products involving the sum or difference of two powers of 2 (for example, 3, 5, 7, 9, 10, 15, 20, 30, 40) may also be considered for this optimization. Note, however, that any significant side effects must be preserved. For example, if the language requires notification of arithmetic overflow, then the generated code should detect bits shifted off the left end of the result and take the same action as an oversize product. Note further that DFA such as range check elimination (as described in Chapter 8) can make many such overflow tests unnecessary.

One particularly interesting optimization recognizes the summation of constant offsets resulting from record field selection or constant array subscripts and the variable offset within its stack or global frame. Even nonconstant array subscripts when the lower bound of the array subscript range is not zero can propagate some constant components of the address out to the variable reference and reduce the runtime arithmetic required. Note that to avoid unnecessary runtime calculation of subscript base offsets, the tree must be transformed so that the product of a constant times a sum or difference involving another constant converts to the sum of a product, as shown in Figure 9.4. The multiplication is then done at runtime with an explicit operator, and the sum is merged with the implicit sum in the hardware variable reference. This transformation could be effected in a constant folding pass over the code tree if the addressing operations are sufficiently explicit [Pittman, 1985], or it could be done in the simulated execution for register code generation, when the virtual stack accommodates an operator and two operands as described earlier in this chapter. The result is the same: a single variable reference with a calculated offset different from the defined offset in the symbol table.

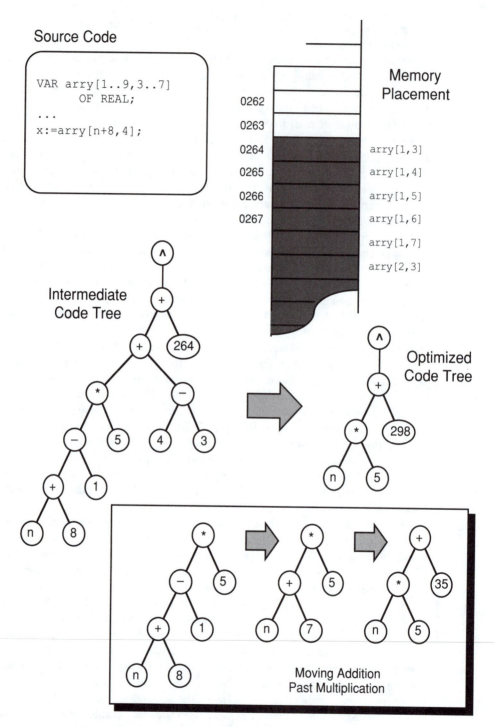

Source Code

```
VAR arry[1..9,3..7]
        OF REAL;
...
x:=arry[n+8,4];
```

Memory
Placement

0262

0263

0264   arry[1,3]

0265   arry[1,4]

0266   arry[1,5]

0267   arry[1,6]

            arry[1,7]

            arry[2,3]

Intermediate
Code Tree

Optimized
Code Tree

Moving Addition
Past Multiplication

Figure 9.4. Propagating constants out of array subscript calculation. Inset shows how addition moves out over multiplication.

Translating array index address references can also improve FOR-loop control variable testing in some computers. Where the hardware supports a test for zero or a sign test in less code than a comparison against another arbitrary value, the compiler may consider adding an offset to the FOR-loop control variable used only for array subscripting, so that its final value is zero. The offset is added back onto each array reference address, which is a compile-time calculation that costs nothing when the program runs.

9.4.2 Strength Reduction

Variable range analysis can also contribute to *strength reduction* in the code generation, if a variable declared generally to be a long integer can be determined at a particular point in the computation to contain a value within the range of the hardware short integer format, where the calculation is faster in the short format. One popular computer, for example, supports the multiplication of two short integers, but not two long integers; the latter requires the sum of the products from three or four short multiply instructions. Knowing that one or both operands is short could greatly speed up the composite operation.

Some computers have instructions to set or clear a single bit in a word, which is useful in the implementation of bitsets. Such instructions, however, are of little help in the generation of a set element range like {x..y}. Assuming that the bitset fits entirely within one computer word, the best code for such a computation requires the construction of the singleton sets xs={x} and ys={y}, then (assuming x≤y) use ordinary integer arithmetic to calculate ys*2-xs, which is exactly {x..y}. In computers without an explicit instruction to set one bit, the singleton one-word set {x} can be constructed by shifting the value 1 left by x bits, or (in some machines faster) by looking up the word in a table indexed by x. With one word for each bit in a bitset, the table is not very large; setting up the shift each time for multiple set calculations could easily take more code than indexing into the table plus the table itself. Note that ys*2 costs no extra to calculate by the table method because it is merely at table index [y+1]. When x and y span separate words in a set, the procedure is slightly more complicated. The first word consists of -xs using two's complement arithmetic, the last word is ys*2-1, and all intervening words (if any) are -1.

A packed bitset is not the only reasonable implementation of a set. In a computer without indexed bit-testing instructions, a set constant such as programmers often use to qualify character variables (as in, IF x IN {"A".."Z"}) may be implemented much more efficiently by storing one set element in each byte, then indexing the array directly by the expression x, followed by a shift or logical AND instruction to test the bit. Up to eight different set constants can be stored in the same table, one in each bit position. When speed is more important than memory space, and a set variable is used mostly in element tests and seldom or not at all in expressions involving union or intersection, the variable could be implemented the same way, one element per byte. Of course, you cannot pack multiple variable sets the way you can with constants, but testing is faster because no shifting or masking is required. The compile-time decision to unpack a set variable is best informed by a statistical analysis of the program.

Even with an impoverished machine instruction set, the opportunities for creative code generation are unlimited. In a compiler whose target machine has a very small memory, one compiler substitutes a memory reference instruction that requires a two-byte address for an unconditional branch over the next two bytes of code: the memory reference instruction is a compare that takes those two bytes as address and fetches from whatever random memory location is so addressed, performs the compare, then ignores the result and goes on to execute the instruction following. The alternate execution path skips over the compare operation code, lands on the first of the two bytes that are its address part, and resumes execution there. We rightly castigate human programmers who embed this kind of code trick in their assembly language, but a compiler can ensure correctness and safety when it does this, or refuse to do it when it would be invalid.

9.5 Specialized Instructions

Computer hardware designers cannot seem to refrain from occasionally yielding to the pressures of expert assembly language programmers who request this or that specialized instruction. The simple compiler will just ignore these baroque filigrees, giving substance to the widely held belief that hand-coded assembly is more efficient than compiler-generated code. With more effort applied to the code generator, the careful compiler designer can engage these arcane instructions in appropriate ways, making the resulting compiler that much more valuable. It is truly an artistic endeavor to make good use of the computer resources in a reasonably fast compiler.

One common microprocessor has several instructions designed to be iterated, and a special "iterate" instruction to effect that purpose. These were intended to support character string data, but they can also be used to effect the assignment of data structures such as records and arrays. The compiler designer should carefully analyze the code required to set up the iterated move, and choose a sequence of individual one-word load and store instructions when that is not longer, because the loop overhead generally costs more execution time than the corresponding unrolled loads and stores.

Another common computer has no iterated or string instructions, but it does support multiple register loads and stores. These two instructions were intended for saving and restoring processor state in interrupt service routines, and for allocating nonvolatile registers on entry to a procedure. They can also be used profitably for moving data structures larger than one or two words. When a structure is substantially larger than the number of available registers will accommodate, it is usually profitable to spill as many registers as possible to memory, then use all of them in multiple loads and stores for a long move loop. The loop overhead is then effectively amortized over all the registers involved, instead of paying full cost on every word moved. With adequate loop analysis, the same technique can be used to unroll array initializations written in the source code with a FOR-loop. The initial value stored into every element of the array can be replicated across some number of registers that divides the array size, then the loop iterator adjusted for the fewer number of times through the loop required. If an exact divisor of the array size is not possible, the nearest convenient size less than the full array is chosen, and the remaining words or bytes filled out at the end, outside the loop. For a nonuniform (nonzero) value to be stored, it will also be necessary to choose a number of registers that exactly spans a multiple of the element size, or add individual store instructions to the loop to even out the block size.

9.5.1 RISC and Pipeline Processor Scheduling

Although not a recent development in computer architecture, paralellism and *pipelining* have become increasingly popular in computer design. A computer pipeline divides the time it takes for an instruction to execute into discrete segments, and stages them in sequential components of the hardware. As the execution advances to the next stage, each component is free to begin work on another instruction. Although the individual operations are no faster, more of them are in some stage of their execution at the same time, yielding greater throughput overall. Unlike the simple computer, however, this means that the result from one calculation may not be immediately available for the next. Consider, for example, the program fragment

```
a := x+y;
b := z*3;
c := a*b;
```

The second assignment could in principle begin executing before the first finished because it does not depend on any results of the first statement, and even its arithmetic operation probably requires different, possibly separate, hardware. The third statement, however, depends both on the results of the two prior lines and on the same arithmetic operation; in a pipelined computer it may be required to wait before beginning its calculation. It is generally the responsibility of the compiler for a pipelined computer to arrange the program steps so that independent calculations can overlap and sequential processes are scheduled to begin when their input data become available. Other computer architectures achieve a similar effect by providing several arithmetic units, and the compiler is obliged to schedule the operations in such a way that the desired arithmetic unit is also available when it is needed. In some computers the hardware will insert delays as needed, but the compiler may be obliged to do so in other cases.

The most radical requirement for scheduling involves a pipelined branch instruction, where the next instruction after the branch begins execution before the branch takes effect. This means that the compiler must arrange for that instruction to be something on which the branch does not depend, or else insert one or more time-wasting instructions.

The scheduling problem is similar in many respects to register allocation, but there are significant differences. Scheduling is usually implemented as a peephole optimization after the code generator completes; except for some of the analysis, it does not submit well to grammar-based tree-transformation implementations. The algorithm described here addresses the scheduling of a single basic block, and assumes the code for the block being scheduled can be generated into a temporary data structure from which operations can be transferred to the final object code file in arbitrary order. As in register allocation, optimal algorithms may require graph-coloring techniques; our simplified approach will often yield very good results in linear time for a large class of pipelined hardware.

The data structure used for scheduling analysis is a directed acyclic graph (DAG), similar to that used in common subexpression elimination in Chapter 8, where an arc represents a computational dependency. Each operation (memory access or arithmetic) is a node in the graph, and it is linked to other nodes on whose results it depends, shown in Figure 9.5 as boxes laid end to end. Associated with each node is a duration time (shown as the length of the box in the illustration), which is based on the hardware process time from start of operation to when the results become available. The graph for an entire basic

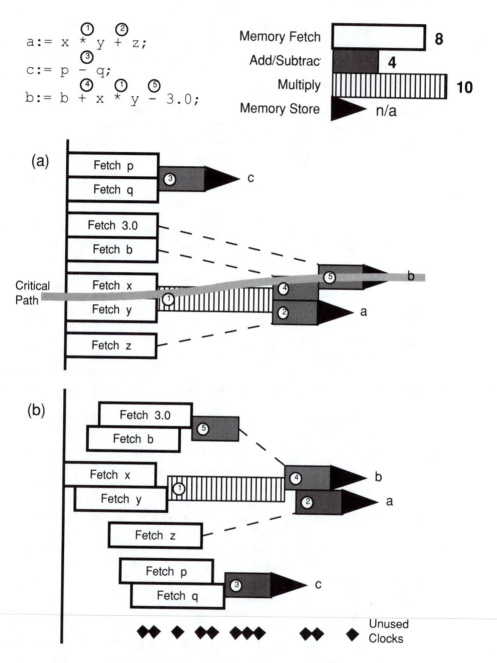

Figure 9.5. Processor scheduling by DAG critical paths. (a) Shows the longest (critical) path; (b) After optimal scheduling.

Code Generation and Optimization   Chap. 9

block will contain one or more independent subgraphs consisting primarily of chains of operation dependencies. There are two independent subgraphs in Figure 9.5; the larger of these joins severally separate chains, then divides again at the end into two chains. The graph is constructed with the nodes or boxes spaced by the execution time through the processor pipeline for each respective operation without consideration of scheduling, so the length of the longest chain through the block represents the "critical path" for resource allocation. Scheduled object code is generated deterministically by choosing the first node in the longest chain not waiting on a previous result; that node is removed from its chain and the proper delay is inserted in its place. As long as processor units are available to start new independent computations, another process can be started in the next cycle, always from the longest remaining path not waiting on an unfinished result. This simplified scheduling algorithm may fail to yield an optimal schedule in a computer with a fixed number each of several different processing units that cannot be reused until they finish. The problem occurs when a secondary chain opportunistically seizes a resource required in the critical path shortly thereafter. The algorithm is optimal, however, for fully pipelined arithmetic hardware, where the computer is always ready to start any new operation. The algorithm's performance at block boundaries can also be improved with a little intelligence from adjacent blocks.

The analysis for resource scheduling can be implemented in a tree grammar which constructs the DAG and identifies the critical paths. The tree nodes may also be decorated with scheduling information, but it is quite awkward to generate code from a tree grammar in scheduled order because sequential operations in optimal execution time may be scattered about several subtrees.

In the example of Figure 9.5 it is also evident that balancing the expression tree can shorten the critical path. The normal left-to-right expression evaluation order originally had both additions in the critical path waiting for the multiplication. By applying the mathematical principle of operator associativity, the difference could be performed in parallel with the multiplication, thereby shortening the execution time. Note, however, that in most computers addition is not strictly associative, and the effects of roundoff in floating point operations may differ between these two evaluation orders. The compiler designer should be aware of the problem in considering the alternatives.

The scheduled execution in Figure 9.5 includes several opportunities for the computer to proceed with other processing, if there were something to do. Many parallel and pipelined computers simply wait for the results to come out of the active processors before proceeding when there is nothing else to do; the software simply issues the next instruction, and if it depends on an active process, the computer waits. More recently a number of very fast computers have been designed where the extra logic to wait for unfinished processes would slow the whole computer down. Generating code for these computers requires that an executable instruction be issued without fail on every clock cycle. Most of the instructions in these computers are designed to execute in a single clock cycle, so there is generally no problem with waiting for a pipeline to clear.

Branches are an exception. To match the speed of the rest of the computer, branches in such a machine must be pipelined. That means the program can issue a conditional branch instruction, but the computer will continue to fetch *and start to execute* one or two more instructions before it finishes deciding whether to branch or not. Therefore, any instructions immediately following a conditional branch must be of such a nature that the pending branch decision does not impact their validity.

Properly generating code for pipelined branches is similar to pipelined functional units, in that the compiler must identify the execution dependency chains through the basic block. The goal is to find a dependency chain (or chain fragment) through the basic block parallel to the chain ending in the final branch instruction, and issue the final operation of the second chain after the branch. Note from the definition of a basic block that a branch instruction is logically the last operation of the block; we do not alter the logical operation order in scheduling the branch this way because the termination of the branch operation remains at the end of the block. If there are no parallel chains at the end of the block, the first operation from one of the successor blocks may be used, provided that it can also be moved into every other predecessor block and creates no side effects than cannot be discarded in case the branch decision goes the other way. If both of these attempts fail, it is necessary to insert one or more NOP (no operation) instructions after the branch. Left-motion hoisting will already have moved code back from the two legs of a fork into the previous block, and that will always be in a parallel chain, safe for postbranch execution. Right-motion hoisted code is also safe for postbranch execution if the hoist is reversed, that is, if some of the hoisted code is moved back from the join into the two legs of the fork. When compiling for a computer with a pipelined branch, the optimizer could mark hoisted code to facilitate subsequent branch scheduling.

Scheduling the branch that returns to the front of a loop is particularly important because most of a program's execution time will be spent in the inner loops. If a parallel chain instruction cannot be found in the final block of the loop, then the first instruction at the beginning of the loop should be moved, both to the end of the loop and also copied into the setup code before the loop start. This assumes, of course, that the result of the first instruction can be discarded when the loop exits (or that the branch at the end is unconditional). Figure 9.6 illustrates the various opportunities for loop branch scheduling.

9.5.2 Vector Processors

Another technique used by computer designers to attain faster execution extends the parallelism to cover the essentially identical processing done in a loop on all the elements of an array or *vector*. The hardware of a vector processor is designed to apply a single or small number of instructions to a sequence of values, either regularly spaced in memory, or else preloaded into vector registers, and produce the results in another memory array or vector register. Another variation has multiple parallel arithmetic processors all controlled from the same instruction sequence, each operating on one slice through the operand arrays. Because the operations are also pipelined, a vector processor can typically restart the calculation on a new array element every clock cycle, sometimes yielding a throughput in excess of the clock rate of the computer.

The performance of scientific computers using these techniques is measured in *megaflops*, or Mflops, which stands for Million FLoating-point OPerations per Second. A vector processor with a clock cycle time of 10^{-8} seconds should be able to attain an average processing rate close to 200 Mflops in a loop like this fragment (where all variables except i are declared REAL):

Code Generation and Optimization   Chap. 9

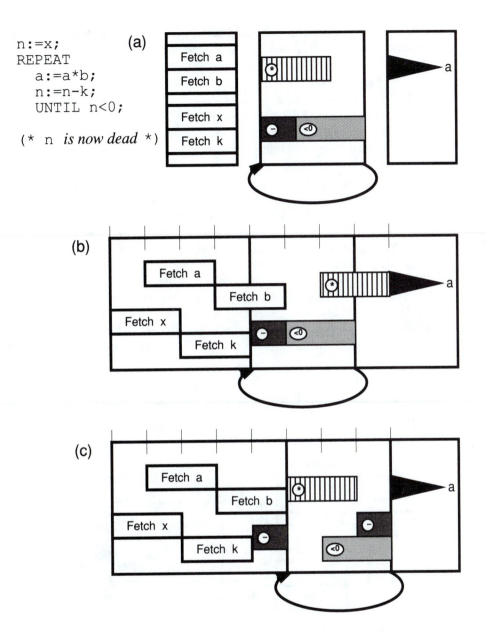

```
n:=x;                    (a)
REPEAT
   a:=a*b;
   n:=n-k;
   UNTIL n<0;

(*  n  is now dead  *)
```

Figure 9.6. Scheduling pipelined loop branches. (a) Unscheduled, after loop constants are moved out (b) Schedule last operation of second chain after branch (c) Move operation from front to after branch, and also to setup block.

```
FOR i:=1 TO 100 DO
   a[i]:=b[i]*c[i]+k
   END;
```

The vectorizing compiler unrolls the entire loop, replacing it with one or two sequences of vector operations (depending on the vector length of the processor). Although the details vary between processors, the sequence of operations is something like this:

1. Start to load vector B from b
2. Start to load vector C from c
3. Load k into a scalar register K
4. Start vector multiplication $D_i := B_i * C_i$
5. Start vector+scalar sum $A_i := D_i + K$
6. Start to store vector A into a

Before the multiplication can begin, the memory fetch of the first elements of the vectors B and C must complete; a good compiler will schedule other processing in that time if possible; a prime candidate might be the continuation of the loop execution when it must be split between two or more vectors segments. The vector sum operation of our example cannot begin until the first product term comes out of the multiplication several clocks later, and the result cannot be stored before the sum completes. But once all vector operations have begun (assuming no conflicts in memory timing), each successive result element will be stored once each clock cycle, as shown in the abstract timing diagram in Figure 9.7. Furthermore, the entire vector operation will continue without further attention from the program, so that as long as processor facilities are available and there are unrelated operations to be done, the computer can continue executing other tasks.

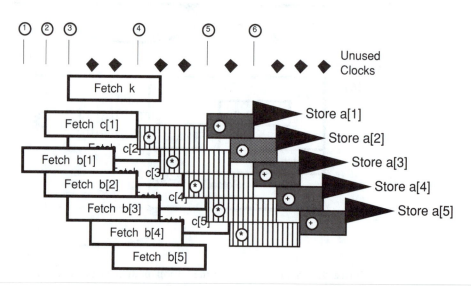

Figure 9.7. Vector processor operation for `a[i]:=b[i]*c[i]+k`.

Compiling vector code combines the problems of pipelined processor scheduling and loop unrolling, with a dash of special-case instruction selection. For example, one vector processor has a facility for adding a scalar to the vector product with no additional timing delays, so the intermediate vector result D_i need not be calculated, but the entire triad product+sum can be directed immediately to the result array. Most vector processors are capable of computing a single scalar result (called a *reduction variable*) such as a sum or product from the elements of vector operands, but the restrictions on how it is evaluated may differ from one machine to the next. Every vector can handle elements of an array in sequential memory locations; some can accept a *stride* (the address increment between vector elements) greater than one, so the compiler must accommodate column-wise (that is, nonsequential) references to multidimensional arrays in some other way for the more limited machines. Even where a larger stride is possible, the distribution of addresses into memory banks could lead to collisions and performance degradation when the stride is a multiple of the number of memory banks. A particularly clever compiler might be able to insert dummy array elements in the lower index ranges to avoid this problem. Thus, if the programmer declares a variable type to be `ARRAY [1..k,1..64] OF REAL`, the compiler might notice that the inner index range is a multiple of the eight memory banks and compile it as if the range were `1..65` (simply ignoring the extra element in calculations). This optimization serves no purpose if there are no inner loops in the program indexing through the array by the first subscript, and may actually be counterproductive if there are diagonal references such as `a[i-1,j-1]` in the same loop with `a[i,j]`.

The vectorizing compiler typically looks for opportunities to convert inner FOR-loops to vector code when all assignments within the loop to variables live on exit are either indexed array elements or reduction variables, and all array subscripts are either loop-constant or linear (sequenced by a constant increment in not more than one dimension). There are several considerations that prevent vectorizing even when these criteria are met, such as order dependencies in the evaluation of array elements. One kind of dependency called *recursion* (although not related to procedure recursion) has array elements calculated within the loop being used again as part of subsequent iterations, as in `s[i]:=s[i-1]*k`. In many cases the compiler may be able to substitute a temporary scalar persistent loop variable for the array element to be used in the next iteration: `t:=t*k; s[i]:=t`, but detecting such an opportunity in other than trivial cases requires serious data-flow analysis. When recursion spans more than one iteration, corrective action by the compiler becomes much more difficult. The burden on the compiler to determine if recursion is even possible increases where array subscripts are evaluated from expressions whose value cannot be known at compile time. For example in the loop

```
FOR i:=n TO m DO a[i]:=a[i+j] END
```

if range analysis on the variable `j` cannot determine whether its value could be negative, then the compiler must not assume this loop is not recursive.

Many loops qualify some of the calculations within the loop by a conditional based on a calculated result either from within the loop or outside it. Conditional branches cannot be vectorized, and processor architects have been quite inventive in coming up with vectorizable alternatives to achieve equivalent results. There are also some steps a compiler can take toward the same end. Loop unswitching has already been discussed as a way to optimize loop invariant condition tests, and it is particularly relevant here. Tests on the loop control variable can also be factored out of the loop. If a single value in an array is to be protected while all others are replaced by the loop calculation, and the subscript of that element is loop-constant, it may be simpler to simply save that one element prior to entering the loop, then restore it after the body of the loop has unconditionally replaced all elements. Similarly, tests on ranges of the control variable may profitably be divided into several shorter loops, each for a full subrange, and each containing unconditional code for that subrange.

Hardware assistance to conditional processing in vectors typically inhibits in some form or another the assignment of a result to a vector element where the corresponding value in another vector satisfies some condition. The controlling vector may be a simple bit vector, with one bit to each vector element, or it may be a sign or zero test in another data vector. Correctly converting a conditional statement within a loop to a vectorized conditional assignment requires careful analysis of a variety of special cases, but it is not beyond the techniques discussed in this book, although somewhat outside the scope of our treatment here. Note that the compiler designer should feel free to allocate a vector temporary for intermediate results (as we did in the example of Figure 9.7), even where the source code or conventional wisdom calls for a scalar value, if that permits a larger part of the calculation to be vectorized. Vector temporaries allocated by the compiler, as well as arrays declared by the programmer but not live on exit from the loop, can safely exist solely in the vector registers of the computer and never be stored into main memory. Apart from setup time and the propagation delays for a single vectorized result, additional vector operations chained into the same calculation are essentially free and can only increase the effective Mflops. Thus, for example, for a source program loop such as this:

```
FOR i:=1 TO n DO
  x:=a[i]*b[i];
  IF x<1.0 THEN r[i]:=b[i]/c[i]
    ELSE r[i]:=SIN(b[i])-x END
END;
```

a prudent compiler might unconditionally evaluate into temporary vectors the expressions $x[i]:=a[i]*b[i]$, $t[i]:=b[i]/c[i]$, and $s[i]:=SIN(b[i])$, and also the composite values $q[i]:=x[i]-1.0$ and $f[i]:=SIN(b[i])-[i]$. The final assignment to the vector $r[i]$ then makes use of a conditional inhibit based on the sign of $q[i]$ to choose between $t[i]$ and $f[i]$. Note that vectorized mathematical library functions will generally return an entire vector of function values in the time it takes to evaluate one function result, plus a tiny multiple of the number of elements in the vector, possibly as little as one or two clocks per element. Thus, even for a fairly low density of false condition evaluations in this loop, it is faster to discard the unused trigonometric results than to separately call the library function for a single scalar result each time it is required.

Nested loops offer another set of optimization opportunities in vector hardware. Multidimensioned arrays where the inner index ranges are fully spanned can be linearized, so that the vector hardware has a larger number of elements to process for each vector setup. The benefits of this tends to diminish, however, when the composite linear array exceeds the length of the vector hardware. Where stride considerations or order dependencies make the vectorization of an inner loop infeasible, it may be possible to invert a pair of nested loops, with the possible result that the new inner loop can be vectorized. Inverting a nested pair of loops may also be desirable if the outer control variable range is significantly greater than that of the inner loop.

9.6 Varieties of Code Optimization

It is customary to partition the consideration of code optimization into two general categories, *machine-independent*, which can be performed on the AST without consideration of the target hardware, and *machine-dependent*, which requires intimate knowledge of the target machine both to implement and even to establish the need, and is usually applied to a low-level quad representation of the intermediate code or the final object code itself. While recognizing such obviously machine-independent optimization as constant folding and loop-constant code motion, we generally hold the less common view that most optimizations depend to a greater or lesser degree on the architecture of the target hardware, and thus we find this distinction less useful. For example, although moving entire loop-constant statements out of the loop is almost surely beneficial, the value of extracting partial expressions to move depends largely on the relative costs of saving and recovering the intermediate results as compared to the cost of evaluation. Depending on the number of registers available for saving intermediate values, the extra time to reload intermediate values from memory when registers cannot be used, and the complexity of the expression to be considered, the decision point may differ substantially from machine to machine.

Another dimension along which it is reasonable to divide the kinds of optimizations is evident from the major distinction between this chapter and Chapter 8, namely that some optimizations submit more readily to a grammar-driven implementation than others. Although there are significant differences along this dimension, it should be pointed out that, like machine-dependency, there is more of a continuum than a binary partition into "haves" and "have-nots." Right-motion hoisting (covered in Chapter 8) is quite awkward in a tree-transformational grammar, but not impossible; range analysis through loops (introduced in this chapter) is easier to implement as a TAG than right-motion hoisting, but not as easy as constant folding or common subexpression elimination.

A third dimension along which one might organize the taxonomy of optimizations is the order in which they are profitably implemented, or a time line. Again, this turns out to be more interesting than practical because many optimizations give rise to opportunities for other optimizations, which might propagate new opportunities back to the initial optimizer. For example, loop-invariant code motion requires a prior constant expression analysis (part of constant folding); after moving out a significant block of code, the loop body may qualify for unrolling, which again raises opportunities for constant folding. There are nonetheless certain optimizations that should be effected earlier in the compilation process, and others that are necessarily later. The back-substitution of procedures called only once should be done as early as possible because the major advantage to this transformation is the opportunities it opens up for other optimizations such as constant folding and CSE. On the other hand, register selection is necessarily one of the last analyses to be performed because any other optimization is likely to invalidate its decisions.

9.6.1 Peephole Optimizations

No compiler book would be complete without mentioning the commonly recognized machine-dependent optimization called *peephole*, although the term actually is applied to any of a variety of late code fixups used mostly to repair lazy or unfortunate choices in code generation. Classical peephole optimization typically includes copy propagation across register loads and stores, strength reduction in arithmetic operators and memory access (that is, address mode selection), and branch chaining. Of these, only branch chaining is likely to be required if a grammar-based optimizer such as we have described is implemented; with the increased memory size in small computers and a continual emphasis on speed, size/speed tradeoffs are more likely to favor speed rather than size, thereby eliminating the last requirement for peephole optimization for all but the tiniest microcontrollers.

The idea behind peephole optimization is that after the code generator has done its work, another pass over the generated code may be able to find opportunities for minor improvements by looking at only a small section of the code at a time (as if peeping through a keyhole at the code, hence the name). For example, a register store, followed by a load to the same register, could be corrected to eliminate the redundant load; a load of constant zero might be replaced by a register clear instruction; and so on. We normally recommend that these substitutions be made at the time code is generated, or even earlier as tree transformations, so there is little requirement to go back to the code file to fix them up. Furthermore, the code fixup is more costly in processor time because branches over the altered code may need correction also.

Summary

During the code generation phase of compiling, the intermediate code received from the optimizer is transformed into machine language code. Code generation is very machine-dependent. Hence, a variety of target machine architectures are considered in this chapter, both in conventional computers and in RISC, pipeline, and vector processors. This chapter deals with two main classes of optimization problems resulting from irregular computer architectures, which affect the design of compilers: (1) memory and register allocation and (2) analysis of loops. Loop optimization problems are largely independent of machine architecture. Storage allocation and analysis of loops may also involve a variety of subproblems.

Acronyms

CSE   Common subexpression elimination.

DAG   Directed Acyclic Graph.

PLV   Persistent Loop Variable.

Keywords

code generation	Produce executable code that has the same semantics as the input (source) program.
computer pipeline	The time it takes to execute an instruction is divided into discrete segments, and stages them in sequential components of the hardware.
induction variable	Any ordinal or temporary variable whose value follows the control variable of a loop in a linear relationship.
pipelined branch	A computer starts the next instruction after the branch (instruction) *before* the branch takes effect.
registers	A small amount of very fast, easily reached memory.
address register	is used to hold main memory addresses.
data register	is used to hold intermediate calculation values.
vector processor	A processor designed to apply a single or small number of instructions to a sequence of values, either regularly spaced in memory, or else preloaded into vector registers, and produce the results in another memory array or vector register.
virtual memory	Disk files used to mimic and extend main memory, but at a slower rate.

Exercises

1. Using the technique shown in Listing 9.3, give the conversion from the IBSM zero-address code to register machine code for each of the following statements to be compiled.

   (a) $a := c*(a+b-c)$ (b) $a := (a+b)*c-3$
   (c) $a := c*(a-c)+d*(a+b)$ (d) $a := (a+b)*(a-b)$

2. Instead of the direct conversion from zero-address code to a hypothetical machine code, simulate (on paper) a code generator for the following statements and give one-address code, which eliminates the register-indirect load and store instructions (replace the corresponding address loads for these instructions with direct loads and stores).

   (a) Listing 9.3   (b) Part a in Exercise 1
   (c) Part b in Exercise 1   (d) Part d in Exercise 1

3. Using the technique shown in Figure 9.2, simulate the execution of the code in the compile-time stack for each part of Exercise 1.

4. Using the technique shown in Figure 9.3, give memory-to-memory code in the virtual stack to simulate execution of a the arithmetic instructions for the assignment statements in Exercise 1. Your answers should be detailed with a clear indication of the value of each of the variables in the virtual stack.

5. Prove that a one-pass loop analysis is safe and adequate in a structured program tree. A one-pass loop analysis is safe when all loop variables are assumed to have ranges no smaller than their actual runtime ranges of values. It is adequate when loop variables are rarely assumed to have a range have a significantly greater range than its actual runtime range. Hint: distinguish between PLVs, which are live on entry to a loop, from variables that are not live on entry.

6. Give a pseudocoded form of an optimal algorithm for making branch address decisions.

7. Show that the optimal algorithm for Exercise 6 has a complexity of n^2 in the number of the branches.

8. A particular Pascal compiler remembers which variable or address is loaded in a register and can sometimes avoid reloading this value. The compiler assigns to any register a value function that estimates the probability of the register's content being used a second time [Jacobi, 1982, p.12]. Suggest an improved optimization algorithm for this compiler. Hint: Consider how register stores might be avoided. Also introduce a technique that could be used to replace probabilistic assignment of a register number.

9. What optimization techniques would be used to handle abstract data types?

10. What form of statistical analysis of a program would be used to make a compile-time decision to unpack a set variable?

Review Quiz

Indicate whether the following statements are true or false.

1. Most execution time for a program is spent in I/O routines and outer loops.

2. Loop unrolling is limited to short loops with an unspecified number of iterations.

3. A **WHILE**-loop of the form

   ```
   WHILE BooleanCondition DO statement END
   ```

   can be partially unrolled.

4. Unrolling the outer loops of a nested set of loops that exactly span a multidimensional array is equivalent to reinterpreting the array declaration as a single-dimension array.

5. Register allocation is basically a graph-coloring problem.

6. Graph coloring adequately addresses the question of allocating registers to expression evaluation.

7. A simple one-pass compiler with no flow analysis can do reasonable code generation for a multiple-register machine by simulating the expression stack in the registers.

8. A vectorizing compiler looks for opportunities to convert inner **FOR**-loops to vector code where all assignments within the loop to variables live on exit are either indexed array elements or reduction variables, and all array subscripts are either loop-variable or linear.

Code Generation and Optimization   Chap. 9

9. The following seven-node tree fragment generates a single machine instruction,

   MOV b,a

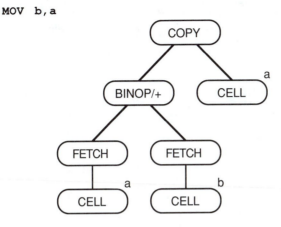

Compiler Project

1. Add loop optimizations to your compiler.
2. Choose a vector computer with which you are familiar, and adapt your compiler to generate vectorized code for it.

Further Reading

Aho, A.V., Ganapathi, M., & Tjiang, S.W.K. "Code Generation Using Tree Matching and Dynamic Programming." ACM *Transactions on Programming Languages and Systems*, Vol. 11, No. 4 (October 1989), pp. 491-516. Introduces a tree-manipulation language used to construct efficient code generators.

Chaitin, G.J. "Register Allocation and Spilling Via Graph Coloring." *SIGPLAN 82 Symposium on Compiler Construction* (1982), pp. 98-105.

Chaitin, G.J. et al. "Register Allocation Via Coloring." *Computer Languages*, Vol. 6, No. 1 (1981), pp. 47-57.

Chow, F. & Hennessy, J. "Register Allocation by Priority-Based Coloring." *SIGPLAN 84 Symposium on Compiler Construction* (1984), pp. 222-232.

Jacobi, C. *Code Generation and the Lilith Architecture*. Ph.D. dissertation, Swiss Federal Institute of Technology, Zurich, 1982. Tells how the Lilith computer was designed to be programmed in Modula-2.

Kennedy, K. "Index Register Allocation in Straight Line Code And Simple Loops." *Design and Optimization of Compilers* ed. R. Rustin. Englewood Cliffs, NJ: Prentice Hall, 1972, pp. 51-64.

Knuth, D.E. "An Empirical Study of Fortran Programs." *Software—Practice and Experience*, Vol. 1, No. 2 (1971), pp. 105-133. Found that most execution time is spent in I/O routines and inner loops.

Pittman, T. *Practical Code Optimization by Transformational Attribute Grammars Applied to Low-Level Intermediate Code Trees.* Ph.D. dissertation, University of California at Santa Cruz, 1985. See appendix, which gives nine grammars representative of the 15-20 needed to implement a full optimizer.

Chapter 10

Nonprocedural Languages

Aims

- Consider problems associated with compiling applicative languages.
- Deal with problem of converting functional recursion into looping structures.
- Develop an applicative programming language (Tiny Scheme) implementation for the Itty Bitty Stack Machine.
- Examine the issues concerning implementation of a TAG-based compiler compiler.
- See a transformational attribute grammar as a nonprocedural programming language used to specify a compiler.
- Examine the four syntactic divisions of a TAG.
- Consider a TAG as a data-flow language in which there are no variables or assignments.
- Consider finite-state automata constructed by a TAG compiler.

10.1 Introduction

Throughout the first nine chapters of this book we have addressed exclusively the compilation of procedural programming languages such as Modula-2. The techniques apply equally to most common programming languages, so there has been little need to bring in other languages for illustrative purposes. Now we are ready to look at some of the particular problems associated with compiling other kinds of programming languages into efficient native machine code. There are three important classes of nonprocedural languages for which compilation is interesting and useful; they are the functional or applicative languages similar to or derived from Lisp, the so-called "fourth generation" database languages, and the nondeterministic reasoning languages related to Prolog. In this chapter we consider an extended example in just one of these language classes to show how the principles of compiler design can be applied.

Although widely accepted as a major advance in programming methodology, object-oriented programming (OOP) presents no distinctive challenges to the compiler designer. The encapsulation of information in "objects" is simply an extension to compilation units of the scoping rules we already addressed in Chapter 5; it is thus equivalent to managing modules in Modula-2. Object classes are record types that include procedure pointers (for the methods) among their fields. The record definition in the symbol table is annotated with references to the procedures that are to be used to initialize the procedure pointers at this scope level. Single inheritance means that the record type is extensible in a new scope. When a new class is defined as a subclass of another, all the field definitions are imported into the new record definition before adding new fields. Overriding a method means that when an object of this class is instantiated (that is, a dynamic variable of this record type is created), a local procedure may be substituted for the one in the defined parent class. Polymorphism refers to the ability of procedures (or operators) to accept a parameter whose type is any of a defined set. The "+" operator in Modula-2 is polymorphic because its operands may be INTEGER, REAL, or a set, which we can readily implement in an attribute grammar. Polymorphism is often thought to be a distinctive of OOP, but it is generally restricted to the ability of an OOP method to accept parameters in the inheritance chain in whose class it lies. OOP languages may thus be implemented at about the same level of design sophistication as Modula-2, so we do not consider them to merit further special attention beyond this brief review.

Finally, no compiler book would be complete without a discussion on automatic compiler construction. Many of our techniques have used transformational attribute grammars (TAGs) as an implementation vehicle. Although Chapter 5 shows a deterministic translation from TAGs to procedural code, a grammar is in principle nonprocedural. A discussion of the implementation of a TAG-based compiler-compiler is thus a fitting end for both this chapter and the book.

10.2 Compiling an Applicative Language

The Lisp programming language was introduced by John McCarthy in 1958 as part of the Artificial Intelligence Project at MIT [McCarthy, 1981]. Lisp is an applicative language which depends on the application of functions without assignments. Compiling applicative languages is essentially the same as compiling expression evaluation and recursive functions in procedural languages, with one important difference. Unlike conventional languages, Lisp and its derivatives permit the direct manipulation of program code, which gives rise to *continuations*, or partially evaluated functions, that can be manipulated as data. In a highly interactive program development environment, an *incremental* compiler is often recommended to provide good turn-around time from user modification to executable code; a language that permits or encourages dynamic code modification makes similar demands on the compiler because new (uncompiled) code can be created at runtime. The compiler in such systems must necessarily be part of the runtime environment.

In Chapter 1 we observed the difference between a compiler and an interpreter. The compiler translates the source code to another language, typically the machine language of the target computer, but does not run the program. An interpreter may do no translation at all, but merely carry out the semantic actions of the source program directly. The language user sees less of a distinction in an interactive system, because an incremental compiler can be as responsive as an interpreter, while yielding some of the same performance advantages of the compiler.

Partial evaluation of functions at compile time consists primarily in the application of constant-folding transformations to the program code. The greater emphasis on function application invites us to investigate folding constant parameters from a class of calls into the called function, creating for each different constant value a new function that takes fewer parameters. The process of folding one or more of the parameters into the function definition so that it can be called with only the remaining parameters is called *currying*, after Haskell Curry, who adapted Schönfinkel's original idea [Curry, 1968; Schönfinkel, 1924]. In a compiler it is most valuable for formal parameters that take a small number of values, when most of the invocations of the function use a constant actual parameter. In each copy of the curried (folded) function, additional constant folding opportunities will usually result from the now-constant parameter. This optimization is possible also in conventional language compilers, but its advantage there is not as great.

In its original incarnation, nonlocal variables (also called *free variables*) in Lisp function definitions were *dynamically scoped*. In a purely applicative language there are no assignments, so there are also no local variables other than the parameters; a reference to an identifier that is not a parameter refers to the nearest definition of that name in the call chain rather than in the source text. The meaning of a free variable reference depends mostly on who called the function. By contrast, Modula-2 and most block-structured programming languages are *statically scoped*, and the meaning of a free variable depends only on where the function is located in the program source text. Although dynamic scoping appears more powerful, in practice it offers little advantage at considerable cost. With static scoping, the compiler can link all free variables to their referents at compile time with only a few machine instructions (see the discussion on display in Chapter 6); dynamic scoping requires the preservation and searching of the symbol table in the execution environment at runtime. With the increasing popularity of compiling Lisp and its dialects, dynamic scoping has fallen into disfavor.

Another common feature of an interpreted language that is much more difficult to implement in a compiled language is dynamic data types. Most computers have different hardware instructions for dealing with floating-point numbers and integers, and with different sizes of each. The most efficient machine code is that where the compiler has chosen the appropriate hardware instructions for the data type to be processed, which requires that the type be known at compile time. The classical languages (Fortran and Basic) distinguished the data types syntactically, by naming conventions; most modern languages like Modula-2 require variables to be declared to be of a particular type, and the information is stored in the symbol table at compile time for the semantic analysis of the program and code generation, as we learned in Chapters 5 and 6. Its long and widespread use without any compiler surely helped the developing Lisp language avoid data type declaration requirements. The result is that any reasonable compiler is obliged to cope with dynamic data types, where the compiled code must examine the data to determine appropriate arithmetic instruction hardware to apply. With extensive data-flow analysis, some of the type analysis code can be eliminated in much the same way we eliminate range-check code, but it is doubtful whether very many compilers actually attempt this kind of optimization.

10.2.1 Some Lisp Concepts

To properly understand the implementation of an applicative language requires a certain familiarity with the programming concepts involved in using the language. This discussion here will be most easily understood by a reader who has used some dialect of Lisp. However, a few elementary concepts should facilitate its comprehension for programmers with no such experience.

Although the name "Lisp" is contracted from the phrase "List Processing," the fundamental data structure in Lisp-like languages is the cell, or *dotted pair*. This amounts to a record type consisting of two pointers to the same type, from which it is possible to construct arbitrary binary tree structures. Lists are constructed by recursively concatenating pairs down the right subtree, as shown in Figure 10.1.

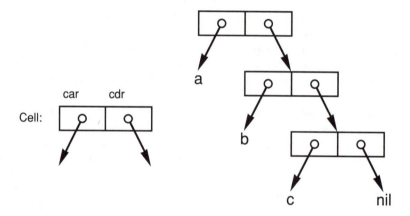

Figure 10.1. Constructing a list (a b c) from dotted pairs.

An *atom* is a single value, usually a character string that serves as an identifier, or else a number. Each component of a pair can either point to another pair, or represent an atom. List construction consists in applying the pair constructor function, *cons*, to two arguments, themselves either pairs or atoms. Two other intrinsic functions, *car* and *cdr* (pronounced "car" and "could-er") extract from a pair respectively the left and right subtrees.

In addition to building arbitrary data structures from lists, lists can be used to define program code. The list, (a b c) interpreted as a program fragment, is a function call or *application*, applying the function named a to the two parameters b and c. Because b and c could themselves be lists, a program can thus be arbitrarily complex. In particular, the function to be applied could itself be a list, so that (at least in a correct Lisp program) the parameters are passed to a function that is the returned value of a function call. This is possible in Modula-2 also, when a procedure returns a result that is a procedure type, but Modula-2 does not allow the returned procedure to be called directly, but requires it to be assigned to a variable first. Pure Lisp has no assignments, and the result of evaluating a program list is some expression value. Expressions (function applications) are evaluated, and the results are passed as parameters to other functions, and so on recursively, until an entire program list is evaluated. The final result is typically printed (displayed) on the user terminal.

In addition to *car, cdr,* and *cons,* Lisp has an instrinsic function that creates a function; it is called *lambda,* after the lambda calculus that forms the mathematical basis of Lisp. In the Scheme dialect of Lisp discussed here, *lambda* accepts two parameters. The first is a list of identifiers that name the parameters of the new function, and the second is a list expression, typically using those parameters. Thus, *(lambda (x y) (+ x y))* is an expression that evaluates to a function that when called with two parameters, returns the sum of those two parameters. The function *(lambda (x) x)* is the identity function; that is, any parameter passed to this function is the parameter itself. Passing a parameter to a function gives the value a name for the body of the function. Recursive functions are thus formed by applying an identity function definition to a function definition; the recursive function becomes the parameter in the identity function, but it acquires a name in the process, so that it can call itself. Function-returning functions are a difficult concept to grasp, only compounded by recursion. Once fully understood, however, the concept is elegant and powerful.

Other intrinsic functions do standard arithmetic operations (for example, + in the example above), permit lists to be written into a program without being interpreted as function applications (*quote*), and permit the conditional evaluation of subexpressions (*if*). Here in Lisp is the factorial function, which returns one if its parameter is zero, and otherwise multiplies the parameter times the result of a recursive call:

   ((lambda (fact) fact) (lambda (n) (if (= n 0) 1   (* (fact (− n 1)))))))

Most dialects of Lisp also define a number of functions that amount to syntactical extensions of the basic lambda calculus form. Some of these look suspiciously like assignments and statement sequences, but most of them can be shown to be equivalent to a lambda expression. For example, the function *define* in the following fragment of a list looks like an assignment because it gives the value three to the name *x* in the subsequent list item:

   . . . *(define (x 3)) (+ x 1)* . . .

The same list fragment can be equivalently written as a lambda expression:

   . . . *((lambda (x) (+ x 1)) 3)* . . .

10.2.2 Tail-Recursion

The lack of sequential control structures such as WHILE loops in applicative languages means that all iteration must be done by means of functional recursion. This makes it desirable for the compiler to convert recursion back to looping structures whenever possible, an optimization that is possible also in conventional languages, but not so important. The conversion is rather direct in the case of *tail-recursion,* where the final step in a computation is a recursive call whose result is returned to the previous caller unmodified. To illustrate this, consider the following factorial function (although written in Modula-2, it is completely applicative):

```
PROCEDURE  fact(n:  INTEGER):  INTEGER;
BEGIN
  IF  n=0  THEN  RETURN  1
    ELSE  RETURN  n*fact(n-1)  END
END  fact;
```

Although this function ends with a recursive call to itself, that is not the last step, because the result must be multiplied by *n* before it is passed on up. This function is not tail-recursive, but it can be rewritten so that it is:

```
PROCEDURE  fact(n:  INTEGER):  INTEGER;
    PROCEDURE  fact2(n,  m:  INTEGER):  INTEGER;
    BEGIN
        IF  n=0  THEN  RETURN  m
        ELSE  RETURN  fact(n-1,n*m)  END
    END  fact2;
BEGIN  (*  fact  *)
    RETURN  fact2(n,  1)  END
END  fact;
```

The inner function *fact2* now returns the result of its recursive call unmodified, all the multiplication having been done on parameters in the call rather than on the function results. Tail-recursion such as this can be readily converted to conventional looping by replacing the entire line containing the recursive call with a simple jump to the beginning of the function; instead of storing the call's parameters into a new activation frame, the new values simply replace the current parameters. The compiler must take due care to prevent overwriting parameters while they are still live (that is, before all the new values have been calculated), but the new values can be assigned to temporary variables, then conventional flow analysis and copy propagation techniques as described in Chapter 8 applied to eliminate unnecessary data movement. The result, viewed as a source transformation, looks like this:

```
PROCEDURE  fact2(n,  m:  INTEGER):  INTEGER;
BEGIN
  LOOP
    IF  n=0  THEN  RETURN  m
  ELSE
      m  :=  n*m;
      n  :=  n-1;
    END  END  (*  of  LOOP  *)
END  fact2;
```

After the optimizer substitutes the function *fact2* back into its call, it is equivalent to the following code, which of course is no longer applicative at all, but that was the goal:

```
PROCEDURE fact(n: INTEGER): INTEGER;
   VAR m: INTEGER;
BEGIN (* fact *)
  m := 1;
   WHILE n>0 DO
     m := n*m;
     n := n-1;
     END;
   RETURN m
END fact;
```

The compiler is not really expected to transform non-tail-recursive functions into tail-recursion, but once existing tail-recursion is identified, it can readily be optimized into iteration.

10.2.3 Implementing an Applicative Language Compiler

A virtue whose praises are too-infrequently sung is the self-compiling compiler, which is a compiler that compiles itself. At first blush it appears to make as much sense as lifting yourself up by pulling up on your own bootstraps — indeed, the analogy is so apt that the term *bootstrapping* is generally used to mean the process of getting a compiler or operating system to the point where it can operate on itself. In the case of a compiler, the first step is to compile a possibly reduced version of the compiler in a different environment. This may involve using the same language that already exists on a different computer, or hand-compiling the compiler into some other available language. Then the first compiler can be used to compile itself for the target machine, and then finally the compiled compiler can compile itself on the target computer. At this point the language can be enhanced to its full capability (if a reduced version was used for bootstrapping) and the enhanced version recompiled. If this last stage includes code optimization that was left out of earlier versions, then two subsequent recompilations of the compiler (each time using the newly compiled version to compile the next) will improve the compiler's own performance. Note, however, the entropic effect of minor code errors, which propagate like their biological counterpart (mutations), and often reduce the recompiled compiler to sterility or uselessness after but a few generations.

The major benefit of implementing a compiler in its own language is that, by its size and complexity, a compiler gives most of the code a vigorous test, making it possible to catch many more errors during development than would be possible with toy programs created for the purpose. As developers are forced to use their own creation, they also become highly motivated to make it convenient and efficient, which amounts to the same benefit at a more abstract level. It comes as no surprise, therefore, that most Lisp compilers are written in Lisp, and that is as it should be. Later in this chapter we concentrate on the development of a TAG compiler, written in a TAG. The main emphasis of this book has been the use of attribute grammars in the implementation of compilers, however, so we back away from the self-compiling compiler goal for our study of a tiny applicative language compiler, choosing rather to discuss the problem entirely in terms of the grammars that define the syntax and semantics of the language.

As with any language, one of the requirements of our compiler design is the specification of the precise source and target languages. For continuity with the earlier chapters in this book, we retain the Itty Bitty Stack Machine as the target language; Chapter 9 has already addressed the issues in which compiling for a commercially available computer might differ from the IBSM. The IBSM is defined as a conventional (integer) arithmetic computer, whereas the basic data structure of Lisp is the list, or more precisely, the dotted pair. It is therefore necessary to define how the dotted pair translates into native IBSM data structures, and for this we choose the machine equivalent of the Modula-2 record type:

```
TYPE
   Cell = POINTER TO Datum;
   Lambda = PROCEDURE (paramlist: Cell): Cell;
   TagType = (code, actf, pair, atom, intn);
   Datum = RECORD CASE tag: TagType OF
      code: fun: Lambda;
            nArgs: CARDINAL;
            itsEnv: Cell |
      pair: ar, dr: Cell |
      iden: offs, lex: INTEGER |
      atom, intn: val: INTEGER END END;
```

We let the *atom* variant contain an index into some unspecified global string table similar to those discussed in Chapter 3; there are better implementations whose complexity need not divert our attention here. Although we define only one numeric data type (integer), we can support others such as rational and *bignum* by constructing them out of pairs or lists of integers. It is a simple modification to add such data types as intrinsics by including their enumerations in the tag type and declaring appropriate machine-level data structures to support them. The pair structure here models the historical form (the names "address register" and "decrement register" referred to components of a machine instruction word in the original implementation).

This data structure also defines a variant for compiled code references. A code reference consists of a pointer to the actual machine code in memory (type `Lambda`), a reference to its symbol table that is to be used if it requires compiling more code within that scope, and the number of parameters it expects to find in its activation record when called. The activation record itself is constructed on the runtime stack from the same symbol table reference, with one cell for each specified parameter. The size of the activation record thus depends on the function definition.

For the source language we choose a tiny subset of Scheme, which is a variant of Lisp with static scoping and fairly regular structures and primitives [Sussman&Steele, 1975; Smith, 1988]. We assume that the compiler is contained within an interactive environment, so that the compiler is invoked whenever there is a functional application of uncompiled code. Uncompiled code will always be in the form of a list, which is a right-recursive linked list of pairs. We develop two grammars, one to parse the source text into lists, and the other to compile a designated list into IBSM code. Although it is beyond the scope of our discussion to go into much detail on the library of intrinsic functions, it is important to distinguish those that the compiler recognizes and compiles into in-line code from those that simply exist as globally defined code. In doing this, we blur the line separating the execution environment from the compiler because a running program can create new lists and present them for compilation. In practice that is the only way the compiler is invoked because that also happens at the top level of user interaction.

The heart of a Lisp interpreter is the expression evaluator. If presented with an atom, it looks it up in the symbol table and returns that value. In the case of a pair, it evaluates the *car* (ar in our record), expecting to find a function reference, and passes to that function the *cdr* (dr in the record) as a list of parameters. In our implementation, the evaluator invokes the compiler and passes it the whole expression, then executes the resulting compiled code. The compiler parses the expression tree according to the grammar of Listing 10.2. Listing 10.1 parses the source text into a tree representation of list cells. These grammars will be more easily understood by a reader already familiar with the Scheme language (or some other dialect of Lisp). Note also that the code sent by the compiler grammar to the code generator EmitIBSM is often packed two or three instructions to a word for compactness; Appendix C explains how this works in the Itty Bitty Stack Machine.

```
SchemeTree ↑theTree:tree
    →  "(" aList ↑theTree ")"
    →  ATM↑strno [ theTree=<atom >%strno]          {ATM returns a scanner token }
    →  NUM↑valu [ theTree=<intn >%valu]            {NUM is a scanned numeral }
    →  "'" SchemeTree ↑aTree
        [theTree=<pair <atom >%–2 aTree >];


aList ↑theTree:tree
    →  SchemeTree ↑aTree
        ("." SchemeTree ↑bTree [theTree=<pair aTree bTree >]
        | aList ↑bTree [theTree=<pair aTree bTree >])
    →  [theTree=<>] ;                              {return nil}
```

Listing 10.1. A Tiny Scheme source-to-tree grammar.

The intrinsic functions that the compiler knows about are identified in the symbol table as atoms with a negative index. One of these functions applied to an appropriate list of parameters will generate native (in-line) IBSM code. Only a few of these functions are shown in the grammar, namely, the integer arithmetic operators, the conditional and functional forms, and the sequence ("begin" in Scheme). The pair decomposition operators *car* and *cdr* could (and should) also be added in this way. Pair composition (*cons*) requires memory allocation, so a library call rather than purely in-line code continues to be appropriate. This compiler knows about three library functions, identified by index to the CallLibe nonterminal, and listed also in Table 10.1. A full implementation might have several other intrinsics and library functions about which the compiler is also aware. Finally, there are some memory management problems that do not concern us here; a complete implementation would have to allocate memory structures for the compiled

CompileExpn ↓cantail:bool ↓env:tree ↓inCode:tree ↑outCode:tree
   → <pair <atom >%n rite > [n<0]   *{negative index is intrinsic}*
         ([n+1=0] rite:DoLambda ↓env ↓inCode ↑outCode
         |[n+2=0] rite:DoSequence ↓cantail:bool ↓env ↓1 ↓0 ↓inCode ↑outCode
         |[n+3=0] rite:DoCond ↓cantail:bool ↓env ↓inCode ↑outCode
         |[otherwise] rite:DoArith ↓env ↓–n ↓inCode ↑outCode)
   → <pair <atom >%n rite > [n>0]   *{positive index is atom}*
         [Lookup ↓env ↓n ↑theTree]   *{find its current definition}*
         ((([theTree :<pair ..>]|[theTree : <iden >]|[theTree :<code ..>])
           [aTree=<pair theTree rite >]   *{substitute it for the atom, }*
            aTree: CompileExpn ↓cantail ↓env ↓inCode ↑outCode *{try again}*
         |[otherwise] rite: CompileList ↓env ↓inCode ↑aCode *{free: stack args}*
            CallLibe ↓env ↓3 ↓n ↓aCode ↑fCode   *{add library lookup reference }*
            CallLibe ↓env ↓2 ↓cantail ↓fCode ↑outCode) *{library ref to call it}*
   → <pair <code theCode > rite >   *{previously compiled code}*
         [GetInfo ↓theCode ↑itsenv ↑nargs ↑addr]
         rite: DoSequence ↓false ↓env ↓1 ↓nargs ↓inCode ↑aCode *{get args}*
         [EmitIBSM ↓894 ↓aCode ↑bCode]   *{push parent frame pointer}*
         ([itsenv>0; EmitIBSM ↓889 ↓bCode ↑bCode@; itsenv@=itsenv−1])*
         ([cantail=true] TailCall ↓theCode ↓bCode ↑outCode *{make tailcall JMP}*
         |[otherwise; EmitIBSM ↓124 ↓bCode ↑cCode]   *{gen subroutine call}*
           [EmitIBSM ↓addr ↓cCode ↑outCode])
   → <pair left:<pair ..> rite >   *{uncompiled function call}*
         rite: CompileList ↓env ↓inCode ↑aCode   *{gen code to stack arg list}*
         left: CompileExpn ↓false ↓env ↓aCode ↑fCode   *{get function code}*
         CallLibe ↓env ↓2 ↓cantail ↓fCode ↑outCode *{add library ref to call it}*
   → <iden <intn >%lex >%offs   *{local param identifier ...}*
         [CurrentLex ↓env ↑cur]
         ([lex=cur]   *{...if the lex level is current}*
           [EmitIBSM ↓892 ↓inCode ↑aCode]   *{code to push its value}*
           [EmitIBSM ↓offs ↓aCode ↑outCode]
         |[otherwise; n=cur–lex]   *{else nonlocal reference ...}*
           [EmitIBSM ↓28633 ↓inCode ↑aCode]   *{code to follow static links}*
           ([n>0; EmitIBSM ↓827 ↓bCode ↑bCode@; n@=n–1])*
           [EmitIBSM ↓28059 ↓bCode ↑cCode]   *{code to push its value}*
           [EmitIBSM ↓offs ↓cCode ↑outCode])
   → <atom >%n   *{assume positive index }*
         [Lookup ↓env ↓n ↑aTree]   *{find its current definition}*
         ((([aTree :<pair ..>]|[aTree : <atom >]|[aTree :<intn >]|[aTree :<code >])
           aTree: CompileExpn ↓cantail ↓env ↓inCode ↑outCode *{try again}*
         |[otherwise; Error])   *{undefined symbol reference }*

Listing 10.2a. A code-generating grammar fragment for Tiny Scheme.

```
  →  <intn >%n                                            {literal number }
         [EmitIBSM ↓28  ↓inCode  ↑aCode]                  {code to push its value}
         [EmitIBSM ↓n ↓aCode ↑outCode]
  →  <code theCode >                                      {code reference }
        [ GetInfo ↓theCode ↑itsenv ↑nargs ↑addr]
        [EmitIBSM ↓28  ↓inCode  ↑aCode]                   {code to push function ref}
        [EmitIBSM ↓addr  ↓aCode ↑outCode];

DoArith  ↓env:tree ↓op:int  ↓inCode:tree ↑outCode:tree
  →  <pair  left <pair  rite <>>>                         {two-param list required}
        left: CompileExpn ↓false ↓env  ↓inCode  ↑aCode    {eval params}
        rite: CompileExpn ↓false ↓env  ↓aCode ↑eCode
        rite: DoArithOp ↓op ↓eCode  ↑outCode              {generate operator code}
  →  atree    {uncompiled param list, so..}
        atree: CompileList ↓env  ↓inCode  ↑aCode          {gen code to stack arg list}
        [EmitIBSM ↓13288 ↓aCode ↑bCode]                   {code to extract & push car}
        [EmitIBSM ↓10105 ↓bCode ↑cCode]
        [EmitIBSM ↓12381 ↓cCode ↑dCode]                   {code to extract cadr}
        [EmitIBSM ↓889 ↓dCode ↑eCode]
        rite: DoArithOp ↓op ↓eCode  ↑outCode ;            {generate operator code}

CompileList  ↓env:tree  ↓inCode:tree ↑outCode:tree
  →  <pair  left  rite >
        left: CompileExpn ↓false ↓env ↓inCode ↑aCode      {compile car of list...}
        rite: CompileList ↓env ↓aCode ↑cCode              {do cdr}
        CallLibe ↓env ↓1 ↓0 ↓cCode ↑outCode              {add library reference to cons}
  →  <> [ EmitIBSM ↓30 ↓inCode ↑outCode];                {push nil at runtime}

DoArithOp  ↓op:int  ↓inCode:tree ↑outCode:tree
  →  atree                                                {operands already compiled}
        ([op=4; EmitIBSM ↓12  ↓inCode ↑outCode]           {add}
        |[op=5; EmitIBSM ↓404  ↓inCode ↑outCode]          {subtract}
        |[op=6; EmitIBSM ↓11  ↓inCode ↑outCode]           {multiply}
        |[op=8; EmitIBSM ↓16  ↓inCode ↑outCode]           {equal}
        |[op=9; EmitIBSM ↓17  ↓inCode ↑outCode]           {less}
        |[otherwise; Error]);                             {unknown operator}

DoSequence  ↓tail:bool  ↓env:tree  ↓cnt:int  ↓limit:int  ↓inCode:tree ↑outCode:tree
  →  atree  [count=limit]                                 {if equal, just one list value}
        atree: CompileList ↓env ↓inCode  ↑outCode {so gen code to stack it}
  →  <pair  left  rite >
        left: CompileExpn ↓(tail&rite=<>) ↓env ↓inCode ↑aCode  {compile car...}
        rite: DoSequence ↓env ↓cnt+1 ↓limit ↓aCode ↑outCode   {do cdr}
  →  <> [outCode=inCode];
```

Listing 10.2b. A code-generating grammar fragment for Tiny Scheme.

AddSymbols ↓inenv:tree ↑outenv:tree ↑nsyms:int
    → <pair <atom >%n rite >   *{symbol required}*
          rite: AddSymbols ↓inenv ↑anenv ↑syms   *{count them to get offset}*
          [CurrentLex ↓anenv ↑lex; offs=–2–syms; nsyms=syms+1]
          [Into ↓anenv ↓n ↓<iden <intn >%lex >%offs ↑outenv] *{insert this name}*
    → <> [outenv=inenv; nsyms=0];

DoLambda ↓env:tree ↓inCode:tree ↑outCode:tree
    → <pair left rite >   *{two lists required}*
          [OpenFrame ↓env ↑newenv]   *{open new frame for params}*
          left: AddSymbols ↓newenv ↑funenv ↑nsyms *{insert them}*
          [EmitIBSM ↓158 ↓<> ↑bCode]   *{gen procedure entry code}*
          rite: DoSequence ↓true ↓funenv ↓1 ↓0 ↓bCode ↑eCode *{gen body}*
          [EmitIBSM ↓188 ↓eCode ↑xCode]   *{add exit code}*
          [EmitIBSM ↓nsyms ↓xCode ↑fCode]
          [MakeCode ↓funenv ↓nsyms ↓fCode ↑theCode]
          [GetInfo ↓theCode ↑itsenv ↑nargs ↑addr]
          [EmitIBSM ↓28 ↓inCode ↑cCode]   *{generate LDC to push ref}*
          [EmitIBSM ↓addr ↓cCode ↑outCode];

DoCond ↓cantail:bool ↓env:tree ↓inCode:tree ↑outCode:tree
    → <pair expn <pair left <pair rite <>>>>   *{three-param list required}*
          expn: CompileExpn ↓false ↓env ↓inCode ↑aCode *{code to eval bool}*
          [EmitIBSM ↓60 ↓aCode ↑bCode]   *{add conditional branch}*
          [EmitIBSM ↓0 ↓bCode ↑tCode]
          left: CompileExpn ↓cantail ↓env ↓tCode ↑xCode *{gen true code}*
          [EmitIBSM ↓1950 ↓xCode ↑cCode]   *{unconditional branch}*
          [EmitIBSM ↓0 ↓cCode ↑eCode]
          [BackPatch ↓bCode ↓eCode ↑fCode]   *{cond.branch comes here}*
          rite: CompileExpn ↓cantail ↓env ↓fCode ↑gCode *{gen false code}*
          [BackPatch ↓cCode ↓gCode ↑outCode]   *{uncond.branch comes here}*

Listing 10.2c. A code-generating grammar fragment for Tiny Scheme.

code, and implement an appropriate garbage collector to recover inaccessible code fragments and other list cells as they become unused. These would normally be invoked within the library routine that supports *cons*.

    This grammar omits two important nonterminals. One of them is CallLibe, which merely constructs appropriate code to call the specified library routines. The details for this would depend somewhat on the mechanism chosen for linking a compiled program to library routines. A simple implementation might store library entry points in a low-memory address vector, and the call could fetch an indexed item from the vector. The other unspecified nonterminal is TailCall, which converts a tail-recursive function call into a jump. In this grammar the advantage of such an optimization is slight, partly because the IBSM procedure call is relatively cheap and the cost of a jump is comparable to it, and partly because most of the new activation frame must be constructed anyway

Intrinsic Function Index

-1 Lambda, used to generate function code.
-2 Sequence, used also to stack parameters for a function call.
-3 Conditional, the standard IF-THEN-ELSE expression form.
-4 Add.
-5 Subtract.
-6 Multiply.
-8 Compare for equal.
-9 Compare for less.

Library Routine Index

1 Construct a cell (*cons*) from left and right (*car* and *cdr*) parts.
2 Construct an activation frame and call an arbitrary function. This is used when the functionality (number of parameters) of the function cannot be determined at compile time, such as when it is compiled at runtime or found from a free variable lookup.
3 Look up a free variable in the symbol table at runtime.

Table 10.1. Key Tiny Scheme intrinsics and library routines

before the parameter values can be safely copied over the old activation frame. If there is a different number of parameters in the procedure being called than in the caller, the position of the return address on the stack must also be shifted. The nonterminal to do all these things (and the specification of a library routine to support it) is left as an exercise.

The compiler outlined in this grammar says nothing about continuations, because there is no tricky code to generate for them. Scheme uses the library function `call/cc` to gain access to continuations, and the entire implementation is buried in that library routine. The effect of evaluating a continuation is to jump to the exit of `call/cc` (again) with a new result. Therefore, the library routine must save the contents of the runtime stack in a data structure, with the code to rebuild the stack from the structure any time the continuation is evaluated. This could happen again and again long after the original stack has been dismissed, so the entire stack must be saved. When there are no longer any references to the continuation, the garbage collector will of course dispose of the structure and release its memory. Note that much of the efficiency in saving and rebuilding the stack depends on the prior conversion of tail-recursion into iteration because each iterator eliminates a stack frame that therefore need not be saved in the continuation.

This grammar also contains no provision for constant folding. We consider this a simple improvement, which is also left as an exercise for the reader. The applicative nature of Scheme brings with it the temptation to generate code too soon for function definitions and calls. Good optimization requires that procedure definitions be left in list form as long as possible, so that constant folding has the opportunity to fold constant arguments in its calls into simplified code. It is rather difficult to develop an appropriate heuristic to decide when to do this in a practical Lisp compiler. With conventional languages, procedure definitions are usually too large to consider substituting back into their callers, and arithmetic and logical operations are not procedure calls at all, so this decision is not generally an issue.

There is considerable research into partial evaluation of programs as a means to turn a general-purpose algorithm into a program that deals with a particular class of problems. Most of this research shows substantial improvements in performance, but it considers only programs in dialects of Lisp. Partial evaluation in this context is equivalent to global constant folding and procedure back-substitution in a conventional programming language. Because Lisp lacks language structures to support application-specific algorithms, these structures must be built up out of low-level nested and recursive function applications. Partial evaluation reduces an abstract Lisp program to the level that a Modula-2 programmer would ordinarily write without thinking too hard, given the compiler optimizations already discussed in Chapters 8 and 9. The advantages of partially evaluating Lisp programs thus appear spectacular only when compared to the relatively poor performance of interpreted or semi-interpreted native Lisp.

10.3 A Transformational Attribute Grammar Compiler

As the specification for a compiler, a transformational attribute grammar (TAG) is a nonprocedural programming language. That is, it can be used as the formal source language to fully specify a program that is a compiler. Therefore, it is reasonable to contemplate a compiler that can generate a functional compiler from a TAG. Programs that compile grammars into code are called *compiler compilers*; YACC ("Yet Another Compiler Compiler") is one well-known example of a compiler-compiler that automates the development of a parser from a context-free grammar specification. Semantics in YACC is specified in the source grammar as embedded fragments of C code with but limited access to a single restricted attribute. The scanner also must be developed in a separate program (Lex). There is considerable research in the development of efficient and productive compiler compilers with varying degrees of integration [see, for example, Leverett et al., 1979, Ganzinger et al., 1977], but because this book has concentrated on TAGs, we limit our discussion in this chapter to the implementation of a TAG compiler that applies the key concepts presented in earlier chapters.

The TAG compiler is developed as a self-compiling TAG, which translates TAGs into standard Modula-2. Predefined functions — generally those useful across a broad spectrum of compilers — are written as a library of Modula-2 procedures that are linked into the finished compiler when it is finally compiled into object code. The source grammar for the compiler is available separately in a machine-readable form, together with object code for a variety of common industrial and academic computers. Many aspects of the compiler described rely on established technology without being particularly innovative. Our purpose is to communicate a workable implementation that can inspire further research and development. Although ongoing research continues to make improvements in the TAG language and its compiler, Appendix B contains the complete syntax and some of the semantics of the version of the TAG compiler described in this chapter; the machine-readable files are generally kept up to date.

In Chapter 3 we developed the algorithms for mechanically constructing an FSA scanner from regular expressions. In Chapter 4 we showed the mechanical construction of a recursive-descent parser from an LL(1) grammar. Chapter 5 extended that parser to encompass attribute evaluation. With less detail, Chapters 6 and 8 discussed code generation and optimization issues in a TAG. Now we are ready to put these techniques together into a single tool that translates a TAG into a functional compiler. As outlined in Chapter 1 (see Figure 1.1 on page 8), there are six components of the compiler to be considered. Of these, the scanner, the parser, and the tree transformer (optimizer) components are represented by separate sections in the source grammar to be compiled. The constrainer and the code generator consist primarily of attribute evaluation functions written into the parser and transformer sections, whereas any desirable peephole optimization is buried in the predefined attribute evaluation functions, as are also the supporting string and symbol table components.

10.3.1 TAG Compiler Parts

A TAG has four syntactic divisions, each defining one separable component of the compiler. A division may be omitted if unused. The first division declares any global attributes visible throughout the TAG, the node names that may be used in constructing trees, and the functionality of a library of predefined functions that may be called from the remainder of the TAG.

The second division begins with the reserved word "scanner" and specifies regular expressions for all the scanner tokens that cannot be specified in a single quoted literal string, or that involve particular scanner semantics. White space and comments are also defined in a similar way, using the reserved word "ignore" as a scanner nonterminal.

The third division begins with the reserved word "parser" and specifies the compiler syntax and static semantic constraints in a context-free grammar extended by attributes and regular expression operators. The final division begins with the reserved word "transformer" and specifies in a context-free tree-transforming attribute grammar any optimization or code generation requirements of the compiler being compiled. Parser rules accept scanner tokens as their input language, and transformer rules operate on tree templates, but a parser nonterminal is allowed to make local tree transformations by calling on transformer rules. Similarly, a transformer nonterminal may call on an empty parser nonterminal (that reads no scanner tokens) for attribute evaluations not applicable to any tree.

Inherited and synthesized attributes in all parts of the TAG are explicitly typed, using one of five reserved type names: "int" for integer numbers, "bool" for Boolean truth values, "set" for variable-length bit vectors, "table" for fixed-length vectors such as hash tables, and "tree" for decorated tree structures. Local attributes within a single nonterminal rule are typed automatically by the TAG compiler based on usage.

A grammar is by nature nonprocedural, but as we saw in Chapters 4 and 5, there is a direct transformation from an attribute grammar to procedural code such as Modula-2 that has the effect of forcing an evaluation order on the grammar beyond that required by the left-to-right ordering of scanner tokens. The transformer section of a TAG makes no reference to input tokens, so in principle the nonterminal references within a transformer rule could be evaluated in any order consistent with the attribute flow. An early version of the TAG compiler actually reordered attribute evaluation functions to eliminate forward reference dependencies, but users found such grammars (and the compiled code) extremely difficult to understand and debug, so the feature has been removed. The current TAG compiler does distinguish attribute evaluation functions that restrict a previously unrestricted attribute to a single value, from attribute assertions that apply further constraints to an attribute already so restricted. It reports an error if the use of regular expression operators such as alternation or iteration render such a decision ambiguous, or if the first assertion to be applied to an attribute fails to restrict it to a single value. Similarly, attributes inherited into a nonterminal or synthesized from a nonterminal must be fully restricted to a single value at the point from which they are passed.

10.3.2 Iterators in a Grammar

The regular expression extensions involving iterators pose a particular problem for attribute evaluation. A TAG is a data-flow language in the sense that there is no such thing as variables or assignment. An attribute evaluation function may restrict the value of an attribute to a single value, but the value of the attribute cannot (in principle) be modified over time by any evaluation function; the most that another evaluation can do is assert further constraints on the same value by comparing it to other attribute expressions or synthesizing *the same value* from another nonterminal reference. Whenever such an assertion fails, the entire rule fails, unless there is another alternative that does not also fail. In a language such as Scheme or Lisp the lack of variable assignments poses no particular problem because there are no iterators as such, only recursion. Similarly, as we have seen in Chapters 2 and 5, grammar recursion can implement iterative concepts and the sequencing of attribute values without resorting to assignments. But how can a grammar cope with the regular expression star operator while (for example) counting the iterations in an attribute? We draw inspiration from the recursive equivalent to the iterator as developed in Chapter 3.

Consider the simple grammar G, expressed here both by recursion and the regular expression iterator:

$$G \to b \qquad\qquad G \to a*b$$
$$G \to aG$$

Assume that a requirement is to synthesize an attribute n for G that counts the number of a tokens in the string. In the recursive form the attribute evaluation is direct:

$$G{\uparrow}n \to b \qquad [n=0]$$
$$\to aG{\uparrow}m \qquad [n=m+1]$$

Each sentential form involving a rewrite of G creates a new instance of the attribute n, with its own unique (fixed) value: 0, 1, 2, ... There is no thought of assignment across nonterminal invocations, as the single value of n is valid throughout the rule at that recursion level. That fixity of value is the key concept, as shown in the layers of Figure 10.2. The attribute n has a fixed value within its layer, but the value synthesized up to the next layer may be different.

Now let each layer in Figure 10.2 represent an iteration instead of a recursion. The local attribute n still has a fixed value within that iteration, and again the value passed up to the next iteration may be different. We can show the transmission of a new fixed value for the local attribute to the next iteration syntactically in the grammar by affixing an "@" symbol to the attribute name. This symbol reflects the transmission of the attribute value across the iteration boundary, and should not be confused with variable assignment, which in procedural languages has no such restrictions. While this expression translates into an assignment in the compiled grammar, the TAG compiler enforces the fixity of values by preventing access of the modified local variable that implements the local attribute. The final value synthesized out of G (in this case) is either the initial value of n (if there were no iterations), or else the final evaluation of $n@$ within the iterator:

$$G{\uparrow}n \;\;\rightarrow [n{=}0] \; (a \; [n@{=}n{+}1])^* \; b$$

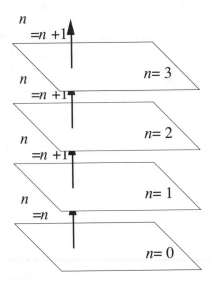

Figure 10.2. Attribute evaluation across recursion or iterations.

10.3.3 Reporting Syntax Errors to the User

Toy compilers that help us to learn compiler concepts tend mostly to be obfuscated by realistic error reporting. We have never eliminated a syntactic or constraint error test, but the normal result of encountering such an error has thus far been "crash and burn" termination of the compilation with no diagnosis other than "Error." This is unacceptable behavior in a production compiler that is to be used by persons other than the compiler writer. It is not particularly difficult to automatically link the occurrence of an error to the production that failed, but the user is unlikely to be any more enlightened by this information. The compiler is more valuable if it reports a probable cause of the failure. As noted in Chapters 4 and 7, sophisticated error recovery and reporting methods have been reported in the literature. We prefer a more direct approach, consistent with our approach of leaving the control of compiler operations to the designer. The TAG compiler therefore, has a syntactic form to specify an error message to be reported when a production rule fails, but the content of the message is defined explicitly by the grammar designer. The error message consists of a specially bracketed sequence of semantic actions that is evaluated only if the immediately following semantic actions or parser syntax fails. The error message applies only to the regular expression form in which it resides, so the final iteration of an iterator can (indeed it must) fail without propagating any error out to the containing structure, unless an error message has been specified within the iterator. Similarly, an error message within the body of one alternative in an alternation construct will not be invoked unless that alternative is attempted by the compiled code, and fails. Error messages are ordered left to right, so that as different semantic actions or tokens in the grammar give rise to different successive opportunities to fail, a sequence of appropriate error messages can be keyed to each separate circumstance. Thus, in the sequence of semantic actions

[*assertionA; errortextB; assertionC; errortextD; assertionE*]

assertionA can fail silently, invoking no particular error message, but a failure of *assertionC* will be reported as *errortextB*, and a failure of *assertionE* will be reported as *errortextD*. If this sequence lies within one alternative of an alternation, or if it controls an iteration, a failure in *assertionA* would simply advance to the next alternative or terminate the iteration, whereas a failure in *assertionC* or *assertionE* would report the respective error and terminate the compile. This makes it possible to construct semantic-directed error messages local to the constraint being checked.

An error message specification in the TAG compiler is set off by enclosing it within a pair of double slash characters ("//...//") inside the brackets that set off semantic actions. Nonterminals cannot be accessed within an error message specification, but any predefined attribute evaluation functions can be used, including reference to attributes that gave rise to the error or are relevant to its interpretation. Quoted text strings within the error message are semantic actions that typically constitute the bulk of the displayed error text.

The grammar fragment in Listing 10.3 illustrates the use of error messages. In this example, the nonterminal TypeClass returns a number reflecting the kind of type represented by the tree etype. Thus, the multiplication operator "*" governs type classes 4, 0, or 3 (set, integer, or real), whereas the divide operator rejects integer, and the integer division operators require it. If none of these constraints fails, then the type of the second operand must be found compatible, and so on.

```
Term !env:table ^etype:tree ^evalu:tree ^iscon:bool
  -> Factor !env ^etype ^evalu ^iscon
     TypeClass !env !etype ^tyc
     (("*" [//"Can't multiply that type"//]
       ([tyc=4; opc=11]|[tyc=0; opc=2]|[tyc=3; opc=7])
     |"/" [//"Can't divide that type"//]
       ([tyc=4; opc=12]|[tyc=3; opc=6])
     |("REM" [opc=5]|"DIV" [opc=3]|"MOD" [opc=4])
      [//"Whole number type required"//; tyc=0]
     |("AND"|"&") [opc=11; //"AND requires BOOLEAN type"//]
       Lookup !env !-2 ^etype )
     Factor !env ^type2 ^valu2 ^iscon2
     [//"Expression term has incompatible types"//]
     Compatible !env !etype !type2
     ...
```

Listing 10.3. Error messages in a TAG grammar fragment.

10.3.4 Automatic Scanner Construction

The scanner section of the TAG source grammar specifies a portion of the scanner for the target compiler; the remainder is specified implicitly by quoted string literals located *in situ* in the parser. For both kinds of scanner tokens, the TAG compiler constructs and accumulates nondeterministic FSA (NDFA) transitions into an unordered list. After the complete grammar has been parsed and converted to an intermediate tree, a tree-transforming nonterminal **BuildScanner** applies the algorithm from Chapter 3 to the list of transitions to create a deterministic scanner, and then translates the FSA tables into executable code.

Four kinds of transitions find their way into the NDFA list. Two of these, the empty moves arising from the structure of regular expressions and the character-read transitions, are normally expected in the construction of an NDFA. In addition to empty moves and character-read transitions, there are also semantic action empty moves and token-emitting halts. A halting state has a semantic action that emits a single token number when it halts; that token number is used in the parser for token lookahead and acceptance. These halts are preserved through the transformation into a deterministic FSA (DFSA); then they are replaced by the equivalent of empty moves to state 0. Of course no empty move can remain in the finished scanner, so each token move spawns a read move (still with the token semantics attached) from the halting state to every state to which state 0 can advance on a read, except that if the halting state has any read transitions out of it, these input characters are omitted from the new transition set. Figure 10.3 illustrates the process with a DFSA built from the regular expression $G \rightarrow ac\ [x]\ |\ b^+\ [y]$. Halt state H emits the token x, and halt state F emits the token y. An empty transition from H to start state S is immediately replaced with transitions to A on a, and to F on b, both retaining the semantic action to emit the token x. Similarly, there would be two new transitions out of halt state F on a and b, except that there is already an existing transition out of F on b, so that character is omitted from the new transition list. Now it can be easily seen that the FSA emits its token, then continues to read the next token instead of halting. In practice the Getoken scanner procedure maintains a static state variable, so that it can return to the parser with each emitted token, resuming from the state where it left off when it is called again to read another token.

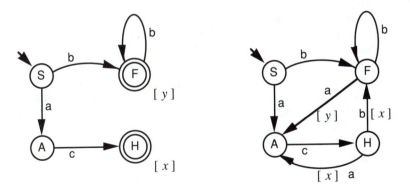

Figure 10.3. Converting halt states into scanner read transitions.

The semantic action transitions are the result of attribute evaluation functions written into the source grammar in the scanner section. These are empty transitions, which must be removed before a deterministic FSA can be built, but the action code cannot be discarded. Instead the construction process transfers the semantic actions from empty moves onto subsequent moves as each empty move is merged with its successor transitions in the transformation. The effect is similar to the result in Figure 10.3, but the transformation takes place much earlier in the construction process. For example, if there is an empty transition from state A to state B with semantic action x, and transitions from state B to states C and D with actions y and z, then the transformed FSA has additional transtions from state A to states C and D with actions xy and xz, respectively, and the original empty move is deleted. It is important that empty cycles be removed first, so that the process will terminate.

When the scanner is finally converted into executable code, there is an entry in the state table for each string of semantic action code. These are given unique identifying numbers, and a CASE statement in the scanner code selects the appropriate code string for execution on each state transition. The identifying numbers are assigned at the beginning of the scanner construction process, then collected into sets to avoid unnecessary replication of the code when states are merged in forming a deterministic FSA. The scanner builder similarly collects characters from the input alphabet into equivalence class sets to reduce the table size. Listing 10.4 shows the structure of the scanner construction part of the TAG compiler, including skeletal nonterminals to build the transition list and to transform that list into code.

The part of the TAG compiler grammar in Listing 10.4 that parses the scanner specification is quite simple. Regular expressions are parsed into character-read transitions connected by empty transitions. Halt states (**tk** nodes) are added to the transition list to be processed later by **BuildScanner**. As the parser section of the TAG is compiled, literal strings are recognized by the **ParseToken** nonterminal, which decomposes them into their individual characters and builds a sequence of transitions from state 0, ending in another halt state.

Most of the compile time in **BuildScanner** is spent in the iterator that constructs the DFSA from the transition list after the empty moves have been removed. The nonterminal in the first line of the iterator finds a state set that has not been converted in the new FSA, or drops out of the iteration when there are no more. The nonterminal **TransSet** in the second line finds all transitions out of any state in the set designated by **stno**, and for each symbol in the reduced input alphabet, creates a state set that it adds to the list **stsets** (and returns the updated list). The new state machine is also augmented by a transition on that symbol to the new state set number.

The scanner constructed for a standard Modula-2 compiler with fully decoded reserved words has an input alphabet reduced to 57 equivalence classes and about 150 distinct semantic action sequences (including all tokens emitted) in an FSA with about 220 states. Reducing the FSA to the minimum number of states would eliminate fewer than 20 states, which is hardly worth the effort, so the TAG compiler omits that step. The resulting state table is quite reasonable in size, compared to the rest of the compiler. If instead of being recognized by the FSA the reserved words were scanned as identifiers and broken out in the string table, the number of states would be reduced by 80% and the

TagCompiler   {*this is the TAG goal symbol*}
    → ... {*initialization, headers*}
        "scanner"   {*start scanner section*}
        (ID ↑name [newelt ↓tokset ↑tokno]   {*get a token number for this*}
          DeriveAttrs ↓env ↓<> ↑attlist ↑nuenv   {*parse its attribute list*}
          "–>" ScanRegExpn ↓nuenv ↓tranlist ↓tokno ↓0 ↑tostate ↑nutran
          [tranlist@=<tk nutran <no >%tostate attlist >%tokno]
          [into ↓env ↓name ↓<tk attlist >%tokno ↑env@]   {*save name*}
          ",")+
        "parser"   {*start parser section*}
        . . .

        "end" ID ↑tagname "."   {*end of source grammar*}
        ["MODULE "; spell ↓tagname; ";IMPORT Library;"]   {*start code generation*}
        BuildScanner ↓env ↓tranlist   {*ready to output scanner*}
        thetree:BuildParser ↓env   {*flatten out parser & xfmr*}
        . . . ;   {*finish up, close files...*}

ScanRegExpn ↓env:table ↓intran:tree ↓tokn:int ↓fromst:int ↑tost:int ↑outran:tree
    → ScanAltern ↓env ↓intran ↓tokn ↓fromst ↑tost ↑outran
        ("|" ScanAltern ↓env ↓outran ↓tokn ↓tost ↑ast ↑atran
          [outran@=<tr atran <no >%ast <no >%tost <> <>>])*; {*empty move*}

ScanAltern ↓env:table ↓intran:tree ↓tokn:int ↓fromst:int ↑tost:int ↑outran:tree
    → [tost=fromst; outran=intran]   {*set up iterator*}
        (ScanTerm ↓env ↓outran ↓tokn ↓tost ↑tost@ ↑outran@)*;

ScanTerm ↓env:table ↓intran:tree ↓tokn:int ↓fromst:int ↑tost:int ↑outran:tree
    → "(" [newstate ↓env ↑ast ; newstate ↓env ↑tost]   {*two new states*}
        [atran=<tr intran <no >%fromst <no >%ast <> <>>]   {*empty moves...*}
        ScanRegExpn ↓env ↓atran ↓tokn ↓ast ↑ost ↑otran
        ")" [xtran=<tr otran <no >%ost <no >%tost <> <>>]
        ("*" [stran=<tr xtran <no >%ost <no >%tost <> <>>]
          [outran=<tr stran <no >%ast <no >%tost <> <>>]
        |"+" [outran=<tr xtran <no >%ost <no >%ast <> <>>]
        |"?" [outran=<tr xtran <no >%ast <no >%tost <> <>>]
        |[otherwise; outran=xtran])
    → CHR ↑lochr [newstate ↓env ↑tost]   {*new state for read tran*}
        [addset ↓lochr ↓empty ↑chset]   {*on all these chars...*}
        (".." CHR ↑hichr
          ([lochr<hichr; addset ↓lochr+1 ↓chset ↑chset@; lochr@=lochr+1])*)
        [outran=<tr intran <no >%fromst <no >%tost chset <>>]
    → "[" [newstate ↓env ↑tost]   {*new state for action tran*}
        SemanticAction ↓env ↓tokn ↑atree   {*build semantic action tree*}
        "]" [outran=<tr intran <no >%fromst <no >%tost <> atree >];

Listing 10.4a. The scanner compiler grammar from the TAG compiler.

ParseToken ↓env:table ↓intran:tree ↑outran:tree ↑thetree:tree
   → STR ↑strno [newstate ↓env ↑tost]   {*strno is string table index*}
      [chno=0; xst=0; atran=intran; length ↓strno ↑len] {*to decompose string*}
      ([chno<len; charfrom ↓strno ↓chno ↑achr]   {*get a string character*}
       [addset ↓achr ↓empty ↑chset]   {*build a read tran on it*}
       [atran@=<tr atran <no >%xst <no >%ast chset <>>]
       [xst@=ast; chno@=chno+1])*
      [outran=<tk atran <no >%xst <> >%strno; thetree=<tk <>>%strno];

BuildScanner ↓env:table ↓tranlist:tree
   → tranlist:ScannerLists ↑thevars ↑theActs ↑chrsets {*extract sets,lists*}
      thevars:VarList ↓true ↓true   {*output scanner **VAR** dclns*}
      tranlist:FindCycle ↓0 ↓0   {*remove empty cycles*}
      tranlist:EmptyMoves   {*remove empty moves*}
      [addset ↓0 ↓empty ↑stsets; nutrans=<>]   {*convert to deterministic...*}
      (AnotherSet ↓stsets ↑stno   {*do another state or fail*}
       TransSet ↓tranlist ↓nutrans ↓stsets ↓stno ↑stsets@ ↑nutran@)*
      nutran:HaltMoves   {*convert halts to moves*}
      nutran:OutStatenCharTables ↓chrsets   {*output finished DFSM table*}
      ["PROCEDURE Getoken;BEGIN REPEAT"]   {*output scanner proper*}
      ["ReadChar(inch);temp:=ChTable[inch];CASE StTable[state,temp] OF"]
      theActs:Flatten ↓env   {*output semantic action code*}
      ["END;state:=StTable[state,temp+1] UNTIL NexToken#0 END Getoken;"]
      tranlist:OutTokProcs ↓env ;   {*do attributed token procs*}

Listing 10.4b. The scanner compiler grammar from the TAG compiler.

input alphabet and semantic action set sizes cut in half, so that a direct code implementation of the FSA may be feasible. With these kinds of figures, however, there is little advantage in choosing a direct execution state machine over the table implementation, even when a perfect hash reduces the reserved word recognition to a single string table comparison. Note also that finding a perfect hash code for a given set of reserved words can take many hours longer than building a state machine recognizer. The TAG compiler spends about half of its time converting the FSA to a deterministic scanner; the other half of its time is divided about equally between parsing the source grammar and generating output Modula-2 program text.

10.3.5 Parsing in the TAG Compiler

Compared to the scanner section, the remaining two sections of the TAG source grammar are compiled into output code in a rather pedestrian way, following the procedures laid out in Chapters 4 and 5. The sections are parsed into an intermediate tree structure that captures the abstract syntax of the regular expression extensions to the underlying context-free grammar. Backward reference to nonterminals takes advantage of the attribute type information already available to set the types of local attributes synthesized from these references. Type-checking (parameter matching) in forward references to nonterminals is postponed until the code output phase.

Slightly less trivial than type-checking is the small amount of flow analysis done concurrently while parsing the grammar, to determine when an attribute assertion is properly an assertion that should evaluate to true or false, or an attribute evaluation that should compile into an assignment. This analysis is supported by a pair of sets, one consisting of all identifiers that have been assigned, and the other the identifiers that may or may not be assigned. An identifier is added to both sets whenever it first occurs as a synthesized attribute returned by a nonterminal reference, or is compared for equality with a defined attribute expression. Subsequent references to the identifer find it in the assigned set, so these references are compiled into equality assertions whose failure aborts the execution of their code segments. When two or more alternatives rejoin at the closing parenthesis, the set of assigned identifiers is replaced by the intersection of the sets from each leg; the second set merges its components by union. A similar merging combines the result of a star iteration with the sets feeding it. Subsequent reference to an identifier in the second set but not the first is reported as an error by the TAG compiler. Another set of identifiers keeps similar track of iteration attributes.

The TAG compiler creates a nondeterministic recursive-descent parser for the transformer and for parser nonterminals that read no input tokens. This permits the construction of semantics-driven parsers capable of handling arbitrarily complex attribute grammars. In particular, the compiler designer can compose syntactically empty nonterminals that check only semantic properties, then build alternatives on the result anywhere the nonterminal is called. If an empty nonterminal fails a semantic assertion without an explicit error message, the execution backs out of the nonterminal and seeks another alternative. If a token has been read before the semantic assertion failure, or if a token read itself fails, or if there is an explicit error message specified for the failure, a syntax error is reported and the compilation terminates.

There are two ways for the code from a compiled grammar to back out of an iteration, alternative, or nonterminal rule on a failed assertion or nonterminal reference. The simplest and most direct is to generate a conditional branch or GOTO that jumps immediately to the next alternative or to the appropriate exit after each potential failure. In a high-level language like Modula-2, this may generally be encoded as a set of nested IF clauses, but doing so has two problems. Most serious is that well-structured code makes it difficult to invoke a second alternative if the *second* assertion of the first alternative fails, especially considering that the second assertion should not even be evaluated if the first fails. Modula-2 explicitly short-circuits Boolean tests in conditionals, so such code is merely awkward, not impossible. A second problem is that many Modula-2 implementations impose limitations on the number of nested statement structures that can be compiled, whereas some reasonable grammars might turn into structures hundreds of clauses deep.

The TAG compiler avoids both of these problems at a slight performance cost by allocating a Boolean variable to hold the current success status. Surrounding the code following each possible failure is a simple test on the variable. Because each test is closed immediately, the flag is tested more often than in the GOTO implementation, but there are no problems with sequencing or nesting. Furthermore, a good optimizing compiler (this is, after all, a book on compiler design) can apply a branch chaining peephole optimization to generate exactly the same (optimal) code as the nested conditional.

Listing 10.5 shows significant portions of the code generation part of the TAG compiler. With liberal reference to Appendix B, the reader should experience little difficulty in constructing a front end to build the tree that this transformer flattens into code; the project is therefore left as an exercise.

BuildParser ↓env:table	
→ <nt link inh der atts body >%name	*{one nonterminal subtree}*
["PROCEDURE "; spell ↓name; "("]	*{generate proc header}*
inh:VarList ↓false ↓(der#<>)	*{inherited attributes}*
der:VarList ↓true ↓false	*{synthesized attributes}*
["):BOOLEAN;FORWARD;"]	
link:BuildParser ↓env	*{do other headers}*
["PROCEDURE "; spell ↓name; "("]	*{generate proc header again}*
inh:VarList ↓false ↓(der#<>)	*{inherited attributes}*
der:VarList ↓true ↓false	*{synthesized attributes}*
["):BOOLEAN;VAR ok:BOOLEAN;"]	
atts:VarList ↓false ↓true	*{output local attribute dclns}*
["BEGIN ok:=TRUE;"]	
body:Flatten ↓env	*{flatten body tree into code}*
[";RETURN ok END "; spell ↓name; ";"]	*{end of proc}*
→ <>; {end of the list}	
Flatten ↓env:table	*{generate a statement}*
→ <ca left right >	*{catenate node...}*
left:Flatten ↓env	*{flatten left subtree}*
["IF ok THEN "]	
right:Flatten ↓env	*{flatten right subtree}*
["END;"]	
→ <al left right >	*{alternation node...}*
left:Flatten ↓env	*{flatten left subtree}*
["IF NOT ok THEN ok:=TRUE;"]	
right:Flatten ↓env	*{flatten right subtree}*
["END;"]	
→ <st body >	*{star iteration node...}*
["WHILE ok DO "]	
body:Flatten ↓env	*{flatten body subtree}*
["END; ok:=TRUE;"]	
→ <tk <>>%tokn	*{string literal token ref}*
["ok:=MatchToken("; number ↓tokn; ");"]	
→ <tk parms:<at ..>>%tokn	*{attributed token ref...}*
["ok:=MatchTok"; number ↓tokn; "("]	
parms:DoArgs ↓env ↓true ↓false ↓<> ↑xx ↑post	
[");"]	
post:Flatten ↓env	*{flatten post-assertions}*

Listing 10.5a. The code generator grammar from the TAG compiler.

$\rightarrow$ <nt send recv >%name   {*nonterminal ref...*}
    ["ok:=nt"; spell ↓name; "("]
    send:DoArgs ↓env ↓false ↓<> ↑coma ↑postx
    recv:DoArgs ↓env ↓coma ↓postx ↑xx ↑post
    [");"]
    post:Flatten ↓env   {*flatten post-assertions*}
$\rightarrow$ <cs link body >%num   {*alternation case selector...*}
    link:Flatten ↓env   {*flatten rest of list*}
    ["|"; number ↓num; ":"]
    body:Flatten ↓env   {*flatten body subtree*}
$\rightarrow$ <as expt thev >   {*assignment node...*}
    thev:GetVarType ↓env ↑tipe
    thev:ShoVar
    [":="]
    expt:Flattex ↓env ↓tipe ↑xx   {*flatten exp'n subtree*}
    [";"]
$\rightarrow$ <mt expt >   {*assertion node...*}
    ["ok:="]
    expt:Flattex ↓env ↓2 ↑xx   {*flatten exp'n subtree*}
    [";"]
$\rightarrow$ <> ; {*no code*}

ShoType ↓needsem:bool
   $\rightarrow$ <ty >%tipe
    ([tipe=1; ":INTEGER"] | [tipe=2; ":BOOLEAN"] | [tipe=3; "Tree"])
    ([needsem=true; ";"])?;

VarList ↓needvar:bool ↓needsem:bool
   $\rightarrow$ ident:<at link tipe > | ident:<vr link tipe >
    link:VarList ↓needvar ↓true   {*do in reverse list order*}
    ([needvar=true; "VAR "])?
    ident:Shovar
    tipe:ShoType ↓needsem
   $\rightarrow$ <>; {*end of the list*}

ShoVar
   $\rightarrow$ <at ..>%name   {*inherit or synth attribute*}
    ["at"; spell ↓name]
   $\rightarrow$ <vr ..>%name   {*local attribute*}
    ["vr"; spell ↓name]
   $\rightarrow$ <tv ..>%varno   {*compiler-gen'd temp*}
    ["tv"; number ↓varno];

Listing 10.5b. The code generator grammar from the TAG compiler.

Flattex ↓env:table ↓mustype:int ↑typex:int   *{gen code for exp'n tree}*
   → thev:<vr ..> | thev:<at ..> | thev:<tv ..> | *{attribute or tempvar ref...}*
      thev:GetVarType ↓env ↑typex
      thev:ShoVar
      [//"Attribute type mismatch"//; mustype*(mustype–typex)=0]
   → <cn <ty >%1 >%num   *{integer constant}*
      [number ↓num; //"This is integer"//; mustype<2; typex=1]
   → <cn <ty >%3 >   *{empty tree constant}*
      ["NIL"; //"This is a tree type"//; mustype*(mustype–3)=0; typex=3]
   → <cn <ty >%2 >%0   *{boolean constant...}*
      ["FALSE"; //"This is Boolean"//; mustype*(mustype–2)=0; typex=2]
   → <cn <ty >%2 >%1
      ["TRUE"; //"This is Boolean"//; mustype*(mustype–2)=0; typex=2]
   → <ng expt >   *{unary negative node...}*
      ["–("]
      expt:Flattex ↓env ↓1 ↑xx   *{flatten subtree}*
      [")"; //"This type is integer"//; mustype<2; typex=1]
   → <ad left right >   *{add node...}*
      ["("]
      left:Flattex ↓env ↓1 ↑tipe   *{flatten left subtree}*
      [")+("]
      right:Flatten ↓env ↓tipe ↑xx   *{flatten right subtree}*
      [")"; //"This type is integer"//; mustype<2; typex=1]
   → <mp left right >   *{multiply node...}*
      ["("]
      left:Flattex ↓env ↓1 ↑tipe   *{flatten left subtree}*
      [")*("]
      right:Flatten ↓env ↓tipe ↑xx   *{flatten right subtree}*
      [")"; //"This type is integer"//; mustype<2; typex=1]
   → <eq left right >   *{equality node...}*
      ["("]
      left:Flattex ↓env ↓0 ↑tipe   *{flatten left subtree}*
      [")=("]
      right:Flatten ↓env ↓tipe ↑xx   *{flatten right subtree}*
      [")"; //"This type is Boolean"//; mustype*(mustype–2)=0; typex=2]
   → ... *{other operators...}*

DoArgs ↓env:table ↓incoma:bool ↓inpost:tree ↑outcoma:bool ↑outpost:tree
   → <ax link expt post >%tipe   *{gen proc arg code...}*
      link:DoArgs ↓env ↓incoma ↓inpost ↑coma ↑postx
      expt:Flattex ↓env ↓tipe ↑xx   *{flatten exp'n subtree}*
      ([post=<>; outpost=postx] | [otherwise; outpost=<ca postx post >])
      ([coma=true; ","])?;
      [outcoma=true]
   → <> [outcoma=incoma; outpost=inpost];   *{end of the list}*

Listing 10.5c. The code generator grammar from the TAG compiler.

The DoArgs nonterminal in Listing 10.5 deserves some explanation. It is used to flatten the list of actual parameters in a procedure call into Modula-2 expressions and variable references. For an inherited attribute, the result is just the flattened expression. For a synthesized attribute, the parser has already determined whether this is a defining reference to the local attribute or an assertion that restricts the synthesized attribute to equality with some expression value. If it defines the value, the expression tree will consist of nothing but the name of the local variable or parameter. Otherwise, the expression tree will be a reference to some compiler-generated temporary variable, and the postassertion subtree will contain the code to assert its equality with the expression specified in the grammar. As the arguments to a procedure call are thus flattened, the postassertions are collected into a tree that is separately flattened for evaluation after the procedure call returns. Each postassertion will normally have the form

$$\text{<mt <eq <tv >\%123 expt >>}$$

which requires the value of the named temporary (number 123 in this case) to be equal to the specified expression value. In context it flattens to a Modula-2 statement something like this:

```
IF ok THEN ok:=(tv123)=(expnvalue);END;
```

The grammar in Listing 10.5 omits two important aspects of TAG compiler code generation: tree transformation and error reporting, both of which are better understood separately.

10.3.6 Tree Transformation

Tree transformation involves three steps: matching the source tree to the grammar template (parsing the source), constructing the replacement tree, and substituting the replacement for the original. Three library routines support these functions in the TAG compiler. Substitution is not particularly difficult, but it is necessary to replace the contents of the root node of the source tree with the contents of the root node of its replacement, so that other references to the source tree will continue to refer to the replacement. The final statement in a compiled tree-transformation nonterminal is a call to the library routine that does this replacement.

Tree construction occurs both in attribute evaluation expressions, which the parser can use to build the original intermediate code tree, and also in specifying a replacement tree in a transformation nonterminal. Construction is facilitated by a single library function that builds one node from the component subtrees. As a function returning a tree node, it can be nested in a structure guided by the structure of the source grammar tree template, which simplifies compiling it. A single assignment in the compiled compiler can build an arbitrarily complex subtree. Assuming a maximum of four subtrees to any node (smaller nodes are built with NIL in the unused subtrees), the library routine has the interface:

```
PROCEDURE  Build(noden,nsubs:CARDINAL;  decor:Tree;
                 s1,s2,s3,s4:Tree):Tree;
```

Recognizing when a given tree matches a template specified in the grammar is the most difficult part of a tree-transformational grammar. Each node in the template to be matched must coincide with the corresponding node in the source tree in both node name and number of subtrees (except when the subtree "don't-care" symbol ".." is specified). Subtrees given an identifier in the template should be assigned to the local variable or parameter with the same name, regardless of whether the name labels additional template structure or not.

There are two approaches to the recognition problem that the TAG might take. The most direct approach parses each node in the structure by assigning to a temporary local variable the pointer to that node, then dereferencing that variable to pick out the parts for analysis. Named tree nodes are assigned to the specified local variable instead of a temporary. The structure of each node must be examined before descending into its internal structure to prevent dereferencing nonexistent subtree pointers. As with backing out of failed alternatives, this poses a small, but not insurmountable, structural problem for the compiled code in a high-level language.

The other approach requires one or more Boolean library procedures to test the individual details of the source tree. The TAG compiler uses a single function TreePart for this purpose, shown briefly in Listing 10.6. It takes a pointer to the root node of the source tree, and a number that encodes a particular path through the tree structure from the root to the detail being tested, and returns **true** if the complete path exists in the target tree and the specified detail matches, and returns **false** otherwise. Because it is a Boolean function, the entire structure can be matched in a single conditional test by conjuncting (with the AND operator) the results of testing every detail. The Boolean short-circuit feature of Modula-2 ensures that as soon as one detail fails to match, the entire test will be aborted. Additional performance gains can be obtained in the library routine by caching the successful path and its intermediate pointers in local static storage, so that each successive test of adjacent deeply nested details can take advantage of path validation and pointer dereferences already done for the previous call. The TAG compiler could also (but does not) save intermediate subtree pointers and base additional tests on these pointers, rather than restarting each test at the root.

The library routine in Listing 10.6 encodes the path as an integer number divided into 3-bit subfields, each designating one segment of the path. Paths up to 10 segments long are possible in a host computer with 32-bit integers, but tree templates nesting more than three or four nodes deep in the grammar source text are unlikely because they would be unreadable. A 3-bit segment value allows the selection of a node name with subtree count, one decoration, or any of up to six subtrees. A string constant or another data type with more bits could be substituted to extend the range if necessary. The TAG compiler version of TreePart returns the subtree at the end of the specified path in a VAR parameter, and accepts in another parameter the value of the node name to be matched.

The parser determines whether a tree template in the source grammar is to be matched or constructed, and builds an appropriate intermediate tree that reflects the template structure. The recursive descent into the tree template when parsing for a match carries down an inherited attribute that builds the encoded path constant with each recursion. Thus, the intermediate code tree already has all the information necessary to generate each individual detail test in a template match conditional.

```
TYPE Tree = POINTER TO Node;
     Node = RECORD
        nodename: INTEGER;
        decor: Tree;
        subtrees: ARRAY[1..6] OF Tree;
        END;


PROCEDURE TreePart (TreePtr: Tree; Pathop, CompareTo: INTEGER;
                         VAR ReTree: Tree): BOOLEAN;
(* PathOp niblets:
     1-6: Select subtree and continue
       7: Return decoration
       8: Return TRUE if node name = CompareTo, else FALSE *)

VAR index: INTEGER;
    result: BOOLEAN;
BEGIN
  ReTree := TreePtr;
  result := TRUE;
  WHILE result AND (Pathop>7) AND (ReTree#NIL) DO
    WITH ReTree^ DO
      index := Pathop MOD 8;
      Pathop := Pathop DIV 8;
      IF (index=0) OR (index=7) THEN result := FALSE
        ELSE ReTree := subtrees[index] END
    END END (* WITH & WHILE *);
  IF result THEN
    IF ReTree=NIL THEN
      RETURN (Pathop=0) AND (CompareTo<0)
    ELSIF Pathop=0 THEN
      RETURN ReTree^.nodename = CompareTo
    ELSIF Pathop=7 THEN ReTree := ReTree^.decor
      ELSE ReTree := ReTree^.subtrees[Pathop] END;
    END;
  RETURN result
END TreePart;
```

Listing 10.6. A library routine to parse one tree template detail.

10.3.7 Syntax Error Halts

Adequate error reporting in a compiled compiler profoundly impacts the kind of code that must be generated for each grammatical form in the source grammar. The TAG source language has a syntactical form for error indications, but the form applies only at the structural level in which it is specified. Consider the grammar fragment

```
[//"ErrorMessage1"//]
DoSomething
(ThisOrThat | [//"ErrorMessage2"//]  OnTheOtherHand )
(RepeatSomething)*
SomethingElse
```

If DoSomething or SomethingElse fails, ErrorMessage1 will be reported, but if ThisOrThat fails, there is no error message unless OnTheOtherHand also fails, in which case ErrorMessage2 is reported and not ErrorMessage1. If RepeatSomething fails, there is no error message at all, because failure of the body of the iterator is the only way to terminate the iteration. Note also that if one of these nonterminals contains its own error message specification, then that error message is used when it fails, instead of the message indicated here. Of course, the nonterminals shown here could be replaced by local semantic evaluation brackets, and the error messages would apply in the same way. That is as it should be.

Achieving a local effect for an error declaration may be done in one of two ways. The compiler can track the scope of the current error message declaration and call up the correct error message on every error test. Or it can define a variable to hold an index designating the error message, then push this variable onto a stack whenever a new structure is entered, and pop it back off again when the structure exits. The code for the stack approach is slower but slightly more compact, and the same stack can be used for other compiler requirements (see Exercise 8).

Summary

This chapter considered compiler design issues for applicative programming language such as Lisp. The compiler design issues relative to applicative languages were explored in terms of Scheme, a dialect of the list-processing language Lisp. As part of the compiler design, this chapter examined some of the problems associated with compiling functional programs. Two Tiny Scheme grammars were presented to parse source texts into lists and to compile lists into Itty Bitty Stack Machine code.

Turning full circle in the coverage of compiler design by attribute grammars, this book concludes with TAG-based automatic compiler construction. A TAG specifies a program that is a compiler. The TAG compiler described in this chapter is a self-compiling TAG, which transforms transformational attribute grammars into standard Modula-2.

Keywords

applicative language	A programming language where function application is the only control structure.
atom	An atomic datum (name or number) in Lisp, not a dotted pair.
call/cc	Stands for *call-with-current-continuation* (in Scheme).

`car`	The Lisp or Scheme function that extracts the left subtree from a dotted pair, or the first item of a list. By convention, the left side of a dotted pair.
`cdr`	The Lisp or Scheme function that extracts the right subtree from a dotted pair, or the remainder of a list without its first item. By convention, the right side of a dotted pair.
`cons`	The Lisp or Scheme function that forms a dotted pair from two values that become the left and right subtrees of it. If the right subtree is a list, *cons* extends the list by inserting the left subtree at its front.
continuation	A partially evaluated function, which may be captured in Scheme with `call/cc`.
curry	To transform a function of more than one parameter into a function that takes less than all of the original parameters and returns another function that can be applied to (one or more of) the remaining parameters.
dotted pair	The elemental data structure in Lisp.
dynamic scoping	Free variables are evaluated in the calling environment.
free variable	Nonlocal variable.
Lisp	Applicative programming language introduced by John McCarthy in 1958. Lisp stands for "List processing"; it is commonly used in artificial intelligence research.
Scheme	A dialect of Lisp from Sussman and Steele [1975]; see also Smith, 1988, for an introduction to Scheme.
static scoping	The meaning of a free variable depends on the program text surrounding a function declaration to determine the context in which the variable is evaluated.
tail-recursion	A function is tail-recursive if the values computed by resursive calls are passed upward without alteration as the recursion unwinds.

Exercises

1. Give the parse tree representations produced by Listing 10.2 for

   (a) `((lambda (x y) (cons y x))`

   (b) `(cons x (cons x (cons y (cons y z))))`

2. Give tail-recursive functions equivalent to the following Scheme functions.

   (a) `(define power (lambda (x y)`
   `    (if (= y 0) 1 (* x (power x (-y 1)))))))`

(b) `(define Fibonacci (lambda (n)`
    `(if (< n 2) 1`
        `(+ (Fibonacci (- n 1))`
            `(Fibonacci (- n 2))))))`

3. Convert the functions from Exercise 2 to conventional looping (iterated) form.

4. Discuss the optimizations of the procedures in Exericse 3. Be sure to include any new or necessary procedures in your discussion.

5. Give the DFSAs built from the following expressions.

   (a) $G = aca\ [x]\ |\ b^+a\ [y]$ (b) $H = a\ [x]\ |\ ba^+c\ [y]\ |\ a^+bc^+\ [z]$

6. Convert the halt states in the DFSAs from Exercise 5 into scanner read transitions.

7. Write a library routine for the IBSM Scheme compiler that copies an arbitrary number of parameters down into the stack offset by a specified number of words (where they would replace the caller's own parameters), then add a nonterminal TailCall to Listing 10.2 that compiles tail-recursion into calls on your routine.

8. Add tree-flattening code to the nonterminal Flatten so that it generates correct code for a Plus iterator. Note that the Plus iteration requires at least one complete iteration (no internal failure) before dropping out of the loop on a failed assertion can be considered successful. Show that your implementation handles nested iterators correctly also. Note also the implementation trade-off between stacking a single loop control variable and allocating multiple temporaries (which requires a flow-through attribute to count them).

Review Quiz

Indicate whether the following statements are true or false.

1. An applicative language allows assignments to variables, but no function calls.

2. Arithmetic operations in Lisp are written using a prefix (Polish) notation.

3. A Lisp compiler must be available at runtime if it is to handle functions created by lambda expressions.

4. Tail-recursion is easily compiled by applying the *cons* function to the parameter list.

5. The TAG compiler creates a nondeterministic recursive-descent parser for the transformer and for parser nonterminals that read input tokens.

6. A TAG is a form of data-flow language.

7. The transformer part of a TAG specifies in a context-free tree-transforming attribute grammar optimizations and code generation requirements of the compiler being compiled.

8. A TAG has exactly two syntactic divisions: scanner and parser.

9. A TAG is a nonprocedural programming language.

10. The function $f(x)$ need not be curried.

Further Reading

Curry, H.B. & Feys, R. *Combinatory Logic*, Vol. 1. Amsterdam: North-Holland, 1968.

Ganzinger, H., Ripken, K., & Wilhelm, R. "Automatic Generation of Optimizing Multipass Compilers." *Proceedings of the IFIP 1977 Congress.* American Horth-Holland (1977), pp. 535-540.

Halstead, R.H. Multilisp: "A Language For Concurrent Symbolic Computation." ACM *Transactions on Programming Languages and Systems*, Vol. 7, No. 4 (October 1985), pp. 501–538. Extends Scheme using the pcall construct for parallel execution (for example, pcall cons x y will concurrently evaluate x and y).

Kessler, R.R. et al. EPIC: A Retargetable, Highly Optimizing Lisp Compiler. *Proceedings of the SIGPLAN '86 Symposium on Compiler Construction*, Vol. 21, No. 7 (July 1986), 118–130. Describes a seven-pass Lisp compiler (each of the passes is described in detail), which is a testbed for a variety of Lisp compilation strategies.

Leverett, B.W. et al. "An Overview of the Production Quality Compiler Compiler Project." Carnegie-Mellon, 1979. An informal collection of optimization ideas for the Bliss-11 compiler.

McCarthy, J. "History of Lisp." *History of Programming Languages.* NY: Academic Press, 1981, pp. 173–197.

Scott, D.S. *Denotational Semantics: The Scott-Strachey Approach to Programming Language Theory.* Cambridge, MA: MIT Press, 1987. See pp. 40–41 for easy-to-read discussion of curried functions.

Schönfinkel, M. Über die Bausteine der mathematischen Logik. *Mathematische Annalen*, Vol. 92 (1924), pp. 305–316.

Smith, J.D. *An Introduction to Scheme.* Englewood Cliffs, NJ: Prentice Hall, 1988. See section 16.2, especially pp. 223–226 for explanation of continuations with Scheme.

Summers, P.D. "A Methodology for Lisp Program Construction from Examples," *Journal of the ACM*, Vol. 24, No. 1 (January 1977), pp. 161–175. Recursive Lisp programs are derived from example specifications by constructing predicate and program fragments for a few input-output examples.

Sussman, G.J. & Steele, G.L. *Scheme: An Interpreter for Extended Lambda Calculus.* MIT Artificial Intelligence Memo, 349, 12 (1975).

Waters, R.C. "User Format Control in a Lisp Prettyprinter." *ACM Transactions on Programming Languages and Systems*, Vol. 5, No. 4 (October 1983), 513–531. This prettyprinter, written in Lisp, provides a general mechanism for printing data structures as well as programs.

Waters, R.C. "Efficient Interpretation of Synchronizable Series Expressions." *Proceedings of the SIGPLAN '87 Symposium on Interpreters and Interpretive Techniques* (June 1987), pp. 74–85.

Wise, D.S. "Functional Programming." *Encyclopedia of Computer Science and Engineering* ed. A. Ralston & E.D. Reilly. New York: Van Nostrand Reinhold, 1983, pp. 647–650.

Appendix A

Itty Bitty Modula Syntax Diagrams

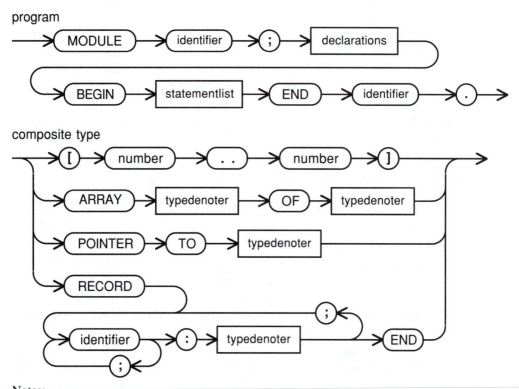

program

composite type

Notes:

1. Although the Modula-2 standard calls for an identifier here and in other places in the grammar, the syntax can permit any type denoter and still reject erroneous programs. The constrainer should reject any composite type anonymously declared here since there can be no type-correct use made of the function value.

2. Identifiers begin with a letter and contain letters and digits; case is significant.

® "Itty Bitty" is a registered trademark of Itty Bitty Computers

expression (operator precedence not shown)

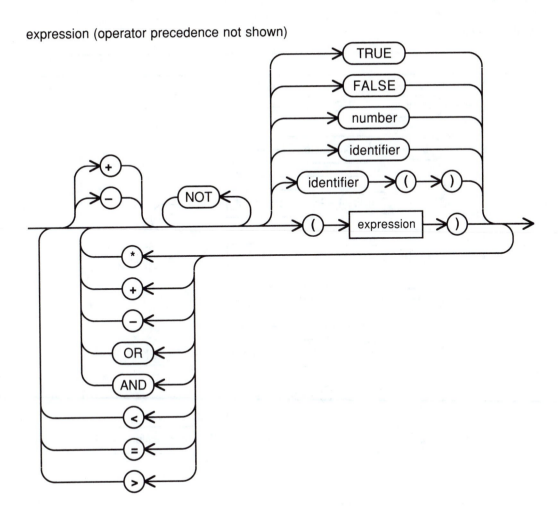

Notes:

3. Operator precedence is:

```
          (   )
          NOT
          *    AND
          +  -  OR
          <  =  >
```

4. Although not shown in this diagram, the relational operators are not associative. This can be easily enforced syntactically.

5. Although this diagram allows it, "- NOT a" is illegal. This is normally considered syntactically correct, but prevented in the constrainer.

6. Comments and spaces are normally removed by the scanner. Itty Bitty Modula comments begin with " (*" and end with "*) " and may contain any characters, including " (", ") ", and "*", but not " (*" nor "*) ".

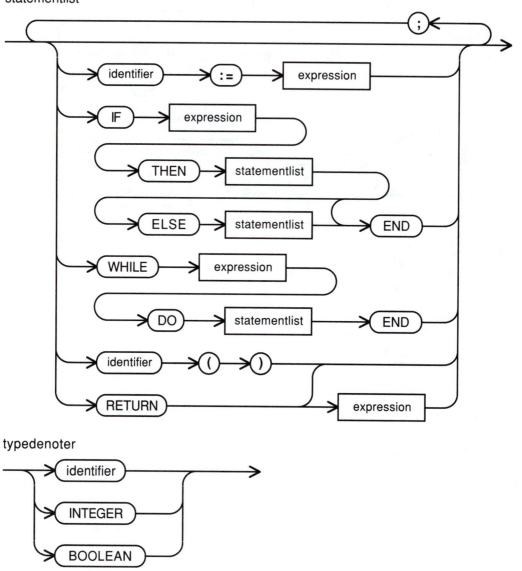

typedenoter

Itty Bitty Modula Syntax Diagrams   App. A

declarations

Appendix B

The TAG Compiler TAG

Although still evolving as a research tool, the TAG compiler searves both as a formal definition of Transformational Attribute Grammars, and as the source code for a compiler to translate TAGs into Modula-2. The listing here completely specifies the TAG syntax and gives enough of the semantics to enable the reader to build a functioning TAG compiler. It also serves as an example of a well-formed TAG.

```
tag TagGrammar:

    {tree node names}
    type node(no, ty, gl, fn, tk, nt, st, pl, qu, tr, ac, at, mt, ot, cn, rt,
    {16}      xf, bt, er, al, ca, qm, dl, rp, dr, vr, as, eq, ls, gr, ne,
    {31}      an, or, ad, su, mp, dv, md, ng, tv, rn, nn, nc, co, sa);

{ node names:
        <ac -- not used                    <dr -- not used
        <al alternation                    <eq equate
        <at param defn, ref                <ls less than
        <bt build tree                     <rp -- not used
        <ca concatenate                    <tr scanner transition
        <cn constant                       <ty type
        <dl dollar iteration               <vr local variable
        <er error code                     <xf transform tree
        <fn function defn, call            <gr greater
        <gl global var                     <ne not equal
        <mt "must true" asserts its subtree  <an and
        <no not, also data structor        <or or
        <nt nonterminal defn, call         <ad add
        <ot output text                    <su subtract
        <pl plus iteration                 <mp multiply
        <pl plus op                        <dv divide
        <qm -- not used                    <md mod
        <qu -- not used                    <ng negative
        <rt recognize subtree              <tv temporary tree variable
        <sa scanner attribute              <rn -- not used
        <st star op                        <nn typecast
        <tk token defn, call               <nc nonterminal call
        <as assignment                     <co type constant   }
```

Listing B.1. The TAG Compiler TAG.

```
funct    {predefined in virtual compiler machine}
   newsetlist ^int;      {allocates set list, returns empty set}
   newnewset !int ^int;  {creates empty set in set list}
   uniquenew !int ^int;  {return first =set, dispose old if dupe}
   addnewset !int !int;  {add value to set in place}
   newinset !int !int;

   settree !set ^tree;
   treeset !tree ^set;
   treeint !tree ^int;   {returns exp from <exp>}
   inttree !int ^tree;
   treetab !tree ^table;
   treecopy !tree ^tree; {to get past tag compiler type fault}
   charval ^int;
   initbl;
   addtbl !int;
   strindex ^int;
   addset !int !set ^set;
   union !set !set ^set;
   intersect !set !set ^set;
   difference !set !set ^set;  {first - second}
   inset !int !set;    {fails if not}
   notinset !int !set;
   newelt !set ^int;   {returns a value not in the set}
   into !int !table !tree ^table;
   from !int !table ^tree;
   nothere !int !table;   {fails if in table}
   length !int ^int;   {length of indexed string or ident}
   charfrom !int !int ^int;  {i,s: char(i) from string (s), 0-based}
   spell !int;    {output identifier or string}
   number !int;    {output decimal value}
   ascii !int;
   opentext;
   closetext;
                                      scanner
ignore
  -> " "|""
  -> "{" ""..."~" "}";
STR ^strg:int
  -> [initbl] "'" (" ".."&"|"("..."~" [charval^this][addtbl!this])* "'"
     [strindex^strg]
  -> [initbl] '"' (" ".."!"|"#"..."~" [charval^this][addtbl!this])* '"'
     [strindex^strg];
ID ^ident:int
  -> [initbl] ("a".."z"|"A".."Z") [charval^this][addtbl!this]
     (("a".."z"|"A".."Z"|"0".."9") [charval^next][addtbl!next])*
     [strindex^ident];
NUM ^valu:int
  -> [valu=0] ("0".."9" [charval^this; valu@=valu*10+this-48])+;

                                      parser
TagGrammar
  -> "tag" ID ^tagname ":"
       [into !1 !vacant !<ty>%1 ^env1]   {int}
       [into !2 !env1 !<ty>%2 ^env2]     {bool}
       [into !3 !env2 !<ty>%3 ^env3]     {tree}
       [into !4 !env3 !<ty>%4 ^env4]     {set}
       [into !5 !env4 !<ty>%5 ^env]      {table}
       [defd=empty; tok=empty; hist=0]
     startoutput !tagname
     (decln !env !defd ^env@ ^defd@)*
     dolibrary !env
```

```
["procedure mainprogram;"; addset !0 !empty ^newtok; trans=<>]

  packattributes !env  !defd   !empty   !newtok !trans !0 ^data
  {attributes: symtable, def'd, redef'd, tokens, trans, histate}

    ("scanner"
      ("ignore"
        ("->" scanre !data !0 !0 ^dtran ^xst
          newtran !dtran !xst !0 !empty !<> !0 ^data@)+ ";")?
      (ID ^name
        [der=<>; newelt !tok ^newtok; addset !newtok !tok ^tok@]
        [//"token name already defined"//; notinset !name !defd]
        [addset !name !defd ^defd@]
        [into !name !env !entry:<tk> ^lenv; env@=lenv]
         (derives !der !data !newtok ^der@ ^data@)*
          entry:redecorate !newtok !der
         ("->" scanre !data !0 !newtok ^data@ ^xst
          der:isdefined !defx
         [inttree !xst ^xstt]
         [trans@=<tk otran xstt <no>%name >%entry])+ ";")+)?

    ("parser" (parsrule !data ^data@)+)?
    ("transformer" (tagrule !data ^data@)+)?
    buildscanner !data ^pdata ^nst ^ncs
    buildparser !pdata ^bdata
    [bdata:<no benv bdef bred btok btran>]
    [//"There is no goal symbol"//; from !tagname !benv ^<nt ..>]
    finishoutput !tagname !nst !ncs
    "end" ID ^endname [endname=tagname] ".";

decln !insym:table !indef:set ^outsym:table ^outdef:set
  -> "type" [outsym=insym; outdef=indef]
    (ID ^tname
      [//"type name already defined"//]
      [notinset !tname !outdef; addset !tname !outdef ^outdef@]
      [into !tname !outsym !tipe:<ty>%tname ^outsym@]
      ("(" (ID^idn
      [//"value already defined"//]
      [notinset !idn !outdef; addset !idn !outdef ^outdef@]
      [into !idn !outsym !<co tipe >%idn ^outsym@])$"," ")" )?)$"," ";"

  -> "global" [outsym=insym; outdef=indef]
    (ID ^consname
      [//"global name already defined"//]
      [notinset !consname !outdef; addset !consname !outdef ^outdef@]
      (":" typename !outsym ^ctype [value=consname]
      |"=" (NUM^value [idn=1] | "<>" [idn=3; value=<>]
          |"false" [idn=2; value=false]|"true" [idn=2; value=true])
      [from !idn !outsym@ ^ctype])
      [into !consname !outsym !<gl ctype value> ^outsym@]
       globalname !consname !ctype ";")+

  -> "funct" [outsym=insym; outdef=indef]
    (ID ^functname [inh=<>; der=<>]
      [//"function name already defined"//]
      [notinset !functname !outdef; addset !functname !outdef ^outdef@]
      ("!" typename !outsym ^ity
        [inh@=<at inh <> ity >])*
      ("^" typename !outsym ^dty
        [der@=<at der <> dty >])*
      [into !functname !outsym !<fn inh der> ^outsym@] ";")+;
```

```
typename !env:table ^atype:tree
  -> ID ^idn [//"invalid or undefined type"//; from !idn !env ^atype:<ty>]
  -> "table"[from !5 !env ^atype]
  -> "set"  [from !4 !env ^atype]
  -> "int"  [from !1 !env ^atype]
  -> "bool" [from !2 !env ^atype]
  -> "tree" [from !3 !env ^atype];

scanre !indata:table !fromst:int !toknno:int ^outdata:table ^tost:int
  -> scanalt !indata !fromst !toknno ^outdata ^tost
     ("|" splitalt !indata !outdata ^xdata
        scanalt !xdata !fromst !toknno ^tdata ^xst
        newtran !tran !xst !tost !empty !<> !toknno ^outran
        joinalt !outdata !tdata ^outdata@)*;

scanalt !indata:table !fromst:int !toknno:int ^outdata:table ^tost:int
  ->    [tost=fromst; outdata=indata]
     (scanterm !outdata !tost !toknno ^outdata@ ^tost@)*;

scanterm !indata:table !orgst:int !toknno:int ^outdata:table ^tost:int
  -> "(" unpackatts !indata ^inenv ^indef ^inred ^intok ^intran ^inhist
        [fromst=inhist+1]
     newtran !intran !orgst !fromst !empty !<> !toknno ^itran
     initer !data ^xdata
     scanre !xdata !fromst !toknno ^odata ^xst ")"
     ([outhist=ohist+1; tost=outhist]
      newtran !xtran !xst !tost !empty !<> !toknno ^otran
      ("*" newtran !otran !xst !fromst !empty !<> !toknno ^ntran
           newtran !ntran !fromst !xst !empty !<> !toknno ^outran [kind=3]
      |"+" newtran !otran !xst !fromst !empty !<> !toknno ^outran [kind=2]
      |"?" newtran !otran !fromst !xst !empty !<> !toknno ^outran [kind=1])
      exiter !kind !indata !odata ^outdata
     |exiter !0 !indata !odata ^outdata
        [tost=xst])
  -> CHR^loch
     unpackatts !indata ^env ^defd ^redef ^tok ^tran ^hist
        [addset !loch !empty ^onch; tost=hist+1]
     (".." CHR^hich ([loch<hich; loch@=loch+1; addset !loch@ !onch ^onch@])*)?
     newtran !tran !orgst !tost !onch !<> !toknno ^ntran
     packattributes !env !defd !redef !tok !ntran !tost ^outdata
  -> [tdata=indata; acts=<>]
     "[" (scanact !tdata !toknno ^tdata@ ^anact [acts@=<ca acts anact >])$";"
     "]" unpackatts !tdata ^env ^defd ^xred ^xtok ^xtran ^hist  [tost=hist+1]
     newtran !xtran !orgst !tost !empty !acts !toknno ^outran
     packattributes !env !defd !xred !xtok !outran !tost ^outdata;

CHR ^char:int
  -> STR ^strg
     [length !strg ^strlen]
     ([strlen=0; char=0]|[strlen=1; charfrom !1 !strg ^char]);

scanact !indata:table !toknno:int ^outdata:table ^anact:tree
  -> ID^name   unpackatts !indata ^inenv ^indef ^redef ^tok ^tran ^hist
     (("@" [notinset !name !redef; inset !name !indef; tenv=inenv]
         [//"invalid iterator reference"//]
          ([from !name !tenv ^thev:<at ..>]
          |[from !name !tenv ^thev:<sa ..>]
          |[from !name !tenv ^thev:<vr ..>])
         [ndef=indef; addset !name !redef ^nred; vtran=tran]
      |([nothere !name !inenv; into !name !inenv !thev:<sa toknno>%name ^tenv]
       |[tenv=inenv; from !name !tenv ^thev:<at ..>; vtran=tran])
         [//"name already defined"//]
```

```
            [notinset !name !indef; addset !name !indef ^ndef; nred=redef])
          packattributes !tenv !ndef !nred !tok !vtran !hist ^odata
          "=" expn !0 !odata ^outdata ^exptr ^expty
            [anact=<as exptr expty thev>]
      |  [//"invalid action call"//; from !name !inenv ^fun:<fn inh der>]
         sends !inh !indata !<> ^sarg ^sdata
         recvs !der !sdata !<> !toknno ^rarg ^outdata
            [anact=<fn sarg rarg >%name]);

parsrule !indata:table ^outdata:table
   ->   [outdata=indata]
        ID^name [der=<>; inh=<>; ldata=outdata]
          (inherits !inh !ldata ^inh@ ^ldata@)*
          (derives !der !ldata !0-1 ^der@ ^ldata@)*
          "->" parsre !ldata ^rdata ^ptree
          ("->" splitalt !ldata !rdata ^xdata
           parsre !xdata ^zdata ^prp
           joinalt !rdata !zdata ^rdata@
           [ptree@=<al ptree prp >])*
          [ttree=<nt <no inh der >%0 ptree >%name]
          ";" datamerge !outdata !rdata ^exdata
          newdefine !name !exdata !ttree ^outdata@ ;

parsre !indata:table ^outdata:table ^outree:tree
   -> parsalt !indata ^outdata ^outree
        ("|" splitalt !indata !outdata ^xdata
         parsalt !xdata ^zdata ^nutree
         joinalt !outdata !zdata ^outdata@
         [outree@=<al outree nutree >])*;

parsalt !indata:table ^outdata:table ^outree:tree
   ->   [outdata=indata; outree=<>]
        (parsterm !outdata ^outdata@ ^nutree
         [outree@=<ca outree nutree >])*;

parsterm !indata:table ^outdata:table ^outree:tree
   -> initer !indata ^ndata
      parsfact !ndata ^odata ^xtree
      ("*" [kind=3; outree=<st xtree >; xdata=odata]
      |"+" [kind=2; outree=<pl xtree >; xdata=odata]
      |"?" [kind=1; outree=<al xtree <>>; xdata=odata]
      |"$" partoken !odata ^xdata ^nutree ^tokn
          [kind=4; outree=<dl xtree nutree >%tokn ]
      |[kind=0; outree=xtree; xdata=odata])
      exiter !kind !indata !xdata ^outdata
   -> ID^tname
      ([from !tname !indata ^<tk der >%tokn]
        recvs !der !indata !<> !0-1 ^rarg ^outdata
        [outree=<tk rarg >%tokn]
      | semantix !tname !<> !indata ^outdata ^outree )
   -> semantix !0 !<> !indata ^outdata ^outree ;

parsfact !indata:table ^outdata:table ^outree:tree
   -> "(" parsre !indata ^outdata ^outree ")"
   -> partoken !indata ^outdata ^outree ^tokn;

partoken !indata:table ^outdata:table ^outree:tree ^newtok:int
   -> STR^strng
      unpackatts !indata ^env ^indef ^redef ^intok ^otran ^hist
      [//"empty token string"//; length !strng ^len; len>0]
      [newtok=strng; outree=<tk <>>%newtok]
      ([notinset !strng !intok; addset !newtok !intok ^outok]
```

```
          [charno=0; xst=0]
          ([charno<len; charfrom !charno !strng ^thisch; charno@=charno+1]
           [addset !thisch !empty ^onch; hist@=hist+1]
           newtran !otran !xst !hist@ !onch !<> !0 ^otran@ [xst@=hist@])*
          [entry=<tk <>>%newtok]
          [inttree !xst ^xxst; outran=<tk otran xxst <st>%strng >%entry]
          |[otherwise; outok=intok; outran=otran])
        packattributes !inenv !indef !redef !outok !outran !hist ^outdata;

tagrule !indata:table ^outdata:table
   ->   [outdata=indata]
        ID^name [der=<>; inh=<>; ldata=outdata]
          (inherits !inh !ldata ^inh@ ^ldata@)*
          (derives !der !ldata !0-1 ^der@ ^ldata@)*
          "->" tagre !ldata ^rdata ^ptree
          ("=>" xformto !ptree !rdata ^rdata@ ^ptree@ )?
          ("->" splitalt !ldata !rdata ^xdata
           tagre !xdata ^zdata ^prp
           ("=>" xformto !prp !zdata ^zdata@ ^prp@ )?
           joinalt !rdata !zdata ^rdata@
           [ptree@=<al ptree prp >])*
          [ttree=<nt <no inh der >%1 ptree >%name]
          ";" datamerge !outdata !rdata ^exdata
          newdefine !name !exdata !ttree ^outdata@ ;

tagre !indata:table ^outdata:table ^outree:tree
  -> tagalt !indata ^outdata ^outree
     ("|" splitalt !indata !outdata ^xdata
       tagalt !xdata ^zdata ^nutree
       joinalt !outdata !zdata ^outdata@
       [outree@=<al outree nutree >])*;

tagalt !indata:table ^outdata:table ^outree:tree
  -> "(" tagre !indata ^outdata ^outree ")"
  -> recogtree !0 !1 !<> !indata !0-1 ^outdata ^comp
       [outree=<mt comp>]
     (semantix !0 !outree !outdata ^outdata@ ^outree@ )*;

xformto !intree:tree !indata:table ^outdata:table ^outree:tree
  -> expn !0 !indata ^outdata ^etree ^exptype
     lookup !3 !indata ^exptype
       [outree=<ca intree <xf etree>>]
     (semantix !0 !outree !outdata ^outdata@ ^outree@ )*;

semantix !idn:int !intree:tree !indata:table ^outdata:table ^outree:tree
  -> [idn#0; indata:<no inenv indef inred intok intran >%inhist]
     lookup !3 !indata ^trtr
     ( ":" ID^ntname
       ( [from !idn !indata ^tren:<vr trty>]
       | [from !idn !indata ^tren:<at lnk vrv trty>])
       ( [trty=trtr] | [trty=<>] tren:retype !trtr )
     | [ntname=idn; tren=<>] )
     ( [from !ntname !indata ^ntdef:<nt <no inh der >%kind ptree >]
       ([ntname=idn; kind=0] | [ntname#idn; kind=1])
     | [inh=<no >; der=inh] )
     sends !inh !indata !<> ^sarg ^tdata
     recvs !der !tdata !<> !0-1 ^rarg ^outdata
     [outree=<ca intree ntree:<nt sarg rarg tren >%ntname >]
  -> "["
       [outree=intree]
     (action !outdata !0-1 ^outdata@ ^nutree
       [outree@=<ca outree nutree >])$";" "]"
```

```
        -> ID^tname   [idn=0]
           semantix !tname !intree !indata ^outdata ^outree ;

initer !indata:table ^outdata:table
  -> unpackatts !indata ^env ^defd ^redef ^tok ^tran ^hist
     packattributes !env !defd !empty !tok !tran !hist ^outdata;

exiter !kind:int !indata:table !exdata:table ^outdata:table
  -> unpackatts !indata ^inenv ^indef ^redef ^tok ^tran ^hist
     unpackatts !exdata ^xenv ^xdef ^xred ^xtok ^xtran ^xhist
        ([kind=kind/2*2; odef=xdef]|[kind>kind/2*2; union !indef !xred ^odef])
        ([kind>0]|[kind=0; //"@-identifiers not in iterator"//; xred=empty])
        [ored=redef] {*** used to be: union !redef !xred ^ored ***}
        [difference !xdef !indef ^nudef; intersect !nudef !xred ^empty]
     packattributes !xenv !odef !ored !xtok !xtran !xhist ^outdata;

splitalt !indata:table !exdata:table ^outdata:table
  -> unpackatts !indata ^inenv ^indef ^redef ^tok ^tran ^hist
     unpackatts !exdata ^xenv ^xdef ^xred ^xtok ^xtran ^xhist
     packattributes !inenv !indef !redef !xtok !xtran !xhist ^outdata;

joinalt !indata:table !exdata:table ^outdata:table
  -> unpackatts !indata ^inenv ^indef ^redef ^tok ^tran ^hist
     unpackatts !exdata ^xenv ^xdef ^xred ^xtok ^xtran ^xhist
        [intersect !xdef !indef ^odef; intersect !xred !redef ^ored]
     packattributes !xenv !odef !ored !xtok !xtran !xhist ^outdata;

newdefine !name:int !indata:table !value:tree ^outdata:table
  -> unpackatts !indata ^inenv ^indef ^redef ^tok ^tran ^hist
        [//"name already defined"//]
        [nothere !name !inenv; notinset !name !indef]
        [into !name !inenv !value ^outenv; addset !name !indef ^outdef]
        [outran=<nt intran value >%name]
     packattributes !outenv !outdef !redef !tok !tran !hist ^outdata;

derives !inatt:tree !indata:table !toknno ^outatt:tree ^outdata:table
  -> "^" unpackatts !indata ^inenv ^def ^redef ^tok ^tran ^hist
     ID^idn ":" typename !inenv ^tipe
        [//"attribute name already defined"//]
        [nothere !idn !inenv; notinset !idn !def]
        [outatt=<at inatt <tk>%toknno tipe>%idn;
         into !idn !inenv !outatt ^outenv]
     packattributes !outenv !def !redef !tok !tran !hist ^outdata;

inherits !inatt:tree !indata:table ^outatt:tree ^outdata:table
  -> "!" unpackatts !indata ^inenv ^indef ^redef ^tok ^tran ^hist
     ID^idn ":" typename !inenv ^tipe
        [notinset !idn !indef; addset !idn !indef ^outdef]
        [//"attribute name already defined"//; nothere !idn !inenv]
        [outatt=<at inatt <> tipe>%idn; into !idn !inenv !outatt ^outenv]
     packattributes !outenv !outdef !redef !tok !tran !hist ^outdata;

sends !formal:tree !indata:table !intree:tree ^actual:tree ^outdata:table
  -> ( [formal:<no>]
       ("!" expn !0 !indata ^tdata ^exptr ^expty
        sends !formal !tdata !<at intree exptr expty> ^actual ^outdata
       |[otherwise; outdata=indata; actual=intree] )
     | [formal:<at nextf vrv tipe >]
        sends !nextf !indata !intree ^xtree ^xdata
        "!" expn !0 !xdata ^outdata ^exptr ^expty
        ([expty#<>; //"attribute type mismatch"//; expty=tipe])?
        [actual=<at xtree exptr tipe>]
```

```
                | [formal=<>; outdata=indata; actual=intree]);

recvs !formal:tree !indata:table !intree:tree !toknno:int
      ^actual:tree ^outdata:table
  -> ( [formal:<no>; tipe=<>] lookup !3 !indata ^trty
       ( "^"
         (ID ^idn
          (":"
           newvariable !true !idn !indata !trty !toknno ^tdata ^thevar ^wasdef ^vartype
           recogtree !0 !1 !thevar !tdata !toknno ^odata ^comp
           [exptr=<ca thevar <mt comp >>; wasdef=<>]
          |newvariable !true !idn !indata !tipe !toknno ^tdata ^thevar ^wasdef ^vartype
           ([wasdef=<>; odata=tdata; exptr=thevar]
           |[otherwise; odata=tdata;
            exptr=<ca thevar <mt <eq wasdef thevar >>>]))
         |newvariable !true !0-1 !indata !trty !toknno ^tdata ^thevar ^wasdef ^vartype
          recogtree !0 !1 !thevar !tdata !toknno ^odata ^comp
          [exptr=<ca thevar <mt comp >>])
         recvs !formal !odata !<at intree exptr vartype> !toknno ^actual ^outdata
       | [otherwise; outdata=indata; actual=intree])
     | [formal:<at nextf vrv tipe >; trty=tipe]
       recvs !nextf !indata !intree !toknno ^xtree ^tdata  "^"
       ( ID ^idn
         (":"
          newvariable !true !idn !tdata !trty !toknno ^odata ^thevar ^wasdef ^vartype
          recogtree !0 !1 !thevar !odata !toknno ^outdata ^comp
          [exptr=<ca thevar <mt comp >>; wasdef=<>]
         |newvariable !true !idn !tdata !tipe !toknno ^odata ^thevar ^wasdef ^vartype
          ([wasdef=<>; outdata=odata; exptr=thevar]
          |[otherwise; outdata=odata;
           exptr=<ca thevar <mt <eq wasdef thevar >>>]))
        | newvariable !true !0-1 !tdata !trty !toknno ^odata ^thevar ^wasdef ^vartype
          recogtree !0 !1 !thevar !odata !toknno ^outdata ^comp
          [exptr=<ca thevar <mt comp >>]
        [actual=<at xtree exptr vartype>]
     | [formal=<>; outdata=indata; actual=intree]);

action !indata:table !toknno:int ^outdata:table ^outree:tree
   -> ID^name                  {assigns or asserts or predeclared function call}
      [indata:<no inenv indef redef tok tran >%hist]
      ( "@" ([notinset !name !redef; asn=true]|[otherwise; asn=false])
        [inset !name !indef] [//"invalid iterator reference"//]
        ([from !name !inenv ^thev:<at ..>]|[from !name !inenv ^thev:<vr ..>]
        |[from !name !inenv ^thev:<sa ..>])
      | ([notinset !name !indef; asn=true]
         ([nothere !name !inenv]|[from !name !inenv ^<at ..>])
        |[otherwise; asn=false]) )
      ( [asn=true]
        "=" expn !0 !indata ^tdata ^exptr ^expty
        newvariable !true !name !tdata !expty !toknno ^outdata ^thev ^ovar ^vartype
        ([ovar=<>; outree=<as exptr expty thev >]
        |[otherwise; outree=<as exptr expty ovar >])
      | [from !name !inenv ^fun:<fn inh der>; //"invalid action call"//]
        sends !inh !indata !<> ^sarg ^sdata
        recvs !der !sdata !<> !toknno ^rarg ^outdata
        [outree=<fn sarg rarg >%name]
      | [otherwise; from !name !inenv ^fun; //"invalid assertion"//]
        ([fun:<at ..>]|[fun:<vr ..>]|[fun:<gl ..>|fun:<sa ..>])
        (":" recogtree !0 !1 !fun !indata !toknno ^outdata ^btree
        |boolex !name !indata ^outdata ^btree)
        [outree=<mt btree >] )
   -> STR^strg                                        {output text}
```

```
             [outdata=indata; outree=<ot >%strg]
    -> boolex !0 !indata ^outdata ^btree               {any assertion}
             [outree=<mt btree >]
    -> "//" [outdata=indata; etree=<>]                 {error action for failure}
       (erract !outdata !toknno ^outdata@ ^btree
       [etree@=<ca etree btree >])$";"
       "//" [outree=<er etree >];


  erract !indata:table !toknno:int ^outdata:table ^outree:tree
    -> STR^strg               {output text}
             [outdata=indata; outree=<ot >%strg]
    -> ID^name                {predeclared function call or assigns only}
       unpackatts !indata ^inenv ^indef ^redef ^tok ^tran ^hist
       ( ("@" [notinset !name !redef; inset !name !indef; tenv=inenv]
          [//"invalid iterator reference"//]
          ([from !name !tenv ^thev:<at ..>]|[from !name !tenv ^thev:<vr ..>]
          |[from !name !tenv ^thev:<sa ..>])
          [ndef=indef; addset !name !redef ^nred]
         |([nothere !name !inenv]
           ([toknno=0-1; into !name !inenv !thev:<vr <>>%name ^tenv]
           |[otherwise; into !name !inenv !thev:<sa toknno <>>%name ^tenv])
          |[tenv=inenv; from !name !tenv ^thev:<at ..>])
          [//"name already defined"//]
          [notinset !name !indef; addset !name !indef ^ndef; nred=redef])
       packattributes !tenv !ndef !nred !tok !tran !hist ^edata
       "=" expn !0 !edata ^outdata ^exptr ^expty
       [outree=<as exptr expty thev >]
       ([from !name !inenv ^iden] ([iden:<vr <>>]|[iden:<sa xtk <>>])
        iden:redecorate !name !expty)?   {I hope this is the same one!}
       | [//"invalid action call"//]; from !name !inenv ^fun:<fn inh der>]
       sends !inh !indata !<> ^sarg ^sdata
       recvs !der !sdata !<> !toknno ^rarg ^outdata
       [outree=<fn sarg rarg >%name]);


recogtree !path:int !depth:int !root:tree !indata:table !toknno:int
          ^outdata:table ^exptree:tree   {*** limit depth to 32 bits ***}
    -> ".." lookup !2 !indata ^exptype {don't care; return true}
             [outdata=indata; exptree=<cn exptype >%1]
    -> ID ^idn  lookup !3 !indata ^tipe
       newvariable !true !idn !indata !tipe !toknno ^tdata ^thevar ^wasdef ^vartype
             [inttree !path ^pathtree; inttree !0 ^compare; wasdef=<>]
          (":" recogtree !path !depth !root !tdata !toknno ^outdata ^comp
             [exptree=<an <rt root pathtree compare thevar > comp >]
          | [exptree=<rt root pathtree compare thevar >; outdata=tdata])
    -> "<>"  {empty tree}
             [inttree !path+9*depth ^pathtree; inttree !-1 ^compare]  {9 sb 10??}
             [outdata=indata; exptree=<rt root pathtree compare <>>]
    -> "<" ID ^idn            {might could take variable node name?  maybe later}
             [//"invalid node name"//]
       lookup !idn !indata ^<co ..>
             [inttree !path+9*depth ^pathtree; inttree !idn ^compare] {9 sb 10??}
             [subtr=<rt root pathtree compare <>>; edata=indata; index=1]
       (recogtree !path+index*depth !depth*10 !root !edata !toknno ^edata@ ^etree
             [subtr@=<an subtr etree >; index@=index+1])* ">"
       ("%" ID ^idn      lookup !3 !indata ^ttipe
       newvariable !false !idn !edata !ttipe !toknno ^edata@ ^thevar ^wasdef ^vartype
             [inttree !path+8*depth ^decorpath; wasdef=<>]
             [subtr@=<an subtr <rt root decorpath compare thevar >>])?
             [exptree=subtr; outdata=edata] ;


boolex !iname:int !indata:table ^outdata:table ^exptree:tree
    -> "otherwise"
```

```
                [//"syntax error"//; iname=0; lookup !2 !indata ^exptype]
                [outdata=indata; exptree=<cn exptype >%1]
    -> expn !iname !indata ^outdata ^exptree ^exptype
       lookup !2 !outdata ^exptype;

expn !iname:int !indata:table ^outdata:table ^exptree:tree ^exptype:tree
  -> boolterm !iname !indata ^outdata ^exptree ^xtype
     (("`" boolterm !0 !outdata ^outdata@ ^btree ^otype         {or}
       checktype !2 !otype !indata  lookup !2 !indata ^exptype
       [exptree@=<or exptree btree >])+
     |[exptype=xtype]);

boolterm !iname:int !indata:table ^outdata:table ^exptree:tree ^exptype:tree
  -> boolfact !iname !indata ^outdata ^exptree ^xtype
     (("&" boolfact !0 !outdata ^outdata@ ^btree ^atype         {and}
       checktype !2 !atype !indata  lookup !2 !indata ^exptype
       [exptree@=<an exptree btree >])+
     |[exptype=xtype]);

boolfact !iname:int !indata:table ^outdata:table ^exptree:tree ^exptype:tree
  -> "~" [iname=0] boolfact !0 !indata ^outdata ^btree ^exptype {not}
     checktype !2 !exptype !outdata
       [exptree=<no btree >]
  -> sexpn !iname !indata ^edata ^etree ^etype
     ("=" sexpn !0 !edata ^outdata ^btree ^etype
       lookup !2 !outdata ^exptype
       [exptree=<eq etree btree >]
     |"<" sexpn !0 !edata ^outdata ^btree ^etype
       lookup !2 !outdata ^exptype
       [exptree=<ls etree btree  >]
     |">" sexpn !0 !edata ^outdata ^btree ^etype
       lookup !2 !outdata ^exptype
       [exptree=<gr etree btree  >]
     |"#" sexpn !0 !edata ^outdata ^btree ^etype
       lookup !2 !outdata ^exptype
       [exptree=<ne etree btree  >]
     | [exptree=etree; exptype=etype; outdata=edata]);

sexpn !iname:int !indata:table ^outdata:table ^exptree:tree ^exptype:tree
  -> ( [iname=0] "+" term !0 !indata ^outdata ^exptree ^extype
         checktype !1 !extype !outdata  lookup !1 !indata ^xtype
     | [iname=0] "-" term !0 !indata ^outdata ^etree ^extype
         checktype !1 !exptype !outdata  lookup !1 !indata ^xtype
       [exptree=<ng etree >]
     | term !iname !indata ^outdata ^exptree ^xtype)
     ( ("+" term !0 !outdata ^outdata@ ^etree ^pltype
         checktype !1 !pltype !outdata  lookup !1 !indata ^exptype
       [exptree@=<ad exptree etree >]
       |"-" term !0 !outdata ^outdata@ ^etree ^mntype
         checktype !1 !mntype !outdata  lookup !1 !indata ^exptype
       [exptree@=<su exptree etree >])+
     | [exptype=xtype]);

term !iname:int !indata:table ^outdata:table ^exptree:tree ^exptype:tree
  -> fact !iname !indata ^outdata ^exptree ^extype
     (("*" fact !0 !outdata ^outdata@ ^etree ^xtype
       checktype !1 !xtype !outdata  lookup !1 !indata ^exptype
       [exptree@=<mp exptree etree >]
       |"/" fact !0 !outdata ^outdata@ ^etree ^xtype
       checktype !1 !xtype !outdata  lookup !1 !indata ^exptype
       [exptree@=<dv exptree etree >]
       |"\" fact !0 !outdata ^outdata@ ^etree ^xtype    {mod}
```

```
              checktype !1 !xtype !outdata  lookup !1 !indata ^exptype
              [exptree@=<md exptree etree >])+
          |[exptype=extype]);

fact !iname:int !indata:table ^outdata:table ^exptree:tree ^exptype:tree
   -> ":" [//"syntax error"//; iname#0]        {named tree}
        fact !0 !indata ^<no env defd redef tok tran >%hist ^etree ^exptype
          [//"tree name already defined"//]
          [notinset !iname !defd; addset !iname !defd ^outdef]
          ([nothere !iname !env; into !iname !env !thev:<vr exptype >%iname ^outenv]
          |[otherwise; outenv=env]
          [//"invalid node name"//; from !iname !env ^thev:<at lnk vrv exptype >])
          [//"invalid named tree expression"//]
          [from !3 !outenv ^exptype; from !iname !outenv ^ref]
          [outdata=<no outenv outdef redef tok tran >%hist]
          [exptree=<ca <as etree exptype thev > ref >]
   -> [iname#0; outdata=indata]
        unpackatts !indata ^env ^defd ^redef ^tok ^tran ^hist
        [from !iname !indata ^exptree]
        [//"undefined identifier"//; inset !iname !defd]
        [//"invalid identifier in expression"//]
        ([exptree:<at lnk vrv exptype >]|[exptree:<vr exptype>]
        |[exptree:<gl exptype>]|[exptree:<sa xtk exptype>])
   -> "<>" [//"syntax error"//; iname=0]         {empty tree}
        [outdata=indata; lookup !3 !indata ^exptype; exptree=<bt <> <>>]
   -> "<" [//"syntax error"//; iname=0] lookup !3 !indata ^exptype
          [//"invalid node name"//]
        ID ^idn  lookup !idn !indata ^<co ..>
          [subtrees=<bt <> <>>; edata=indata; index=1; decor=<bt <> <>>]
        (fact !0 !edata ^edata@ ^etree ^xxxtype          {*** not LL(1) ***}
        {*** also, the xxxtype needs repair so it compares it to exptype ***}
          [subtrees@=<ca subtrees etree >%index; index@=index+1])* ">"
        ("%" sexpn !0 !edata ^edata@ ^dtree ^etype
          [decor@=<nn dtree etype exptype >])?
          [exptree=<bt subtrees decor >%idn; outdata=edata]
   -> "false"
          [//"syntax error"//; iname=0; lookup !2 !indata ^exptype]
          [outdata=indata; exptree=<cn exptype >%0]
   -> "true"
          [//"syntax error"//; iname=0; lookup !2 !indata ^exptype]
          [outdata=indata; exptree=<cn exptype >%1]
   -> "empty"
          [//"syntax error"//; iname=0; lookup !4 !indata ^exptype]
          [outdata=indata; exptree=<cn exptype >%0]
   -> "vacant"
          [//"syntax error"//; iname=0; lookup !5 !indata ^exptype]
          [outdata=indata; exptree=<cn exptype >%0]
   -> NUM ^value
          [//"syntax error"//; iname=0; lookup !1 !indata ^exptype]
          [outdata=indata; exptree=<cn exptype >%value]
   -> ID ^name
          [//"syntax error"//; iname=0]
          [indata:<no env defd redef tok tran >%hist]
        ("@" [//"invalid use of iterator"//; inset !name !redef]
        | [//"invalid use of iterator"//; notinset !name !redef])
        fact !name !indata ^outdata ^exptree ^exptype
   -> "(" [iname=0] expn !0 !indata ^outdata ^exptree ^exptype ")";

newvariable !chktyp:bool !name:int !indata:table !tipe:tree !toknno:int
           ^outdata:table ^thevar:tree ^oldvar:tree ^vartype:tree
   ->      [name<0]
        unpackatts !indata ^inenv ^indef ^redef ^tok ^tran ^hist
```

```
     packattributes !inenv !indef !redef !tok !tran !hist+1 ^outdata
         [thevar=<tv tipe >%idn; oldvar=<> vartype=tipe])
  -> [name>0]
      unpackatts !indata ^inenv ^indef ^redef ^tok ^tran ^hist
    ("@"                          {** what about call from assignment? **}
         [//"invalid iterator reference"//; inset !name !indef]
         ([from !name !inenv ^avar:<at lnk xvrv exty>]
         |[from !name !inenv ^avar:<vr exty>]
         |[from !name !inenv ^avar:<sa xtk exty>])
         ([chktyp=true; tipe#<>; exty#<>;
         //"attribute type mismatch"//; exty=tipe])?
      (  [inset !name !redef; oldvar=avar]
       newvariable !chktyp !0-1 !indata !exty !toknno ^outdata ^thevar ^xvar ^vartype
       | [otherwise; addset !name !redef ^nred]
      packattributes !inenv !indef !nred !tok !tran !hist ^outdata
         [thevar=avar; oldvar=<>; vartype=tipe])
     |( [inset !name !indef]
         ([from !name !inenv ^oldvar:<at lnk xvrv exty>]
         |[from !name !inenv ^oldvar:<vr exty>]
         |[from !name !inenv ^oldvar:<sa xtk exty>])
         ([chktyp=true; tipe#<>; exty#<>;
         //"attribute type mismatch"//; exty=tipe])?
       newvariable !chktyp !0-1 !indata !exty !toknno ^outdata ^thevar ^xvar ^vartype
       | [otherwise; addset !name !indef ^ndef; oldvar=<>]
         ([nothere !name !inenv; vartype=tipe]
         ([toknno=0-1; into !name !inenv !thevar:<vr tipe>%name ^tenv]
         |[otherwise; into !name !inenv !thevar:<sa toknno tipe>%name ^tenv])
         [exty=tipe] packattributes !tenv !ndef !redef !tok !tran !hist ^outdata
         |[otherwise; tenv=inenv; from !name !tenv ^thevar:<at lnk vrv vartype>]
         packattributes !tenv !ndef !redef !tok !tran !hist ^outdata
         ([chktyp=true; tipe#<>; //"attribute type mismatch"//; vartype=tipe])?)))
  -> [otherwise]
     ID^idn
     newvariable !chktyp !idn !indata !tipe !toknno ^outdata ^thevar ^oldvar ^vartype;


lookup !name:int !data:table ^value:tree
  -> [data:<no env defd redef tok tran >%hist; from !name !env ^value];


checktype !mustbe:int !typ:tree !data:table
  -> [//"wrong type"//] lookup !mustbe !data ^typ;


newtran !intran:tree !fromst:int !tost:int !onch:set
        !actn:tree !tokn:int ^outtran:tree
  -> [inttree !fromst ^frtree; inttree !tost ^totree; settree !onch ^ontree]
     [outtran=<tr intran frtree totree ontree actn>%tokn];


datamerge !ldata:table !rdata:table ^outdata:table
  -> unpackatts !ldata ^inenv ^indef ^redef ^tok ^tran ^hist
     unpackatts !rdata ^xenv ^xdef ^xred ^xtok ^xtran ^xhist
     packattributes !inenv !indef !ored !xtok !xtran !xhist ^outdata;


uniqueset !oldlist:tree !theset:set ^setno:int ^newlist:tree
{find or create a set item in the list, =theset, return index}
   -> [alist=oldlist; newlist=oldlist; setno=0; settree !theset ^asett]
      ([asett#<>]
       ([alist:<no link tset >%ixt; treeset !tset ^aset]
        [alist@=link; difference !theset !aset ^dif1]
        [difference !aset !theset ^dif2]
        ([dif1=dif2; treeint !ixt ^ixn; setno@=ixn; alist@=<>])? )*
       ([setno=0]
        ([oldlist:<no ..>%lxt; treeint !lxt ^lxn]|[otherwise; lxn=0])
        [setno@=lxn+1; newlist@=<no oldlist asett >%lxn+1])? )?;
```

```
nothertranxx !atran:tree !frosty:int !tosty:int !aset:set !actor:int ^trans:tree
  -> [inttree !frosty ^frtree; inttree !tosty ^totree]
     [settree !aset ^seton; inttree !actor ^acton]
     [trans=<tr atran frtree totree seton acton >];

scannerform !thelist:tree !defalts:set !inchs:tree
           ^chrsets:tree ^outacts:tree ^actno:int ^matchtoks:tree
{thelist is a list of tk&tr nodes built in scanner & newtran}
{defalts is the set of all chars, diminished by any particular }
{ chars along the way, to become "anychar" in strings & comments}
{inchs accumulates disjoint character subsets, which becomes }
{ chrsets on the way out, sets of which tag revised transitions}
{outacts is a list of unique action sequences, one each per tran}
{matchtoks is an isolated list of tk nodes, from which to build }
{ the matchtok procedures} {trans is a cleaned-up list of tr }
{ transitions, including converts from tk "on char 256"}
  -> [thelist:<tr link frtree totree ontree acts >; elt=0; nelts=0]
     [treeset !ontree ^onset; unset=onset; treeset !<> ^emty]
     ([onset#emty]
       ([elt<256; anelt=elt; elt@=anelt+1]
        ([inset !anelt !onset; nelts@=nelts+1]
         ([notinset !anelt+1 !onset; elt@=260])? )? )* )?
     ([nelts<64; difference !defalts !onset ^redefs]
     |[otherwise; redefs=defalts])
     [alist=inchs; nxlist=inchs]
     ([onset#emty; alist:<no slink tset >%ixt; treeset !tset ^aset]
       [difference !onset !aset ^dif1; difference !aset !onset ^dif2]
       [intersect !onset !aset ^dif0; onset@=dif1; nlist=slink]
       ([dif2#emty&dif2#aset; nlist@=alist] alist:deleteitem
        uniqueset !nxlist !dif0 ^setn0 ^xlist
        uniqueset !xlist !dif2 ^setn2 ^nxlist@ )?
       [alist@=nlist])*
     uniqueset !nxlist !onset ^setn1 ^inchex
     scannerform !link !redefs !inchex ^chrsets ^inacts ^nactn ^matchtoks
     [csets=chrsets]
     ([acts=<>; actno=nactn; outacts=inacts; actor=0]
     |[otherwise; actno=nactn+1; actor=actno]
      [outacts=<no inacts <no <> acts >%actno >%actno])
     ([nelts<64; bset=emty]|[otherwise; addset !0 !emty ^bset])
     ([csets:<no clink csett >%cnot; treeint !cnot ^cno]
       [treeset !csett ^oset; csets@=clink]
       [intersect !unset !cset ^qset]
       ([qset#emty; addset !cno !bset ^nset; bset@=nset])? )*
     [treeint !frtree ^frosty; treeint !totree ^tosty]
     nothertran !frosty !tosty !bset !actor

  -> [thelist:<tk link frtree nmtree >%acts; treeset !<> ^emty]
     scannerform !link !defalts !inchs ^chrsets ^inacts ^nactn ^machs
     (([nmtree:<no ..>; acts:<tk ders >%tokno]
       [matchtoks=<tk machs frtree nmtree >%acts]
      |[nmtree:<st>%tokno; ders=<>; matchtoks=machs])
      [addset !3 !emty ^cset; actno=nactn+1]
      [outacts=<no inacts <no <> <tr ders >%tokno >%actno >%actno]
      [treeint !frtree ^frosty; treeint !tokno ^tokn]
      nothertran !frosty !0 !cset !actno
     |[otherwise; matchtoks=machs; actno=nactn; outacts=inacts])

  -> [thelist:<nt link ontree >]
     scannerform !link !defalts !inchs ^chrsets ^outacts ^actno ^matchtoks
  -> [thelist:<nc link ontree >]
     scannerform !link !defalts !inchs ^chrsets ^outacts ^actno ^matchtoks
```

```
    -> [thelist=<>; outacts=<>; actno=0; matchtoks=<>]
       [treeset !<> ^emty; addset !0 !emty ^rets; ones=inchs]
       [addset !32 !emty ^spas; settree !rets ^rett]
       [addset !256 !emty ^mgss; settree !mgss ^mgst]
       [settree !spas ^spat; settree !defalts ^deset]
       [csets=<no <no <no <no <> deset >%0 rett >%1 spat >%2 mgst >%3]
       ([ones:<no olink osett >; ones@=olink; treeset !osett ^oset]
        uniqueset !csets !oset ^nsetx ^csets@ )*
       [chrsets=csets];

findcycle !trans:int !headst:int !here:int !looky:set
{if you find an empty to headst, convert all statenos of trans }
{ in looky to headst; if from=to then delete; err if acts#<>}
  -> [flist=trans; addset !here !looky ^looking; treeset !<> ^mtset]
     (getatran !flist ^frono ^tono ^chrs ^acts ^flist@
       ([frono=here&chrs=mtset]                {flist,frono,tono,looking}
        ([tono=headst; alist=-1]
         (getatran !alist ^afro ^ato ^achrs ^acta ^alink
          [rev=false]                          {##alist,afro,ato,achrs}
          ([inset !afro !looking; afro@=headst; rev@=true])?
          ([inset !ato !looking; ato@=headst; rev@=true])?
          ([ato=afro&achrs=mtset]    fixatran !alist !-1 !-1 !mtset !-1
          [//"Empty cycle action"//; acta=<>]
          |[rev=true]    fixatran !alist !afro !ato !achrs !acta )
          [alist@=alink])*
        |[notinset !tono !looking]
          findcycle !-1 !headst !tono !looking ))? )* ;

matchlist !atree:tree !btree:tree    {fails if different}
   -> [atree=btree]
   -> [atree:<no alnk acode >%adec; treeint !adec ^anum]
      [btree:<no blnk bcode >%bdec; treeint !bdec ^bnum]
      [anum=bnum]  matchlist !alnk !blnk;

cataction !oldact:tree !act1:int !act2:int ^act3:int ^newact:tree
{find or create action list act1;act2 (no dupes), return id# tree}
   -> [alist=oldact; blist=oldact; newact=oldact; sub1=<>; sub2=<>]
      [got=false; hino=0]
      ([act1=0; act3=act2]
      |[act2=0; act3=act1]
      |([alist:<no alnk aseq >%axt; treeint !axt ^axn]
        ([act1=axn; sub1@=aseq])? ([act2=axn; sub2@=aseq])?
        ([hino<axn; hino@=axn])?  [alist@=alnk])*
       sub1:catlist !sub2 ^sub3
       ([blist:<no blnk bseq >%bxt; blist@=blnk; treeint !bxt ^bxtn]
        (matchlist !sub3 !bseq [act3=bxtn; blist@=<>; got@=true])? )*
       ([got=false; act3=hino+1]
        [newact@=<no oldact sub3 >%act3])? );

buildscanner !indata:table ^outdata:table ^highstate:int ^hicharset:int
   -> unpackatts !indata ^envt ^indef ^inred ^intok ^intran ^inhist
       ["CONST MuchTooBig=262143;TableHigh=32767;"]
       ["TYPE BigRange=[0..MuchTooBig];TableRange=[0..TableHigh];"]
       ["StateTableAry=ARRAY BigRange OF TableRange;"]
       ["StateTable=POINTER TO StateTableAry;"]
       ["VAR TokenPreview,CurrentState,ncharsets:INTEGER;"]
       ["scannextch:CHAR;StateTablePtr:StateTable;"]
       ["chartrans:ARRAY CHAR OF INTEGER;"]
       [treetab !envt ^env; treeset !<> ^mtset; allset=mtset; tch=1]
       ([tch<256; nch=tch; tch@=tch+1]
        ([nch#32&(nch<8`nch>13); addset !nch !allset ^allset@])? )*
```

```
            scannerform !intran !allset !<>
               ^trans ^chrsets ^actsets ^actnx ^matchtoks
{@}        [atran=trans; change=true]    {actsets...}
           actsets:findvars !env !mtset ^xset
           ["errno:INTEGER;"]
           ["PROCEDURE NewStateTable(nitems:BigRange);"] {generic}
           ["VAR ix:BigRange;BEGIN NEW(StateTablePtr);"]
           ["FOR ix:=0 TO MuchTooBig DO StateTablePtr^[ix]:=0 END END;"]
           ["PROCEDURE doerr;VAR ok:BOOLEAN;"]
           ["BEGIN ok:=TRUE;CASE errno OF 0:|"]
           actsets:finderrs !env !1 ^lasterr
           ["END;IF errno>0 THEN abortit ELSE errno:=0;END;(*doerr*)"]
        {remove empty cycles}
           (getatran !atran ^cyc0 ^cyc1 ^chrs1 ^acts1 ^link1
             ([chrs1=mtset] findcycle !link1 !cyc0 !cyc1 !mtset )?
             [atran@=link1])*
        {remove empty moves, transfer action to successor moves}
{~}        ([change=true; change@=false; btran=trans]
           (getatran !btran ^from3n ^froto ^chrs3 ^acts3 ^link3
             ([chrs3=mtset; ctran=trans; change@=true; chng=false]
               (getatran !ctran ^tofro ^tost4n ^chrs4s ^acts4 ^ctran@
                 ([froto=tofro]
                  cataction !actsets !acts3 !acts4 ^acts34 ^actsets@
                  ([chng=false]
                    fixatran !btran !from3n !tost4n !chrs4s !acts34
                  |[otherwise]
                    nothertran !from3n !tost4n !chrs4s !acts34 )
                  [chng@=true])? )* )?
             [btran@=link3])* )*
        {convert to dfsm (no reduce)}
{ }        [chrsets:<no ..>%hinot; treeint !hinot ^hino; nxchs=chrsets]
           [newsetlist ^stsets; newnewset !stsets ^firstset]
           [addnewset !0 !firstset; doing=firstset]
           [more=true; newsetlist ^usacts]
           ([more=true; more@=false; alln=0]    {:doing,alln}
             ([alln<hino+1; oldtr=trans; newnewset !stsets ^alls]
             [newnewset !usacts ^user]
             (getatran !oldtr ^frstn ^dest ^chrs8s ^actor ^oldtr@
               ([inset !alln !chrs8s; newinset !frstn !doing]
                 ([actor#0; addnewset !actor !user])?
                 [addnewset !dest !alls])? )*
             [uniquenew !alls ^destn; uniquenew !user ^actno]
             ([destn>firstset; dests=(destn-firstset)/4]
             |[otherwise; dests=0])
             ([dests>0`actno>3; "(*"; number!(doing-firstset)/4]
             [","; number!dests; ","; number!alln; ","]
             [number!actno/4; "*)"; ascii!0]
              notherdetran !(doing-firstset)/4 !(destn-firstset)/4 !alln !actno )?
             [alln@=alln+1])*
{n}        ([alls>doing+4`destn>doing; more@=true; doing@=doing+4])? )*
        {transmogrify halt/block transitions}
{^}        [etran=-1]
           (getadetran !etran ^frost ^tost5 ^ch5 ^acts5 ^link5
             ([ch5=3; ftran=-1; gtran=-1; chg=false; nset=mtset]
               (getadetran !ftran ^from6 ^tosey ^ch6 ^acts6 ^ftran@
                 ([frost=from6&tosey#tost5; addset !ch6 !nset ^mset; nset@=mset])? )*
               (getadetran !gtran ^froy ^tost7n ^ch7 ^acts7 ^gtran@
                 ([froy=tost5; notinset !ch7 !nset]
                  [newunion !acts5 !acts7 ^acts57]
                  ([chg=false; chg@=true]
                    fixadetran !etran !frost !tost7n !ch7 !acts57
                  |notherdetran !frost !tost7n !ch7 !acts57 ))? )* )?
```

```
                [etran@=link5])*
        {output dfsm}
{%}     ["PROCEDURE scanstateitem (st,ch,ac,ns:INTEGER);"]
        ["VAR ix:BigRange;BEGIN ix:=st;ix:=(ix*ncharsets+ch)*2;"]
        ["StateTablePtr^[ix]:=ac;StateTablePtr^[ix+1]:=ns END scanstateitem;"]
        ["PROCEDURE ScannerFill;VAR ix:CHAR;BEGIN"]
        [htran=-1]
        (getadetran !htran ^frost8 ^tost8 ^ch8 ^acts8 ^htran
          ([tost8>0`acts8>3; "scanstateitem((("; number!frost8; "),"]
           [number!ch8; ","; number!acts8/4; ","; number!tost8; ");"]
           [ascii!0])? )*
        {output rest of scanner code}
{"}     ["FOR ix:=CHR(0)TO CHR(255)DO chartrans[ix]:=0 END;"]
        ["FOR ix:=CHR(8)TO CHR(12)DO chartrans[ix]:=4 END;"]  { :=6; }
        ["chartrans[CHR(13)]:=2;"]
        ([nxchs:<no nxlnk achsett >%setnt; treeint !setnt ^setno]
         [nxchs@=nxlnk; ixc=0; treeset !achsett ^achset]
          ([ixc<256]  ([setno>0; inset !ixc !achset; "chartrans[CHR("]
            [number!ixc; ")]:="; number!setno*2; ";"; ascii!0])?
           [ixc@=ixc+1])* )*
        ["END ScannerFill;PROCEDURE Getoken;VAR ix,errno:INTEGER;ok:BOOLEAN;"]
        ["BEGIN ok:=TRUE;errno:=0;IF Debugging THEN writeC('"; ascii!34; "')END;"]
        ["REPEAT NextToken:=TokenPreview;TokenPreview:=0;"]
        ["IF LastCharacter>CHR(0)THEN writeC(LastCharacter)"]
        ["ELSIF NOT Debugging THEN writeSln END;LastCharacter:=scannextch;"]
        ["IF EOF(source)THEN scannextch:=CHR(255);"]
        ["ELSIF EOLN(source) THEN READLN(source);"]
        ["scannextch:=CHR(0)END ELSE READ(source,scannextch)END;"]
        ["ix:=CurrentState*"; number!(hino*2+2)]
        ["+chartrans[scannextch];"]
        ["CASE StateTablePtr^[ix]OF"; ascii!0]
        [newnewset !usacts ^usual; using=usual-4]
        ([using>usacts; number!using/4; ": "; gots=mtset]
{:}      [aclist=actsets; hitok=0; toktr=<>]
          ([aclist:<no aclnk actup >%listr; treeint !listr ^lino]
            ([newinset !lino !usacts]
              ([actup:<no zlnk coder >%itmt; treeint !itmt ^item]
                ([coder:<tr ..>%tkno; treeint !tkno ^tknn]
                  ([tknn>hitok; hitok@=tknn; toktr@=coder])?
                 |[notinset !item !gots]  coder:flatten !env
                  ["|"; addset !item !gots ^git; gots@=git])?
                 [actup@=zlnk])* )?  [aclist@=aclnk])*
           ([hitok>0; ";"]  toktr:flatten !env )?
           ["END;"; ascii!0; using@=using-4])*
        ["0:END;CurrentState:=StateTablePtr^[ix+1];"]
        ["IF CurrentState=0 THEN TokenPreview:=-1 END"; ascii!0]
        ["UNTIL NextToken<>0;IF Debugging THEN IF NextToken<0 "]
        ["THEN writeS('"; ascii!34; " ?? ')ELSE writeC('"]
        [ascii!34; "')END END END Getoken;"; ascii!0]
        ["PROCEDURE InitializeScanner;BEGIN "]
        ["ncharsets:="; number!hino+1; ";TokenPreview:=0;"]
        ["scannextch:=CHR(0);LastCharacter:=CHR(0);"]
        ["CurrentState:=0;NewStateTable("]
        [number!(doing+1)*(hino+1)*2; ");ScannerFill;"]
        ["NEW(StringTable);StringTable^[0]:=CHR(0);"]
        ["EndStrings:=1;Getoken END InitializeScanner;"; ascii!0]
        ["PROCEDURE MatchToken(tkno:INTEGER):BOOLEAN;"]
        ["BEGIN IF tkno=Nextoken THEN Getoken;"]
        ["RETURN TRUE ELSE RETURN FALSE END END MatchToken;"; ascii!0]
        ([matchtoks:<tk klnk ontree <no >%tknam >%entry]   {/ders}
         [entry:<tk ders >%tokno]
         [treeint !tokno ^tokn; treeint !tknam ^toknam]
```

```
                      ["PROCEDURE MatchTok"; number!tokn]
                      ([ders#<>; "("]  ders:paramlist !true !false ^osemi  [")"]
                      [":BOOLEAN;"]
                      ["BEGIN IF NexToken="; number!tokn; " THEN "]
                      ([ders:<at dlnk vrv vty >%namt; ders@=dlnk]
                       ["at"; treeint !namt ^name; spell!name; ":=sa"]
                       [number!tokn; spell!name; ";"; ascii!0])*
                      ["IF Debugging THEN writeS('='; spell!toknam; "');"]
                      ders:showdeprams    ["writeSln END;"; ascii!0]
                      ["Getoken;RETURN TRUE ELSE RETURN FALSE END END MatchTok"; number!tokn; ";"]
                      [ascii!0; matchtoks@=klnk])*
                      [hicharset=hino; highstate=doing];

buildparser !indata:table ^outdata:table
  ->     [outdata=indata]    indata:checkntcalls !inenv;

startoutput !name:int
  ->     ["MODULE "; spell !name]
         [";FROM InOut IMPORT ReadChar,ReadLn,WriteStr,WriteLn;"];

finishoutput !goalname:int !name:int
  ->     ["BEGIN InitializeScanner; IF nt"; spell !goalname]
         [" THEN WriteStr('Success')ELSE WriteStr('Failed')END END "]
         [spell !name; "."];

globalname !name:int !itstype:tree
  -> ["v"; spell !name; ":"] itstype:showtype [";"];

dolibrary !env:table
  -> ;
      {output the predefined routines}


                                          transformer

redecorate !decor:int !subtree:tree
  -> <vr ..>
  => <vr subtree >%decor
  -> <tk ..>
  => <tk subtree >%decor
  -> <nt ..>
  => <nt subtree >%decor
  -> <tv ..>
  => <tv subtree >%decor
  -> <sa toknno xtyp>
  => <sa toknno subtree>%decor
  -> <tr link fromst tost chrs acts >
       [inttree !decor ^atree]
  => <tr link atree subtree chrs acts >;

retype !subtree:tree
  -> <vr <>>%decor
  => <vr subtree >%decor
  -> <at next vrv <>>%decor
  => <at next vrv subtree >%decor;

isdefined !defset:set
  -> <at next vrv tipe >%idn
     next:isdefined !defset
        [//"undefined attribute "; spell !idn //; inset !idn !defset]
  -> <no >;
```

```
checkntcalls !env:table
  -> <tr link fst tst chs act >|<tk link fst chs >
     link:checkntcalls !env

  -> <nc link <nt snd rcv trn >%name >
     link:checkntcalls !env
        [//"not a nonterminal: "; spell !name //]
        [from !name !env ^<nt <no inh der >%tgf rightp >]
     ([trn=<>; //spell !name; " is not a parser nonterminal"//; tgf=0]
     |[trn#<>; //spell !name; " is not a transformer nonterminal"//; tgf=1])
     snd:actualformal !inh !name
     rcv:actualformal !der !name

  -> <nt link rpt >%name          {do nonterminals as functions}
        [from !name !env ^<nt <no inh der >%tgf rightp >]
     makeforward !name !env !inh !der !tgf
     link:checkntcalls !env
     rpt:doflatten !name !env !inh !der !tgf
  -> <> ;

makeforward !name:int !env:table !inh:tree !der:tree !tgf:int
  ->     ["PROCEDURE nt"; spell !name]
     ([inh:<>; der:<>; tgf=0]
     |[inh:<>; der:<>; tgf=1; "(thetree:tree)"]
     |[otherwise; "("
       inh:paramlist !false !false ^isemi
       der:paramlist !true !isemi ^dsemi
       ([tgf=1; ";thetree:tree)"]|[tgf=0; ")"]))
        [":BOOLEAN;FORWARD;"];


actualformal !formal:tree !name:int
  -> <>
     [//"too few actual attributes, calling "; spell !name //; formal:<>]
  -> <at link exptree:<vr expty>%idn <>>
     [formal:<at nextf vrv tipe >]
     [//"attribute type mismatch calling "; spell !name //]
     ( [expty=<>] exptree:redecorate !idn !tipe
     | [otherwise; expty=tipe] )
     link:actualformal !nextf !name
  => <at link exptree tipe >
  -> <at link <ca exptree:<tv expty>%idn mtt> <>>
     [formal:<at nextf vrv tipe >]
     [//"attribute type mismatch calling "; spell !name //]
     ( [expty=<>] exptree:redecorate !idn !tipe
     | [otherwise; expty=tipe] )
     link:actualformal !nextf !name
  => <at link <ca exptree mtt> tipe >
  -> <at link exptree expty >
     [//"attribute type mismatch calling "; spell !name //]
     [formal:<at nextf vrv tipe >; expty#<>; expty=tipe]
     link:actualformal !nextf !name;

paramlist !needsvar:bool !insemi:bool ^outsemi:bool
  -> <> [outsemi=insemi]
  -> ident:<at link vrv tipe >%name
     link:paramlist !needsvar !insemi ^tsemi
        ([tsemi=true; ";"])?
        ([needsvar=true; "VAR "])?
        [outsemi=true]
     ident:shovar !false !false !true !true !empty ^xset;


showdeprams
```

```
       -> ident:<at link vrv tipe >%name
          link:showdeprams
              ["Sho"] tipe:showtype  ["("]
          ident:shovar !false !false !false !true !empty ^xset  [");"]
       -> <> ;


doflatten !name:int !env:table !inh:tree !der:tree !tgf:int
    -> <nt <no ..>%kind body >
           ["PROCEDURE nt"; spell !name; ";var ok:boolean;t0:tree;"]
          body:findvars !env !empty ^xset
              ["errno:INTEGER;PROCEDURE doerr;VAR ok:BOOLEAN;"]
              ["BEGIN ok:=TRUE;CASE errno OF 0:|"]
          body:finderrs !env !1 ^lasterr
              ["END;IF errno>0 THEN abortit ELSE errno:=0 END;"]
              ["END doerr; BEGIN ok:=TRUE;errno:=0;"]
          (  [kind=1; "t0:=thetree;"]|[otherwise; "t0:=NIL;"])
              ["IF Debugging THEN writeS('+"; spell !name; "');"]
          (  [kind=1; "Shotree(t0);"])?
          inh:showdeprams   ["writeSln END;"]
          body:flatten !env
              ["IF NOT ok THEN doerr END;"]
              ["IF Debugging THEN writeS('-"; spell !name; "');"]
              ["IF ok THEN "]   der:showdeprams
              ["ELSE writeS('  ----')END;Shoboolean(ok);writeSln END;"]
              ["RETURN ok END nt"; spell !name; ";"];


findvars !env:table !indone:set ^outdone:set
  -> <> | <ot > | <tr ..>  [outdone=indone]
  -> <al left right > | <ca left right > | <no left right >
     left:findvars !env !indone ^tdone
     right:findvars !env !tdone ^outdone
  -> <st body > | <pl body > | <dl body tokn > | <er body >
     body:findvars !env !indone ^outdone
  -> <tk params >
     params:argvars !env !true !indone ^outdone
  -> <nt snd rcv tre> | <fn snd rcv >
     snd:argvars !env !false !indone ^tdone
     rcv:argvars !env !true !tdone ^outdone
  -> <mt expt > | <xf expt >
     expt:expnvars !env !indone ^outdone
  -> <as expt exty thev >
     thev:shovar !true !true !true !false !indone ^tdone
     expt:expnvars !env !tdone ^outdone ;


expnvars !env:table !indone:set ^outdone:set
  -> <ca stm exp>
     stm:findvars !env !indone ^tdone
     exp:expnvars !env !tdone ^outdone
  -> <bt exp1 exp2 >
     exp1:bldvars !env !indone ^tdone
     exp2:expnvars !env !tdone ^outdone
  -> (<or exp1 exp2 >|<an exp1 exp2 >|<eq exp1 exp2 >
     |<ne exp1 exp2 >|<ls exp1 exp2 >|<gr exp1 exp2 >|<ad exp1 exp2 >
     |<su exp1 exp2 >|<mp exp1 exp2 >|<dv exp1 exp2 >|<md exp1 exp2 >)
     exp1:expnvars !env !indone ^tdone
     exp2:expnvars !env !tdone ^outdone
  -> (<no exp >|<ng exp >|<nn exp >)
     exp:expnvars !env !indone ^outdone
  -> <rt nod pth cmp <>>
         [outdone=indone]
  -> <rt nod pth cmp var>
     var:shovar !true !true !true !false !indone ^outdone
```

```
   -> (<>|<cn ..>|<vr ..>|<at ..>|<gl ..>|<tv ..>|<sa ..>)
        [outdone=indone] ;

bldvars !env:table !indone:set ^outdone:set
  -> <ca stm exp >
       stm:bldvars !env !indone ^tdone
       exp:expnvars !env !tdone ^outdone
  -> exp:<bt ..>
       exp:expnvars !env !indone ^outdone
  -> <> [outdone=indone] ;

argvars !env:table !uparo:bool !indone:set ^outdone:set
  -> (exp:<vr ..>|exp:<at vlnx <> vty>|exp:<at vlnx <tk> vty>
     |exp:<gl ..>|exp:<sa ..>)
        [uparo=true]
       exp:shovar !true !true !true !false !indone ^outdone
  -> <at nexta exptr expty >
       nexta:argvars !env !uparo !indone ^xdone
       ( [uparo=true]
         exptr:argvars !env !uparo !xdone ^outdone
       | [otherwise]
         exptr:expnvars !env !xdone ^outdone )
  -> <ca exp stm >
       ( [uparo=true]
        exp:shovar !true !true !true !false !indone ^tdone
        stm:findvars !env !tdone ^outdone
       | [otherwise]
        exp:findvars !env !indone ^tdone
        stm:expnvars !env !tdone ^outdone )
  -> <> [outdone=indone] ;

shovar !usesa:bool !needsem:bool !tytoo:bool !allvars:bool !indone:set ^outdone:set
  -> <tv vty >%numb ["tv"; number !numb; outdone=indone]
        ( [tytoo=true; ":"] vty:showtype
        ( [needsem=true; ";"])?)?
  -> <gl vty >%name
        ( [allvars=true; "gl"; spell !name; addset !name !indone ^outdone]
        ([tytoo=true; ":"] vty:showtype
        ( [needsem=true; ";"])?)?
        | [otherwise; outdone=indone])
  -> <at lnk vrv vty>%name
        ( [vrv:<tk>%toknno; toknno#-1; usesa=true;
          notinset !name*20+toknno !indone; "sa"; number !toknno;
          spell !name; addset !name*20+toknno !indone ^outdone]
          ([tytoo=true; ":"] vty:showtype
           ([needsem=true; ";"])?)?
        | [allvars=true]
          ["at" spell !name; addset !name !indone ^outdone]
          ([tytoo=true; ":"] vty:showtype
           ([needsem=true; ";"])?)?
        | [otherwise; outdone=indone])
  -> <vr vty >%name
        ( [notinset !name !indone; addset !name !indone ^outdone]
          ["vr"; spell !name]
         ([tytoo=true; ":"] vty:showtype
        ( [needsem=true; ";"])?)?
        | [otherwise; outdone=indone])
  -> <sa toknno vty>%name
        ( [notinset !name*20+toknno !indone;
          addset !name*20+toknno !indone ^outdone]
          ["sa"; number !toknno; spell !name]
          ([tytoo=true; ":"] vty:showtype
```

```
                ([needsem=true;  ";"])?)?
       |  [otherwise;  outdone=indone]);

    showtype
      -> <ty >%typeno
         ([typeno=1;  "INTEGER"]
         |[typeno=2;  "BOOLEAN"]
         |[typeno=3;  "tree"]
         |[typeno=4;  "tree"]
         |[typeno=5;  "table"]
         |[typeno>5;  "INTEGER"]);

    finderrs !env:table !inerno:int ^outno:int
      -> <> | <tr ..> | <ot > | <tk ..> | <nt ..> | <fn ..> | <mt ..> | <xf ..> | <as ..>
         [outno=inerno]
      -> <al left right > | <ca left right > | <no left right >
         left:finderrs !env !inerno ^midno
         right:finderrs !env !midno ^outno
      -> <st body > | <pl body > | <dl body tokn >
         body:finderrs !env !inerno ^outno
      -> <er body >
         [number !inerno; ": "]
         body:flatten !env
         ["|"; outno=inerno+1]
      => <er >%inerno ;

    flatten !env:table
      -> <>                 {no code}
      -> <ca <> right >
         right:flatten !env
      -> <ca left right >
         left:flatten !env
         ["IF ok THEN "]
         right:flatten !env
         ["ELSE doerr END;"]
      -> <al left right >
         ["push(errno);errno:=0;push(Taken);Taken:=0;"]
         left:flatten !env
         ["IF NOT ok THEN doerr;ok:=TRUE;errno:=0;"]
         ["IF Taken>0 THEN SyntaxError END;"]
         ["IF Debugging THEN writeS('|')END;"]
         right:flatten !env
         ["IF NOT ok THEN doerr;IF Taken>0 THEN SyntaxError END;"]
         ["END END;Taken:=Taken+pop();errno:=pop();"]
      -> <st body >
         ["push(errno);push(Taken);WHILE ok DO "]
         ["errno:=0;Taken:=0;IF Debugging THEN writeS('(')END;"]
         body:flatten !env
         ["IF Debugging THEN writeS(')*')END;"]
         ["IF Taken>0 THEN IF ok THEN push(Taken+pop())"]
         ["ELSE SyntaxError END END END;"]
         ["Taken:=pop();errno:=pop();ok:=TRUE;"]
      -> <pl body >
         ["push(errno);push(Taken);push(0);REPEAT "]
         ["Taken:=0;errno:=0;IF Debugging THEN writeS('(')END;"]
         body:flatten !env
         ["IF Debugging THEN writeS(')+')END;"]
         ["IF Taken>0 THEN IF ok THEN push(pop()+pop()+Taken);"]
         ["push(1) ELSE SyntaxError ELSIF ok THEN "]
         ["push(pop()+1)END END UNTIL NOT ok;ok:=pop()>0;Taken:=pop();errno:=pop();"]
      -> <dl body tokx>%tokn
         ["push(errno);push(Taken);push(0);REPEAT errno:=0;Taken:=0;"]
```

The TAG Compiler TAG   App. B

```
            ["IF Debugging THEN writeS('(')END;"]
    body:flatten !env
            ["IF Debugging THEN writeS(')$')END;push(Taken+pop)"]
            ["UNTIL NOT ok OR NOT matchtoken("; number !tokn; ");"]
            ["Taken:=pop;IF NOT ok THEN doerr;"]
            ["IF Taken>0 THEN SyntaxError END END;"]
            ["Taken:=Taken+pop;errno:=pop;"]
  -> <tk <>>%tokn
            ["ok:=matchtoken("; number !tokn; ");"]
  -> <tk params:<at ..>>%tokn
            ["ok:=matchtok"; number !tokn; "("]
    params:doargs !env !true !false !<> ^needs ^post
            [");"]
    post:flatten !env
  -> <nt snd rcv tre>%name
            ["ok:=nt"; spell !name]
    ([snd:<>; rcv:<>; tre:<>; ";"]
    |[otherwise; "("]
      snd:doargs !env !false !false !<> ^sneed ^postx
      rcv:doargs !env !true !sneed !postx ^rneed ^post
      ([tre#<>]
       ([rneed=true; ","]|[rneed=false])
       tre:shovar !true !false !false !true !empty ^xset)?
       [");"])
    post:flatten !env
  -> <fn snd rcv >%name
            ["ok:=fn"; spell !name]
    ([snd:<>; rcv:<>; ";"]
    |[otherwise; "("]
      snd:doargs !env !false !false !<> ^sneed ^postx
      rcv:doargs !env !true !sneed !postx ^rneed ^post
       [");"])
    post:flatten !env
  -> <mt expt >
            ["ok:="]
    expt:flattex !2 !env ^extx [";"]
  -> <as expt <> thev >
    thev:getvartype ^<ty>%exty
    thev:shovar !true !false !false !true !empty ^xset [":="]
    expt:flattex !exty !env ^extx [";"]
  -> <as expt <ty>%exty thev >
    thev:shovar !true !false !false !true !empty ^xset [":="]
    expt:flattex !exty !env ^extx [";"]
  -> <ot >%txtno
    ([txtno>0; "writeS('"; spell !txtno; "');"]
     ["IF Debugging THEN writeSln;writeS('\'"; spell !txtno; "'')END;"]
    |[txtno=0; "writeSln;"])
  -> <xf body >
            ["replacetree(thetree,"]
    body:flattex !3 !env ^extx [");"]
  -> <tr ders >%toknot
            [treeint !toknot ^tokno; "TokenPreview:="; number!tokno; ";"]
  -> <er ..>%erno
            ["if not ok then doerr;errno:="; number !erno; ";"];

getvartype ^vartype:tree
  -> <tv vartype>
  -> <gl vartype>
  -> <at lnk vrv vartype>
  -> <vr vartype>
  -> <sa toknno vartype>;
```

```
flattex !mustype:int !env:table ^istype:int
  -> <rt root pth comp nvar>  [from !1 !env ^itype]
       ([nvar:<vr vty>]|[nvar:<at vlnx vlv vty>]
       |[nvar:<gl vty>]|[nvar:<sa toknno vty>]|[otherwise;vty=<>])
       ([itype=vty; "treeparty("]|[otherwise; "treepart("])
       ([root=<>; "thetree"]
       |[otherwise] root:shovar !true !false !false !true !empty ^xset)
       [","; treeint !pth ^path; number !path; ","; treeint !comp ^con]
       [number !con; ","]
       ([nvar=<>; "t0"]
       |[otherwise] nvar:shovar !true !false !false !true !empty ^zset)
       [")"; istype=2; //"boolean type expected"//; mustype=2`mustype=0]
  -> <bt <> <>>
       ["NIL"; istype=3; //"tree type expected"//; mustype=3`mustype=0]
    -> <bt subs decor >%ndn      ["build("; number !ndn; ","]
         [istype=3; //"tree type expected"//; mustype=3`mustype=0]
      decor:flattex !3 !env ^exty
      subs:buildtree !env ^nsubs    [nnn=nsubs]
      ( [nsubs<8; ",NIL"; nsubs@=nsubs+1])* [","; number !nnn; ")"]
  -> <nn expr:<vr exty> <> <ty>%toty>|<nn expr exty:<ty> <ty>%toty>
      exty:castype !toty ^itsty
         ["("; istype=toty; //"type mismatch"//; mustype=toty`mustype=0]
      expr:flattex !itsty !env ^extx  [")"]
  -> <or left right >    ["("; //"boolean type expected"//; mustype=2`mustype=0]
      left:flattex !2 !env ^exty [")OR("]
      right:flattex !2 !env ^extz [")"; istype=2]
  -> <an left right >    ["("; //"boolean type expected"//; mustype=2`mustype=0]
      left:flattex !2 !env ^exty [")AND("]
      right:flattex !2 !env ^extz [")"; istype=2]
  -> <no left >    ["NOT("; //"boolean type expected"//; mustype=2`mustype=0]
      left:flattex !2 !env ^exty [")"; istype=2]
  -> <eq left right >    ["("; //"boolean type expected"//; mustype=2`mustype=0]
      left:flattex !0 !env ^exty ["="]
      right:flattex !0 !env ^exty    [")"; istype=2]
  -> <ne left right >    ["("; //"boolean type expected"//; mustype=2`mustype=0]
      left:flattex !0 !env ^exty [")<>("]
      right:flattex !0 !env ^exty    [")"; istype=2]
  -> <ls left right >    ["("; //"boolean type expected"//; mustype=2`mustype=0]
      left:flattex !0 !env ^exty [")<("]
      right:flattex !0 !env ^exty
         [")"; istype=2; //"invalid magnitude compare not int"//; exty=1]
  -> <gr left right >    ["("; //"boolean type expected"//; mustype=2`mustype=0]
      left:flattex !0 !env ^exty [")>("]
      right:flattex !0 !env ^exty
         [")"; istype=2; //"invalid magnitude compare not int"//; exty=1]
  -> <ad left right >    ["("; //"integer type expected"//; mustype<2]
      left:flattex !1 !env ^exty [")+("]
      right:flattex !1 !env ^extz    [")"; istype=1]
  -> <su left right >    ["("; //"integer type expected"//; mustype<2]
      left:flattex !1 !env ^exty [")-("]
      right:flattex !1 !env ^extz    [")"; istype=1]
  -> <mp left right >    ["("; //"integer type expected"//; mustype<2]
      left:flattex !1 !env ^exty [")*("]
      right:flattex !1 !env ^extz    [")"; istype=1]
  -> <dv left right >    ["("; //"integer type expected"//; mustype<2]
      left:flattex !1 !env ^exty [")DIV("]
      right:flattex !1 !env ^extz    [")"; istype=1]
  -> <md left right >    ["("; //"integer type expected"//; mustype<2]
      left:flattex !1 !env ^exty [")MOD("]
      right:flattex !1 !env ^extz    [")"; istype=1]
  -> <ng left >          ["-("; //"integer type expected"//; mustype<2]
      left:flattex !1 !env ^exty    [")"; istype=1]
```

```
    -> thev:<vr <ty>%vty> | thev:<gl <ty>%vty> | thev:<at xx vrv <ty>%vty> |
        thev:<tv <ty>%vty> | thev:<sa toknno <ty>%vty>
            [//"identifier type mismatch"//; mustype=vty`mustype=0; istype=vty]
        thev:shovar !true !false !false !true !empty ^xset
    -> <co <ty>%tipe >%idn
            [//"identifier type mismatch"//; mustype=tipe`mustype=0]
            [number !idn; istype=tipe]
    -> <cn <ty>%2 >%0
            [//"boolean type expected"//; mustype=2`mustype=0]["FALSE"; istype=2]
    -> <cn <ty>%2 >%1
            [//"boolean type expected"//; mustype=2`mustype=0]["TRUE"; istype=2]
    -> <cn <ty>%4 >
            [//"set type expected"//; mustype=4`mustype=0]["NIL"; istype=4]
    -> <cn <ty>%5 >
            [//"symbol table type expected"//; mustype=5`mustype=0]["NIL"; istype=5]
    -> <cn <ty>%1 >%val
            [//"integer type expected"//; mustype<2][number !val; istype=1]
    -> <cn <ty>%cty >%val
            [//"invalid constant type"//; mustype=cty`mustype=0; cty>5]
            [number !val; istype=cty] ;

doargs !env:table !uparo:bool !insemi:bool !repost:tree
        ^outsemi:bool ^post:tree
  -> <> [outsemi=insemi; post=repost]
  -> <at nexta exptr expty:<ty >%tyno >
        nexta:doargs !env !uparo !insemi !repost ^xsemi ^postx [outsemi=true]
        (  [xsemi=true; ","])?
        (  [uparo=true] exptr:splitarg !postx ^post
        |  [otherwise; post=postx] exptr:flattex !tyno !env ^xty );

splitarg !pre:tree ^post:tree
  -> <ca exptr thep >
        exptr:shovar !true !false !false !true !empty ^xset    [post=<ca pre thep >]
  -> thev:<vr ..> | thev:<gl ..> | thev:<at ..> | thev:<tv ..> | thev:<sa ..>
        thev:shovar !true !false !false !true !empty ^xset    [post=pre];

buildtree !env:table ^nsubs:int
  -> <bt <> <>> [nsubs=0]
  -> <ca next extr >
        next:buildtree !env ^nmos [","; nsubs=nmos+1]
        extr:flattex !3 !env ^xty ;

castype !wanty:int ^typeno:int
  -> <ty >%typeno
        ([typeno=1; "int"]|[typeno=2; "bool"]|[typeno=3; "tree"]
        |[typeno=4; "tree"]|[typeno=5; "tree"]|[typeno>5; "int"])
        ([wanty=1; "int"]|[wanty=2; "bool"]|[wanty=3; "tree"]
        |[wanty=4; "tree"]|[wanty=5; "tree"]|[wanty>5; "int"]) ;

deleteitem {delete from list, replace with its link}
  -> <no link aset >
  => link
  -> <tr link fromst tost chrs acts >
  => link;

catlist !tail:tree ^result:tree        {cats tree to tail}
  -> <> [result=tail]
  -> <no link code >%deco
        link:catlist !tail ^midlist  [result=<no midlist code >%deco];

end TagGrammar.
```

Appendix C

Itty Bitty® Stack Machine Instruction Set

The Itty Bitty Stack Machine is a hypothetical stack computer with a simple instruction set and only one addressing mode. This makes it easier to generate object code for it when compiling a high-level language like Modula-2, and also clarifies some of the code optimization issues. The computer effectively has three registers, none of them directly programmable (that is, there are no load or store instructions for altering the register contents). The three registers are the program counter, the stack pointer, and the frame pointer. A fourth register (Limit) protects the user from stack overrun, but is not generally alterable. All four registers are given initial values from memory on startup.

The program counter (PC) advances through the machine code as the program executes, and three of the instructions alter the sequence of instruction execution by changing the contents of the program counter in other ways.

The stack pointer (SP) always points to the top of the expression and control stack. Unlike many modern computers, the IBSM stack grows in the positive direction, toward increasing memory addresses. Most instructions cause the SP to increment or decrement as the stack grows or shrinks, respectively. Two instructions affect it more radically as part of entering and exiting a procedure.

The frame pointer (FP) is the base address for the two memory reference instructions. It is also altered implicitly as part of entering and exiting a procedure, and not otherwise.

The IBSM is designed to operate approximately the same with any word size, except that with larger machine words, more instructions can be packed into a single word. Each instruction is five bits, so three instructions may be packed into a 16-bit word (a fourth instruction consisting of one significant bit can fit into the 16th bit). With a 32-bit word, the compiler could pack six or seven instructions in. The IBSM runs just fine with only one instruction per word, also, as described in Chapter 6. When packing multiple instructions per word, the least significant five bits of a word are executed first, then the next five bits, and so on, until there remain no non-zero instructions. Branches and procedure calls (as well as returns) always cause execution to continue beginning with the first instruction of the addressed word. The IBSM has no byte addressing as such; the word is atomic.

® "Itty Bitty" is a registered trademark of Itty Bitty Computers

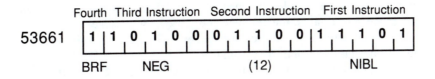

53661

| 1 | 1 | 0 | 1 | 0 | 0 | 0 | 1 | 1 | 0 | 0 | 1 | 1 | 1 | 0 | 1 |

BRF   NEG   (12)   NIBL

Figure C.1. The IBSM Instruction Word (16 bit version).

On startup, the IBSM reads a single address out of (absolute) memory location 0; this becomes the starting stack pointer. From the top of this initial stack the IBSM pops three words (counting down, so that the three words are at locations n, $n-1$, and $n-2$), that become respectively the stack limit (to prevent stack overrun), the initial frame pointer, and the initial program counter. In Listing 6.1 these are set to

SP	3 (initially, before popping)
Limit	100
FP	0
PC	100
SP	0 (after popping the other three words)

If it is necessary to run larger programs (requiring more stack growth than 100 words), the first line in the object file can be altered by systematically replacing the three "100" values by a larger number.

Some of the instruction codes are reserved for multitasking applications, and are not relevant to compiler design principles. Others are reserved for future research The remaining 28 instructions are defined in Table C.1. The instruction codes in this table are given in decimal.

An interpreter exists for the IBSM, coded in a moderately portable subset of ISO Pascal. Several of the procedures can be sped up by resorting to "dirty tricks," and are so marked. This interpreter accepts a text file containing the IBSM code and load information as decimal numbers. Except when the load address is explicitly changed, loading the virtual machine memory begins with address 0 and continues sequentially, one number per word.

The number "−1" is used as an escape code. If followed by another −1, that value goes into the next word and loading continues. If the next value is positive and a valid address, loading continues from that address with the next number in the file. If the next value is larger than the greatest valid address, it signals the end of file, and execution begins by fetching the SP from address 0 and popping the remaining registers.

If the number following the −1 escape is negative but not −1, four of the low five bits of that number are used to set some trace-enable flags, then execution begins normally. The significant trace enable bits are as follows:

0 (1)	(Reserved)
1 (2)	Trace writes to memory (ST instructions)
2 (4)	Trace any change in sequential execution
3 (8)	Trace only procedure entry and exit
4 (16)	Trace every instruction

The respective trace enable bits are set when the corresponding bits of the negative number are zero (that is, the complement is used), so a value –31 enables all tracing whereas –9 only traces procedure entry and exit. To set a particular trace level, add the selected bit values and subtract the sum from –1.

The instruction trace shows a instruction "cycle" count, the address of the current instruction, then the SP and the value on the top of stack and the FP after the instruction executes. Sequence change and memory write traces identify the respective addresses involved, and in the case of a write, the data stored there.

Listing 6.3 includes decimal codes that can be generated at the beginning of a procedure entry to build a display. Listing C.1 shows the machine mnemonics for this operation.

00	Nop	No OPeration. Used as a filler for partially-filled instruction words.
01	BrFalse	BRanch if False. Pop two numbers off the stack, and if the second one is zero, add the first to PC and continue with the first instruction of that word. Otherwise take the next instruction in sequence. This can be the fourth instruction packed into a 16-bit word.
02		(Reserved)
03	Call	Call a procedure whose (absolute) address is on the top of the stack, by exchanging the top of the stack with the PC. A procedure that does not use ENTER can also return by using this instruction, though the caller must discard the top of stack if so. The PC value pushed as a return address is always the address of the next instruction word, even if there remain unused instructions in the current word.
04	Enter	Enter a procedure. Pop the top word n off the stack and replace it with the current contents of the frame pointer (the dynamic link to a procedure using this in its header), repoint the frame pointer to the static link (assumed to be the second word below the dynamic link), then adjust the stack pointer upward by n words (to reserve local variable space).
05	Exit	Exit a procedure that was entered by the ENTER instruction. Pop a value n off the top of the stack, set SP to point to the dynamic link (which is the value in FP, +2), then pop the dynamic link into FP, pop the return address into PC, and finally pop and discard n more words (which were parameters to the procedure, now unneeded).
06,07,10		(Reserved)
08	Dupe	Duplicate the top of stack, by pushing a copy of the top word.
09	Swap	Swap the top two words on the stack, reversing their relative position.
11	Mpy	Multiply the top two words on the stack, replacing them with a single-word product. If the result is greater than one word, the excess high-order bits are lost.

Table C.1a. The IBSM instruction set (part 1).

12	Add	Add the top two words on the stack, replacing them with their sum. If the result overflows, it will have the wrong sign.
13	Xor	Perform a bitwise Exclusive-Or on the top two words from the stack, replacing them with the result.
14	Or	Perform a bitwise Inclusive-Or on the top two words from the stack, replacing them with the result.
15	And	Perform a bitwise logical And on the top two words from the stack, replacing them with the result.
16	EQUAL	Compare the top two words on the stack, replacing them with the value True (1) if they are equal and False (0) otherwise.
17	Less	Compare the top two words on the stack, replacing them with the value True if the first is greater than the second, and False otherwise.
18	Greater	Compare the top two words on the stack, replacing them with the value True if if the first is less than the second, and False otherwise.
19	Not	Complement every bit of the top word on the stack.
20	Negate	Replace the top stack word with its Two's Complement negative.
21,22,23		(Reserved)
24	Stop	Stop execution of the IBSM. This is usually reserved for error halts.
25	Global	Subtract the FP from the top word on the stack. If it is an absolute address in memory, this converts it to be relative to the FP so that LD and ST work correctly.
26	Store	STore variable. Pop the top two values off the stack and store the first into the memory location addressed by the sum of the second and the FP. This gives simple access to local variables addressed relative to the FP.
27	Load	LoaD variable. Pop the top value off the stack and replace it with the contents of the memory location addressed by the sum of that value and the FP.
28	LoadCon	LoaD Constant. Push the value of the word pointed to by the PC, and increment the PC. Note that additional instructions in the current instruction word will continue to execute, but the next instruction word will follow the constant word.
29	Nibble	Load short constant. Push the value of the next five bits of the current instruction word onto the stack as a word, and do not execute that part as an instruction. If there are additional instructions after the five-bit constant, then continue executing them; otherwise continue with the next word pointed to by the PC.
30	Zero	Load zero. Push 0 (False) onto the stack as a word.
31	One	Load one. Push 1 (True) onto the stack as a word.

Table C.1b. The IBSM Instruction Set (part 2).

28828	Entry:	LoadCon	#nvars	; *the number of local variables*
		Enter		; *allocate variable space on stack*
		LoadCon	#lex	; *the number of display cells*
44968	Loop:	Dupe		
		Nibble	#11	; *offset to* **Done**
		BrFalse		; *quit if no more cells to build*
13288		Dupe		
		One		; *increment copy of remaining count,*
		Add		; *...so last item quits immediately*
30		Zero		
21481	UpLevel:	Swap		; *chase static links for this item*
		One		; *decrement count, go to* **GotIt** *if* 0
		Negate		
268		Add		
		Dupe		
1149	Here:	Nibble	#3	
		BrFalse		
26473		Swap		; *load next static link (parent frame)*
		Load		
		Global		
7102		Zero		; *branch unconditional back to* **UpLevel**
		Nibble	#6	
52		Negate		
		BrFalse		
32044	GotIt:	Add		; *dispose of zero by adding to TOS*
		Swap		; *insert this link below count*
		One		; *decrement count, then go to* **Loop**
31124		Negate		
		Add		
		Zero		
53661		Nibble	#12	
		Negate		
		BrFalse		
	Done:			

Listing C.1. Code to Build a Display on the IBSM Stack.

Appendix

Code Generation Tables
for Four Computers

Chapter 9 includes sample source code for a table-driven module that translates Itty Bitty Stack Machine code into register code for four popular computers. This appendix lists the data in the two large tables. The tables should be read vertically, that is, the column of data for one computer is selected and the other three columns discarded. These tables do not include procedure entry and exit blocks, nor the code to call a procedure, which are left to the reader.

OpCodeIndex:	(11)	(86)	(370)	(68000)
(Nop)	0,0,0,	0,0,0,	0,0,0,	0,0,0,
	0,0,0,	0,0,0,	0,0,0,	0,0,0,
(Load)	0,7,15,	0,7,14,	0,7,14,	0,8,16,
	23,31,39,	22,30,0,	23,32,0,	24,32,39,
(Store)	0,0,57,	0,0,38,	0,0,39,	0,0,47,
	23,0,0,	22,0,0,	23,0,0,	24,0,0,
(Cmpr)	0,65,73,	0,46,54,	0,0,48,	0,55,63,
	0,81,0,	0,62,0,	0,57,0,	0,71,0,
(Add)	0,89,97,	0,70,78,	0,0,64,	0,79,87,
	0,105,0,	0,86,0,	0,73,0,	0,95,0,
(Subt)	0,113,121,	0,94,102,	0,0,80,	0,103,111,
	0,129,0,	0,110,0,	0,89,0,	0,119,0,
(Mlpy)	0,137,145,	0,0,118,	0,0,96,	0,127,135,
	0,153,0,	0,126,0,	0,105,0,	0,143,0,
(Neg)	0,0,0,	0,0,0,	0,0,0,	0,151,159,
	0,161,0,	0,134,0,	0,112,0,	0,167,0,
(And)	0,0,0,	0,142,150,	0,0,119,	0,175,183,
	0,0,0,	0,158,0,	0,128,0,	0,191,0,
(Or)	0,169,177,	0,166,174,	0,0,135,	0,199,207,
	0,185,0,	0,182,0,	0,144,0,	0,215,0,
(Jump)	0,0,193,	0,0,190,	0,0,151,	0,0,223,
	0,0,0,	0,0,0,	0,0,0,	0,0,0,
(Bcc)	0,0,200,	0,0,197,	0,0,159,	0,0,230,
	0,0,0;	0,0,0;	0,0,0;	0,0,0;

Table D.1. TargetMachine code indexes for four popular computers.

OpCodeTable values:	(11)	(86)	(370)	(68000)
Nop (all modes)	2,0,0, 0,0,1, 160,	1,0,0, 0,0,1, 144,	2,0,0, 0,0,1, 7,	2,0,0, 0,0,2, 78,113,
Load r,#con	4,0,1, 2,2,2, 192,21,	3,0,1, 1,2,1, 184,	4,1,16, 2,2,1, 65,	6,0,2, 2,4,2, 32,60,
Load r,mem	4,0,1, 2,2,2, 64,23,	4,1,8, 2,2,2, 139,134,	4,1,16, 2,2,3, 88,0,208,	4,0,2, 2,2,2, 32,46,
Load r,@r	2,0,1, 0,64,2, 0,18,	2,1,8, 1,1,2, 139,4,	4,1,16, 1,1,3, 88,0,208,	4,0,2, 2,16,2, 32,54,
Load r,r	2,0,1, 0,64,2, 0,16,	2,1,8, 1,1,2, 139,192,	2,1,16, 1,1,1, 24,	2,0,2, 1,1,1, 32,
Load r,cc	12,11,1, 0,128,12, 2,0,38, 10,142, 10,1,1, 38,10, 128,21,			2,1,1, 0,1,2, 80,192,
Store r,mem	4,0,64, 2,2,2, 53,16,	4,1,8, 2,2,2, 137,134,	4,1,16, 2,2,3, 80,0,208,	4,1,1, 2,2,2, 45,64,
Cmpr r,#con	4,0,1, 2,2,2, 192,37,	4,1,1, 2,2,2, 129,248,		6,0,2, 2,4,2, 176,188,
Cmpr r,mem	4,0,1, 2,2,2, 64,45,	4,1,8, 2,2,2, 59,134,	4,1,16, 2,2,3, 89,0,208,	4,0,2, 2,2,2, 176,174,
Cmpr r,r	2,0,1, 0,64,2, 0,32,	2,1,8, 1,1,2, 59,192,	2,1,16, 1,1,1, 25,	2,0,2, 1,1,2, 176,128,
Add r,#con	4,0,1, 2,2,2, 192,101,	4,1,1, 2,2,2, 129,192,		6,0,2, 2,4,2, 208,188,
Add r,mem	4,0,1, 2,2,2, 64,109,	4,1,8, 2,2,2, 3,134,	4,1,16, 2,2,3, 90,0,208,	4,0,2, 2,2,2, 208,174,
Add r,r	2,0,1, 0,64,2, 0,96,	2,1,8, 1,1,2, 3,192,	2,1,16, 1,1,1, 26,	2,0,2, 1,1,2, 208,128,

Table D.2a. TargetMachine code for four popular computers.

OpCodeTable values:	(11)	(86)	(370)	(68000)
Subt r,#con	4,0,1, 2,2,2, 192,229,	4,1,1, 2,2,2, 129,232,		6,0,2, 2,4,2, 144,188,
Subt r,mem	4,0,1, 2,2,2, 64,237,	4,1,8, 2,2,2, 43,134,	4,1,16, 2,2,3, 91,0,208,	4,0,2, 2,2,2, 144,174,
Subt r,r	2,0,1, 0,64,2, 0,224,	2,1,8, 1,1,2, 43,192,	2,1,16, 1,1,1, 27,	2,0,2, 1,1,2, 144,128,
Mlpy r,#con	4,0,1, 2,2,2, 192,117,			6,0,2, 2,4,2, 193,252,
Mlpy r,mem	4,0,1, 2,2,2, 64,125,	4,1,8, 2,2,2, 247,166,	4,1,16, 2,2,3, 92,0,208,	4,0,2, 2,2,2, 193,238,
Mlpy r,r	2,0,1, 0,64,2, 0,112,	2,1,8, 1,1,2, 247,224,	2,1,16, 1,1,1, 28,	2,0,2, 1,1,2, 193,192,
Neg r	2,0,1, 0,0,2, 0,11,	2,1,8, 1,1,2, 43,192,	2,1,16, 1,1,1, 27,	2,0,2, 1,1,2, 144,128,
And r,#con		4,1,1, 2,2,2, 129,224,		6,0,2, 2,4,2, 192,188,
And r,mem		4,1,8, 2,2,2, 35,134,	4,1,16, 2,2,3, 84,0,208,	4,0,2, 2,2,2, 192,174,
And r,r		2,1,8, 1,1,2, 35,192,	2,1,16, 1,1,1, 20,	2,0,2, 1,1,2, 192,128,
Or r,#con	4,0,1, 2,2,2, 192,85,	4,1,1, 2,2,2, 129,200,		6,0,2, 2,4,2, 128,188,
Or r,mem	4,0,1, 2,2,2, 64,93,	4,1,8, 2,2,2, 11,134,	4,1,16, 2,2,3, 86,0,208,	4,0,2, 2,2,2, 128,174,
Or r,r	2,0,1, 0,64,2, 0,80,	2,1,8, 1,1,2, 11,192,	2,1,16, 1,1,1, 22,	2,0,2, 1,1,2, 128,128,
Jump mem	4,0,0, 2,2,1, 119,	3,0,0, 1,2,1, 233,	4,0,0, 2,2,2, 71,240,	4,0,0, 2,2,1, 96,
Bcc c,mem	6,0,128, 2,2,3, 2,0,119;	3,0,1, 1,2,1, 112;	4,1,16, 2,2,1, 71;	4,0,1, 2,2,1, 96;

Table D.2b. TargetMachine code for four popular computers.

Index

→ (arrow) 3 14 **20**
⇒ (double arrow) **21 226**
∈ (empty string) **20**
⊥ (end of string) **108**
Δ (delta) **57**
δ (delta) **58**
Σ (sigma) **19**
Σ* (sigma star) **20**

A

abbreviated addressing 170 311
absolute address 172 314
absolute branches 314
absorption 50 51 91 281
abstract 19 321
abstract machine 24 42 319 320
abstract tree 264 320
abstract-syntax tree (*see also* parse tree) 7 10 11 13 14
    22 42 136 222 **223** 224 225 226 227 231 234 235
    236 267 268 277 281 332 333
abusive 213
accent 77
accept **25** 27 40 **48** 58 59 69 73 78 90 91 **100** 121
    174 191 206 213 353 357
access, memory 160 178 249 293 294 311 325 334
accountants 3
accumulator **160** 170 193 311
action, parser 15 213
action, semantic *see* semantic action
activation record, *see* stack frame
active nonterminal 39 277
active process 327
active register 277 294 295
actual parameter 265 341 365
acyclic graph, directed 16 254 325 327
Ada (programming language) 150 235
add (instruction) 160 162 165 179 185 187 263 290
    293 296 312 321 327
address expression 184 253
address mode 161 253 290 293 **311** 313 314 334

address offsets 172
address register 178 293 335 346
address space **293** 311 313
address vector 350
address, target machine (*see also* memory address)
    160 172 174 176 177 189 293 295 319 323 324
aged (information) 308
aggregate (*see also* data structure) 185 238
algebra of regular expressions 48 **50** 91 92
algebraic properties 50 51 55 57 92 165 169
Algol 6
algorithm 60 72 82 84 195 203 212 243 245 254 259
    273 293 298 310 314 320 325 327
alignment 183
allocate (variable) 161 166 168 176 179 182 **183** 184
    361 370
allocation (resource) 176 248 **292** 294 295 308 311
    325 327 332 347
alphabet (input to scanner) **77** 78 92 358 360
alphabet (of a grammar) 4 **19** 21 34 41 48 52 103 121
    224 227
alphabet (of an automaton) 24 **60** 72 100 **103** 119 121
    209 213 215
alternation (*see also* bar) 4 **49** 50 56 71 91 **114** 118
    119 122 193 354 356 361 366
alternative code 287 311 321 327 331
ambiguous 6 7 23 30 **32** 35 41 104 **114** 122 127 136
    183 210 224 354
American (*see also* ASCII) 162
analysis of machine code 264 324
analysis, data-flow, *see* data-flow analysis
analysis, lexical 4 **9** 15 **48**
analysis, loop 244 249 **264** 288 290 291 324
analysis, range **250** 288 289 291 323 331 333
analysis, semantic, *see* semantic analysis
anonymous (temporary) variables 161
anonymous tree templates 228
apostrophe 118
application, function 340 **342** 343 346 347 352
application, production 11 21 28 30 37 41 106 203 215
    226 236 280
applicative language 339 340 **342** 345 351 368

applying compiler theory 33 190 340 352 357
appropriate code, choosing 80 81 142 160 161 166 188
    190 216 262 296 321 324 341 347 350 358
arc, graph 59 67 243 325
architecture, machine 13 **160** 168 176 190 236 242
    287 293 312 325 331 333
arguments (*see also* parameter) 177 342 351 365
arithmetic laws 50 162 169 263
arithmetic operators 36 138 160 166 183 188 235 288
    294 298 310 311 320 325 328 334 342 343 347
    352
arithmetic overflow 321
arithmetic, two's complement 323
array 73 82 84 86 91 139 152 176 179 184 **186** 190
    191 250 273 288 290 291 298 321 324 328 331
arrow 4 14 20 21 40 66 118 133 140 226
art 5 33 **39** 288 324
article 4
artificial intelligence 160 340
artificial language 24
ASCII **19** 40 77 78 86 140 183 224
assembler **2** 3 12
assembly language **2** 3 12 163 287 320 324
assertion 5 **131** 136 137 138 140 142 145 153 186
    228 236 263 276 354 356 361 365
assignment 5 139 142 144 145 150 **164** 168 174 182
    184 188 189 190 223 237 239 240 242 244 250
    254 258 261 265 289 290 294 296 311 312 320
    324 325 331 340 343 344 354 358 361 365
associative law 50 **51** 56 57 **169** 263 327
AST, *see* abstract-syntax tree
asterisk **20** 59 79 110 113 114 115 166
atom **342** 346 347 368
attribute assertion, *see* assertion
attribute evaluation 5 **132** 136 137 138 142 144 150
    152 175 190 215 227 230 240 252 256 276 280
    353 354 356 358 361 365
attribute evaluation order, *see* evaluation order
attribute flow, *see* evaluation order
attribute grammar (*see also* transformational attribute
    grammar) 13 **132** 138 **151** 160 169 172 184 223
    227 236 240 340 345 353
attributed code generation 166
attributed graph 230
attributed tree transformations 227
automatic 4 5 13 19 33 144 161 213 298 320 340 352
    353 355 357
automaton (*see also* finite-state automaton, linear-
    bounded automaton, push-down automaton, Turing
    machine) **24** 223
automaton, finite-state, *see* finite-state automaton
automaton, linear-bounded, *see* linear-bounded
automaton, push-down, *see* push-down automaton
available expressions 254
axiom 263 281

B

back end **12** 14 90 **159** 190 234
back-substitution 13 71 333 344 351
backing out of failed alternatives 193 **235** 276 361 366
backpatching **172** 174 175 193
Backus, John 6
backward DFA (*see also* data-flow analysis) 237 239
    243 244 262 298 308 310 311
backward jumps **175** 313 314 360
balanced expression tree 327
bar (*see also* alternation) 4 **49** 50 56 57 118
barbarisms 339
baroque instructions 160 288 312 320 324
base offsets, subscript 186 321
base type 149 183 184 237
Basic (programming language) 191 341
basic block **242** 247 264 310 325 327 328
batch computer 213
bignum 346
bilingual 2
binary node 230
binary numbers 133 136 191
binary operator 50 96 254
binary tree 342
binding 50
biological 345
bite 234
bitset 188 231 241 323
block (code, memory, or file) 86 177 273 314 324 333
block-structured language 142 145 151 172 177 179
    215 **241** 341
block, basic, *see* basic block
blocked (automaton rejects) **25 58** 59 69 73 75 78 100
    103 105 202 203
BNF 6 14
body (of program structure) 13 38 115 118 142 145 149
    231 244 264 266 279 290 291 332 333 343 356
    368
Boolean 12 73 75 131 139 144 156 163 169 170 173
    183 186 188 223 230 235 240 250 261 264 276
    353 361 366
bootstrapping 345
bottle 198 199
bottom-up 11 15 **32** 109 118 132 133 135 136 **198**
    213 215 217 230 259
Bottom, lattice **237** 253
boundary, block 150 152 310 327 355
bounds (array, loop, or subrange) 186 188 250 273 288
    290 291 321
boxes 60 325 327
braces 116
bracket (grammar metasymbol) **80** 81 134 139 165 190
    226 228 355 368

branch (of a tree) 11 15 23 162 239 249 252
branch instruction **169** 171 176 242 248 256 266 312 314 319 324 325 327 329 331 334 344 350 351 361
break (in C) 241 289
break, line, *see* line break
bucket **82** 84 152
buffer 78 173 188 190
build (compiler code), *see* construct
build (data structure) 7 86 151 179 184 190 211 212 216
build (tree) 7 11 15 30 85 216 222 234 250 268 342 360 365
burden 188 331
buried 351 353
burn, *see* crash and burn
Burroughs 227
business 3
bypass 179
byte 73 78 168 183 187 191 293 323 324

C

C (programming language) 118 139 149 176 177 178 187 210 216 235 242 264 289 293 294 352
cache 292 366
cafeteria 27
calculation 84 108 110 113 119 168 173 175 182 186 215 253 290 292 293 308 310 314 321 323 325 328 330 344
calculus, *see* lambda or predicate
call (procedure or function) 8 119 144 149 150 164 **176** 177 179 188 190 231 269 276 310 340 341 343 347 350 365
candidate 239 256 258 259 294 308 311 330
canonical **30** 41 198 199 215
capability 2 33 135 273 320 321 331 345 361
capacity 311
capital letters 20
capture 49 67 193 204 312 360
car **342** 343 347 369
cardinal numbers 35 237 273
careful 4 6 29 119 136 320 324 332
Carrol, Lewis 130
carry 66 140 144 145 172 188 193 206 207 210 211 228 230 232 245 249 295 298 308 320 341 366
CASE statement 75 80 216 250 256 **319** 358
castigate 324
catch 22 39 345
category 20 132 136 210 249 333
catenate, *see* concatenate
cause 13 66 78 215 279 293 309 311 355
cdr **342** 343 347 369
cell 163 165 166 296 298 312 **342** 346 347 350

certain 20 34 39 131 132 138 249 264 285 333 342
CFG, *see* context-free
chain (branch or call) **314** 319 334 341 361
chain 67 152 179 180 185 327 328 332 340
challenge 150 340
chance 213
change (*see also* exchange, unchanged) 8 16 29 37 55 62 64 73 115 142 168 213 231 236 240 243 256 273 314
CHAR 149 182 183
character 5 7 9 10 11 19 20 24 25 33 48 50 51 52 72 77 78 82 83 84 86 87 90 99 107 139 150 166 183 186 189 215 250 323 342 357
characteristic 3 7 18 23 32 36 39 50 131 162 254
characterize 3 160
chase frame links 152
chauvinism 162
check, range, *see* range-check code
check, type, *see* type-checking
child 234 261
choice 21 22 35 59 104 105 106 109 110 114 138 160 161 202 203 209 264 287 298 309 320 334
Chomsky hierarchy 19 **24** 25 26 29 33 39
Chomsky, Noam 24
choose 4 21 28 30 35 50 54 59 82 104 110 114 135 160 189 199 202 207 293 311 324 327 332 341 345 350 360
chronicle 312
circle 59 145 368
circuit, short, *see* short-circuit
circular **135** 279
circumflex 140
circumstance 100 227 356
clarity 71 173 179
class of automaton (or language) 11 18 19 23 **25** 28 91 100 118 203 204 224 325 339
class of optimization 237 248 **249** 264 288
class, equivalence, *see* equivalence class
class, object-oriented 340
class, type 149 356
classic 5
classical 13 132 138 170 230 236 243 334 341
clause 6 114 314 319
clean 1 5 10 48 160 169
clear 64 102 114 191 310 323 327 334 339
clever (compiler) 262 320 331
client 273
clock 327 328 330 332
closed 53 145 151 185 320 361
closure 20 51 **52 204** 205 207
clue 183
clusters 293
cluttering 138
Cobol 3 320
Cocke, John 253

code file (*see also* text file) 166 175 314 325 334
code generation 7 11 12 **14** 159 163 **166** 182 194 226
    234 236 240 249 264 287 295 299 308 310 314
    319 323 335 341 347 353 362
code motion (optimization), *see* hoisting
codes, *see* condition codes, hash codes, operation codes
coerce 320
coincide 250 366
collapse 65
collect 7 9 56 57 78 79 118 137 138 166 207 216 231
    236 237 259 263 358 365
collector, garbage, *see* garbage collector
collision **82** 83 86 92 152 331
colloquial 339
colon 116 118 189
color 131 293
coloring, graph **293** 310 325
column 59 65 66 163 175 331
combination 4 52 122 132 153 170 312 320 339
combine 11 14 66 169 198 218 234 236 241 311 330
    361
comma 5 19 182 188
command 2 3 108 121 172 191
comment 6 7 10 50 76 **78** 116 163 164 175 223 353
commercial 254 320 346
COMMON (global data in Fortran) 177
common left-factors **112** 113 114 118
common subexpression elimination 249 **253** 256 258
    289 291 294
communicate 2 352
commutativity **50** 51 56 57 263
compact 49 51 132 207 237 311 347 368
compare instruction (*see also* condition codes, string
    compare) **163 170** 171 264 313 323 324 351
compatible types 149 321 356
compel 35 36 132 145 235
compilation unit 150 237 243 245
compile time (*see also* run time) 10 13 29 171 177 179
    186 215 236 239 249 250 256 268 288 290 296
    331 341 351 358
compiler compiler (*see also* self-compiling compiler)
    1 5 12 72 76 81 **116** 118 122 213 216 227 230
    234 280 340 **352**
Compiler, TAG, *see* TAG Compiler
complement 170 249 323
complex arithmetic 321
complexity 3 4 18 20 24 33 85 114 135 138 144 149
    160 163 166 168 182 183 186 188 190 192 203
    210 231 235 242 258 269 289 292 293 294 295
    296 312 314 319 321 323 333 342 345 346 361
    365
complexity, computational 25 230
component 4 5 7 9 19 36 57 73 100 121 140 141 142
    144 186 188 190 228 234 236 242 243 254 261
    293 320 321 325 335 342 346 353 361 365

compose 2 20 134 165 171 174 190 255 291 361
composite 78 108 228 230 255 256 323 332 347
compound 33
compounded 293 343
comprehension 342
compromise 75 191 288 320
computability 25 320
computation 25 75 83 162 168 172 186 231 254 262
    323 327 343
computational dependency 325
compute 3 12 82 84 108 150 159 161 165 204 210 225
    253 256 320 331
concatenate 49 **50** 51 52 53 56 57 62 104 107 108 115
    342
concentrate 13 90 149 152 162 176 198 234 345 352
concept 4 6 13 30 37 39 81 131 133 138 139 144 152
    163 175 176 193 204 222 288 290 293 342 343
    352 354 355
concern 3 10 12 34 48 55 72 75 82 84 136 139 141
    142 159 163 176 177 193 228 237 238 240 243
    249 259 265 289 292 319 347
concurrent 85 136 249 361
condition codes **170** 310
conditional branch (*see also* unconditional branch)
    170 171 242 256 313 327 328 331 361
conditional expression 259
conditionals 6 72 73 75 102 150 170 171 175 182 223
    230 239 240 241 244 250 256 263 265 276 290
    331 332 343 347 351 361 366
configuration **58** 59 66 69 **100** 102 104 105 122 203
    206
conflict 139 266 330
conflicting states **206** 207 210 211 212
conjunct 366
connect 4 6 11 13 49 65 72 114 179 223 224 230 279
    358
cons **342** 343 347 350 369
conservative 130
consist 2 4 8 12 19 22 24 25 26 30 33 34 36 37 38 49
    59 72 80 83 103 107 108 119 130 131 134 140 177
    179 184 191 203 215 224 242 244 249 250 254
    259 313 323 327 341 342 346 353 355 361 365
consistency check 142 190 268
consistent 10 130 136 138 149 183 190 230 243 268
    353 355
console 189
constant factor, same 263
constant folding 225 228 229 234 249 **250** 253 263
    265 289 291 296 321 333 341 351 352
constant identifier 182 183 225 227 228 230
constant increment 331
constant propagation 237
constitute 119 244 288 356
constrainer (*see also* constraints checking) 7 **11** 13 15
    39 82 **131** 138 150 154 235 237 250 321 353

constraint 132 138 193 262 354

constraints checking (*see also* type-checking) 11 118
    142 145 150 234 236 250 356

construct (compiler code, *see also* compiler compiler)
    4 5 7 13 18 33 37 72 75 78 81 90 102 118 119
    202 204 210 227 276 340 353 **357** 361

construct (tree), *see* build

construct, language, *see* structure

containing procedure, *see* nested procedure

contents (of register or variable) 13 73 163 176 178 237
    249 255 256 310 351

context **29** 136 230 235 249

context-free 1 6 19 **27** 28 **35** 41 49 90 100 103 111
    114 118 131 133 162 166 226 352 353 360

context-sensitive **26** 28 29 **38** 41 130 132 159 233

contiguous 86 237 238

contingency 261

continuation **340** 351 369

control structure, *see* structure

control variable 5 265 288 289 290 291 323 331 332

conversion, type 320

cookie 234

copy propagation 237 249 **256** 334 344

correctness, formal 6 33 48 75 121 159 166 241 249
    290 314 324

cost (*see also* fast) 6 75 77 82 176 190 231 234 235
    249 250 253 256 288 290 293 314 324 332 333
    334 341 350 361

counter, *see* location counter, program counter

counting (in a grammar) 33 34 **35** 168 354

crash and burn 213 215 355

creation 159 345

creativity 39 323

criteria of goodness 160

critical path 327

CSE, *see* common subexpression elimination

CSG, *see* context-sensitive

current state 57 73 75 170 179 182 209 294

Curry, Haskell 341 369

currying 341

cut 22

CYCLE node 264

cycle, clock, *see* clock

cycle, empty **64** 358

D

DAG, *see* directed acyclic graph

data structure (*see also* structure) 82 86 138 151 184
    188 194 224 230 237 250 253 267 279 298 311
    314 320 324 325 342 346 351 353 360 366

data-flow analysis **237 240** 243 244 245 247 248 256
    262 272 276 280 281 288 289 291 295 298 **308**
    310 331 342 344 361

data-flow language 354

database language 340

dead code (*see also* live) 13 248 **250** 329

deallocate (*see also* allocate) 178 188

decimal number 49 144 168 175 179

decision point 114 **115** 122 203

declaration, identifier 7 9 12 29 38 130 136 138 **141**
    145 152 159 166 168 172 178 182 185 186 188
    189 235 272 292 323 332 341

decoration **7** 162 228 230 **231** 235 240 245 249 250
    268 281 321 327 366

decrease 243 265

decrement 308 309 346

define (in Lisp or Scheme) 343

delay, timing 325 327 330 332

delimiter 7 79 116 228

demand allocation (*see also* allocation) 294 295

dependency 135 325 328 331 332 353

deprecated 264

depth-first (*see also* tree walk) 255

dereference, pointer (*see also* pointer) 184 185 294 295
    366

DeRemer, Frank 210

derivation 11 **21 30** 32 38 41 100 106 199

derived attribute (*see also* attribute) **132** 134 136 139
    141 144 **150** 153 173 175 230

derived induction variables, *see* induction variables

destination, *see* assignment, branch instruction, quad,
    store operation, transition

deterministic (*see also* nondeterministic) 5 11 28 39 **57**
    59 60 64 67 71 76 79 81 87 100 101 106 115 116
    122 130 198 203 210 276 357 360

DFA, *see* data-flow analysis

DFSA, *see* deterministic, finite-state automaton

diagnosis 355

diagonal 331

diagram, syntax 11 372

dialect (of Lisp) 179 341 342 343 347 352

digit 34 49 77 78 85 116 133 136 144 189

Digital Equipment PDP-11 160

digits 34 45 49 78 86 93 134 195 254

Dijkstra, Edsger 169

dimension (of arrays) 6 75 188 213 292 331 332

directed acyclic graph 16 254 325 327

discard (execution results) 328 332

discard (grammar tokens), *see* panic mode

disjoint 109 207

disk 73 273 292

display 176 177 **179** 182 190 193 341

dispose 268 273 351

distributive law **50** 51 56 57 92 112 263 264

divide operation (*see also* modulo) 83 144 169 195 321
    356

dominoes 39

dotted pair **342** 346 347

double arrow 21 226
double quote 44
double slash 356
dual, mathematical 237 249
dump, memory 175
duplicate code 75 263 266
dynamic links (*see also* static links) 178 **179**
dynamic scope 179 **341**
dynamic variables 184 268 272 295 341 342

E

editor 192 215
efficient (*see also* inefficient) 8 9 10 12 19 39 48 75 82
    84 91 132 135 151 161 176 186 190 198 212 213
    227 264 267 268 273 323 324 339 341 345 351
    352
elegant 191 248 249 343
element (array or vector) 84 102 162 179 184 187 188
    190 311 324 328 330 336
ELSE 6 33 114 127 171 174 223 239 240 241 250 256
    266 319
ELSIF 314 319
elusive 39
embedded C code 216 352
emit 8 10 79 166 172 190 263 310 314 319 320 357
    358
emphasis 224 334 341 345
empty cycle, *see* cycle
empty language **30**
empty move, *see* empty transition
empty nonterminal or production 26 27 **28** 55 56 71
    106 112 113 137 141 166 168 353 361
empty range 247 253
empty set **51** 237 243 273 298
empty stack **100** 102 105 121 205 296
empty string 20 26 **30** 50 **51** 69 105 112 115 119 136
    193
empty transition **59** 61 64 67 68 92 357
encapsulation 150 340
encode 11 19 73 75 80 90 138 141 144 165 168 170
    191 213 319 366
end of file 108 110 207
end of line, *see* line break
end of string, *see* end of file
enforce 7 34 138 140 236 242 269 355
English 2 6 11 19 49
ensure 2 244 324 366
enter (instruction) 164 176 182 400
entropic 160 345
enumerable, recursively 25
enumeration type 12 73 78 80 182 183 186 250 346
environment 25 136 150 160 273 340 341 345 346
equality assertion 137 140 142 361 365

equivalence class 54 64 **68** 77 78 92 203 358
equivalent automata **58** 59 64
error reporting 9 11 **75** 78 82 142 150 161 **213** 239
    250 354 355 361 365 **367**
evaluation order 134 135 **136** 140 161 215 227 **229**
    327 353
exclamation point 140
executable code 73 169 269 327 357 358
execution dependency, *see* dependency
execution order (or path) 11 162 170 178 189 237 239
    240 249 255 289 291 310 319
execution time, *see* run time
exhaustive search 320
exit (from loop) 231 244 245 264 289 292
exit (IBSM operation) 164 176 **178** 400
expense, *see* cost
expert (assembly language programmer) 320 324
exponential time 230 290
export 150 268
expression complexity 161 242 294 295
expression evaluation 13 **161** 164 171 183 188 223
    249 294 295 327 340 343 347
expression tree 224 228 231 235 240 250 253 289 327
    347 365
extended grammar **114** 118 122

F

factorial 343 344
failed assertion or production 234 276 354 361 368
fall-through, branch, 243
FALSE 141 163 **169** 171 182 264
fast (*see also* cost, run time, slow) 75 253 288 292 311
    323 327 328 332
fetch, memory 160 165 169 185 190 308 324 327
field, record 184 **185** 190 231 267 321 340
file management 150 273
file type 188
final state **25** 27 40 48 **57** 59 66 68 70 73 78 81 92
    100 102 119 121 203 205 357 358
finite-state automaton 24 **29** 33 48 **57** 60 64 67 **72** 73
    75 78 80 82 90 92 119 139 202 207 209 213 352
    357 360
first pass, *see* two-pass
first sets 106 **107** 109 113 115 204 206
fixup, code 334
flag 12 38 39 152 183 188 240 250 273 310 361
flatten 234 249 263 319 362 365
floating-point 5 183 321 327 341
flow analysis, *see* data-flow analysis
flow graph 243 244 245 254 264
flow-through attribute 134 136 215 240 288 295
fold, constant, *see* constant folding
follow sets 106 **107** 109 113 115 204 206

Index

fork 243 248 252 256 266 311 328
formal parameter 176
format (of file or text) 6 166 192
Fortran 3 5 6 10 14 176 177 178 235 242 247 264 295
    341
forward branch **171** 175 313
forward DFA (*see also* data-flow analysis) 237 244 249
    265 308 310 312
forward move error recovery 215
forward reference 172 235 353 360
frame pointer, *see* stack frame
frame, stack, *see* stack frame
free variable
free, *see* cost, nonlocal variables
front end **12** 14 18 48 **159** 190 193 234 362
frontier **23** 41 216
FSA, *see* finite-state automaton
function application, *see* application
function-returning function 343
function, attribute evaluation (*see also* attribute
    evaluation) 5 **132** 134 137 139 142 144 145 **150**
    153 175 190 240 253 256 352 353 354 356 358
function, *see* procedure
functional programming language, *see* applicative
fusion, loop, 248 288

G

G_2 **21** 22 26 27 30 31 32 36 109 110 113 114 139 163
    169 199 207 208 209 210 212
Ganzinger 227
garbage collector 350 351
gather information 229 230 236 249 259 290
generative grammar 227 228 241
Giegerich 227
global attributes 136 353
global flow analysis, *see* data-flow analysis
global instruction 164 182 **185** 400
global variables, *see* nonlocal variables
goal symbol 19 **20** 21 22 26 28 29 32 35 54 55 103
    108 109 **118** 133 140 152 199 206 227
goto (*see also* branch) 76 169 192 194 241 242 244
    289 361
graft (tree operation) 231 232 233 249 256 258 259
graph coloring **293** 310 325
graphical FSA representaion 58 61 66 67
grave accent 77
greater (instruction) 163 164 400
grow (stack or table) 27 100 144 151 230 295

H

hacker 139 160 287
halt (error) 367

halt state, *see* final state
handle (in LR parse) 205
handwritten code 11 31 72 90 114 118 121 190 267
    308 320 324 345
hardware 2 13 73 160 166 169 176 178 183 187 235
    237 264 273 288 291 295 321 327 332 335 341
hash code **82** 92 151 152 254 353 360
head, loop or procedure 145 179 232
heap 184
heuristic 215 234 310 311
high-level language 1 **3** 5 13 139 176 236 242 294 320
    361 366
HLL, *see* high-level language
hoisting 248 249 **256 258** 265 279 328 333
homonyms 144

I

IBSM, *see* Itty Bitty Stack Machine
idempotent property 91
identifier 10 29 38 42 48 49 78 82 86 130 136 138 142
    145 151 168 172 182 185 189 223 227 228 230
    235 237 240 249 254 343 361
identities, *see* mathematical laws
identity function 343
IF-THEN-ELSE 33 75 76 169 **171** 223 242 244 256
    351
ignore (TAG component) 324
implementer 7 13 213 291
improvement 5 8 13 75 84 86 129 152 160 236 249
    266 290 291 292 311 320 323 334 345 351 352
in-line code 184 234 347
inaccessible 66 185 256 350
INCL procedure 149
incremental compiler 340
indirect address mode 161 295
induction variables 248 **265** 288 **290** 291 335
inefficient (*see also* efficient) 10 12 25 82 105 137 139
    155 207 293 295
infix expression 162 169
inheritance (object-oriented) 340
inherited attributes **132** 136 138 142 145 150 154 168
    173 179 193 215 227 230 233 235 250 261 353
    365 366
inner loop 247 249 288 291 311 328 331 332
input file, *see* source text
input/output 189
instruction, machine 2 8 12 13 73 119 160 161 163
    164 175 177 185 190 287 293 295 310 311 320
    323 325 327 334 341 342 346 347
instrumentation 311
integer 11 12 34 49 78 79 82 131 134 136 138 141
    142 144 169 183 186 191 235 250 321 323 341
    346 347 353 356 366
interactive environment 215 340 341 346 347

interlocking loops 244
intermediate code (tree) 224 **234** 241 264 308 310 320
  321 333 357 360 365 366
interpreted execution **3** 15 108 191 341 347 352
interpreter, *see* interpreted execution
interrupt 293 324
intersection (*see also* union) 188 **237** 239 240 243 248
  265 273 323 361
intrinsic functions 190 252 256 342 343 346
invariant, loop, *see* loop-invariant
invocation (procedure or function), *see* call
invocation, nonterminal, 173 175 230 341 354 356 361
irregular 234 288 334 339
isomorphic 58 212
item 203
iterated DFA (*see also* data-flow analysis) 243 245 246
  254
iteration **50** 54 57 62 72 115 324 343 351 **354** 358
  361 368
Itty Bitty Stack Machine 163 **164** 170 173 174 178
  181 184 187 189 242 258 263 284 287 296 308
  335 346 350 **400**

J

join (of a fork) 171 243 256 310 311 319 327 328 361
jump, *see* branch

K

kernel **204** 207 211 212 217
keyboard 72 189
keyhole 8 334
keyword (*see also* reserved words) 5 141 149 176 223
  281
Kildall, Gary 243
kill **240** 244 246 247 256 261
Kleene star **20** 21 49 50 53 56 354 361
Kleene, Stephen Cole 20
known constants 237
Knuth, Donald 133 202 217 227 295

L

L-expression **184** 188
label (target of branch) 171 242 319
LALR(*k*) **211** 215
lambda calculus 343
lattice **237** 243 249 253 281
laws, mathematical, *see* mathematical laws
LBA, *see* linear-bounded automaton
leaf (*see also* tree) **23** 33 162 224 225 227 235 259

left factor **112** 122
left-linear grammar **29** 41 **72** 111
left-recursion 110
leftmost derivation 11 14 **31** 41 199
leftpart 60 108 118
leg (of a fork) 240 256 319 328 361
length (of vector or string) 19 34 37 82 106 109 134
  139 179 191 193 205 330 332 353
less (instruction) 163 164 400
letter 4 14 **19** 20 21 35 38 49 77 78 85 86 116 191
lexeme 9
lexical analysis **9** 10 15 **48**
lexical grammar **4** 5 9 10
lexical level 99 142 **144** 149 151 177 **179** 180 182
  188 194 340
library procedure 149 150 189 190 321 332 346 350
  351 352 353 365 366
limits (compiler or hardware) 27 139 151 161 191 254
  273 291 293 295 311 320 331 361
line break (*see also* space) 9 108 116 168 190 223 281
linear 29 82 84 151 186 224 264 290 310 314 325 331
linear-bounded automaton **26** 38 130 233
linearize arrays (*see also* unroll loops) 152 186 248 288
  292 332
linguist 24
link (after compile) 82 172 350 352
linked list (*see also* static links) 82 84 139 150 152 178
  272 279 298 319 325 342 346 350 357 365
Lisp (programming language) 179 339 340 **342** 345
  351 354
list, *see* linked list
literal (constant) 34 49 90 353 357 358
live variables **239** 244 254 262 265 290 293 308 311
  331 344
LL(*k*) **105** 110 112 118 121 169 193 198 202 210
LL(*k*) criterion **105** 110 114
load (instruction) **163** 164 166 169 179 184 190 264
  295 310 311 324 334 400
load constant (instruction) 163 164 171 185 190 400
local variables (*see also* nonlocal) 142 145 149 176
  177 179 185 190 215 273 295 311 355 365 366
location counter 173
location, memory 10 12 119 131 160 163 166 168 170
  172 175 178 189 279 293 294 311 324
logical operation (AND, OR, NOT instruction) 188 237
  264 294 310 323 352
lookahead **106** 107 109 110 115 118 119 136 193 199
  202 204 207 209 211 213 310 357
lookup, table 2 75 77 86 254
loop constant 231 234 265 **266** 276 279 288 290 291
  329 331 333
loop fusion 248 288
loop-invariant 288 331 333
LR(*k*) **202** 203 210 213 215
Lukasiewicz 162

M

machine language code (*see also* target machine) 2 7 12 13 14 75 119 150 159 163 166 168 175 186 264 273 296 308 310 320 321 325 327 333 339 341 346 352
machine-(in)dependent 7 13 168 264 288 291 295 333
machine-readable 352
machine, *see* finite-state automaton, target machine
mainframe 77 213
manipulate 50 114 268 272 340
manual 9 13 67 76 144 160 198 213 280
mapping 90 118 150 153 227 273 294
market 13 160 287 320
mathematical laws 50 51 55 56 57 112 165 198 248 262 263 327
maximal munch 234 263
McCarthy, John 340
meaning 2 5 10 33 50 138 163 237 261 341
mechanical 1 5 13 60 116 118 119 132 269 276 280 293 352
mechanism 24 144 149 150 250 256 350
megabyte, *see* byte
megaflop 328 332
member (of a set) 58 59 71 228 237 239 243 262
memory allocation 168 **177** 183 215 273 **292** 347
memory management, *see* memory allocation
memory reference 179 253 292 298 323
memory-mapped I/O 189
merged (moves, sets, or states) 64 211 217 236 244 253 358 361
metasymbols 40 41 50 54 55 80 114
method, OOP 340
methodology 3 4 340
Mflop, *see* megaflop
Micro-Modula **139** 142 150 154 166 168 179 192
microcomputer 191 324 334
mirror 72 262
mnemonics 163
mode, address, *see* address mode
model 25 59 121 190 243 319 346
modern 1 3 10 29 39 76 90 116 130 139 149 166 169 176 184 212 264 273 294 312 341
modified variables 231 254 265
Modula-2 (*see also* Micro-Modula) 6 29 73 78 85 87 118 136 140 142 149 166 176 179 182 187 213 235 254 264 272 276 289 294 308 320 339 341 343 346 352 353 358 360 361 365
MODULE 150
modulo 83
monotonic **243** 244 247 254 289
multidimensional arrays (*see* dimension)
multipass, *see* pass

multiply operation 36 79 141 162 166 169 187 255 262 290 312 321 323 327 356
mutations 345

N

native code, *see* machine language
natural (human) language 2 3 4 6 18 24
NDFA, *see* nondeterministic
NDPDA, *see* nondeterministic
negative **163** 175 179 263 289 331
nested (procedure or structure) 6 33 142 145 151 177 179 180 184 247 269 290 292 319 332 352 361 365
nondeterministic (*see also* deterministic) **59** 60 63 66 67 91 100 101 103 105 122 124 130 233 235 340 357 361
nonlocal variables (*see also* local variables) 118 145 176 177 179 182 190 254 273 295 311 321 341 369
nonprocedural 339 340 352 353
nonrecursive 37 56 73 109 113
nonterminal 19 **20** 28 42 54 60 103 106 109 110 118 131 133 137 167 204 224 226 350 353
nonterminal invocation 174 175 341 354
nonvolatile registers 295 324
nullable 115

O

object code, *see* machine language code
object-oriented programming 340
oddness 34
offset 170 175 179 182 185 253 314 321 323
operand 8 160 161 162 164 166 183 191 235 237 240 242 254 264 293 294 311 312 320 323 328 331 340 356
operating system 49 86 108 121 183 188 268 273 295 345
operation codes 2 264 299
operator 8 16 32 36 50 72 79 99 114 138 141 162 166 169 171 183 185 188 191 224 227 235 240 242 253 264 267 273 283 288 295 298 311 320 327 334 340 347 353 366
operator precedence 36 162 193 224
opportunistic 227 311 327
optimize 7 12 13 14 119 136 151 186 188 224 230 231 **236 247** 249 256 **287** 288 296 311 320 325 **333** 341 345 353 361
or-bar, *see* bar
ordinal 83 149 150 189 237 290
orthogonal 160 287
output file, *see* text file

overflow 84 321
overhead 273 291 324
overlap 325
overload, operator 166 183 188 235

P

pack 11 82 144 168 169 176 188 190 293 323 347
packet 216
pair, dotted, *see* dotted pair
palindrome 36 37
panic mode 215
parallelism 325 327 328
parameter 13 39 142 149 153 176 177 179 188 216
    236 247 269 295 311 340 341 343 346 351 360
    365 366
parent frame pointer, *see* stack frame
parent node 133 216 233 261
parentheses 33 36 50 79 100 114 144 162 189
parse tree (*see also* abstract-syntax tree) **22** 23 30 32
    114 131 134 136 162 169 172 215 223 230
parser 1 **4 99** 116 118 119 139 150 160 190 198 **202**
    210 211 213 215 226 234 235 236 321 353 355
    361 366
partial evaluation **249** 263 340 341 352
Pascal 6 29 32 33 49 78 79 114 116 118 131 136 138
    142 144 149 166 172 176 177 179 182 187 188
    189 190 223 235 237 264 272 294
pass, one- or two- 12 29 134 137 **172 190** 193 235
    243 245 254 258 265 290 295 310 312 321 334
path, execution, *see* execution path
Payton, T 227
PDA, *see* push-down automaton
peephole 8 13 319 325 333 353 361
Pennello, Tom 215
perfect hash (*see also* hash code) 152 360
performance 13 75 85 152 160 213 247 249 254 287
    290 320 327 331 341 345 352 361 366
persistent loop variable **265** 281 288 289 291 311 331
phase 11 13 230 320 334 360
phrase structure 4 7 9 11 99 122 130
pipeline processor 287 **325** 327 328 330
PLV, *see* persistent loop variable
pointer (*see also* dereference) 11 80 82 139 152 176
    184 188 254 267 273 294 340 342 346 366
Polish notation 162 169 224
polymorphic 149 150 268 340
pop, stack (*see also* push) **27** 100 121 162 163 206
    209
popular 49 86 118 161 170 191 299 323 325 341
port, I/O 189
porthole 233
position-independent 170
positional notation 132

postorder 162 223 241
power of two 133 237 262 321
powerful 14 28 49 231 341 343
practical 13 19 25 86 132 139 151 184 215 216 230
    231 272 291 320 333 351
practice 12 13 27 36 79 86 135 139 233 259 268 288
    294 295 314 341 347 357
predefined 46 136 138 139 142 149 191 352 356
predicate 131 **132** 137 138 140 150
predictive parser 105 199
prefix 106 224 228 343
pretty-printer 192
private 7 185
procedural language 339 340 353 355
procedure (or function) 80 118 142 145 149 151 **176**
    180 188 216 237 258 268 273 294 311 324 340
    343 351
product 32 113 141 161 169 186 256 263 289 321 330
production (commercial) compiler 268 308 355
production (grammar), *see* rule
profitable, *see* cost
program counter 73 75 76 170
programmer 3 132 150 161 213 242 291 293 320 323
    324 331 352
programming language 1 3 9 13 19 29 71 76 87 99 112
    116 121 130 137 139 142 149 176 189 191 210
    235 264 339 341 352
Prolog (programming language) 340
propagation, copy, *see* copy propagation
properties 23 113 136 139 144 149 166 169 191 228
    230 361
proximity 310
prune (*see also* graft) 249 250 256 258 259
pseudocode 171 174 186 187 308
punctuation 19 50 223
push-down automaton 27 35 **100 119** 122 130 132
    161 204 207
push, stack **27** 100 121 162 163 177 182 205 209 215
    295

Q

quads 131 **242** 243 264 333
question mark **50** 115
queue 82 314
quick brown fox 72
quotation mark 114
quote 343

R

random-access 273
range-check code 186 188 249 253 288 321 342

rational numbers 346
read head 25 27 203 207
readable 6 10 51 132 138 366
recognizer 33 76 77 205 360
recompile 213 345
record (structure) 132 139 144 149 151 184 **185** 190
    231 238 250 254 267 273 277 298 321 324 340
    342 346 347
recursive descent 100 **118** 119 123 150 190 213 223
    226 230 276 353 361 366
recursive function or procedure 118 177 180 182 272
    340 343 352
recursively enumerable 25
redeclared 87 151 152
reduce step (in LR parse) 205
redundant 13 65 119 334
reference (VAR) parameter 149 150 177 236 247 269
    295
register allocation 262 **293** 294 295 **308** 310 **311** 312
    325 332
registers 13 73 160 176 178 186 189 249 256 262 264
    288 **292** 298 308 310 312 320 321 324 328 332
    334 346
regular expression **49** 50 51 54 **61** 79 111 114 354
    357 360
relative addressing 170
relocate 170
REPEAT 182 245 247
replication 151 176 249 263 291 324 358
research 4 13 24 39 135 160 213 227 234 242 293 352
reserved words (*see also* keyword) 3 15 46 87 90 98 116
    182 196 223 353 358 360
resource 248 262 288 324 327
responsibility 321 325
reward 5 288
right-linear grammar **29** 42 55 56 72 80 111
rightmost derivation 11 14 **31** 38 41 198 199
rightpart 35 39 56 60 106 110 114 118 132 134 166
    199 202 205 207 209 215 226 227
Ripken, K 227
RISC 325
root 11 133 134 227 245 253 289 365 366
roundoff 327
routine 2 149 150 166 168 190 273 308 321 324 350
    365
row 8 59 66 68 217
rule 4 20 25 29 34 36 54 60 62 64 71 100 103 109 110
    112 114 116 118 131 132 137 149 166 168 182
    199 202 215 224 226 227 234 236 250 259 263
    276 320 340 353 355 361
run time (*see also* compile time) 13 48 168 186 188
    191 240 249 256 262 266 288 291 321 324 325
    327 328 340 346 351

S

save 27 67 75 78 82 115 121 161 176 185 245 253
    256 264 295 310 331 351 366
scalar 183 186 188 250 288 330 331 332
scale factor 133 134 135
scanner 4 6 19 21 34 48 59 68 71 81 87 90 99 116 118
    138 142 152 169 173 213 235 352 **357**
scheduled instructions 325
Scheme 343 346
Schönfinkel 341
Schwartz, J 253
scope level, *see* lex level
search 82 84 90 107 145 150 152 179 185 215 235 254
    310 320 341
segment 170 272 273 291 292 293 325 330 361 366
Select (set) 109 111 115 119 209
selection, code 160 248 249 **264** 266 282 288 294 298
    311 **312 320** 330 333 358 366
self-compiling compiler 345 352
self-relocating 170
semantic analysis 11 123 138 227 290 291 311 323
    325 327 333 341 342 366
semicolon 116 118 207 215 240 279
sentence 2 4 5 19 22 23 30 38 48 100 114 131
sentential form **22** 23 28 31 103 198 199 200 201 203
    354
set constants 73 119 323
set element 107 112 115 237 240 243 246 272 273 323
shift 190 **205** 262 **321** 323 351
short-circuit 289 361 366
skip 171 191 215 324
slash 356
slow (*see also* cost, fast, run time) 11 83 262 287 292
    293 321 327 368
SLR(k) **210** 215
small 1 8 33 60 73 77 82 84 145 159 161 163 183 189
    194 215 228 237 241 243 249 254 259 272 289
    290 291 292 308 311 314 321 323 328 334 336
    341 361 365
software 3 273 293 321 327
source text (input file) 7 9 10 30 48 86 189 214 230
    235
space characters (*see also* line break) 5 9 10 19 78 79
    166 191 193 223
sparse 273
speed (*see also* fast, slow) 5 75 86 160 258 287 311
    314 319 323 327 334
speed/space tradeoff 13 75 160 256 262 264 272 314
    319 323 334
spelling 4 7 9 10 12 19 36 39 82 90 139 140 151 163
    223
spill registers **294** 295 298 310 311 324

square brackets 81 134

stabilize 243 244 314

stack frame (*see also* push, pop) **177** 179 180 182 185 188 190 215 321 344 346 350 351

star operator, *see* Kleene star

start state **24** 25 57 59 60 66 67 68 73 82 102 121 204

start symbol (of grammar), *see* goal symbol

state machine, *see* finite-state automaton

statement 5 6 7 33 75 80 119 144 164 173 177 181 191 215 216 223 239 240 241 249 250 259 294 296 309 319 325 332 343 358 361 365

static links (*see also* dynamic links, parent pointer) **179** 180 182

static scoping (*see also* static links) 142 179 194 **341** 346

storage (*see also* memory...) 27 29 73 176 256 268 293 294 310 320 334 366

store (instruction) 164 **165** 168 179 184 264 295 296 310 311 312 324 334 400

strategy 13 31 100 135 151 262

strength reduction 248 262 263 264 323 334

stride 331 332

string compare 11 82 84 85 86 151 360

strong 5 130 138 142 149 150 183 212 235 268 294

structure, program (*see also* data structure) 5 12 76 169 177 179 192 215 234 242 245 264 269 289 319 343 352 355 361 368

style 39 83 197 241 247

subdivide 70 293

subexpression 56 138 140 161 228 248 250 253 262 289 291 294 296 325 333

subgraph 250 279 327

subrange 183 186 237 250 332

subroutine 8 176 308 320

subscript 104 134 184 186 187 188 190 250 253 290 291 292 321 323 331 336

subset 19 20 32 57 78 79 118 121 138 224 293 295 346

substitute 5 13 57 71 121 204 215 288 291 314 319 323 331 333 334 340 344 351 352 365 366

substring 35 38 69 107 134 136

subtract operation 79 164 165 169 186 187 263 290 291 312

success, successive 7 35 67 105 112 114 215 314 320 328 330 356 358 361 366

surprise 7 150 224 320 345

symbol table 7 **12** 15 39 82 **138** 144 149 166 168 172 177 182 188 190 216 228 230 235 250 253 256 261 321 341 346 351 353

synonym 163

syntactic 4 20 99 118 138 144 156 159 179 183 189 220 222 235 267 339 341 343 352 361 367

syntax-directed 149 **160** 162 166 183 188 189 190 192 194 236 263

synthesis 12 232 266

synthesized 132 150 172 173 215 227 230 232 234 250 259 319 353 354 360 361 362 365

system, operating, *see* operating system

T

TAG Compiler, (*see also* compiler compiler) 90 116 118 123 142 144 166 280 340 352 **353** 354 357 360 365 366

TAG, *see* transformational attribute grammar

tail-recursion **343** 344 345 350 351 369

tape 24 25 26 27 29 33 57 72 73 106

target machine (*see also* machine language) 12 34 138 159 163 168 170 183 190 295 312 319 321 323 327 331 333 342 345

task 11 13 190 268 293 330

technique 1 32 33 100 160 198 215 241 254 258 268 290 324 325 328 339 340 344 353

technology 287 352

template **226** 227 228 230 234 235 269 276 321 353 365 366

temporary 27 73 161 242 253 259 266 290 293 294 298 325 331 332 344 365 366

terminal (*see also* nonterminal, token) **19** 30 43 49 103 106 112 119 131 139 203 226

terminate 5 21 25 30 37 73 75 82 85 109 110 113 115 116 118 121 178 205 213 215 243 291 355 356 358 361 368

terminology 3 132 206

terms 11 50 56 57 73 75 100 104 114 152 169 249 253 263 287 345

text file (output, *see also* code file, source text) 12 168 172 190 192

THEN 171 173 223 239 240 241 250 256 266 319

theory 1 9 13 18 25 48 79 132 237

threaten 294 295

throughput 325 328

Tiny Basic 191

Tiny Scheme 346

token 8 **9** 19 34 48 **79** 87 118 357

tool 5 25 33 118 132 230 231 234 268 353

trace 11 36 145 189 199 209 237

track 13 172 199 250 361 368

tradeoff, *see* speed/space

tradition 4 12 24 160 163 242

transcription 76 276

transfer 13 118 132 170 189 325 358

transformational attribute grammar 90 **227** 240 281 288 340 352

transformer 267 269 273 276 353 361 362

transition (*see also* rule, finite-state automaton) 25 **57** 60 61 63 71 73 79 100 204 357

translation 3 4 5 13 86 119 162 220 222 227 234 242 269 276 340 341

translator 2 3 160
traverse 203 244 248
tree walk 162 203 223 226 227 228 232 234 240 245
    249 250 253 254 259 321
trend 170 215
trie 85
triples, *see* quads
TRUE 141 163 **169** 182 264
tuple 19 20 57 100 119 227
Turing Machine 25 **27** 320 321
Turing, Alan 27
tutorial 118 133 163
two's complement 323
type-checking (*see also* constraints checking) 39 139
    140 145 149 153 168 169 183 185 186 189 **235**
    360

U

unambiguous, *see* ambiguous
unary 364
unconditional branch 170 171 176 242 313 314 324
    328
undefined 73 237 238 239 348
unfortunate 7 37 110 169 183 189 230
uniform 268
union (*see also* intersection) 52 53 68 103 107 110 156
    188 212 218 **237** 239 243 248 251 253 257 273
    323 361
unique 10 11 80 82 86 87 138 139 140 142 189 231
    235 237 250 354 358
unit 144 150 183 189 237 243 245 325 327 340
Unix 49
unpack, *see* pack
unrolling, loop 248 288 **291** 292 324 330 333
unstructured, *see* structure
update 243 250 252 265 296 310 358
use-definition flow analysis 239 240 244
useful 9 25 39 63 114 131 170 222 225 236 247 249
    253 290 308 323 333 339 352
useless 30 240 248 262 345
user 6 149 190 213 215 340 341 343 347 353 355

V

valid 4 9 11 12 59 66 73 79 118 167 310 354
validate 8 34 145 186 189 366
VAR parameter, *see* reference parameter
variable reference 145 149 169 179 185 190 236 237
    240 261 265 273 298 308 310 311 321 331 341
    361 365
variant 172 258 267 268 298 346
variation 25 188 210 215 294 328
vector 152 179 193 237 238 245 268 273 287 288 328
    330 350 353
vectorize 291 331 332 337
Venus 5
verification 131 189 241
virtual 150 159 268 273 274 275 276 292 296 297 298
    311 312 313 319 320 321
visible 131 149 177 178 185 243 254 353
visit 162 241 243 244
volatile 295

W

walk, *see* tree walk
white space (*see also* space, line break, comments)
    9 353
Wilhelm 227
Wirth, Niklaus 6 7 176 321
Wittgenstein, Ludwig 18
workstations 215
world 2 77 78 99 189 249
worms 130
write 1 2 5 6 22 25 26 33 36 37 54 60 68 71 80 110
    114 116 132 133 134 135 140 150 163 166 240
    243 320 352

Y

yacc 118 352
yield 39 68 104 151 203 206 288 290 320 324 325
    327 328 341